BILL GRAHAM PRESENTS IN NEW YORK
LED ZEPPELIN
WOODY HERMAN
AND HIS ORCHESTRA
DELANEY & BONNIE
AND FRIENDS
JOSHUA LIGHT SHOW
INDICA
MUSIC PRODUCTIONS, INC
presents
LED ZEPPELIN
JOHN BONHAM
ROBERT PLANT
JIMMY PAGE
JOHN PAUL JONES
TUESDAY
MAY
13,
1969
CIVIC AUDITORIUM
7:30 P.M. • $4.50 advance $5.00 at door
BATH FESTIVAL
FLEETWOOD MAC
JOHN MAYALL
TEN YEARS AFTER
LED ZEPPELIN
THE NICE
CHICKEN SHACK
JOHN HISEMAN'S COLOSSEUM
MIKE ABRAHAM'S BLODWIN PIG
KEEF HARTLEY · GROUP THERAPY
LIVERPOOL SCENE · TASTE
SAVOY BROWN BLUES BAND
CHAMPION JACK DUPRE
CLOUDS · BABYLON
PRINCIPAL EDWARDS MAGIC THEATRE
IN CASE OF BAD WEATHER THERE WILL BE A SUBSTANTIAL AMOUNT OF UNDER COVER ACCOMODATION
REFRESH-MENTS AND HOT SNACKS WILL BE AVAILABLE ALL DAY
12 NOON TO
FREDERICK BANNISTER IN ASSOCIATION WITH PETER GRANT PRESENTS
LED ZEPPELIN
AT
KNEBWORTH 1979
OFFICIAL PROGRAMME 90p
BATH FESTIVAL OF BLUES
SAT. 28 JUNE
RECREATION GROUND
JERRY WEINTRAUB/CONCERTS WEST
AND S&L B.V.
PRESENT
AN EVENING WITH LED ZEPPELIN
SUN. APR 10 1977 8:00P .M.
CHICAGO STADIUM
1800 W. MADISON
NO REFUNDS OR EXCHANGES
BOX
PRICE
$10.00
ENTER
AISLE
SECTION
ROW
SEAT
HAPPENING
SUN., 27 FEB.
2.00 p.m.
Chrysalis
in association with Peter Grant
presents
LED ZEPPELIN
In concert with their friends
LIVERPOOL SCENE
AND
BLODWYN PIG
BIRMINGHAM, Town Hall, Friday, 13th June, at 7.30 p.m.
MANCHESTER, Free Trade Hall, Sunday, 15th June, at 7 p.m.
NEWCASTLE, City Hall, Friday, 20th June, at 7.30 p.m.
BRISTOL, Colston Hall, Saturday, 21st June, at 7.30 p.m.
THURS. AUG. 21
THE LED ZEPPELIN
& ORPHEUS
FRI. AUG. 22
DAVID RUFFIN
SAT. AUG. 23
JOHNNY WINTER
SUN. AUG. 24
ENZIO STUARTI
PHONE RESERVATIONS: 872-3577
Mail Orders to FRANK CONNELLY'S
Carousel Theatre
3 PERFS. JAN. 20-21-22nd
MON.-TUES.-WED. at 8 P.M.
Swan Song in association with
Jerry Weintraub/Concerts West
Present An Evening With
Led Zeppelin
Prices: $8.50, $7.50, $6.50
TICKETS GO ON SALE AT BOX OFFICE
DEC. 15 and ALL TICKETRON OUTLETS
CHICAGO STADIUM
1840 West Madison, Chicago, Illinois 60612
For Information Call (312) 733-5300

Led Zeppelin

Whole Lotta Love

A People's History

First published in Great Britain 2024
by Spenwood Books Ltd
2 College Street, Higham Ferrers, NN10 8DZ.

A CIP record for this book is available from the
British Library.

ISBN 978-1-915858-35-1 (hardback)

Design by Bruce Graham, The Night Owl

Rear cover images: (clockwise from top left) Stacey Katsis; Stacey Katsis; Stuart Whitehead; Steve Acri; Stuart Whitehead

All other image copyrights: As captioned
Thom Lukas's photographs can be found at thomlukas.com

LED ZEPPELIN: WHOLE LOTTA LOVE

A PEOPLE'S HISTORY

Richard Houghton

Spenwood Books
Manchester, UK

ABOUT THE AUTHORS

Richard Houghton is the author of more than 20 books about music, including authorised publications on Jethro Tull, Simple Minds, The Stranglers, Orchestral Manoeuvres in the Dark, Shaun Ryder, Fairport Convention, The Wedding Present and The Ukrainians. He can be reached at iwasatthatgig@gmail.com

Dave Lewis is the world renowned Led Zeppelin chronicler and author of many highly acclaimed books on the band and editor and publisher of the *Tight But Loose* Zep magazine from 1978 to 2019. For his regular online updates visit www.tightbutloose.co.uk

SPECIAL THANKS

Wayne Lee Sales; Mike Adams; Ren Hudspith; Marci Connelly; Kevin Jarrell; Jenzi Silverman; Judith Jones; Daniel E Smith; Steve Thorp; John Oldham; Fran Hickman; Dylan White; Michael Adler; Bill McGowan; Dawn Fox; Bonnie Richardson; Stacey Katsis; Norm Alberts; Mark Brady; Andreas Stocker; Michael Ruggieri; Dan Paterson; Darla Watlet; Daniel Rogers; Randy Bailey; Norman Wilson; Donald Fuller; Edward Ortiz; Doreen Sympson; Sue-Ellen Downie; Ty Williamson; Carmel Wilkinson; Craig Goldenberg; Dan Bowyer; Doris Walsh; Gary Bodrog; Martial Mason; Jim Messina & Jim Martinez; Nick Smithers; John Larson; Andrew Greaves; Malcolm Goode; Suzi Schmidt; Derek Peplau; Jamie Pipe.

GOT A CONCERT MEMORY?

If you have a concert memory you'd like to share, please send it to iwasatthatgig@ gmail.com.

FOREWORD

When the four members of the band that would soon be known as Led Zeppelin travelled to Copenhagen in early September 1968 for their first tour dates, the art of rock presentation was in its infancy.

It says everything about their humble beginnings that the first gig that Jimmy Page, Robert Plant, John Paul Jones and John Bonham performed together was staged in a school gymnasium in Gladsaxe, Denmark.

Their early UK dates consisted of one night appearances at such choice venues as the Fishmongers Arms Hall in Wood Green, The Toby Jug in Tolworth, Farx Club at The Northcote Arms in Southall and the Nottingham Boat Club.

Led Zeppelin emerged out of the remnants of The Yardbirds. When the band split in the summer of 1968, Page was left with the rights to the name and with the task of assembling a new unit. On the recommendation of Terry Reid, he and Grant travelled to the Midlands to see a local-based singer by the name of Robert Plant. It was immediately apparent to them both that he was the man for the job. As was drummer John Bonham – a friend of Plant. Page saw him at a Tim Rose gig and instantly offered him the job. The line-up was complete with the addition of a much-respected session musician, John Paul Jones.

Having signed a mega record deal with Atlantic Records, maverick manager Peter Grant and guitarist Jimmy Page had their sights set on the American market. In their final months together, The Yardbirds had established a strong reputation on the ballroom touring circuit, notably at Bill Graham's Fillmore East and West venues and The Boston Tea Party. It was these venues that the fledgling Led Zeppelin took by storm on their first US tour in early 1969.

Whilst their US success was instant, the UK was something of a slow burn but by the end of 1969 and with the release of their second album, Led Zeppelin II, they were more than ready to move into the big league. Significant 1970 milestone appearances at the Royal Albert Hall and a bill-topping appearance at the Bath Festival cemented their position as the world's top band – a status that was confirmed when they replaced The Beatles to win the prestigious *Melody Maker* readers' poll.

Back in the US, they were soon selling out the likes of New York's vast Madison Square Garden over multiple nights. Similar demand followed wherever they appeared, notably in Japan and Australia.

By 1973, more people wanted to see Led Zeppelin perform live than practically any other band. This was more than evident when they opened their US tour in May of that year by playing to 49,000 in Atlanta and the next night to 56,000 in Tampa. In doing so they laid the template for the type of single act mega stadium show that paved the way for the likes of the Rolling Stones and The Who.

Led Zeppelin – Whole Lotta Love – A People's History tells the Led Zeppelin story from the place they functioned best – live on stage – and it's told by the people that mattered the most – the fans...

Their studio albums were only the starting point – on stage the band extended their repertoire in a totally unique way and their improvisation skills ensured no two concerts were ever the same.

Visually, they went from the jeans and plimsolls look to lavish stage presentations taking in dragon suits, complex light shows and lasers. As manager Peter Grant told me in 1993, 'When Led Zeppelin played a concert, it wasn't just a concert it was an event.'

These concert events are now dissected by the book's many contributors – all of whom were fortunate to have been right there as the action was unfolding. I count myself very lucky to have attended 15 of their shows, going back to 1971.

Led Zeppelin – Whole Lotta Love – A People's History brings together 750 first hand reports from across the globe. In doing so, it offers a unique insight in to what made Led Zeppelin such an engrossing live act and how they developed during every stage of their remarkable career.

So let them take you there…

Dave Lewis
August 2024

BEGINNINGS

Jimmy Page is an established session player in London. Robert Plant sings in various bands around the West Midlands, doing odd jobs to make ends meet, including spreading 'half the asphalt on West Bromwich High Street'.

CLUB LAFAYETTE
1965, WOLVERHAMPTON, UK

I WAS THERE: DAVE BRADDOCK

About fifty years ago the Club Lafayette was principally a discotheque but occasionally the management would splash out on a live band and I saw Robert Plant perform on several occasions. The regular crowd were very clothes orientated – this was the era of the Mods – and I remember Robert Plant distinguished himself with a pair of yellow trousers with a large reel overcheck, which were quickly named as his 'Rupert Bear' pants. At the time I felt he was trying a little too hard to please a very discerning audience. On stage, he was very animated and belted out numbers at high volume but the Lafayette crowd wanted to hear the sounds that generally came on imported records of the Tamla Motown type so they didn't always appreciate his hard work. I don't recall the name of his group in those days but I don't think it was Led Zeppelin! Nevertheless, he has persevered and obviously found a style that brought success, although I suspect it is in spite of and not because of his Rupert Bear pants. A local boy made good.

ST JOHN'S HALL
1965, STOURBRIDGE, UK

I WAS THERE: DEREK THOMAS, AGE 14

Robert was a grammar school kid who went to King Edward VI School in Stourbridge. He was a Mod. He had his hair cut like a Mod. Apparently, he used to follow the Small Faces everywhere around the country and would try and get in the dressing rooms. They used to chuck him out. He was quoted as saying, 'For fuck's sake, all I wanted to be was Steve Marriott.' Hence 'You Need Loving' by the Small Faces and 'Whole Lotta Love' are the same song. When Marriott heard him singing that and copying Marriott's voice, he apparently said, 'Good on yer, Bob.'

I come from a village called Wordsley, three miles from Stourbridge, and I used to take myself off to town and what not. All my mates were playing cricket and football and that wasn't for me. I went to town to meet other people. The first time I encountered Robert Plant, he was sitting on as wall just outside Stourbridge bus station with a local beatnik called Frosty. Frosty was well known to me because I used to hang around town all the time. Frosty was playing guitar and Bob

Plant was playing harmonica, sat down by him. He was wearing a college scarf, which a lot of kids did because it was the trend. I was a young Mod and a Stones fan and Bob sounded brilliant. I wasn't awe-struck but, 'Whoah! Real live music' you know? I played around with my guitar at home and had Bert Weedon's chord book but he was much, much better than me, even then. From then I'd see him knocking around town, and I'd say 'hi' to him.

I was still at school when I went to a dance at a place called St John's Hall, Stourbridge and there was Bob Plant fronting a band. The band was called Black Snake Moan. Named after a Blind Lemon Jefferson song, they were playing blues and R&B, Marvin Gaye and stuff like that. Bob was always around. If there were any local gigs on with local musicians, up would pop Bob and he'd take over lead singing or join in the band. I even saw him at a New Year's gig at Dudley Town Hall. Roy Harper was there, all nice and gentle, and up pops Bob. At the end of the evening, he and Roy were singing 'Auld Lang Syne' to us.

THE WOOLPACK
1966, WOLVERHAMPTON, UK

I WAS THERE: PETER SMITH

I saw the band Listen at the Woolpack in Wolverhampton with Robert Plant on vocals and with a great friend of mine, John Crutchley, on guitar. Robert ran through the audience dressed in an afghan waistcoat waving a tambourine to great effect. I was hooked; he had a superb presence and a great blues voice. They became the Band of Joy, with John Bonham on drums, and they played frequently around the Midlands. Robert used to visit the Milano coffee bar in Wolverhampton often as well as the very posh Beatties store cafe lounge, so he was often about. Packies in Wednesbury was also a regular place to be seen in those days. His style of wear was always noticeable and very flamboyant. It was obvious even then that eventually he'd succeed in the rock world. As the years rolled on, Led Zeppelin played at the Belfry in Sutton Coldfield around 1969, just after they'd slayed America. Noddy Holder was there. He used to work for Robert, fetching and carrying, a sort of roadie. I wonder what happened to him?

In 1966 Page moves from session man to handling guitar duties for The Yardbirds, initially on bass and then alongside Jeff Beck on guitar before Beck leaves the group.

NEW SOUND DANCE CLUB, RACINE YMCA
3 AUGUST 1967, RACINE, WISCONSIN

I WAS THERE: JON PARIS

I started out playing drums in The Chevelles (with David Zucker on rhythm guitar) in 1963, pre-British Invasion. We played rock 'n' roll (Chuck Berry, Bo Diddley, Buddy Holly and Eddie

Cochran), the same repertoire as the rest of the world, but also played some blues (Jimmy Reed, Freddy King, Bobby Bland and Tommy Tucker). In 1966 I joined The Walkers (with Bob Metzger and Jerry Harrison) playing bass guitar and harmonica. We were becoming big blues fans, whether it was the real guys (Muddy Waters, Howlin' Wolf, John Lee Hooker and BB King) or the Brits (the Stones, The Animals, Manfred Mann and The Yardbirds). When we caught The Yardbirds in Chicago in August 1966, we couldn't figure out who was on bass. It looked like Paul Samwell-Smith's bass, but it didn't look like Samwell-Smith. Turns out it was Jimmy Page, who we knew little or nothing about. By the time we caught The Yardbirds in Racine, Page was beginning to make a name for himself.

Almost exactly one year later, Bob Metzger and I drove from Milwaukee to Madison to catch The Who open for The Blues Magoos at Dane County Coliseum. We left right after The Blues Magoos' first song (sorry, Peppy) and arrived in Racine just in time to catch The Yardbirds go on using the opening band's battered Vox and Fender equipment. I remember Page had a Telecaster and a Tone Bender pedal, and them doing 'I'm a Man' and especially a long improvisational number we'd never heard before – 'I'm Confused' (which became 'Dazed And Confused'). I still use a couple of harmonica riffs I 'stole' from Keith Relf that night.

After their set, Bob and I followed them downstairs to their dressing room, hoping to get to talk with them. Jim McCarty, who I became friendly with years later, was with a young woman and wanted nothing to do with us. Keith Relf and I talked about harmonica influences, and Bob got to ask Chris Dreja about Eric Clapton and Jeff Beck. Jimmy Page was aloof, kind of unapproachable, but as soon as he heard the conversation, his ears perked up and he asked, 'What do you know about Jeff Beck? What do you know about Eric Clapton?' He seemed very competitive. I also remember that they looked pretty worn out for their age; touring the States was probably not as glamorous as many might think, with few if any nights off and no fancy hotels or luxury tour buses. I'd often wondered why a well-known British band with chart hits was doing a gig at a local YMCA dance; I guess they had to fill as many dates as possible while they were Stateside.

After a show several years ago at Tramps in New York City with what remained of The Yardbirds and The Animals, our friend Giorgio Gomelsky and a couple of the musicians held a Q&A session. Giorgio spoke about how he and The Yardbirds toured the States in two station wagons; and how they stopped, while on tour, to record at Sun in Memphis and at Chess in Chicago. Pioneers.

By the end of their final US tour in 1968, The Yardbirds have completely abandoned the Mickie Most leanings towards pop. The last third of the tour develops into what one critic describes as 'stirring exercises in blues-laden psychedelia'.

ANDERSON THEATER
30 MARCH 1968, NEW YORK, NEW YORK

I WAS THERE: ARNIE GOODMAN

I saw The Yardbirds' Anderson Theater show, which I guess a lot of people consider the first

Led Zeppelin gig in New York in a lot of ways. It was an interesting period. The place was probably half empty. There really was not much interest in it. A lot of big shows, even Fillmore shows, historical as those shows were, weren't always that well attended. The Yardbirds, for all intents and purposes, were a blues pop band and Jimmy Page was bringing them in a different direction. It was an all-right show. It wasn't one of those shows where you came out and said 'hey, this was a great show' and the audience was going nuts. It was an acceptable show. The show became legendary because the record got taken off the market. That had more to do with the making of the legend than the actual show.

The whole idea with Zeppelin really came from that first Jeff Beck record. There was a competitive thing between Jimmy Page and Jeff Beck. I think Jeff was a little pissed at the time. All the ideas of stretching out these blues numbers that he was doing was pretty much a model for Zeppelin. That first Jeff Beck band was really the prototype. He had Rod Stewart in the band. It was a charismatic band. Peter Grant was managing Jeff Beck as well and he took Page along to take a look at him. The Jeff Beck Group did a tremendous show in New York with Mountain and Savoy Brown.

A lot of British blues guitarists have no respect for Jimmy Page at all. When Jimmy did that first record and took all the Willie Dixon stuff and didn't give him credit? That really kicked the other British blues players in the balls. They didn't like it; because they thought Page nicked some stuff that he should at least have given some credit to, which he seems to be totally against. In the late '80s or early '90s there was talk of Jimmy Page doing a tour with Chris Farlowe and others and Alvin Lee nixed it when he heard it was with Jimmy Page. He didn't want to be a part of it.

MANDEL HALL, CHICAGO UNIVERSITY
8 APRIL 1968, CHICAGO, ILLINOIS

I WAS THERE: PETER RUDOFSKY, AGE 10

The concert was billed as The New Yardbirds with the Otis Rush Blues Band opening for them. They played songs like 'Dazed And Confused' and 'How Many More Times'. I was surprised they didn't play any usual Yardbirds songs.

MONTGOMERY INTERNATIONAL SPEEDWAY
4 & 5 JUNE 1968, MONTGOMERY, ALABAMA

I WAS THERE: JIMMY LEE, AGE 12

I met The Yardbirds on their very last gig. Every summer, from 1963 to 1972, I stayed with my uncle and aunt at our stock car track outside of Montgomery, Alabama. In June of 1968, I sat in my uncle's office and looked at all the upcoming events at the racetrack, which my uncle was promoting. A county fair held at the racetrack that particular year was to feature The Yardbirds.

I examined the band's promotional photo intently, as I always did when my uncle had national and international bands play at the facility. I recognised Keth Relf, Chris Dreja and Jim McCarty, but not the fourth member, a skinny guy with rather short hair.

A month later the road manager for The Yardbirds, Richard Cole, arrived at the facility two days ahead of the band. I rode around with Richard obtaining the equipment needed for the show – a flatbed trailer for the stage, PA equipment, light show, etc. The overwhelming memory I have is of Richard Cole being a racist dickhead. Dr King had been assassinated the previous April and as I rode around with Richard, I began apologising for the racist nature of the South in that era. With that, Richard said something like n***ers weren't my people and that I should stand by my people. I told him that black people were my people far more than white racist assholes and for him to take me back to the track. And I told him he should cut his hair lest someone mistake him for somebody who was cool. I never spoke to the motherfucker again.

When the band arrived at the facility, I met them all, along with Peter Grant. Jimmy was cool, as were the rest of the band. They used my aunt and uncle's bedroom as their dressing room. My sister wanted to steal Jimmy's Zippo but thought better of it. Peter Grant wasn't happy with anything and cussed a lot. They played the gig. Within just a few weeks of that show at our racetrack, Page had recruited and was jamming with Robert Plant, John Paul Jones and John Bonham. Six months later, *Led Zeppelin I* was released featuring all the tunes played that night at the track.

GERRARD STREET
19 AUGUST 1968, LONDON, UK

The four members of what would become Led Zeppelin meet in a basement below a record shop.

John Paul Jones: We all met up in this little room to see if we could stand each other.

TEEN CLUB
7 SEPTEMBER 1968, GLADSAXE, DENMARK

The band perform their first ever show together, as The New Yardbirds.

UNKNOWN VENUE
12 SEPTEMBER 1968, STOCKHOLM, SWEDEN

The band's second ever performance is curtailed when the speakers shut down.

POP CLUB
12 SEPTEMBER 1968, BRØNDBY, SWEDEN

The band's second show of the night. A reviewer later suggests that 'Robert Planto's... (sic) dancing needed work'.

STJARSCENEN CLUB
15 SEPTEMBER 1968, GOTHERBURG, SWEDEN

The band complete their Scandinavian tour.

OLYMPIC STUDIOS
27 SEPTEMBER 1968, BARNES, LONDON, UK

The band begin recording Led Zeppelin I. *The album is recorded, mixed and ready to be mastered in just nine days.*

Robert Plant: What I heard coming back to me over the cans while I was singing was better than the finest chick in all the land. It had so much weight, so much power, it was devastating.

MAYFAIR BALLROOM
4 OCTOBER 1968, NEWCASTLE, UK

The band make their UK debut.

155 OXFORD STREET
14 OCTOBER 1968, LONDON, UK

Forced by contractual implications to stop calling his group The New Yardbirds, Peter Grant makes a series of phone calls to the press to unveil the name Led Zeppelin.

MARQUEE CLUB
18 OCTOBER 1968, LONDON, UK

Their first London appearance and their first live review in the UK. **Melody Maker** ***magazine describes the band as 'very much a heavy group', advising that 'there seems to be a need for Led Zeppelin to cut down on volume a bit'.*** **New Musical Express** ***writer Keith Altham later complains to Peter Grant that he left a Zeppelin gig after three numbers because 'they were far too loud'.***

LIVERPOOL UNIVERSITY
19 OCTOBER 1968, LIVERPOOL, UK

The band play their last gig as The New Yardbirds.

UNIVERSITY OF SURREY
25 OCTOBER 1968, GUILDFORD, UK

The band appear for the first time as Led Zeppelin.

EWELL TECHNICAL COLLEGE
26 OCTOBER 1968, EPSOM, UK

I WAS THERE: MARTIN LEYDEN

The show was billed as The New Yardbirds and the first time I heard the Led Zeppelin name was at the show. The friend I was with asked Jimmy Page what the new album was going to be called and he said, 'Probably 'Led Zeppelin Plays'.' I can't really remember what they played, other than that it was quite loud. I guess it must have been all the material off *Led Zeppelin I*.

COLLEGE OF TECHNOLOGY
16 NOVEMBER 1968, MANCHESTER, UK

I WASN'T THERE: JOHN PEAKE

Were we there? Unfortunately for me and my mates, we weren't. That Saturday evening, four of us were walking back down Oxford Road in Manchester, disconsolately and unusually having failed to gain admission to Manchester University's Owens Park to see whichever band was playing there that night. We were all still at school, so didn't have student union cards, except that one of us did and somehow we usually managed to get ourselves in. But not on this occasion.

Anyway, one of us piped up with, 'There's a band called Led Zeppelin on at UMIST tonight. Anyone fancy going there?' It was only a few minutes' walk away. We all said, 'Nah, never heard of 'em,' as we trudged back to the train station. Little did we know that they'd just recorded what would become one of the most influential rock albums of all time. What a bummer!

Led Zeppelin's debut in the United States opening for Vanilla Fudge, initially unbilled. A press review for this show read, 'The concert was cranked off by another heavy, the Led Zeppelin, a British group making its first US tour.'

AUDITORIUM ARENA
26 DECEMBER 1968, DENVER, COLORADO

I WAS THERE: DENNIS GAMEROS, AGE 18

When I saw Zep's first ever American show in Denver, Colorado, the ticket sold for $3.50. The hall was packed and it is a huge room. I went – alone – to see Spirit. I had never heard of Zeppelin before. They played their first album and blew everyone away. I believe this is the tour that led to Spirit claiming Zep plagiarised the riff from 'Stairway To Heaven'.

They had a huge sound for a three-piece band with a singer. I had never heard a singer hit higher sustained notes than Robert Plant. They gave 100 per cent. Page established a guitar sound that would influence every rocker after him, using a violin bow on his guitar. In those days, we could smoke weed in the Denver Auditorium Arena. It was an incredible experience. Bonzo was the loudest drummer ever.

Everyone was fairly well spent before Spirit came on. They played a regular show, knowing they could not compete with Zeppelin. Right after that, I heard Zeppelin's first album and we played it over and over. They were young, fresh and full of energy. I'll never forget it.

I WAS THERE: DENTON FRENETTE

I was at Led Zeppelin's very first US appearance. Barry Fey of Feyline Productions was the promoter, and also on the bill were Spirit and Vanilla Fudge. Led Zeppelin played pretty much just English blues – 'Stairway' hadn't been written yet – but we thought it was a great show anyway. Vanilla Fudge and Spirit both kicked in $1,500 of their fee and gave it to Led Zeppelin in order that Led Zeppelin could go on first. So Zeppelin earned $3,000.

PACIFIC COLISEUM
28 DECEMBER 1968, VANCOUVER, CANADA

I WAS THERE: FRED TAIT

They were the backup band for the Vanilla Fudge. I had never heard of the Zeppelin at that point but I was totally blown away by them. I saw them again in Amsterdam in October 1969, with Steamhammer as back up. Great band!

I WAS THERE: TRICIA NOBLE

In those days it was all festival seating and I was about two feet from the stage. I saw them twice more in Vancouver, and again in Seattle, and they were the best four live concerts I ever saw. Back then I was young and acid was involved but when I listen to their music now it is like being back in time. They changed music for me forever.

KENNEDY PAVILION
30 DECEMBER 1968, SPOKANE, WASHINGTON

I WAS THERE: SCOTT D SMITH, AGE 13

Mom worked in the record department of Valu-Mart (later to become Fred Meyers) and got demo albums for new bands. We had an album introducing Led Zeppelin on one side and Cream on the other. I got to go because my sister wanted to go, had just got her driver's license and Mom and Dad said she had to take me too. Tickets were $5 in advance and $6 on the door. I remember being mesmerised watching the band and the reactions of all the older kids. This was my first rock concert – and it was a blast! When they advertised the concert, the band were billed as 'Len Zefflin'.

WHISKEY A GO GO
2-5 JANUARY 1969, LOS ANGELES, CALIFORNIA

I WAS THERE: STEVEN RADILOFF

I had been a big fan of The Yardbirds, where I discovered Clapton as a teenager. Beck followed when Clapton left, and immediately on Beck's departure came Page. It's extraordinary that one band had three of the greatest lead guitarists of all time. I hadn't heard anything new from The Yardbirds in quite a while and didn't know that they had broken up and gone their own way.

One day I saw in the *LA Free Press* that 'The New Yardbirds' would be playing at the Whiskey A Go Go, a venue of only 500 seats. Wow! I immediately called and bought four tickets. On the night of the performance, Alice Cooper was on the same bill as the opening act. When Alice's band had finished their set there was a short break and The New Yardbirds came out and set up. I recognised Page, but none of the other guys. The drummer was as big as his drum set, and there was a skinny, long-haired guy at the microphone and a bass player. As I remember it, the minute they began, every jaw in the place dropped opened and stayed that way for over an hour. The first several songs were Yardbird classics, but then they played songs I had never heard before, which eventually were on the first Zeppelin album. By the time they went to London, they had renamed the band. Bonham almost blew the roof off the Whiskey.

I WAS THERE: ROBERT KNIGHT

I had started as a photographer in the summer of '68. The first artist I ever photographed was Jeff Beck and Rod Stewart, and after a couple of shows we became friends and Jeff said, 'You're not going to believe this band Jimmy's put together. I don't know the name of it yet but it's going to be something. I've heard some of the tracks' so I had a heads up. I knew Jann Wenner over at *Rolling Stone* and I knew that the band were going to do a date in California. I went in and tried to sell Jann on sending me down to LA and eventually talked him into giving me a letter so that I could get in to shoot the band.

I showed up at the box office and the woman there said, 'How old are you?' I told her and she said, 'You can't come in. You gotta be 21.' I said, 'Well, I'm with *Rolling Stone* magazine, I gotta shoot the band. What are you gonna do?' So she picked up the phone and called the Chateau Marmont Hotel, where the band were staying, got Jimmy on the phone and Jimmy said, 'Come on over to the hotel'. So I spent the entire day with Jimmy and Robert and everybody, talking. He was saying, 'Call your friends in Hawaii.' I called them up and he was talking to my friends in Hawaii. The band were very excited that someone was interested in them.

They brought me in to the show as road crew. I had to stay away from the floor but I was able to shoot the show. They were opening for another artist but we didn't stay around to watch them. At the time, I didn't pay any attention but I remember Jimmy saying, 'It's some chick band.' Years later, Alice Cooper came up to me and said, 'Did you shoot that first Led Zeppelin show?' and I said, 'Yeah'. He said, 'Do you know who they were opening for?' I said, 'Jimmy said a chick band.' Alice said, 'Dude, they were opening for me!'

We became friends. I even followed them up to San Francisco. I shot the show in San Francisco and at that point quit my school because I wanted to join the circus. I called the promoters in Hawaii and convinced them they needed to book Led Zeppelin. When the band came in, I met them at Honolulu Airport because the promoter said, 'Well, they know you, why don't you go out there?' So I went and shot that famous picture of them holding the master tapes of *Led Zeppelin II* in their arms. They were recording it as they were travelling on the first tour.

I don't think they came over to Hawaii to do a show. I think they were just coming to relax, or were on their way to Japan or something, because I ended up hanging out with them for over a week. I drove them around Honolulu and took them to dinner. FM radio was becoming a big deal at that point. A buddy of mine was a deejay over there and I said, 'Hey, do you guys want to do an interview on FM radio?' and they said 'sure'. I brought Robert and Jimmy over to the recording studio and they did an interview. I also remember telling Jimmy, 'You know there's an album coming out called *The Yardbirds Live At The Anderson Theater*?' And he completely freaked because he hadn't known about it and it had songs on it that were actually similar to the new Led Zeppelin album. I think that's when they got that restraining order put in place, to stop that record from coming out.

I had worked with Jimi Hendrix a couple of months before that, so I shot Jeff Beck, Jimi Hendrix and Led Zeppelin in my first six months of being a photographer and my career just took off from there. I still see the guys from time to time in different places. I had breakfast a couple of mornings with John Paul Jones in Los Angeles while he was doing the Them Crooked Vultures album, and we hung out and talked at length, although we never talked about Led Zeppelin. I knew not to bring the subject up. I brought Tyler Bryant to meet Robert in Nashville and we hung out for a few hours in a coffee shop. And then I saw Jimmy at Jeff Beck's wedding. Jason Bonham I see every once in a while too.

A reunion isn't going to happen. It's not Led Zeppelin without John Bonham.

FILLMORE WEST
9 JANUARY 1969, SAN FRANCISCO, CALIFORNIA

I WAS THERE: KENNETH LISS

They opened for Country Joe and the Fish and Taj Mahal. The cool thing for any Bill Graham show back then was each band played two sets each night. They also played the following night. He'd have the same shows on Friday and Saturday nights. The two sets meant that the concert would go until around 3am, with Led Zep playing, then Country Joe, and then Taj, and then Led Zep, Country Joe, and Taj a second time. It was great for those of us who took acid or some other psychedelic substance at the shows we went to back then.

Jimmy Page: We'd come on and hit them like an express train. After the San Francisco gig it was just – bang!

Led Zeppelin ***is released in the United States on 12 January 1969. The UK release is not until March 1969. The album comprises their live set at the time of its recording.*** **Rolling Stone** ***magazine is less than complimentary: 'Robert Plant sings notes that only dogs can hear.'***

GRANDE BALLROOM
19 JANUARY 1969, DETROIT, MICHIGAN

I WAS THERE: KEVIN KELLY, AGE 16

I saw Zep three times, the first time at the Grande Ballroom in Detroit. I loved The Yardbirds and all I really knew about Zeppelin was Jimmy Page. I was just getting started in sex, drugs and rock and roll. Being a guitarist led me to hanging with older 'bad influences'. Me and a couple friends were riding around in a 1961 Chevy with no place to go. It was a turd of a car; but we had a big bag of weed. There was not a lot happening because it was so fucking cold, like ten degrees Fahrenheit. We were in a very crime-ridden part of town. In Detroit a couple of years after the race riots, many of the buildings in the area were gutted by fire.

There on the empty sidewalk was a white girl, not dressed for the weather, walking the wrong way to be out of danger. We pulled over to see what she was doing there. She said she was from San Francisco, following Robert Plant across the country and trying to find the Grande. We gave her a ride and thought we might as well go in. Led Zep, $2.50 admission. I knew Jimmy Page was in The Yardbirds so thought it might be good.

There weren't many people there, maybe 300 to 400 people for a venue with 1,200 capacity. We thought Plant was gay, which was not widely accepted in those days. Page seemed reckless to me, because I worshipped Clapton who never played a clunker in his life. Pagey stretched to reach untilled pasture. We didn't like them very much – my honest opinion is that they were a bit sloppy – but they started to grow on me from listening to the album that everyone soon had. I thought it was much better than that live performance.

I WAS THERE: DAVID LAABS

Their first album had only been out a week or two. They were great. The ticket cost $3.50 or maybe $4.50. Bonham did a drum solo with his hands. Page played great and used his violin bow. I thought the tremolo in Plant's voice was going to shake the roof of the old building down.

BOSTON TEA PARTY
23-26 JANUARY 1969, BOSTON, MASSACHUSETTS

I WAS THERE: CLEMENT PORTER

The Boston Tea Party was an old white wooden church from which all the pews had been removed. Once inside you sat on the floor. My friends and I were the first ones in line and we made a beeline to the front of the stage, which was almost floor level. When the band came out and started to play, I was sitting about eight feet from Jimmy Page. After the first song, people started throwing LSD tabs and joints up on the stage.

Rumours were that the band would gobble them up, get higher than the sky and send everyone to nirvana. Of course, that wasn't true but Plant and Page brought the house down and it was magical. I had met Jimmy Page at the Comic Strip in Worcester when he was with The Yardbirds. He came across as shy and something of a perfectionist.

I WAS THERE: IVAN LIPTON, AGE 13

I became a Led Zeppelin fan before their first LP had even been released. I would frequently tape music off the radio, using an old Wollensack reel-to-reel tape recorder that had been my dad's. An FM radio station in Boston called WBCN was one of the coolest stations in the country at the time, playing all the new underground rock sounds. They received an advance copy of the unreleased first album and played it straight through. There was then some sort of cease-and-desist order to stop them from playing it again. I happened to record it, so had taped the entire Led Zeppelin album off the radio at least a month before it was released anywhere. I played it constantly, and turned some of my friends onto it. I bought the album as soon as it came out and played it even more.

Later that month we heard that Led Zeppelin were playing at the Boston Tea Party, where all the UK and American underground rock bands played. I went with two friends, Rene Merghart and Peter de Lafemina. I remember being in school and talking about how we were going to see Led Zeppelin and other kids in school asking, 'Who the hell is Led Zeppelin?'

We lived in a suburban town about 20 miles west of Boston, and either hitchhiked or got a ride to the closest train station from our parents. We rode into the city on the MBT, got off at the Arlington T-stop and walked to the Tea Party club and waited in line to buy tickets. When we were only about five people away from being admitted they announced the show had sold out. Luckily it was a multiple-night engagement (four nights, I believe) and they were playing again the next night, so we bought advance tickets for that and came back again to see them on the Sunday. I don't have my ticket stub to the show, so I don't remember how much the ticket cost, but shows at the Tea Party were generally around $3.50 to $4.50.

The Boston Tea Party was a converted temple that had become the ultimate psychedelic rock ballroom, with swirling light shows in the temple building and a very small balcony way up in the back. For some reason we wound up in the small balcony and my most vivid memory is of plaster cracking off the ceiling and falling on our heads. We feared the entire balcony would fall down.

I believe there was an opening act that night called Raven, but I honestly don't remember them. Maybe we missed their set. Led Zeppelin were incredible, absolutely mindblowing. They did 'Train Kept A Rollin'', 'Communication Breakdown', 'Babe I'm Gonna Leave You', 'White Summer' and an absolutely incredible and long 'Dazed And Confused', where Jimmy Page did extensive playing with the violin bow.

Their initial set was almost two hours. But this was the legendary show where they came back for an encore and played for hours and the audience would not let them leave the stage. After they came back for the 'encore', Robert Plant said something to the effect that they'd already played their whole repertoire, so they were just going to jam and play a bunch of songs they knew. They proceeded to play a seemingly endless medley of cover songs, running through portions of dozens of rock and roll classics and contemporary hits. I recall bits of 'I Saw Her Standing There' and various Chuck Berry and Elvis hits.

Unfortunately, we had to catch the last train home or we would have been a bunch of 13 and 14-year-olds stranded all night in Boston, plus it was a Sunday night and we had school the next day. The city of Boston was a very early-to-bed city with no late night club scene and the final train on the subway system was somewhere around midnight. So tragically we had to depart in the midst of what subsequently has become one of the most legendary concerts ever. The rock and roll medley had been going on for at least 40 minutes when we left, and I have no idea how much longer Led Zeppelin played for. Some reports have said they played for four hours that night, so if that's true we missed a lot! My friend Peter remembers we had to make a mad scramble out of the balcony to run to the last train, and in order to get through the crowd we had to walk down the stairway by walking up on the handrails.

I WAS THERE: CHARLOTTE EPPS-FLETCHER

The first time I saw Led Zeppelin was in the winter time of '69 around Brookline, at a nightclub that did not serve liquor called the Boston Tea Party. They just looked like a smaller regular group and I totally fell in love with them. It was very psychedelic inside, with videos playing on the walls. There was really no place to sit down but it was great. Just one year later they played at the Boston Garden, a huge venue that is still around today. I saw them a couple more times after that.

I WAS THERE: DIANNE BENTLEY

I started going to the Tea Party when I was 16. I took the subway in at least four or five times a month and saw everyone in the day back then. Zep stood out for me because of Bonham. I had never heard drums hit like that before. As usual, I was very close to the stage, with the audience on my left and the stage on my right and it was amazing. The show was very soon after *Led Zep I* was released. I think the Berkeley Street location was mobbed and I had a better time when they played Lansdowne Street. That was mobbed as well, but I got a better spot on the floor.

For their visit to New York's Fillmore East, Zeppelin's manager Peter Grant persuades Bill Graham to bump Zeppelin up to second on the bill. Iron Butterfly, having only just become headliners themselves and aware of Zeppelin's burgeoning reputation, threaten not to play. Grant's response is that Zeppelin will simply play for longer. Zeppelin play for 90 minutes.

FILLMORE EAST

31 JANUARY & 1 FEBRUARY 1969, NEW YORK, NEW YORK

I WAS THERE: DONALD SZTABNIK

I was in love with The Beatles and completely immersed in the British Invasion. So many great bands, so many great songs. One of my favourites were The Yardbirds. I couldn't get enough of this guitar-driven blues that brought us Eric Clapton, Jeff Beck and Jimmy Page. They epitomised the way guitars could and should be played. After Clapton left, Beck continued and was joined by Jimmy Page – remember the great scene in *Blow Up*? Eventually Beck bailed and Jimmy Page soldiered on as the Guitar Face of The Yardbirds. After a short period as the New Yardbirds, they suddenly re emerged – or should I say exploded – as Led Zeppelin. Heavy and light simultaneously? I didn't pause for analytics as I was knocked out by what the debut album contained. The most incredible noise my rock and roll ears had heard to date, with a British accent. I could not stop listening to this great album with the burning Zeppelin on the cover art. It burnt my ears and my soul. Jimmy Page's guitar was a sound that we had only dreamed of, and now we basked in this fever dream.

Shortly afterwards, Led Zeppelin stood before me on the stage at the Fillmore East. There they were: John Bonham, John Paul Jones, Robert Plant and Jimmy 'Yardbird' Page. He seemed so small... so much hair; a low-slung Les Paul and an attitude that knocked me out. And they hadn't even played a note. But I was ready. I had played their debut album at maximum volume and was still processing 'Good Times Bad Times', 'Dazed And Confused' and 'Communication Breakdown' as if a new language was being spoken – loudly! I was in the third-row centre stage at the Fillmore when suddenly, without warning, Led Zeppelin kicked out their first song in 'real life'. We were stunned. It was beyond our belief. It was heavier than the air I was breathing.

Remember this, the shock of the new.

These songs were fresh and still unknown and were what they were to become. I knew it was exactly where I was supposed to be. Exactly where I wanted to be. Exactly where I had to be. I could not believe Jimmy's guitar sound and the equally insane voice of Robert Plant. The drums and bass of John and John were tectonic plates moving. I stood my ground and leaned into the sound. I did not want this concert to end. Every song was complete and perfect. This was my first Led Zeppelin encounter, followed by another soon after at the New York Pavilion at the former World's Fair in Flushing, New York. I never had a desire nor the opportunity to see Zeppelin again after those early shows. I heard something that for me was complete and satisfied my desire completely. The New Yardbirds morphed into Led Zeppelin and I was very, very happy.

I WAS THERE: PAUL FAHRENKOPF

Iron Butterfly were top billed and they blew Butterfly out of the water. Led Zeppelin were in another stratosphere. I remember they did 'Dazed And Confused' and 'Communication Breakdown'.

I WAS THERE: DOUGLAS A FINLAY. AGE 15

I was fairly tanked on booze. We would pour whiskey into a large Coke or 7UP bottle and get away with it. I may have danced in the aisles, up in the mezzanine. It was the early Friday night show and Iron Butterfly were headlining. There was a hold up to Led Zeppelin coming out. The story was that John Paul Jones had left his bass back at the hotel although I've read elsewhere that Robert Plant had split his trousers and needed to get them mended. Whatever the reason, Jimmy Page opened their set by coming out and sitting on his white captain's chair and playing 'White Summer', which is a complete rip-off of Davey Graham's '63 exploration of 'She Moves Through The Fair'. At one point Plant took his jacket off and threw it at the light show screen. Perhaps the trousers held? Someone else at that show said they walked out after the Led Zep set. They were so mesmerised by Zeppelin that Iron Butterfly sounded terrible.

I WAS THERE: ANTHONY STEELE, AGE 14

The first concert I ever went to. The day before I had got the first album. Scott Muni played it on his WNEW show, *Things From England*. I remember the first note of 'Good Times Bad

Times'. I just get chills talking about it. The first time I heard it I was like, 'Oh my god, what is this?' because I had already been into Hendrix and Jeff Beck. A bunch of kids on the block used to go to concerts all the time. My parents wouldn't let me go. But when the kids got tickets for Led Zeppelin, my mom knew all the kids on the block and said 'all right'. We got to see the early show that night. I was living on Long Island and had to take the train to Manhattan. I remember walking in and just seeing what was going on. All of a sudden, they came out. Robert Plant was wearing a ginny t-shirt with a pair of grey pants and no shoes on. Jimmy Page had hair halfway down his back and his guitar was down to his knees. I was like 'holy shit!' The one song I wanted to hear that they didn't play was 'Good Times Bad Times'. But they did everything else. I was stunned. They played for almost two hours.

About two years later they headlined the Garden for three days. We went two nights and they played everything. A bunch of us had gotten tickets to go see 'em and we were running late. I said, 'There'll probably be an opening act.' As we walked in the door I heard the 'Immigrant Song' going and I said 'oh shit'. We just ran up to our seats and stood there. They must have played eight songs in a row and then Robert Plant goes 'good evening'.

The sound, the equipment, the look. The attitude. Those licks that Jimmy Page played? Him, Jeff Beck, Clapton and Hendrix were my idols. You always saw Jimmy Page with that sunburst Les Paul. We would party all the way to the show and party all the way home afterwards.

I WAS THERE: GREGORY JACKSON, AGE 16

In 1968 going into '69 a lot of stuff happened in this country – MLK, RFK, the Democratic Convention. But in NYC I was a long-haired bass playing hippy. A friend asked if I'd like to go see Jimmy Page's new band, opening for Iron Butterfly. I said 'sure.' The Fillmore was my haunt by then. I sat in the balcony on Page's side when they came out. I was tripping on acid. Plant had on a black velvet outfit, and that hair! They looked like rock stars compared to our hippie bands like the Dead, the Airplane, etc. It was a life altering experience and to this day, 'How Many More Times' is a favourite song.

I WAS THERE: BRUCE COHEN, AGE 18

I saw them second billed at the Fillmore East. I didn't even know they were playing there. We just walked up, bought tickets at the door and got seats. They only had their first album out, so most of their set was from that album. They opened with 'Train Kept A-Rollin'', left over from when they were calling themselves The New Yardbirds, plus a song by Love, although I can't remember which, and 'Long Tall Sally'. The highlight was 'Dazed And Confused', with Jimmy bowing the guitar.

Later that same year I saw them in the Quaker City music festival in Philly, not yet headlining. And then I was heading to Woodstock with five friends and heard on the radio, 'Tonight at Asbury Park Convention Hall, Led Zeppelin!' so we headed there instead. Joe Cocker opened up for them before playing his star-making performance the next day at Woodstock. After that, I saw Led Zeppelin play on every tour until they stopped touring. They never failed to amaze me, but those early concerts will always be my favourites.

I WAS THERE: ELLEN FRISHBERG, AGE 15

Some teens went to the movies on dates. I was fortunate to grow up in Brooklyn, New York, where a subway token and $2.50 bought a balcony ticket to the Fillmore East. I was in high school from 1968 to 1971, coincidentally the same years that Bill Graham ran that rock palace. In 1969 I wanted to hear 'In-A-Gadda-Da-Vida' by Iron Butterfly. I knew nothing of Led Zeppelin. But they opened the show and I was hooked. The crowd booed Iron Butterfly when they came on and chanted that they wanted Zeppelin back.

We went to Flushing that summer of '69 to see them again at the New York State Pavilion, an outdoor arena in the old World's Fair grounds. And then once more before I graduated and left NYC at Madison Square Garden, which was not on Madison Avenue, was not square and was not a garden! I remember an amazing psychedelic show. It was 1970, my senior year of high school, I was doing LSD and 'Dazed And Confused' was an anthem! One of the best shows ever, and I saw many.

I WAS THERE: JOSEPH ANGIER, AGE 15

I saw one of the two early shows. I went at the suggestion of friends who were more ardent followers of Jimmy Page than me and who were anxious to see his new band. I certainly wouldn't have chosen that show based on Iron Butterfly, a band I didn't care for. Jimmy Page was quoted as saying, 'By the time we reached San Francisco, the other groups on the bill just weren't turning up. Country Joe and the Fish backed out of playing with us on the West Coast and Iron Butterfly didn't turn up on the East.' I don't know if or when that occurred, because at the show I saw Iron Butterfly headlined as advertised. I thought Led Zeppelin were pretty good that night, but since that was the one and only time I saw them, you could say that's a reflection of my ongoing lack of enthusiasm for their music. It is strange to think that I was able to buy a ticket at the last minute for Led Zeppelin in a 2,600 seat theatre.

The other thing I remember is that in the middle of the show Robert Plant announced that he'd 'split his trousers' and had to go fix them. I was watching the show standing in the lobby in the rear of the orchestra (my actual seat was way up in the balcony) and Plant came around looking for someone to help him stitch up his pants while his bandmates continued playing on stage. That also would have been unthinkable just a couple of years later; when he was a super-duper megastar.

I may not have been bowled over that night, but I do recall hearing them perform 'Whole Lotta Love' which was very exciting. I didn't have *Led Zep II*, which had only just come out, so that was the first time I heard that song.

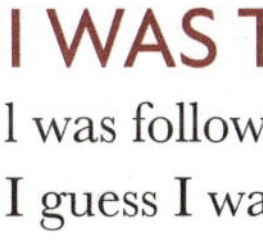

THE ROCK PILE
2 FEBRUARY 1969, TORONTO, CANADA

I WAS THERE: JJ CLARKE, AGE 21

I was following The Yardbirds music and Eric Clapton and Jeff Beck. Then it was John Mayall. I guess I was just following guitar players. I came across Jimmy Page by accident through that.

The first time I saw Zeppelin was at the Rock Pile in Toronto. I drove there on a 1969 BSA motorcycle. Damn, it was so hot in that building it was like a heatwave.

KINETIC PLAYGROUND
7 FEBRUARY 1969, CHICAGO, ILLINOIS

I WAS THERE: CRAIG BARROWS

All our information on bands came from *Rolling Stone* magazine or the liner notes on albums. We knew about Page from The Yardbirds but that was about it. When my buddy dropped the needle on *Led Zeppelin I*, my life changed. Mostly for the good. Listening to The Beatles? That was over. The first time I saw them was their first trip to Chicago, at a converted roller-skating rink called the Electric Theater. We sat on the wooden floor, very close to the riser. It was very loud and very intimate. This was in the days before huge arena rock. They played their first album and parts of *Brown Bomber* (the second album) and an encore. They were digging the Chicago vibe, as we knew what we were listening to, and they did a bunch of standards, Chuck Berry, etc. That was a hell of a show.

After the show, I'm in the men's lavatory taking a leak and Plant comes in – bands used public lavatories back then – and takes a leak next to me. He asked me, 'How do we sound tonight?' and bummed a cigarette. My moment next to a hero!

I saw them there again, maybe six months later. And then I was living in Los Angeles and saw them at the Forum. That show was not as intimate or as spontaneous. It certainly wasn't the same feeling as years earlier in Chicago.

I WAS THERE: DENIS RYLE

It was 1969, The Beatles were ending, and having spent our teenage years listening to them, most of us were sad. But then I saw Led Zeppelin at the Kinetic Playground. They opened with 'Communication Breakdown' and I was a lifelong fan from that moment. Their music is just amazingly powerful. *Led Zeppelin I* is one of my top ten albums. It's very rare to have an album that you play both sides of. *The Dark Side Of The Moon* is another. *Zeppelin II* was more of the same and *III* was a change, more blues and sit-down music than before.

I saw them at Chicago Stadium three times. The first time they sat down during a show was so different. The audience became so quiet as the Zeppelin spell took over. When *Zoso* (*Led Zep IV*) came out, we were in the eleventh row at Chicago Stadium. That was the first time we heard that music, and it was fantastic to hear 'Stairway', 'Rock And Roll' and 'When The Levee Breaks', with Robert's harmonica playing. The Zeppelin blues was very addictive. The day after the concert, there was a line two blocks long outside Rolling Stone Records, with people queuing up to buy *Led Zeppelin IV*. They sold out in hours.

I WAS THERE: BOB HOLLIS

The first time I saw Led Zeppelin they were at the Kinetic Playground in Chicago, opening for

Vanilla Fudge. The other opening band was Jethro Tull. I had not heard of Led Zeppelin or Tull at that point, but I had seen Jimmy in The Yardbirds in Aurora, Illinois in 1967. I remember that the lead singer, Keith Relf, had abscessed teeth. Jimmy brought out his Danelectro guitar and just went at it. My friend and I were so close to him that he was sweating on us.

I WAS THERE: THOMAS FILIP, AGE 16

I saw them three times – twice at the Kinetic Playground in Chicago in 1969 and once in 1975, touring *Physical Graffiti* at the Chicago Stadium. I was a senior in high school living in a small town, Algonquin, in the suburbs of Chicago. My friends and I had just gotten the first Zep album after hearing all the lead-up to its release and a few cuts on radio, plus I was a huge fan of The Yardbirds, so the release was greatly anticipated. The Kinetic Playground was Chicago's version of the Fillmores, the Boston Tea Party, et al. It was only open at weekends. Bands had Friday and Saturday as residency, while Sunday was local bands only, and admission was always $5 at the door. It wasn't a large venue; I'm unsure of the capacity but don't think it was more than 3,500 and that may be on the generous side.

There were many eclectic bills, such as The Who and Buddy Rich. My friend Don LaRocco was always my KP travel buddy; we'd met and bonded at school and he was two grades ahead so had already graduated and was working. Plus, he had the best car – a new Plymouth Road Runner which he'd recently bought. Being just 16 (Don was 18), there was a curfew where it was mandated all under 17-year-olds were supposed to be home by 1am. As my mom liked and trusted Don, and knew we were going to dig the music and not cause trouble, she didn't jam me up about being out 'after curfew' as the shows didn't usually end before 2am, as many times the bands played two sets. Sadly, though, this was not always the headliners. Don and myself saw many bands at the KP, just about any and everyone who was popular during that era as it was the only place for touring bands to play.

Zep were the opening act on the bill and Vanilla Fudge the headliner. This tour is where Fudge's drummer Carmine Appice and Bonzo apparently began their friendship (Bonzo was a fan of Carmine's playing) and is how Carmine got Bonzo an endorsement with Ludwig drums, which he played until his death. On the following Monday, I raved to all and sundry at school about the group.

I WAS THERE: ELLIOTT STURM

Some of the bands who played there were just on the cusp of fame – The Who, The Grateful Dead, Zeppelin. It's mind blowing to think we had the opportunity to see these bands, two or three in one night, for the admission fee of $5. If we got there early, we were close to the stage. There were no chairs so we just sat on the floor. Plant always had his shirt open to the waist and we were in awe of his voice. Jimmy Page playing the double-neck guitar with the bow was mesmerising, and watching as Plant matched the guitar with only his voice was something that still gives me chills.

I WAS THERE: GLENN CHRISTENSEN, AGE 17

The Kinetic Playground was Chicago's 'underground' club, sort of our Fillmore, I guess (although I never went to the Fillmore). Zeppelin's first album had only been released about three weeks prior. I have a vague memory of one of my friends mentioning it, or them, at lunch in high school. Anyway, I guess I bought the album right away because I was familiar with their songs already when I went to see them. The Kinetic was a round-shaped room encircled by white screens onto which videos and/or colours were projected when the bands weren't playing. They'd feature three bands a night for five dollars.

There was an area outside of the actual room where the bands played where drinks or whatever could be bought, and they had a small separate bar area where they sold albums, and they had meditation booths! The room in which the bands played only held three or four hundred. There was no seating. Kids sat next to each other on the floor, jammed together knee-to-knee. I managed to get within about ten feet of the stage.

The night I went, Jethro Tull opened, Zeppelin played second and Vanilla Fudge were the headliner. I had no clue who Jethro Tull was when I went there but was amazed and delighted at how good they were. They still wore the tattered clothes and I seem to recall they greyed up their hair. I was a drummer at the time and spent much of Zep's set watching John Bonham, who was great. The only songs I specifically remember them doing are 'Dazed And Confused', 'You Shook Me', 'How Many More Times', 'Communication Breakdown' and 'White Summer/Black Mountainside'. I can't swear to it, but I think I also remember 'Babe I'm Gonna Leave You'. I had seen the Jeff Beck Group there in October 1968 and I have a specific memory of watching Robert Plant perform and thinking that he struck me as a Rod Stewart wannabe – but not as good a singer!

The band went over really well, getting a rhapsodic reception, and people were really cheering Jimmy on, which was interesting, because at that point they were a new band who hadn't yet achieved 'rock god' status. But I guess word about them had spread quickly through the underground hippie grapevine before they appeared.

The way things worked at the Playground, the first band played a 45 to 50-minute set, then after equipment changes the second band played their 45 to 50 minutes and then the third band did the same before the whole process began again, each band playing in order: Tull, Zeppelin, Fudge. Unfortunately, because I was seventeen and Chicago operated a curfew for under eighteen-year-olds, which was loosely enforced by my parents if not by the City, I didn't stay for the second round of sets.

I really enjoyed seeing Zeppelin on the way up, before the bloat set in. There was no endless jamming. The songs were tight and they weren't yet jaded by the distractions of the road. But one problem for me was that, other than Hendrix and a couple of other great bands, I got to see practically everyone there from ten or twelve feet away, three bands for five bucks. It didn't give me a huge incentive to see bands like Zeppelin or The Who at some enormodrome six months or a year later, sitting two hundred feet away!

I WAS THERE: STEVE HILL, AGE 17

I saw them in Chicago on their first American tour. Jethro Tull opened, Zeppelin were the second band (touring on the strength of Jimmy Page having been in The Yardbirds) and Vanilla Fudge were the headliners. This was all for $5! We were all sitting on the floor as the venue had no seats, and at one point they brought the volume of the music down and Robert Plant went up to the mic and let out what would later become one of his trademark screams. Everyone around me immediately put their hands over their ears, me included. It was piercing! Jimmy

Page used a violin bow on 'How Many More Times', and I went out and bought Zeppelin's first album on the strength of that song. It's still my favourite album of theirs. Although I enjoyed Tull more on the night, I didn't buy Tull's first until many years later.

Led Zeppelin's first US tour comprises 36 shows in total and concludes with an appearance in Baltimore.

CIVIC CENTER
16 FEBRUARY 1969, BALTIMORE, MARYLAND

I WAS THERE: BARBARA NELSEN

They were on the bill with Vanilla Fudge and the Paul Butterfield Blues Band. I'm not sure what order they played but they weren't well known at that time yet. My best friend had a crush on Robert Plant and I was mad about John Paul Jones. I still can't believe we did this, but we tracked down the band after the show to the Holiday Inn (which shows they weren't famous yet!) around the corner from the arena. After the show, we were by the side doors and I saw John Paul coming out. It was a cold February night and he was all bundled up in this gorgeous big fur coat. He walked past us and we said 'hi'. He smiled and said hello and started walking across the street. That's where we got the idea to see if they were staying in the nearby hotel. We got Robert Plant's room number just by asking the clerk. We went up to Room 304 and knocked and he opened the door bare-chested, in a pair of blue velvet low ride pants and with that mass of curly hair. Oh, that image will never leave my mind! We were so startled to see him in person that we both immediately became tongue-tied. We sort of stammered out how much we loved the band, their performance that evening and wished him continued success. He was very gracious and thanked us. Then we took off!

Robert Plant: I realised what Zeppelin was about around the end of our first US tour... I started getting this little light glowing inside, and I began wiggling me hips and realising that it was all a fantastic trip.

Returning to Europe after making their mark in North America, between 1 March 1969 and 17 April 1969 the band play 18 UK dates, some one-off dates in Denmark and Sweden and a host of TV appearances.

DE MONTFORT HALL
13 MARCH 1969, LEICESTER, UK

I WAS THERE: STUART LANGFORD

Led Zeppelin played as part of Leicester University's rag week with Ferris Wheel and the

Decoys as support. My mate Mick and I ran the disco that day; our speakers were tiny compared to everyone else's! The band arrived during the afternoon, and they were such nice guys. They hung around with us during the afternoon playing records from our rock selection – lots of Moby Grape and blues stuff – and then set up their equipment. No roadies in those days; they carried their own gear in from the van.

It was late afternoon, early evening, and Mick and I saw Jimmy Page kneeling on the stage. He'd opened one of the dips – they're the little hatches in the middle of the stage under which there are live sockets, so you don't need to run long cables across the stage, which is dangerous. I heard this 'zzzzzzzzz' noise, and saw Jimmy trying to wedge the bare ends of his amplifier lead into a 15-amp round socket under the stage. This was before the days of earth trips and RCD leakage devices that would cut the power off if you did anything stupid. For some reason, they'd taken the plugs off their amps and were just wedging the wires in with matchsticks.

So, there was Page, hardly able to see in the dark, reaching under the stage, feeling around, with the bare wires of his amplifier cable catching the odd spark, going 'zzzzzzzzz' and with the smell of singeing in the air. I literally pulled him away. I can genuinely say he was within moments of electrocuting himself. And I said, 'Jimmy, don't do that! Mick and I will give you a plug for your amp.' So we gave him a round-pin plug from our toolbox of spares. And he said, 'Oh lads! Thanks ever so much. I'll give it you back at the end of the night.' Did he hell!

But they were fantastic. They played for three hours. Mick and I paid them, because we were a part of the college business side, 175 quid cash, and they held the money in their hands like school kids. 'Look at this, lads. We're rich! Let's go get egg and chips somewhere!' I got their autographs, all except John Paul Jones. I eventually sold them to a Finnish journalist, and he met up with John Paul Jones and asked him to add his signature to the three. Apparently, he got quite tearful remembering the days when the whole band was together.

ARGUS BUTTERFLY
23 MARCH 1969, PETERLEE, UK

I WAS THERE: HENRY RACE, AGE 15

I saw them seven times. The first time was at the Argus Butterfly pub in Peterlee in County Durham, with my friend Ian Anderson. I had read about them in the *NME* or possibly *Disc & Music Echo* or *Melody Maker* because they'd done the tour of Scandinavia and America at the back end of '68. I was a fan of The Yardbirds and I was quite intrigued. No one had heard of John Paul Jones or Bonham or Plant but it was just following Jimmy Page through. The *NME* was talking in really enthusiastic terms about the New Yardbirds shows they'd done in Scandinavia and the States. Perhaps I heard a track or two off the first album on John Peel, because it was out in America but wasn't released in the UK until the end of March. But we'd seen the reviews and the accounts in the *NME* and we'd seen that they were playing at the Argus Butterfly. I saw Taste there, and Family. It was that kind of gig, with local prog groups. It was a function room off the side of a pub in Peterlee, a little industrial town between Durham and Teeside. It might have held a couple of hundred people. I'd like to say there was only me and Ian and a couple of other blokes and a dog there, but it was pretty full. The stage was only 18 inches high.

Ian was a year younger than me. It was a half an hour or 40-minute bus ride from where we lived and I said to Ian, 'Do you fancy going down?' We didn't have advance tickets. You couldn't really do that then. We paid at the door. I was 15 and he was 14 and it was a pub gig. How we got in I don't know. We tried to pretend we were 35, saying, 'We've just come here to see the band. We're not going to cause any trouble.' The guy on the door said, 'Well, okay, but don't try to buy any drinks from the bar.' I've seen a putative set list online – 'Train Kept A-Rollin'', 'How Many More Times' – but I can't remember any individual songs. I do remember they were fucking loud. Having done two American tours by then they were as tight as all fuck. They were a proper band, really loud. They bashed it out. Jimmy Page was playing his Yardbirds Telecaster with all the paintings and etchings and stuff on. I don't remember walking home. We can't have walked home, because Peterlee was a fuck of a long way from where we lived. Ian died in 2017.

I WAS THERE: JO FOSTER

I was there that night, albeit asleep in my bedroom upstairs. I was nine months old and my mum and dad, Joan and Jim Foster, ran the Argus in those days. I only found out about the gig, and the many others they put on there, years later.

FARX CLUB, NORTHCOTE ARMS
30 MARCH 1969, SOUTHALL, LONDON, UK

I WAS THERE: BARRY JUDD, AGE 16

I saw them in a pub in Southall in West London. It was packed, with condensation dripping from the ceiling, which I thought was someone flicking beer around. Two things stick out in my memory: Jimmy Page's use of the violin bow and a feedback device that was on top of his amp and had an aerial. I saw them again at the Royal Albert Hall in '69 or '70 and witnessed one of the infamous 25 minute – I exaggerate – Bonham drum solos. Bless him.

TOP RANK CLUB
2 APRIL 1969, CARDIFF, UK

I WAS THERE: GARETH HICKERY

I first came across Led Zeppelin around the beginning of 1969 when I was in Form 5, studying for my O levels. A school friend convinced me to go to the Top Rank in Cardiff to see 'The New Yardbirds', as he called them. I was only allowed to go as it was half term, midweek and not a school night. When they took the stage, it was nowhere near full, with maybe a couple of hundred at a venue that could take a lot more. I was surprised to see no Jeff Beck. However, they started and I was completely blown away, and probably everybody there was. I think they started with 'Good Times Bad Times' and they certainly played 'Communication Breakdown' early in the set. I remember 'Dazed And Confused' and 'Babe I'm Gonna Leave You' and it was about an hour set. I was now a fan. The only other band that hit me that hard live were The Who, around the time of *Live at Leeds*.

I WAS THERE: ANDY SHEPHERD

Four 19-year-old electrical apprentices – me, Ron 'Duke' Davies, Mike 'Spike' Potter and Gerald 'Jecca' Williams – climbed into a slightly battered and more than slightly rusty light green Mini van (they were all light green) to travel from the western valley town of Newbridge to Cardiff. Suited and booted, we walked in through the entrance. I say 'suited and booted' because in those days it was only possible to gain entrance to the Top Rank if you were smartly dressed. This was somewhat alien to a Zep fan but, never mind, we were in. Part way through the performance, Robert Plant could see that his audience were all dressed in suits, jackets and ties and began to take the mickey. A few of them tried to explain to him that it was due to the venue's dress code but it made little difference.

None of us were strangers to live bands but when Zeppelin began to play we were blown away, almost literally. We had never heard a band play so loud! You not only heard the sound they made, you almost wore and tasted the sound. We had never seen anything like them before. Some of us sat on the edge of the stage while they performed and Plant chatted to the audience. It seemed so informal compared to the gigs of today. It changed our take on what a live band could sound like.

ROUNDHOUSE

5 APRIL 1969, DAGENHAM, EAST LONDON, UK

I WAS THERE: DAVID JOHNSON, AGE 18

It was ten days before my 19th birthday. There were supposed to be three of us going – myself, John and Glen had a bedroom guitar band – but Glen said he couldn't afford to go. Me and John left work from Rolls-Royce in Derby on Friday afternoon and caught a coach to London. On arriving in London, we made our way to the Marquee to see who was on – Jeff Beck! Only when we went back later, he had cancelled and Steamhammer were on instead. After the gig we spent the night touring London's cafes.

We spent the next day hanging around Carnaby Street and some record shops. We saw both Lulu and Steve Marriott there. Later we got the Tube to Dagenham and queued to get in. We were quite early and at a cost of around 2s 6d (12½p) secured our wooden seats on the front row with our feet resting on the 18-inch high stage. It is nearly 50 years ago and memories fade, but I vividly remember the call and response section of 'Dazed And Confused' and the 'electronic aerial' and someone in the audience letting out a few 'aaahhhs!' It was a brilliant gig. The album had only been out a couple of months. Our friend who didn't go bought it that day.

CHERRY TREE
8 APRIL 1969, WELWYN GARDEN CITY, UK

I WAS THERE: DAVE BARBER

They played most of the tracks from *Led Zeppelin I* and *Led Zeppelin II*. Tickets for the concert were 7s 6d (37½p). The band were just unbelievable live. I stood in the front row, right up against the small, low stage in front of Robert Plant. He appeared to be very shy, but once he started singing he became a giant. Although using just two Marshall 4x12 columns, his stunning vocals shone through – what an amazing vocal range he has. Their live version of 'Dazed And Confused' was incredible, as was John Bonham's drum solo in 'Moby Dick', using his bare hands as well as drum sticks. Led Zeppelin were so tight and powerful. One of the finest live performances I've ever seen and heard.

I used to be in a band called Coda. Coda's Colin Fretcher helped John Paul Jones join Led Zeppelin. Colin had a dance band gig in the Continental Restaurant in Bush Hill Parade in Enfield and John stood in on bass guitar. John asked Colin if he could help find some arranging jobs. Later Mickie Most asked Colin if he could do a string arrangement for a Herman's Hermits song, possibly 'I'm Henery the VIII I Am'. Colin was too busy at the time so he recommended John Paul Jones instead. At Mickie Most's office, John met Peter Grant, the future Led Zeppelin manager, and the rest is history.

I WAS THERE: COLIN FRETCHER

I only played in a restaurant with him and then recommended him to Mickie Most, where he met Led Zeppelin's manager. I haven't seen him since!

TOBY JUG
9 APRIL 1969, TOLWORTH, LONDON, UK

I WAS THERE: JOHN LETHBRIDGE

I saw Led Zeppelin at the Toby Jug in Tolworth just after they changed their name from 'The New Yardbirds'. I remember the gear came in a Ford Transit because I put a business card for our recently formed light show on the windscreen in the naive hope they might book us. Several years earlier, around 1965, I had tried to form a band and our guitarist, who lived in New Malden, went round to Jimmy Page's house to buy a guitar from him. Our band never took off. I was the drummer and the other three kept failing to come to my house to practice.

I WAS THERE: MARTIN LEYDEN

After the first time I saw them, I saw them again at the Toby Jug in Tolworth, between *Led Zep I* and *Led Zep II*. The *Rolling Stone* issue about groupies had just come out and someone in the crowd asked Robert about the Chicago Plaster Casters. He looked a tad embarrassed and said (re Jimmy), 'Well, he did it too'. I also saw them at the Royal Albert Hall in 1969, the Bath Festival and Earls Court. It's the first two shows that stick in my mind.

KIMBELLS BALLROOM
13 APRIL 1969, SOUTHSEA, UK

I WAS THERE: PETER FORD, AGE 16

I was there with my mate, Roger Shipp. We were both 16. This wasn't my first gig but it is one I will never forget. There were no seats. Standing or sitting on the floor was the order of the day. There was a bar at the back of this quite small dance floor and the stage was in the front. Being quite young we decided to make our way to the front where we managed to sit cross legged in front of the stage and what appeared to be an enormous banks of speakers. Sitting waiting for the band to come on, we thought nothing of it. Then the mighty Led Zeppelin came on and what a sound they made. I was partially deaf for at least a week after. I often blame my slightly impaired hearing in my advanced years on them.

Led Zeppelin's second North American tour kicks off in April 1969 with four nights in San Francisco, two each at the Fillmore West and Winterland. Achieving top billing, the band are able to command appearance fees four times what they earned on their first tour. They sometimes appear without a support act, one of the first ever acts to do so, but also coheadlining with larger acts. The band's anthemic 'Whole Lotta Love' receives its first airings at the San Francisco shows.

WINTERLAND
25 & 26 APRIL 1969, SAN FRANCISCO, CALIFORNIA

I WAS THERE: TOM BRODY

The opening act was Brian Auger and the Trinity with a girl singer, Julie Driscoll. She was on stage drinking from a glass of water and said she did not like the water in San Francisco. When it came to Led Zep, at one point Jimmy Page brought out a chair and sat on it and played a guitar solo. I thought it was unusual for a guitar player in a rock 'n' roll band to bring out a chair and sit on it. The only other thing I remember is Robert Plant's singing. I did not like his excessive groaning. I thought he groaned too much in 'Whole Lotta Love'.

I was at this concert with a boy from my high school, Pacific High in San Leandro, called Pat

Gardner. He complained that l did not seem excited by the concert. There were two reasons why l was not excited. The first is that I was not familiar with the music and had never heard their records. The second reason is that we were far away from the stage, up in the balcony.

Bill Graham always had a jazz act included in the line up along with two rock 'n' roll bands. So along with Jefferson Airplane and the Grateful Dead, for example, we got Mongo Santamaria, a Cuban percussionist. In the past 40 years this practice seems to have been discontinued. It's such a loss that people who go to rock 'n' roll concerts are no longer exposed to jazz acts and, as a result, are culturally deprived.

I WAS THERE: WALTER KENNEDY

A friend and myself were looking for something to do on a Friday night. A man on Sutter Street said there was a band playing at Winterland and we all took a bus there. It was Led Zeppelin, and the opening act was Brian Auger. Led Zeppelin were pretty unknown at that point – well, we had never heard of them – and you could just walk in and buy a ticket. Winterland held about 5,000 people and because it was a relatively small crowd and a relatively small venue, we ended up right at the stage. For some reason, John Bonham was placed at the front of the stage for the show and at one point he did a ferocious extended drum solo. I ended up in a kind of call and response with him during the solo, me clapping once and him responding with one beat, me clapping twice and then three times, etc. It was lots of fun and very dramatic and it probably only lasted 20 or 30 seconds if that. Needless to say, it was a great show. I saw them there twice more, before they could only play huge arenas.

I WAS THERE: LYNNE FISK

Bill Graham was one of the finest producers in America as far as rock 'n' roll shows were concerned. You knew that you were going to get more than your money's worth when you went to one of his shows. Winterland was a huge place that held five or six thousand people. It was an old ice rink. The building ran east and west. The load in area had a big roll up on the north west corner of the building. That's where the line formed to go around the building to the east side where the doors where and where they took your tickets. My ex and I were sitting there. I had two hits of acid in my little watch pocket and this limo pulled up and all four members of Led Zeppelin got out. I pulled these two hits of acid out into the crook of my finger and one of them dropped on the sidewalk. I said to my girlfriend 'play it up' and I got down on my hands and knees and said, 'I lost my contact lens, I lost my contact lens.' And three members of Led Zep – everyone except John – got down on their hands and knees with about half a dozen other people, looking for a contact lens. I never found the hit of acid and I don't know who did.

They turned the stage at Winterland so it was across it lengthwise. They turned all the lights off during the show. Jimmy Page left the stage and came back on in a solid white satin outfit. They put one spotlight on him, a black light (UV) spotlight, and it was like he was glowing in the dark.

FILLMORE WEST
27 APRIL 1969, SAN FRANCISCO, CALIFORNIA

I WAS THERE: STEVE PARISH

There are many other takes on the four nights in late April '69 that Led Zeppelin spent in San Francisco. All I have to do is listen to *Led Zeppelin I* and I'm blessed with the wondrous amazing recall of their Fillmore West concert, which was not too long after their first album hit. Me and two friends sat on the edge of the hardwood floor and watched music taken to the next level. I had been to many concerts at the Fillmore West and at Winterland, but that evening with Led Zep was very different. I had just smoked some pot and had a couple of drinks of wine and I was really in a good state of mind – in control of my enjoyment. The music was 'next level' for almost all consumers. This was a packed house as normally, based on my time of arrival, we would have been right up front. But everyone remained seated on the floor throughout the show. The music played and the spirit in the house that night was of another world. It was 'a new music' experience witnessed by an experienced audience. I have a vivid recall of the crowd leaving the Fillmore West that evening. It seemed like a mass of people were walking down the stairs in a trance. This was a powerful experience. The group was way more about music than the glitz then. The glitz came later!

CRAWFORD HALL
1 MAY 1969, IRVINE, CALIFORNIA

I WAS THERE: JON C GARNER

I was pretty young and pretty high. UC Irvine used to have great shows with Janis Joplin, Buffalo Springfield, Lee Michaels, Canned Heat and of course Led Zeppelin. On the rare occasions I studied, when I was a freshman in college, I'd smoke some pot and then listen to *Led Zep II* with the headphones on. No wonder I didn't do so well! I was always a blues guy and I still play quite a bit, but Led Zeppelin were innovative and they were great. The only bad thing is that Robert Plant's screaming was copied by many subsequent rockers – and not very well!

I WAS THERE: RICK NABERS

California in the sixties and seventies was the place for live music. I bought the first Zeppelin album the day it came out at a place which is now long gone, called the LSD (London Sounds Distributors) in Newport Beach. When we saw them at University of California Irvine, no one knew who they were. After seeing Jimmy Page that night we were huge Led Zeppelin fans.

I WAS THERE: RICHARD DEAN PURDOM

My friend and I decided to go see them on a whim. We walked right up to the ticket window and bought the tickets. I think they were $8. Real cheap. It was a good concert. They mostly did stuff from the first album but they also did some older years' stuff too. Lee Michaels opened for them. It was a pretty small venue so we had great seats.

I WAS THERE: MICHAEL ADLER

This was the only time I saw Zeppelin. But I've seen Robert Plant four times since.

ROSE PALACE
2 MAY 1969, PASADENA, CALIFORNIA

I WAS THERE: CATHY ANDERSON KILPATRICK

Five of us went. It was a blast. We were not in chairs but standing. I was up on this guy's shoulders for a while, but we were all jumping and dancing. They were so good, and better than anything we'd seen. They were different than The Beatles, much more insane and we loved it. Oh yeah, and we were all smoking weed.

THE GARDENS
9 MAY 1969, EDMONTON, CANADA

I WAS THERE: TIM DANCY

The first of two times I saw them was one of the great events of my teenagehood. What was originally a Yardbirds tour became a Led Zeppelin introduction across North America. We were stunned by Page and John Bonham particularly. They had great presence. As a stage crew member, we saw it all up close and became immediate fans. Within days their first album was flying off the store shelves.

I WAS THERE: ALLAN LEVIN, AGE 15

My great, late father had bought a brand new Grundig German component stereo, the first one I ever saw. I bought the first album after hearing one of their tunes on radio. As we all know, LZ begs to be played loud. I put it on my Dad's brand new stereo and – yep – blew the speakers. Boy, was I in trouble? But I was also hooked on Zeppelin for the rest of my life.

I went to my first show at the Edmonton Gardens with a good friend. The concert was delayed as Led Zeppelin's equipment was caught up in customs. Once they came out – Jimmy Page was sitting on a chair, playing an acoustic guitar with the spotlight on him on a dark stage – the place exploded with voice and sound and the stage lit up with enormous energy. The Gardens were on fire with heavy rock and blues for the first time ever and the fans were mesmerised. I saw them live three times. The second time was with Redbone, Frank Zappa and The Turtles and the last time was at the Kinsmen Field House in Edmonton with Vanilla Fudge and Deep Purple. That was a great concert – and great memories, although they have faded a little.

GRANDE BALLROOM
16 MAY 1969, DETROIT, MICHIGAN

I WAS THERE: GARY GALUSKY, AGE 15

I saw them three times. The first time was my fifteenth birthday, when they were promoting the first album, and then in June 1972 (promoting *Led Zep IV*) and July 1972 (for *Houses Of The Holy*), both at Cobo Hall. They were great all three times except for Bonham's solo, which was Godawful boring. He was terrific in the context of songs, but a lousy soloist. Clive Bunker from Jethro Tull played circles around him. That said, all three Zep shows were fabulous. The first time was $5 and we bought tickets at the door. Golden Earring opened up, and they were so-so.

KINETIC PLAYGROUND
23 MAY 1969, CHICAGO, ILLINOIS

I WAS THERE: THOMAS FILIP

Having seen them in February, I caught them again at the KP, headlining. The support groups were Illinois Speed Press and Pacific Gas & Electric.

MERRIWEATHER POST PAVILION
25 MAY 1969, COLUMBIA, MARYLAND

I WAS THERE: JUDY GREENBERG

It was a beautiful evening. Led Zeppelin were the opening act, with a very young and bare-chested Robert Plant. I was there with my high school boyfriend but the real reason for us to be there was to see The Who perform *Tommy*. Led Zeppelin were pretty much nobodies. The crowd just milled around smoking dope during their set. It was dusk and the crowd really didn't pack in until The Who took the stage. My little sister became the Led Zeppelin fan in the family but I'm not even sure she had their first album then. The Who were great.

I WAS THERE: MAC MCMULLEN

The Who did the whole *Tommy* album and Led Zep did their whole second album along with most of their first. To this day it was the best show I've seen!

I WAS THERE: BARBARA NELSEN

I saw Led Zep again a few months later at the Merriweather Post Pavilion, where they were the lead-in act for The Who. It was a fantastic music scene that night!

I WAS THERE: SLIM MANICOTTI

They opened for The Who at Merriweather Post Pavilion, the first and only time that happened. I met Robert Plant a few years ago at a funky old grocery store in a not-so-great section of Nashville. He was in line behind me and nobody recognised him. I asked him about that Who show at the Merriweather. He told me they didn't want to do the show; they thought they were better than The Who!

I WAS THERE: LEE SMITH

l came for Bonzo, and left during the first Who song, because I was never a fan of Moon's playing. I was one of millions of instant fans who bought the first LP on the strength of Page's history, Then l was totally floored by the content. As a drummer, Bonham completely made me rethink my approach to playing. His legendary status is based on merit, regardless of the hype associated with Led Zeppelin.

I WAS THERE: PAUL WOLAVER

I saw Zeppelin several times. The first time was an epic show at the Merriweather Post Pavilion in Columbia, Maryland. The Who were on their very first *Tommy* tour and Zeppelin were the opening act! They were playing material from their first album, which had been released, and new material from their yet-to-be-released second album. They were not yet a huge cultural presence, but they were well known to those of us who listened to FM radio and who were plugged in to the underground music scene. Back then, concerts were a very special event for those of us who were young. We were part of this new culture and it was almost like our music was our very special secret that we shared, and that the larger, older, American society was not yet fully aware of. The night was electric for me – I had taken my share of psychedelics – and being a huge fan of both Led Zep and The Who, this concert was an astonishing experience. Even to this day, some of my old chums and I reminisce about this event: 'Did we really see that?' There was a bit of a riot at the venue, with fences being trampled and stuff smashed up. (Being so close to Washington DC, there were many 'counter culture' youths who were becoming somewhat used to rampaging.)

In 1971, I moved to Colorado, where I saw them a couple more times at the Denver Coliseum. LZ's very first US show was in Denver, in December of 1968, at the Denver Auditorium Arena. They were fitted onto the bill at the last moment and opened for Vanilla Fudge. Nobody had any idea who they were, although we knew who Jimmy Page was from The Yardbirds.

I WAS THERE: BO BEDFORD

When The Who took the stage, Daltrey said, 'We'd like to thank Led Zeppelin for what they did to you!' We looked at each other and said, 'What did they do to us?' with fear in our voices. It was fantastic. Psychedelics may have been involved.

FILLMORE EAST
31 MAY 1969, NEW YORK, NEW YORK

I WAS THERE: JERRY MCGUIRE
It was a great show. The opening acts were Delaney and Bonnie, and the Woody Herman Orchestra, who the audience liked. That billing was down to Bill Graham. He often had an unusual act open for big name artists, so the audience would be exposed to different types of music.

I WAS THERE: NIC REEGER
I was driving in the mountains in California when 'Good Times Bad Times' came on. I knew this was something else. The power I felt in that was unbelievable. I raced to the nearest record store and bought not only the LP but an 8-track for the truck. I slapped on the tape and drove on California grass to an album that changed the blues. When I came home to New York in April of '69 and found out Zep would be at the Fillmore East in May, I got tickets. This was a band that really delivered. I sat in awe of these four guys. They closed their set with The Beatles' 'I'm Down', which I've never heard them do again on a bootleg or elsewhere. I went home exhilarated.

Led Zeppelin return to the UK for a 13-show British tour beginning on 8 June 1969 and ending 21 days later. Blodwyn Pig and The Liverpool Scene are the support acts.

TOWN HALL
13 JUNE 1969, BIRMINGHAM, UK

I WAS THERE: LAURENCE HIPKISS
Blodwyn Pig were on the same bill and as I recall both bands were incredible. I would've been 16 and was just a lucky s-o-b to see them for free. The mother of a friend worked at the Town Hall and consequently we saw a few gigs that year. I have great memories of that gig but to be honest it was just one great gig amongst other great gigs that year. I saw Floyd the week after Zeppelin and they filled the place with coloured smoke and someone in a huge green lizard costume brushed past me as he ran around the audience as part of the act. Sadly, because my mate's mom got us in for nothing, I have no ticket stubs from those gigs!

FREE TRADE HALL
15 JUNE 1969, MANCHESTER, UK

I WAS THERE: PAUL WELSH, AGE 16
Because the Manchester Free Trade Hall was home to the Halle Orchestra and was the main

venue for classical music recitals, tickets for all their events were sold through a shop on nearby John Dalton Street called Hime and Addison. The shop specialised in classical music, selling both vinyl and sheet music. The staff was made up of elderly gentlemen in suits, shirts and ties. Consequently, when a rock gig was imminent you would invariably find a queue of 'heads' wearing an assortment of denim, leather and studded belts with long unkempt hair snaking through the shop all the way to the door. The Zeppelin audience was no exception.

I attended the Free Trade Hall gig with Blodwyn Pig and The Liverpool Scene as support and I can remember Adrian Henri doing 'The Woo-Woo'. Robert Plant looked unnaturally thin with his mane of hair. I remember the band still doing their encore as the Free Trade Hall lights came on. The mums and dads who'd come to collect their kids were standing by the internal doors and I remember thinking what must all these old people be thinking, seeing this band and seeing Robert Plant.

A friend of was rather upset to discover that the vocalist's name was Robert Plant and not, as he'd previously thought, Robert Planet. 'Robert Planet would have been a much better name!'

CITY HALL
20 JUNE 1969, NEWCASTLE-UPON-TYNE, UK

I WAS THERE: KEVIN CRUICKSHANKS, AGE 14

They were supported by Blodwyn Pig and The Liverpool Scene. But the support bands were completely forgotten about once Zeppelin came on stage. The hairs still stand up on the back of my neck when I listen to the first album.

I WAS THERE: HENRY RACE

Three months after the Argus Butterfly show they played City Hall, promoted by Chrysalis. Led Zeppelin supported by The Liverpool Scene and Blodwyn Pig. I remember Planty was wearing a pair of really tight black and white striped pirate's trousers. He was coming out to emcee the bands, introducing them and coming out afterwards and asking the audience to 'give a big hand for The Liverpool Scene' and all that stuff. It was only when Led Zeppelin came on and we saw the same guy with the stripey trousers that we went, 'Oh, it's Planty.' I've still got the shitty little programme they were selling.

COLSTON HALL
21 JUNE 1969, BRISTOL, UK

I WAS THERE: RICHARD EVANS

It wasn't sold out! Many fans were a little bemused by the extended guitar solos and vocal histrionics. I saw them again the next year at the Royal Albert Hall just after the release of *Led Zeppelin II*. Now that was just amazing, and for me ranks alongside The Beatles and Dylan, who I also saw at the Colston Hall in Bristol (although not together!), and Cream at Bristol Corn Exchange.

PLAYHOUSE THEATRE
27 JUNE 1969, LONDON, UK

I WAS THERE: NIGEL MOLDEN

I was studying for a Sociology degree at the Polytechnic in Regent Street, London. I had been elected to be the Social Vice President for the college and was promoting a wide range of top bands, such as Fleetwood Mac and The Who. Almost at the end of the academic year, a small group of us got hold of tickets for a live recording to take place for the BBC at the Playhouse Theatre in Northumberland Avenue in London for a programme to be called *One Night Stand*. The band was Led Zeppelin and it was a full house. It was not a normal performance and we were in the balcony, but they did play a number of the compositions with which they were to become closely associated, including 'Communication Breakdown' and 'Dazed And Confused'. I recall Jimmy Page coming to the front of the stage and sitting down to play the final number or two from the set. The recording was to be broadcast by the BBC some six weeks later, on Sunday 10 August 1969.

I remember the performance particularly well because the agency that we used at the Polytechnic had sent a booking agreement in the name of The New Yardbirds without having referred to us. We were a little put out by this, which I made clear to them. They were surprised when we declined the booking. Of course, the band made no more than a handful of appearances as The New Yardbirds and we could have had one of them. I did not even keep the proposed booking agreement!

BATH FESTIVAL OF BLUES
28 JUNE 1969, BATH, UK

I WAS THERE: BARRIE GLENN

I remember holidaying in Canada and hearing 'Communication Breakdown' being played at a record store and the guy looking at me kinda strange when I asked him who was playing. Their first album was released in America before it came out in the UK so I kind of knew who they were when I saw them at the Bath Blues Festival. It was an open air festival. I went with my old friend Steve Baker. The weather was perfect.

They came on late in the day, and I guess not many people knew who they were as there was not much of a crowd and l was able to get really close to the stage. Jimmy did his solo acoustic thing but Plant took the show. He was in great form with powerful vocals and, just as you thought he couldn't sing any higher, he sang higher; but not thin and weedy like some when in the upper register but thick and powerful.

When 'Whole Lotta Love' came out I was hooked. I never saw them live again – they were too expensive. That was my thing in the sixties – seeing bands. I saw the Rolling Stones, The Who (when they were The High Numbers) and Johnny Kidd and the Pirates, with the great Mick Green on guitar – one of the best Telecaster players. I also saw many of the great visiting black blues guys – Sonny Boy Williamson, Howlin' Wolf (what a voice!), Jimmy Reed and many more. That era was the best.

I WAS THERE: PETER CLINICK, AGE 17

This one-day festival was a festival for those of us who had seen a Bath festival of classical music every year, with the likes of Yehudi Menuhin and others, but nothing for the teenagers. That changed with this festival. It caused a bit of a stir as it was held on the Recreation Ground, next to the River Avon and close to the city centre and Pulteney Bridge. I attended with a group of friends. We bought all day tickets for 22 shillings and sixpence (£1.12), purchased on the gate entering via the Victorian ticket booths at the Pulteney Street (North) end of the Rec. The two stages were side by side to help the flow of bands – 21 were billed to appear in eleven hours – and were at the far end of the Rec by the car park for the Pavilion. This is where the Bath Sports Centre and the Thatcher's Stand (named after the cider producers, not the misery producer) now are.

On the day, the weather was really good and the atmosphere great. Before the bands started and in between each act, records were played and I remember how Jeff Beck's 'I Ain't Superstitious' with the wah-wah fuzz guitar echoed off the surrounding buildings and hills. As the bands started up, we wandered around the site taking a few photos. We were waiting for the bands we were fans of. For me, it was Taste, who I had previously seen in the Pavilion and was to see again at the 1970 Isle of Wight Festival, and a new band, Led Zeppelin.

Some billed bands did not appear and some who were not billed did. I moved closer to the stage when The Nice were due and was able to snap a picture of Lee Jackson with John Peel about to announce them. As The Nice played, I got ready for the arrival of the main reason for us being there, the band whose great first album we had been playing constantly since its release just under three months before this appearance.

By the time Led Zep arrived on stage, I was right up at the stage edge and able to get some reasonable photos considering my camera was a cheap black and grey plastic Kodak Brownie 44A and that I was using black-and-white 127 film. I was amazed by their performance, so true to the album we had all been playing to destruction. Page's guitar and Plant's shrieks reverberated around the surrounding buildings and hills, just as – ironically – Jeff Beck's record had earlier in the afternoon. At the time, all the talk was of Led Zep 'stealing' songs such as 'You Shook Me' from *Truth* for *Led Zep I* when in fact many were actually stolen from black blues players.

At the end of their performance, I was able to make my way backstage in time to see Robert Plant and Jimmy Page. I took a photograph of Jimmy Page. Due to my basic camera and the backstage area being in shade of trees, the photo didn't turn out as well as I hoped. They stopped to talk to a girl and sign an autograph for her. I approached them all and asked for an autograph. I didn't have a pen with me but as they had just signed for the girl, they asked her to lend me her pen. She refused, which elicited a response from Jimmy along the lines of 'selfish bitch'. They then said, 'If you can find a pen, then we're in the artist area. Come in and see us and we'll sign for you.' I said, 'Thanks, but there's no chance they will let me in.' I went back to my friends.

After Led Zeppelin, we decided that Ten Years After, John Mayall and Fleetwood Mac were not going to be able to top their set, so we went off to our local pub for a few illicit pints and to regale other friends who didn't go with tales of what they had missed and what we had witnessed.

ROYAL ALBERT HALL
29 JUNE 1969, LONDON, UK

I WAS THERE: CHRIS GREEN

I saw Zep live twice. At the Albert Hall, they were on with Blodwyn Pig and The Liverpool Scene. Needless to say, they were magnificent and, as this was the first time I had been to such a venue, the whole experience was rather overwhelming. Jimmy with his bow on the guitar and a band that was playing brilliantly together.

Led Zeppelin return to North America for their third concert tour in July 1969, completing 46 dates and starting with the Atlanta Pop Festival.

ATLANTA POP FESTIVAL
4 JULY 1969, HAMPTON, GEORGIA

I WAS THERE: ALAN KAUFFMANN

The crowd was estimated at 150,000. The band was still relatively new at that time. The first album was released in January 1969 and *Led Zeppelin II* would not be released until October of that year. Consequently, as popular as they already were, no one really knew what to expect. Their performance was part of a collage of recording acts, most far more well known at the time than Zeppelin. They played the second night, between Spirit and Janis Joplin. Although these two acts were big draws for the festival, when Zeppelin took the stage they instantly captivated the entire audience and simply took control. To say they were absolutely mind-blowing is an understatement. The festival was plagued by power problems. The fact that Zeppelin mesmerised a crowd of this size, under the crippled conditions, was a musical milestone of the ages. They played a perfect set of songs from both albums with several strong blues breaks in the mix.

I WAS THERE: RICK ALLEN LIPPERT, AGE 16

I don't really remember much about them, but I do remember my buddy being intrigued that Jimmy Page was playing the same Silvertone guitar as his.

I WAS THERE: GARY SMITH, AGE 17

I went specifically to see my favourite bands like Spirit, Johnny Winter, Blood Sweat & Tears, Booker T – and Led Zep. It was hot. Very hot.

I WAS THERE: KENNY LUCAS, AGE 17

They were touring hard and heavy in 1969. I saw them at the Atlanta Pop Festival, at the Texas Pop Festival and twice in Dallas within the span of about six months. It was a cool time to be 17. I knew who The Yardbirds were, of course, but I was a little sketchy on Led Zeppelin. A guy in the crowd at Atlanta Pop kept raving about 'em, and by the time they hit the stage they had my attention. Page came out wearing a white fedora and they ripped into some song and the rest was history. The guy who kept raving about them passed out and missed their whole show. We bought our tickets at a Sears store and they gave each of us a poster. I still have the poster. The people I went with are all dead!

I WAS THERE: BERT BARRY

I remember sitting around on the ground waiting for a group called Led Zeppelin to introduce their first album to the multitudes of stoned-out hippies. What a crowd response, with everyone around me asking, 'Who are these guys?'

I WAS THERE: ROD NORWOOD

I was deep into The Yardbirds. I was 17 or so. I had gotten the *Little Games* album (the first Yardbirds album featuring Jimmy Page, released in July 1967). I really liked Jimmy Page, who I wasn't aware of prior to that because he was just doing session work. In 1969, Zeppelin had a series of pop festivals in the US. Atlanta is about 400 miles from Memphis. Zeppelin were booked to play there and were one of the primary reasons I went, particularly to see Jimmy Page. They were fairly low on the bill and it was still daylight when they started.

They came out and Robert Plant asked if anybody in the crowd had a bottleneck. Apparently, Jimmy had lost his. They opened with 'Train Kept A-Rollin'' by The Yardbirds. It was fantastic. Fierce guitar work. But it was 1969.

Everybody was doing LSD – I was in an altered state of mind myself – and the entire crowd was just fucked up. It started getting scary and weird and really eerie. Up front, by the band, it was just like this pit of people in pain, out of their minds. It was still good clean rock and roll but I remember feeling a bit of apprehension.

We got to 'Dazed And Confused' and all fucking hell broke loose. That slow riff just felt menacing to me. It was very, very strange. It was scary. I was looking at the crowd and they were just mad people up front, like whirling dervishes, all naked and crazy. Then some crazed, naked long-haired hippy jumped up on stage. He was out of his mind and he started throwing himself into the drums. It was insane. Nobody knew what was going on. Finally, a couple of Zeppelin roadies picked him up, one by the arms and one by the legs, and they swung that fucker out into the crowd. It was so bizarre to see him flailing in the lights and he was just consumed by the crowd.

Then I looked over to the right of Jimmy Page and they went into the fast part of the song and there were a bunch of crazy sons of bitches just dancing. I really felt like the ground was going to split open and we were all going straight to hell. I had never read anything about black magic or devil worship but I felt a sense of evil. I attribute 99 per cent of it to the drugs but it's weird that I felt that, having read nothing about the band's supposed satanic roots. I really felt like this was going too far – too weird, too scary. I went back to the camp site after that. I was done for the evening. To this day I don't think I've seen anything as intense as that. I don't think the band were tripping, but everybody else was.

I bought the second album and liked it, but not as much as the first album. I think he's a cool guy but Robert Plant's voice started getting on my nerves. He screeches too fucking much. I really lost interest by the third album. I did get to meet Jimmy Page. I had a guitar shop here in town and I spent about an hour with him, talking not about Led Zeppelin or even The Yardbirds, but about the Cyril Davies blues band and all that early English blues stuff. We talked about a bass player called Cliff Barton, who died really young. He was the cat in England who is the reason that all the English guys were such great bass players, because they all learned from him.

I WAS THERE: CHRISSY BEAN, AGE 21

I was a college student in Florida and their first album knocked me sideways, upside down and inside out. I could not play it enough. So along came this event called the First Atlanta Pop Festival, a month or so before Woodstock. There had been a few festivals before that but all smaller than this one turned out to be – something like 400,000 very stoned freaks! No one knew how to prepare for something like this. We decided to go with just the clothes on our backs.

Other greats were on the bill like Janis, Joe Cocker, Spirit, Creedence, Canned Heat and Sweetwater, but it was Zep I wanted to see. There was a general idea of what bands were playing on what days, but times weren't even thought about – everyone was very high! Zep were to be on the stage on day two. I lost my companions early on the second day but I didn't care. When the skies turned dark, the buzz was going around that Zep would hit the stage soon. I wound my way from the back of the extremely stoned crowd of hundreds of thousands of people, determined to get right in front of the stage. I was so wrecked that I thought the music coming out of the loudspeakers was a band playing onstage, but that was just the roadies. When I hit front centre stage, I realised that and it freaked me out. But I had no idea who they were setting up for.

Around 9pm, first out was Robert Plant. He was maybe ten feet away and ten feet up from me. I pretty much zoned totally out for the next two hours. I was aware of nothing but Plant's unreal vocals and the booming drums of Bonzo. I was in ecstasy. They were out of this world and I knew I was witnessing something that I would remember all my life – and I'm 71 now! Robert was scintillatingly hot, shining like a lion, master of his vocal range, wearing a tight t-shirt and even tighter jeans. He was commanding everyone, 'Hear me, watch me!' Oh Lord, that voice! There was nothing like it in this world. They played every song on the first album and were having a great time. I was in heaven.

Then Robert said that they were about to put out a second album and would we like to hear it? They then proceeded to sing every one of those songs, which had never been heard before, at least in the USA. For two hours those guys played and sang and had the crowd whipped into a total frenzy, many of whom hadn't heard much from them before that night. How they had missed them, I don't know, just different tastes in music or something. I never took my eyes off Robert Plant. He remains seared into my brain forever. Oh yeah, he 'shook me'.

When Zep finally ended their set, I was in a swoon of joy. I could still hear them. I could not move for about 15 minutes, but time meant nothing on good, heavy acid. Eventually a huge roar went up and Janis Joplin stumbled out – literally. She was so wasted she couldn't walk. For many, she was the big star of the show; they had waited for her. For me, it was just too much. I was Zepped out. I had the best 'seat' in the house (of course, there were no seats and everyone just stood up most of the time), front row, centre stage, but I had to get out of there or I'd go crazy. I felt like Led Zeppelin had crashed into all the cells in my body. And I loved it. I still do.

NEWPORT JAZZ FESTIVAL
6 JULY 1969, NEWPORT, RHODE ISLAND

I WAS THERE: JANN M SCOTT

I had their first album so I knew their sound. But to hear them live at Newport was something else. We got there on the Saturday. Friday had turned out to be a riot and there was the smell of tear gas everywhere. The jazz festival was transforming from strictly jazz to rock. Led Zeppelin came on about 9pm. We were sitting on the hillside and they had a big sound system. The festival had a huge number of attendees. People were overflowing from the seats in the amphitheatre to the hillsides all around. We were sitting on a blanket, drinking some wine, smoking some dope, dropping some LSD-25 and listening to Led Zeppelin tear up the night sky.

I WAS THERE: FRANK MARTINELLI

They entered the stage very late. I think it was about 1am. I remember a concert-goer sitting on the top of the fence yelling out, 'Jimmy Page, turn up your amp!' He must have said it ten times. Finally, Jimmy turned up his amp and the rest is history. What a great performance. Tickets were $5.

I WAS THERE: DAVE LIVINGSTON, AGE 14

The show was at Festival Field. There was a tall fence surrounding the property but we watched for free on a large grassy hill that overlooked the stage. We were young but liked what we heard. Lots of rock bands showed up at the jazz and folk festivals in Newport, such as Jethro Tull and Sly and the Family Stone. Those were magical times. I went to two other Zep shows – the next one was in Providence, Rhode Island and they opened up with 'Rock And Roll'. Jimmy Page was just awesome.

LAUREL POP FESTIVAL, LAUREL RACETRACK
11 JULY 1969, LAUREL, MARYLAND

I WAS THERE: CAROLYN TRAVIS

I discovered their music when I was a freshman at the University of Miami. They played at a club there in early '69. I was out of town that night, but everyone who went was talking about them, so I bought the album. I saw them along with Johnny Winter, Jethro Tull and Al Kooper. The second night was Sly and the Family Stone, Jeff Beck, The Guess Who and a couple of others. It was the very early days of music festivals, so it's a bit of a blur of seeing so many acts I loved in one place. I remember being pretty close to the front. The whole venue only held 14,000-15,000 people and the tickets being $10. The energy in their live performance was the thing that sticks in my mind.

I WAS THERE: BARBARA NELSEN

The Laurel Pop Festival was held over two nights at the Laurel Racetrack. This was loads of fun because the bands just kept coming, one after another. There was hardly any security so I wandered around the backstage area and met members of several bands, including Jimmy Page. He was very intimidating – he just did not seem happy to be there. I said 'hello' and he sort of waved me into the band tent but then I saw one of my favourite musicians, Al Kooper, walking by so I just waved back at Page and took off to talk to Al.

I WAS THERE: MARC CLARK

The venue was the centre of a horse race track. There was a large stage on the field and rows and rows of folding chairs. There were many other entertainers and groups playing at this gathering. However, the Zep were the major draw and the closing act.

Prior to Zeppelin's opening song, the lights surrounding the performance stage and their equipment went totally black. What was stranger was that the entire crowd became eerily silent. A hush fell over the everyone. Then things erupted. The lights flashed on and bigger than life stood Robert Plant, Jimmy Page, John Bonham and John Paul Jones.

The world changed in an instant. Hard driving, wild moving, over the top guitar playing, faster than lightning drum rhythms, bass notes equally as fast as the lead guitar and vocals from another realm. It was an incredible display of talent, raw and pumping from the heart. Once the group started playing, the audience were brought to their feet and no one sat down again.

Zep played for close to an hour before the authorities came on stage and told the concert-goers that due to a sound ordinance the concert would be ending. The power to the stage was turned off and the music stopped. However, with the power off the lights went off also and no one could leave the concert area. When the lights were turned back on to aid people in finding the field exits, Jimmy Page immediately went into playing 'Communication Breakdown' and the place went wild. They stretched this song to 30 minutes. My second-row centre seat cost me $14. What an experience.

SPECTRUM POP FESTIVAL
12 JULY 1969, PHILADELPHIA, PENNSYLVANIA

I WAS THERE: STAN DENSKI

I remember Al Kooper in a sort of rhinestone Elvis suit playing a Gibson Flying V guitar for part of his set. I remember Ian Anderson prancing. I remember Jimmy Page playing the dragon Telecaster with the violin bow. I don't remember any songs specifically. I do remember the crowd's ecstatic response to their set.

SINGER BOWL
13 JULY 1969, NEW YORK, NEW YORK

I WAS THERE: NIC REEGER

After the Fillmore East in May, I saw a show at the Singer Bowl, which was the World's Fair site from 1964 in Queens, with The Edwin Hawkins Singers, Ten Years After, The Jeff Beck Group with Rod Stewart and Ronnie Wood and headliners The Vanilla Fudge. When Jeff Beck came on, he did amazing stuff from *Beck-Ola* and was joined on stage by Carmine Appice, Alvin Lee's drummer Ric Lee and Jimmy Page, Robert Plant and John Bonham! Four drummers playing! I had to pinch myself to see if I was dreaming. They did 'Train Kept A-Rollin'' and Bonzo stripped down to his Union Jack briefs and had to be carried out on his drum stool because he wouldn't stop playing. He was still swinging his drumsticks!

The last time I saw them was at Sheep Meadow in Central Park. I smoked a lot of hash that day so I don't remember too much other than 'Whole Lotta Love' and 'The Lemon Song'. Plant's voice back then was other worldly. I did see John Paul Jones about ten years ago, when *Zooma* came out, and he's just an amazing musician who I believe wrote some of the best Zeppelin riffs.

I WAS THERE: STEPHEN WARNE

I wanted to see the Jeff Beck Group with Rod Stewart and saw that they were playing this gig at Singer Bowl. Vanilla Fudge headlined and the opening act was a gospel group called the Edwin Hawkins Singers – famous for 'Oh, Happy Day' – followed by Ten Years After. The show started in the late afternoon and went on into the evening, finishing around 11pm. When Jeff Beck came out it suddenly seemed to get dark and the spotlights came on making it appear like a polished kind of performance. Right towards the end of their set they started to play 'Jailhouse Rock'. Jeff Beck wandered behind his amplifiers and brought a guy out and it was Jimmy Page, holding an old-fashioned martini glass. Zeppelin were really new at the time but I had seen them at the Fillmore East the previous winter. Jeff Beck put one of his guitars around Jimmy, who began laughing and put his cocktail down and started playing. So now they're both playing guitar and who steps out but Robert Plant? So now Robert Plant is sharing the microphone with Rod Stewart.

Then John Bonham came out. He must have been pretty wasted because he was falling all over the drum kit. He started playing drums but also taking his clothes off. So he's playing and laughing and throwing his shirt off, and then he started taking his pants off revealing the black stretch shorts he had on for underwear. It looked like a bathing suit. He carried on playing, sat down at the drum kit, and then someone came up behind him and pulled his shorts down, so now his ass was hanging out. It was just this cacophony of colours and sounds.

I WAS THERE: REGINA M WILEY, AGE 18

I went with a friend and we met the photographer Neal Preston whilst waiting on line to enter the venue and he invited us to sit in the press box. Led Zep played first, opening for Ten Years After. After Page played, he came over to the press box and asked if he could sit with me. Neal took our picture and it was shown in *Creem* magazine.

KINETIC PLAYGROUND
18 JULY 1969, CHICAGO, ILLINOIS

I WAS THERE: THOMAS FILIP, AGE 17

The third Zeppelin show that year, and the best of those I saw, had Jethro Tull, Savoy Brown and The Litter in support. Kim Simmonds told me some years later, after a Savoy Brown show, how he and Plant got into a punch up backstage, as apparently RP was telling all how he was the 'real deal blues singer' and everyone else a pretender. Kim rightfully took exception. I think it was this show where Zep introduced 'Heartbreaker' and I was absolutely gobsmacked watching Page play the middle part (well, actually the entire song but especially the breakdown) as I'd never seen anyone play guitar in that manner. To this day I can see it in my mind's eye and it remains my favourite Zep song, which is not easy to say as there are so many.

I WAS THERE: STEVEN CHARLES, AGE 17

I have very powerful, life-changing memories of the night I saw them. It was in a cool psychedelic club in Chicago, kind of like our version of the Fillmore, but it wasn't so much a theatre as an experience. Everyone sat on the floor, and they had a circular light show booth just under the ceiling in the middle of the showroom, so it was a 360-degree light show, as they had projectors placed all around the booth. The club even had some smaller, more private 'meditation rooms'. I don't remember if there was a bar, as I was too young to drink.

But I did drop acid, that very night, for the first time... I went there by myself (as I often did, during that year and a half or so, I'd drop acid and then attend a concert), because while tripping, it was useless for me to attempt a conversation, and I didn't want to be distracted from just soaking in all the sound and energy coming off the stage...

I don't remember which band I most came to see. It was probably Zep, as their incredible first album had been out for a while, with the second one just about to drop. The line-up was Jethro Tull, Zeppelin and then Savoy Brown headlining! Quite a pair of opening acts... and all for a whole five bucks!

Tull were awesome – once I got over just how totally weird they all looked, dressed as lumberjack leprechauns with their bushy hair, beards and flannel shirts. Ian, of course, was on fire as were the band. I loved their very first album. It was pretty jazzy as well as rocking.

Zeppelin just totally blew me away. I was sitting on the floor, maybe 15 or 20 feet from the stage, on my first acid trip, so the deep heaviness of their psychedelicised version of the blues resonated deep within my body and psyche.

Even though I had seen Jimi Hendrix the year before, this was something else altogether, not better, but on the same level and with their personal flavour. I still remember the slowly descending, booming bass notes of the intro to 'Dazed And Confused' and how intense Plant's singing was to begin with and, as the tempo picked up, him adding some wailing riffs, egging on Page's fiery soloing.

I don't even remember what Savoy Brown played, or what I thought about their performance, as Tull and Zeppelin were so amazing.

Watching old Zeppelin videos, you'd have to call some of what they were doing 'jazz', just as with Cream and some others, because the freedom and abandon and the spontaneity of the interplay between Plant and Page was similar to an improvisational jazz singer and an instrumentalist. Zeppelin's first album will remain my all-time favourite. It's the most blues influenced and was recorded while they were still hungry and while Plant was stretching and growing.

SCHAEFER MUSIC FESTIVAL, CENTRAL PARK
21 JULY 1969, NEW YORK, NEW YORK

I WAS THERE: ARNIE GOODMAN

This was a show where they blew the roof off. It was the best show that I ever saw them do and I used to see them pretty much every time they came through town or the New York area. In June 1972 they did two shows at the Nassau Coliseum. Central Park and Nassau Coliseum were the best two shows I ever saw them play. I went to two of the nights where they recorded the live record at Madison Square Garden – those shows didn't kill me.

I saw two Page and Plant shows at the Meadowlands in New Jersey and I thought they were very disappointing. The shows, with the orchestra, didn't have the energy of Led Zeppelin. I thought that took away from what Led Zeppelin were about. Robert Plant? On the one hand here's a guy who doesn't want to do Led Zeppelin but on the other hand he's still doing Led Zeppelin songs.

The thing I like about Led Zeppelin, especially that period in the early seventies, was that they'd come on and they'd sit down and do that acoustic set in the middle – and they were doing a long set. One of my favourite bootlegs of theirs was the *Blueberry Hill* bootleg. My favourite Led Zeppelin record was the first album. You could go to clubs like the Marquee or Eel Pie Island and see a lot of these bands around at the venues.

Led Zeppelin are one of the few bands that have somehow crossed over to a younger generation. Some bands draw people but not a younger audience. If Led Zeppelin toured again, they would draw a younger audience.

PNE AGRODOME
26 JULY 1969, VANCOUVER, CANADA

I WAS THERE: CHRISTINE BURSEY, AGE 13

I saw them three times. My favourite memory is of the first concert, when Jimmy Page used a bow on his guitar in the song 'Dazed And Confused'. The echo was unforgettable.

I WAS THERE: LAURA PASSENGER

I went to a lot of concerts back in the day and that Zeppelin concert was by far the most memorable. Even after they had turned on the house lights after the encores, the audience continued with the standing ovation and applause. Apparently the band were about to leave the building, but came back again to do one more song. They were very tight, with no flaws with the music or performance. I'll never forget it.

SEATTLE POP FESTIVAL, GOLD CREEK PARK
27 JULY 1969, WOODINVILLE, WASHINGTON

I WAS THERE: ERIC LAWRENCE, AGE 16

I had heard them on the radio quite a bit and was already a fan when I saw them at the Gold Creek Dome, which was quite a small venue. A friend bought tickets. I remember the crowd was fun and everyone was psyched for the show. I had seen a few concerts before, but this was the best and it actually got me into playing music. I took my brother to see them the next time they came, in '77 at the Kingdome in Seattle. A favourite song? I love 'Kashmir', 'Dazed And Confused' and 'Achilles Last Stand'.

KINSMEN FIELD HOUSE
29 JULY 1969, EDMONTON, CANADA

I WAS THERE: TIM DANCY

I saw them at the Gardens then in Edmonton the following July at a different, terrible venue. They shared billing with Vanilla Fudge. It was a great show once again. Top tickets were under $4.

I WAS THERE: LES VAUGHAN, AGE 16

They were the opening act for Vanilla Fudge, who were riding high on their hit 'You Keep Me Hanging On'. Tickets were $3 (Canadian) and I attended with my buddy Chris Walker. We purchased tickets at the door. I'd already heard of them through shortwave Radio Luxembourg. From that show on I bought every Zeppelin release on vinyl. I still have them!

I WAS THERE: ROSS CABLE

The venue was a sports field house and the crowd was about 5,000 strong, small by today's standards. I had a heightened sense of awareness due to some white blotter LSD, but remember the show very well. It was festival seating, so we could stand in front of the stage or sit in bleachers. The band absolutely blew me away. They were promoting their second album and played most of the first. What sticks in my head to this day is 'How Many More Times'. Vanilla Fudge were also on the bill and their drummer, Carmen Appice, sat in on the last part. The intro just shook the building and had us all on our feet. Fudge went on after Led Zep, but it should have been the other way around. Both bands were great and were two of my favourites but Led Zep were rock gods. No question. They had appeared in Edmonton two months prior in a different venue and got better reviews for that show, which they headlined. I'm pissed to this day that I missed it.

'Dazed And Confused' also rings in my brain like it was yesterday. Watching Jimmy Page wield a violin bow was mesmerising. None of us had ever seen anything like it.

The show was so close and so personal on every level, it was like we were at a private party with the biggest band in the world. It was an awesome experience I will take to my grave, happily and with gratitude for having experienced these legends before they became the monster band we all know today. It was inspirational. I went home and put both *I* and *II* on the turntable, cranked it, and learned both albums to the best of my ability on my drums. I still occasionally put on both albums, crank the hell out of it and dance around the house like a little kid!

CIVIC AUDITORIUM
2 AUGUST 1969, ALBUQUERQUE, NEW MEXICO

I WAS THERE: CARMINE RUSSO

I saw them twice in Albuquerque and there was a huge difference in the two shows. In 1969 my older brothers had just come home from spending the summer in New York, and they brought the Jimi Hendrix Experience, The Doors, Janice Joplin, Cream… and the first Led Zeppelin album. After hearing that and then hearing that they were coming to town, I got tickets. In their first show, they were like any rock band... no glitter and glam, just casual dress. They only had the one album, and they played it all, but it wasn't enough material to get them through the night, so they ended up jamming on a few cover tunes, like 'Johnny B Goode' by Chuck Berry. To me that was extra special, since after 1969, they'd never need to do that again. They were relaxed and had fun.

The Civic Auditorium could hold up to 6,000 people and it was basically sold out; not many sat behind, or on the sides of the stage, but those who did walk around back there could get up very close to the band on stage... about 50 feet away. I'm guessing that there were about 5,000 people at that show. The Civic was round, and the building was built for basketball and had a round 'floor space' surrounded by chairs upstairs, so those who went down the circular ramps to the floor could get all the way up to the stage, about six feet high above the people on the floor, and some got to see the show just ten feet away from the band. From when Vanilla Fudge opened the show to when Led Zeppelin ended it, the crowd was treated to a great time and people were up and dancing in the aisles.

The warm up band was Vanilla Fudge, who were also fabulous. This show was one of the few that had John Bonham using a double bass drum kit, and both bands used the same drums, so they may have belonged to Carmine Appice. Sometimes one of Albuquerque's many top-notch bands was the support act, and other times the warm up band was quasi-famous.

After four years and with a few more albums to add to their first, Led Zeppelin came back to Albuquerque. They sold out again, but this time they were playing at the PIT Stadium. The excitement in the air was thick. It was the basketball area for the University of New Mexico so there were over 14,000 people there and only the space to the sides and back of the stage were roped off. I don't remember who opened the '73 show, but when Zep came out, everyone was getting high just from all the secondhand pot smoke that filled the building, and when the main lights went out, the crowd started screaming. When they came on stage you could see by how they were dressed that they had become very successful, with lots of glamour. It was a fabulous show from beginning to end.

I WAS THERE: CODY SAUCEDO

I was a junior in high school. About three of us had heard of them. 'Communication Breakdown' was my favourite song. Vanilla Fudge opened for them. There were a lot of empty seats. They came back next year to a full house.

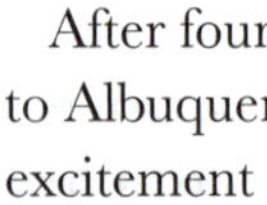

STATE FAIR COLISEUM
4 AUGUST 1969, DALLAS, TEXAS

I WAS THERE: JOYCE BRASWELL-KAFER

Me and a bunch of friends saw Led Zeppelin for the first time on the front row at the horse arena at the State Fair of Dallas, Texas. It's the only time I saw a group in the horse arena and that's why it's so memorable. Plus, after hearing them for the first time, I said, 'These guys are going to make it.' I'm glad I saw them, but Robert's hair was so long I couldn't see his face!

SWING AUDITORIUM
8 AUGUST 1969, SAN BERNADINO, CALIFORNIA

I WAS THERE: TONY KING

I lived, and still live, half an hour from the Swing Auditorium site, where loads of big rock bands played. If we couldn't afford to buy a ticket we would go and hang out in a big grassed area right outside. Lots of people would do this, a big party of people who loved music and smoked pot and had a great time. We were all peaceful, never causing any trouble. Honestly? We weren't all crazy that Led Zeppelin were playing because we got to see so many big rock bands play. But they definitely rocked the place.

My older brother had his first car with an 8-track tape player and we didn't have much money to buy tapes so for quite a while he only had two that we totally wore out playing over and over – Creedence Clearwater's *Bayou Country* and Led Zeppelin's first album. To this day, I can't hear any of those songs and not think of being in high school in the late sixties. Good times, for sure. Our parents feared that music that we loved. Nowadays, looking at all we did, it seems pretty darned harmless compared to today's world. We never harmed anything or anybody. And here I am now at 64 sitting in my garage listening to classic rock. It is the best era in music ever!

I WAS THERE: MIKE LOPEZ, AGE 14

My friends and I had seats front row and centre stage. I recall seeing Jimmy Page swinging and dancing across the stage with his Les Paul. They played a lot of material from the first album. I also saw Led Zeppelin at the Inglewood Forum twice in 1973, and Jimmy Page and the Black Crowes at the Greek Theatre in Los Angeles. I have a man cave featuring hundreds of items of Led Zeppelin memorabilia and tattoos of the four symbols of each member on my upper right arm. My most valuable Led Zeppelin item is a song sheet of 'Stairway To Heaven' with a certificate of authenticity. There are a few moments in my life I will always remember. The most memorable might be when I was in the audience at the Ace Hotel in Los Angeles in 2014 and saw the personal interview with Chris Cornell and Jimmy Page. I got my Jimmy Page book and his personal stamp autograph of Zoso.

ANAHEIM CONVENTION CENTER

9 AUGUST 1969, ANAHEIM, CALIFORNIA

I WAS THERE: CHAD J REYNOLDS

Two months later I was going to be in the US Army headed for Vietnam training, but I was there in August 1969. This show is my first love. Zeppelin were still hungry. To kick it all in gear, Jethro Tull were opening, and both bands had only two albums out at the time. I saw Zep in '75 and '77 in LA as well, and Page and Plant ripped the roof off. But because Tull were there in '69, the roof was already gone so Zep flattened the perimeter walls!

I WAS THERE: ALAN BUFFINGTON

I was going to high school at Corona Del Mar High School in Newport Beach, California. My friend had an older sister who told us to go and see a band that was going to play at University of California for free on lawn by the dorms. It was the late sixties, and music was our life in a period of creative expansion. Bob Romney and I went over to UCI (University of California Irvine) a couple of miles away. As we walked up on the crowd of about 300 to 400 people, we heard them. Nothing could have prepared you for the musical transformation we witnessed. There were the aged Beatles, The Young Rascals, Beach Boys, Motown, and the Stones. 'Communication Breakdown' floored us. Wide-open throttle music that was impossible not to enjoy.

The next night I was on a date with my girlfriend Cathy. We were driving around her home town of Anaheim looking for a movie or friends to hang out with. As we went by the Anaheim Convention Center I saw the billboard 'Jethro Tull and Led Zeppelin'.

The show had already started but we decided to go and managed to scrape together enough for the tickets. Since it was already underway, we got lucky and were seated five rows back from the stage. Jethro Tull was an amazing first act with a unique style that still stands up to this day. When Led Zeppelin came on, many weren't aware of what was to happen next. The future of rock and roll displayed talent that may never be matched. We sat a little off centre in front of Jimmy Page. From that moment I knew I wanted a Gibson Les Paul and to figure out how he made a guitar sound so good. When he brought out the violin bow on 'Dazed And Confused', it was an example of creative expertise. I went out and bought the black and white album the next day. I bought two more after wearing out the first with non-stop playing.

I WAS THERE: BOOM BAKER, AGE 22

I first discovered Led Zeppelin when I visited a record store in Hollywood, California that specialised in English imported albums. They turned me onto Cream before the American release of their first album hit the stores. The first time I dropped a needle on 'Good Times Bad Times', I was blown away by Jimmy Page's guitar chords. When the rest of the band kick in, it takes you into the stratosphere. It was unlike any musical performance at that time. It was like you were hearing a new kind of music that was also very familiar with its roots steeped deep in the blues. You felt this was something special.

My college roommate went with me to the Anaheim show. Tickets were $6.50 purchased at Wallich's Music City in Hollywood. Many who attended the Anaheim Convention Center concert have hailed this show as one of the best concerts ever experienced at the time. It was because everything lined up for an over-the-top, highly charged show. No one wanted to open for Zeppelin because they were blowing everyone off the stage. Yet Jethro Tull opened that night and because they were courageous and even a bit unusual with their eccentric front man, Ian Anderson, they pulled it off and set the stage for Led Zeppelin to take their show to another level. And did they ever!

Anderson led Jethro Tull through a seven-song set with five songs off their forthcoming album, *Stand Up*, and two songs from their first album, *This Was*. He bobbed and weaved like a contortionist, often playing the flute while standing on one leg, all the while swaying to and fro. By the time Led Zeppelin took the stage, the crowd was fired up with excitement and anticipation. We were still reeling from the exceptional set Jethro Tull had just performed. The Zeppelin boys picked up on the energy in the room right away with their opening number, 'Train Kept-A-Rollin''. Next up was a slow Willie Dixon blues song, 'I Can't Quit You Baby', with Page playing a sunburst Gibson Les Paul. This song had some inspired bottom end drumming and bass.

'Dazed And Confused' started out with a mournful bass from John Paul Jones and Page using his wah-wah pedal with his Fender Telecaster guitar. Then Page kicked in with distortion on his guitar like we had never heard. What followed were some power chords and back to the distorted lead, with Plant giving the song full force vocals. Next was the moment you had to put on your seatbelt, when Page started playing his guitar with a violin bow, creating sounds that were sonically out of this world. Then the tempo picked up with everyone playing in hyperdrive but all in sync. As the song was building, they turned on the house lights so the band could see the audience. The place was about to exploded with excitement. Bonham's drumming was like nothing you had ever experienced. I thought Ginger Baker of Cream was a great drummer but man, oh man, Bonham was coming from some place magical.

During 'White Summer/Black Mountain Side' the band left the stage and let Jimmy Page sit with his Danelectro guitar and simply impress us with his guitar skills. What a tour-de-force! Next was the Willie Dixon song, 'You Shook Me', which opened with Plant playing harmonica with some very nice slide work from Page. There was a wonderful call-and-response with Page's guitar and Plant's vocals on this one.

Plant was wearing a fringed vest with no shirt and tight pants that rode low on his hips. The song 'How Many More Times' started out, with Page playing some mighty fine power chords. Plant's voice and Page's guitar were running on the same railroad track, just moving slowly and sultrily down that track, and they picked up speed. The song morphed into several other songs – 'Rosie', 'The Hunter' and several John Lee Hooker songs.

During Page's guitar solo later in the song, Plant started a slow gyration with the mic hanging from his hand just below his waist band. Because he was wearing such tight pants, it became apparent his flaccid manhood was now becoming semi-erect and bulging. The woman dancing with her boyfriend in front of me was so moved that she slid off her panties and flung them towards the stage. The energy and the erotic atmosphere were something like I had never experienced. Plant went into a trance and sang, 'Everybody wants it...old people want it, young people want it... oh my baby... no there's another thing, just one little thing that everybody needs and everybody needs so bad… I want ya, I need ya... squeeze my lemon until the juice runs down my leg... that's what my momma said… I said you can do it so hard... I'm pretty sure you gonna knock 'em dead.' Then the song slowed down: 'Now... now... now... I've got you in the sights.' The song seemed to go on for ever.

The song culminated into a musical orgasm. By the time the band dosed with 'Communication Breakdown', we were all spent. The vibe in the audience was that we had gone on a journey to a far, far, faraway place and it felt wonderful.

I WAS THERE: IAN ANDERSON, JETHRO TULL

The interesting reality is that the bands who made it big in America back then didn't give a shit. First of all, Cream. They barnstormed across the USA. They didn't give a shit whether the Americans liked or loathed them. They went on stage and did their show, and didn't seek approval. Same thing with Zeppelin. They were a bunch of Viking raiders, pillaging and plundering. They didn't care what people thought. They just went on and did their show as if they were doing it for them.

During our second North American tour in the summer of '69, we supported Led Zeppelin on some shows, and during the next couple of years we again appeared as an opening act with Led Zeppelin. It was a good opportunity to see a band that was a year ahead of us in terms of building a reputation in the USA. You couldn't watch Led Zeppelin and not pick up some useful tips. The most useful tip I picked up was don't try to be Robert Plant. I didn't look like him, I didn't do that kind of strutting cockrock vocalist thing and there's no way I could have sung anything remotely within his range. Robert Plant was in a very unique stratosphere of his own when it came to his vocals. Led Zeppelin really knew how to create excitement with a dynamic range and the impetus they got from quiet passages suddenly becoming symphonic loud. I watched them a few times, not from the wings but from somewhere in the venue, and it was always an illustrative experience to see how they worked.

It didn't always go well. Zeppelin had bad nights, the same as Jimi Hendrix had terrible nights. They weren't all great shows. And you learn what it is that went wrong and how it affected the band and how they responded to the difficulties, whether they were technical or being upset with something musically, or the audience or whatever. It was interesting and educational to see how things could go wrong even for great talents. You would expect every night would be a winner, but it wasn't always like that.

I WAS THERE: CHAD REYNOLDS

Just after I graduated from high school in June 1969, I was given tickets to see the mighty Zep with Jethro Tull as a warm up band. Each had only one album out at the time and were promoting their second. I thought nobody could follow Ian Anderson and Mick Abrahams. The lights went down and a single light focused on a mass of blond hair. Plant grabbed the mic and said 'good evening'. Zep then proceeded to rip the roof off. l saw Zep two times after that, in San Diego in 1975 when it was general admission and I was about five feet from Page's feet, and then Los Angeles Forum in 1977. This show is probably the best live performance I ever saw.

I WAS THERE: STEPHEN PEELER, AGE 15

The live show was soooo much different (and better) than the record, even the records that I loved. I have been to thousands of concerts since but this show still ranks at or near the top. My girlfriend's parents drove us. The Anaheim Convention Center is a medium-sized venue that seats about 7,500. Our tickets cost $2.50. After Tull's set, I thought, 'Wow, this is crazy and this great.' Anderson was already the consummate entertainer. Then Zep came on. It was crazy loud. The cheap seats turned out to be great seats.

We were four rows up from the stage and directly behind the stage. Luckily for us, Page spent a good portion of the show with his back to the audience and facing us! 'White Summer/Black Mountain Side' was Page alone in a chair on stage. Unbelievable. More unbelievable was the back and forth between Page and Plant during 'You Shook Me'. Plant would do a multi-octave scream and Page would play the exact notes. Page would do a screaming solo and Plant would sing it. Like the album, 'How Many More Times' was a medley of a bunch of other songs including some that weren't on the album. 'Communication Breakdown' killed it to end the night. I couldn't sleep that night, my ears were ringing so badly. 49 years later they still are.

SPORTS ARENA
10 AUGUST 1969, SAN DIEGO, CALIFORNIA

I WAS THERE: BEA GREEN

The *San Diego Union-Tribune* ran an ad that Led Zeppelin would be performing at the San Diego Sports Arena. I trotted myself over to Chula Vista to get tickets. The anticipation was incredible and almost unbearable. I had to find the perfect thing to wear. It was a beautiful tunic top with fringe on the sleeves and around the bottom, bell bottoms and the perfect leather sandals. So when the day of the concert came I was looking hot and ready to get blown away by the music.

We were walking around outside the grounds of the arena and I remember slipping my wallet with the tickets in it into my pocket. When we got to the ticket booth my wallet was gone. A multitude of expletives escaped my lips, and panic and a cold sweat ensued. I managed to tell the guy in the ticket booth what section, row and seat numbers we had. Yes, I had all the information memorised! He told me he would be on the lookout if anyone tried to claim the seats. I decided then and there I was not going to miss the concert. I started panhandling, telling people that my wallet had been stolen. After an hour of panhandling, I had enough money to get us back in. I went back to the ticket booth and found out that no one had claimed the seats. The guy let us in on my word alone.

What happened after that was a total mind-blowing concert to end all concerts.

Jethro Tull were on stage with Ian Anderson rocking the place with his flute, vocals and amazing ballet moves. The air was thick with the smell of weed. The joints were being passed down the rows, one after another, and the cops didn't care.

When Led Zeppelin came out on stage, the place went wild and the magic began. Robert Plant's voice was commanding. Jimmy Page's guitar riff simply blew you away but when he brought out the bow and started dragging it across his guitar strings there was this audible gasp of realisation that it was this that made that incredible sound in the song 'Dazed And Confused'. It was a real 'holy shit' moment. I remember Robert Plant being congenial but because of the density of the smoke in the place and my need to breathe I can honestly say I have no idea what he said. We were all so wrapped up in the music (and the smoke) he could have yelled 'bomb!' and no one would have moved.

They finished their set but the audience wouldn't let them go. They came out and played another song. After the concert we went out to dinner on my panhandling funds and relived the concert. In October of that same year, my wallet was mailed back to me in El Paso with my tickets still in it but minus the $50 I had in there.

HEMISFAIR ARENA
15 AUGUST 1969, SAN ANTONIO, TEXAS

I WAS THERE: DAVID SUMNERS

The opening act was Jethro Tull and they were fantastic, incredibly tight with a great sound.

Zep sounded like a garage band. They were sloppy, missed changes and had a messy sound. To compound their problems, a local radio station was getting picked up through their amps on stage, which was very distracting and Jimmy Page was not happy. To their credit, at the end Robert Plant walked to the edge of the stage and said to the audience, 'I'm sorry we sounded so bad. Jethro Tull was much better than us and we will try harder next time.' Kudos to him for being honest.

I WAS THERE: RON DOOLITTLE

They had a problem with the sound system so they didn't play much. Thankfully, the warm-up group, an up and coming band called Jethro Tull, blew us away.

CONVENTION HALL
16 AUGUST 1969, ASBURY PARK, NEW JERSEY

I WAS THERE: PHYLLIS FOX, AGE 16

Growing up, I spent every summer at my uncle's hotel in Asbury Park, New Jersey. We heard that Led Zeppelin and Joe Cocker were coming to do a gig at Convention Hall on the Boardwalk. All of my friends went there, bought tickets and waited for their limo to drive up to the stage entrance door. One of my girlfriends was tall, blonde and gorgeous! As they pulled by us the limo stopped, the rear window rolled down and Jimmy Page reached out to my friend. She hopped in the limo and about 20 minutes later came over to us and whispered in my ear, 'I just gave Jimmy Page a blowjob.' Then she shouted it out for everyone to hear!

I WAS THERE: GLEN PARTUSCH, AGE 12

For the first show you could just walk up to the door and buy a ticket for $5.50. The second show was pretty much a sell-out.

I WAS THERE: PAM DELISA

I kept the ticket. I couldn't believe someone had scribbled on the back of the ticket (Jimmy and Robert had written 'Love to Pam'). I must have been so excited about getting kissed by Robert Plant that I forgot I had gotten the autographs.

THE ROCK PILE
18 AUGUST 1969, TORONTO, CANADA

I WAS THERE: MIKE PETRONIS

I saw Zeppelin at the Rock Pile. It was the same weekend as Woodstock. I say 'saw' but we didn't get into the venue as we didn't have the money, but we were outside at the back door with about three thousand other people, just listening to the music. They were so loud. One guy climbed up the south wall and onto the second floor with help from the people up there. They pulled him up as the cops tried to grab his legs but he made it. The crowds cheered! That was awesome...

I saw them again at Maple Leaf Gardens in 1971. This time I was front row centre, rocking on with five thousand other people. At one point during the concert, Plant pointed at me as he was wailing out a tune. He looked at me and smiled and then kept on singing and bouncing around the stage. I'm sure he did that at every concert many times, but for it to happen to me still felt so cool.

And in 1985, Robert played at the CNE Grandstand with the Honeydrippers. There was nobody outside because everybody was inside at the concert. I was there with my girlfriend and my German Shepherd, Doug, when Robert's limo cruised silently up towards the back gate. He actually stopped the limo, my dog walked over to the car and Robert put his arm out and patted her and then went off on his way. Wow!

CAROUSEL THEATRE
21 AUGUST 1969, FRAMINGHAM, MASSACHUSETTS

I WAS THERE: TOM BRUNEAU

I was with a friend smoking hash on the hill behind the tent. They started with 'Train Kept A-Rollin'', and we ran down the hill and into the tent. We were in the last row of the front section, pretty good seats. They played the first album. It was jaw dropping. During 'Dazed And Confused', when the spotlights lit the band after the intro, I saw my little brother sitting on the stage next to Jonesy. I remember they had acoustic bass bins. The show was great. I saw them at the old Tea Party too. I had to leave after about three and a half hours because our ride was leaving. Zephyr opened the show and they were great too. That was a great year for rock and roll in Boston. There were venues everywhere and cool shows all the time. It was all good until the drugs and all the crime it brings ruined things in the early seventies.

I WAS THERE: DANA TETON, AGE 14

I was young, really young, and about five years into my barely post-pubescent, post-Beatles/Ed Sullivan lifelong musical odyssey. Framingham was about 30 miles from my teenage suburban home in Randolph, Massachusetts. This was way before the day when everybody had the sum of all past and current world knowledge in the palm of their hand, so how I found out about this concert, or ended up with tickets, is anybody's guess.

It's funny the things you do and don't remember. I remember the precise moment Led Zeppelin first seeped into my consciousness. This was about six months after the first album was released, around the time of this concert. There are not many records I've purchased over the years solely on the LP artwork and band name alone, but this was one of them, in the record department of the now defunct Lechmere's in Dedham, Massachusetts.

My memory is that me and my friends were driven by one of their parents to this show and that my dad had the return trip covered. But my friend Steve remembers that my dad took us there and back in his Mustang. There were four, or maybe six, of us.

Steve recalls that it was me, him, his then girlfriend Rhonda, my 'date' Karen and the now deceased Eric. Rhonda ultimately dumped Steve and married Eric. Steve believes I somehow got these tickets, but I have no memory of the logistics involved.

I do remember the concert, but filtered through the eyes of a musical neophyte 14-year-old whose grasp of what he was seeing had no historical context, and years before I had ever heard of The Yardbirds. One definitive, iconic image always comes up – Jimmy Page playing electric guitar with a violin bow in a circus tent in Framingham, Massachusetts. Soon to be wielding the Hammer of the Gods in massive arenas around the world. That definitely focused my attention. Watching old videos, this still blows my mind to this day.

The other very specific image I associate with this show is that my father had come to pick us up a bit early. I very distinctly remember him leaning up against a wall at the entrance/ exit, waiting to transport the suburban rat pack back to the peace and quiet of Randolph, and probably wondering what in the name of Satan was this dark vision?

'You Shook Me' indeed! That was the one and only time I ever saw Led Zeppelin, a few months before they took over the world. I don't think too many people can claim Led Zeppelin as their first concert. That was more likely to be a high school battle of the bands. I'm such a pack rat, I basically still have everything since the day I was born. So where's the ticket stub? Steve still has his.

I WAS THERE: ROBIN DEXTER

The Carousel Theater was a tented circular venue owned or booked by Frank Connolly, who later would become an early Aerosmith manager. We were in the front row. I mostly remember Robert Plant's flowing blond hair and them doing songs from the first album. It was the summer before I went to college. I must have purchased the tickets at a record store, or perhaps a ticket outlet located in a department store near the venue. At the end of the show, when the band was packing up, John Bonham was picking up a broken drumstick. I was already leaving and I looked to my left and my friend put out her hand for the drumstick and John handed it to her. I remember thinking, 'Why didn't I do that?' She still has the drumstick, but gave it to her brother for safe keeping.

I WAS THERE: IVAN LIPTON, AGE 14

Having seen them once at the Boston Tea Party, I was lucky enough to have a chance to see Led Zeppelin a second time later that summer. The Carousel Theater was a tent theatre that for many years had been used for what was known as 'summer stock' theatre, basically musical theatre productions. But they also booked musical acts, beginning earlier in the sixties with fairly middle-of-the-road acts who appealed to a straight adult audience. From around 1967, the Carousel began to mix in shows from lots of cool rock acts. In the 1967 and 1968 seasons, I had seen the Lovin' Spoonful, Jimi Hendrix, Soft Machine, Vanilla Fudge, the Mothers of Invention and probably a few others.

I went to this show with my older brother, who was 15. We lived two miles away in Cochituate, which was a village part of the larger town of Wayland, bordering Framingham. We may have hitchhiked to the show or possibly even walked there, and most likely our parents picked us up afterward. I don't have the ticket stub but I do have my Jimi Hendrix stub from the previous year, for which I paid $4.95, so my guess is Led Zeppelin was about the same.

The theatre was a fairly small tent located at the back of an expansive dirt parking lot. There were two small buildings at the edge of the parking lot, one where tickets were sold and another with concessions and possibly rest rooms. Behind the tent was another small building or trailer which was connected to the back of the tent and which served as the band's dressing rooms. A small hill surrounded the back of the venue, and local kids would often line the hill and listen to bands playing. The tent would become very hot in the summer, so they would roll up the outer side flaps of the tent to allow air flow. This allowed the music to be heard easily outside, and it also made it a very easy venue to sneak into. Several friends snuck into many shows there, including this one.

Inside the tent, the seating was on a tiered concrete foundation that circled around the stage, declining down to the small stage in the centre. The aisles radiated out from the centre, so each section was five seats across at the front row, but wider at the back. There were only about 30 rows of seats. I've seen sources that said the capacity was 2,500 to 3,000, but my guess is it was less than 2,000 people. There was a small orchestra pit on one side of the stage that was used for the musical theatre, and some of the aisles had ramps that went right across the pit up onto the stage.

Some bands who played the venue simply made a row of speakers across one side and played to one side of the venue. Everyone seated on the opposite side then had to come around and fill the aisles or find a place to watch the show from. This had been the set up when I sat in the front row and saw Jimi Hendrix the previous summer. But other bands attempted to set up 'in the round', positioning themselves and the amps so there were views of the band from all sides, and Zeppelin did this.

We had aisle seats in the second row, right in front of Robert Plant. We were on the side of the circular stage with no orchestra pit, so there were only about five feet between us and the lip of the very low stage, putting us close to the musicians. The emcee for the show was a deejay named JJ Jackson, one of the radio personalities on WBCN. Years later, when MTV first launched, he became nationally known as one of the original five MTV 'veejays'. I remember him speaking to the crowd several times throughout the evening.

The opening act was Orpheus, based in Worcester, Massachusetts and part of the local Boston underground music scene. They had had a fairly successful radio hit with the soft-rock song, 'Can't Find The Time' but I honestly don't recall anything of their set.

Led Zeppelin's set was incredible. Many of the recording sessions for the next album had already occurred and they played several songs from *Led Zeppelin II*. I recall 'What Is And What Should Never Be' and them saying it was the first time they had ever played it live. They also did 'The Lemon Song'. As when I saw them before, I distinctly remember where Jimmy sat down and played solo and did 'White Summer' and/or 'Black Mountain Side'. While he was playing, the other musicians lingered around beside the amps, some lighting cigarettes.

When the band finished, they did not immediately depart the stage but lingered around. Some of them tended to their gear, while JJ Jackson came back out and talked to the audience. I went up to the edge of the stage and shook Robert Plant's hand. I remember how sweaty it was!

That was the last concert I attended at the Carousel. I don't think they continued with music concerts much beyond 1969. The front building where the ticket office was burned down and the venue went out of business. But the remains of the seating and stage area remained on the site for the next decade. I visited it several times in the seventies and a talented photographer girlfriend even took some great pictures that showed the ruins of the staging, the seating, the tent poles, the dressing room building, etc. In the early eighties the site was razed and corporate office buildings built on it. It became the headquarters of Prime Computers and, after they went out of business, it was known as Carousel Office Park.

I WAS THERE: JIM MORIN

The combined indoor-outdoor setup made for great, balanced sound and its 3,000 or so seating capacity for an intimate experience. The hill next to the theatre was used by those not having tickets and this night it was totally packed, alarmingly so. My brother wanted to beat the traffic by leaving the show before the encore, 'Communication Breakdown'. It was my favourite track from the first album. It was a while before I forgave him.

I WAS THERE: STEVEN POFCHER

In elementary school and junior high, I was friends with Kane Roberts, who has played guitar for Alice Cooper and has his own solo career. His older brother turned us onto good music, including The Yardbirds. I was excited to hear that Led Zeppelin were coming to the US with Jimmy Page. I think they were called The New Yardbirds then. A few friends and I drove to the tent in Framingham. We had no tickets but knew that we would not need any. We were experts in sneaking into concerts. We had done it many times before. We had even snuck into Boston Garden to see the Rolling Stones. We thought the tent would be easy. We parked the car, walked to the back of the tent and rolled under it. It was a great show.

I WAS THERE: DANA SMITH

In high school, I was the keyboardist for a smalltown rock band that mostly played cover tunes. All the band members were constantly bringing in new music to consider. We all liked Jimmy Page's guitar work when he was in The Yardbirds so when Led Zeppelin appeared we thought that was fantastic. I played that record over and over. The day of the concert, one of my band mates and I hitchhiked 25 miles to get to the Carousel Theater. We went without having any tickets, figuring it was in a tent and the music would be loud enough to hear outside. I remember sitting on a fence before the show and a woman walked up to me and said, 'My friend couldn't attend the concert so I have an extra ticket.' I thought she'd wanted to sell it for an outrageous price but, no, she gave it to me for free! I turned to my friend and said 'see you later!' He understood, since it was one of my last concerts before going into the army. The show was sold out so he couldn't purchase a ticket that close to the show. Tickets were $5 to $7.

The woman who gave me the ticket was seated next to me and she only stayed for the opening band, Orpheus. I could not believe it! I was mesmerised when Led Zeppelin started to play. Every bit of that show was phenomenal. After their encore number, John Bonham threw his sticks into the audience and I managed to retrieve one.

I WAS THERE: STEVE BREMNER

I remember a three-hour long show, and the crowd attempting to rush the stage at the end. The security was sufficient to keep the boys safe, fortunately. As for the music, it was the first two albums they played. It's all kind of hazy now, but I remember I had a great time.

PIRATES WORLD
22 AUGUST 1969, DANIA, FLORIDA

I WAS THERE: RICK RYAN, AGE 15

In 1969, trip and go to shows is what we did. Pirates World had bands weekly and bands that played at Pirates World played both Friday and Saturday night. Led Zeppelin were no exception. We had decided we were going to see Led Zeppelin without really knowing who they were. We paid $4 for tickets in advance and went to the Friday night show. Those were heavy LSD times for me. Tripping, I was totally mesmerised. The venue was outdoors, so the sound wasn't one to be contained by a room. And the lighting. The blue spot lights on Jimmy Page and Robert Plant were mesmerising and unforgettable. The songs were also mesmerising. I can't use that word too much. We had to go again to see to the Saturday night show. Again, I was mesmerised. I have since discovered an audio of that very show that takes me right back there.

I WAS THERE: STEVE STACY, AGE 14

I saw them in 1969, at Pirates World, and in '72 or '73 at the Miami Beach Convention Center. The '69 concert was the first time I noticed a Les Paul as a guitar. It was after heavy rains so the grounds were wet and muddy. We were tripping (I was turning 15 that summer) and my overall impression was one of awe mixed with mystery because that was how important and mysterious that first album was to me.

JACKSONVILLE COLISEUM
24 AUGUST 1969, JACKSONVILLE, FLORIDA

I WAS THERE: CHRISSY BEAN

I saw them live only one more time, a month after Atlanta Pop. I drove the 60 miles from Gainesville, Florida with two other women. They didn't hammer me like they had in Atlanta, but I had not done drugs because I was driving, and I was literally right under them in Atlanta whereas the Jax Coliseum had chairs and the first row was quite a distance from the stage. One of the women in my trio was a writer for the college newspaper and had front row tickets. They were way off to stage left, but still. But of course they were awesome.

The two girls I was with were very much Jimmy's 'type' – exotic-looking, with long dark hair, darkish skin and huge dark eyes, seemingly sensual. The reporter had a back stage pass and tore back there as soon as the band was done. She came back a bit later and told us that Jimmy Page had invited us to his motel (not hotel!) room. Zep didn't travel in limos back in those days, and Jimmy had no clue where the place was. He just knew the name. Of course we went, but I had to stop at some gas station and get directions. This was a small place, only one floor and a couple wings of rooms. I wanted to meet Robert, but it didn't happen.

We all sat in Jimmy's room for at least an hour talking, and he asked if we wanted him to play us a couple of tunes. His accent was so thick we could hardly understand him, but so what? He played and did he ever. He was obviously quite smitten with my two very sexy companions, and I was wondering if I'd be asked to leave but I wasn't. The entire time Robert, who was in the room next door, was banging on the wall and telling us to shut up. Rude! I saw a side of Robert that many know – he is not always a nice guy. But Jimmy was beyond gracious and wonderful – just a total gentleman.

We sadly bid Jmmy adieu and I drove home in a trance, Led Zeppelin songs screaming in my brain. I never saw them live again, but I honestly think that my two experiences of seeing them were about as good as it ever gets or got with them. It was very early in their career, when they were still travelling coach on planes and using vans and regular cars. They were still humble, except Robert, and Jimmy was not into the hard stuff yet.

I saw many of the greats back in the day but nothing and no one ever came close to the majesty and power of Led Zeppelin. It was a great time to be alive, and I am lucky I survived it. There were lots of drugs, but I was always the damn driver.

JACKSONVILLE INTERNATIONAL AIRPORT
25 AUGUST 1969, JACKSONVILLE, FLORIDA

I WAS THERE: ROBERT LAROCQUE, AGE 17

I had the extreme pleasure of meeting the members of Led Zeppelin at approximately 2am in the Jacksonville, Florida airport. They had performed in Jacksonville the night before and I was lucky enough to be in their path as they moved on to another performance. A friend and I were returning to Long Island in the US via Jacksonville after a short vacation in Nassau, Bahamas during our summer break from high school. We arrived at our gate probably ten hours before our scheduled flight home with no money and only our return airline tickets to New York so had to sleep in the airport. Anyone who has ever tried to sleep on those chairs in the waiting areas understands how difficult that is. You find yourself waking up many times and really getting no sleep at all.

Upon waking up, at about 2am this time, I noticed a few guys who looked like the members of Led Zeppelin walking toward the snack bar near our gate. I rubbed my eyes to make sure I wasn't dreaming, woke my friend and we realised it was them. Jimmy Page and Robert Plant were in the lead, John Bonham and John Paul Jones were following close behind, and Peter Grant was behind them. I distinctly remember Robert Plant's long, curly, golden hair which confirmed to me that this band were the 'gods of rock and roll'.

I was very nervous but figured I should approach them as they stopped in the snack bar. I didn't know what to expect but I was very happy that they did not mind my visit. I think because there were very few people in the area, only two of us realising who they were, they felt comfortable. They all said 'hello' and that was enough to give me the courage to start a conversation. Jimmy Page, being the oldest member, seemed to take the lead. I remember his voice was very soft. Robert Plant chimed in when he had something to add. I asked them how their show went, as we understood they were performing in Jacksonville, and they said they were very happy with the performance and the response from the crowd was appreciated. I mentioned to them that I had attended their show the past May at the Fillmore East in NYC and they said 'thanks' for that.

I asked them if they would mind if we took some pictures with them and they, and Peter Grant, said it would be okay. My friend had to get assistance from someone in a back room to retrieve his camera from our bags that were being held for us until our flight. While he was gone, I continued my visit with them. They indicated that they were in the process of recording *Led Zeppelin II* while they were on this tour of North America and that it would be released, they thought, in September or October. My friend returned with his camera and started taking pictures of me with the band. After this short photo op, they indicated they needed to move on but I couldn't let them get away without getting their autographs.

The only thing I had that I could use for this purpose was my airline ticket holder which had enough white space for their signatures. After borrowing a pen from a gentleman standing in our 'sleeping' area, I hurried back to them and they proceeded to sign for me. It was time for them to leave and I thanked them for their time, autographs and the great music. I watched as they continued on to their gate and was still thinking that this was all a dream.

When we got back home, I reminded my friend to get his film developed as soon as possible because I really wanted the photos to prove I had met my favourite band.

He always had an excuse as to why he did not have the photos developed. He kept 'forgetting', he 'lost the disposable camera', he 'hasn't had the time'. I don't remember a flash going off each time he took a picture, so maybe underexposure was the real problem and he did not want to admit it because he knew I needed to have those pictures. 40 plus years later, I still have no pictures. But I have an experience I will never forget and the autographs have been well protected in my home in a steel box and each time I move house they have been close at hand so I never lost track of where they were.

I was able to attend another Led Zeppelin show at the Singer Bowl, only five days after meeting the band, and I was still having difficulty comprehending what I had experienced in Florida. 'Would they remember me if they saw me in the crowd?' Probably not, but I will never forget how gracious they were that early morning in Jacksonville. The greatest rock and roll band in the world.

SINGER BOWL MUSIC FESTIVAL
29 & 30 AUGUST 1969, FLUSHING, NEW YORK

I WAS THERE: JOSEPH DEVITO

We were sitting on the floor. About an hour and 20 minutes in, John Bonham kicked over the drums and they left. I thought it was gonna be a riot, but we all left peacefully. They were great. That was my first time.

I WAS THERE: LEN CAMPANELLI

I saw Zep five or six times. In the summer of '69, we heard they would be performing at the New York State Pavilion at the old World's Fair site. My friend scored tickets for several of us and what a mind-blowing show it was. Page at that time was still using his Tele. They were so fantastic we went back again on the Saturday night. We couldn't score any tickets so we bought some colour enhancements and sat outside on the grass and listened, since it was basically an outdoor concert just enclosed by a short wall. We heard everything just as well, maybe better, and they rocked! I saw them several times subsequently, including the day after the death of Jimi Hendrix. They were very cool and respectful and dedicated the show to him.

In the early '70s I worked at Alex Musical Instruments on 48th Street, the music Mecca of the time. Jimmy Page and John Paul Jones came in and really liked our selection since we specialised in vintage collectables. Jimmy liked me enough to actually find time to hang with me while I worked on one of my own guitars. While watching me adjust the guitar, he noticed I installed two extra height adjustment nuts under the bridge, very tight to the body. He asked me why I did this and I explained it improved sustain and bridge rigidity. He asked me to do the same mod to the '58 Sunburst he bought from us and I was glad to oblige. Years later, I saw one of the first Page model Les Pauls in a music store and saw that the stock model included the same mod I did for Pagey. I'm still proud and amused by this!

Jimmy also brought John Paul Jones around. He was a very quiet reserved gentleman. Amongst other pieces, he bought a late '50s Gibson double-neck guitar and mandolin original black from me and was quite pleased and gracious as well. I was lucky enough to be invited to Electric Lady Studios by Pagey and observed him mixing the drum solo from 'The Song Remains The Same'. What an incredible experience it was watching him work in the studio. At one point, he took a break from the control room and came into the studio where I was hanging with a few friends. There was a guitar on the piano where we were seated and I was riffing around on the guitar, playing 'Since I've Been Loving You'. He walked right over, which stopped me cold. He looked at me and said 'go on!' Which I did, incorrectly. Very matter of fact-like, he put his hands out for the guitar which I readily handed over to him. In a most friendly way, he then proceeded to show me the correct fingerings which I remember and use to this day. I must say that every time I ran into that gent, he was friendly and cordial.

TEXAS INTERNATIONAL POP FESTIVAL
31 AUGUST 1969, LEWISVILLE, TEXAS

I WAS THERE: MICHAEL MULLEN, AGE 18

They didn't make it to Woodstock. Two weeks afterwards, most all of the bands packed up and came to Dallas to duplicate the experience for three days. I went with a friend who was just starting out as a roadie for a new bunch for an up-and-coming musician named Leon Russell.

I WAS THERE: SALLY ESHNAUR PRENTICE

My friends were all about the same age. We were sharing a house in Kansas City, Missouri. One friend bought their album for us to hear. We didn't have much as far as furniture or food, but we had an awesome stereo. I had been going through a rough time, but when I heard 'Dazed And Confused', I was just blown away. Someone in our group had heard of a music festival that was a lot like Woodstock but at a racetrack near Dallas, Texas, an eight-hour drive away. Six of us gathered all our money and left for Dallas.

We arrived at the festival site. There were more than 200,000 people there, way more than we expected, but it made the experience even more exciting. There was a lake with campgrounds close to the festival site and we stayed there. Led Zeppelin played on the second night. They were late taking the stage for various reasons and went on around midnight, being introduced as, 'The Led Zeppelin, a new band from England'. It was just the most unbelievable experience. The crowd was mermerised. 'Dazed And Confused' had us all under their spell. I can still remember being there, with the cool summer night's wind, feeling that this was really something special.

I WAS THERE: ELAINE BENDER

l was right at the front of the stage and the sun began to sink. The weather was so hot and there was Page in his purple velvet pants. I felt sorry for them because we were all in our shorts and t-shirts. The biggest surprise was that they sat down quietly and did an acoustic set before launching into 'Whole Lotta Love' and the hits we all had come to hear.

I WAS THERE: JERRY GUTHRIE, AGE 13

I was wearing bellbottoms and had bright red hair down to my shoulders. I worked myself next to the right side of the stage and was only a few feet from their drummer. What a view! Suddenly he broke a drum stick and it landed three feet from where I stood. I picked it up, we made eye contact and he kept playing. I ran as fast as possible to my older brother and his friends and gave them the stick. Sadly, I've no clue where it is today, but the memory lives on.

Led Zeppelin undertake a short European tour in the autumn of 1969, to promote* Led Zeppelin II*, consisting of four shows in mainland Europe and one in London, England.

LYCEUM THEATRE
12 OCTOBER 1969, LONDON, UK

I WAS THERE: AL PATERSON, AGE 19

This is one of the most psycheclelic concerts I've ever been to. A bunch of us were living in a big flat in Earls Court and we all went together. We rode the Tube in and, when we arrived, ushers showed us to our places on the carpeted floor. All the seats had been removed. While the band played, they showed cartoons behind them and on the ceiling. It was insane. We were loaded to the max and loving it all. When we all exited the hall, we flowed in one big mass of stoned out hippiedom through the streets of London. I have no idea how we all made it back home.

Commencing on 17 October 1969, Led Zeppelin undertake a single leg 20 show tour in North America including a 15,000 capacity show at the Boston Garden, leading manager Peter Grant to observe that, 'This performance makes me realise that we can be bigger than the Stones and the Beatles.'

CARNEGIE HALL
17 OCTOBER 1969, NEW YORK, NEW YORK

I WAS THERE: VINCENT AUSTIN

My high school friends and I saw the infamous Carnegie Hall show. John Bonham had that giant gong and Jimmy whipped out that famous violin bow for 'Dazed And Confused'. The band was dressed in ripped jeans and t-shirts and of course rocked Carnegie Hall! I was pleasantly buzzed on reefer and port wine but had to stay on point because my friends were blazing on Orange Sunshine. NYC wasn't the safest place at the time, with lots of losers and hustlers.

I then caught them a second time at Flushing Meadow Park in NYC, Bill Graham's summer venue at the old World's Fair Grounds. I was blazing on microdot and remember Jimmy's hair blowing, tripping in the wind. I was pretty gonzoed but I loved the show!

I also had the pleasure of meeting Jimmy while he was mixing at Electric Ladyland Studio on Eighth Avenue and shared some nice French wine with him. He was very nice and cordial, a very pleasant person. I caught him one more time when he was playing at Jones Beach with the Black Crowes. He broke his wrist and cancelled the Madison Square Garden show. He probably broke it slinging that heavy ass Les Paul around.

I WAS THERE: MICHAEL KULICKE, AGE 14

I probably had a Kinks album and a Rolling Stones album or two plus Steppenwolf, Hendrix and Led Zep, purchased from a neighbourhood record store up on Broadway. I won a ticket on the FM rock station WNEW to see them at Carnegie Hall. My buddies were impressed – we regularly trekked to the Fillmore East on Friday or Saturday nights for concerts. I went alone, and faintly recall taking the #5 bus in front of my house, which went down Riverside Drive and across at 72nd and 59th to get to 5th Avenue as this went close to Carnegie Hall. Jimmy Page used a violin bow. They really were a great blues band. I knew every note of their album and live they were every bit as good as the record.

OLYMPIA STADIUM

18 OCTOBER 1969, DETROIT, MICHIGAN

I WAS THERE: CAROLYN PETERS, AGE 19

It was a Saturday and I went with a friend. I probably got tickets at Hudson's department store. I remember we paid $6 for the most expensive floor seats, but couldn't see very well as we were quite far from the stage. I also remember Robert Plant being so thin and us thinking he was on speed. The best moment was Jimmy Page, all in white sitting under a spotlight, with the rest of the stage and the stadium dark and everyone quiet while he played 'White Summer'/'Black Mountain Side'. What a great concert!

KINETIC PLAYGROUND

19 OCTOBER 1969, CHICAGO, ILLINOIS

I WAS THERE: GARY SPEARS, AGE 17

Some fool sold me a handful of used 8-track cassettes for $5, total. These were little played rejects from the seller's personal collection, no doubt purged from association with the likes of 1910 Fruitgum Company and Brother Love's Travelling Salvation Show. Two of the cruelly dismissed albums were Blind Faith and Led Zeppelin. I was instantly hooked and determined to see a Led Zep concert if at all possible. When my chance came, I hitchhiked from Ottawa, Illinois to my friend Larry's Chicago apartment. I don't remember his address, but I took the Belmont exit from Lake Shore Drive to get there, hoping he'd join me for the three o'clock Lighthouse/Santana/Led Zep show at Aaron Russo's Kinetic Playground. Alas, Larry had another commitment but his roommate decided to go with me.

We took a CTA bus to the Playground. Seating was first come, first served – there were no chairs and it was a bare hardwood floor. The afternoon attendance was, no doubt, less than the evening concert, but certainly no disadvantage, since the space was small. The room was dark except for stage lighting and it was hard to tell how many people were there. My guess is there were under 1,000. It was truly intimate.

I barely recall the Lighthouse segment. Santana, on the other hand, were incredible. It was hard to imagine how Led Zeppelin, or any other band, could be anything but anti-climactic after such an overwhelming performance but when Jimmy Page launched into 'Communication Breakdown', all doubt was instantly removed. There may be some disagreement about the set list order, and the sequence may have been different between the afternoon and evening shows, but that opening guitar hammer riff is etched into my brain.

It wasn't long before the roommate guy who accompanied me stood up and walked out. He said the volume was too loud. Too loud? Led Zep? How many living people would be willing to admit, 'I purposely walked out of a Led Zeppelin concert, and I wasn't having a medical crisis'?

If I hadn't already been sitting there, I would have been knocked to the floor. Jimmy wore a cream-coloured frock coat and was a haunting figure with violin bow on guitar. The volume was indeed cranked. If they survived, surely those who were hugging the speaker stacks for the entire concert have long since lost their hearing. I also recall a continual stream of little, hand-rolled cigarettes being passed throughout the crowd. No one, to my knowledge, took more than one puff before handing it off to a neighbour – for immediate disposal, of course. One might conclude that fire-code enforcement was somewhat less than robust in those days.

The only disappointment associated with my first – and last – Led Zep concert is that I had no friend sitting next to me, although I recently found out that a friend from Ottawa attended the evening concert. Even so, the experience was truly a community one, held together by the common focus and intense appreciation of a relatively small group of fellow early Zep fans. Unforgettable!

I WAS THERE: KATHY MORRISON

I discovered them as a hippie in the sixties, right before they released their second album. Moving blobs were projected on the wall and moved to the beat of their music. We sat on the floor with our knees touching. Jimmy Page did 15 minutes of controlled feedback. The auditorium smelled of marijuana and people passed around bottles of wine infused with LSD.

Led Zeppelin II ***is released on 22 October 1969 in the USA and nine days later in the UK. It was the first Zeppelin album to reach number one in the US (where it displaced*** **Abbey Road*****) and the UK, where it stayed on the charts for 138 weeks. Certified 12 times platinum by the Recording Industry Association of America for exceeding 12 million sales, the album also yielded a 45 in the shape of 'Whole Lotta Love'. Released only in America, this reached number 4 on the*** **Billboard Hot 100.**

BOSTON GARDEN

25 OCTOBER 1969, BOSTON, MASSACHUSETTS

I WAS THERE: PAUL ROBINSON

I saw them three times. The first time was at Boston Garden with MC5 and Johnny Winter as the opening acts. My seats were at the far end of the stage and I don't remember much save for a fight on the floor between some Hell's Angels and the MC5's set. The second time was in 1970 at the Bath Festival – I was living in the UK at the time. It was the time of the third album and I recall them doing 'Immigrant Song' and some others off the album.

MUNICIPAL AUDITORIUM
31 OCTOBER 1969, SPRINGFIELD, MASSACHUSETTS

I WAS THERE: BETSY STEPHENSON

I was in high school and hung around with some older hippie boys who turned me on to Zep. I immediately bought *Led Zeppelin I*. I saw them at Symphony Hall (previously the Municipal Auditorium) and paid $5 at the door. I wish I saved the stub! I don't believe tickets were sold in advance back then. I really can't recall who I went with but I do remember I wore bell bottom jeans with an inch of purple flowered ribbon that I hand sewed to the bottoms; that was the in thing to do. My favourite song from *Led Zeppelin I* is 'Thank You'. I listened to it over and over. When I married in 1983, that was our song and my brother played it on our turntable just after our vows. We didn't write our own vows back then, and 'Thank You' expressed what I would have written, and what I still feel today. My husband, a Vietnam vet, passed in 2005, after a 13-year illness contracted in Vietnam. I listened to 'Thank You' a few times the other day, and cried and cried.

I WAS THERE: RON BURATI, AGE 16

It is October 31, 1969. Hallowe'en. Led Zeppelin's first album is out and getting considerable airplay on underground radio and *Led Zeppelin II* is to be released in weeks. This tour is taking them through Springfield, Massachusetts where I live. My friend Larry and I attend high school in downtown Springfield. We are 16 and we have tickets to the Led Zeppelin concert at the Springfield Auditorium tonight.

As we leave school, I suggest that before heading home on a city bus we walk to the auditorium to see if we can peek at the equipment being set up. We walk the five or six blocks but we find the place appears locked up; there is no activity that we can see. We walk around the back of the building to the loading dock and rear stage entrance. Everything seems locked up tight there too, so we decide we should just go home. But just then a limo turns the corner and pulls up to the kerb, feet from where we are standing. Out jump Robert Plant, John Bonham and John Paul Jones. They act rowdy, make-believe wrestling with each other. A passing black and white cruiser pulls up and the officer yells from the passenger window 'knock it off or there'll be no show tonight'. The three of them freeze. The cruiser pulls away and Mr Plant leans over toward me and says, 'I think the constable is upset with us.' To which I reply, 'Yeah, they're... just like that.'

An awkward moment later, a big yellow Ryder box truck rounds the corner and pulls up. The guys cheer and pretty soon the doors are open and they start loading in the band gear. Since the doors are wide open, Larry and I wander in and take a couple of seats near the front to watch the gear getting set up. This is what I wanted to see. And it was cool to encounter those guys on the sidewalk outside.

But while we're sitting there Mr Plant comes out and sits sideways in the seat in front of us and starts chatting away. Narragansett Brewing is sponsoring this tour and a large banner is hoisted above the stage. Mr Plant speaks in apologetic terms about the tour being sponsored by 'beer'. He goes off on a tangent about how, unlike some people, he gets mellow and happy when he drinks. We nod in agreement. I am gobsmacked and have no idea how to talk to him.

I had recently acquired a small amount of weed and I get the idea to offer him some for later, incorrectly figuring that these guys can't possibly have stuff while travelling. I ask him if he'd like some little pot for afterwards. He says, 'Sure, come see me after the show.'

We leave for home and I roll up a half dozen reefers. But I'm afraid to carry them with me to the show so I leave them at home.

The show is good. Springfield native Taj Mahal is the opening act and the Zeppelin set would be the only time I would see Jimmy Page. But I am horribly distracted by thinking about how this is going to transpire.

Afterwards, Larry and I go out back to the stage door. How else would I see him after the show? We aren't the only one there. There are about 30 other people hanging around outside the door, some of whom I recognise from school.

A while later the door finally opens and Mr Plant comes out, holding a bouquet of red roses in his arms. He sees all the excited people and I manage to get his attention and he comes straight over and says, 'See Cole (referring to Richard Cole), our road manager, he'll bring you up.' He leaves in a car. A lot of people are now staring at me.

After the truck is loaded, I stop Cole as he's getting in the cab and tell him that Robert told me to see him because 'I have some pot for you guys.' He says to climb in, so we get in the truck and I say, 'I don't have it on me. We have to go get it at my house.' He says 'where is that?' I tell him it's a few miles and direct him to my street. (It was actually about a twelve-mile round trip.)

My parents are watching *The Tonight Show* when we pull up to the kerb in front of the house. I run inside, grab what I came for and tell my folks I'll be back later.

We arrive at the Sheraton Inn in downtown Springfield about 12.30am. When we arrive at the room there is already quite a party happening. Turns out they really didn't need what I brought at all. We enter and a crew places a rolled-up towel at the bottom of the door. I give my humble offering to one of the guys in charge of the refreshments. Mr Plant asks me if I ever had a Jamaican spliff. I say 'no' and he instructs someone to make one up for us. He proceeds to roll up an enormous spliff, using four or more large papers, and fills it with cigarette tobacco and I believe hashish. He lights it and hands it to me. Not being a tobacco user, I take a drag and think my lungs are on fire. I do my best not to cough and feel the effects very quickly.

Now Mr Plant is reclining on the bed. Larry and I sit in a couple of chairs next to the window by the bed. There is a great deal of activity in a darkened adjoining room involving other bandmates, maybe the crew and some young women. We sit and Mr Plant talks about missing being home with his young family. I listen but am not in any condition to contribute to the conversation.

An hour or so later, people are running out of steam. I certainly am. Things have quieted down in the adjoining room. Mr. Plant is close to nodding off. I say 'we need to be going' and thank everyone (I think). Larry and I walk out the front door of the Sheraton. It's almost 3am and the late October night air is sobering. It is then that I realise that the city buses are not running this late. I hadn't thought this far ahead.

A moment later, a very pretty blonde college-age girl walks out of the hotel. I had seen her upstairs. She says, 'You guys need a ride anywhere?' I say 'sure!' She has a very new Mustang. On the drive she explains that her father is an executive at Narragansett Brewing and that she's tagging along on the tour for fun. She drops us off near at the corner of my street and we head to our homes. Unfortunately, I still have very little recollection of the concert itself.

ONONDAGA COUNTY WAR MEMORIAL
1 NOVEMBER 1969, SYRACUSE, NEW YORK

I WAS THERE: BOB HOLZ, AGE 11

Seeing Led Zeppelin as a 'peace, love and music' child shaped and guided the outcome of my life journey through music. My first concert was Jimi Hendrix, also at Onondaga County War Memorial. But the Zeppelin show was different and drew a larger attendance. I was eleven going on 18. My mom took me and a group of childhood friends. But my mom, being the hip lady she was, fitted right in. The opening act, the James Gang with Joe Walsh, was huge. They had just released 'Funk #49'. When the headliners hit the stage, I loved Zeppelin's uniqueness, originality and power. Each member of the band was featured during the performance. The acoustic guitar performance of 'Black Mountain Side' was epic as Jimmy Page played the piece seated in a chair.

John Bonham's drum solo that night shaped who I am. I was impressed with his big sound, powered by his Ludwig drums. Yes, he was fast, especially his bass drum foot. But he was also rock solid in his beats and always had a perfect blues rock feel. I feel fortunate to have seen John live. His playing has been a huge influence on me. I followed my dream in life and became a professional drummer and, even though I've established myself as a jazz rock fusion artist, and listen primarily to that genre, I can still put on a Zeppelin tune and it still sounds totally fresh and relevant. Their music is timeless.

I WAS THERE: JOHN OLMSTEAD

There were approximately 3,000 people there. It was raw, up close and personal – and incredible! They are one of two of my favourite all-time bands, and I'm proud to have been able to see them at such an early stage of their career.

I WAS THERE: RON CARUANA, AGE 18

I went with a group of friends. The venue was a good size, with a seating capacity of 8,000. The James Gang were relatively unknown at the time and opened for them. I remember they were using small amplifiers, which looked so funny on a large stage. But they were miked up and everything was really loud and sounded great. It was the first time I heard 'Funk #49'. Led Zep performed their second album, but overall my friends and I were just as impressed with the James Gang.

I WAS THERE: SALLY BARRY

I was 20, maybe 21. We were all into rock 'n' roll music in the late sixties and early seventies and we knew good music from junk. The first time I ever heard Led Zep their music gave me chills down the spine! I was dating the one and only cool boy I had ever met. He was cold and mysterious and just utterly sophisticated. He travelled back and forth from my city to NYC and knew a lot of musicians and people in the underground scene. He sold his gorgeous chestnut-colour leather jacket to get money for tickets to Led Zeppelin for us. We didn't drive and so took the bus downtown to the War Memorial. It was the loudest concert I had or have ever been to. It was just absolutely thrilling and we enjoyed it so much. I remember we walked the five miles from downtown back to his mother's house, where he was staying, on what was a chilly night. He then called me a cab so I could get the other five miles back to my mother's house.

I don't think Robert Plant has aged very well. But my husband and I love his later work and I am glad he is still alive and working!

O'KEEFE CENTRE
2 NOVEMBER 1969, TORONTO, CANADA

I WAS THERE: DAVID GORDON

I saw them twice in Toronto. The first time, we were hearing 'Whole Lotta Love' and the rest for the first time. Page was wearing purple pants and they were simply outstanding. The next time I saw them was at Maple Leaf Gardens when they toured the fourth album. Hearing their new song, 'Stairway To Heaven', live for the first time was memorable.

MEMORIAL HALL
5 NOVEMBER 1969, KANSAS CITY, KANSAS

I WAS THERE: GEORGE BOJE

I was hitchhiking in Overland Park, Kansas and the driver who picked me up had an 8-track tape of Led Zeppelin's first album. I was knocked out. I had not heard of them prior to this. I looked for the album in the Kansas City area and couldn't find it. I was in St Louis a few weeks later and found it at Target in Florissant, Missouri. It is still my favourite Led Zeppelin album. I only had the first two. I didn't really care for their other albums.

I saw them at Memorial Hall. I was in the fourth row, centre, and very excited about the show. Unfortunately, John Bonham was so wasted he didn't really play. He would get up and leave the stage in the middle of a song. Roadies would lead him back to the drum throne, put sticks in his hand and move his hands up and down to get him started. He would play for maybe 30 seconds and then leave the stage again. I don't know how many times they tried this, but eventually he left and did not come back.

Jon Paul Jones was very pre-occupied with reflecting the spotlight off his Fender bass hardware into the faces of audience members. He eventually got so in to it that he stopped playing and he too left the stage and did not return. Page and Plant finished the show alone, with Page playing his guitar with a violin bow and Plant answering Page's lines in an extended but not impressive version of 'Dazed and Confused'. Overall, the concert was very disappointing. I was anticipating a great show and got much less.

I WAS THERE: DAN SMITH

The Led Zeppelin show was sold out so quickly that the promoters added a second show that same night. I went to the second show and, anticipating a warmed-up band that was ready to kill it in front of adoring fans, I witnessed a train wreck. As a young drummer who wanted so bad to see John Bonham blow me away, I was shocked to see him come out before the set, obviously drunk, mumbling on a microphone something about the police and then being escorted off before returning with the band and all but passing out behind the drums in short order. The abbreviated set deteriorated into a vocal and guitar jam session between Jimmy Page and Robert Plant while John Paul Jones mostly watched a roadie, sitting behind Bonham on a chair, occasionally kick Bonham's drum stool, prompting short bursts of percussion before resting his head back on his snare. Bummer.

I WAS THERE: SALLY ESHNAUR PRENTICE

I think there were some things that happened due to management decisions and planning that contributed to all the chaos. The promoter that booked the concert scheduled the concert to be two shows, at 7pm and 9pm. They were assuming that concert goers for the first show would leave promptly when Zeppelin were finished. That didn't happen. Half to three quarters of the kids at the 7pm show decided they wanted to stay so the 9pm show was absolutely packed. The second big problem was Zeppelin's equipment manager either forgot or didn't know about the Kansas City show, so all of their equipment was sent to San Francisco.

One of the local music stores was able to provide exact duplicates of their gear. Page, Plant and Jones were okay with this but Bonham was very upset. He wanted 'his drums'. Three or four local bands performed short sets before Zep. Bonham was in the front row at the 7pm show, watching the local bands while drinking a bottle of whisky. He continued to drink throughout the first show and through the break. By the time the second show started, he had downed the whole bottle.

A friend of mine who was working backstage said it was pretty obvious he was in no condition to drum, but the other guys insisted he go on. By the time they had played a couple of songs, Bonham was having trouble sitting up at his kit. The stagehands would try holding him up but things just got worse. Finally, he fell on the floor, out cold. Stagehands had to drag him off stage and left him passed out in a hallway. Page, Plant and Jones continued with the concert and did the best they could. Occasionally Plant would walk over and bang on the cymbals or a drum. The show was not one of their best, but it was still Zeppelin!

I WAS THERE: EVAN JOHNSON

I was a drummer in a band. We discovered Led Zeppelin's first album and did a couple of their songs in our set. We then heard they were coming to Memorial Hall. They played two shows that night and that I attended the second one. Unfortunately, they were wasted for the second show, especially Bonham. It was a poor performance. People who attended still talk about it with disappointment. They were an amazing and innovative group whose songs and style have certainly endured. It's too bad their live show that night didn't go well. Real fans forgave them, though, and love their music still!

I WAS THERE: RICH FAVREAU, AGE 16

I was at the second show. It was my first concert and my first exposure to large amounts of weed – secondhand! The story goes that Bonham drank a bottle of Jack Daniels starting mid-afternoon as he and the band felt the show would not go on because they had lost their equipment. My biggest recollection is that it was loud and raw but that's what everybody wanted. I was not in tune enough to realise how bad Bonham was for that second show, but Jimmy Page and the others were aware and they were not happy. I kept my ticket stub. It was not bad entertainment for $3.50, despite the equipment and alcohol issues.

I WAS THERE: HERB BAIN

This is the worst show I ever saw! I had third row centre seats to both shows in Kansas City and paid $3.50 for each. Bonham was drunk during the first show and passed out on his snare drum during Page's 'How Many More Times' solo. The band quit and walked off stage. I lost all respect for them and never went to see them again and never bought another record. It was very disrespectful of them to their fans in Kansas City. I guess we don't matter much here in the middle of the country. Added to all that, they weren't that good live. I've heard better local garage bands.

I WAS THERE: TOM BLAKE, AGE 19

It's the worst concert I ever saw, because John Bonham was smashed drunk. He laid on the snare drum a good part of the show.

I WAS THERE:JOHN J DAILY

It was a disaster because Bonham passed out on his kit and was dragged from the stage by one foot. He only managed three songs. I was in the second row. It was my first good look at Page, who was spectacular. I also heard them play for three hours in Seattle in 1973. There's a bootleg album of what was a great show. The last time I saw them was in St Louis in '77. It was a good night, not a great one, but I'm glad I caught up with them.

I WAS THERE: NELSON CLARK

I was the bloke that held John Bonham up on his drum stool so he could finish the concert at the Memorial Auditorium when he became too drunk to play. Zep had rented equipment from the music store that I managed, Mission Music, because their equipment was being flown from the West Coast to the East and KC was a quick stopover for them. We provided a Marshall stack and a Ludwig drum kit to their specifications. John was either upset or celebrating and proceeded to drink a fifth before going on stage. He managed to make it through the first concert but was totally inebriated for the second performance. Page was kicking at him, trying to get him to perform, and John upchucked.

I was concerned about our equipment and the promoter, a friend of mine, was concerned they couldn't finish the set and we would have to return attendance fees. They asked me to hold him up so they could finish a set, and so that's what I did. Zep gave me a large autographed poster which was later stolen out of my music store, but the story lives on.

I WAS THERE: MIKE BROCKMAN

John Bonham was so drunk that he could not play. They had someone behind him trying to prop him up but to no avail. The fans booed all night. I don't think they ever played Kansas City again. A friend and I stuck our heads into the dressing room after the show and Bonham was laying on the floor – passed out! Page and Plant were just sitting there talking and they did not seem too concerned.

WINTERLAND

6-8 NOVEMBER 1969, SAN FRANCISCO, CALIFORNIA

I WAS THERE: DIXIEANN TIETJE, AGE 17

I was a senior at Fairfield High in Fairfield, California. It was my first rock concert. My folks were Country and Western fans. I saw quite a number of shows with them, even some at the Grand Ole Opry. But I had never experienced anything like the magic of the Zeppelin show. The sounds were everywhere, the crowd nearly hypnotised by the light show. However, nothing hit me like the amazing sound of Jimmy Page's guitar dancing through the air with Robert Plant's voice. That show changed my perspective on music.

I WAS THERE: CHERYL T-REBEL, AGE 16

I was just a kid. I lied to my parents, telling them I was spending the night at a girlfriend's house, but instead I drove my 1956 Chevy to San Francisco and saw them at Winterland in 1969. They were great and I was so smitten with them.

I WAS THERE: DON MAHLMAN, AGE 18

I grew up with The Beatles all through high school. Their last album came out the day I graduated from high school, and then we started with the heavy stuff. The second wave of the British Invasion was incredible. When The Beatles ended in '69 we had Zeppelin and Black Sabbath debuts. I was 18 years old so my timing was perfect. I realised those bands in real time. If you live in California, it's a long state. San Francisco was only two-and-a-half hours' drive for us.

After Bill Graham closed the Fillmore in '69 because it was too small, we went over to the Winterland which was originally a skating rink. It was frantic. The vibe was so electric back then. Everybody was so young. It was so exciting, waiting outside because they wouldn't open the doors. Everybody had got there early in the day and we were all sitting out front of this old ballroom. Right across the street were a fish and chips place and a Kentucky Fried Chicken. People would go across the street and bring food back. The temperature was real cool so there was no heat. But the anticipation was almost overwhelming.

Everybody sat on the wooden floor. It had bleachers upstairs, so you sat Indian-style on the floor. You had to be a young man to do this! We weren't as excited for the Zeppelin show as we were for Black Sabbath but we all went. We didn't get down as close as we wanted to. We got there early. It didn't matter if we were in the end of the line or at the front of the line, we nearly always ended up right in front because, once everybody stood up, the people with the energy could just move to the front.

I think it was the last show where they played that small a venue. The Winterland only held 3,000 people. They had the stage elevated that night. They would move it for different shows, because it was an oval-shaped building. For the Black Sabbath shows they had the stage at the end of the ballroom. For Zeppelin, they moved it over lengthwise so it was longer.

My good friend got arrested that night, because we all did LSD and people were handing it out. He got too high and left the ballroom and ran out on the street and the San Francisco police arrested him. But they let him go. It was a wild time, because everybody was smoking marijuana. What were they going to do? Arrest everybody?

I don't remember what they opened with. I can't remember what songs they played. It was so long ago and I was so high on LSD, pot and a drink of whisky. But that show was like a religious experience. All I can remember is it was a great show and it went by real quick. When we came out of there – maybe it was the LSD – we were saying, 'What did we just see? What did we witness?' because it went by so quickly. The highlight of the show was when Jimmy Page pulled out that bow and started playing. We had never seen anything like that. My memories have faded. I'm not proud of it but I did do a lot – a *lot* – of drugs back then.

I WAS THERE: STEPHEN DEVINE, AGE 15

I was a big British Invasion fan and also a fan of the British blues scene. I had heard of Jimmy Page from the Immediate LP collection, *Dealing With The Devil*, and knew he was the top session guitarist in England. The Bay Area music scene was evolving at the same time, and we had our own big-time bands and guitar players as well. I took advantage of this by attending as many shows as I could, including lots of free concerts in Golden Gate Park. Even at the age of 15, I knew Altamont was going to be a bad scene. My rule was that when the Hell's Angels showed up, it was time to go home.

Bands like Blue Cheer and Vanilla Fudge were getting my attention. During my sophomore year in high school, the buzz about this new super blues/rock band featuring Jimmy Page started to circulate. Then every party had Led Zeppelin on the turntable and every car had it on the 8-track. 'Good Times Bad Times' just floored everyone. Even the most popular girls were all over it! The Led Zeppelin buzz was all over my school and the Bay Area. This wasn't your brother's Grateful Dead. This was 'my' band! ZEPPELIN RISING! When I was in the presence of 'the gods' I never took my eyes off them. I knew the band was that special. Did I have a story to tell at school the next day?

The band undertake a UK tour. There is no support, except at Edinburgh's Usher Hall where Barclay James Harvest are the warm-up act.

COLSTON HALL
8 JANUARY 1970, BRISTOL, UK

I WAS THERE: PAUL LEWIS

I went on a bus from Hengoed in Wales. It started snowing. I was cold, man, wearing crushed velvet flares, shirt and waistcoat on the bus to Bristol. Plant was late but it was a really good, rocking show.

I WAS THERE: MIKE MURTAGH, AGE 16

My schoolfriends and I had formed a rival music society at school as an alternative to the 'establishment' version – The Progressive Music Society. It gripes me a bit to see what became known as 'prog rock'. Originally, progressive music was an effort to create for our young selves a new genre which would espouse a more serious approach to rock/popular music, in which the standards of musicianship were raised to more conventionally respectable levels. The emphasis was on the musical content and not the spectacle, the antithesis of mass-appeal popular music at any time. The 'prog rock' that it morphed into, with its emphasis on overblown and self-indulgent stadium shows and costumes, is the very triumph of image over substance that we were trying to get away from in the early days. Cream were admired by Igor Stravinsky and Leonard Bernstein, and this was exactly the sort of recognition and respect we craved.

Led Zeppelin, at least for their first two albums, were real game-changers. From the first, blasting chords of 'Good Times Bad Times', it was quite clear that they were The Next Big Thing! Because we lived in what seemed to be a top band touring desert, our little school society would organise trips to the nearest big touring venue, the Colston Hall in Bristol, to see prominent bands. Zeppelin's gig there was one such occasion.

About eight of us took the train to Bristol that very cold January day. I remember little detail about the gig itself but I am convinced they did an Eddie Cochran number as one of the encores, although this is not reflected in online setlists I have seen. I've retained an overall impression of being absolutely blown away by this band's raw energy and creativity – and the volume! It made my sternum vibrate and I had ringing ears for a long time afterwards.

Jimmy Page stole the show, displaying breathtaking virtuosity at times. It was the first time I'd seen an electric guitar being played with a violin bow. However, it would be invidious to single out one of the band over another; they all excelled on what was an astonishing and exciting gig.

ROYAL ALBERT HALL
9 JANUARY 1970, LONDON, UK

Jimmy Page: Albert Hall was a massive gig for us, and we really wanted to do the best we could. It was a magic venue. It was built in Victorian times, and you go in there thinking about all the musical history that has preceded you. On top of that, it was something of a homecoming for John Paul Jones and I, because we had both grown up around there.

USHER HALL
17 FEBRUARY 1970, EDINBURGH, UK

I WAS THERE: ANNE GALLOWAY

I was a student nurse in Edinburgh and my boyfriend was at Heriot-Watt University. He had something to do with arranging the gigs that the university put on. I knew of their music before then so was a fan. I remember the sound system failing as Robert Plant was singing. Despite this, he could still be heard up in the gods. I went backstage to meet them all and have a drink. I got all their autographs in green ink on my programme. I still have it all these years later. I saw an unsigned one for sale on eBay over 10 years ago and it sold for $500.

I WAS THERE: ROB COLE-HAMILTON, AGE 21

I was at art college, and I probably went with some stoner pals who will have got the tickets. *Led Zep II* had just been released, so their set was awesome. Robert Plant's mic failed at one point and he could still be heard right up in the gods where we were sitting. A combination of too much weed (then) and senile decay (now) has rendered most of that evening a blur. I heard *Led Zeppelin I* quite early on and bought the LP. It still makes my blood tingle, listening to it now.

After the Spring 1970 UK tour, Led Zeppelin play 16 shows in Europe before returning to North America for a fifth time, playing 28 shows in the USA and Canada in four weeks with only one night off.

PACIFIC COLISEUM
21 MARCH 1970, VANCOUVER, CANADA

I WAS THERE: ED BILAWCHUK

Led Zeppelin played in Vancouver four times. I saw the 1970 and 1971 shows. After they finished 'The Immigrant Song' at the 1970 concert, I remember Robert Plant announcing that it was off their new album, *Led Zeppelin III*, and that they hadn't played it live before that, anytime or anywhere. I mainly went to shows with the crowd I hung out with as a teenager in Prince George, where we all thumbed a ride to the concerts. It really was the beginning of my life as I was leaving high school. I began both going to gigs and starting 20 to 25 years as a drummer in many bands. Nothing that made any of us rich, but we had one hell of a time crossing British Columbia a few times.

MEMORIAL COLISEUM
23 MARCH 1970, PORTLAND, OREGON

I WAS THERE: JERRY GREENE

In 1969 I was in high school in Portland, Oregon. A friend of mine called me up to come over and listen to his new album. At the time I think the only two albums I had were *Meet The Beatles* and *The Doors*. I remember us lifting the lid on his floor standing record player and setting the needle on the first track. We were mesmerised by the entire album and moved the needle to replay various tracks. The depth of creativity was just amazing; a song with tablas, a song with acoustic guitar, and then the rocker, 'Good Times Bad Times'.

Not that long after, my friend got tickets for us to their concert at Portland Memorial Coliseum. We were pretty naive; we had never been to a concert before. I remember sitting in the upper rows, like everyone else politely sitting in our seats; this was long before mosh pits. Near the end of the show my friend said, 'Let's go down and try and get right in front of the stage'. I tried to say 'no' but finally he convinced me, and we stood up to start walking down the stairs. It seemed like about a third of the audience got the same idea at the same time, and I can remember a wave of excited fans rolling down the stairs to get on the main floor. That moment, maybe more than anything for me, was a loss of innocence.

By the next Zep concert in Portland, I had grown my hair, had a tie dye t-shirt and was in a band. I'm still playing guitar to this day, and consider Jimmy Page and Jimi Hendrix my two main influences. I especially like Page on 'Whole Lotta Love' live at Madison Square Garden, where he is using the tape echo.

MEMORIAL AUDITORIUM
28 MARCH 1970, DALLAS, TEXAS

I WAS THERE: LISA OLIVE, AGE 14

I saw them every year prior to Robert Plant's son dying. They used Dallas, Texas as their practice shows and based our reactions on them for the rest of their tour, so it was a real treat for us. The light shows they put together were awesome. I remember one such laser light that was golden and it formed into a stairway while they performed 'Stairway To Heaven'. The whole band, and we, just partied during each concert. Unfortunately, the tours stopped after Robert's son, and then John, died.

CIVIC ARENA
30 MARCH 1970, PITTSBURGH, PENNSYLVANIA

I WAS THERE: JIM POOBAH GUSTAFSON, AGE 18

When I was 16 or 17, my college age neighbours had *Led Zep I* and played it for me. I bought every official release from then on. Jimmy Page had such an advanced guitar sound at the time. Being a recording artist myself, I loved his technique. I saw them on the *Led Zep III* tour in Pittsburgh. I loved the band, but was somewhat confused as to why the promoter had such a weak PA system. I had seen The Who not long before this and they had a great sound system. I still enjoyed seeing Zeppelin but it seemed like too small a sound system for a large place, and the band were not very loud.

CIVIC CENTER
2 APRIL 1970, CHARLESTON, WEST VIRGINIA

I WAS THERE: ALAN L BURGE

I had fifth row seats. The band were terrible. They were so high they couldn't even play together. At one point Bonham got up from his drums and went around to the front of his kit and started dancing and laughing, and it took the other band members several minutes before they realised there was no one playing the drums. Page couldn't even play the 'Whole Lotta Love' solo correctly. He really botched it. By the end of the show people around me were booing loudly. It was shameful.

MACON COLISEUM
3 APRIL 1970, MACON, GEORGIA

I WAS THERE: JULIA CASEY, AGE 20

I went with my husband who was a local musician. We drove from Columbus, Georgia to Macon and back to attend this concert. It was one of their first American tours and I had seats on the eighth row. I purchased tickets by mailing the promoter. I have always been into music. I used to lie on the floor between the stereo speakers and listen to 'Whole Lotta Love'. My daughter went to see Page and Plant in Atlanta in the '90s. She remembers that there was always music in our home and calls her husband's childhood, where there wasn't, 'musically challenged'.

I WAS THERE: JODY HUSSEINI, AGE 15

My first ever concert. I bought a ticket on the first row, so close that the stage partially obscured my view of John Bonham playing the drums. Their set was drawn from their first two albums and followed by an encore of the 'Immigrant Song'. The performance was full of energy and the sound was incredible, even though the acoustics in the stadium weren't the best. It gave a reverb sound off the back wall every time Page slapped his strings with the violin bow. I still remember Page and Plant going back and forth, Plant's vocals imitating the guitar work on 'Dazed And Confused'.

BALTIMORE CIVIC CENTER

5 APRIL 1970, BALTIMORE, MARYLAND

I WAS THERE: BARBARA NELSEN

They were a solo act by this time and there was no support. John Bonham played the longest drum solo I ever heard. I actually had to leave my seat for a while. He was giving me a headache!

DORTON ARENA

8 APRIL 1970, RALEIGH, NORTH CAROLINA

I WAS THERE: ALAN OGUS, AGE 23

I discovered their music in 1968 when it was played on the North Carolina State University's Student FM radio station. I went with my good friend Bert Palmer (now deceased) and we purchased tickets at the Dorton Arena box office. It was a long time ago but I do remember Jimmy Page using a bow on his guitar. My favourite song? 'Communication Breakdown'!

I WAS THERE: MICHAEL DEANGURY, AGE 15

My father was stationed at Seymour Johnson Air Force Base in Goldsboro, North Carolina. Most of us kids would hang out at the Teen Club on base and the base would occasionally provide buses with chaperones to accompany us to concerts. Led Zeppelin was one of those concerts. 15 years young at the time, I had never been to a concert before. Many of the older kids were riding high by the time we arrived at the concert. Our chaperone was the father of several of the kids attending and came equipped with earplugs. Some of the kids started peaking on the drugs they were taking and thought it would be a good idea to go outside of the concert venue. Unfortunately for them, they did not realise how difficult it was going to be to get back in, especially while peaking on LSD. Fortunately, our chaperone came to their rescue and got them back in.

The concert itself was unreal. It was more like attending a life event than it was a concert. I knew I was in the presence of something very special and inspiring.

I WAS THERE: BILL BARNES

I was a senior in high school and had two seats, stage left on the front side area. Raleigh was a bit behind the rest of the country in terms of musical taste but was rapidly catching up. Amongst touring acts it had the reputation of being a difficult place to play if you weren't an R&B act. Zeppelin were fresh and in top form and the crowd was definitely enthusiastic. At one point, Plant paused in the show to say, 'North Carolina has come a long way.' I remember how amazed I was that they could bring off 'Dazed And Confused' live. But even after springing for Zeppelin tickets, I still didn't get to third base with my date, Caroline Pigott.

I WAS THERE: KELLY CRAVEN, AGE 17

My first concert was Strawberry Alarm Clock, Buffalo Springfield and The Beach Boys in 1967 in Greenville, North Carolina. That made an impression, but not nearly as much as seeing Led Zeppelin up close. I drove to the show alone because I didn't know any of my friends were going. It was one of the first times I had driven on a long trip out of Greenville. It wasn't until years later I found out a couple of friends, Richard Tucker and Luther Rowe, also went. My ticket cost $5 with a $2 service charge. They were reserved seats, marked on folding chairs. I was dead centre in the floor of the arena, under the huge hanging American flag. Everyone stood up to see, and I'm pretty short and so I couldn't see. Eventually I walked up to the front, and made my way to the front edge of the stage, where I was able to stay until the show was over.

My memory is that Jimmy Page played through two Sound City amps, sitting side-by-side on a table, with four ratty old Marshall speaker cabinets, but after all these years I saw a picture that showed the amps and they were Hi-Watt, so I was wrong. Jimmy Page at that concert was the best guitar player I've even seen live. This was before the drugs and alcohol and the broken finger set him back. I don't think he had that 'something' later; no matter how good he still was.

I'm a drummer. I was just starting out back then, and watching Bonham from about ten feet away was very influential. Another memory is the drumming on 'Whole Lotta Love'. Some of the guys on the road crew came out and were banging on things as percussion instruments. One of the guys was beating on a stove top percolator. Yep, a coffee pot.

I WAS THERE: STEVEN BURGESS

In the late sixties every spring, Dorton Arena at the North Carolina State Fairgrounds hosted a band that was most popular at the time. In 1969 I saw the Jimi Hendrix Experience and in 1970 I saw Led Zeppelin. It was billed as 'Spend an Evening with Led Zeppelin'. They played for over three hours with nobody backing them up. *Led Zeppelin III* had not yet been released so in reality they only had two albums' worth of music to entertain us with. They played a couple of tunes from the third LP but mostly the first two. The songs were very long. 'Dazed and Confused' lasted for what seemed to be 30 minutes and there was a lot of improvisation. My two friends, Chuck and Terry, and I sat by the side of the stage, stage left. We were right at the stage so we could see Jimmy Page's guitars lined up waiting to be played. I remember he had a Danelectro, exactly like the one my cousin had. I don't remember which song he used it on. It was a great show.

CURTIS HIXON HALL
9 APRIL 1970, TAMPA, FLORIDA

I WAS THERE: MIKE ROYAL

I saw them three times, beginning with downtown Tampa at a venue with a 3,500 capacity and then in 1971 outside of Orlando, Florida at the Orange County Cow Palace, where they also held rodeos and which had a capacity of 2,500. I also saw the 1975 at Tampa Stadium where they set a record for the largest crowd at a single act concert at that time. They were onstage saying, 'We're bigger than The Beatles,' because they broke the Shea Stadium record. Led Zep never had an opening act when I saw them.

I WAS THERE: PAUL STREICHER, AGE 16

This was my first concert, with my first true love, Cheryl. I remember standing nervously outside the doors waiting for them to open so we could go in and grab some seats. Upon the doors opening, we made our way in and into the concert hall where we found that most of the seats were already taken. We sat down in the middle of the second back row. There was this little stage set up with shiny instruments that sparkled in the stage lights. The huge brass gong was a treat to see. I couldn't wait to hear it played, even though it was only a smack or two for one song that escapes this 64-year-old mind. (It's been a long time since I have listened to any Led Zeppelin, or any music from those years.)

The band started a few minutes before the hour. People were muttering and you could feel excitement in the air. This was truly an amazing moment in our little town. The band began to play one song after another and I sat there stiff, not wanting to miss one beat of the music that I had only been hearing on the radio and on the one album I had of theirs.

I got a nudge on my right arm. I turned to see a long-haired freak offering me a hit from his hash pipe. I was deathly afraid of drugs at the time from the films we were shown at school so I said 'no, thanks'. I turned to my girlfriend, Cheryl, and she gave me a funny look. We turned our attention back to the band.

The band went through their set and soon it was all over and we were getting up and walking out with the crowd. Outside everyone seemed to be in a daze, wandering around, glancing at each other and muttering things like 'amazing' and 'can't believe this just happened'. Yes, we were all hypnotised from the sounds we had just heard for ourselves in person and not on the radio this time. I would go off to sleep thinking about that night for many days thereafter.

I got one more chance to see Led Zeppelin play, at the stadium in Tampa in 1973. Our football stadium was offering concerts now that the Convention Center was no more. That was the day they broke the attendance record.

KIEL AUDITORIUM
11 APRIL 1970, ST LOUIS, MISSOURI

I WAS THERE: BARBARA MARCHIANDO HERRIES, AGE 17

I found their music on a St Louis radio station, KSHE 95. I went with a group of boys from the neighbourhood I had grown up with who also loved Led Zeppelin. An ad for the concert was placed in the *St Louis Post-Dispatch* newspaper. We just hopped in the car, drove to St Louis and bought the tickets the night they played. It was awesome to be able to walk right up to the ticket booth and purchase tickets. I don't think it was a sell out. I remember thinking Robert was so very tall and the music very loud. It was still very foreign to me since this was my very first concert. They played music from their first and second albums, and from *Led Zeppelin III* as well. I was totally in love with Zeppelin. Unfortunately, I never saw them again due to money issues. That was a big mistake.

I WAS THERE: FAYE CRAFT, AGE 17

I first heard them on KSHE 95. They had their second album out and they sounded great. There was no fancy light show and I had one of the best times. I went with my sister. I was in awe of them. I worked at a place called Roberts Records, owned by United Artists. I used to get tickets to concerts and cocktail parties. Known people would come through there to see how records were selling. It was great to go to concerts then because it was general admission. Also, people wouldn't get crazy. You would just really enjoy the music!

MET CENTER
12 APRIL 1970, BLOOMINGTON, MINNESOTA

I WAS THERE: JEFF MILETICH, AGE 17

The Met Sport Center was a hockey arena. It has since been torn down and an IKEA store is there now. I went with my then girlfriend and 16-year-old brother. And with my mother, who drove us and who liked Zep, most popular music and was big on reggae. She'd go to Negril, Jamaica for two to three weeks at a time until she was in her late seventies. This was the first big show I attended where a large number of people were smoking weed. They did a few songs from *Led Zep III* which was released four to five months after we saw them. The sound system was horrible. You couldn't hear any vocals on the first song.

I WAS THERE: STEVE KRAHN

Led Zep was the first rock concert I saw. The music we listened to on mainstream radio was insipid on the most part. We had to drive out of town late at night to pick up on our car radio an underground radio programme called Beaker Street all the way from Arkansas. I likely heard about Led Zeppelin for the first time on this show. I gave a friend of mine

Led Zeppelin I as a birthday gift, not knowing the music well at all. I may have bought it just for the cool graphics on the cover. Listening to it was like a bomb going off and I realised immediately that this music was definitely out of the ordinary. It was powerful with off-beat driving rhythms, strong vocals and great lyrics. We loved it and got tickets immediately when we learned they were coming to our hometown. I don't recall if there was a warm up band but if there was, memories of them have been obliterated by the show Led Zeppelin put on. I particularly remember 'Dazed And Confused' being so loud and filling the 16,000-seat arena. We were awed by this show and how a great recorded album sounded even better live.

FORUM
13 APRIL 1970, MONTREAL, CANADA

I WAS THERE: PAUL MASSICOTTE, AGE 15

It is my first visit to the Forum. After seeing Richard Cole unboxing Jimmy Page's gear (the Tone Bender and the Les Paul with its case covered with international flight tags), CJMS's Robert Arcand and Roger Scott/CFOX, the radio men who introduced us to Led Zeppelin, come on stage to announce the Montreal Pop Festival, taking place the following month and bringing together Grand Funk, Robert Charlebois and La Nouvelle Frontière as well as the Cream movie, *The Farewell Concert*. They then introduce Led Zeppelin. Jimmy Page quickly goes up on the stage and shakes a few hands, Robert Plant does the same and then the roof explodes! My head explodes too.

Towards the end, people lit their lighters. It seems that this was the first time Led Zeppelin had seen an audience do this. Plant asked the group to stop playing and thanked Montreal. There were four encores. This show is engraved on my memory forever.

CIVIC CENTRE
14 APRIL 1970, OTTAWA, CANADA

I WAS THERE: ANDRE BOYER, AGE 21

Tickets were only $4. There were only 8,000 people there and everyone and anyone who knew anything about Led Zeppelin in Ottawa and the surrounding area was there. I had their two albums and spent much of my time learning about them and so many other British bands of that era by listening to Radio Luxembourg. I saw them again at the Silverdome in 1977. The concert in Ottawa was better. It was full but it was much easier to hear them and interact at such a concert!

MID-SOUTH COLISEUM
17 APRIL 1970, MEMPHIS, TENNESSEE

I WAS THERE: DENNIS K RUSSELL SNR

I saw them twice in Memphis. My late friend, who I grew up with, was with me and we were nuts over them. Their first three albums were the best. We actually smoked pot during the concert in the Coliseum, like everyone else did. Back then, pot was so mild compared to today. The sound there was great – my God, I can still feel the vibes. 'Dazed And Confused' was the best. Jimmy Page was a bad ass in his day and the loud sound was so clear that the guitar strings ran chills all over me, one by one. I never wanted that day to end. I've seen so many top bands at the Coliseum, but nothing to compare to the great Led Zeppelin.

I WAS THERE: DAVID A DUTTON, AGE 14

Just as I decided to approach the stage, Jimmy Page sat down to play the instrumental version of 'White Summer' on his Danelectro black guitar. I couldn't get as close as I wanted because the volume was incredibly loud.

I WAS THERE: GENTRY JONES

I was up in the nose bleed seats. There were some serious hillbillies sitting behind me from Arkansas and one of them tapped me on the shoulder and asked, 'Which one of them fellers is Led?'

I WAS THERE: WENDY NUNEZ, AGE 21

The main floor was general admission, so my sister and I just worked our way to right below the stage. We were up close and standing right below Robert. It was a great show. I'd first heard 'Dazed And Confused' blasting at one of the head shops. They were different from everyone else.

I WAS THERE: MIKE GAINES

The first concert I ever attended was one of the Dick Clark *Caravan of Stars* tours that featured a large number of acts performing two or three songs each, including The Yardbirds with Jeff Beck in November 1966. I saw The Yardbirds again with Jimmy Page on lead. I have a polaroid snapshot of him and his fiddle bow. While I don't remember the song, it was likely an early version of 'Dazed And Confused' that I know The Yardbirds were playing on tour about that time.

Back to 1970. That Friday had been a school day. My friends and garage band mates were tenth and eleventh graders at North Little Rock High School in central Arkansas. I, the oldest, was a college freshman. We loaded into one of our parents' cars as soon as school was out and made the three-hour journey to Memphis, Tennessee. Led Zeppelin were scheduled to play a two-hour concert sponsored by Memphis radio station WHBQ at Mid-South Coliseum, which had previously hosted concerts by Elvis Presley, James Brown and The Beatles.

Our freeway trip up Interstate 10 from Little Rock to Memphis took us close to several seminal small towns and sites integral to the history of rock and roll and the Delta Blues – a connection to Led Zeppelin that was totally lost on our carload of five young men. We arrived at Mid-South early and were among the first few thousand concert goers to make our way inside and locate our reserved seats, some 20 or so rows back and to the left of the stage. The stage was already set up with amplifiers, mic stands, a Hammond organ and John Bonham's sizeable drum kit and huge gong. It was going to be a very exciting evening.

About 8.30pm, the Coliseum went dark but for the well-lit stage. A local disc jockey made the following announcement to the 11,000 attendees: 'Let's hear it for Led Zeppelin!' Thus began a most memorable concert. John Paul Jones, with his sunburst Fender Jazz bass, walked across the stage. Jimmy Page, in black velvet pants and a black flowered shirt, his sunburst Les Paul slung low, plugged in and took his place to the right. John Bonham climbed behind his gold-coloured kit and Robert Plant strutted to mid stage. The opening song was a cover of an old soul tune by The Drifters, 'We're Gonna Groove'. It was loud and Led Zeppelin made it their own. 'Dazed And Confused' followed and the crowd erupted.

During the extended version of what was already a classic, I noticed a few fans approaching the stage with cameras. The uniformed security was being fairly accommodating, allowing a few camera flashes before moving in and directing folks back from the stage. Seeing my chance, I moved up toward the stage with my camera. I was able to snap several shots, including some of Jimmy Page using his violin bow and interacting with Robert Plant.

'Heartbreaker' was next, followed by 'Bring it On Home', with Robert Plant on harmonica. At mid-stage, Jimmy Page sat on a chair with his black and white

Danelectro. He played 'White Summer' and 'Black Mountain Side' and, at the end, the entire crowd was on its feet. I had ventured up to the stage again and was able to get a shot or two of the seated Page before the police officer sent me back to my seat.

After 'Since I've Been Loving You', John Paul Jones seated himself behind the Hammond organ, his bass still strapped over his shoulder. The band played 'Thank You' and Jones' organ solo earned another standing ovation. Next came 'What Is And What Should Never Be', then 'Moby Dick' with a long and frenetic drum solo that brought John Bonham his standing ovation. The audience was at its rowdiest during a 30-plus minute version of 'How Many More Times', standing on chairs and with large numbers moving toward the stage. In the midst of the song, the band added snippets of several other songs, ranging from 'Tobacco Road' to Ravel's 'Bolero'. Midway through the song there was a brief pause and Robert Plant belted out, 'Long distance information, give me Memphis, Tennessee'. The crowd roared to the strains of Chuck Berry's 'Memphis'. Toward the end, the house lights went on and Plant urged the crowd to calm down and not stand on the chairs. They finished with Elvis Presley's 'That's Alright Mama', the conclusion of 'How Many More Times' and a quick 'thank you and goodnight'.

The lights came on and the crowd roared and clapped. After what seemed like forever, they came back on stage. Their encore was 'Whole Lotta Love'. Jimmy Page produced a bizarre wooden box with antenna (now well known as his theremin) and regaled us with the truly weird 'Whole Lotta Love' sounds. It was an amazing finale to an amazing two hours.

We loaded up the car and headed back across the Arkansas delta toward Little Rock. *Zeppelin*

I was cranked loud on the 8-track. Back home, our band soon added 'Dazed And Confused', 'Heartbreaker' and 'How Many More Times' to our set list. I was proud to be playing a 1965 Fender Precision bass that looked very much like Jones' Jazz bass, and we were blessed to have something of a teen prodigy on lead guitar who could carry the difficult Page licks quite well. Many concerts have come and gone over the past decades, but Led Zeppelin in Memphis that night in 1970 will always be one I will remember as one of the very best.

SANTA BARBARA BOWL
22 APRIL 1970, SANTA BARBARA, CALIFORNIA

I WAS THERE: CLIVE BUNKER, JETHRO TULL

I think it was on the third tour that we did a theatre where we were top of the bill and Led Zeppelin were billed as support. They had taken off really, really fast, so I went into their dressing room and said to John Bonham, 'Look, we're top of the bill, but why don't you go on last, because you're more popular than us now.' Bonham went and had a chat with the others and I could hear them laughing, so I thought, 'Here we go.' They were really good fun, that mob. But Bonzo came back and said, 'Nah, let's leave it as it is,' laughing his head off. I thought, 'Oops.'

I went back to Ian and everyone and said, 'They want to leave it where we're top of the bill.' And we said, 'Okay we'll just be stupid about it all. We'll go for it.' The Zeps went on and went down unbelievably well. Then we went on, and it was amazing. The audience went berserk. When we finished the gig, I went into their dressing room and said to John Bonham, 'Thanks for warming them up for us.'

The band undertake a six-date summer tour including four German shows, an appearance at the 1970* Bath Festival of Blues *before an audience of 150,000, and starting with an appearance in Iceland that inspires Robert Plant to write the lyrics to 'Immigrant Song', debuted at Bath just six days later.

LAUGARDALSHÖLL
22 JUNE 1970, REYKJAVIK, ICELAND

I WAS THERE: HALLDÓRA KRISTĹN MJÖLL KRISTINSDÓTTIR

Me, my boyfriend and our friends went to the Led Zeppelin concert in Laugardalshöll. It was on a Monday evening at 10.30pm. There had been another show in the concert hall immediately beforehand, so they had to empty the concert hall before the Led Zeppelin concert could be held. The workers at the concert hall were on strike, so my boyfriend and his friends along with a lot of other people that were going to the concert helped tear down the stuff in the concert hall from the previous show. Me and my friend, Inga, were downtown a couple of days before the concert, walking up a street called Skolavordustigur, when we suddenly saw the boys from Led Zeppelin walking towards us. We did not expect this, but there were Robert Plant, Jimmy Page and John Paul Jones being followed by a couple of fans. Inga and I stood there for a while shocked. Unfortunately, we didn't have a camera with us!

We did not have a camera at the concert either, but there were some photographers there from the newspapers who shot a lot of pictures. We were almost right up against the stage at the concert, which was packed. All of a sudden, people from the back of the hall started pushing to the front and me and my boyfriend and our friends managed to squeeze our way out so that we wouldn't be squashed up against the stage. We all thought the concert was amazing. We had the time of our lives.

BATH FESTIVAL OF BLUES
28 JUNE 1970, SHEPTON MALLETT, UK

I WAS THERE: HENRY RACE

Their performance was a big thing. Zappa was on. Pink Floyd were on. My favourite at the time, the Jefferson Airplane, were on. But there was a real crackle when Zeppelin came on. They were the only band I took photographs of on my Kodak Instamatic camera and I might as well not have bothered. We were quite a way away from the stage. Everyone stopped what they were doing when Zeppelin came on. I remember them playing 'The Immigrant Song' and Planty doing his 'aa-aa-aah!' I remember peering at the stage from quite a long way away and trying to decide whether it was in fact Jimmy Page, because he had a big tweed overcoat on and a big tweed sou'wester hat. And he had a beard as well. We thought, 'What's going on there?' It wasn't a very rock 'n' roll style of dress, dressed up in brown tweed. We were thrilled to see Zeppelin. They were the headliners. The Bath Festival in 1970 was the biggest festival, bigger than the Isle of Wight. It was an event.

I WAS THERE: PETER CLINICK

I had been to the previous Bath Festival in 1969, a one day event that included Led Zeppelin. Like 1969, the 1970 Shepton Mallet festival was a Freddy Bannister promotion. The site was three and a half miles south of Shepton Mallet, on the site of the (now Royal) Bath and West Farm Show, and a real pain to get to. My mother took me and a friend as close as she could, which was by the Babycham factory in Shepton Mallet. We walked the last two-and-a-half miles. I don't recall how we got the tickets. It was probably on site. Lots of so-called security were letting people in for a 'fee', but I still have a ticket or pass out somewhere, so we must have paid officially.

The site was far from adequate to cope with the approximately 200,000 people that turned up. In one field, there was a line of toilet pans lined up in the open air, not plumbed in to either water or sewage. There was a guy with his trousers down sat on one, a surreal sight. Other toilets were of the chemical-type, basically dustbins in old caravans that were divided in two. They had not bothered to level them so when the dustbins were full, they simply overflowed. Nobody seemed to empty them.

The first morning, I woke up in our crappy little tent wheezing badly. I suffered with asthma as a kid, and occasionally in later years, and I needed my inhaler which I'd forgotten. I walked slowly to the nearest phone box at Cannard's Grave, a small hamlet between the site and Shepton, and rang home. My mother agreed to bring my inhaler, got stuck in a queue of traffic on her way down, saw a motorbike cop and explained she needed to get an inhaler to her son suffering an asthma attack. The cop gave her an escort with his lights and siren going to Cannard's Grave!

The line-up was startling for those days, with many US bands. I was keen to see Johnny Winter and Santana. The rumour on site was that Led Zeppelin were paid over £20,000 and had flown in from the US especially for the festival, exactly one year to the day after appearing at the previous Bath Festival. When they came on stage, the reception was loud and enthusiastic. I was stood at the front but on the extreme left-hand side, which meant I could not see the rear of the stage. Even though it was meant to be summer and the weather was occasionally sunny, it was cold and damp at times, especially at night. The wind blew in strong gusts across the front of the stage. Jimmy Page made the most of the fashion of the day, wearing a knee-length top coat and hat and looking like a local farmer or landowner.

The sound power was more than adequate, but the gusts of wind made the sound fluctuate. I recorded the performance on a Phillips mono portable cassette recorder and the fluctuating sound was very evident. The C90 cassette I used later snagged whilst I was playing it back and I threw it away. How I wish I still had it now, damaged or not. There really should be an official release of any soundboard recording if it exists.

They played a lengthy set, most of which I loved, especially my favourite songs 'Since I've Been Loving You' and 'Communication Breakdown', with a few encores. One song that stuck in my mind the most was 'The Immigrant Song', which I had never heard before. I was not that impressed by it. I was used to hearing and loved the songs off the first album, as played at the festival on the Bath Rec.

This was the last time I saw Zeppelin. I was just too fond of their first album songs. Although there are definite highlights on other albums, none had the same impact on me as *Led Zeppelin I*. In those days, as soon as a band became too popular my group of friends and I dropped them, seeking out new sounds and bands. It was more fun and cheaper to see them in the smaller venues we grew up with locally.

I WAS THERE: ALLAN BOSLEY

One of the most memorable sets that I ever heard. Bath had a spectacular line up – and a couple of inevitable duds – but Zeppelin were outstanding. I can still hear Jimmy Page using the violin bow on the guitar strings for 'Whole Lotta Love'. It was a great set, the highlight of the festival and a memory for ever.

I WAS THERE: TERRY ANDREWS

I saw so many groups that weekend. In my scrapbook I just wrote 'great!' and gave them an A. A mate saw them at the first Bath Festival and had the first LP, which I loved, so I knew about them. They took the prime early evening spot – rumour had it they paid Canned Heat to take their spot. I remember being surprised at Jimmy's appearance as he had cut his hair and was wearing a bush hat and a herringbone overcoat. The only thing I didn't enjoy was 'Moby Dick', which went on forever and included Bonzo hitting the drums with his hands. I clapped him for his stamina. I kept the *Disc* review of the festival which I must have agreed with and will now defer to:

Led Zeppelin clearly had more fans than anyone else. Would the crowd have been so big had they not been on? As soon as Zeppelin ripped into their first number the living field of people exploded. Zeppelin immediately seemed to be in top gear but then they don't use any lower ones. (Led Zeppelin) were on stage for nearly two hours and long before the end they were in overdrive. Zeppelin brought the festival to a peak and a lot of people fought their way out of the ground when it was over.

Back in those days of pocket money as sole income, if your mate had a record you didn't buy it – you borrowed it. But I did buy my own copies of *Led Zeppelin I* and *Led Zeppelin II* after seeing them live. It was just one crunching classic after another, and when they ran out of songs, they did a rock and roll medley. This was deemed the band's break out gig, and they went stratospheric afterwards!

I WAS THERE: CHRIS DAWSON

Also playing that day were Donovan, Santana, Flock, Frank Zappa, Hot Tuna, Dr John, Country Joe, Moody Blues and Jefferson Airplane. Led Zep came on after Frank Zappa and played for approximately two hours, including around five encores, and finishing about 11.30pm. They were the highlight of the day and really got through to the audience, though the sound wasn't good from where we were sitting.

I WAS THERE: GARETH HICKERY

The 1970 Bath Festival had an estimated 250,000 crowd. There was some fabulous music and, as badly organised as it was, those are the memories that remain. My memory is that after a great Sunday afternoon of It's A Beautiful Day, Zappa and the Mothers and Santana, The Flock took the stage. An excellent set, but as a fan even I thought they were overstaying their welcome when somebody (Peter Grant, I later learnt) starting pulling out the plugs. I was about 50 yards away, slightly to the right of the stage.

It was what everybody had been waiting for all weekend. Led Zeppelin took the stage and started with 'Immigrant Song'. I remember Plant's polka dot shirt and Page's overcoat and hat. I remember an acoustic type set midway through and at least two encores with a lengthy rock and roll medley to finish. Unfortunately, after that our driver, a part-time roadie for a local Cardiff band, said, 'That's it, I have to be in work tomorrow, not like you college boys!' and we were off. Meaning I missed the Byrds and Dr John. And, I heard later, a torrential downpour.

As a coda (yeah, I know) I've lived in Adelaide, South Australia since 1978 and a couple of friends who went to see Led Zep on their only visit in 1972 talk about how bad they were, under the influence and generally disinterested. In those days, Australia was a long way away, not just in distance terms, and it seemed to be a common theme from Led Zeppelin to the Beach Boys and a few others.

I WAS THERE: CHRIS GREEN

The second time I saw Led Zep was at the Bath Festival. Approximately 150,000 people were there, which made this a bit of an endurance test but the band were superb. Also on that bill, making it probably one of the best line-ups possible at the time, were Santana, Johnny Winter, Pink Floyd, John Mayall, Steppenwolf, Moody Blues and many more.

I WAS THERE: IAIN WOLSTENHOLME

My friend Alan and I got into the press enclosure as he had taken his dad's camera, which was posh enough to gain entry. No pass or wristband in those days, just a load of bluff by holding it aloft and shouting 'press!'

I WAS THERE: JAN HEWITSON

Me and a friend hitchhiked down from Fishguard in Pembrokeshire. Amazingly, we met up with some friends just as Zep came on stage. I vividly remember Robert Plant strutting about the stage, his wonderful hair blowing in the wind, singing 'Dazed And Confused'. We were all mad for them as we'd just discovered *Zep I*. After the festival we started hitching back with not a hope of getting a lift because there were so many people hitching, but amazingly we got a lift with two great guys whose van was decked out with sheepskin rugs and all sorts of hippy-type drapes. They gave us food and drink and we slept all the way to Cardiff. We were wiped out.

I WAS THERE: JEFF LEWIS

I saw Led Zeppelin live three times, the first time at the legendary 1970 Bath Festival, which featured the top American rock acts of the day and their British counterparts. An impromptu line-up, led by Zeppelin guitar technician Joe Jammer, even played a set.

Zeppelin themselves performed on Sunday evening, as dusk approached driven by a cold summer wind, hence Jimmy Page taking to the stage wearing a greatcoat and country yokel hat. All that was missing were a couple of pieces of straw between his teeth. Move over Worzel Gummidge and let the guitar maestro take over.

The music, to quote fellow Bath performers Steppenwolf, was true 'heavy metal thunder' driven along by the three musicians and topped off by Robert Plant's blues-wailing rock shrieks. In the following week's music papers, the majority of the rock critics agreed that Zeppelin's majestic and savagely raw set had produced the outstanding performance of a very special rock festival weekend.

I WAS THERE: JOHN FLETCHER

Bearing in mind some of the other groups there – I recall waking up on Sunday morning to Canned Heat, having slept in front of the stage – the one outstanding gig was Zep, with mind-blowing stuff from Jimmy Page. In fact, we were stunned by the music from just three instrumentalists and vocals. And, having previously seen Cream twice live, I took a bit of impressing. My first taste of 'Whole Lotta Love'. Brilliant!

I WAS THERE: JULIE LONG, AGE 18

I went with my friend from college, Penny Stewart. The first song I heard was 'Good Times Bad Times'. I thought then that they were going to be mega.

I WAS THERE: DEREK THOMAS

I was stood at the top of the hill in this great natural amphitheatre. They were headliners. It was an absolutely incredible sound. I can remember Robert singing 'What Is And What Should Never Be.'

I WAS THERE: MIKE MURTAGH

I set off from Swansea with a group of school friends. One of us was lucky enough to own a green Minivan, so we chipped in for petrol and piled in. What should have taken a few hours ended up taking many. We stopped off for a while in Bath, where we had an interesting chat with an American drug-dealer. He was short-haired and very smartly turned out in an effort not to attract the attention of the police. It seemed to work. He gained a lot of kudos with us with his claim that he had been at Cream's legendary *Wheels Of Fire* gig at Fillmore West.

It was early evening by this time, so we thought it a good idea to get ourselves to the festival site. The roads were fine until just outside Bath, on the road to the site at Shepton Mallett. We soon hit the tail-end of a queue of traffic, imagining a small tie-up just ahead. How wrong can you be? Once we rounded the corner we could see from the tail lights ahead that the traffic stretched for miles. Still, it was far from a tedious trip. It seemed we were quite an attraction ourselves, as the locals lined the roads to see this strange procession disturbing their peace, although the mood was good amongst all concerned.

We arrived at the site very late after taking several weary hours to get to the Showground at Shepton Mallet where the festival was being held. We soon lost touch with each other in the throng and in the dark. Early on, I was with my mate, John. Neither of us had much money and we had no food but we had heard that smoking cigarettes (straights, that is) made you feel less hungry, so we shared the price of a packet of 20 Embassy, thereby starting an eight-year habit! It worked, though. I don't remember being particularly hungry there.

I remember the weather being dreadful on one day. The line-up suffered, too, with the continuing traffic problems significantly delaying many bands. Donovan performed a sort of Cliff-Richard-at-Wimbledon service by entertaining the crowd for three hours while those who had been delayed struggled to arrive. Not my cup of tea, but you have to hand it to the guy.

There was a lot of bad acid at Bath and some people became seriously ill with it. I never touched chemicals, so this was not a problem for me, but I had bought a quite large 'quid deal' from our American acquaintance earlier and the two of us managed to persuade someone a bit more experienced (for a slight share) to roll us a massive five-skinner joint, which we smoked with relish. Unfortunately, this made me massively stoned, to such an extent that I became very unwell. I decided I needed to go to the medical tent and, as I staggered through the crowd, I managed to throw up copiously onto some poor sod in his sleeping bag.

I made my erratic way along the path to the medical tent but collapsed on the way and was tended to by a very kind hippy couple who, thinking I was on bad acid, crammed my mouth full of oranges, a supposed cure for a bad acid experience. I never made it to the tent, though. I became convinced that I'd be arrested if I went inside, so I crashed out on the grass outside the tent until I'd recovered sufficiently to make my way back to the main crowd. Needless to say, I'd lost all my friends by this stage.

Zeppelin were headlining on the Sunday, along with Frank Zappa, and it seems that this, for them, was a seminal gig. I remember it as being exceptionally enjoyable with the expected thrilling riffing but offering something a lot more sophisticated than the bastardised heavy-rock offerings of bands like Black Sabbath, who seemed to offer a sort of lowest common denominator as far as the standard of musicianship was concerned. Plant and Page had now developed to the point where they dominated the stage in a way that they had not done before. They weren't for everyone, though. I remember a group of Fairport Convention fans heckling Zeppelin during their performance and yelling, to Robert Plant's apparent consternation, 'You're fucking hopeless! Bring back the Fairports!'

I never saw – or wanted to see – Zeppelin after this. As far as I was concerned they, like Pink Floyd and many others, strayed into the self-indulgent, style-over-substance excesses of what became known as prog rock. I think I saw them at their best at those two gigs in 1970.

I WAS THERE: SHARON DELANEY, AGE 16

I lived in a Welsh coastal village that my parents had moved to two years previously – and I hated it. All girls of my age seemed to want to go into their family hotel trade or farming whilst I wanted more adventures in life. I didn't fit in at all – being five feet nine and looking far above my age. But unlike 16-year-olds nowadays who seem to want to look like older versions of themselves, l wanted to be individual. I had been buying records for a couple of years, my first album being by Bert Jansch, but I collected many more of various types, including Led Zeppelin! I read in the *New Musical Express* that a festival was coming up and I wanted to go, but only a few of the older boys from the village were interested in going, and they were certainly not interested in a 16-year-old kid tagging along, so I thought no more of it.

The day after I had finished my exams, a Friday, I packed my kit bag (no rucksacks back then) taking very little with me apart from a little money saved from my Saturday job. I told my mother that I was going back to Birmingham to sec my gran. I had been brought up to be very independent and there was no problem with my going alone and so I set off, not sure quite where I was really going.

I hitched a ride in a lorry that was going to Bristol and when we stopped at Aust Service

Station the place was packed with young people. When I asked why they were there, they said they were 'going to the festival near Shepton Mallet'. That was it – the same one I'd heard about. I asked who was on and when told it included Led Zeppelin, Pink Floyd, Santana and Canned Heat, that was where I was going!

I got to an almost empty field early on Saturday morning and started talking to a very good-looking guy whom I later learned was Rory Gallagher. A little later, the place was filling up and it started to rain so I retreated under my fleecy army blanket and started playing my jew's harp. I got a kick in the back and someone asked if I wanted to share their plastic. There were no tents other than those rented out by the management, let alone glamping, so some enterprising boys had taken large plastic sheets to keep dry under. I shared the sheeting and later shared it for 16 years with my future husband, who was one of those boys!

How naive was I to ask what was going to be played on the side screens and believed when told cartoons (yes, they did show The Archies playing 'Sugar, Sugar'). Everything was really badly managed, with few food outlets and a disgusting toilet block miles away from the main seating areas but, despite everything, everyone was happy and good natured. Even when you trod on someone, which was inevitable with almost 250,000 people there, they only commented with a smile or friendly word. We saw some great bands, got rained on again and again, slept little – in case we missed someone – and had a wonderful time.

The highlight of Sunday was Led Zeppelin – the sun was going down and I'd made it! We sat up on the packed hill, with everyone around us happy. A lad in front of us was so stoned that he dropped his joint and almost set himself on fire. The band played and were brilliant. I still remember Robert Plant strutting around stage with his hair flowing and shirt open, screaming and singing songs both from their forthcoming album and some favourites. I was a teenager in heaven. Everyone went mad about their set and they were called back on stage time and time again.

We saw a huge number of fantastic groups over that extended weekend. I was still watching Dr John early on Monday morning, and I have to say that it changed my life. I was an impressionable young girl, surrounded by happy people, fantastic music, seeing Led Zeppelin on one of the best weekends of my life. There was nothing quite like that festival line-up ever again.

I WAS THERE: CHRISTOPHER MADDOCK

Born in Cornwall in 1950, I started going to UK rock concerts and festivals in about 1968. One of my first was the Bath Festival of Blues in 1969, followed by the Shepton Mallet three-day event in 1970, the Bath Festival of Blues and Progressive Music. I was a junior reporter on *The Kentish Times* and I managed to get in the press area in front of the stage. Led Zeppelin followed Flock on stage. Flock were obviously very stoned and their set was cut a bit short, much to their stoned bemusement. This apparently happened on the orders of the Zeppelin team, who wanted Zeppelin on stage at their preferred time of dusk. While Zeppelin played, members of their crew continually jumped into the packed press area and barged through to rip cassettes out of cassette recorders that they had spotted, with no argument permitted. I suppose that was fair enough in a way, with bands' concerns about bootlegs.

On Led Zeppelin's website on the page referring to the Shepton Mallet show, manager Peter Grant is quoted as saying: 'Some people were trying to videotape the Bath festival and they'd already been told beforehand they couldn't, so I had no qualms about throwing a bucket of water on to the tape machine which blew the whole lot up. Whoosh! It made a horrible smell and then it melted.' I did not see this incident, metres as I was from the stage. Ah, the wisdom of hindsight. It would be great now, wouldn't it, to have all those destroyed video and cassette tapes?

I WAS THERE: DA LA

This was the year after the original Woodstock festival in the States, which event lives on through having been recorded and filmed. Sadly, no one thought to archive the Bath Festival for posterity. Tickets for the weekend were 30 shillings (£1.50) to see Canned Heat, Steppenwolf, Colosseum, the Mothers of Invention, Floyd and, late on Sunday afternoon, Zeppelin. And it didn't rain. I was sober, as myself and two friends had only one bottle of sherry to share the whole weekend. All the pubs in the area had run dry and I had to walk two kilometres to the nearest pub. Sherry was all they had left.

I WAS THERE: GRADY JOHNSON

I went to the Bath Blues Festival in 1969, then to Shepton Mallet in 1970. I saw Zeppelin present their first album at the first festival, and their second album at the second. I was still at school but as a young guitarist I'd seen loads of concerts. I'd seen Jeff Beck playing the material from *Truth* at Wolverhampton Polytechnic in 1969, so I had a lot of interest in what such guitarists as Beck, Page, Gallagher, Green and Clapton were playing and who their influences were. I thought Page to be far from the strongest of this bunch. That said, his presentation of Zeppelin at the Pulteney Street concert was extremely impressive.

A PUB
SOMETIME IN 1970, STOURBRIDGE, UK

I WAS THERE: DEREK THOMAS

We had a local pub that was halfway from my village to Stourbridge. I was 17 or 18 by this time, and Robert used to pop in there regularly. He had his little flock with him, the hangers on, but one thing that did make me smile was him walking up to the juke box – he was already in Led Zeppelin at this time – and putting 'Whole Lotta Love' on. I thought, 'Come on mate, a bit self indulgent.'

He's a really nice guy. He lived near where we came from, near Stourton, and my mate Geoff was driving his motor down the road and all these sheep were in the road. He stopped the car and there was Robert Plant and he said to him, 'Can you give me a hand to round these up?' Which Geoff did. And they went back to Robert's house and he said to Geoff, 'You're welcome to come here any time, any time you want. But please don't bring hordes of people with you.'

The Summer 1970 North American tour starts in Hampton, Virginia after planned shows in Cincinatti are rescheduled due to John Paul Jones' father being ill. 25 shows are performed altogether. The band also mixes* Led Zeppelin III *at Ardent Studios in Memphis during the tour.

HAMPTON ROADS COLISEUM
10 AUGUST 1970, HAMPTON, VIRGINIA

I WAS THERE: KEVIN LEE, AGE 12

My older brother played Led Zeppelin in our home. One particular friend was a drummer in our junior high school band and introduced me to the works of John Bonham. When we found out that Led Zeppelin were coming to our hometown, we agreed that we had to go and see this guy. I gave Joe the money for the concert.

I remember distinctly how out of dress I was for the show, with my starched collared shirt and dress pants, but I was at a rock concert and I was being cool. The show was loud, even for our reserved seats halfway back in the auditorium. There was a distinct drum solo during the performance of 'Moby Dick' that seemed to last for a half an hour, which satisfied our main purpose of attending the show – Bonham on drums! 'Whole Lotta Love' led to the house lights going up and the rest of the night was 'open air'. I remember strange smells coming from around me but was not interested in the concert-enhancing refreshments at the time. As much fun as I had at this, my first concert, almost exactly five years later I was witness to the 'messiah of rock 'n' roll', Bruce Springsteen. Both shows left lasting impressions as I travelled through the magical world of live concerts, establishing the criteria to be measured against and raising the bar.

I WAS THERE: ALAN HOSHOR, AGE 19

It was the only time I saw Led Zeppelin. Jimmy Page bowed his guitar, which I had never seen before and haven't seen since. I know a lot of people think they're rock gods, but I haven't listened to them since 1971. I ended up more of a David Bowie/Roxy Music kind of guy. I still am. It was a shame about Bonham as he was legendarily talented.

I WAS THERE: ALAN VANCE

I was a guitarist in a seven-piece rock/horn band. We all got special seating, just behind and above the group and looking down on them. I wasn't sure what to expect and they were much more of a jam blues band than I expected. When they completed their set, we were blown away, so much so that we went back and started covering some Zep tunes in our set!

YALE BOWL
15 AUGUST 1970, NEW HAVEN, CONNECTICUT

I WAS THERE: ANTHONY PEDEVILLANO

In 1970, the New Haven Pops produced a bunch of summer concerts held in the huge open-air stadium, the Yale Bowl, including Peter, Paul and Mary and Three Dog Night on a bill with the James Gang, Chicago with Terry Kath (my all-time favourite guitarist) and, on 15 August, Led Zeppelin. The sponsor was Silly Putty, of all things. I got my tickets at a record store called The Music Box for a whopping $6.50 a pop. I had just graduated high school and this was my last summer before college. Led Zeppelin were dynamic and opened with the 'Immigrant Song', capturing the crowd's enthusiasm, which stayed high for the entire set. I don't remember an opening act, but Led Zeppelin were 'on' and in great form all night.

I WAS THERE: BILLY TEE-TOMLIN, AGE 24

I played bass and backup vocals in rock bands and went with a few band members along with a few other musicians. We were in a circle of Connecticut musicians along with a couple of rock deejays and so had an 'in' when it came to tickets. The concert was amazing.

I WAS THERE: DAN MOROZ, AGE 17

I grew up in a very small rural town and only knew Led Zeppelin through records or 8-track cassettes. I had just graduated from a small high school in rural Connecticut. My girlfriend at the time, Gretchen, talked me into going. She had a connection with the local rock and roll FM radio station where her older sister was a deejay and got us two tickets. When we arrived, the crowd was not allowed inside the open-air football stadium as the band started to play. The bass notes hung in the air as Page was screaming riffs. As we found our seats they started up. I remember Bonham hitting his large gong. It set the stage for the evening, as Plant's voice rang out the lyrics with Jones's bass.

The music was pure and hard as they rocked through their set. I had never been high before and the folks seated next to us offered us some good pot. So, as I became high for the first time, I also experienced my first rock concert which probably changed my course in life from a country bumpkin to a music lover. It also expanded my mind from naive to a seasoned explorer of my mind, relationships and the world. It freed my mind and soul as it was so impressive! My lasting memory is of the end of the concert, as they boarded a helicopter to leave the venue. So cool.

My heart, soul and being for my college years and adult years were shaped from that concert onward. To this day I stop everything I do and turn the volume up to eleven when I hear an old Zeppelin song. Such pure rock and roll!

I WAS THERE: FRANK L ROBERTS

If I remember correctly, they were played on by Leslie West and Mountain. Both of them were outrageous shows but Led Zeppelin was the better show. They were promoting *Led Zep III* but playing *I* and *II* also.

I WAS THERE: TOM ZELANIN, AGE 15

It was the summer between my freshman and sophomore year of Catholic high school. I came from a very conservative family, who probably would never let me go to my first rock concert, but they had attended shows of fifties music there and assumed things were similar. A classmate fell jumping the fence, fracturing his skull, resulting in a cast that looked like a light bulb, hence the nickname 'The Bulb'. There were huge stacks of speakers, where my friends and I could see a little orange glow being passed back and forth by non-band members. There was a bit of a cloud above the Bowl that night.

I WAS THERE LISA GIANFREDO CARFORA, AGE 11

It was a mob scene. I went with my cousins who were all older than me – Natalie who is ten years older, her husband, cousin Tony, his now wife Roseanne and my cousin Marie and Sandy, both deceased. We all listened to music all the time. At a young age, I fell in love with Robert Plant's voice and I still love his voice today. We had seats on the second level bleachers, across from the stage. There was pot smoke everywhere, and lots of people doing drugs. The music was awesome. It was like a dream.

MUNICIPAL AUDITORIUM
19 AUGUST 1970, KANSAS, MISSOURI

I WAS THERE: CLAIRE PRINGLE LENZ

I went with a high school friend who passed away about 20 years ago. It was at the Municipal Auditorium, Kansas but that's about all I remember. We were into LSD at the time, so that killed my memories of a lot of things. Blurry memories? Blurry is right!

I WASN'T THERE: DAN SMITH, AGE 18

Their second and last trip to Kansas City, this time on the Missouri side, was considered a triumph. It was my eighteenth birthday and I had four tickets to the show. The bad news was that my boss at a neighbourhood grocery store would not let me take the day off. So, in a mad dash to collect my friend and our dates, whose parents insisted that we come in and hang for a spell, we arrived at the steps to the hall just in time to watch hundreds of smiling faces exit the venue and realise it was all over. Except the crying.

STATE FAIRGROUNDS ARENA
20 AUGUST 1970, OKLAHOMA CITY, OKLAHOMA

I WAS THERE: DAVID BREWER

I had a ticket in the nosebleed seats but as soon as the lights went down I ran and dropped down from a wall that separated the floor seats from the upper levels. I wrangled my way to the stage and stood right in front of Robert Plant. Jimmy Page was to my right. What a show! It may have been my first concert and I will never forget how they rocked the house. I was way high from the second hand smoke, which just made it super-duper great. Page inadvertently taught me a load of riffs as I watched him thrash that double-neck Gibson guitar.

TARRANT COUNTY CONVENTION CENTER
22 AUGUST 1970, FORT WORTH, TEXAS

I WAS THERE: PHILLIP JONES

I had discovered sex, drugs and rock and roll in a big way that summer. We had floor seats and they cost me $6.50 each, which was a strain on my minimum pay income bagging groceries. I don't recall what they opened with, but I do remember suddenly hearing Page, Jones, Bonham and then seeing an angel appear from the smoke and haze – Robert Plant! I was mesmerised by that voice and the dynamic energy being created by one of the greatest bands in the world. The high point of the night was the mind blowing 20-minute jam on 'Dazed And Confused'. I still get goosebumps thinking about it. I saw them perform three other times and, while all were great shows in their own right, nothing compared to that first one. It made me a lifelong fan and I mark it as the point in life that I became who I am today.

MUNICIPAL AUDITORIUM
25 AUGUST 1970, NASHVILLE, TENNESSEE

I WAS THERE: NEAL HOOTEN, AGE 17

They were the first band I saw to say 'fuck' on stage. As they came on stage, Plant asked a couple of times that they turn off the mezzanine lights that were lighting up the portals which were in turn lighting up the arena. After being ignored he said, 'If you don't turn those fucking lights off, we will not play.' The crowd started to get rowdy and the lights were turned off. I remember they started with 'Immigrant Song'. Page had a full beard. He used a violin bow during his solo on 'Whole Lotta Love', and they took an intermission followed by an acoustic set. They came back to do more electric songs and did a few rockabilly songs at the end.

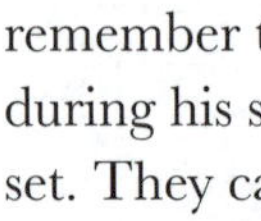

OLYMPIA STADIUM
28 AUGUST 1970, DETROIT, MICHIGAN

I WAS THERE: PERRY DROR, AGE 16

The show was amazing musically. I don't know if it sold out, but the stadium was full. Tickets cost somewhere between $5 and $8. Those were the days! I remember being put off by Jimmy Page's smug facial expression, but there was no doubt that he was a great guitarist, and I did enjoy his playing. Robert Plant's voice was spot on. Also, I remember really enjoying it when Plant sat down to play mandolin on 'That's The Way'. Bonham and Jones were rock solid. I had a memory of their having played 'Stairway To Heaven'. But after looking up the history of the song, it doesn't seem possible.

I WAS THERE: RANDY ROY

I had been to a lot of concerts back then, and this was one of the worst. Sonically they were terrible, like they mailed it in. It really changed my opinion of them. I never bought another one of their albums. Great studio band, but terrible live. It was very disappointing.

MAN POP FESTIVAL, WINNIPEG ARENA
29 AUGUST 1970, WINNIPEG, CANADA

I WAS THERE: RON SIWICKI

It was originally supposed to be outside in the Winnipeg Stadium but halfway through – before the headline bands – there was a downpour and it got moved inside to the Arena, right next to the Stadium, and delayed by hours while a new sound system could be set up. Led Zeppelin weren't going to play until Dianne Heatherington, a gutsy singer like Janis Joplin, insisted. Everyone was jammed in and soaking wet and The Youngbloods, Iron Butterfly and The Ides of March played before Led Zeppelin.

I WAS THERE: MARK NELLIGAN

Their concert was moved into the arena adjacent to the outdoor stadium when it started to rain. There was no opportunity for a sound check and they totally sucked.

MILWAUKEE ARENA
31 AUGUST 1970, MILWAUKEE, WISCONSIN

I WAS THERE: JEFF CRIM, AGE 16

I along with five other friends made the drive from Green Bay, Wisconsin. Our tickets were $5. This was the first major concert we attended. The music and atmosphere were so amazing. Seeing Jimmy Page play guitar with a violin bow without any prior knowledge of him doing this was awesome. The same can be said of seeing John Bonham play part of a drum solo with his bare hands. A female fan made her way onto the stage and jumped up and put her arms around Robert Plant's neck. She was hanging on while Robert continued to sing and then she was gently removed from him and the stage.

OAKLAND COLISEUM
2 SEPTEMBER 1970, OAKLAND, CALIFORNIA

I WAS THERE: THERESA PARSON

It was one of those nice summer nights that the San Francisco Bay Area is blessed with every year. Myself and my hippie tribe were doing what we did every Friday night, sitting in Tom Lutz's blacklight, lit with back-to-back neon posters, swilling cheap warm Olympia beer and passing around a joint. The room was so thick with cigarette smoke that my eyes were watering. We inherited this room every week when Tom's mom would go spend the weekend with her boyfriend.

After playing Led Zeppelin's self-titled first album through two times, we turned the radio to KSAN, the FM alternative station. This station was like the Holy Grail to its listeners. It played the latest rock albums from both the US and the UK from beginning to end. Every band that came through San Francisco stopped at KSAN for an in-depth, call-in interview. The lights on the switchboard lit up like Christmas lights and it was nearly impossible to get on. But if you did, you could find yourself chatting with the likes of Mick Jagger, Jerry Garcia or Bonnie Bramlett.

KSAN was always the first to hear about any new concerts that were coming to town. So imagine our stoned and slightly excitement when the deejay announced that Led Zeppelin were coming to the Oakland Coliseum. We whooped and hollered, played the album again and made plans to buy our tickets the next day. When 9am rolled around, we pulled up to Al's Records and joined the line waiting for the store to open. Our town was so condensed that everyone knew everyone in that line!

The wait seemed eternal, but finally September 2 arrived. Us girls spent the day pin curling our long hair and then sat under our mothers' hair dryers to achieve that curly singlet look. We worked diligently to put together our lace and velvet vintage-style dresses, exchanging accessories until we were satisfied with our look. The guys picked us up at 5.30pm. We stopped at Jack in the Box for dinner and lurked outside the liquor store until we found someone willing to buy us beer and cigarettes. Lutz had already secured the weed so we were ready to rock!

When we got to the Coliseum, the parking lot looked like a huge tailgate party, so we got out our provisions, cranked up the radio, which was playing nearly non-stop Zeppelin, climbed into the car and joined the fun. We knew we'd never get the beer into the venue so we made sure we drank every drop before we went to line up. The roving drug dealers worked the line, and soon there were joints being passed in every direction.

Finally, they opened the door and everybody rushed in looking for their seats. Ours weren't the best, but we could see pretty clearly whatever was about to go on onstage. As for the PA, we weren't even worried about that. The band sauntered onto the stage and the place shook with stomping and applause. We were on our feet. We weren't going to miss a thing! There was Plant with his long wavy blond hair and jeans so tight you could see a perfect outline of his package.

And then there was the beautiful Jimmy Page, decked out in a velvet coat that hung over velvet pants and a striking white shirt with an ascot at the neck and ruffled sleeves. The music started as they barrelled through 'Dazed And Confused', 'Immigrant Song', 'What Is And What Should Never Be', 'Good Times Bad Times', 'Communication Breakdown' and 'I'm Movin On' before hitting some covers like 'Blueberry Hill' and 'Long Tall Sally'.

Each song was met with wild appreciation and Jimmy Page had hundreds of air guitarists backing him up. John Bonham was a whirling dervish. It was like his sticks were a part of his hands. Running between the bass and keyboard, and playing both flawlessly, John Paul Jones never missed a beat. And Plant. That voice, screaming and growling, then dropping down until he was hardly heard and then throwing his head back and letting go of a guttural primal scream. It was like riding a vocal rollercoaster. By this time, we had managed to move a few aisles down. Our goal was to get to the floor, even though it was already blanketed in assigned seated metal chairs.

All too soon the show was over and the band filed off the stage. They had brought us to a musical peak so high we couldn't see down, and we wanted one more ride. In unison we screamed, banged chairs in the floor, lit our lighters and refused to give up. The crowd on the floor had tossed aside the folding chairs. There wasn't enough security to stop us, so everyone streamed down from their seats and inched closer to the stage.

For their encore they did 'Whole Lotta Love' and that's when holy hell broke loose. Hundreds stormed the stage, knocking each other over and crawling over each other's backs. It could have turned into a tragedy, but fortunately it didn't.

On the way home we put on the Led Zeppelin 8-track. The guys talked about every note, fret and whatever other technical thing that went into the show. They marvelled over the brands of the equipment that the band used. It was all Greek to me. Us girls? What did we talk about? The size of Plant's package of course!

I saw Led Zeppelin again at the all-day festival, Day On The Green, in Oakland. The place was packed and the sound excellent, but it couldn't compare to the first show. I think concerts are like losing your virginity – the first time is always the best!

INTERNATIONAL CENTER ARENA
6 SEPTEMBER 1970, HONOLULU, HAWAII

I WAS THERE: EVERETT L MCINTOSH

People in Hawaii smoked a lot of weed at concerts in those days and there was no hassle. And there was a lot of acid, mescaline and psilocybine. I saw Janis in Hawaii about two weeks before she died. The cops tried to calm the crowd down from her antics at the HIC. She started calling them pigs, sobs, etc. It was very close to a total riot. She was gulping a bottle of bourbon and threatened to take it into the street if they didn't get off the stage and hassling her fans. It was wild.

BOSTON GARDEN
9 SEPTEMBER 1970, BOSTON, MASSACHUSETTS

I WAS THERE: STEVE EISLER

I saw them with friends. They opened with Robert Plant announcing a new song called 'The Immigrant Song' and played all the music from the first two albums. I grew up with the music of the fifties and sixties. I fell in love with the 'new rock' and the blues. I became a Jeff Beck fan immediately, and when Zep arrived, I was absolutely in love with the music they made that embraced all of these. As a drummer in a band, we were early Zep tributees. Their first two albums are among the top ten best albums produced. I'll never forget this concert.

I WAS THERE: JIM MORIN

My second time of seeing them. My brother and I had tickets for the early performance but we were told the show was cancelled. Rumour was this was due to lacklustre ticket sales. Peter Grant insisted travel problems were to blame. Nevertheless, we were given the same seats for the late show which started around 9pm. By now they had become international superstars and were not nearly as good as the previous year's show at the Carousel. They seemed disinterested and sloppy. The lousy sound at Boston Garden didn't help.

I WAS THERE: LINDA BEAGAN, AGE 21

It was my first concert ever. My dad did not speak to me for six months afterwards because I came home late. I was so exceptionally drunk during the concert that I almost fell over the balcony. My first boyfriend held onto my ass and saved me from going overboard.

I WAS THERE: PETER MARINOW, AGE 15

I first got into Led Zeppelin when I was 14. I heard the radio edit of 'Whole Lotta Love' on the radio. I loved it and bought *Led Zeppelin II* at the first opportunity. I put it on my turntable and was blown away when I heard the full uncut version of 'Whole Lotta Love'. About a year later, Led Zeppelin scheduled two shows on the same night at the Boston Garden. A friend and I got tickets to the first show, the very first concert I attended. My dad drove us to Boston and dropped us off. Much to our chagrin, we learned that the first concert had been cancelled due to insufficient ticket sales. However, our tickets would be honoured for the second show, and we actually got upgraded to floor seats. I don't remember exactly how close we were to the stage, but it was fairly close and off to the right. We had a pretty good view.

Zeppelin opened with 'Immigrant Song', which Page said was from their forthcoming album. The rest of the concert is mired in memory haze for me, but three things stand out. During 'Dazed And Confused', Page used the violin bow to point to each corner of the arena. During one solo, Page wandered to the edge of the stage, kicked one leg out and someone on the floor grabbed his foot and attempted to pull him into the crowd. Roadies or security were right there and grabbed Page and the fan, pulling Page back onto the stage. I was amazed that he never missed a note. And I had never seen a theremin, nor knew what one was, until Page used it during 'Whole Lotta Love'. Overall, it was a thrilling event and it remains my favourite concert ever.

MADISON SQUARE GARDEN
19 SEPTEMBER 1970, NEWYORK, NEWYORK

I WAS THERE: MIKE J LOGAN, AGE 16

Before seeing them live, I wasn't impressed but went with my pals because it was something to do. We scored an ounce and rolled 13 joints, expecting to light up as soon as the lights went down, but before we could three girls sat to complete our row and lit up 26 nicely rolled numbers one after the other. After seeing Led Zep I loved them – and their audience! When they played 'Since I've Been Loving You' I was hooked. I've been to the Garden a lot and never heard it go silent before or since.

I WAS THERE: VERONICA LEE CASCINO

I saw Zeppelin so many times in concert I've lost count. I saw them each time at Madison Square Garden. I also saw them in New Jersey once I moved to Delaware. What fun times, standing on our chairs and singing along to their music and clapping our hands.

Recorded between January and July 1970,* Led Zeppelin III *is released in October 1970.

The Spring 1971* Back to the Clubs *UK and Ireland tour is a conscious decision to play smaller venues to reward British fans with gigs in a more intimate setting, despite less income from fewer ticket sales.

ULSTER HALL
5 MARCH 1971, BELFAST, UK

I WAS THERE: NOEL THOMPSON, AGE 16

I had been a complete convert since *Led Zeppelin I*. They were the only band I wanted to know about, and I can remember the excitement we felt when we heard they were coming to Belfast. Two friends and myself went. I don't think it was that difficult to get tickets or there being a queue. We just went down to the Ulster Hall.

We had great seats. The Ulster Hall has seats that envelop the back of the stage so we were side on to the band, and it was an amazing experience from start to finish. At the end of the gig, they played 'Stairway To Heaven' for the first time. We didn't know what it was. It was just, 'We're going to play one of our new songs off the new album.' It got a fairly rapturous response, although it was the first time anyone had heard it anywhere in concert.

At the end, my friends and I sneaked onto the stage and snipped a little bit off Jimmy Page's amplifier lead. That was sellotaped onto the back of my wardrobe door in my childhood bedroom, which my mother lived in, until three years ago. It was there the whole time and it was our booty of war, along with the ticket which I also kept.

Jim Aiken, the promoter that night, staged a 30-year memorial concert in the Ulster Hall with a Led Zeppelin tribute band and I went with the same people and got the same seats. The tribute band were quite good, but what was amazing was the age range of people there, from twelve to 90. It was a whole rock and roll family night, which showed the enduring legacy of Zeppelin.

They met my expectations one hundred percent back in 1971. It's still the best concert I was ever at. Every time I listen to Led Zeppelin, I think I should write to Robert Plant and just say, 'Thank you for the incredible joy you have brought to my life.' I believe he has the best white blues voice ever. I was in the West Country a few years ago and we were in one of the villages near Ludlow. Plant had been in for tea with the family the previous afternoon and I thought, 'Damn it, I just missed him'. If he'd been sat at the next table I'd have said, 'Thank you. You can't believe what an influence and what a pleasure your voice has brought me over 50 years. And it still does today.'

I WAS THERE: PHILIP HOGG, AGE 15

I had just turned 15. I was gobsmacked when I was able to get my hands on the ticket, which cost £5. The seat was perfect, on the balcony on the left-hand side near the stage. I couldn't have been any more than 20 feet from the band and had a great view. I still remember the spine tingles I got when Zep launched into the 'Immigrant Song' for their first number. It was heady stuff for a young fella from the small town of Larne, about 20 miles from Belfast. And that night was the first outing for 'Stairway To Heaven'. My mum was a bit nervous letting me go to Belfast on my own but she realised how important it was to me. Thank God she did. I wouldn't have missed it for the world!

I WAS THERE: ALAN BECK

I can remember queuing up outside with some mates. It may have been raining. Once inside, the house lights were on and the place was humming. The atmosphere inside the place was electric, and there was a terrific sense of anticipation as we waited. I can remember seeing Jimmy Page's Les Paul sitting on stage with its back towards the audience. I distinctly remember the back and neck were cherry red. And I think John Bonham's drum kit was green or possibly orange sparkle!

The lights went down and suddenly they were on stage. I can't remember the exact play list but I do remember 'Dazed And Confused' with the violin bow and them sitting at the front of the stage on chairs and doing an acoustic set from *Led Zeppelin III*, playing 'Bron y Aur Stomp', 'That's The Way', 'Gallows Pole', etc. Then Page produced this Gibson twin neck SG and Plant said 'this is from our forthcoming album.' What followed was the first public performance of 'Stairway'. I remember thinking at the time 'this is something special, I'll have to remember this on the new album.' The audience reaction was tremendous.

For an encore they did 'Whole Lotta Love'. I can remember Jimmy doing all that stuff with the theremin etc. Suddenly it was all over and they were gone. Apparently, Bonham went for a drive up the Falls Road and got lost!

I have been to many concerts in the Ulster Hall before and after Led Zep but that rates as one of the best ever. People were actually hanging over the balcony and standing in the aisles. I have never seen it so packed as on that night. I have two cousins who were also there that night but they had seats directly behind the band on the stage. Lucky them!

NATIONAL BOXING STADIUM
6 MARCH 1971, DUBLIN, IRELAND

I WAS THERE: BRIAN FLYNN, AGE 19

I only saw Led Zeppelin once but I would argue that I saw them at the very, very peak of their powers, before things got a little bit too flash but after they had bedded themselves in as top class. It was quite a small venue (2,400) so we got the full experience.

I first heard about Led Zeppelin very early on in their career. I used to go round to a friend's house to listen to music. He lived near me in the town I came from called Athlone. He'd buy an album every week and he had a record player as well, which I didn't have at home. On this particular week that I was down he said, 'I've got two records today.' One was *High Tide And Green Grass*, which was the Rolling Stones' greatest hits at the time, and the other was *Led Zeppelin I*. He played a little bit of *Led Zeppelin I* and we were chatting away and nothing really hit me too dramatically, but then 'Communication Breakdown' came on and there was something about that track. I knew there was something special about them from that moment.

Ireland was a wasteland from the point of view of gigs. None of the big acts ever came because of the state of war in Northern Ireland. There were bombings and murders and all that. The only big star who came was Rory Gallagher, who was Irish. He came home every Christmas and it was a huge big thing and maybe he did a festival in the summer. But apart from that, nobody came. And then suddenly the biggest band in the world were coming. We were the generation that read the *NME*, *Melody Maker* and *Sounds*. We knew that Led Zeppelin were the biggest band in the world, even though they didn't get the kind of publicity that the Rolling Stones got. We couldn't believe that they were coming to play in Dublin.

There was an outlet where you'd send in your money and you'd get your tickets sent to you. There was no scramble to get tickets like there is today. I went with my brother and two schoolfriends. We were all music nerds from the same town, down the country. I had left secondary school the year before, after doing the leaving certificate, and they were all coming up to doing their A levels that year or the year after. So they were kids really; one was 16, 17. We were very young. I had seen Rory Gallagher's band Taste live a couple of months prior so I knew what a rock concert would be like, but the boys had no idea whatsoever.

We knew that Zeppelin had a great reputation and we had devoured the first three albums but nothing could have prepared us for what we witnessed that night. Nothing could prepare you for actually being there as they walked out on stage and that wall of sound. We'd never seen footage of them so we didn't know what to expect. Zeppelin never did *Top Of The Pops* at any point, which is ironic given that 'Whole Lotta Love' became the theme tune for the show. You never saw Led Zeppelin except in the music papers. Kids took music very, very seriously. The live format was the big thing. Maybe 30 per cent, 40 per cent of the crowd just sat back in amazement at what they were seeing, but the rest knew what to expect. We were very cool kids. We were music mad. We knew what was happening. We had the records. A lot of people there that night hadn't heard *Led Zeppelin III* because *Led Zeppelin I* and *Led Zeppelin II* were what really brought them to attention but a Dublin audience would be quite smartarsed, like a Liverpool or Glasgow audience maybe, but also a very good audience. They were with the band from the beginning.

They walked out and said 'good evening'. It was no more showbiz than that. And then Robert Plant just said 'can we have the house lights down please?' That's how low key it was in those days. And they went straight into 'Immigrant Song'. From the moment it started it was just – bang! You knew there was something special going on and they never let up.

I don't know how long they played for, maybe two-and-a-half, maybe three hours. Somebody had a cassette player and they made a recording of it which you can hear on YouTube but it's pretty low quality. But it was an experience and if you were there, you'd never ever, ever forget it. At the end of the gig, I remember everybody was hugging each other. It wasn't that hippie an audience really. But there was definitely magic in that hall that night.

UNIVERSITY
9 MARCH 1971, LEEDS, UK

I WAS THERE: JEN MCCONNELL, AGE 17

I queued with my friend Gina for eight hours to get tickets, armed with money from all our friends. We got to the front to find the allocation was one ticket per person, so our eight-hour wait was rewarded but our friends were disappointed. When you bought the ticket, which I think was around eleven shillings or just over 50p (a lot of money back in the day), the back of your hand was stamped with indelible ink to stop you joining the queue again. Not that I would have waited another eight hours once I'd got my precious ticket!

The big night came and we got a great spot to watch. They opened with 'Immigrant Song'. I was smoking at the time and lost my cig as my jaw dropped at the amazing sound of Robert Plant's voice belting out. The whole set was electric. I could not pick a best bit out as it was all incredible. I say it was mind blowing because when the gig had finished, we were on our way home and I challenged my friend to sing 'Happy Birthday' or the National Anthem and neither of us could get any tune as we had just seen the most mind-blowing band.

I have seen hundreds if not thousands of bands, been to all the festivals in the day, and even seen Plant and Page a few times, but that 1971 gig remains the best. It is in my will that when my time comes to depart this world, my family are to play 'Stairway To Heaven' at my funeral service as loud as possible so people can rock in the aisles. My daughter is threatening to play the Rolf Harris version. I have promised to come back and haunt her if that happens!

SOUTHAMPTON UNIVERSITY
11 MARCH 1971, SOUTHAMPTON, UK

I WAS THERE: JEFF LEWIS

After seeing them at Bath in June 1970, in late September I went to Southampton University on a three-year law course. During Freshers' Week, I joined the student union Events department and became an assistant to the events treasurer, Sue Donovan, and was given the role of head of ticket sales. Because I had a large and eclectic record collection, I was also event DJ at many of the student union gigs. The acts that performed on campus during my first term included Deep Purple, Steeleye Span, Chicken Shack, Supertramp and Genesis, plus a band called Bronco, led by Jess Roden and Robbie Blunt. The latter was in a pre-Zeppelin group with Robert Plant.

Towards the end of my first term, the aforementioned Sue Donovan resigned from her post and I was elected Events treasurer. In 1971 Led Zeppelin embarked on a *Back to the Clubs* tour. At the time we used Chrysalis as our booking agents and, against fierce opposition from small venues all over Britain, we were able to book Zeppelin for £100. The gig sold out within minutes of the tickets going on sale.

In the early 1970s, Southampton University was quite a radical campus. In the days leading up to the March Zeppelin date, the students took over the prestigious Nuffield Theatre, on the campus site next to the law faculty. The student union was in dispute with the university authorities over the way they held and used data concerning students' personal details and academic records. This sit-in lasted quite a few days. It was rumoured that beneath the Nuffield Theatre was a Cold War control room governmental regional bunker. The student union was threatened with legal action if they did not leave the theatre. At first the students would not be moved. Indeed, the committee which was formed to run the sit-in asked me, as the only member of the Events department taking an active part, to organise a concert in the Nuffield to emphasise our defiance.

Paul McCartney had just formed Wings, who had yet to perform a concert, and I was able to get McCartney's phone number from Les Perrin, who was a bigwig PR man in the entertainment business. I rang the McCartney abode and the phone was answered by Linda. I explained the Southampton student union stance regarding the sit-in and asked whether Wings would come down and perform a special one off gig for the cause. She said that she would run the proposition past Paul and asked me to ring back the next day. Next day, Linda answered the phone again and explained that whilst she and Paul supported the stance, we were taking they had been advised that playing at the Nuffield would be perhaps too controversial.

So it was time to ring Les Perrin again and this time ask him for George Harrison's number. Les however was unwilling to get George involved with what was becoming a hot potato of a gig. Perhaps we were aiming too high, so I decided to give the Edgar Broughton Band a go. They were up for it but the threats of legal and other action were getting quite nasty and, with the Zeppelin gig fast approaching, the sit-in was brought to an end. Nobody wanted to miss the Led Zeppelin concert or do anything to jeopardise it happening.

The gig itself was held in the Old Refectory, one of the places on campus where students could eat. It had no stage so a concert required all the tables and chairs to be moved aside and a makeshift stage built. This was then taken down and stored after the gig finished. This herculean task was performed by the stage administration wing of our Events department.

Led Zeppelin were probably the biggest rock band on the planet. They had honed their act to perfection in the larger auditoriums of the USA and they ran a slick, no-nonsense operation. Their road crew had a reputation for being hard-nosed arrogant sons of bitches. Imagine my surprise when one of them turned out to be a guy who I had played in a fledgling band with at school. Indeed, one of the numbers we murdered as a band was 'Communication Breakdown'.

This guy was Trevor Martin, who had been used as a model on the debut Uriah Heep LP cover, *... Very 'Eavy ... Very 'Umble*. He worked for the Bron music organisation and usually roadied for Uriah Heep, but had wangled his way into a bit of freelance work with the Zeppelin road crew. That I knew one of them helped to smooth things over whilst the copious amounts of equipment were being unloaded and set up.

Jimmy, John Paul, Bonzo and Robert soon arrived. The first three were on their best behaviour, Page being particularly polite. However, Mr Plant had a king bee in his bonnet and boy was he buzzing. On entering the student union building he started raving and ranting about how his exorbitant taxes were paying for us lazy left wing revolutionary students. He started to deface BUNAC posters advertising cheap subsidised student trips to the USA, writing the slogan 'Who pays – I do' on them. I have always been one to fight my own corner so I pointed out to him why, if he was so down on students, was his band doing a tour which featured several university gigs? 'Peter Grant,' he grunted, as he was ushered towards the group's dressing room, which was our Events office that backed onto the makeshift stage.

I was present at the sound check and a by now more amiable Robert Plant came over and we had a brief chat about the college music scene. I mentioned that I was a big fan of the American West Coast scene and bands like the Jefferson Airplane, Love and Moby Grape. He admitted that he used to listen to them but had moved on to other artists. I replied that he should give the Californian bands another listen. He just shrugged his shoulders, shook his shaggy lionesque mane of hair and headed back to the dressing room. Fast forward the clock 20-odd years and I am watching the *Later With Jools Holland* show on TV and his special guest is Robert Plant. Jools asks Robert what he is listening to these days. Plant tells him that he has been going back to his sixties roots and is listening to the Airplane, Love and Moby Grape. Well, to quote Adam Faith, 'Don't that beat all.'

Zeppelin were epic that night. Within the confines of a small, intimate room with the narcotic smoke producing a thick fug, a fog of reefers were passed amongst the audience who sat crosslegged on the floor, transfixed and totally hooked on the mesmerising power of the musicians and singer – both as individuals and as a group. Zeppelin were truly a band bonded by some alchemistic secret power. Page's mastery of his various guitars was awe inspiring. John Paul Jones' bass playing was truly enigmatic, powerful and yet under stated, with the notes he didn't play just as important as those he did. His keyboard playing was both melodic and concise.

As a poor excuse for a drummer myself, I paid particular attention to the percussive muscle of John Bonham, gong and all. He was effortless perfection that night whether playing with his sticks or his bare hands. As Sandy Nelson would say, he was 'drumming up a storm'. The world had never seen a drummer like Bonham before. Nor have they since.

Robert Plant was at the top of his game. His blues-zapped soulful rock yaps were masterful, with siren-esque squeals powered on by the avalanche of unrelenting riffing from Jimmy Page. A good time was had by all. After the gig, Plant seemed genuinely bemused that 90 per cent of the audience were male. It was as if all his testosterone fuelled vocals were being misdirected. He said that in the States the audience consisted of a much larger female contingent. I told him that when Sandy Denny's group Fotheringay had appeared in the Old Refectory the previous term, there was a much larger proportion of the fairer sex in attendance. On the mention of Sandy Denny, his eyes sparkled and he admitted that he was a big admirer of the lady both as a singer and as a person. Enough said. All there was left to do was pay the band.

We never normally paid cash on the night – it was always a cheque to the agency within a stipulated time following the date of the performance. But Zeppelin had insisted in their contract that they wanted their hundred quid on the night so cash it was. The day after the Zeppelin gig, we had a Mott the Hoople concert in the Old Refectory. They were contracted to play for a fee of £400. It was a case of 'after the Lord Mayor's Show'. The Old Refectory was not even half full. The performance was enjoyable but the atmosphere was flat. Let's face it, there were precious few acts who would even contemplate trying to upstage Led Zeppelin in 1971.

The week before the gig, Elton demanded that his fee be increased and we told him 'No way, Jose' so he never showed.

PAVILION
13 MARCH 1971, BATH, UK

I WAS THERE: PAUL SHEPPARD

Bath Pavilion's capacity is for about 1,000 souls. It's an old building dating back to 1910 and catering for all manner of entertainments. Led Zeppelin first played the venue on 16 December 1968 when they were still trying to make a name for themselves. In 1971, as part of their *Back to the Clubs* tour, the Pavilion was once again selected as a venue for the band. At 75p at a ticket I couldn't turn this down, even though 75p was a lot of money to a non-working schoolboy at the time. Having immersed myself in the three albums the group had released to date, I was pretty sure they'd open with 'Immigrant Song'. They didn't disappoint on that score but, boy, were they loud! I read years later that they had brought their stadium sound system with them, so the Pavilion shook to some 400 watts that night.

My specific memories centre firstly on the band's apparel, dressed as they were in very casual clothes. Bonzo was notable as he wore dungarees, a style he would later extrapolate into the 'droog' look used by the characters in the film *A Clockwork Orange*. John Paul Jones was, as always, the quiet one but attention was focussed on him briefly when his keyboard failed during 'Since I've Been Loving You'.

A surprise for me, as I had no prior knowledge of the band's live history, was the inclusion of acoustic numbers and the playing of new songs from their forthcoming untitled fourth album. Highlights were 'Heartbreaker' and the 'Whole Lotta Love' medley, packed full of rock and roll standards, including lines from the Nashville Teen's 'Tobacco Road'. Also notable was Robert's sense of humour with his reference to 'The Pushbike Song', a chart hit for The Mixtures. I was partially deaf for three days afterwards and it is with regret that I never managed to see the band a second time.

Nevertheless, this was a landmark in the musical soundtrack of my life and Led Zeppelin are my favourite band still, bar none!

TRENTHAM GARDENS
14 MARCH 1971, STOKE-ON-TRENT, UK

I WAS THERE: ALAN JERVIS

My wife Susan and I attended both of the gigs at Trentham Gardens, in 1971 and again on 15 January 1973. I don't remember a great deal about either gig other than that Led Zep were fantastic live. We were a few minutes late attending the first one and they were already playing 'Immigrant Song', which blew my socks off. As they closed their performance at one of the shows, John Bonham flung both of his drumsticks spinning into the crowd, possibly at someone's great peril. My wife seems to remember that it cost around £3 each for the tickets.

I WAS THERE: MICHAEL JONES

We were late in arriving but managed to get a good view in the 3,000 capacity Trentham Gardens which, from memory, had an excellent reputation for its acoustics. The set list for the gig was something like 'Immigrant Song' leading through to 'Heartbreaker', 'Stairway To Heaven', 'What Is And What Should Never Be', 'Whole Lotta Love' and 'Communication Breakdown'. The sound was so loud but excellent and in keeping with the venue's reputation. However, towards the end the performance smoke suddenly appeared from the stage and it was quickly apparent that it wasn't stage effects but the equipment had caught fire! The performance abruptly came to an end for safety reasons and soon we were back out in the fresh cool evening air and on our way home.

I WAS THERE: PETER ALCOCK

This was two-and-a-half hours of Zeppelin at the top of their game. They kicked in with 'Immigrant Song' and Robert's voice was so powerful I thought he would break the windows of the venue. They did all the old favourites – 'Heartbreaker', 'Since I've Been Loving You',

'Dazed And Confused', 'Whole Lotta Love', 'That's The Way', 'Thank You' and 'Moby Dick'. They also did three new tracks from their up and coming LP: 'Black Dog', 'Stairway To Heaven' and 'Going to California'. They encored with 'Communication Breakdown'. I'll always remember one of the amps catching fire near the end of the performance.

I WAS THERE: DAVID POINTON

I was at both Trentham Gardens gigs but the 1971 show was particularly memorable for me, as it was the first gig I ever attended. Bands generally used to tour before album releases, so this would have been the first rendition we'd heard of material from the fourth album. I remember the following day talking with some other guys who had been to the gig and one of them commented, 'Hey, that 'Stairway To Heaven' was good, wasn't it?' Of course, I had to agree, but in retrospect, I don't think I realised what a legendary anthem it was to become. The evening's entertainment was all provided for the princely sum of 50p. The tour had been billed as 'cut-price' so that probably explains why one of the amplifiers apparently caught fire!

I WAS THERE: TIM DIGGLES

I'd listened to their albums but was thoroughly disappointed by them live. In fact, I can probably say I was bored. Most of it seemed to be long acoustic pieces and after that I never bothered listening to them unless someone else was, in the college common room. A few days later I saw Black Sabbath and they were amazing. Maybe there are times we expect too much. I remember seeing Crosby and Nash in Manchester and realised how much Stills and Young made that band. That was a dreadful, long evening. My father, who'd now be 114, saw a real Zeppelin flying over Derby when he was a boy!

I WAS THERE: STEVE KELLY, AGE 16

It was the talk of the week in the school breaks. It was a time when we were just discovering music, and Zeppelin were one of the biggest bands. I went with my girlfriend and all my schoolmates. It was in a proper ballroom with all the fanciness. I first discovered their music on an LP called *Age of Atlantic*, a 99p sampler with 'Communication Breakdown' on it. I also remember the single 'Whole Lotta Love'. I couldn't afford LPs but my girlfriend had *Led Zeppelin IV* when it came out. I still like the earlier stuff. I remember seeing Robert Plant in Kidderminster High Street in the early eighties with his wellies on.

MAYFAIR BALLROOM
18 MARCH 1971, NEWCASTLE-UPON-TYNE, UK

I WAS THERE: ROBERT MARTIN

I went with my then girlfriend. We were so into the performance that we decided to stay until the very end of the show, which meant missing the last buses and train back to our home town of Sunderland, 15 miles away. After a great night's entertainment, we started walking home.

We were a bit strapped for cash in those days and a taxi was out of the question. However, we did manage to hitch a lift after trekking about eight miles along the road. We got dropped off in Sunderland town centre so I just had to escort my girlfriend home and proceed on to my childhood home. I don't remember what time we got in but it was very late, as I remember being knackered when my mother got me up for work the next morning.

I WAS THERE: HENRY RACE

The venue probably held about 2,000 people and I still have my ticket. I remember it being absolutely jammed. I can't remember anything about the show.

BELFRY HOTEL
20 MARCH 1971, SUTTON COLDFIELD, UK

I WAS THERE: PETE SMITH

I saw them at the Belfry in Sutton Coldfield. I still see Robert around. He's an avid Wolves supporter, and a truly great rock star.

BOAT CLUB
21 MARCH 1971, NOTTINGHAM, UK

I WAS THERE: RICHARD TURNER, AGE 17

I was a cadet oarsman at the Boat Club when Led Zeppelin returned, having first played there in April 1969. As a member it was our club so, along with those privileges, everybody was expected to lend a hand with bar work, etc. When the tickets for the gig went on sale, I watched from the Boat Club balcony as the queue formed and eventually reached and travelled along Trent Bridge. I had discovered Zeppelin by then and had a couple of albums, but the heavy metal genre was not my favourite.

On the day of the concert, a handful of us volunteered to help the roadies. When their lorry pulled up, a couple of guys got out. I remember being relieved that they were pleased for us to be there. In addition to the usual amplification and boxed equipment, the most notable item was a very large gong which it took two of us to negotiate the narrow turning stairs to the club stage.

I think we must have dispersed after we unloaded, as my next recollection is of the stage being packed with glittering equipment, tended by a couple of guys adding the finishing touches. The band were already in our scruffy and slightly whiffy changing room.

Now it was time for us to get a pitch. We had a blank canvas. Where were we going to stand? The decision had to be made before the fans were upon us. There was a gap between the top of the bar and the ceiling, with just enough room to sit or crouch. The handful of us would also be able to repel hostiles from there. So I had a perfect spot, 20 feet from the stage.

My recollection of the concert is initially of the noise, which was considerably louder than any other concert I had experienced. A couple of songs into the set, Plant asked to have the lights put on and he spoke to the fans. He said that they had been playing in large faceless venues and were keen on returning to playing where they could see people, and back to where it all started. It was clearly nostalgic for him. The most memorable number for me was 'Moby Dick'. As an audio visual experience, it was stunning. The effort and feeling that went into Bonham's performance was nothing short of Olympian, at one point throwing down his drumsticks and playing bare-handed. I had seen quite a few bands by that time but nothing compared to the enthusiasm and aggression he showed, like a dog unleashed. The aftermath of this extravaganza was evident when we came to clear up and move the equipment downstairs. I was surprised to see several discarded, cracked, blood-stained drumsticks along with a blood-smeared cymbal. I secreted a pair of drumsticks away and later took them home.

The band had returned to the changing room where an interview attempt was being made by a reporter via a hand-held Dansette tape recorder. His progress was delayed with his failed attempts to press play and record simultaneously with one hand. Whilst this was going on, Jimmy Page was vigorously complaining about his missing t-shirt. I remember thinking that this wasn't very rock and roll. Couldn't he afford another one? Ironically, t-shirts going missing was a familiar complaint emanating from our shower room.

Seeing Zeppelin at such close quarters was a lifetime experience. I took it for granted, not realising just how privileged I was. Now I can see what a significant effect it had on broadening the spectrum of my life's musical appreciation. Not fully understanding their historical significance, I lent the drumsticks to my much younger step brother who was going through a 'I want to be a drummer' stage. He lost them.

MARQUEE CLUB
23 MARCH 1971, LONDON, UK

I WAS THERE: ANDY MORRIS

I saw Zeppelin at the Marquee Club. It was a big deal because you had to queue up all night for tickets. I queued up with a mate of mine from north London. We were really lucky because you'll never see a band like that again in a small club. I remember Plant had a beard and I think Jimmy did too. And Plant was wearing an Indian kaftan. It was magical, an amazing show. I saw them a couple of years later at Alexandra Palace and in Madison Square Garden on their last tour of the US. They're my favourite band. I've been a huge fan of theirs ever since they released their first record. There were no bands out there that sounded like Zeppelin. You put those four people together and they were equally as important as each other. It wasn't just 'Plant had a great voice' or Jimmy was great'. John Paul Jones? What a master of keyboards!

MOUNTFORD HALL, LIVERPOOL UNIVERSITY
10 MAY 1971, LIVERPOOL, UK

I WAS THERE: JAN MERSEY, AGE 18

We called bands 'groups' in those days and gigs were 'concerts'. This was a birthday present from my then boyfriend and my friends. I was so happy, as it was the best present I'd ever had. Tickets were about 50p, which was quite a lot then, and then there were the drinks on top! We were all working – I was a student nurse – but nights out could be quite expensive. I don't have the ticket any more as they tore them up at the door so you couldn't go out and cheat. I do however still have the poster I got from one of the roadies, a local lad who my boyfriend knew. I'm not sure what the capacity was for that first gig, possibly not more than 400 or 500, but they did let more people in. We sat on the floor most of the time and then stood up for the heavier songs, and especially 'Whole Lotta Love' at the end. I was so in awe I don't remember a hell of a lot about it. I was drunk too, it being my 18th, but I remember Jimmy Page was wearing a horrible Fair Isle yellow-brown tank top waistcoat thingy. He and Robert both had beards. The first few numbers were creaky and the amps were up too high so there was a lot of feedback, but they got better.

They were loud even then, and the acoustics in there with the low ceiling in the room weren't great. They did 'Communication Breakdown', 'Dazed And Confused' and most of the songs from the first two albums, plus some blues numbers I didn't know at the time but got to know later. The violin bow on the guitar was a fabulous solo which lasted for between eight and ten minutes.

I WAS THERE: RODDIE GILLIARD, AGE 16

May 10th 1971 was the day before my 17th birthday. I'd left secondary school in the summer of 1969 and started a Painting and Decorating apprenticeship that September, spending most of my wages on records and going to live concerts. It was a golden time for gigs as all the bands were constantly touring and Liverpool had several venues like the Empire, Liverpool Uni Mountford Hall, the Stadium, the Philharmonic and St George's Hall. There was also Liverpool Polytechnic and smaller clubs like The Mardi Gras and The Cavern. I was lucky enough to see The Who four times, Deep Purple, Black Sabbath, Free, Mott and so many more, usually for between 60p and £1. And I got to see Led Zep twice within the space of six months.

Amongst my circle of friends, we owned most all of the classic albums of the time and spent time at each others' houses, listening to them all constantly. There were so many albums by so many bands it was impossible to own them all personally. It was not unusual to buy a ticket to see a band you didn't own albums by as chances were that one of your mates had them. Other times you would go to see a band you didn't know, sometimes out of curiosity. It was a time of great musical adventure. There were several ticket kiosks where you would see listings of bands coming to town.

I saw that Led Zep were playing at Mountford Hall at Liverpool University and bought a ticket. I seem to remember I went on my own. At that time, I didn't own any of the three albums that had been released, but several of my mates had copies so I was well aware of the band. I think the ticket was 60p. Mountford Hall was a modern hall in the Uni complex – long and fairly narrow with a flat floor, no seating with a low stage at one end. It was normal for everyone to squeeze in and sit on the floor, until it was rammed and everyone would then have to stand up. It probably held about 1,500 people. I remember there was a kind of 'programme' which was a single sheet of thick paper, maybe about nine inches wide and 15 inches long, printed on both sides. I also remember that the ink came off on your hands! They started with 'Immigrant Song', which was instantly recognisable by the vocal intro, and the rest of the show featured songs from the three albums, and possibly some of the new songs from the forthcoming album, although I'm afraid everything is a bit vague after so many years.

Led Zeppelin's 1971 North American tour, their seventh visit to the continent, starts on 7 August 1971, included two European warm-up shows and concludes on 17 September 1971. Comprising 26 shows in total, it is designed to coincide with the release of* Led Zeppelin IV*, but the album's release is delayed. The tour grosses over $1 million.

PACIFIC COLISEUM
19 AUGUST 1971, VANCOUVER, CANADA

I WAS THERE: SHAWN DUGGAN, AGE 11

The Pacific Coliseum was built for house our NHL hockey team and doubled as a concert venue for years. It was my first concert. My folks let my older sister act as a chaperone. It was a sunny day and a 'smoky' environment. About all I remember is that they played songs off the first three albums.

I WAS THERE: BRIAN BINGHAM

It was a Thursday. I still have my pink ticket stub to prove it, general admission ticket stub #12526.

SEATTLE CENTER COLISEUM
20 AUGUST 1971, SEATTLE, WASHINGTON

I WAS THERE: RUSTY WILLIAMS

I'm playing guitar in a local Seattle band called Bighorn. The band is rapidly gaining popularity and we are able to afford a two-man road crew. The two guys we picked up were pros – we thought. They had been touring with Led Zeppelin. How could they have any better credentials? They and we were pretty consistent partiers. But the roadies took it a step further. They liked white port and lemon juice along with 'Red Devils', which were pretty strong barbiturates. Zep were in town, playing at the Coliseum. The roadies were going down to hang with their old mates in the band and the crew. We just wanted to see the concert.

It was following the release of *Led Zep IV* and we knew it would be great. And it was. When we got back to the band house, the roadies were already there and they were hitting a 30-gallon keg of beer pretty hard. 'Hey! A keg! Where did you get it?' we asked. 'We snagged it from the band's dressing room while they were playing. We missed the show but we got a keg!' They were already pretty snowed under. Evidently Reel Devils go with beer too, so we put a nasty dent in the keg and toasted Zep repeatedly. They played great and they supplied us great beer. The roadies didn't last too long with Bighorn either. Imagine being too rowdy for rock and roll bands.

I WAS THERE: CONRAD T JEMSLAND, AGE 15

Tickets were $3, capacity was 20,000 seats and it was sold out. It is a night I will never forget.

FORUM
21 & 22 AUGUST 1971, LOS ANGELES, CALIFORNIA

I WAS THERE: DAVID FRESHMAN

I saw Led Zeppelin five times. 1971 was my first time and they were explosive and powerful. Witnessing 'Immigrant Song', 'Heartbreaker', 'Celebration Day', 'Black Dog', 'That's The Way' and so much more was such an incredible experience for me. They mostly seemed to be playing music from *II*, *III* and *IV* plus 'Communication Breakdown' and 'Dazed And Confused' from *Led Zep I*. *Led Zeppelin Ill* was a misunderstood LP. In 1971, at the Forum, we got to see this music debuted for us and I personally loved it. They also did 'Weekend', an Eddie Cochran song. This was when l realised how much Led Zep loved music from the fifties.

I WAS THERE: LESLIE C MILLER, AGE 14

This was my first rock concert. I went with my older sister and three girls from the neighbourhood. We had great seats and Led Zeppelin were awesome.

I WAS THERE: MARCOS FERNANDES. AGE 14

I was living in Japan and my American classmate had bought Zep's first album for a couple of dollars at the Navy Exchange. But he didn't like it and offered to sell it to me for ¥100, at a time when albums cost ¥2,000. It was a bargain I couldn't refuse. I bought it, took it home and slapped it on the turntable. 'Good Times Bad Times' started and I honestly don't know what hit me. I played it again and again every day for quite some time.

In August 1971, I was in Los Angeles with my folks to attend my sister's wedding. My childhood buddy, Ricardo Alonso, called me up and asked me if I'd like to go see Led Zeppelin. l said yes and so I caught their second night there. I was seeing the band live for the first time and this was also my first concert experience in America, so the whole thing was quite overwhelming. We had excellent floor seats and people kept passing joints around. Though we didn't indulge, I'm sure just breathing the air in that arena would get you high. The performance was loud and raunchy. I was blown away, just like the first time I heard them blast out of my stereo speakers. But live they were so much more intense.

I WAS THERE: KIKI

After the concert, we were backstage and I spoke a little to Jimmy Page. Then, as Robert Plant was walking off the stage, he kept staring at me and we happened to meet at the bottom of the stage steps. I told him I enjoyed the show and he answered that it was pretty nice except at certain points. He said, 'I have to go' and touched my shoulder. He also kissed me on the cheek.

As we were walking up the driveway, the limo sped past and then suddenly it stopped and Robert flew out of the door, ran straight to me and asked if I'd meet him at the Whisky. He said there was no room in the car but that he'd see me in front or leave my name. When we got there, they hadn't arrived yet so Jean and I had to walk around.

Finally, we saw them. Jean went in and brought him out to get me. We left in my car and went back to the Hyatt House. He opened doors for me and allowed me to go into the elevator before him. He was so polite. He called room service for some Coke. Someone called and he informed them that he was entertaining a young lady so to please excuse him as he must hang up. Some chick called. He said 'this is not Jimmy's room' and then rang the front desk and told them not to allow any calls to come through from now until eleven in the morning. No interrnptions. His voice continues to bother him. He says every now and then Jimmy and the others and himself pack up and stay out in the country for awhile to get back down to basics.

He decides he'd like to take a shower. We talk some. He questions my everyday activities, tells me to explain to him fully. We stand out on the balcony for awhile. Touching me, kissing now and then. He offers me some whisky. Few sips. We lie on the bed for awhile. He gets up to take a shower. Requests a washing of his back. I agree.

He undresses in the bathroom. I stand before the window, gazing out to the street. He comes in, naked, says my name very boyishly, innocently. I come over to him. Hugs. I say, 'I have to go to my car and get some things.' He says couldn't I do it in the morning? I say no. He gives me the key to the door. There is a 'Do Not Disturb' sign on the door when I return. John Bonham, Buffy and Candy see me before Robert's door so they journey down the hall and knock after Robert lets me in. He is now wearing a simple white hotel towel around himself. They enter and then comes Willy, a flunky, a business associate and three guys from Britain who are in a group. They're all extremely polite and nice to me, seeing that Robert reacts to me surprisingly well. He'd put his feet on my feet or shoes, I took them off at one point. One guy hypnotises Robert. By 3.30pm, he asks me to come into the bathroom for a private tete-a-tete in which he tells me of the hypnosis he just underwent and that he is tired and that the guy told him he should sleep deeply now. I ask, should I leave? He replies, 'Will you call me tomorrow?' I ask when. He replies, 'Midday.' I consent and smile politely and all. Everyone leaves. He kisses me goodbye. I am delirious with joy. The next day I ring about three times before I reach him. He says, 'How are you? Come up now – I'll be in my room.' I get there in about 45 minutes. He is not in. Scared, insecure, after about 10 minutes of going up and down I decide to leave for awhile for

I find out everyone is to be back at the hotel by 6.15pm. As I leave down Sunset I see him drive in. I turn around and he is not in his room. I stay on the mezzanine for awhile. Go back to his door. Knock. He asks, 'Who is it?' I say my name. He opens. He is getting ready to leave. I sit out on the balcony, reading *A Season in Hell* (at least, trying). He's busy dressing. He comes out and comes up from behind and kisses my head. Looks to see what I'm reading. Asks me to cut a tag off his shirt. He begins to scent himself with patchouli oil, asks if I'd like some. I accept, placing some on my wrist. He puts some right above my nose on the forehead. He says he'll put my name on the guest list. I leave. Already have ticket. Get backstage. I see him. He wanted to get me a front-row ticket. No more left. See him afterwards. Says he is tired but to drop in next time they come and 'be jolly and bring some more silly literature [Rimbaud]'.

TARRANT COUNTY CONVENTION CENTER
23 AUGUST 1971, FORT WORTH, TEXAS

I WAS THERE: MOKSHA JO EFSEA, AGE 16

I went with friends from high school. I was an anti-war hippy and I still am! I saw them four times in total. I remember 'Whole Lotta Love' and 'Stairway To Heaven' best. It was during 'Stairway' that they first used the rainbow machine. Tech was really old school back then, so the rainbow was a real surprise. I was also at the first concert where they used laser beams. The lasers blew our minds. We had never seen anything like them! Tickets for the first show were $4, $5 and $6, a lot of money then! I did a lot of acid back then and saw them twice on LSD. The acid didn't dull my experience. It enhanced my memories.

I saw them live on TV during *Live Aid* too. My employer allowed me to run home every six hours to change my video tape and I was home during their set, with Phil Collins on drums.

MEMORIAL AUDITORIUM
24 AUGUST 1971, DALLAS, TEXAS

I WAS THERE: STEPHEN FLOYD

At Christmas 1970, my older sister gifted me a *Led Zeppelin III* album. Unwrapping it, I noticed the cardboard wheel on the inside of the front cover which you could turn, giving you the ability to change the album cover. I still enjoy turning that wheel on that same album some 40 years later. Dropping the needle down on my portable turntable, I heard the distinctive sound of the needle touching the vinyl. Then the now familiar guitar intro, the beating of the drums, that powerful bass line and, unexpectedly, that incredible voice, like a man in the wild calling out. 'Immigrant Song' would be the standard by which I would judge other albums for quite a long time. The first two albums blew me away but there was something different about *Led Zep III*. It stirred a new emotion that had been hiding in a corner of my mind waiting patiently for me to release it when the time was right. The time was right. I was hooked for life!

The next summer, I was hanging out with friends in a haze of smoke and we were listening to our favourite radio station. They advertised that there would be a special announcement and it came that same afternoon – Led Zeppelin were coming to Dallas. It was going to take planning, money, co-ordination and a whole lot of luck to buy tickets so we hoped the Golden God was sending positive vibrations.

The closest place to buy tickets was 50 miles away in Fort Worth. Once that was accomplished, we would then have to figure out how to get the money for gas so we could make the 200-mile round trip and get our parents let us go to Dallas, when the oldest in the group was 18 years old. We had never before saved, done extra chores and picked up and sold empty glass bottles. Nor would we ever again! The price of tickets was somewhere between $8 and $12. But whatever it would take, we were going. We pooled our money and – bingo! – we had enough. Boe drove the three of us to Fort Worth and we unbelievably scored four tickets to the concert. We were celebrating all the way home!

Coming from a town of 15,000 people in central Texas, when we entered the Coliseum I was taken back by the gigantic size of such a place. I remember the infectious joy and positive vibes emanating from the entire building. We were joined together as one and with one goal – to rock! Our seats were in the back of the facility, about midway up. We were sitting there anticipating and discussing what we hoped they would play when, all of a sudden, the lights went down and the crowd erupted – wham!

There it was, that familiar guitar riff, that exploding drum beat, that perfect bass line. I couldn't believe it. It was live right in front of me. One deep yellow beam of light radiated down on Robert Plant. He was turned sideways, leaning back, head cocked, his beautiful, long curly golden hair hanging loosely on his shoulders and that perfect rock star stance. With the microphone in front of his mouth, he was opening his mouth and that incredible voice projected that opening scream of 'Immigrant Song'. It was fucking unbelievable! The joy, the excitement, the disbelief. My vinyl record was live and in person. It was Led Zeppelin heaven from then on.

Hearing them play 'Communication Breakdown', 'Heartbreaker', 'Black Dog', John Bonham's thunderous solo on 'Moby Dick', 'Going To California', 'Dazed And Confused', my favourite Led Zeppelin song ever, 'Thank You', 'Since I've Been Loving You'. Then, when you thought it couldn't get any better, 'Whole Lotta Love' with Jimmy Page's guitar solo on a double-neck guitar melted every other guitar solo I had ever heard into dust. I never knew there was such a thing as a double-neck guitar. And it was playing the most famously familiar guitar solo ever!

With the last note still ringing throughput the building, they walked off stage. I was startled when people unexpectedly started clapping and screaming and banging on the seats, hollering 'more, more!' It felt as if the building was going to implode at any moment. I seem to recall there being three encores. On the last encore, I remember Robert Plant saying they were going attempt to play a song they had never performed live. Whether that was true or not didn't matter – it was true for me! I can't remember if I had heard it before but I will never forget the undeniable and most startling notes of 'Stairway To Heaven'. I've seen over 300 concerts and to this day I remember that show, those feelings, and the excitement of that evening as if it were yesterday!

MUNICIPAL AUDITORIUM
29 AUGUST 1971, NEW ORLEANS, LOUISIANA

I WAS THERE: BARBARA JONES GOODE, AGE 13

Led Zeppelin was the first concert I ever went to. An older cousin was visiting and he talked my dad into letting him take me. It blew my mind! After seeing Zeppelin live, I was no longer interested in the teen heartthrobs of the day. I can't list all my favourite Zeppelin songs because there are too many. It might be easier to say which are my least favourite – 'Heartbreaker' because I heard it too much and 'Stairway To Heaven' because the radio stations played it to death!

ORLANDO SPORTS STADIUM
31 AUGUST 1971, ORLANDO, FLORIDA

I WAS THERE: TIM LINEHAN

I discovered Zep's music when I was about 13 years old. A year later a friend got tickets to see them and invited me to tag along. Words cannot begin to describe the feeling that I had, seeing these rock gods performing right before my eyes. It is something I will remember for the rest of my life. It was the best of many concerts I have attended.

I WAS THERE: BILL CHADWELL

Sometime in the fall of 1969, I heard 'Whole Lotta Love' on the AM radio and it blew me away. I was 13 and it quickly led to my purchasing the album at a local music store, which I played on a very cheap hand-me-down stereo from my mother. I'm sure she came to regret that decision. *Led Zeppelin II* was the first album I ever purchased, and may have been only the second record. (I purchased 'Touch Me' by The Doors sometime in early 1969.) In any case, listening to *Led Zeppelin II* turned me into a hard-core Zeppelin fan, and I soon followed that up with the purchase of their first album. I played those records over and over and over again. I had never heard anything like it. Up until then, I had only listened to music via AM radio, and those stations only played the hits. There was nothing comparable on AM. As I later came to realise, there was very little comparable anywhere in the world.

Through the rest of 1969 and most of 1970, my friends and I waited expectantly for their next album and when *Led Zeppelin III* was released, I bought it the first chance I had. It was… different. It took some getting used to, but I came to love it as well.

Nearly a year after *Led Zeppelin III*, I heard via an ad on the radio that they were playing a show in town at the Orlando Sports Stadium. I somehow convinced my mother to let me go, and one of my friends went along with me. It was my first concert and was like nothing I had ever seen or heard before. The band just roared. Although their fourth album hadn't been released yet, the highlight of the show was when they previewed 'Black Dog' and 'Stairway To Heaven'. I couldn't believe 'Stairway', which remains to this day one of the most impactful songs I've ever heard. The only down side is that now that I've listened to it probably over a million times, it doesn't have quite the impact it did then.

While the fourth album was released only a couple of months after their concert in Orlando, at the time it seemed like I had to wait for years. I bought it as soon as I could, and it joined the rotation of being played over and over and over.

I continued my Zeppelin fandom through the rest of their albums, of course, and then in 1977 had the opportunity to see them again, this time at 'the big sombrero' – Tampa Stadium. The sky was darkening with an impending thunderstorm when they came on. They sounded even better than they had in 1971. And then the heavens let loose. I got to hear them play three songs, and then the show was over. That was the last time I saw Led Zeppelin, although I did get to see Jimmy Page and Robert Plant when they toured in support of *Walking Into Clarksdale.*

MADISON SQUARE GARDEN
3 SEPTEMBER 1971, NEW YORK, NEW YORK

I WAS THERE: MIKE ADAMS, AGE 15

My best friend and I lived to hear Led Zep. I loved them from the very first spin of their first LP. I must have played it ten dozen times after I purchased it. I had heard some of their songs on WNEW-FM. But when at the record store the cover caught my attention. It screamed 'buy me... this shit is great!'

But seeing Led Zep live was the pinnacle. This was the first proper concert that I attended. It was exhilarating. My friend and I paid $5.50 to see them at Madison Square Garden. Although we were in the mezzanine, it did not impact the thrill. I remember the stage broke down when Zeppelin moved into their first of three encores and Robert Plant encouraging the crowd to back off or the show would end. All the while, he was bouncing up and down the plywood planks as if it were a trampoline. They were an excellent live band. I also saw them on the succeeding tours in 1973 and 1975 at the same venue.

MAPLE LEAF GARDENS
4 SEPTEMBER 1971, TORONTO, CANADA

I WAS THERE: JJ CLARKE

I was seated with my girlfriend and two other friends about ten rows from the stage. It wasn't until we walked out of the building that we realised we could hardly hear anything going on outside on the street. The concert had numbed everyone's hearing and it took about ten minutes before we could hear each other talking at normal volume again. But we had a great time, and my hearing is now working fine!

I WAS THERE: JOHN CLERKIN, AGE 17

The bow on the guitar I remember. The rest is a blur. I still have the stub. My ticket cost $3.50 plus $0.35 tax!

INTERNATIONAL AMPHITHEATRE
5 SEPTEMBER 1971, CHICAGO, ILLINOIS

I WAS THERE: BEN MASKA, AGE 16

I saw them in '71, '75 and '77, all in Chicago. They were great shows, each around two-and-a-half hours long. I took a couple of photos in 1971 using a small Kodak Instamatic camera with a flash cube. I photographed Page when they were doing their opener, 'Immigrant Song'. I had managed to get to the front of the stage but then security told us to move back. The last encore in '71 was 'Communication Breakdown'. Page's amp went out right before the solo. He waved his arms around like he was dancing and as soon as the amp was fixed, he motioned to John Paul and Bonzo to circle back to the chorus so he could do his solo.

In '77, the band came out with all the stage lights on. They got a standing ovation before they even played. The only reason it stopped was because Jimmy got his double neck on and they started playing 'The Song Remains The Same'.

BOSTON GARDEN
7 SEPTEMBER 1971, BOSTON, MASSACHUSETTS

I WAS THERE: PAUL ROBINSON

The third time I saw them was in 1971, after the release of *ZOSO*. The set drew heavily from that album. My memory is of the scent of pot in the air, them playing 'Black Dog', 'Rock And Roll' and 'Stairway To Heaven', and it being very loud.

HAMPTON ROADS COLISEUM
9 SEPTEMBER 1971, HAMPTON, VIRGINIA

I WAS THERE: KATHIE DUVALL BEACH, AGE 13

I was a teeny bopper that liked uplifting pop music. My boyfriend turned me on to the likes of Led Zeppelin and I was changed almost overnight. Their music was unlike any I had ever heard and

I didn't know how to take them. I bought their albums and listened alone in my room or blasted my ear drums at parties. Their music was three dimensional and caused visions. Led Zeppelin was the second live concert I saw. Back then we went to see live concerts for the price of movies today. I saw all the big ones, except Janis, Hendrix and The Doors. I missed the chance to catch a ride to Woodstock because I had a healthy fear of my dad. I was in seventh grade after all! My friend ran away to go, and said it was worth the six month restriction that followed.

I WAS THERE: MICHAEL MONAHAN

We had an old record shop that was a combination news stand where I bought the first issue of *Rolling Stone* magazine, with John Lennon from *How I Won The War* on the cover. It was a folded paper publication then, and my gateway to music that I hadn't truly discovered yet. It was from the pages of that publication, and from the airwaves of our first FM radio station, that I stumbled onto the music that I still listen to almost exclusively today. *Nazz Nazz* on red vinyl, The Zombies' *Odyssey And Oracle*, Blind Faith and *Led Zeppelin I*. I was dating my first true love, a girl who was shockingly out of my league, and playing guitar in my first band. The day that my best friend and I brought home the Led Zeppelin album we knew nothing of it other than it had a really cool cover, and that the guy at the record shop said it was his favourite new release.

My parents were out of town, so we had the girls over and put on side one. Something about that record just oozed sexuality, and it put us all into a very heavy kissing and petting mood. We played the album back to front, flipping it over on the turntable every 20 minutes or so, several times that afternoon. Heavenly!

Fast forward a couple of years. *Led Zeppelin II* was out and was also a favourite. With The Beatles gone, Led Zeppelin was the band that I was most drawn to. Like The Beatles, their new records were 'events' that warranted dimmed lights and hours of listening. By 1971, I had started playing and singing professionally, and it was through one of my bandmates that I heard about them coming to the Hampton Coliseum. We went and stood on line the morning tickets went on sale and scored sixth row seats for the show.

I remember staring in awe at the size of John Bonham's drum kit. I'd never seen anything like it, and behind it all was this massive gong. I don't remember if he ever hit it during the show. They were the most powerful act I had ever seen on a stage, every member just dominating the stage. They kicked the show off with an extended 'Immigrant Song' and transitioned quickly from that into 'Heartbreaker'. The highlights of the evening for me were the acoustic set, which they opened with a new song, 'That's The Way', and 'Moby Dick'.

Oh my God, 'Moby Dick'. What a solo! Bonham sounded like six drummers at times. The show ended with 'Whole Lotta Love' and Jimmy Page striking his Les Paul with a violin bow, pointing it to the left of the auditorium and hearing it echo there, then to the right, and then back to the left. Just brilliant. I have read that the soundboard bootleg of this show is one of their most coveted performances. We were, after all, a small out of the way town compared to a lot of the other venues they played in. The speculation is that they were just a little more relaxed, a little more free, and that Page's playing in particular was some of the best ever recorded live. What a thrill to know I was at that show. They were absolutely spellbinding and we left with our jaws dragging the ground in full awe of the band we had just seen in concert. I vividly remember that weekend afternoon whenever I hear any of the tracks from that first album – that girl, those kisses and that amazing music.

I WAS THERE: PAMELA LAMBIASE, AGE 17

I had just graduated high school and we were living on our own. My best friend and roommate worked for a radio station and we got good seats. It was my first really big concert with such an awesome band. It was just an incredible experience, and when Robert Plant came out solo on stage and sang 'Stairway To Heaven' it was unbelievable! The entire audience lit their lighters and swayed and hugged, and it was just… wow! I was so lucky to have the memories even if it was a bit smoky in there (if you get my drift!). It's hard to believe it was so long ago. I wore that Zeppelin album out. Robert Plant still is making really good music, but I'm so glad I got to see the band that was such a part of my life back then.

I WAS THERE BUT THEY WEREN'T: GEORGE IRVING

My girlfriend was working the front desk at the Holiday Inn, next to the Hampton Roads Coliseum where Led Zeppelin played. Beth came home one night and said Zeppelin's road manager had called and asked if it was possible to book most of one floor. It was possible. Beth told me where and when Zeppelin would be at the suites so I thought the best thing to do was to not go to the show but to be on that part of the floor they had paid for. I was on the floor and waited for a few hours and then waited a few more hours. Then I realised they might not return. They didn't.

ONONDAGA WAR MEMORIAL
10 SEPTEMBER 1971, SYRACUSE, NEW YORK

I WAS THERE: DAVID FATTA

They performed material from their fourth album shortly before its release. Robert Plant was reluctantly apologetic about their new musical direction but said they could not 'ahah-ah-ah' ('Immigrant Song') forever.

I WAS THERE: CHRIS TZETZIS, AGE 14

I was into rock music at the age of twelve. The first Zeppelin album I bought was *Led Zeppelin II*. I went back and bought *Led Zeppelin I* and became a huge blues fan. *Led Zepplin III* had been released but *Led Zeppelin IV* was not out yet. I went with my friend, Marc Zeppetello. We were junior high school friends and boy scouts together. Imagine watching 'Stairway To Heaven' for the first time. As a kid I didn't comprehend what I was watching.

I WAS THERE: WENDELL BIGGS, AGE 22

When Zeppelin came to town I had to see them. They put on a great show. When Page put the violin bow to his guitar, the sound shook the building and my mind was blown. They even did a small Elvis set that really showed Plant's vocal diversity. I loved Page's acoustic guitar and the songs from the second side of their third album.

Led Zeppelin undertake a short Japanese tour in September 1971, comprising five dates.

BUDOKAN
23 SEPTEMBER 1971, TOKYO, JAPAN

I WAS THERE: MARCOS FERNANDES

Having seen them at the LA Forum, I was fortunate enough to catch them again upon my return to Japan. I remember Jimmy breaking his first string on the opener, 'Immigrant Song'. And things just kept getting more intense throughout the evening and over the years. I moved to California to attend university in 1973 and caught them on every tour thereafter, including their final LA Forum concert.

Recorded between December 1970 and February 1971, Zeppelin's untitled fourth album goes under various names – **Led Zeppelin IV, Four Symbols** ***and ZOSO – and is released on 8 November 1971. Recorded at Island Records' Basing Street Studios in Notting Hill, London and at Headley Grange in Hampshire using the Rolling Stones Mobile Studio, it features 'Black Dog', 'Rock And Roll' and 'Stairway To Heaven'. The album sells 37 million copies.***

Jimmy Page: 'We needed the sort of facilities where we could have a cup of tea and wander around the garden and go in and do what we had to do.'

Tickets for the 1971 UK Winter tour sell out despite going on sale less than a week before the start of the tour.

CITY HALL
11 NOVEMBER 1971, NEWCASTLE-UPON-TYNE, UK

I WAS THERE: PETER SMITH

For an old guy like me, who grew up listening to rock music in the late sixties and early seventies, Led Zeppelin were *the* band. Their early albums are absolute classics of blues rock, and their live shows were simply the thing of legend. Everyone I knew had a copy of *Led Zeppelin II* and would bring it to school to play at the record club, proudly displaying it as a badge of honour. I'd so wanted to see Zeppelin live since I'd heard my friend's older brothers talk about how great they were. They had been lucky enough to see them at Newcastle City Hall and Newcastle Mayfair in the late sixties, and they came back from those gigs so excited, full of tales of Plant's screaming vocals, of Page's amazing guitar and how he 'played his guitar with a violin bow'. In those days such tricks seemed almost unbelievable to a teenager like me.

So when Zeppelin toured in late 1971 it was my turn to see them for the first time. I was determined to make the most of the opportunity, and was lucky enough to end up seeing them twice in two days, on the first two nights of their UK tour, when they played in Newcastle and Sunderland. The concerts took place in the week that *Led Zeppelin IV* was released. Zeppelin were at the peak of their powers, simply an awesome, electric live act.

I already had a ticket for the Friday night concert in Sunderland but just couldn't wait so I decided to try and see them at Newcastle the night before. The City Hall gig had been sold out for weeks, with people queuing all night for tickets, but I wasn't going to let that stop me. I got home quickly after school on the Thursday night, had something to eat, and then set off on the train to Newcastle to try and blag a ticket outside the venue.

I managed to buy a ticket for a pretty ropey seat up in the circle, paying £1, which was twice the 50p face value. This may sound cheap now, but it seemed quite expensive at the time. But – hey – I was in, and although my view wasn't great, I was going to see Led Zeppelin for the first time! I took my seat and waited.

There was no support act; soon the lights went down and the guys stormed out, Robert Plant greeting us with a simple 'good evening! Here we are again.' Then it was straight into 'Immigrant Song', with Plant's screaming wails roaring above Jimmy Page's guitar. Page was wearing his guitar low, down around his knees, prowling around the stage while Plant posed and played the rock god at the front. John Paul Jones stood quiet and calm, providing the bass rhythms, while John Bonham pounded and bashed away at his massive drum kit. For the next couple of hours, I sat completely mesmerised by this band. I couldn't take my eyes off Page and Plant.

The set unfolded, featuring old favourites and tracks from the new LP. There were so many highlights: the opening 'hey hey, mama said the way you move / gonna make you sweat, gonna make you groove' lines of 'Black Dog'; the mystical beauty of 'Stairway To Heaven'; the back to their roots rhythms of 'Rock And Roll'; the exquisite blues guitar and blood-tingling vocals of 'Dazed And Confused'; the acoustic guitar interlude for 'That's The Way', 'Going To California' and 'Tangerine'. And Jimmy Page did play his guitar with a violin bow, and he had this strange aerial which he waved his hands at and, as if by magic, made weird spacey, spooky sounds. (I later learned that this was called a theremin.)

The concert was quite long, over two hours, and LOUD (which was good; for me the louder the better), even up in the circle where I was sitting. Just perfection; the greatest rock 'n' roll band in the world. I caught the late train home, the music still ringing in my ears, still buzzing and knowing that I'd experienced something very special. I couldn't wait to see them again the next night, and bored everyone at school with how great they were.

I WAS THERE: NEIL THOMPSON, AGE 12

My cousin taped the second album on a reel-to-reel and played it whenever we went to their house. 'Whole Lotta Love' was played on Radio 1 all the time in late '69, so me and my brother decided to go to Sunderland as he was going to buy it. We went to every record shop in Sunderland and at the very last one that we tried (the Co-op) the woman pointed at a small leaflet that was stuck next to the counter. It read something like 'The Led Zeppelin single 'Whole Lotta Love', although being played a lot on the radio at the moment, is not commercially available to buy' so that was that!

Zep were playing at Newcastle City Hall and Family were there a couple of nights later. My brother went to Newcastle to get tickets for both gigs. I remember him stepping off the bus. For some reason I'd been waiting for him at the bus stop. 'Well, the Family ticket was 75p.' 'Aah, that's okay.' 'But the Zep ticket was 90p.' I went mad. '90p? That's most of my pocket money gone then, isn't it?'

Four of us went and we sat quite near the front. They were selling some strange album in the foyer with no writing on the sleeve. I presumed it was some religious album they were giving away (this was quite common in those days). At one point Plant said, 'We have a new album out today' and loads of people held this album in the air! 'Aah, that's what it is!' It was *Zep IV*. I quite enjoyed the concert. I'd love to have seen it a bit later on in my life.

Years later, in 1994, I was doing some recording at a rehearsal studio in Kings Cross called The Depot. I was having a break and chatting to one of the workers there about Sabbath, Purple, Zep – the usual chat – and he says, 'Zeppelin are in later.' I walked back upstairs and I was thinking 'Zeppelin are in later? What on earth was he talking about?' Anyway, I finished the recording and I'm walking downstairs and here's Plant and Page standing at the bottom of the stairs. Now I quite like Zep, but if I was a fanatic this would been like a dream come true. They were rehearsing for the *No Quarter* album and it was news to me (or anyone) that they were working together again. They were chatting away but sort of looked up to me as I was walking down the stairs. 'Goodbye, then,' I said. Plant looked at me and smiled and said, 'Goodbye.' Great stuff!

I WAS THERE: HENRY RACE

I've still got the ticket. I remember this one because I recorded it. 15 or 20 years ago, there was a guy called Simon Pallet who did the *Led Zeppelin Concert File* book, and I helped him out with some of the dates. I said, 'I've got this little Led Zeppelin tape. Do you want a copy of it?' I didn't want anything for it. He said, 'Listen, lots of people would be interested in this.' With his help, we got about 20 digital copies made and sent them out to trusted people that Simon knew in the Led Zeppelin collectors network and they each burned 20 to 40 copies. They were all given away, and dropped on the same day, just to make sure that no one could get this bootleg and sell it. It's called the *Newcastle Brown Ale* bootleg, because it's got a mock up of the Newcastle Brown Ale label on the cover. No other recordings of that concert exist as far as I know. I recorded 'Whole Lotta Love' on one side of a separate C60 tape and that has been lost over the years. That will turn up in a box somewhere, I'm sure.

LOCARNO
12 NOVEMBER 1971, SUNDERLAND, UK

I WAS THERE: JOHN HENDY

I used to drink in the Argus Butterfly in Peterlee and went there now and then to see groups, although I missed Zeppelin's appearance at the jazz and folk club in the pub's ballroom in 1969. I was in the Argus lounge one night in November 1971 when a friend came in and told a group of us that he'd heard Led Zep were on at the Locarno in Sunderland. He offered to get tickets as he worked in the town. We were sceptical because nobody had heard about this show, but told him to get them if he could. Next night in the pub, in he came with five tickets. Other friends were not happy on finding out that we were going and then finding out that they couldn't also get tickets!

I remember getting into the Locarno early and being about ten yards from the front of the stage. We sat down cross-legged and waited. Some reports suggest the van bringing Zep broke down and that they were late starting but I don't remember that. As soon as they came on stage, everyone jumped up and went to the front and I distinctly remember Robert Plant saying that this was only their second time in the north east and that the first was in a little pub down the road.

I saw some great bands in that old pub – Family, Medicine Head, Quintessence and many others – and travelled to Sunderland and to Durham to see Deep Purple and Free (on the same bill). I also saw the Groundhogs, Argent and Lindisfarne around that time. One of my outstanding memories of seeing Zeppelin was Jimmy Page playing his twin neck Gibson with a violin bow. It was magical. To top it off, it was my birthday the week after and a friend bought me *Led Zep IV*.

I WAS THERE: HENRY RACE

Everyone used to call it the Mecca. Friday nights everyone went to the Mecca and everyone played there – Family, the Edgar Broughton Band, The Groundhogs. I saw Ginger Baker there. Geoff Docherty was the local promoter in Sunderland who used to bring all the bands in, including Free. There's a story in Geoff's book, *A Promoter's Tale,* about how he was promised Led Zeppelin by Peter Grant. Peter Grant broke the deal and Geoff Docherty said, 'I used to go down to London on a weekly basis on the train and knock on Peter Grant's door and say 'you owe me a gig in Sunderland'.' And in the end his persistence paid off.

I went with my girlfriend at the time, Alison, and a few others. I have the tickets but I have no memory of seeing Led Zeppelin on two consecutive nights, in Newcastle and then in Sunderland. The 11th November one was 70p and the one at the Mecca Ballroom was 75p. The Mecca was absolutely jammed. It was Sunderland. It was a shitty little town and Led Zeppelin were playing there.

I WAS THERE: PETER SMITH

Having recovered from my Zeppelin experience at Newcastle City Hall the previous night, I was ready to see the band again at our local ballroom the Sunderland Locarno (or The Mecca, as we knew it). Local ace promoter Geoff Docherty had been promising us a Zeppelin gig in Sunderland for some time. By 1971 the band were massive, and it seemed unbelievable that they would come and play at our local Mecca ballroom.

But Geoff was true to his word, and delivered the rock gods to us on a Friday night in November. Tickets had been on sale at Bergs record shop in Sunderland for all of 75p. Like many others, I rushed home from school and got over to the Mecca early, to join the queue and get a good spot down the front near our idols. By the time the doors opened there was a massive queue right down the ramp which used to lead into the venue, along the street and over the road to the Wheatsheaf pub, which stood on the corner. Everyone I knew was going; there were lots of friends in the queue with us. I was full of stories of the previous night's gig and how great Zeppelin were.

As soon as we got in, we took our places on the dance floor. Those were the days when you would sit cross-legged on the floor watching the band. The Mecca was a medium size ballroom holding perhaps 1,500 or so people. The dance floor had wonderful plastic palm trees at either side, and there was a revolving stage, although for bigger bands like Zeppelin a wooden platform was built above that.

Zeppelin came on stage quite late and the crowd immediately rose to their feet and surged to the front, forming a terrible crush. There was some concern about taking photographs. I think they searched us at the door on the way in and were confiscating cameras. I remember a guy trying to take a photo of Robert Plant just as they came on stage and the bouncers waded into the crowd to get his camera. Robert intervened and told the bouncers to leave off the guy to a great cheer from the crowd. The set list was similar to the previous night, but the atmosphere was so much better. I was right down the front close to the band; I could almost touch them and the atmosphere was electric.

They played an extended version of 'Whole Lotta Love', incorporating a medley of rock 'n' roll standards such as 'Hello Mary Lou'. I managed to stay down the front for about half of the set, but I was too hot, sweaty and getting crushed. In the end I gave up and made my way to the back of the hall to spend the latter part of the concert up in the balcony. It was an evening of pure magic which I remember to this day. Many of my friends still talk about this concert as one of the best they ever witnessed.

Sadly, the Mecca was demolished a year or so ago, and in the spot now stands a massive supermarket.

I WAS THERE: ALAN ROUNTREE

I remember this gig as though it was yesterday. Me and my friends paid 19 shillings (95p) for a ticket. When Zep came on stage and started up, the hairs on the back of my neck stood on end. The riff from 'Communication Breakdown' still gets me going now, not that I can jump about like I did in those days, mind. And me and my friends didn't need any drugs or anything like that to enjoy those nights, just a few pints of the local ale. Which, can I add, was watered down most of the time!

Somebody said 'if you could go back in time what era would you like?' I say 1969 to 1973, because those days will always be fresh in my mind. I saw many bands in that era thanks to Geoff Docherty, a local promoter who started off at the Bay Hotel and then moved on to the Locarno. Zeppelin were always a favourite for me. I can understand why Robert Plant was a sex god to women – he looked the part! That night you wanted the music to go on forever, the atmosphere was that good, ie. hot and sweaty. A friend I had at the time got mistaken for Robert Plant when he was going into the Locarno due to him having long blond hair. He was over the moon for months after about it. Sadly, he passed away a few years ago. If you're looking down, Tom Newby, I mentioned you.

I saw many bands over the years at both the Bay Hotel and the Locarno, including Pink Floyd, who still are my favourite band now, Free, Jethro Tull, Blind Faith, Wishbone Ash and many more. Heady days.

I WAS THERE: ROBERT MARTIN

Several months after I saw them in Newcastle, the band were due to play at Sunderland's Locarno Ballroom. My girlfriend and I both managed to get tickets. I recall she bought a really cool hippy/early Goth-style dress and coat outfit in black. I remember loving it on her. Again, we had a perfect night's entertainment provided by the boys. But at least this time it was much easier to get home and we woke fully refreshed in the morning with magic tunes still ringing in our ears as we made our way to work.

The promoter who organised both the Newcastle and Sunderland shows was a local guy called Geoff Docherty. He brought many top bands in the late sixties and early seventies to Sunderland Locarno and also to the Bay Hotel, many of which I attended including Pink Floyd, Traffic, Free, The Who, Ginger Baker's Airforce and Family. That girlfriend of mine back then is now my wife. 47 years on, we are both still rocking along to this legendary music.

I WAS THERE: PHIL OLIVER

Led Zeppelin I was the first record I bought. I was there at the Mecca in 1971 and what a great night it was. I can't remember where I bought the 75p ticket, but I do remember how excited I was about seeing them live. The place was packed out and we had to go upstairs. It was rocking and I ended up standing on a table with my hands on the ceiling so I could see but try not to fall off. The balcony was vibrating with the beat. 'Stairway To Heaven' was amazing but I was looking forward to 'Whole Lotta Love', 'Black Dog' and 'Rock And Roll'. I went home with my ears ringing for the next couple of days.

I WAS THERE: STEPHEN BREWIS

I remember that night as though it was yesterday. Me and my mate, Steve Kershaw, left Wearside College, where we were both studying Shipbuilding Craft Studies, to go down to the Mecca. We joined the queue at the bottom of the ramp leading to the entrance of the Mecca, and I was checking every five minutes that I still had my precious ticket in my pocket. Within half an hour, the queue was literally a mile long and about ten deep, past the Wheatsheaf pub.

The doors opened and in an orderly fashion we started going in and getting our 75p tickets scanned under an ultra violet light to check that they were legit. Once in, and after buying merchandise, we got a position about midcentre. The natives started to get restless and when Led Zeppelin finally came out on stage there was an almighty surge from behind and I was pushed right to the front and into the safety rail. It was a state of pure euphoria and adulation.

The noise was amazing. Robert Plant called for calm and eventually everyone settled down. Then the band launched into 'Immigrant Song' and everyone went wild again. I remember standing right in front of Jimmy Page – he must have been all of six feet away. You couldn't move from your position. If you went to the loo, you lost your place. It was probably the best concert that I have ever been to, and I've been to a good few. The pure energy of the band was transferred to the fans and you've got to say that Led Zeppelin were, and still are, the best band ever. I went and bought a copy of the fourth album the next day. I've still got all my Led Zeppelin albums and a few singles and a couple of, shall we say, 'unofficial' albums. The whole show was absolutely brilliant and I will never ever forget it. I still have the ticket stuck on my copy of *Led Zeppelin III*.

CAIRD HALL
13 NOVEMBER 1971, DUNDEE, UK

I WAS THERE: DOUG BISSELL, AGE 16

I had seen both Rory Gallagher and then Deep Purple with Ritchie Blackmore at the Caird Hall, so the possibility of seeing Jimmy Page there was magical. But the show was a sell-out. However, an hour before the show started, fate intervened and I went with our friend, Roddy Ogilvie, in place of my brother Billy. Dundee United FC were playing Celtic at Tannadice Park that Saturday and Billy, a fervent United fan, had attended the match. At some point Billy, who could be vocal and cheeky, got into a fracas with rival supporters and was arrested with others and held at police headquarters in Bell Street, Dundee. No charges were preferred but the group was held for a cooling off period and not released until around 10pm. Fortunately for me, Billy's Led Zeppelin ticket lay on the mantelpiece and, after the police phoned my parents around 6pm, they informed me what had happened and I took the ticket.

I recall with great clarity the almost electric atmosphere and feeling of anticipation as the lights went down. The chap who introduced the band spoke with nervousness and hesitation which seemed to be in keeping with the great occasion. The concert was fantastic. The stand out moment for me was Jimmy Page playing his guitar with a bow on 'Dazed And Confused' and using it like an outstretched wand as he fired sound bullets which seemed to bounce and echo off the walls. It was an unforgettable day. And Billy? Not only did he get arrested and miss Led Zeppelin but Celtic thrashed Dundee United 5-1. So it was an unforgettable day for him too, but for different reasons.

I WAS THERE: MICHAEL JONES

I was at both Zeppelin shows in Dundee, in 1971 and 1973. My brother, back from Australia on holiday, came with me. He had never been to a concert before. As Zeppelin appeared on stage, he uttered the immortal words, 'Will it be like the record player turned up full?' My reply was, 'And then some!' As the group crashed into 'Immigrant Song' I turned to see my brother virtually blasted back into his seat.

I WAS THERE: JIM LONG

The Zeppelin concert was the first I'd been to since seeing the Rolling Stones at Caird Hall in 1965. I was only ten then, and a bit scared when all the girls started screaming. I queued up from 4am with my friend Colin outside Largs in Whitehall Street for Zeppelin tickets and we managed to get two. My friends and I were all really brought up on T. Rex, Bowie, Deep Purple and Led Zeppelin. What I remember about the day itself is the amazing anticipation of the crowd, Robert Plant strutting about the stage like a peacock, shirt unbuttoned, and Jimmy being incredible on the night and playing guitar with a violin bow. The crowd were shouting for 'Heartbreaker' the whole night and I'm sure they did it as an encore. *Volume IV* was just out and 'Rock And Roll' was amazing. They did 'Stairway To Heaven' in two parts. It was truly an amazing night, head bopping to 'Whole Lotta Love' whilst playing air guitar. It was the second best concert I've ever been to. Nothing beats front row at the Bowie concert in May 1973.

I WAS THERE: DUNCAN LEITH, AGE 18

My two mates and I were lucky to get front row tickets for this one. Drink was a new toy to us so we started the evening at the Phoenix Bar and bought a carry out of a few cans to smuggle into the gig. Time seemed to fly and we missed the start of Led Zep's only Scottish date on this tour. We sheepishly skulked our way down the aisle to the three conspicuous empty seats, right in the middle of the front row. We thought nobody would notice as the place would be rocking but it wasn't. It was eerily quiet. Robert Plant and Jimmy Page were sitting together on stools at the front of the stage doing an acoustic section. They had a spotlight on them which now heavily featured the three of us as well. Oh, well. In for a penny, in for a pound. We all cracked open a can of McEwans in unison and bid our heroes on stage good health. They both gave us a smile and a ripple of laughter passed through the audience.

Fast forward to 1985. Me and a pal are cycling from Land's End to John O'Groats. We have arranged to stop at Monmouth for a night where a chap called Roy Andrews, who used to come up to Dundee for the Six Nations rugby and watch the games in our local, The Scout Bar, was mine host at the Royal Oak. Roy says to me, 'Duncan, boyo. You're going to meet a good friend of mine in here tonight. Robert Plant!' He had a recording studio near there. I then told Roy about the Caird Hall episode and I'm reckoning Robert might well remember us. Alas, Roy gets word that Robert has had to fly to Geneva that day.

I WAS THERE: SANDY FRASER

I attended both Led Zep's Dundee concerts. I was at Logie Secondary School in 1971 and Harris Academy in 1973. On both occasions, I went with my friends Billy Griffin, Ed Black and Martin Donnelly. Dundee around the seventies was a fantastic place to be if you were a rock fan. I remember seeing a whole raft of bands around that period: Jethro Tull, Yes, Black Sabbath, ELP, Queen and the Sensational Alex Harvey Band. But none were larger than Zep and they were the only band of the time that had such longevity. So much so I was privileged enough to be one of the very lucky ones to attend their final concert at the O2 Arena. My colleague and I, who were at the time senior managers with a large multi-national company, cancelled a fairly important managers meeting and arranged a trip to a large customer in London so that it coincided with the concert. The lengths you will go to.

I WAS THERE: STEVE SCOTT, AGE 18

I first heard them at a friend's house in 1969. His older brother had bought the first album. He was out of the house, so we sneaked into his room, found it in his collection and put it on the record player. I thought my head was going to explode when I heard the first few notes of 'Good Times Bad Times'. We played the album three or four times, one after another. I had never heard anything so powerful in my life! From Plant's singing to Page's guitar playing, JPJ's bass and Bonham 's powerful drumming, I was stunned. I had been to other gigs at the Caird Hall, most memorably The Who, but a friend had managed to get a couple of Zep tickets and I remember to this day how excited I was at the thought of seeing them. There was no support. They came on, opened with 'Immigrant Song', ended with 'Whole Lotta Love' and encored with 'Communication Breakdown'. Plant had to tell some of the more excitable sections of the crowd to calm down a bit as it threatened to get out of hand. They were in their pomp and just fantastic.

I WAS THERE: NEIL STIRLING, AGE 15

The tickets were sold at a small office in Exchange Street, Dundee. Fans came from across Scotland as it was the only Scottish gig on that tour. There was a Celtic football match on that day and when the concert finished, Celtic and Zeppelin fans mixed. My friend, who got the tickets, left the concert with me very sharply after it finished and got Page's autograph on an album as Page was getting into a black limousine at the front of the Caird Hall. The *Dundee Courier* review of the Zeppelin gig commented on how loud the band were.

I WAS THERE: RAYMOND MEYER, AGE 16

I was at my local youth club in St Andrews, the Cosmos Centre. A friend of mine arrived and informed me that Led Zeppelin were going to be playing a one-off Scottish gig at the Caird Hall in Dundee and that the tickets were going on sale the following morning at 9am. I didn't believe him! He told me that he had read about it in that morning's edition of *The Courier* newspaper so I asked the youth leader if he happened to have a copy of the newspaper. Luckily, he did and there it was in black and white.

Tickets were priced at £1 each and limited to five per person. I informed the youth leader that I was going to get the next bus from St Andrews to Dundee and queue up overnight to secure a ticket. He had an idea. If we could get a few more people to join me, he would pay for a taxi to take us to Dundee and give us £5 each so we could each buy five tickets and then sell them through the youth club. But first I had to go home and let my parents know where I was going that night.

In 1971, I had just turned 16 and my parents didn't have a phone, so I ran home and informed my parents of my intentions. They both knew I was Led Zeppelin daft by then and they gave me their permission to go. Back at the youth club, two taxis ferried eight of us to Dundee, arriving at the ticket office at around half past midnight.

There were already about 30 people queuing up when we arrived and we duly took up our place in the queue. Luckily that night the weather was kind to us and it didn't rain, but it was really cold. With each passing hour more and more people joined the queue until it stretched the whole way round the block by the time the box office opened at 9am. We each got our five tickets and then a bus back to St Andrews just after noon. We were tired but elated. We were going to see Led Zeppelin live!

The night of the concert arrived and we all met up at the youth club before making our way to Dundee. The youth club had hired a minibus to take us to and from Dundee but it had to make two trips because of the number of people. I was on the first trip over to Dundee and the second coming back after the concert.

We arrived at the Caird Hall, where the corner of our tickets was torn off on entry. The atmosphere inside the hall was electric. The lights went down and Led Zeppelin arrived on stage, torches lighting their way. The stage lights went on and Led Zeppelin ripped into 'Immigrant Song'. For the next three hours, we were mesmerised. We never sat down. In fact, even although we were only ten rows from the stage we stood on the chairs so we wouldn't miss a thing. A few people right at the front of the stage were giving the bouncers a bit of trouble by trying to get onstage with the band, but apart from that the concert was a total success and Led Zeppelin lived up to the hype of being the greatest live band ever. And boy were they loud. My ears were still ringing hours after the gig.

Of course, we were the first Scottish audience to hear 'Stairway To Heaven' played live. But as the fourth album hadn't been released at that point, we didn't know that we had just witnessed hearing the greatest rock song of all time. The highlight was Jimmy Page playing the guitar with a violin bow during 'Dazed And Confused' as none of us knew he do this and it was just breath taking.

As we waited outside the Caird Hall for the minibus to return to take us back to St Andrews, two black limousines pulled up and down the stairs in front of the Caird Hall came manager Peter Grant and the four members of the band. Robert Plant and Jimmy Page briefly shook hands with me before hurriedly jumping into the awaiting cars, but John Bonham engaged with the waiting fans and signed the back of my ticket, which I still have to this day. A night I'll never forget.

I WAS THERE: GRAHAM KENNEDY

This is still the best concert that I have ever attended. Having queued all night in the cold and rain to get a ticket, the excitement was electrifying. There was no support band and the equipment on stage didn't look that much but it was all very high-powered stuff. The lights went down, a row of big bouncers lined up in front of the shoulder high stage and then Zeppelin simply walked onto the stage.

Robert Plant shouted 'good eeevening!' which got a loud 'good evening' back, Jimmy Page plucked a few notes on the old Gibson, Percy nodded to Jimmy and then we were off into 'Immigrant Song'. A wall of sound hit you in the chest – oh my God it was loud – and without as much as a pause they went straight into 'Heartbreaker'. There were a few minutes of chat to introduce the new songs off the new album. It was during this chat that Percy explained that they had wanted to play elsewhere in Scotland but the halls were all booked up when very loudly from just behind us came 'oh, fuck the bloody halls and get on with it.' 'You what?' replied Percy, and the message was repeated so Percy introduced a new number off the new album, 'Black Dog', swiftly followed by 'Rock And Roll'. The new album had only been released the day before so none of us had heard these songs but the whole place had gone apeshit by now and those bouncers were causing a bit of trouble at the front.

The acoustic set was wonderful and we heard 'Stairway' for the first time. It was also the first time we'd seen the double neck Gibson. I'm sure that 'Celebration Day' was played that night as it's a favourite of mine. The internet suggests otherwise but it does appear on the setlists for other nights around this date. I'd read that Bonzo had tired of playing 'Moby Dick', so between songs I shouted for it! Percy turned around, walked over to Bonzo and then said 'by special request – John Bonham – 'Moby Dick'.

The concert ended after an amazing 'Whole Lotta Love'. The house lights went on but the crowd wouldn't move. The bouncers were pushing folks about at the front too. Then the crowd rushed the stage and the bouncers were forced to jump onto the stage – well, all bar one who got a bit of a doing over, which served him right. The bouncers were lined up along the edge of the stage when Zeppelin returned after what seemed like an age. Percy waved them to get off the stage and the big man (Mr Grant) watching from the side of the stage obviously got the message through to those idiots to clear off.

'Communication Breakdown', another song I'd been shouting for, was the encore and it was brilliant. Jimmy paid a compliment to the Dundee crowd about having 'a great little world of rock appreciation here' and then off they went again. It was on with the house lights and the end of the concert, or so we thought, but the crowd wouldn't move and kept on shouting for more. After a very long wait, Zeppelin returned and Percy asked the crowd to calm down and not give the bouncers any excuses to cause any more trouble. The final encore was the old Eddie Cochran number, 'Weekend', which was very apt as it was the weekend. Then it was all over.

Percy recalled the troubles in 1971 at the 1973 concert when they returned, but in an interview in 1972 prior to the 72/73 tour, Jimmy Page recalled the concert as being 'phenomenal... fantastic.' He was right. It was.

ST MATTHEW'S BATHS HALL
16 NOVEMBER 1971, IPSWICH, UK

I WAS THERE: GRAHAM DAY

This is the most memorable event I have ever been to. St Matthew's Baths Hall in St Matthews Street was a Victorian indoor swimming pool in the summer months but in wintertime the pool was covered over by boards to enable different events to take place. A fine Public Hall had been destroyed by fire many years earlier and the former Hippodrome Theatre, which became the Savoy Ballroom in the early 1960s, had been converted into a bingo hall. The Baths Hall was therefore the one big space which could be used for dances and gigs.

During the 1960s, a husband-and-wife partnership named Nanda and Ron Lesley brought their Bluesville Club to Ipswich. They ran similar clubs in places such as Aylesbury. In the summer time, they promoted the Monday Clubs in the smaller Manor Ballroom and in the winter at the St Matthew's Baths Hall. One of my neighbours and school friends was Eric Fleet. He had an almost encyclopaedic knowledge of rock and blues, honed by listening to albums in his bedroom. After a while, he somehow became the spinner of discs between bands at the Bluesville Club, and was on duty when Led Zeppelin appeared.

It was Eric who told me the story behind Led Zeppelin's appearance in Ipswich. Apparently, Nanda and Ron had booked the band in their early days as a band but, by the early 1970s, were contemplating retirement. To return a favour, Zeppelin agreed to do the gig so that all the proceeds went to the promoters. It must have been a good return, as the Lesleys were able to retire to Torquay.

I could not believe that the band were coming to Ipswich. Bluesville had staged many acts, from John Mayall and Chicken Shack through to The Equals and Rod Stewart when he was part of Steampacket (with Julie Driscoll and Long John Baldry), but no one with the high profile and international reputation of Led Zeppelin. I was working at the old East Suffolk County Council in Ipswich at the time and walked along to the box office at the Baths Hall to buy my tickets. The tickets cost the large sum of £1. I had a former girlfriend who worked in County Hall. One of her friends, Sally, worked in the County Education Department and had recently split up with her boyfriend. As I was unattached, I asked her if she would like to come to the concert and she agreed. I kept this quiet from my workmates in the local land charges office. This was until she popped her head around the door and asked if I had got the tickets. I then had five very jealous and envious colleagues to work with, and I was persona non grata for several weeks afterwards.

The day of the concert arrived; a dark and chill November day. I picked Sally up. I remember wearing a long grey coat and Sally a long maroon velvet one. We stood on the floor of the hall waiting for them to come on stage. There was no support. All of a sudden, they appeared to enormous cheers and launched into 'Immigrant Song'. They rocked on, making the fabric of the Hall tremble with the volume of their music. The combination of Jimmy Page's guitar, John Bonham's thunderous drumming and Robert Plant's vocal explorations were a real unforgettable joy. The floor shook – remember, the swimming pool was covered – as the audience danced and jumped up and down. All too soon, the final two songs were played as the encore, 'Weekend' and 'Gallows Pole'. Then it was all over and we emerged exhausted into the cold November air.

No other gig has surpassed that moment. It lives long in the memory and the concert still has legendary status in Ipswich and Suffolk. Seven or eight years ago, a bootleg tape of the concert was discovered at a Sunday car boot sale in Portman Road, Ipswich, opposite the football ground and a stone's throw from the Baths Hall. I read a biography of Peter Grant where it said that, if he found bootleggers at a gig recording his band, their equipment would be destroyed and the person doing the recording would be in mortal danger of their life. Obviously, someone was very lucky indeed!

For many years, I worked with French students who came to England to learn English. I used to get them talking about music, and someone always mentioned Led Zeppelin. This was around the time of the O2 reunion. I'd tell them I'd seen Led Zeppelin for £1 and there would be looks of astonishment on their faces!

I WAS THERE: ERIC ALLARD

I was there with a few friends. There were one or two problems with the acoustics to start with, with mics feeding back, but once these were sorted the sound was amazing. We were treated to some expected favourites, but a lot of the set included tracks from the *Four Symbols* album which was about to be released, so we were hearing them for the first time. I was especially blown away when I heard 'Stairway To Heaven' with Jimmy Page playing his double-necked Gibson guitar. Awe-inspiring, and such a great night!

I WAS THERE: JANE HALL (NEE KEER), AGE 16

What fantastic memories I have of that concert. I somehow finagled my parents into letting me go. I think my dad even drove into Ipswich to pick me and my friends up as we lived in Sudbourne back then. Half the time I was scared to death as the dance floor went up and down with the weight of so many people jumping about and I thought it would cave in and I would drown in the pool! Was there really a pool underneath?

I WAS THERE: WILLIAM MARTIN

I arrived in the afternoon without a ticket but went to the box office and bought one for £1. I saw Robert Plant and Jimmy Page arrive in a green Rolls-Royce. After a quick wave to the crowd, they disappeared around the back of the hall. While waiting to go in I saw Peter Grant, Led Zeppelin's manager, with the road crew. I also saw Robert Plant walk by again.

The concert was very loud with the hall packed out. They came on stage at eight o'clock and played for over two hours including tracks from *Led Zeppelin IV* which was just coming out and including 'Stairway To Heaven'. I was very near the front. I could not hear for hours afterwards as it was so loud. This concert has gone down as one of the greatest concerts ever in Ipswich and one I will never forget. I also saw them at the Bath Festival, at Earls Court in 1975 and Knebworth in 1979. Great memories.

I WAS THERE: ANDREW SQUIRREL, AGE 19

I was heavily into the music of the Stones, Led Zep and Pink Floyd – I still am! The concert was staged on top of a covered over swimming pool. I went with a friend who lived in Ipswich and who managed to get the tickets fairly close to the day they played for £1 each. (By way of contrast, I paid £400 to see the Stones in 2012.) We were quite near the front and when they first started playing 'Immigrant Song' after a brief chat to the audience, I thought the volume was about right. It wasn't until Plant started singing that the full force and volume of the group hit home. We were then treated to two hours or so of classic Led Zeppelin songs, some of which we weren't to know would become classics, eg. 'Stairway To Heaven'. My ears used to ring after gigs but usually stopped a few days later. This time it carried on, so I believe this concert contributed to me getting tinnitus, although being a farmer and working with loud machinery didn't help. My friend and I still talk about the gig and it was very much a case of 'we were there' to anybody who cares to listen. (Most of my friends start yawning!) It's also still very much a big event in the history of sleepy Ipswich; the local paper often mentions it. I managed to get hold of a dodgy three CD bootleg recording of the concert years ago and now I see it's all over YouTube.

EMPIRE POOL
20 & 21 NOVEMBER 1971, WEMBLEY, LONDON, UK

I WAS THERE: MARK BRADY, AGE 14

I saw them five times in all. The first time was at Wembley Empire Pool in 1971 and the second at Ally Pally in December 1972. My older brother took me to both these shows. Ally Pally seemed rather empty, cavernous and extremely cold and damp, and I seem to recall that the sound was not great and sort of reverberated around the lofty building. The Wembley gig had some sort of circus acts performing on stage, and the sound was much better and the overall atmosphere more like an exciting gig than Ally Pally. The other gigs I went to were in May 1975 at Earls Court, where I managed to see them twice, and Knebworth.

I WAS THERE: ROSIE BLISS

My late husband Eddie and I watched them from the side of the stage at Wembley and sang Christmas carols with them after the concert, backstage in their dressing room. We were friends with their tour manager then, and still are, and Jimmy lived in my village, Pangbourne, in the seventies. We had some great times in their company. It was so easy and uncomplicated in those days!

PUBLIC HALL
23 NOVEMBER 1971, PRESTON, UK

I WAS THERE: STEVEN THORP

I attended both Led Zeppelin's gigs in Preston. I still have the ticket stubs. The best live band ever in my opinion.

FREE TRADE HALL
24 NOVEMBER 1971, MANCHESTER, UK

I WAS THERE: WILL BLAKE

I saw Led Zeppelin a few times back in the day, including twice in Manchester in 1971 – at the Free Trade Hall and a few days later at the King's Hall, Belle Vue. At the Free Trade Hall, Robert Plant told the audience he had a cold and a couple of wags threw toilet rolls on the stage. They opened with 'Immigrant Song' and 'Heartbreaker' and closed the show with 'Thank You'. At Belle Vue, they played a similar set but opened with 'Black Dog', and during 'Dazed and Confused' Jimmy Page's violin bow snapped so he threw it into the audience to a lucky recipient. I also saw them in 1972 at the Hardrock in Manchester, where they opened with 'Rock And Roll', but I don't remember too much else about that show.

I WAS THERE: GRAHAM WILKINS

I was studying civil engineering at Salford University. Tickets went on sale on a Sunday about three weeks before the concert. The only place to buy tickets was a music shop called Hime and Addison in Manchester. Tickets varied between about 65 pence and £1 each. I got there at about 7am and the queue was already about a quarter of a mile long. At about 1pm, we finally got into the shop and managed to get three tickets, one for me and one each for my flatmates, Ian Stephenson and Les Wentland. You were happy to get whatever was left after you'd been queueing on the street for about six hours.

The concert set list contained much of the material from the recently released *Led Zeppelin IV*. It was the first time I'd seen the four band members logos, which were on the amps and drum kit. Nobody really understood what they were supposed to mean, if indeed they meant anything at all.

The concert was in two halves, each half being about an hour and 20 minutes with an interval between. The performance was incredible, better than anything I'd seen before. The audience were going wild. At the end of the first set, Robert Plant advised us to shove some bog paper in our ears for when they came back on as it was going to be even louder. The whole performance was about three hours with the interval, and remains one of the most memorable and electrifying concerts I've ever been to. Page was on top form, showing his total mastery of a variety of guitars, whilst Plant's screams into the microphone left my ears ringing for days afterwards.

I WAS THERE: PAUL WELSH

I went to see them again at the Free Trade Hall in 1971. I've found something I'd written after the gig: 'Plant and Page really amazing, especially with 'Black Dog'.' About 20 years ago a guy that I used to work with, who was also a drummer in a local rock band, was intrigued by what he'd heard about Led Zeppelin and went to HMV to purchase the band's first two albums. After listening to them he returned them to the shop and asked for a refund as, according to him, they were crap! There's no accounting for taste.

PERCY GEE BUILDING, UNIVERSITY
25 NOVEMBER 1971, LEICESTER, UK

I WAS THERE: STUART WHITEHEAD, AGE 16

Even though I went to Alexandra Palace in December 1972, all five nights at Earls Court in May 1975 and Knebworth in August 1979, the one that started it all for me was Leicester University in November 1971. It is hard to imagine now, but even though the fourth album had been released just days earlier, they were playing in what can only be described as a school hall at the Percy Gee Building at Leicester University. Tickets were only available to Student Union members, which I wasn't. I resorted to hanging around the ticket sales area and tried to second guess which students would not be interested in Led Zeppelin and who might buy a couple of tickets on my behalf. Bingo, a very studious-looking guy strolled by me. I explained my dilemma and he was only too happy to help. The ticket was a beautiful silver Zeppelin-shaped affair.

When the day arrived, my friend and I stood at front of the queue waiting for the doors to open. All day whenever we saw anyone with long hair I would joke 'look, there is Robert Plant.' My friend by this time was not even listening to me anymore when a side door opened and... you guessed it – it *was* Robert Plant! He was taller than I had anticipated, and now clean shaven after sporting a beard since 1970. He came out to quickly check out the queue and disappeared again.

As the doors opened, we made our way to the front with surprising ease. The students seemed too 'cool' to be excited, and in those days, people sat cross-legged on the floor like at school assembly. The stage was a normal-looking school stage and leaning on it I was feet away from Jimmy's double-necked Gibson. This was already well worth the £1 ticket price.

They came on and Robert said very politely 'good evening' and, after a bit of tuning up they were off, straight into 'Immigrant Song' followed by 'Heartbreaker' with no break and then what we all thought was 'Out On The Tiles' but no, wait, it stopped and turned into 'Black Dog', and then 'Since I've Been Loving You' and 'Celebration Day'. Then it was time for them to sit down as they went into the acoustic set, with Jimmy playing his odd-looking Giannini guitar that looked like a giant mandolin, and John Paul Jones with his tiny mandolin for 'Going To California', 'That's The Way', 'Tangerine' and 'Bron-Y-Aur Stomp'. It was back to the electric guitars for 'Dazed And Confused', then Jimmy picked up the double neck for one song, 'Stairway To Heaven'. Next up was 'What Is And What Should Never Be', 'Whole Lotta Love' and then they went off. They came back on refreshed and it felt like 'Rock And Roll' and 'Communication Breakdown' were openers rather than encores.

I went in not really knowing how they would be. There was no footage back then to give you a preview of what you were about to experience but they were even better than I could have imagined. It was my first taste of the counter culture and the underground nature of what Led Zeppelin represented back then. And it tasted pretty good.

LIVERPOOL STADIUM
29 NOVEMBER 1971, LIVERPOOL, UK

I WAS THERE: RODDIE GILLIARD

It only seemed a few months after their Liverpool Uni appearance that they were billed to play at Liverpool Stadium. In those few months the band, along with many of their contemporaries, seemed to gain in popularity. The tickets that had been 60p were now £1. We had to queue to buy tickets. The Stadium was an old boxing stadium, cavernous and dusty, rectangular with the boxing ring in the centre. Normally bands would play on the boxing ring and the audience would be around three sides, with the other side – behind the stage – being empty and in darkness. For the Zep show, they removed the boxing ring and set a stage high up over one end of the hall, enabling a bigger audience. (I'm told they did a similar thing when T. Rex played there around that time.) Behind the stage were draped the four large *Zoso* symbols. This time the show was much longer and included the acoustic section, which I can't recall them doing at Mountford Hall.

Where the audience at the Mountford Hall had been a mix of student types and prog types, the Stadium gig seemed younger and rowdier. Concert going was becoming more and more popular and the big bands were becoming too big for the venues available. It was only a few years later that 'stadium rock' became the thing, much less intimate and much more commercial.

During the early 1970s, I attended several of the large festivals, where you would see and hear tons of bands back-to-back, bands who became household names a few years later. I'm glad I saw these bands at the time.

Around this time, I acquired a copy of the first Zeppelin album. It remains my favourite, although I find many similarities to the material recorded on Jeff Beck's *Truth* album. I bought *Houses Of The Holy* on its release and also a copy of the *Blueberry Hill* bootleg.

Sometime later, I became (and remain) friends with Steve Hardstaff, who did tons of artwork for bands and promoters. I found out that he had been heavily involved in the *Zep III* artwork and had produce the wonderful Electric Magic poster. Steve also worked alongside Peter Grant on other promo stuff for the band.

I WAS THERE: JAN MERSEY

We queued in the rain for between four and six hours for tickets, which were £1. I still have mine. It's yellow and black and it has the four runes from *Led Zep IV* on it. It's a work of art. They tore up the tickets on the door at that show but I managed to keep hold of mine as I hid behind my friend and sneaked in while the guy on the door was taking hers. Then we found one on the floor so she had one to keep as a souvenir too – result!

We were on the right side of the stage, standing beside the amps. I couldn't hear at all when we left but we were so close it was wonderful. This was the best of the three Liverpool shows I saw. 'Dazed And Confused' was even longer, going on for almost 15 minutes, and Bonzo did his drum solo for a good ten minutes on 'Moby Dick'. There was lots of *Led Zep IV* this time and it was the first time I heard 'Stairway To Heaven'. 'Immigrant Song' and 'Gallows Pole' also stood out.

KINGS HALL, BELLE VUE
30 NOVEMBER 1971, MANCHESTER, UK

I WAS THERE: JILL WARBURTON, AGE 15

Four extremely excited 15-year-old girls (Vicky, Lorraine, Ann and Jill) set off in on a chilly late November evening to the Kings Hall. It was the first time I'd been to a music event there – it was usually a wrestling venue! We were all dressed up in our mini-skirts, mini-jumpers, platform shoes and handbags, thinking we looked great. It was a bit of a shock to get there and find that everyone else was in denim, but what can I say? We were rock concert virgins!

We'd been fans for about 18 months, and only got into them because some boys we fancied (one of whom, Brian, is now my husband of 40 years) kept talking about how fantastic they were. I actually thought Robert Plant was the ugliest thing I'd ever seen – but we listened to them... and suddenly... wow! I was instantly in love with their music and them, especially Robert Plant. Did I say ugly? He was now the sexiest thing I'd ever seen – and still is!

We took our seats, just to the side quite near the amps. The familiar opening bars of 'Immigrant Song' started and Robert's wail, so loud and powerful, nearly knocked me sideways; it was dizzying. There wasn't much security in those days and we were up, standing leaning against the chest high stage, still near those amps. I don't know how my hearing survived. I remember leaning and stretching my hand onto the stage when Robert danced near us, hoping he would stand on it! He wore white tennis shoes. The fourth album had just come out, I think, and Robert introduced 'Stairway To Heaven', which was amazingly just another song then. I think it was during 'Dazed And Confused' that Jimmy brandished his violin bow, his playing so enthusiastic that he actually broke it. They had no support act that night and played for three hours including three encores. That was great value for the ticket price of £1. My diary entry for that wonderful night simply says, 'Led Zeppelin were fantastic! Robert Plant and James Page are beautiful. Oh, I feel awful.'

I also saw Zeppelin at the Hardrock in Manchester in 1972, at Earls Court in London in 1975, at Knebworth and at the reunion concert at the O2 in London in 2007. I still go out to see Robert whenever he's in town or nearabouts, and I met him after a gig at the Manchester Apollo. People crowded round wanting autographs but he didn't have a pen so I lent him mine. After all those years, all I managed to say to him was 'I've got a pen'!

CITY HALL
20 DECEMBER 1971, SALISURY, UK

I WAS THERE: BAZ MORT

This show had to be rescheduled because Jimmy Page had the flu. I'd seen Led Zeppelin at Bath cricket ground and then the Shepton Mallet festival. This was to be a more intimate show and, more importantly given the time of year, it was inside. Led Zeppelin had been on a tour of the USA playing huge stadiums, so to witness one of my favourite bands at a venue like this was not to be missed.

Myself and four friends drove from Winchester, about 25 miles away, and arrived about half an hour before the show started. I remember going in to the hall, which was filling up pretty quickly. All the tickets had sold out and we had to hustle to find a good spot about centre stage. These were the days before pre-booked seats. I don't recall any seating. Unlike nowadays, it was a case of plonking yourself on the floor. I really didn't take much note of whether there was a support band. In those days getting a drink had priority over anything else!

Led Zeppelin came on around 8.30pm and kicked off with 'Immigrant Song'. My God, it was loud. To see the Zep this close was an awesome experience. Bearing in mind that I'd seen them before, nothing could compare to this full-frontal assault on the senses. No wonder my hearing has suffered over the years. They followed up with 'Heartbreaker', 'Black Dog', 'Since I've Been Loving You', 'Celebration Day' and 'Stairway To Heaven'. They then did an acoustic set of about four songs before it was back to the heavy stuff – 'Dazed And Confused', 'What Is And What Should Never Be', 'Rock And Roll' and 'Whole Lotta Love'. For an encore they delved back in time for a rock and roll medley comprising 'Boogie Mama', 'Hello Mary Lou', 'Lawdy Miss Clawdy' and 'Mystery Train'. Two-and-a-half hours of the loudest, most exciting music on earth in 1971. What's more – it only cost a quid!

I WAS THERE: PAUL MUNNS

I got into the band on the release of the second album. I had, up until this point, been a devout Stones fan, plus all the old blues artists like Howling Wolf and Leadbelly. To hear heavy re-workings of songs I had already liked was great. My future wife, Anne, and I were reading the local paper, the *Salisbury Journal*, when we saw a small advert purporting to be selling tickets to see Led Zeppelin for £1 at the City Hall. We were a bit perturbed at the low price and being asked to send money to a council house in Harnham, a part of Salisbury. Much to our surprise two very flimsy paper tickets arrived.

I can't remember the date of the gig but, within days, it seems we had notification that the gig was cancelled and to await further news, I thought immediately that I was right to have been worried and mentally wrote off the £2. However, a little later we were told to turn up at the City Hall with the old tickets on the new date in December and we would be admitted.

Still thinking it might be a hoax, we walked there to be met by the biggest queue I had ever encountered, stretching way down Fisherton Street towards the city centre. When we finally got in, the only space available was standing right at the back of the auditorium behind the tiered seating. I was told later that about 3,000 tickets had been sold and the official capacity was 1,700. I can believe the first figure, as there wasn't space to move an inch once everybody was in.

I can't remember the set list, but a lot of the songs were off the *Four Symbols* album. Every song was elongated and very loud. 'Stairway To Heaven' was met with stunned silence for quite a few bars as it seemed so out of character and there was even a shout of 'We want Johnny Reggae', whatever that meant. My personal favourite was, and still is, 'Black Dog', Bonham playing with real power. The only problem that I can recall is that Anne is not a fan of drum solos, whereas

I could listen to them all night. After the gig we headed home. At the junction of St Paul's Road and Fisherton Street, which is the A30 and at the time the main route from London to the west country, we stepped off the pavement without looking and were very nearly run down. We hadn't quite realised how deaf we were from the concert and had not heard the oncoming traffic. It could have been the end of a loving relationship that has since lasted nearly 46 years, as we got engaged just after the gig and married a year after that.

In those days, nobody seemed to know where Salisbury was and you used to have say, 'It is close to Stonehenge'. Now, of course, we are too well known as Novichok City. It still seems unreal that Led Zeppelin came to little Salisbury.

I WAS THERE: KAREN CANNINGS, AGE 16

I was one of the first six girls lucky enough to be chosen to go to Dauntsey's School for the sixth form, an all-boys day and boarding school. It was quite a hedonistic time, in which us girls were made to feel very special and extremely popular! We were invited by some of the lads to join them on adventures to listen to various bands in Portsmouth, Salisbury and Reading such as Genesis and Mott the Hoople. The Led Zeppelin concert was the first really big gig that I had been to. About a dozen of us from Dauntsey's were on the floor directly in front of the band. The hall was packed to the brim. Robert Plant's voice was just so distinctive and 'Stairway To Heaven' has been ingrained on my aural memory! I ended up marrying a Dauntsey boy which didn't last. However, in 1998 I met a Salisbury-born and bred man, Richard, who I ended up marrying. Richard was at the same Zeppelin concert.

I WAS THERE: GRAHAME CHUBB, AGE 18

I cannot recall how and when we purchased the tickets. I went with a friend – we both liked heavy rock music and the chance to see Led Zeppelin in our small local entertainment venue was an opportunity not to be missed. It was my first major rock band concert. The hall was crammed full. I was just starting my drumming career and watching John Bonham was awesome. It was a memorable performance. I loved the 'Immigrant Song' and they did a fantastic rendition of 'Stairway To Heaven'. The music was very loud and my ears were still ringing the day after.

I WAS THERE: STEVE MANN

I had been at the Bournemouth gig a couple weeks previous, which was possibly the best I've ever seen. The encore included a great rendition of 'Johnny B Goode'. At Salisbury, the band were just as good, but the audience was cold and totally different to Bournemouth. I remember them coming back to do the encore and clearly just going through the motions, as disappointed as I was about the atmosphere in the hall. I don't think they bothered with 'Johnny B Goode' this time.

I WAS THERE: SEAN RICE, AGE 17

We came away with our cars ringing. The power and musical might was truly awesome. They ripped through 'Heartbreaker', 'Black Dog' and 'Dazed And Confused'. It was raw musical muscle. I was already a big fan, and my favourite number was 'Since I've Been Loving You'. So it was a treat to see it live, with Jimmy Page ringing every ounce of emotion out of his guitar. Salisbury City Hall was quite an intimate venue and, with the lights subdued, the band brought out stools and sat down for an enchanting acoustic set which featured 'Going To California', 'Tangerine' and possibly 'That's The Way'. *Led Zeppelin IV* had had only just come out. A girlfriend had already acquired it and we listened intensely to 'Stairway To Heaven' on the turntable. When they performed this number, they held the whole audience spell-bound. They ended the evening with 'Whole Lotta Love'. Having been a Beatles fan at school, I was now drawn to this new form of heavier rock. I saw Free, Jethro Tull, Genesis and many others in the months that followed. But Zeppelin remained supreme.

I WAS THERE: SUSAN HAYWARD

My husband Roger was in a local covers band and used to buy some of his kit from Sutton's Music shop in Salisbury. Pete Coombs, who worked in the shop, organised the gig, mostly by pestering their manager until he agreed. When we bought the four tickets, for ourselves and the lead guitarist and his wife, Pete told us to keep it secret. The gig was never advertised and by the time that the news was out, the tickets were all sold.

On the day of the show, we queued down the side of the City Hall and the crowd was very excited when a large car passed by and word spread that the group was in it! We had seats because I was six months pregnant. I had never heard anything so loud in my life. I swear you could feel the force of the sound against your face. My baby started to kick wildly and continued for the whole concert. It was quite a relief when they played 'Stairway To Heaven'. My son Justin was later very proud of the fact that he had been to a Led Zep concert, albeit in the womb. Needless to say, my husband's group soon had a lot of Led Zep on their playlist. My husband and I still play in a little group in our church.

I WAS THERE: PETER COOMBS

When I was only 16, I was in a band that opened for Van Morrison when he was the singer with Them in '65. I was doing some promoting at Bournemouth and Salisbury with a very old friend of mine called David Strand. I booked The Crazy World of Arthur Brown, Rory Gallagher, Free, Heads, Hands and Feet with Albert Lee, and people of that sort of ilk. I did it because I'd been in a band in London for twelve months between 1969 and 1970 and met one or two people up there. We lived very close to Peter Townshend so you just bump into people.

We realised that the tour promoting *Led Zeppelin IV* was going to be something special. Somebody mentioned, 'If you want to get hold of Peter Grant, you really ought to contact Mickie Most' and said that he'd be a natural bridge to get to Peter Grant. So I went up to see them in a very modest office above Millets in Oxford Street in London and they said, 'Yes, we can introduce you to Mr Grant. Would you like to come up?'

We went up a few days later. We met Mickie Most, Peter Grant and Richard Cole, who was their tour organiser. It was obvious to me they did business in a rather maverick sort of way, but they came across as being honest people and gave me a piece of paper saying, 'We will come to the City Hall. We're happy for you to have ten per cent of the gross profit and we will not let you charge more than £1 admission.'

I think it was one of the few promotions we did where we never needed to do any posters. We did have a wonderful souvenir poster for sale, which has become iconic, but which we got nothing out of.

The show was scheduled for 15 December but was cancelled after Jimmy Page contracted flu. Very near the due date, I had a phone call from Mr Grant, saying, 'I'm awfully sorry, but we're going to have to pull out because Jimmy is poorly.' My heart sank because I thought I was going to be lynched, because I'd taken money off all these people. It delighted the sceptics, who said that the band would never play Salisbury. But Peter Grant paid for the hall to be used that night so that local fans could still enjoy a show. He said to me, 'Find some decent local rock bands and I'll pay their expenses. We'll pay for the hall and we'd like you to find a couple of decent local bands that play in the style of Zeppelin, which will be a free concert on us.'

So the two bands that did a concert were Marble Orchard and a young band called Jerusalem, one Ian Gillan from Deep Purple was very helpful to. Everybody who had a Led Zeppelin ticket was able to come in and see that concert and they put on a very good free show. There would have been about 1,200 people there that night. Everyone enjoyed it – and I wasn't lynched!

Mr Grant also said, 'If you can find out from the City Hall when we can have an alternative date, I'm sure by then Jimmy will be fit and we'll do a gig for you.' The tickets remained valid for the rescheduled date, and six days later Zeppelin landed in town. Even then, they were the hottest band in the world and people were sceptical that I – at 22 years of age – was going to put them on. And Salisbury is very little, and very conservative with a small c.

On the day, a seven-ton truck – large by the standards of the day – turned up outside the music shop I was managing and they said, 'We're looking for Peter. Can you tell us where we're playing?' I jumped in the truck with them and we went to the City Hall.

They did 'Battle Of Evermore' and 'Going To California' as part of an acoustic set, with the mandolin and with John Bonham playing tambourine.

After the gig, we took them to Edward and Jerry Moss's restaurant where they did a super supper. When we arrived at the restaurant at eleven thirty at night, they'd cleared all their kit away and their roadies were with us. At the door on street level, the journalist from *The Times* tried to worm his way into the supper. Mr Grant, who was not a small man, looked down on this journalist and said, 'There is only one man in the world tonight who could invite you to this private party and Mr Coombs doesn't want you at the party so please go away.' Those weren't the exact words he used! It made me feel ten feet tall.

We had a very pleasant supper. I saw no sign of drugs, no unpleasantness and no drunkenness. It was a very civilised evening, a very un-rock and roll party. Robert Plant has a reputation for eclectic tastes in music, particularly leaning towards the pastoral. During the post-gig meal, he made a tantalising suggestion to which we would still love to see an outcome. He, being interested in early history, said to me, 'If ever (what is now) English Heritage said they would consider a folk-inspired outdoor gig at Old Sarum, please let me know.' I don't think I even thought it was worth talking to anybody from English Heritage, because how do you crowd control for someone like Led Zeppelin at Old Sarum (an Iron Age fort)? It was absolutely out of the question.

One of the local crew from the Zeppelin show had a lift home to remember. The young man, Tim Simons, was from Bishopdown and was helping that night. He'd pretty much been the senior steward at the City Hall that evening. He got chatting to John Bonham at the meal and said, 'I know it's a bit cheeky but any chance of a lift home?' Bonzo said something along the lines of 'why do you want a lift home with me?' And Tim, who was 17, said, 'Well, you're the only man I know with a white soft top Rolls-Royce Corniche. I live on a council estate and I would feel great if you took me home.' So Bonzo took him home in his white Roller and made Tim's evening.

It's either feast or famine in the music business, if you're in a band. You either earn just enough to buy food or, like Jimmy Page, you end up worth £150 million. There's no middle road. No middle road at all.

1972 begins with Led Zeppelin's only visit to Australasia. They perform six shows. A seventh show is cancelled when Zeppelin are not allowed to disembark from their aircraft at Singapore due to local laws banning males from having long hair. Another victim of the ban that year is British pop star Cliff Richard.

SUBIACO OVAL
16 FEBRUARY 1972, PERTH, AUSTRALIA

I WAS THERE: GARY CLYNE

Led Zeppelin IV had been released about four months earlier. They started with 'Immigrant Song' and the sound was phenomenal. After the concert they visited a fish and chip shop in my neighbourhood. If only I'd known! A drummer friend got to hang out with them in their hotel in Scarborough and said they were all great guys. Outside the concert there was a riot with people trying to get in for free.

MEMORIAL DRIVE
19 FEBRUARY 1972, ADELAIDE, AUSTRALIA

I WAS THERE: NEVILLE QUIST, AGE 20

I will never forget the day – or rather, the evening – in February 1972 in Adelaide, Australia when music changed for me forever. It was a perfect balmy 25C night and the pungent smell of incense and herbal fragrances gave an exotic feeling to our sleepy town and the sounds of 'Dazed And Confused' mesmerised this 20-year-old. Jimmy hypnotised us with his violin bow and Robert Plant's vocals were clear for all to hear on a still night in an outside concert on the banks of the River

Torrens. The rhythm section with John Bonham pounding the drums with his bare hands left the crowd in awe. Across town all my friends had gone to see Creedence Clearwater Revival perform and it was impossible to explain to them later what they had missed out on. I chose to leave it as a personal experience and I knew at some time later they would get it. I have seen so many hundreds of amazing gigs around the world, yet this still remains my favourite over all these years.

KOOYONG STADIUM
20 FEBRUARY 1972, MELBOURNE, AUSTRALIA

I WAS THERE: EUGENE OGILVIE, AGE 19

ln 1971, it was announced that Led Zeppelin were coming to Oz in the summer of 1972. The tour was to consist of five shows in Australia, at each of the state capital cities (except Hobart in Tasmania), and one in Auckland, New Zealand. I made sure to purchase tickets to the Melbourne show once they went on sale. The gig was being held at the Kooyong Tennis Stadium which was the venue for the Australian tennis open until 1986. Accompanying me to the gig on the big day was my youngest sister Julia, aged 14, my 16-year-old cousin, Peta, and a family friend, Gabrielle. We ended up with seats on the lawn area, in front of the stage and about halfway back. The weather on the day was somewhat inclement, with a fair bit of wind and rain threatening, and with Kooyong being an open-air stadium, I was concerned that the weather might interfere with the show.

The gig started at about 3pm. My recollection of the initial part of the concert is that the wind had an effect on the sound. However, I didn't care. I was just enjoying the fact that l was actually at a live Zeppelin concert. I loved the acoustic set of four songs in the middle of the show – where Page, Plant and Jones all sat on little chairs – and then came 'Dazed And Confused', which just seemed to go on forever. When Page produced the violin bow, I was just blown away. At the end of 'Dazed And Confused', there was a bit of rain and Plant said they may have to go off as he once had a friend who played guitar in the rain and he was no longer a friend. He also added that the 'first to get a shock onstage and we're off!' After the next song, 'Rock And Roll', they actually did go off stage due to the rain.

I'm not sure how long they were off for but when they came back, they launched into 'Whole Lotta Love', with the medley additions of 'Let That Boy Boogie' and 'Let's Have A Party' in the middle. Unfortunately, with rain threatening, they cut the show short with Plant saying, 'We've gotta go... water and electricity don't mix!'

And that was it. No encore, and the gig lasted probably under two hours. And even though I loved the gig, I had a sense of disappointment that we hadn't seen the full Zeppelin onslaught and that they had been constrained by the conditions.

I WAS THERE: DALE MCCABE

What I remember most besides the quality of music, the showmanship of Page and Plant and Bonham's drum solo, was the number of instruments that John Paul Jones played. With all the accolades directed at Page and Plant, and to some extent Bonham, I feel that the musical genius of John Paul Jones is often ignored.

At that concert, they did a fairly substantial set of acoustic numbers during which Page, Plant and Jones sat on chairs at the front of the stage. Plant sang, Page played guitar and JPJ went through an array of stringed instruments that were lined up beside him on the stage. I think there was a guitar, banjo and ukelele and when you add the bass and keys, it was that concert that made me realise that if it was not guitar or drums and it was on a Zep recording it was Jones who played it. The exception is the mouth organ, which Plant played.

This show was staged at an outdoor tennis centre seating about 12,000 and – of course – it was sold out. It was only a few songs in and Plant called out to the people outside the stadium asking them if they were enjoying the show. There was a roar from outside and then Plant said, and I quote him, 'Well, why the fuck don't you come in?' I was sitting in the back row and could see outside. There were a couple of hundred people there, and hearing Plant's invitation they all ran down the bank to get in. It was quite funny watching two security guards trying to stop them. They had no hope. From then on not only was every seat filled but the aisles were also filled up.

I remember the concert going for over three hours and them finishing with a medley of old rock 'n' roll songs, and Page playing his guitar with a violin bow and a theremin, from which he extracted some weird and wonderful sounds by waving his arm around during 'Whole Lotta Love'.

It was a windy day which played havoc with the sound at times and it also rained a couple of times. The rain was only a light drizzle but Plant explained that they had to stop as they did not want to get electrocuted. During one of the stops Page and Plant sat on the front of the stage chatting to people in the front rows. I was so jealous but in retrospect, I realise that it was unlikely that either of those guys would be lining me up for a visit to their hotel after the show.

The news reports the next day told of people complaining about the noise two suburbs away.

I WAS THERE: SUELLEN BAYLY, AGE 15

As a bit of a wannabe hippie teenager, I was already a Led Zep fan. This was my first concert and it's still my favourite. I didn't have a ticket but thought that, as it was outdoors, I'd be able to hear them. Someone had cut a hole in the fence and crowds were going in so – yep – through the wire fence I went. I sat right down near the front, centre stage. I mainly remember 'Rock And Roll' and then the thunderstorm that put an end to it. But that just added to the magic and drama!

Led Zeppelin had a large influence in shaping my psyche (along with a huge dose of Tolkien, some LSD and weed experiences – which were par for the course in the 1970s – and the magic of the Aussie bush, deserted beaches and waterfalls with glow worms). My head was all music, words and magic. It's a pity life didn't let me drift totally into that magical world. I was never hooked on the groupie type of side of things (although Robert Plant was ultimately sexy to a young girl); it was all about the music. After playing piano and keyboards in a jazz band later in life, I had a huge appreciation of the quality of their musicality. I still view the world through that otherworldly lens created by Tolkien and Led Zeppelin. And I still play Zep today.

WESTERN SPRINGS STADIUM
25 FEBRUARY 1972, AUCKLAND, NEW ZEALAND

I WAS THERE: LLOYD WILSON, AGE 14

I was introduced to the music of Led Zeppelin by a rascal by the name of Nick Gane. Nick hailed from Auckland but had been in trouble so was sent down to live for a year with his uncle and auntie in Levin in the hope a change of scenery would help change his behaviour, and he became part of our third form crew at Horowhenua College. Nick brought with him an attitude and a heavy rock record collection; Black Sabbath, Deep Purple, Uriah Heep and Led Zep. Our gang soon adopted a passion for the counter-culture music and we became converts to the long hair and screaming vocals, and membership of the mail order World Record Club saw my own collection grow with *Zep III* and *IV* being early purchases. Then came the news that Led Zeppelin were coming down under. It seemed too good an opportunity to miss!

I somehow convinced my parents to let their 14-year-old son travel unaccompanied to Auckland for a rock concert. And I can't recall how I purchased the ticket, but the package I shelled out included a non-stop round trip on the 2ZM train and admission to the concert. However, the train was not scheduled to stop in my hometown of Levin. But with providential timing, on the day before the concert our school was taking a bus trip to Palmerston North to see the movie *Nicholas and Alexandra* as part of our Russian history course. After the film I got picked up by a friend of my dad, stayed at his place that night and he dropped me down at the railway station very early the next morning en route to his shift work. There I caught some more sleep on one of the benches before the early commuters turned up.

Later that morning the 2ZM train rolled in and I joined a few other locals for the ride to Auckland. I must have been one of the youngest passengers on board, but I found a seat next to a new friend, James, from Wellington, who had just 'retired' at 21 years of age, and he took me under his wing for the trip.

The adventure continued north – the train guards and even some policemen that drew the short straw to travel with the group were hopelessly outnumbered. There was the odd serious scuffle on the train, but pillow fights were common so there was kapok everywhere, supplemented by toilet rolls being tossed from one end of the carriage to the other. It got to the point where, if you needed to go to the loo, you grabbed some paper from carriage decorations and took it with you.

There must have been a more serious incident, as the train temporarily ground to a halt as we were travelling over the Raririmu Spiral. I recall there being vegetation close to the train, and this being grabbed by passengers to add to the cabin décor. Another recreational activity involved the heavy-duty NZ Railways china plates being used as frisbees off the train, especially as it crossed the Mangaweka Viaduct.

At Taumaranui, there was the traditional pie stop and a chance to use clean toilets. We were warned not to leave the station, but despite restrictions on alcohol on the train, some headed straight to the local bottle store. Not returning before the train rolled out, the rumour was the culprits grabbed a taxi and drove ahead to a railway crossing to be able to force their way back on the train.

On our eventual arrival at Auckland Railway Station, there were huge queues for the food outlets and we were concerned we wouldn't have a chance to get food in time before the buses taking us to Western Springs were due to leave. However, by stroke of luck two good-looking teenage girls that somehow knew James saw him in the crowd and offered to go get us some takeaways, returning quickly with burgers, milkshakes and chips. I'd never seen them before, nor since, but their generosity and hospitality were appreciated, and the result was we were well fed while others were still queueing.

It was only a short bus ride to Western Springs Stadium, the legendary stock car track that was being used as venue for the concert, but anticipation levels were tangible. From the first primeval screams of 'Immigrant Song' the concert itself was electric. 'Black Dog' remains a favourite of mine, but with every song the concert just kept cranking up in atmosphere, climaxing with 'Whole Lotta Love' followed by the encore. As a 14-year-old, the whole deal was just surreal – like all my friends, I'd never been to a large concert, yet alone to a rock one 25,000 people strong.

After the concert came to a close, we made our way back to the buses, arriving there before the drivers, who weren't impressed that we gained access in their absence. I seem to remember that one coach had even been hot wire started, and certainly lights were on. They rushed us back to the railway station – no doubt keen to unload us before the buses were subjected to the same treatment as the railway carriages!

Once back to the station, we were immediately escorted back onto the train. The post-concert buzz died down as we travelled into the night and tiredness overtook us. However, I remember freezing in the unheated carriage. In true '70s style I was wearing jeans, a tank top, ex-WWII battledress jacket and Roman sandals – cool-looking for the time but hardly appropriate for travelling through the Waiouru/Desert Road area in the middle of the night! Again, the train back to Wellington was not scheduled to stop in Levin but I somehow managed to get the conductor to arrange for it to do so long enough for me to disembark and give a tired wave to my fellow travellers, bonded by the whole experience.

I don't recall debriefing my parents about any of the tour adventures – I probably figured it was safer for them not to know more than they needed to. But I remember going back to school on the Monday morning with all of my class being aware, and in many cases very envious, that I had been the first to go to a rock concert.

To Nick – wherever you are now – thanks for broadening my music tastes all those years ago!

I WAS THERE: SCOTTY CUNNINGHAM, AGE 16

There was no PG warning on the ticket. They blew my mind! I saw them again at Knebworth in 1979. Again, they were spectacular, with the laser pyramid and Jimmy Page with his violin bow. I was with a German girlfriend and she leaned across and said, 'You know this band? They really fuck you!'

SHOWGROUND
27 FEBRUARY 1972, SYDNEY, AUSTRALIA

I WAS THERE: DIANNE VICKERS

They opened with 'The Immigrant Song' and I will never forget Robert's wail at the beginning of it. John Bonham's drum solo seemed to go on for such a long time. I was amazed he could keep it up for so long. The other thing I remember is how many people were there. I went with a girlfriend and we were on the grass in front of the stage. I needed to go to the loo but knew that if I went, I would never get my spot back again. I just had to live with it!

I WAS THERE: GORDON MACKIN, AGE 18

I had hair down to my arse! I went with four mates. We first heard the first Led Zeppelin album when we were all 15. At the time here in Australia, they were not commercialised – there was nothing on the radio, etc. One of my mates used to go into the record shops, put the headphones on and just listen. If he fancied something, he'd buy it. Being 15, we didn't have cars. Every weekend we lobbed up (dropped in) at his parents' place. Every weekend his parents had a weekender and stayed there. Being surfers, we would literally stay up till just before dawn. Well, he brought home *Led Zeppelin I* and we wore it out. The first side would finish and one of us, or more to the point all of us, would say 'turn it over!' In other words, we listened all Friday night and all Saturday night.

The same mate got the tickets. We were ecstatic. They didn't disappoint. They obviously had the equipment already tuned up because they came on stage to a screaming crowd and just started straight away with the 'Immigrant Song'. We were fortunate to be close to the front and had an unobscured view. Halfway through John Bonham did a solo that went on for ten minutes. The first five minutes was with the sticks and the next five with bare hands. I know this because one of the lads was an upcoming drummer and he timed it.

Another incredible memory is of Jimmy Page grabbing a violin stick, striking his guitar and pointing it to our right. We could hear this crystal clear quiver in that direction. He struck it again and directed that to our left. Then he pointed straight down the middle and everyone's hair stood up like we had stuck our finger in a power socket. And we all said before the concert that Robert Plant couldn't possibly have that same voice live. Oh yes, he did! That Led Zeppelin concert is by far the most awesome entertainment I've ever had the pleasure to witness.

I WAS THERE: JENNY HARRIS

As an 18-year-old who had a transistor radio glued to her ear for several years, I drove across the Sydney Harbour Bridge in my tiny Mazda hoping to hear Led Zeppelin from a distance. Arriving at the Sydney Showgrounds, I gathered with a small group of others on the grass outside the entrance. 'Hey hey mama, said the way you move, gonna make you sweat, gonna make you groove…'. I could hear them!

A guy crossed the grass towards our small group of tragics and said 'you wanna go in? Ten bucks!' Yes! Money handed over, a side gate opened and we went down the side and easily hopped over a low wire fence into the mosh pit area at the front of the stage – although I had no idea what that was, this was my first ever proper concert and it was Led Zeppelin!

Being small, I worked my way through the crowd until I reached the stage, right in front of Robert Plant. My hands and chin were on the edge and I was transfixed. The voice coming out of this tall young man with long, curly hair was astonishing. At one stage he dropped the microphone and just lifted his voice – I was there I saw it and heard it. Considering the noise coming out of the gigantic speaker on stage, it seems unbelievable, but I could still hear him. I note that many women's recollections seem to be all about Plant's looks, body and the bulge in his pants – I was all about his voice. Pure, clear, in tune and acrobatic and – most of all – live!

Behind Robert, John Bonham dominated the stage. What an artist! His playing was intricate and the centrepiece of the band. At one point he performed a long drum solo – the others gave him the stage with deference. Robert Plant appeared in the middle with a video camera and filmed the crowd – that film is still out there.

Jimmy Page – what can I say? To see a guitar genius live changed my life. I've been fascinated with watching the intricacies of guitar playing ever since and identifying styles and individual tones created by notable guitarists such as Ritchie Blackmore, Eric Clapton, Brian May and Prince. To me, on that day in Sydney, Page seemed quite theatrical and very close with Plant, who seemed to take cues from him. Jimmy didn't really speak, yet seemed to me to be the leader of the band.

Lastly John Paul Jones. Sadly, he didn't make much impression on me compared to the other three members of the band. I now know how essential he was as the backbone of the band, yet to me on that day, he was just quietly there.

My overall impression of that summer day is of being immersed in the music of my favourite band. Led Zeppelin changed my world on that day and it remains the most favourite musical memory of my life.

I WAS THERE: SUE SMITH. AGE 23

The tickets were only $4. I went with my boyfriend at the time, and my brother and his girlfriend. Anyone could sit anywhere so we stood down the front. The music was loud and fabulous and Robert Plant was beautiful.

I WAS THERE: EUGENE OGILVIE, AGE 19

Sometime after the Melbourne gig, I made up my mind to travel to Sydney for the show there, which was taking place exactly a week later. On the Sunday, I got a bus to the venue and was there nice and early. I wanted to be close to the front of the queue to get in and secure a good vantage point as there were no allocated seats. The biggest issue, and one that made me extremely uneasy that morning, was the fact that, while it was quite warm, it was raining. I was convinced that this was going to be a disaster, with the band not being able to play. I do not recall whether I bought the ticket for the show – for the princely sum, at the time, of a little over $4 – in Melbourne or Sydney, but I do remember that I entered via the official entrance and not over the fence as a lot of other punters did.

Once the gates opened, everyone took up their seats in the stands. Miraculously, not long before the scheduled 2pm start the rain stopped, the sun broke through and it did not rain again for the entire concert. They started with 'Immigrant Song', which was amazing. Once it started, people just flooded the lawn area in front of the stage. The cops tried to stop them but had no hope. I was a bit too slow to make the decision to join them, so stayed in the stands. The official crowd was put at 28,000 but if it was actually 35,000 to 40,000 in size that wouldn't surprise me.

The set list was similar to Melbourne but with the addition of five extra songs, including a bigger medley set in 'Whole Lotta Love' and 'Moby Dick', where Bonzo was phenomenal and at his brilliant best and the crowd went wild. I couldn't believe what I was seeing – no sticks! Between 'Heartbreaker' and 'Black Dog', Robert said, 'If it rains, we're gonna have to stop... and that's a fact, because we'll blow up!' This was similar to what he had said in Melbourne. However, thankfully the rain stayed away.

At the Melbourne concert, Page had a beard, but in Sydney he was clean shaven! Everyone got into 'Bron-Y-Aur Stomp', clapping in unison. 'Dazed And Confused', 'Moby Dick' and 'Whole Lotta Love' between them went on for over an hour. Plant got the crowd to join in singing the final bit of 'Whole Lotta Love'. '26,000 larynxes,' he said.

I managed to sneak a cassette deck into the concert and taped it, and I have still got the tapes to this day. The quality leaves a little to be desired but it is a lasting memory of the day. The gig went for about three hours. It was awesome. The band were extremely tight at this concert, and the sound was much better than in Melbourne.

I WAS THERE: DAVID BRUCKSHAW, AGE 16

Dad was a musician and played a 24-string triple-necked guitar, so he was very interested in listening to Jimmy play. He pushed me up onto our roof so I could see and hear them. Dad was also a promoter and was on the front page of *Pix-People* magazine in 1964, billed as the unluckiest man in Australia. He knew Brian Epstein and Brian sent him a letter asking him to find gigs for a new band he'd just signed. Dad couldn't find anyone to take on The Beatles in Australia at £1,000 a week…

I WAS THERE: NORM ALBERTS

I was 15 going on 16 and got backstage before the gig with a mate through knowing the stage manager, Ray Arnold. He ran the Sydney Amp Centre above Chequers nightclub, where he was also stage manager. (The story goes that Bonham hit on Ray's girlfriend at Chequers after the Sydney gig and a punch up ensued, with Ray clobbering John!) I hit one of Bonham's tom-toms as I was walking across the stage to the mixing booth. I didn't know they were already live, and the crowd went mental thinking the band was coming on. But no, it was just me and I threw a double peace sign as I walked across the stage. I wish there was footage!

My mate and I asked to plug our Akai reel-to-reel into the mixing desk. In unison, Page and Plant said 'fuck off!' So we went into the stands where a food truck let us plug into their power supply and we were able to tape the show. The recording was okay on the tape but it lost a lot in transition to vinyl. We only had 200 copies pressed, at Festival Records in Sydney, and it was titled *Rockin' the Showground*. I no longer have a copy. I lost contact with my friend over the years.

He owned the equipment and I wouldn't be surprised if he still has the original tapes from back then. We bootlegged a lot of shows. The only gig we couldn't get a recorder into was the Stones. My mate even wore a pair of Channel 7 overalls!

I WAS THERE: PETER BOSZ, AGE 16

The tickets were under $10. I was just busting to go. I went with my girlfriend. The major sponsor was 2SM radio station, which is now no more. We were in the upper grandstand. From where we were sitting the sound wasn't brilliant but just being there was nuts. The opening song was 'Immigrant Song', and one of my favourite songs, 'Since I've Been Loving You', was a part of the set but they played all the big ones including 'Stairway' and 'Dazed And Confused'. It was a sell out and more wanted to get in. Some fences were broken by the crowd. 'Whole Lotta Love' was the last song, which they played as a medley and during this we raced down, jumped the barrier and tried to get close to the stage. We had no chance but it was fun trying! The concert was amazing. I don't have any photos but I still remember it like yesterday.

I WAS THERE: REGINALD WEST

I first heard Led Zeppelin whilst listening to the radio. The song was 'Whole Lotta Love' which I heard first because *Led Zeppelin II* was released in Australia before the first Led Zeppelin album, the Australian government having in their infinite wisdom placed an embargo on international imported music from early in 1969 that lasted for about twelve months. Shortly after, I saw a film featuring many bands called *Supershow*, in which Led Zeppelin performed 'Dazed And Confused'.

I bought the albums and once it was announced that they would be touring, I purchased tickets for myself and my good mate, Greg 'Muzza' Murray, to their Sydney gig for the princely sum of $3.80 each.

It was a balmy summer's Sunday afternoon. Rain clouds had threatened all morning but thankfully the rain never materialised. Muzza and I jumped on the train and headed into the city. We arrived at Central Station and walked the couple of miles to the Sydney Showground, which was more accustomed to holding rodeos and such rather than rock concerts. Thousands of people had gathered, with the numbers estimated at somewhere between 26,000 and 28,000.

They threw the gates open about 15 minutes before it started. The stage was set back about 50 yards from the boundary fence and the stands were full. There was a handful of VIPs sitting on the grassed area and several fans tried to join them but they were tackled by the cops and escorted back to the stands.

The band ripped into the 'Immigrant Song' and pandemonium broke out when we charged on to the field. The cops didn't know what had hit them and gave up the chase. But as fast as it started it ended, with everybody just stopped and sat down all at once for a few seconds before they then started going off the field. We were about ten yards from the band, centre stage. After a couple of songs, Robert said, 'Hello Sydney, I hope it doesn't rain and we have to stop. If we don't, we'll all blow up!' and the throng erupted.

One of the many highlights was when they played 'Bron-Yr-Aur Stomp' and the whole crowd clapped along with the chorus in perfect time. It was a real 'you had to be there moment'. I left there with a feeling that I was part of something special that day and it only seems like yesterday, even though it is now more than 50 years ago that The Mighty Led Zeppelin landed in Oz.

FESTIVAL HALL
29 FEBRUARY 1972, BRISBANE, AUSTRALIA

I WAS THERE: JOHN PETER O'NEILL

I was gobsmacked by the incredible sound, and as I was a drummer myself in those days, I was absolutely blown away by Bonzo. The crowd would not calm down when they sang a ballad – I think it was 'Stairway to Heaven' – and I remember Robert Plant telling them to 'shut the fuck up', which they promptly did. It was, and probably still is, the loudest concert I have experienced and I feel privileged to have done so.

***Led Zeppelin return to North America for their eighth visit, a month-long tour comprising 21 shows. It sees the band at their peak. The recordings from the 25 June LA Forum and 27 June Long Beach Arena shows are later remastered by Jimmy Page for the album* How The West Was Won.**

COBO HALL
6 JUNE 1972, DETROIT, MICHIGAN

I WAS THERE: MARTIN POTTINGER

I did a tour with Led Zeppelin as road crew on their 1972 North American tour. I read *Hammer Of The Gods*, the 'definitive' Led Zep story, and it was fairly rubbish. I turned to 1972, where he said the tour kicked off in Denver and I thought, 'Hang on, it kicked off in Detroit.' He got the first two letters right but if you can't get that kind of fact right... Maybe I'm being picky, maybe it was just the one error in the book.

My friend Iain Nicholson and I played in a band when we were architecture students in Aberdeen. Back in 1969, we played at the Plumpton Jazz Festival. We were almost famous – but we never actually got to the fame bit! You always have a mix of people in your year at university and there's always an English public schoolboy or two. We went to London because his father's friend ran the Marquee Club. So I was there and I knew the people who ran Van der Graaf Generator, because one of our connections knew them, and I drove a white Transit for them for about a year. They broke up and so I went back to repeat a year of my studies in Aberdeen and finish my architecture degree. Then I went back to London and played drums for a while.

The girlfriend of the drummer in Van der Graaf Generator knew the secretary who worked in Led Zeppelin's office and, because I'd driven a van for Van der Graaf Generator, in May 1972 I got a call saying, 'Are you doing anything? Led Zeppelin are putting a crew together for an American tour. Are you interested?' 'Yessss, of course.'

So I found myself at Stargroves in Berkshire, the big house that Mick Jagger owned, with the Stones Mobile. Led Zeppelin were all there recording some music (for *Houses Of The Holy* and *Physical Graffiti*) and I thought, 'Well, this is really all quite amazing.' Of course, I had nothing to compare it to.

The Zeppelin tour was chaotic in various ways. I think Peter Grant liked the idea of having four British road crew out there. One of them stayed behind and he was pretty much their tour manager and looked after them and obtained all the bad things that rock and roll bands want. The chief roadie was Mick Hinton. I got on okay with Mick. I didn't really have a job. I was originally told I was going to be doing John Bonham's drums but then that didn't happen. I was kind of Robert Plant's personal roadie, so I made him the lemon and honey tea that he took before he went on stage. He's a really nice guy. I hung out with him and picked him up from the station, as I did Jimmy Page very occasionally in London.

I had as little to do with John Bonham as possible because he was really quite a nasty drunk when he was drunk. The first time I met him, at Stargroves, he was pissed and there was new crew there and he was bumping into you trying to get a reaction so he could whack you. This is the sort of guy you don't want to see in a pub, a big guy with big hands. He and I didn't get on, which was fine because I was going to leave at the end of the tour anyway. But he got in first and they fired me.

They did two warm up gigs, one in Amsterdam and one in Brussels. We got to America, to Detroit, and they had a sound company called Tycobrahe based in Dallas. I thought 'this is weird' because there were no artics, no big trucks, just two or three big box transits and the car that we drove around in was the owner of the thing's own car. You think, 'There's so much money going round on this tour. Why does he have to cut things so fine we're driving his own big station wagon with Texas number plates?' It was very odd.

The tour started and they were great, fantastic, from the first gig. You didn't need effects because Led Zeppelin were such an amazing band, although they made the odd mistake. You just stood back in awe. The crowds of 20,000 in the American stadiums loved it. You think, 'Yes, this is going to be good.' We didn't have to load or unload any of the trucks. That was all done by the American crew. They used to set it all up. The stage was really bare, just backline, a huge PA and a few lights. No effects, nothing.

On the east coast, the band were based in New York and they flew to the gig every time. So we didn't really see the band at all other than on stage. They'd do the set and they were out the back door of the stadium within two minutes and gone with a police escort. So we'd help clear up and we'd occasionally help load the van. We'd stay in the hotel or a Holiday Inn, or embark upon some monstrous drive.

The excesses of rock and roll were there but we were not with the band. We were Led Zeppelin's road crew. There was obviously going to be some interest. But you're working. You've got to drive from Detroit to Montreal overnight. Then you've got to drive from Montreal to

North Carolina in a day. And then you drive back up to Buffalo in New York State again. You're just driving and doing gigs and not being groupies. That's the one thing that you never ever do. And you're not awestruck by them.

So we didn't see the excesses, except you knew there was something going on. When Bonham did his 20-minute drum solo and the rest of them all disappeared, we weren't allowed into the dressing room. You think you know what's going on but I know for a fact that Robert Plant did not take white powders because they're really bad for your voice. John Paul Jones? You'd just never see him and you never spoke to him. Jimmy Page and Bonham were probably the bad boys for doing things with girls and white powder in the back.

But we settled into the kind of routine of it all and I still didn't really know what my exact role was. I worked the echo machine on the side of the stage where the guy was mixing the sound. I was looking after Robert Plant and nobody had told me what to do. One of the microphone leads went mid-way through a show and he turned and looked at me and I went, 'I don't know where the microphones are. Nobody told me.' Somebody else had the microphone. It was that kind of chaos. But we survived.

Then we ended up in New York for three or four days, because you could do places like Philadelphia in easy drives, and so the band were there. They were recording stuff in Electric Lady Studios and I got to hang out there. That was pretty cool.

The promoters on the east coast were called Concerts East. They were all Italian, all heavily connected to organised crime and nothing ever went wrong. You see the performance. What you don't see is the security and everything that's being done to make things go smoothly. At the end of every gig, as you always do, you collect your cash. In Zeppelin's case that would be about $250,000. There was one occasion, not on my tour, where that was put in the safe deposit box at the hotel they were in and it went missing.

I remember we went to a reception in New Jersey or Brooklyn. We were invited on a Sunday afternoon to go and hang out with the promoters, these heavy guys. You'd be drinking wine and these guys would say, 'Anything you want, *anything* you want, just have a word.' And we thought, 'Oh, okay.' We never did.

In the background I think it was really quite heavy. You're not Led Zeppelin and touring America without having a lot of security and a lot of things going on. They had the Mafia and they had the cops in control. The unions had to move everything on stage. It fell to me to buy them off. 'You don't mind if we move all the equipment?' 'No, that's cool.' We used to have to buy them off with $400 or $500.

Robert Plant and Jimmy Page were really good to me. They were interested in the fact that I was an architecture student. Jimmy invited me to his house in Sussex that was owned by Aleister Crowley. My little theory is that they were both grammar school kids. Robert Plant was training to be an accountant and Jimmy Page wanted to do something and I think they were just pleased to have someone to talk to, because there were a lot of heavy guys, lots of London geezers, around. Peter Grant could be very heavy, although he was absolutely fine with the crew.

From New York we flew to Seattle and did two nights there. My relationship with John Bonham worsened, particularly when he tried to throw my suitcase out the window when he was pissed. I think he thought I was some little twat, which is fine because I thought he was a complete arsehole and not a nice person at all. He took a dislike to me. John Bonham did throw a bucket of water on my hotel bed. I wasn't in it, and it wasn't aimed at me.

Mick Hinton used to play the congas at the back on 'Whole Lotta Love'. He said to me, 'You go and play them'. I said, 'I don't mind.' So I went and played them, and I don't think Bonham liked the idea that I was behind him, playing the congas for him on 'Whole Lotta Love'. I wasn't being picked on. He was just an arsehole and I rubbed him up the wrong way.

Then we did an epic drive from Seattle to Denver over the Rockies at night. We were driving the trucks then. It was dark so I never really saw the Rockies. But you come down into places like Wyoming and say 'wow!' It's what you see in cowboy films. This was my first trip to America so I was a little bit struck by it all. The east coast is familiar to everybody from Europe. You have pavements and buses and you can walk around. But the west coast is a whole different place. If you walk anywhere there, you're looked at as weird or a burglar. We ended up in Los Angeles for a week. And we always stayed in the same hotel which was the famous 'Riot House', the Hyatt on Sunset.

We survived. The tour finished. Myself and one of the other guys thought we'd stay on and spent the money that we'd made, so we just hung around and then came home. There were no bonuses. I've worked with other bands, like the Stones, and at the end of a big tour you'd get a bonus of £1,000 which in the early seventies was a lot of money.

I was still employed by them and I thought 'I've really got to end this' because when you're not touring there's not a lot to do. We were asked to help Peter Grant move house from south London to Sussex. And then you're moping round in studios waiting to do this, move that, so I was quite happy to depart.

So that was it. Driving. Not setting things up on stage. Twiddling a knob at the side of the stage. Driving back. Listening to the band, however many gigs that was. I remember thinking every single time, 'Wow! 'Stairway To Heaven' and 'Whole Lotta Love'.' This was pretty bloody good.

Having done that tour and left, I was then in a loop. I went back to my parents' place in Edinburgh to recover. Then I went back to London intent on being an architect yet again, for the third time, and then I got a phone call saying they'd sacked a driver and 'Do you want to go and drive a truck for Wings? Can you fly to Oslo tomorrow?'

There were bands that came across from America and promoters put them on here and they just brought the guitars over. They didn't bring all the equipment. I found myself touring Europe with Ike and Tina Turner, and Isaac Hayes, and interesting bands like that.

Then I went back to being an architect and then I got another phone call in August '73: 'Martin, we're putting some people together for the Stones European tour. Are you interested?' 'Give me five minutes. I'll call you back.'

I then did a big European tour with the Stones. After that, I stopped doing it and went back to being an architect. Those tours gave me a perspective on the Zeppelin tour. The Rolling Stones were such a different tour to Zeppelin. Everybody had a job. Everybody knew what they were doing. It was much more organised than Zeppelin.

I finished my diploma in London. I was living a slightly rock and roll lifestyle after the Stones tour. My friends were all in that area. Nobody was particularly over impressed by it because we were all doing things. We were all a bit rock and roll. Robert Plant moved to Primrose Hill, where I lived, and I could sit in a pub and have a pint with Robert Plant because he's that kind of guy. Robert would buy his round, despite most people in the pub going, 'Bloody hell, that's Robert Plant!' It was when my children were growing up and got into their early teens and told their schoolmates, 'My dad roadied for Led Zeppelin' that everybody was really impressed. They were all starting little bands. Suddenly I found myself being hero worshipped by my kids. And then you think, well this is quite amazing.

MONTREAL FORUM
7 JUNE 1972, MONTREAL, CANADA

I WAS THERE: KEVIN ROWE

I was right against the stage, at the base of Robert's mic stand. They opened with 'Immigrant Song' and it was an incredible show! My photos are on the Led Zeppelin website.

BUFFALO MEMORIAL AUDITORIUM
10 JUNE 1972, BUFFALO, NEW YORK

I WAS THERE: MICHELLE CAREY SIRIANNI

I saw Led Zeppelin at the Old Aud in Buffalo, New York and they were phenomenal. I also saw Robert Plant with the Honeydrippers there years later. Robert sounded amazing, singing these old songs like 'Sea Of Love'. I ran into him at the Hyatt Regency Hotel after the concert. I said hello and told him how great the concert was. He smiled very nicely and thanked me.

BALTIMORE CIVIC CENTER
11 JUNE 1972, BALTIMORE, MARYLAND

I WAS THERE: BARBARA NELSEN

By the last time I saw them they were selling out everywhere they played. My friend and I ended up in the cheap seats in the upper concourse, next to an amplifier! I don't think I heard properly for days after, and still don't now. I feel so lucky to have been able to see and hear all those now classic rock groups. My friends and I thought nothing of hopping up to NYC to the Fillmore East a few weekends every month or travelling anywhere on the east coast to see our favourites.

I WAS THERE: TOM RIFFE

I saw Led Zeppelin three times – in 1972, 1973 and 1975. The first two concerts were in Baltimore and the last Washington, DC. My good friend in the ninth grade at school in 1969 had turned me on to *Led Zeppelin I*. The big takeaway with the live concerts was the electrifying energy levels as the audience anticipated the opening of the show. In 1972, with a sudden onrush of sound, Zeppelin opened with 'Celebration Day'. It was sheer pandemonium as Jimmy Page locked in with John Paul Jones, John Bonham and Robert Plant and it was so magical to finally see my rock heroes!

NASSAU COLISEUM

14 JUNE 1972, UNIONDALE, NEW YORK

I WAS THERE: FREDERICK AHNE

I saw them eight times, first at the Coliseum in Nassau in 1972. They played for four and a half hours, from 8pm on the dot until 12.30am and did four encores. It was named 'Four and a half hours of madness' and indeed it was. They made the venue switch the house lights off, and I quote: 'Shut off those fucking lights, we're not done yet.' The worst was the '73 show at the Garden. The music was okay but the cameras being used for filming what became *The Song Remains The Same* were annoying and ruined the ambience. I saw them four times at the Garden in 1977. My problem with the later shows is that the jams started getting longer and longer.

I WAS THERE: TOM LEMAIRE, AGE 17

My mother gave me a quadraphonic stereo for Christmas when I was 13. With it she bought a bunch of albums. One of them was *Led Zeppelin I*. I was hooked. This show was right before I graduated. I went with high school friends who spent the night in line to purchase the tickets. The band went on at 8pm and didn't walk off until close to 1am. They came out for five encores!

SEATTLE CENTER COLISEUM

19 JUNE 1972, SEATTLE, WASHINGTON

I WAS THERE: GARY ALLAN

I saw LZ twice. The first concert, in 1972, was at the Coliseum with 14,000 fans. I had a good buzz on from weed, as did most everyone else. One of the friends I was with was quite tall and we would follow him as he pushed his way through the crowd on the floor, giving nose hits to those in our path so that after five minutes we were very close to the stage. I remember the audience roaring the loudest when they started 'Stairway To Heaven'. And I remember Bonham's drum solo for what seemed like 30 minutes. Awesome.

FORUM
25 JUNE 1972, LOS ANGELES, CALIFORNIA

I WAS THERE: DAVID FRESHMAN

This show became the ultimate LZ show for me and it was properly captured on the DVD *How The West Was Won*. They debuted much of what was to become *Houses Of The Holy*, including 'Dancing Days', 'Over The Hills And Far Away' and 'The Ocean'. We were overjoyed to hear new Zep songs. The opening one-two punch started with an ominous drone (I believe in the key of F#) that led straight into 'Immigrant Song'/'Heartbreaker'. 'Immigrant Song' is in the key of F#. I also recall the powerful 25 to 30 minutes of wonderful acoustic music that Zeppelin shared with us with 'Tangerine', 'That's The Way', 'Going To California' and 'Bron-Y-Aur-Stomp'. What struck me most is how important JPJ's work was to the acoustic side of Zeppelin. His mandolin playing was superb. I had always found his bass work top notch. Seeing how he and Mr Page played together reminded me of the great British psychedelic folk band Pentangle, or perhaps Fairport Convention. The concert was so long, very close to four hours, with three or four encores. I can't recall exactly. I was wrecked on Red Columbian!

LONG BEACH ARENA
27 JUNE 1972, LONG BEACH, CALIFORNIA

I WAS THERE: STAN FEES

I was in the US Navy, stationed in Long Beach. I paid $6.50 for my ticket and the seats were floor level on the 26th row. It was my first real rock 'n' roll concert and it was awesome!

OLYMPIC STUDIOS
SUMMER 1972, LONDON, UK

I WAS THERE: ANDY MORRIS

I started in the music business working at Dick James Music in New Oxford Street and worked for Elton John and John Reid, his manager at the time. Then I got an interview at Olympic Studios and took the job of coffee boy, where I was brought in to do sessions for jingles. About five months into working there, I got put on the Zeppelin session and subsequently other bands that worked there.

Led Zeppelin were at Olympic doing some mixes and overdubs on *Houses Of The Holy*. Keith Harwood was working in the studio with them and I was put on a bunch of sessions, just for a few mixes and some overdubs. Jimmy and Bonham came in a few times and they were working on some stuff, and the whole band came in for about a week doing some overdubs on 'The

Ocean'. They were in and out the studio quite a band. It was pretty bizarre, because the whole studio had these amazing bands that were all in at the same time. Zeppelin were in for a week and they'd go and come back a month later, and then The Eagles would be in there with Glyn Johns, working on their first album.

Zeppelin play six dates in Japan between October 2 and October 10 1972.

The 1972/73 UK tour kicks off in Newcastle. Box offices open simultaneously, with tickets at £1 each (except Manchester, where they are £1.25), and 110,000 tickets sell out in four hours. It is to be the band's last full UK tour.

CITY HALL
30 NOVEMBER & 1 DECEMBER 1972, NEWCASTLE, UK

I WAS THERE: PETER SMITH

A year after my first live Zeppelin experience, the band were back out on tour in the UK again. This was the first show of their 24-date UK tour. The tour sold out in four hours – a total of 110,000 tickets – which was some sort of record at the time. The 1972 tour was Zeppelin's longest ever UK tour and consisted of stops at concert halls around the UK including two nights at the massive 6,000 seater Alexandra Palace in London and two nights at the City Hall in Newcastle. I had tickets for the first night. I can't recall how I got them; I guess I must have queued at the City Hall. However, get them I did as we had pretty good seats, about half way back downstairs. All tickets for the tour were £1, which was very reasonable, particularly given the popularity of Zeppelin at the time.

I went along with three mates, a couple of whom had been at the Sunderland show the year before. We were all excited about the show; Led Zeppelin were at this point the biggest band in the world, and they had a lot to live up to. It was an amazing show. They were introduced by promoter Tony Smith with a simple 'what can I say? Led Zeppelin!'

Robert Plant came out wearing a pair of silver shoes, and the whole band looked great! In those days, the City Hall would sometimes let people sit at the back of the stage behind the band, and this happened at this gig, with around 100 lucky people being allowed to pay on the night to take their place on some raised steps just a few feet away from the band. 'Stairway To Heaven' was dedicated to Roy Harper who was in hospital at the time. The set included four numbers from the new album: 'Over The Hills And Far Away', 'The Song Remains The Same', 'The Rain Song' and 'Dancing Days'. It was another extraordinary night in the company of one of the greatest bands of all time! This was to be their last tour of the UK. From then onwards, it was an arena in London and an open-air show at Knebworth.

I wish I'd gone both nights.

I WAS THERE: COLIN PETERSEN

In the early 1970s you queued up for a ticket, sometimes for a few hours, and normally the gig was just a few weeks later. These days you can book tickets up to a year in advance (I've had Steve Hackett tickets for about seven months and there's another five months to go) plus it's all done online. I cannot remember the last time I went to a box office, other than to collect tickets ordered online. Led Zeppelin at Newcastle City Hall was my fifth concert, the first three being Free and, for the sake of my street cred, I'm not owning up to number four. Much as I still love Free, it was now time to play with the big boys!

I was late for school due to the trip to Newcastle on the ubiquitous number 39 to buy the tickets. Two tickets for me and Jim Welsh; other mates sorted their own. Jim's recollection is that I went through early morning, probably on the first bus, and he joined me later, possibly even having been to registration at school; we were 14. The first question we had to resolve was which night to attend – first or second? A problem that didn't arise for Dave 'I'll go to both' Pitt. I think the decision on which night to attend was determined by ticket availability. Jim and I plumped for the first night as we could get tickets in row A, over to the right of the stage. How jealous were the others?

We arrived at the City Hall on the night and located the seats. 'Dear me' or some similar expletive emanated from Jim, 'this is a tad bit close to the amps and speakers!' A quick chat with other mates at the gig and Jim relocated himself to the safe environs of row S while Clem came to join me in row A.

In those days it wasn't uncommon for bands to tour and promote a new album in advance of release, The Who with *Quadrophenia* and *Tales From Topographic Oceans* by Yes being two examples I attended. My recollection is that *Houses Of The Holy* wasn't released until a couple of months after the concert, so about a quarter of the material was totally new to the audience.

My abiding memories of the concert are Jimmy Page standing on my hand, which was on the front of the stage, and the volume, which was ear-shattering. I've seen lots of other loud bands but this was by far the nearest I've been to the speakers.

Zeppelin were awesome. I know we can have retrospective rose-tinted-glasses syndrome, but it just all seemed spot-on. Much as I would have loved to see them in the *Physical Graffiti* era, this was exceptionally high calibre fare. They started with 'Rock And Roll', then something new followed by 'Black Dog', plenty from *Led Zep IV*, a few from *Houses Of The Holy* and the expected classics such as 'Dazed And Confused' and 'Since I've Been Loving You'. I was disappointed they didn't play 'When the Levee Breaks', but that seems a small gripe in hindsight.

Although I have a slight preference for Free, Zeppelin had a superior stage presence and seemed significantly more professional and polished, an opinion probably supported by the fact that Free were almost in their death-throes when I saw them. While Paul Rodgers looked like more of a street-fighter – a typical northern bloke! – Plant had a magical stage presence, more handsome, with Nordic-type features and more sensual-looking. He owned the stage, an arrogance born of someone clearly aware he was at the top of his game.

JPJ was quiet and understated, almost unnoticed at times but such an integral and essential part of the band on bass and organ. Bonham was and is still the most awe-inspiring drummer

I've seen in 46 years of concerts. There have been many pretenders to the throne since, but in my mind Led Zeppelin have never been bettered in their genre.

I WAS THERE: PAUL HINDESS, AGE 15

We used to play truant from school and one of my friends had a really good record deck in his bedroom, so we'd play truant to listen to Led Zeppelin. I went to the first of the two nights they played at City Hall with Linda. It was our first date and we've been together ever since. Me and my friends had bought the whole of the fifth row. We queued up overnight to buy the tickets when the tour was announced. We didn't realise that the box office wouldn't open until 10am. When we got back to school, me and the lad who was in my class were caned in front of the class for being late by the technical drawing master and deputy head, Mr Dodds.

In those days I couldn't listen to Led Zeppelin sitting down. If rock and roll was playing, I had to get up. But bouncers used to drag you down. It was only my second ever gig. I'd seen Deep Purple the year before. I was getting hammered by the bouncers. They were going to throw us out. But every time a new song started, I couldn't sit down. I remember, during the concert, Robert saying to me 'sit down, boy', but I can't find it on the bootleg.

We didn't think of buying tickets for the second concert. We didn't think about them playing Hull or Sheffield or Leeds just down the road. Later in life, with a bit of money, you'd tour the bloody country. But in them days, the second gig you've ever been to, you're still at school. Linda remembers that, as was always the case at City Hall, we had to leave before the end of the encores to catch the last bus from Worswick Street bus station back to where we lived, in Washington. We probably had to leave before the end, although I don't remember that. But I do remember having an aching neck the next day.

I WAS THERE: JULIE SHANKS, AGE 14

I went with my brother, Larry Page, and some friends. It was amazing. Practically everyone sat and listened to them until the end, when some at the front crowded around the stage. It was my first ever live concert and I couldn't hear properly when I came out!

I WAS THERE: HENRY RACE

The last time I saw them. The ticket was £1. I went with my girlfriend, Alison. I still have both tickets. It sounds so blasé to say that I saw Led Zeppelin so many times it all merges. I reached a stage with Led Zeppelin where I thought, 'You know what? You've stopped being interesting.' After that I went, 'I'm kinda done. You've turned into something quite unpleasant, quite fat and not really pertinent to what's going on.' I'd lost interest by the time of Earls Court in '75. I didn't buy *Houses Of The Holy*. Friends had it and I heard it and I said, 'Neh.' I didn't want to go and see them at Knebworth. They just got a bit bloated, a bit up themselves. When they announced the reunion people said to me, 'You're a big Zeppelin fan. Are you going to try and get tickets?' I went, 'I've got no need. I saw them a few times when they were good.'

I WASN'T THERE: NICK VAGG

The queue stretched twice round the block. My parents wouldn't let a ten-year-old go on his own!

APOLLO THEATRE
3 & 4 DECEMBER 1972, GLASGOW, UK

I WAS THERE: BILL MCGOWAN

I was a daft 16-year-old at the time and all I can remember was that the gig was just knockout. The band were so tight, with Robert Plant's vocals at their very best. I don't know what track Jimmy Page used the bow on his guitar, but I do remember thinking 'wow'. His guitar work was the best I had ever heard. Living in Glasgow I was spoilt in having such an iconic venue on my doorstep as it attracted all the top acts.

I WAS THERE: PATRICK MAGUIRE

I've got the ticket somewhere. It cost something crazy like £2. Led Zeppelin were the best rock 'n' roll live band ever.

I WAS THERE: KEVAN JAMES

I saw them on the Monday night, and with the old place due to close, fans were not chuffed at lack of encores – apparently, they did several on the Sunday – and started trying to rip up seats in the balcony in protest, but I loved Page playing 'Scotland The Brave' on the guitar with his violin bow.

I WAS THERE: JOHN GIBSON

I was at the first night. There was a two ticket per person limit at £1 a ticket, so five of us slept out on the street in Glasgow to get ten tickets for the balcony front row.

I WAS THERE: TOM MARLEY

I remember taking the morning off work to line up in the freezing cold to get a ticket, but it was worth it. Plant's voice was incredible live.

I WAS THERE: BOB POLLOCK

I was there with two friends, my first and the best gig ever. I had travelled through from Dunfermline. I believe the set was the same as was used in the film of the Madison Square Garden concerts, *The Song Remains The Same.*

I WAS THERE: JOHN MCHUGH

Robert Plant came onto the stage in his fringed suede waistcoat and suede trousers with a kipper tie. He produced a pair of scissors and cut the tie in half to a big cheer from the assembled crowd. It turned out he had been refused entry into the hotel restaurant for his evening meal at St Enoch's Hotel. The gig was amazing. I thought the Stones and King Crimson gigs couldn't be beaten but I was wrong. I'm still listening to Zeppelin to this day and I'm 71.

I WAS THERE: GERRY ROSSI

We started out queuing all night for tickets when they went on sale a few months before and were lucky to get a ticket each for the two consecutive nights they were playing. On the day of the first concert, we sneaked out of school at lunchtime to do what we often did, which was try to ingratiate ourselves with the roadies by helping them carry a few things in and asking them to let us in to meet the band at the end of the show.

The first night was great, and they played for well over two hours. After the show finished, we managed to sneak into the dressing room and meet them which was very exciting. I had my *Led Zeppelin III* album cover with me which they all signed. We got talking to Robert about music and *The Lord of the Rings*, which had clearly influenced his lyrics. He was enjoying all the attention.

Jimmy Page seemed a little bit out of it – but still floating around. JPJ was chatting to others and seemed very contained and not too extroverted. They had a case of German Blue Nun wine, which we each managed to get a paper cup full of, which again was generous of them. We asked them to play 'When The Levee Breaks' the following night. RP said they hadn't played it recently but they would see what they could do. They didn't play it the next night, but they probably played about a third of different material from the previous night, which just shows how versatile and loose things were with them. They were captivating and so exciting.

A year later, we packed into the back of someone's Transit van and went down to see them at Earls Court, staying the night at a friend of a friend. That show was great too but the place had nowhere near the atmosphere or intimacy of the Apollo.

We had a band at school and uni and played quite a few of their songs – 'Stairway', 'No Quarter', 'Over The Hills', 'Dancing Days', 'In The Light', 'Kashmir' and 'Ten Years Gone', but not all at the same gig!

I still listen to them.

HARDROCK
7 & 8 DECEMBER 1972, MANCHESTER, UK

I WAS THERE: MELVIN HEMINGBROUGH

We got into Led Zeppelin around 1970. We were listening to the Moody Blues and the Rolling Stones and stuff like that. I was at college and a guy brought this record to college. He said, 'Take that home and listen to that and tell me what you think.' I took it home, put it on and I was absolutely blown away by it. That was *Led Zeppelin I*. It was like nothing that you'd ever heard before. We used to listen to a bit of Floyd and a bit of certain other bands, but when you heard this heavy rock for the first time, and how Bonham used to hit those drums and that drum beat, it was just something completely different. We immediately went out and bought *Led Zep II, III* and *IV*. I've been listening to them ever since. You might go a couple or three months without listening to Led Zeppelin and then you just put it on one night at home or when you're in the car, and then you might have a Led Zeppelin bash.

For some reason we didn't see them in Leeds. We managed to get to the Hardrock after jumping the train from Leeds to Manchester. We got there early, about five o'clock at night. There was hardly anyone there. We were able to buy two tickets off a tout almost immediately. We went in when the doors were opened and sat in the front row, cross-legged on the floor and very close to the stage, eight to ten metres away, if that.

Before they came on, everybody was shouting 'Wally' for some reason. But then over the tannoy somebody said, 'Look, Wally's trying to get in so can everybody shuffle forward? We're trying to get more people in.' So we moved further forward and then we were really near the stage. And the stage wasn't really raised up. It was good acoustics in there. The ceiling wasn't very high and the stage wasn't very high either, perhaps three feet, so we had a fantastic view.

When we were sat cross-legged on the front row, we didn't know what we were going to see. We'd seen bands like Deep Purple and the Faces before. We thought we were just going to see another band that was going to come on and play a bit of heavy rock. To sit that close to that low stage, with Robert Plant and Jimmy Page there, was mind blowing. We were a bit taken aback at first but by the end of the show we were just absolutely mesmerised by what we'd seen.

As it got to the end of the show, we had no train home, no bus or anything like that. It was gone half past ten or eleven. But the lads that were sat near us were from Huddersfield and we managed to wag into them giving us a lift back to Leeds in their car.

I WAS THERE: PAUL NASH

In all honesty I can't remember too many details about the Hardrock gig. I seem to remember that in 'Whole Lotta Love' Robert missed the high note where he goes 'looooove…'.

I was down at Earls Court when they played there in May 1975. Five of us drove down in a Vauxhall Victor estate and crashed out for the first night in the car and for the second night at a squat in an old disused fire station somewhere near Fleet Street. Driving down we stopped at a service station on the M1 and, as England were playing Scotland that weekend, there were a lot of Scottish fans wearing tartan. One of the guys with us thought they were Bay City Rollers fans!

And I was at the first Knebworth concert. I hired a Transit and drove down with eight people sat in the back. Who cared about seatbelts in those days? There was a couple in the crowd who got married that day and they were in their wedding outfits – dress and suit.

I WAS THERE: GORDON MACDONALD, AGE 15

The Hardrock was near Old Trafford, Manchester United's football ground. It hasn't existed for years and years now. It later became a supermarket. It was industrial looking. It didn't exude a great atmosphere from the outside and it was only a venue for a couple of years. But inside it had absolutely no windows and was dark. There was no seating in front of the stage, so it was a proper music venue rather than a theatre-cum-music venue and quite different to the other big

Manchester venues, the Apollo and Belle Vue. Me and Phil Gummerson went, slightly more at Phil's behest. He said, 'Do you fancy going and watching Zeppelin?' I said, 'Yeah, I'm not doing anything else that night.'

It was a pain in the arse getting the tickets. We had to go to Manchester and into a record shop, in a basement, to get the tickets a few weeks before, and then go back to Manchester for the gig. But we got them.

I hadn't got all their albums. I was a bit more taken by some of Zeppelin's folkier stuff, because at that time I was into Joni Mitchell, Neil Young, Sandy Denny and people like that. I was also coming into music from the heavier end, predominantly through the blues. That's what I was listening to. It was only later, looking back at the credits on Zeppelin's LPs and things like 'When The Levee Breaks', credited to this woman called Memphis Minnie, and then finding out who she was that I got into her music.

It was close to Christmas time. We got the train in from Wigan, fresh-faced and pretty much an alcohol-free evening, straight to the gig. We probably caught a bus from the station to the venue. I remember being very excited but with not much sense as to what we were going to see. Two real stand-out moments from the gig were Jimmy Page playing the guitar with a violin bow on 'Whole Lotta Love' and me thinking, 'Well, I've not seen that before and probably won't see it again.' That was a bit special. I also have a vivid image of Robert Plant being Robert Plant, very commanding of the stage with an incredibly strong voice. You've got to have a strong voice to play over the drums, bass and the guitar of Led Zeppelin but he could do it. He could almost overpower the band, he was that strong. How do you get to sound that powerful while being that good? I remember being a bit in awe of the solid nature of that sound. Although each of them were very powerful players, and Plant was a powerful singer in his own right, the whole lot came together.

The other thing I remember is that I was dying to go to the toilet. There must have been an interval because I remember queuing up to go to the toilet, bursting for a pee, getting to the urinal and then behind me were these huge tough-looking Hell's Angels, bearded guys with denim jackets on and leathers. Could I piss? I just couldn't do it. So I came out of the toilet still bursting to go. I had frozen with the pressure of the Hell's Angels waiting for a piss behind me.

I was quite chuffed that they played what was effectively Led Zeppelin's greatest hits: 'Black Dog', 'Immigrant Song', 'Whole Lotta Love', 'Communication Breakdown', 'Rock And Roll', and 'Stairway To Heaven' of course. They were churning these iconic tunes out one after the other. I never knew how much of this is improvised as opposed to rehearsed, but it came across as a lot of freewheeling through it but not messy freewheeling, still keeping it pretty tight. It was a pretty gobsmacking evening.

At the back of my mind was the practical consideration that I was a 15-year-old kid in Manchester and it was getting late and I didn't know whether I was going to make it back for the last train. But we stayed to the end. It was one of those gigs where you've got that sensation of it first starting and those opening chords and next thing you know it's all over and it's 'thank you and good night'. It felt quick, but I'm sure we got our money's worth out of them.

It had quite a low ceiling and quite a low stage. I remember a raised stage with us beneath it so we're standing there looking up at the band. From the outside you're thinking, 'This is not much.' But it was a great place for creating atmosphere internally. It's the opposite of a cavernous place like the Manchester Arena, which some bands can still carry. Led Zep in their prime would probably be one of them. But seeing these great bands in that tight, close sweaty environment? Well. there's no better way to see rock bands than that. I vividly remember looking up at them. You're looking up to these guys in all sorts of ways and there you are, perched at their foot level, looking up at them on the stage. It adds to the feel of them being rock gods, giving it all they've got.

I WAS THERE: JEREMY WILSON

There was no seating. They didn't do 'Immigrant Song', which I was disappointed by, but 'Stairway' made up for it.

I WAS THERE: JOHN OLDHAM

I first got into Led Zeppelin when I was about 16 or 17. I heard 'Whole Lotta Love' and thought it was amazing, so I started trawling old record stalls on markets and shops for their albums. I bought *Led Zeppelin I* and *II*, but to be honest Hawkwind were my main band. I loved them. Me and my mates used to go to rock concerts nearly every week, mainly at the Free Trade Hall in Manchester. However, I saw Led Zeppelin at the Hardrock in Stretford, Manchester, just after *Led Zeppelin IV* had been released.

That album is what got me back hooked into them. It was, and still is to me, one of the best albums and pieces of rock music ever produced. It left such an impression on me that whenever I hear it, and particularly 'Stairway To Heaven', I am taken right back in time to the very place I first listened to it, which was in a mate of mine's house. It's an awesome album, although I think *Houses Of The Holy* is up there with their best work.

Unfortunately, I only saw them live the once, but at least I saw them in their prime and with their original line-up. And I also saw Sabbath and Hawkwind at the same venue. As I went to the bar after that gig, I was stood there waiting to get served and Robert Plant came and joined the queue right next to me!

I WAS THERE: GEORGE MASON

I was at the concert at the Kings Hall, Belle Vue in 1971 and the two at the Hardrock in Stretford the following year. All three were brilliant. It was packed out at the Hardrock whereas the King's Hall hadn't been, with quite a lot of empty seats at the back of the hall.

At the Hardrock, they were on for about three hours. It was a very small stage and we were right at the front. I bet we were only six feet away from Robert Plant. He looked down and nodded at our lot. I didn't know until after the concert but an old school mate of mine was the manager. We asked if we could go backstage but he said we couldn't. But we saw him and some of the staff taking their rider into the back, and there was very little to it. It was a funny place. It had a revolving floor, and when Zep went off it revolved and turned into a disco.

I WAS THERE: NEIL COSSAR, AGE 14

At 14 years old I was a huge Beatles fan. I'd lent a copy of *Abbey Road* to a friend at school who returned the album and, as it wouldn't fit in my school bag, I found myself walking around going from each class with it tucked away under my arm. This guy stopped me in a corridor and asked was it any good. I told him I thought it was the best album I'd ever heard to which he replied, 'Have you heard of Led Zeppelin?' I mumbled something like I thought they were a bit 'heavy' and he said he would bring an album in the next day and do a swap. He did and the following afternoon after school I placed *Led Zeppelin II* on my dad's turntable, turned up the amp and sat back. From the opening riff of 'Whole Lotta Love' until the end of 'Thank You' I was transfixed.

Zeppelin didn't sound like anything I heard before. Also, I was listening on my dad's new hi-fi which, as he was an electronics wizard, he had built himself, buying the parts for the amp from *Practical Wireless* magazine. 50 watts per channel through 12-inch Wharfedale speakers and a Garrard SP25 deck sounded amazing. I was so in love with side one of the album I didn't listen to side two for three days. I kept listening to side one over and over. When I did flip the album over, I wasn't disappointed! 'Heartbreaker', 'Ramble On' and 'Bring It On Home' were just brilliant.

Two years later with my new Zeppelin friend, Pete, we bought tickets for the show at the Hardrock in Manchester (which later became a B&Q DIY store but has since been demolished). This was one of my first ever gigs. I'd seen the Faces twice and Status Quo but nothing prepared me for this. The things that have stuck with me from the night are the smell of weed in the hall and that when Zeppelin took to the stage, almost everyone put their hands over their ears for the opening of 'Rock And Roll'. They were so fucking loud!

It was a killer gig and to see Zeppelin in such a small venue was amazing. The sit-down section was especially good as it was so different. I remember sitting in Maths the next day at school with a very loud buzzing in my ears, which lasted into the next day.

I've remained a fan all my life. A friend who worked at Warners very kindly managed to blag a pass for me to see the sound check at the Ahmet Ertegün Tribute Concert at the O2 in 2007, but sadly not to see the gig. I watched from the side of the stage as Page, Jones and Jason Bonham ran though parts of 'Trampled Underfoot', 'Kashmir' and 'No Quarter'. Robert Plant didn't sing. He was stood on the floor in front of the stage sipping tea, with the string on his teabag hanging over the side of his cup. I've taken my tea the same ever since.

A couple of years back I was at the BBC in London (working as a radio plugger) and Mr Page was also in the building recording a radio show. I noticed a small crowd gathering outside the building, which was made up of fans and photographers. Walking to the BBC canteen for lunch, I mentioned to a colleague how great it would be to bump into Jimmy, as I was such a fan. It turned out my colleague had worked with the guitarist in the past, so he said jokingly, 'If we bump into him, I'll introduce you.'

After lunch we stood waiting for a lift. The doors opened and there was Jimmy, who immediately greeted my friend by shaking his hand. My friend kept his word and said to Jimmy, 'Meet a good friend of mine, Neil Cossar, who is a huge fan of yours.' Jimmy held out his right hand – the hand that had played 'Rock And Roll' a thousand times, the hand that came up with the riff to 'Whole Lotta Love', the hand that had composed 'Stairway To Heaven'. 'Lovely to meet you,' said Jimmy, squeezing my hand in a firm but friendly handshake. I think I mumbled 'great to meet you'. We all had a quick chat and off he went. Over the next few days, I told anyone who would listen my tale. And I didn't wash my hands for two days... I'd met my guitar hero.

CAPITOL THEATRE
11 & 12 DECEMBER 1972, CARDIFF, UK

I WAS THERE: ANDY SHEPHERD

After the Top Rank in 1969, I saw them again in 1972. Once again they were excellent. My one overriding memory of that gig was when Plant grabbed the mic and stand and performed one of the tracks carrying the stand and dancing across the stage with it. When he finished, he said, 'It's only me and Rod Stewart can do this.' I also saw them at Knebworth. Knebworth was great and had its own atmosphere, but at the Rank and the Capitol I felt more at one with the band because of the closeness and the enclosure of the gig. They were definitely the more magical shows.

I WAS THERE: MALCOLM TAWTON, AGE 19

Mc and my brother went. I was already a huge fan but after this gig I was so stunned. All the people coming out were open-mouthed and saying, 'What have we just seen?' Well, what we saw was a two hour and 15- minute set with 35 minutes of encores and the best live gig I've ever seen. I thought The Who in *Rock at the Oval* couldn't be beaten, but Zep's gig surpassed it by a long way. The pure energy of 'Whole Lotta Love' and the lovely, mellow 'Ramble On' will stay with me forever, as will the memory of the look on people's faces as they left.

After the gig, we went to an old Cardiff venue called the Moon Club and saw a young Pino Palladino playing guitar before he changed to bass. Everyone there spoke of the Led Zep gig. It's a shame the Capitol's gone. It had the best acoustics ever.

ODEON THEATRE
16 & 17 DECEMBER 1972, BIRMINGHAM, UK

I WAS THERE: CARRIE WHITE, AGE 16

This was once a concert venue for many bands. T. Rex was my first, in 1971. I had just left school. Me and a few friends bought tickets, but unfortunately we couldn't get seats together for the gig, so I wasn't sure where my seat was. As my ticket was only for one single seat, I walked right past where my friends were sitting and down to the seventh row from the front. How chuffed was I? The gig itself was high in energy, with Plant and Page running about the stage, playing to a very enthusiastic crowd. They went down really well with the audience. There was time for an encore after a really psychedelic 'Whole Lotta Love' and they played 'The Ocean' from the upcoming new album. We all left with smiles a-plenty.

DOME
20 DECEMBER 1972, BRIGHTON, UK

I WAS THERE: CHRIS DAWSON

The second time I saw them was at Brighton Dome. This was very different from the first. My memories are based on what I wrote in my diary at the time. It was one of the few gigs that I have ever walked out of before the end. I have always loved rock music, and of course it needs to be at a certain volume, but this was so loud it was literally painful to listen to. It was also a lot of over-indulgent nonsense. 'Bron-Y-Aur Stomp' was excellent, as was the start of 'Dazed And Confused', but the rest was just a ghastly heavy loud noise as far as I was concerned.

I WAS THERE: PAUL JOHNSTON, AGE 16

They played two or three songs from the forthcoming album, *Houses Of The Holy*. 'Dancing Days' was one I do recall. There were the usual Zep features with Bonham's 20-minute solo, played partly with his hands and without sticks, and a seemingly endless violin bow guitar solo, which was a little boring. But that minor criticism aside, it was electric. I always wonder how I managed to obtain tickets as this was obviously before the internet and Ticketmaster and credit cards and touts were the norm, but having seen Elton, Bowie, Humble Pie, ELP, Derek and The Dominos, Genesis and many others in the early seventies, I guess it was just a case of going to the box office!

I WAS THERE: TONY MARTIN, AGE 18

Tickets cost £1. I don't remember much about the gig, but the general consensus amongst my friends was that it was a bit disappointing. I think Led Zep were banned from ever playing the Dome again because they or their roadies churned up the adjacent Pavilion Gardens by riding vehicles across them.

ALEXANDRA PALACE
22 & 23 DECEMBER 1972, LONDON, UK

I WAS THERE: IAN NICHOLSON

I first saw Led Zeppelin at Alexandra Palace on the 1972/73 UK tour, and then four of the five nights at Earls Court in 1975. This was my second ever gig, after seeing Alice Cooper supported by Roxy Music at the Empire Pool. When the tour was announced, my friends and I were really excited at the thought of seeing the mighty Zeppelin in the flesh. The day the tickets went on sale, a group of us made our way over to Harlequin Records in the Haymarket, London. We expected a queue but it was relatively quiet. I believe other shops selling tickets had large queues – we were lucky. We bought tickets for the Friday night. Well done to Zeppelin for making the whole tour a uniform ticket price of £1. On refection, I wish that I had bought tickets for the second night too!

The night of the gig, my mates and I made our way from Peckham in South London over to Wood Green in North London. When we arrived at the Ally Pally, our unperforated tickets were simply torn in half and half was dumped on the ground. It was disappointing to have our precious ticket ruined this way! The Ally Pally was a cavernous and cold place, especially on a December night just before Christmas. But as there were no seats, we could cram together sitting on the floor in front of the stage, patiently waiting for the band to kick off their set. We managed to get to within 25 feet of the stage, on the left-hand side where John Paul Jones would later stand.

The show kicked off with the excitement of 'Rock And Roll', one of rock music's great opening numbers. As the show went on, it was great to hear new Zeppelin material for the first time, as they treated us to four songs from the as-yet-unreleased *Houses Of The Holy*. We were introduced to 'Over The Hills And Far Away', 'Dancing Days', 'The Song Remains The Same' and 'The Rain Song'. They all sounded great and made me very excited about the upcoming new album, which was still a few months away. One song that got me particularly excited, as it was a favourite of mine, was 'Bron-Y-Aur Stomp'. I clapped along with my hands in the air, much to the annoyance of the person behind me, who had a go at me. If you were the person sat behind a long-haired teenager wearing glasses and a maroon velvet jacket, well I'm sorry, I just got carried away in the moment!

We were treated to a fantastic set that night – 'Dazed And Confused', 'Stairway To Heaven', 'Whole Lotta Love' with a rock and roll medley, 'Immigrant Song' and 'Heartbreaker'. Stupidly, I left after 'Heartbreaker', only to find out the next day from a mate who had stayed that they came back and played 'Thank You' as a final encore. On the way out, we were met by the sight of piles of the torn half tickets strewn across the floor. People tried to match the torn pieces with what remained of their own tickets, but it was a difficult task.

I WAS THERE: DEE (TWEETY PIE)

For me it started with buying *Led Zep I* on Carnaby Street in 1969. I was blown away. I went to New York as Mum lived there and saw Zep when they played Madison Square Garden in September 1971. It was mind blowing. I ran into Bonzo in the lobby of the Drake Hotel, me with an English accent which Americans loved, and Susan Prechtel, who was a stunning American girl. We had the nicknames Henry Cooper and Tweety Pie. He invited us up to their floor, where it was chaos. There was Robert, Bonzo,Jimmy (initially) and stunning girls and black guys. It was great fun! We left at 5am. I also met Peter Grant, Richard Cole and Mick Hinton.

Then we flew to San Francisco and saw them at the Berkeley Community Theater in

September 1971. Peter Grant let us in for free, mainly as I was an English girl – and cute! We followed them to Oahu and saw them at the Civic Auditorium in Honolulu. Again, Grant let us in. Then they went to Japan and Susan didn't have a passport so we went back to New York.

Then I saw them in London in 1972, at Alexandra Palace. I went with two girlfriends that night, Liz Harper and Sally Tyoran (RIP). It was an incredible gig. Robert used to get used to seeing me at the front of audiences, and sang 'Since I've Been Loving You' to me. That was one of the best nights of my life, next to my son being born.

CITY HALL
2 JANUARY 1973, SHEFFIELD, UK

I WAS THERE: IAN STEPHENSON, AGE 17

I queued for five hours in the freezing cold for the tickets. I went alone. I had long curly, wavy hair over my shoulders, an Afghan coat, an earring and liberal amounts of patchouli oil. I would have been wearing orange, stripy bell-bottomed jeans. I had some herbs under my hair, secreted behind my ear. You could go to jail in those days for having a joint. It was the most amazing concert ever. I was about 30 feet from the stage. It was a life-changing experience. A young girl removed her bra and passed it to Robert Plant who hung it onto Jimmy Page's guitar whilst he played. She was invited backstage to collect it when the concert finished. Being a few feet away from 'Stairway To Heaven' being played is inexplicable. As an introduction, Robert Plant told of a bunch of skinheads chasing the band the last time they appeared in Sheffield. A big hiss went throughout the City Hall.

There were lots of fake t-shirts being sold illegally on the steps outside. Their manager came out and gave the sellers a hard time, quote: 'You're fuckin' rippin' off my band.' I don't remember him being very big, but I do remember him being not very happy. I'm from Rotherham and had to walk home afterwards, which probably took two and a half hours.

I WAS THERE: NORMAN WILSON, AGE 15

When the tickets for this tour went on sale, the whole of my year group from school seemed to be in the queue at Wilson Peck's music store in Sheffield. A couple of us arrived and shamelessly joined friends who had queued overnight. The seating plans for the City Hall at the ticket desks showed no seats available for sale in the front centre blocks but, given our position in the queue, we secured decent seats for just £1 each.

On arrival at the gig, we saw that the front centre blocks of seats had been removed and replaced with a scaffolding rig in an attempt to stop fans getting up to and onto the stage. However, once the house lights were down myself and quite a few friends were soon up against the scaffolding and within a song had worked our way through the scaffolding and were up against the stage. Security couldn't get to us because of the crowd and the criss-crossing scaffolding poles. Pole position, I guess you would call it.

It was so loud. The opening 'Rock And Roll' metaphorically pushed us back ten feet. Being directly in front of Page's amps and stack was obviously the greatest view in the house, but boy did my hearing pay for it later. They introduced four new songs from the much awaited fifth album which was eventually released months later: 'Over The Hills…', 'Dancing Days', 'The Song Remains The Same' and 'Rain Song'. In the course of the latter, I made a huge mistake. During a quieter, mellow moment when Page was standing at the very front of the stage playing on the twelve-string of the double neck, I strummed the six-string open chord. He was not happy and threatened to kill me if I did it again. I never did it again!

The new songs were pretty memorable, as I was able to recall the tunes and melodies when first hearing the new album when it was released, especially 'Dancing Days'. But the highlight was the extended 'Dazed And Confused'. They had dispensed with the acoustic set due to Plant's voice being shot and Page took the reins in 'Dazed And Confused' to unleash a riff-filled magnum opus. 'Stairway' and 'Whole Lotta Love' completed the show to a euphoric crowd.

As the band left the stage, I realised I could barely hear anything. For three more days my hearing did not improve and it was weeks afterwards before I could hear normally again. Jimmy's revenge?

EMPIRE THEATRE
14 JANUARY 1973, LIVERPOOL, UK

I WAS THERE: JAN MERSEY

Tickets were again £1. Mine was pink. I was in seat Q1 in the stalls. I am not a huge fan of *Houses Of The Holy*, and 'The Song Remains the Same' and 'Rain Song' are the only ones I really like. This time they sat down with an acoustic guitar and with JPJ on mandolin and did 'Tangerine' and 'What Is And What Should Never Be' slow. It was lovely. I found sitting in an allocated seat weird after standing and being able to move, dance and head bang at the first two shows. The bouncers were quite aggressive at times and I felt restricted. We all did. We did go into the aisles at the end and they couldn't get us all to sit down then, but it spoilt the atmosphere for me. All three of the Liverpool gigs I saw were intimate, even though the Empire holds 2,500. Earls Court was vast. Knebworth was far too many people.

TRENTHAM GARDENS
15 JANUARY 1973, STOKE-ON-TRENT, UK

I WAS THERE: ALAN MAITLAND, AGE 14

It seems that long ago now that it's like a dream. We all sat on the floor near to the front. Robert Plant was sipping a lemon and honey drink and saying it helped his vocals. When the concert came to an end, we hung back to watch the roadies start to pack away and Robert Plant came within a hair's breadth of where I was standing. I was struck dumb and could not move or speak. He was saying something about how the concert had gone and about the sound. I always think back to then and wonder why I didn't say something? Perhaps because I was 14 at the time and very shy.

I WAS THERE: ANDREW SHERLOCK

It is probably the best concert I attended at Trentham, including seeing The Who, Pink Floyd, Deep Purple, T. Rex and the rest. It was a week night and I was an apprentice and had to be at work at 8am the next day. The tickets were a quid each. My wages in 1973 were £10.34 per week. It's sad that I can remember such trivia! The first song was 'Rock And Roll', and when it kicked in it nearly took the roof off, because Trentham was a great venue for the loud bands. It seemed to go on for hours. The finale was 'Whole Lotta Love' and that went on for a long time. I recall walking back home, up Longton Road, with my ears buzzing with the noise until the next day.

I WAS THERE: MICHAEL MASSEY

I ran The Place discotheque in Hanley from about '63, when all the groups were coming out and were nobodies – Rod Stewart, Elton John, the whole lot. Kevin Donovan used to book the acts. Kevin had booked Led Zeppelin when they were virtually nobody, when they had just started, and we'd even got as far as advertising that they were on at The Place. But then their management got in touch and asked if there was any chance that we could release them from the contract because they'd got this massive tour of America, which was obviously going to be their first big tour. So Kevin said 'yes' and let them off the date. Then, years later, they got in touch with Kevin and said, 'We're so pleased that you let us off and it was so important to us, we'll do you a date for nothing.'

The Place wasn't very big. It had a downstairs and an upstairs. The stage measured about 20 feet by ten. Kevin said there was no way they could appear there because they wouldn't get half their equipment in, and asked if there was any chance we could hold it somewhere else? They agreed, but they would put a stipulation on the price we could charge.

We booked Trentham Gardens Ballroom, which held 2,000, and they appeared there. I've got a ten by eight taken on the night of the group and myself and a girl. The girl had won an LP in some competition so they agreed they would present it to her. They're stood in a line with me, and the girl has the LP in her hand. I was walking around as top dog. But I had very little to do with the group other than that photograph.

I WAS THERE: ROY SMITH, AGE 16

My lasting memory is of the end of the drum solo. I've been remembering it as being 'Moby Dick' but having just checked the set list online it doesn't appear to have been in the set that night so it must have been during something else. Anyway, it was memorable as I had gone with a school friend of mine, Richard Barnes, and when John Bonham finished his solo, he threw his drumsticks out into the audience. One came straight towards us and hit Richard on his eyebrow. He bled quite dramatically but was more concerned and annoyed that the drumstick bounced off his head and that someone else caught it! I subsequently saw Zeppelin at Earls Court and both Knebworth shows. And my son managed to get us tickets for the O2 reunion.

I WAS THERE: SUE WARDLE

I attended with my friend. I don't recall very much apart from sitting on the floor and a (rather too long for me) drum solo. I drank rather too much at these events when I was young and so sadly do not remember much about the iconic bands I saw at the time at local venues. My diary entry for that day just records the concert details and the note 'super'.

KING'S HALL
16 JANUARY 1973, ABERYSTWYTH, UK

I WAS THERE: DAVID PIDWELL

The gig took place at the King's Hall rather than the bigger students' union because of some dispute between the uni Ents manager and the band's management. It wasn't quite a sell-out – I walked up to the venue on the night and bought a ticket on the door. I was in the small balcony which gave a great view. There was a delay mid-concert while they wired up the mandolins, so we just sat there. The encore included an Elvis number. As Plant stepped off the stage he said, 'Elvis Presley has left the building.'

I WAS THERE: BRYN JONES

I moved down from Caernarfon in North Wales in 1971. My old man was a vet and he became the divisional veterinary officer so he moved to Aberystwyth. We moved to school here. In 1973, I was in the first year Sixth at school and I was still in contact with my mates in Caernarfon. I was going up to play rugby on a weekend. We lived in a caravan for about a year and then we'd go back to my mum in Caernarfon on the weekends.

Eventually the whole family moved to Borth. I remember getting a phone call from my mates in Caernarfon saying, 'Led Zeppelin are playing in Aberystwyth – get tickets!', so me and my sister queued one morning before going to school and bought six tickets. It's funny that my mates knew about them playing Aber before I did. My mates came down for the weekend and we all went to see the gig. I remember John Bonham starting with 'Black Dog' and the hi-hat cymbal start. That was brilliant.

I also remember Robert Plant and Jimmy Page telling everyone a story about why they were playing in the King's Hall. It was because Robert went to the Aberystwyth University student union and they wouldn't let them in because they didn't have student union cards. So it was two fingers to the university and the students union, and that's why they wanted to put on a gig in the town 'for you lot'. The whole place erupted. There's always been that kind of town and gown thing in Aberystwyth.

They were *the* band when I was a lad. For them to come to my little home town and play in the King's Hall was just phenomenal. It's gone now. It's been flattened and they've built some flats. But on the front there's a restaurant called Baravin and they've got some pictures on the wall, including a massive black-and-white blow up of the audience at the concert that night. I've been there many a time. The photo is in the corridor on the way to the loo and I swear I can see my long hair and dark glasses in that crowd. We were down near the front. But I bet there's a lot in Aber who point at that photo and say, 'That's me there!'

My wife worked in the Belle Vue, the big hotel on the front, as head receptionist. She used to get complimentary tickets because most of the bands stayed there. I remember The Boomtown Rats, Slade, Ian Dury and The Blockheads. They all stayed there and played in the King's Hall. But Led Zeppelin was a big deal.

Robert Plant comes to Borth a lot. He's got a place out in the hills. He comes down to the Vic, the pub on the front, a lot. We used to have a massive carnival in Borth. In those days there used to be a carnival dance down in the old hall. And the old man turned up at the carnival dance with Robert Plant. He said, 'I've just seen this guy in the pub and I've brought him down to see you.' Because Robert got talking to him because the old man was a vet. My old man with a bike, walking in with Robert Plant, for Chrissakes.

I WAS THERE: DAVID HUGHES

I was at that Zeppelin gig – an amazing experience – and also had the unusual experience of reciprocating (in a *very* minor way) when Robert Plant turned up at a gig my uni band was playing in Borth. He was living in the area at that time. We chatted to him in the interval and he regaled us with details of his last gig – at Madison Square Garden. Quite a contrast! If I remember correctly, we were playing on a Sunday (licensing laws were strict in Cardigan at the time) and he had brought his own booze, which probably explains the large numbers at the gig.

Coincidentally, many years later I taught two of his grandchildren when I taught in Bath.

ST GEORGE'S HALL
18 JANUARY 1973, BRADFORD, UK

I WAS THERE: CHARLES PRIESTLEY

I'd sneaked out of work with my friend Duncan a couple of months before to queue for the tickets. It was a long queue, so we finished up with poor seats, two floors up down the side. If you're familiar with St George's, you'll know the sightlines are terrible but the acoustics are good. There was no online booking in those days, and no rip-off ticket agencies either. The gig was delayed a couple of weeks because Robert had a close of flu. I think he was still a bit below his imperious best when they eventually performed. I went with my fiancée (now my wife of 45 years) but she's a Cliff Richard fan, so I might as well have saved the money for her ticket. I don't remember too much of the set list, but I do remember being a bit disappointed.

Like many young Zepheads, I was originally drawn to the band by the powerful blues rock which characterised the first two albums. By the time I saw the band, albums *III* and *IV* and *Houses Of The Holy* had all been recorded, and the gig was, shall we say, a bit less loud and bombastic than I had hoped. Actually, the local paper had warned us in advance that this was a 'very loud' band, but the warning wasn't really necessary. I do clearly remember 'Bron-Y-Aur Stomp', which Robert sang sitting on a stool, his right foot pounding to the beat of Bonham's relentless bass drum. And of course we got 'Whole Lotta Love', complete with the medley of rock 'n' roll standards which was a highlight of their live gigs. I never got to see them again, sadly, but I can still tell my grandchildren that I saw Led Zeppelin in their 1973 pomp. Trouble is, they won't have a clue what I'm on about.

I WAS THERE: MELVIN HEMINGBROUGH

After the Hardrock in Manchester we then saw them in Bradford which was absolutely fantastic. Plant was starting to do a bit of impersonating Elvis Presley and ad libbing. He said, 'I've never done this before.' They must have had a really good night that night.

OLD REFECTORY, UNIVERSITY
22 JANUARY 1973, SOUTHAMPTON, UK

I WAS THERE: STUART JOHNSTON

January 1973 – was it really that long ago? My memory is understandably hazy, as was my brain on the evening in question. The hippy period had stretched on to the early seventies and Led Zeppelin still personified, in my mind at least, the 'turn on, tune in and drop out' mentality. This is not to say that Led Zeppelin 'dropped out' during this concert. They were tight, and that is an understatement. They were, however, definitely 'turned on and tuned in'. I can only recall one track with much clarity, this being the wonderful 'Whole Lotta Love'. I recall the familiar guitar riff, the heavy pounding drums and Robert Plant's searing vocals, all interspersed with Page's screeching violin interludes. Combine this with the unique atmosphere of a fairly small, smoky, intimate student union gig at Southampton University and I have a great memory of one of the world's greatest rock and roll bands in their prime.

I WAS THERE: JEFF LEWIS

At the end of my second term at uni the entertainment secretary, one Alan 'Mac' MacIndle, resigned. This meant an election for the position of Entscom (entertainments committee) secretary in the student union. I stood and was duly elected, a position I held for the remaining seven terms of my university career and I booked dozens of acts working alongside first Ed 'Dr Z' Zaluska, then Nick Ralph, later a booking agent for the Circle agency, editor of the cult rock magazine *Dark Star* and then owner of the record label Mdnight Music. After Nick, I worked with fellow law student Clive Fisher who became a booking agent for Bron, went on to work for Phonogram via Polydor and became executive vice president of Universal Music in the UK. In my last seven terms, I booked dozens of acts including The Who, Jeff Beck, King Crimson, Captain Beefheart, The Velvet Underground and ELO. I was still working for the student union in 1973 and I also booked Led Zeppelin.

Every lunchtime members of the events team would congregate in our events office, which was always a scene of organised chaos. One particular lunchtime, the phone rang and it was Peter Grant, the manager of Led Zeppelin. He stated that the band had really enjoyed playing in the Old Refectory back in March 1971 and that they were impressed with the intimate atmosphere and the quality of acoustics. They thought it would be the ideal venue for the band to record a live album at. The band had booked a UK tour of larger venues which included a date at Southampton's Gaumont (now the Mayflower) Theatre on Sunday 21January. What Grant proposed was that the band would play a gig at the Old Refectory without charging a performance fee if we agreed to allow the Rolling Stones mobile studio to record the event. As they were going to waive their fee they wanted us to provide them with a free bar.

Back in those days the only regular rider clauses that appeared in our contracts was for us to provide a Steinway piano if any of the acts that we booked required a top of the range piano. Drinks rider clauses were unheard of in our neck of the woods. Most of the acts we booked preferred a smoke to a drink. Although the San Francisco group The New Riders of the Purple Sage – an offshoot of the Grateful Dead and Jefferson Airplane – both smoked and drank copious amounts but were still able to play an amazing set.

There had been a problem with The Who when they demanded a top of the range bottle of brandy, which was not mentioned in the contract when I booked them. The said bottle of brandy would have cost more than two weeks of my student grant money so I refused to buy them one, pointing out that the one thousand pound fee which we were paying them represented the highest fee that the students union had ever paid any act. (This would be eclipsed in May 1973 on FA Cup Final day when we paid Captain Beefheart £1,200.)

The Who got quite snotty, particularly their lighting manager John Wolfe who, with his gleaming bald head, was an intimidating figure. I stood firm against them despite all sorts of threats but the sell-out gig went ahead and they played a brilliant, savage set. It was probably the first time on that tour that they had played sober.

Following the phone call from Led Zeppelin's office, we convened an events committee meeting and agreed that we would put on the gig. Tickets were rapidly printed and a rather fetching poster produced by our publicity team. The design of this poster nearly caused the gig to be cancelled. The poster featured a scantily clad lady in stockings and suspenders wearing a top hat, standing behind a World War Two German soldier on a military motorbike and next to a German army officer in leather trenchcoat. When Peter Grant saw the poster, he went berserk. He did not want his band portrayed as Nazis.

The general feeling at our end was that Grant was being a bit of a hypocrite, especially when one considers the cover artwork of *Led Zeppelin II* which hinted heavily towards a German teutonic macho theme. The album cover had Lucille Ball. Our poster had a good-looking lady in her underwear. Grant threatened to pull the band out of the performance unless we removed all the posters from public display. But we never needed to advertise the gig anyway.

We refused to destroy the posters and they were given away to members of our Events team. I was left with several dozen which I gave away over the years to friends on the Isle of Wight. For years, one was on the wall of the first record shop that I owned on the Isle of Wight. When I sold the business to travel in the USA, I left several of my rock posters on the wall of the shop.

Eventually the new owner of the shop business had sold it to a well-known local heavy rock musician who was a Zeppelin fanatic. He kept it for several years before selling it for a four figure fee.

The January 1973 Refectory gig was even better than the one in March 1971. All four band members were in mellow mood. The road crew were more user-friendly than at the previous gig. The band brought a large management team with them this time, plus various young ladies who been conspicuous by their absence at the 1971 gig. Amongst the entourage was the ebullient tour manager Richard Cole and PR madcap BP Fallon. Also there, if my memory serves me well, was Rod McSween, then working for Bron and now I believe working for the renowned ITB – International Talent Booking – the booking agency for Robert Plant and The Who plus dozens of other top rock acts.

When Zeppelin hit the makeshift Old Refectory stage, they were even tighter and more powerful than when they had performed there in 1971. The rendition of 'Black Dog' was a particular stunner. Their performance of 'Stairway To Heaven' was also poignant. The classic 'Whole Lotta Love' was dedicated to Alan Whitehead, who the previous year had been student union president. Although still a student at Southampton Uni, he was no longer involved with Events department activities. But there were a few people who didn't agree with Alan's politics and someone had written on the men's loo wall, 'Alan Whitehead is a wanker.' Plant had seen this piece of graffiti when he had visited the men's room, hence the tongue-in-cheek dedication. Alan still lives in Southampton. Back in 1973, he had hair longer than any member of Led Zeppelin. (From 1997 to 2024 he was the MP for Southampton Test, representing the Labour Party.)

The gig finished with 'Communication Breakdown'. For years after the gig, those who were lucky enough to be present waited for the mooted live album to come out. To date it hasn't emerged officially, although the gig can be heard on a bootleg CD that has been doing the rounds of record fairs in recent years. And talking of rounds, the band ran up a bar bill of over £200. By today's prices it sounds like small beer but back in those days, when a quid would buy you several pints at our subsidised student union bar, two hundred smackers was a lot of money. But who were we students to complain? In two years, our Events Department had put on two epic rock concerts by the greatest rock band in the universe for a total of three hundred odd pounds.

Earlier this century, it was rumoured that Richard Branson had offered the band £200 million plus to get back on the road with the late great John Bonham's son Jason on the drums. Of the original members, it was Robert Plant who declined. Good on you, Robert. Unless Branson can come up with a Tardis as a tour bus, those heady dazed and confused days of the early seventies can never ever be replicated.

I WAS THERE: PAUL MAY

My very good friend Stuart Johnston, who at that time was Entertainment Secretary for the Isle of Wight College, asked me if I was interested in going to a Led Zeppelin gig at Southampton University, which he knew about through his friend Jeff Lewis, who had booked them as the university's Entertainment Secretary. Led Zeppelin and the Stones were my two favourite bands of the time so of course I had to be there. On the day, Stu and I travelled over on the ferry to Southampton and made our way to the Uni building to meet Jeff. Jeff showed us around a bit and eventually we made our way to an empty hall with a fairly low stage with the band's equipment on it.

The hall started to fill up and the atmosphere was electric. I was sitting on the floor in the first row with my face at about stage height, perfectly positioned to see and hear the band. The lights were switched off so that all I could see were the red lights from the amplifiers and speakers. Then shadowy figures started to slip into view past the red lights. I recognised the beginning of 'Rock And Roll' and John Bonham's thunderous drumming. The lights came back on and Page and John Paul Jones were playing away and Robert Plant started singing 'been a long time since I rock and rolled…'.

I was in rock heaven that evening. Through the mists of time, what I remember is that, as an amateur drummer who had tried drumming along to Led Zep LPs, I focused very much on John Bonham, who was in front of me and behind Robert Plant. His drumming was so fast that at times I could barely see his arms moving, and yet he was so powerful too. To this day he is my favourite drummer. Jimmy Page seemed to play more different ways on guitars than I'd ever seen and the sounds he created were awesome. The violin bow was just magical too.

JPJ seemed to really help drive the band along and I was really impressed with his keyboard playing. I can still picture Robert Plant – tall, skinny and with his great mane of long hair – dancing in a side-stepping way and singing and howling like I'd never heard before, often using his voice like an instrument, duelling or harmonising with Page's guitar. The band were so tight. It all fitted together so well, sounded astoundingly good and almost overloaded my senses. I can honestly say that it was the best gig I have ever been to and I have seen many over the years.

GAUMONT
23 JANUARY 1973, SOUTHAMPTON, UK

I WAS THERE: GLYN AMOS, AGE 20

I had just left the family home for the first time to move into shared lodgings with other people. As you do, I made friends with the other guys around my age. There were around eight to ten others who wanted to see them and I was persuaded to go along to the Gaumont. I was not a huge fan of prog rock at the time. I do remember how loud it was in the theatre. 'Stairway To Heaven' was included in the set, and stands out as a pretty long rendition. With the passage of time, I now know what a great group they were – and are – and Robert Plant has one of the best voices ever!

MUSIC HALL
25 JANUARY 1973, ABERDEEN, UK

I WAS THERE: BOB DOUGLAS, AGE 18

I remember the camaraderie in the 5am queue for tickets, all great-coated, chilly and damp, lining up outside Telemech at 25-27 Marischal Street, clutching our one pound sterling and waiting for the doors to open to purchase the hard card ticket. I cannot recall many details about the show other than how blown away I was, parked in the fourth row of the tiny municipal hall with its 1,500 seats. I saw them again at Knebworth. They were nowhere near as good.

I WAS THERE: DAVID FINDLAY

I had to wait two hours to get a ticket, because they went on sale at 9am and I had to attend a lecture. I managed to get one of the last tickets. I remember being pushed back into my seat by the sonic blast of John Bonham's intro to 'Rock And Roll'. It was a tremendous concert, but I'll always remember Robert Plant asking if there were any fishermen in the audience to a silent reply, all the boats being out. I also remember the sinister, massive hooded figure of Peter Grant skulking up and down the aisles, looking for folks with cassette recorders. He would scare the life out of anybody.

I WAS THERE: COLIN BLACKHALL

The performance was not particularly good. Aberdeen Music Hall was never noted for good acoustics and I swear I was deaf for two days afterwards. I don't believe Led Zeppelin really gave their all that evening; you can sense when a band is 'hot' and the atmosphere was pretty stilted in spite of three encores. Arguably, the overly enthusiastic review from the local paper, *The People's Journal*, was not properly objective. Aberdonians were culturally starved at that time and few observers wanted to knock any top line band's performance. David Bowie visited two months later at the height of his Ziggy phase and he was even worse!

I WAS THERE: GORDON HULSE

The gig was over two hours long, perhaps two and a half. It's so long ago I can't remember. It was already sold out, but I was determined to see them and bought a ticket outside. I recognised the guy from the record shop, Telemech, who sold the tickets. He had obviously held tickets back or bought them from his day job and was trying to sell them for more than face value outside, just like your touts do today. I said, 'I am only paying the price of the ticket or I will report you to the bobby just up the street.' He grudgingly took the two quid and I got a really good seat, second row from the front.

I remember how good the concert was. Robert Plant stood out a mile. He was a real showman. Jimmy Page is a great guitarist and the only one I've seen play a double neck guitar. The whole group just stood out. A decade or so ago, I sold my ticket and programme for 50 quid at a pop music memorabilia auction. It was good money at the time but now I wish I had kept them!

I WAS THERE: MALCOLM WILSON

As a teenager growing up in Buckinghamshire, I became obsessed with the popular music of the day. I was 13 years old in 1967 when somebody walked into the school library with a newly purchased copy of *Sgt. Pepper's*. It was a turning point. I began buying the *Melody Maker* and *New Musical Express* to read about the new releases of my idols; the music scene was so vibrant. I recorded friends' LPs on an old reel-to-reel tape recorder as I couldn't afford to buy albums.

When I was 14, my family moved to Scotland and a small village about 60 miles from the relatively big city of Aberdeen. I managed to make the journey with school friends on coach trips organised by the fifth and sixth formers to catch acts visiting Aberdeen Music Hall. In those days, quite big stars would play small venues rather than the vast arenas or football stadia like today. I remember seeing a young and hyper Elton John, Yes, Ten Years After and Tyrannosaurus Rex at this small venue during these after-school coach trips. And as an 18-year-old, I left home to study at the University of Aberdeen, thus bringing the Music Hall within walking distance!

Music was an even more vital part of my life. Getting my rather basic hi-fi system installed in my halls of residence bedroom at Crombie Halls was the essential and first step at the beginning of each term. I had some early Led Zeppelin sessions that I'd recorded from the BBC and I'd managed to record some of their albums, thanks to more wealthy friends!

I made friends with other music fans that I'd met at the halls of residence and when we heard that Led Zeppelin were visiting the Music Hall, tickets were obtained via the old fashioned queuing process. There was no Ticketmaster in those days! I think a ticket cost about £1. I used to say that at the University Union you could get drunk for a pound as a pint cost less than 20p. Could you see a top rock band today for the price of five pints? No chance! In those days, acts made their money from album sales, or at least the record companies did.

Deciding that Led Zeppelin outranked getting drunk, and accompanied by Alan Main (nicknamed Kang) and Mike Collins, we got the tickets and made our way to the Music Hall. The venue is Victorian and designed for a string quartet rather than rock gods. We had seats in the middle of the stalls and they played an amazing set that both deafened and amazed us. They looked a bit like us, with long hair and scruffy jeans, and we were mesmerised by their musicianship and authenticity. When the encores were over, we exited onto a cold grey Aberdeen Union Street and made our way back to the halls of residence in a state of euphoria. Kang was so entranced that he followed them to their next concerts in Dundee and Edinburgh. I wish I'd done the same!

I tried to recreate the feeling recently by going to a cinema in Aberdeen just close to the Music Hall and watching the Led Zeppelin reunion concert. It was quite eerie to realise that, apart from the sad death of Bonham, they were just the same and could still play like gods while I sadly am about to become a pensioner! When I explain to younger folk today that I was and am a music fan, I just have to say, 'I saw Led Zeppelin at the Music Hall' and I gain instant respect. Age has some benefits.

I WAS THERE: MARION ANDERSON, AGE 18

I went with my pal, clutching my *Led Zep IV* album and hoping that I could perhaps meet my heroes and get a few autographs. I was dressed in a black maxi skirt, black boots and a black curly short jacket. The excitement was palpable as the packed venue cheered on the best rock band that I have ever seen. The set was spectacular, opening with 'Black Dog', and the final ovation was filled with loving emotion and great respect. I will never forget it. My friend knew one of the security guards on the stage door, and after a long queuing process, we were allowed in to meet the band. The one member of the band who remains in my mind is Jimmy Page. He took time with people, made sure that my album cover was autographed by all, and he will always be remembered as thoroughly nice fella. I left when the squad of groupies entered. My autographed album is still my pride and joy, and to this day, I maintain it was their best album.

I WAS THERE: PATSY FRASER-MACKENZIE, AGE 20

I was training to be a teacher and my boyfriend George, now my husband of 40 years, was an Agri student, so we didn't have much money, but saved enough and couldn't believe our luck when we got tickets for the concert. We were so excited to be there. I well remember the huge volume of sound as they went through their repertoire. It was like being somewhere that was not of this earth and we knew we were in the presence of something very special. When the set finished, the Aberdonians were not keen to let the band go and, amazingly, we were treated to an encore that went on for another hour. What a gig and what an amazing group. When it was finally over, we went outside into the night onto Union Street. Our cars were ringing with the noise and we couldn't hear what anyone was saying. We both looked at each other in disbelief at what we had witnessed, and were so thrilled to have been part of something very special. For days afterwards we lived it over and again and my ears finally recovered – a bit! That Led Zeppelin gig will live forever in my memory. Now, unfortunately, I am suffering from a bit of deafness, but I would probably do it all over again. I definitely could wear the 'I might be old but I saw all the best bands' t-shirt!

I WAS NEARLY THERE: DONALD MORRISON

I didn't manage to get a ticket but went to listen from outside. It turned out that another 2,000 people had the same idea! Incredibly, at the ends of the concert proper and before the encores, the doors were opened and the masses flooded in. There were police in attendance but no attempt was made to deprive us of our moment of glory on health and safety grounds. We were treated to no less than five encores. I can't remember what they played but it was incredible to have witnessed the band in their prime and for free. Now that's what I call a great night out for an Aberdonian!

CAIRD HALL

27 JANUARY 1973, DUNDEE, UK

I WAS THERE: GRANT MACKIE, AGE 17

We queued up for hours to get tickets from Largs, a well-known music shop in Whitehall Street, Dundee. All the tickets seemed to go on sale there at the time. At least you knew if you had a certain place in the queue, you'd get a half decent seat, although the seats were seldom needed. Music was much more accessible then and the real fans could usually work out a way to get there, even in a small venue like the Caird Hall. I remember going to the Led Zeppelin concerts with a mate from our school, Morgan Academy, and Plant and Page were rock gods to us, particularly by the time of the 1973 gig. They were electrifying live and really charismatic. Not many bands sound better live but they did. The great thing was you didn't have to wait six months for the concert and things moved at a faster pace. By the time they took the stage the anticipation and atmosphere were unbelievable.

It's pretty hilarious when you look back at those days. My mum and dad were in despair at the length of my hair. We had a budgie at the time that was a great mimic and my dad taught the bird to say 'get your hair cut' every time I came into the room. He thought it was brilliant but the novelty wore off with me after a while!

I WAS THERE: RAYMOND MEYER

A little under two years after the first Caird Hall show and Led Zeppelin announced a full UK tour, again playing at the Caird Hall. I was working as an apprentice electrician and had no way of getting tickets for this concert. A work mate mentioned that his girlfriend worked for Dundee council and he would ask her to get tickets for me. I never thought any more about it until a few weeks later; whilst having our tea break, he told me he had something for me. He then produced three tickets for the Led Zeppelin concert. I about fell off my chair! I was going to see Led Zeppelin once more.

I persuaded a friend of mine to smuggle his portable cassette tape recorder into the concert so we could record it. We had side balcony seats with a great view overlooking the stage. My lasting memory of this concert was the powerhouse drumming of John Bonham. The whole band were on top form and again it was an amazing concert. When I got home, I played the recording of the whole concert over again into the wee small hours.

Unfortunately, I gave a friend the tape to listen to and he recorded over the whole of the second side of the tape. I could have killed him! The tape also got chewed up in someone else's machine but I did manage to salvage some of it and it can now be heard on various bootleg CDs including one entitled *Dundeeism*. I later travelled down to London in 1975 to see the first night of their Earls Court concerts and also saw them at Knebworth in 1979. The best band ever!

I WAS THERE: GORDON CAMERON. AGE 17

It was memorable not only for being a great concert but because one of my mates, Dennis, decided not to come back to Perth with us after the concert. Rather, he wanted to hang around and see if he could meet the band. He appeared the next day in the pub at lunchtime, the Sally aka the Salutation Hotel, saying that not only did he get to meet the band but that he got a lift back to Perth from Jimmy Page who was driving up to Loch Ness after the gig. According to Dennis, Jimmy had a house overlooking the loch that used to be owned by the occultist Aleister Crowley. True or not I can't say, but Dennis certainly gained a good few beers that afternoon on the back of that story.

I WAS THERE: GERRY BROADFOOT, AGE 16

I was living away from home for the first time. I went on my own. Tickets had sold out months before and were hard to get. I only got one as a college friend had to go home and he wasn't able to attend. He sold me the ticket at face value, £1.10, but I would have paid more. I was offered a fiver for the ticket as I was queuing to go in but politely declined. About four places ahead of me was a granny who was also queueing. She was drawing quizzical looks from the bouncers and the rest of us, but in she went.

I was ten rows centre from the stage and there was no support act. I don't remember much of the show as I must have been high on the adrenaline of the night. Bonham's drums seem to overpower Plant's vocals. Jimmy Page was just mesmerising. I once saw a pirate recording of the show but was unable to get a copy. I remember that they left Bonham on stage by himself while he did a ten-minute drum solo.

MY WIFE WAS THERE: IAN MCALLISTER

I saw Led Zeppelin at the Caird Hall. I didn't know her at the time but my wife Dianne blagged her way into the dressing room. Her friends were hanging around the Caird Hall during the day and the roadies just shouted 'hey guys, come and give us a hand to get the gear in,' which they did. That evening, Dianne and a friend were invited to the gig by these guys and she toddled along with them and they got free passes and everything. They got an acknowledgment from Robert Plant as the band walked across the stage prior to the performance. She didn't even know who Robert Plant was, but she remembers he was dressed head to toe in tartan.

I WAS THERE: JOHN MCLEISH

My friends and were driving to the Dundee gig from Glasgow. We had stopped in a lay by (there was no motorway then) when a green Rolls drove past. Right away I saw Plant in the back seat! We chased after the car, caught up with it and maybe because of our 'La Cucaracha' air horns sounding over and over, or maybe because the driver wanted to avoid an accident, they stopped in another lay by. We couldn't believe it.

Bonham and John Paul Jones sat in the car but Robert got out to talk to us. He asked if we were off to the concert and then opened the car boot, which had a load of Newcastle Brown Ale which he dished out. He asked who owned the Cortina GT and my friend said it was his. Plant said, 'You must be Peter then,' as he had made a big perspex sign with his name which was stuck on the dash. When we drove off, we were in front of the Rolls and paid their toll over the Tay Bridge!

At the concert, Plant dedicated 'Rock And Roll' to 'a car called Peter which drinks a lot of beer!' We went nuts up in the circle. What a day, what a night. Incredible!

(clockwise from top left) Dennis Gameros saw Zeppelin's first ever American show; Kenneth Liss thought acid enhanced seeing Led Zep; Ellen Frishberg was hooked on first seeing an unknown Led Zeppelin; Zep in action at the Grande Ballroom, Detroit (Kevin Kelly); Donald Sztabnik saw Zep in action at the Fillmore East

KODAK SAFETY FILM
KODAK TRI-X PAN

Opposite page (clockwise from top left): Tom Brody did not like Robert Plant's 'excessive groaning'; Paul Fahrenkopf thought Zeppelin blew the top-billed Iron Butterfly out of the water; Craig Barrows was in the men's room when he met Robert Plant; Gregory Jackson was tripping on acid when he saw Zep; Elliott Sturm got the chills from watching Zeppelin; Richard Bean photographed Zep at the Carousel Theater in Framingham, Massachusetts; Joseph Angier remembers Robert Plant splitting his trousers

This page (clockwise from top left): Listening to *Led Zep I* takes Steve Parish back to the Fillmore; Paul Wolaver first saw Zeppelin in 1969; Chrissy Bean was at the Atlanta Pop Festival; Paul Welsh's mate thought RP was called 'Robert Planet'; Barbara Nelsen's ticket for the Laurel Pop Festival; Slim Manicotti bumped into Robert in Nashville

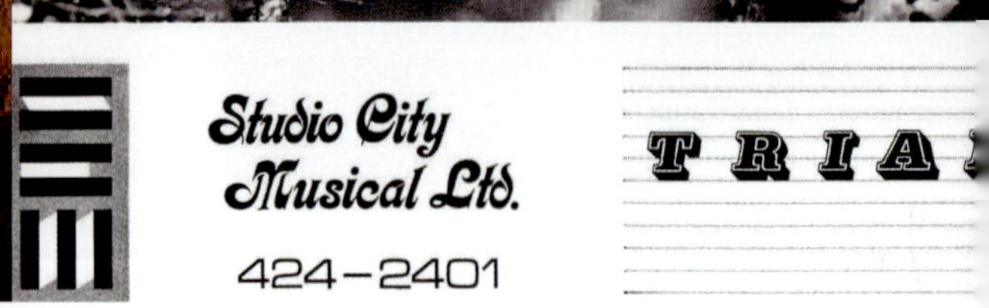

(clockwise from top left) Carolyn Travis was at the Laurel Racetrack; Christine Bursey's ticket for the PNE Agrodome; Ross Cable's band: he thought seeing Zep was like being at a private party; Boom Baker discovered Zeppelin at a specialist import store; Joyce Braswell-Kafer predicted success for the early Zeppelin; Christine Bursey's pic of JP on stage in 1969

'Zeppelin' takes off at Carousel

By NATHAN COBB
Globe Staff

Led Zeppelin is the British rock quartet whose appearance at the Newport Jazz Festival last month was an off-again, on-again affair. It seems the producer of that show, in an attempt to get gate crashing rockers out of town, denied that the group would ever appear; yet, in the end, it did.

Apparently the Carousel Theater's Frank Conley had so such trepidations last night, even with the massed lurking on the hill that overlooks his Framingham tent. Before a packed house of 2600, the Zeppelin proved to be made of something more than but air.

The first half of the program featured Orpheus, a Boston based group that is turning up everywhere these days. A sort of East Coast (hard) version of the Beach Boys, they ran through a tight set that featured rich vocal blendings.

Then the Zeppelin flew in, total theater of blues-rock, lead singer Robert Plant was the shrieking flight engineer, guiding the ship (imagine, if you will, a male Janis Joplin). Lead guitarist Jimmy Paige was the orange-bedecked pilot, the man really in charge. Drummer John Bonham was the engine, always roaring lest the Zeppelin crash. And bassist John Paul Jones was the passenger, seemingly along for the ride.

Most of the tune's came from the group's album (Atlantic SD 8216). There was Willie Dixon's Down and Dirty Blues, "I Can't Quit You Babe," featuring a fine Jimmy Paige solo. Later came Paige's own earthy "Dazed and Confused," to be greeted by a standing ovation. Next there was a zinging Indian-influenced solo tune by Paige again; then "But What Is and What Should Be" (never before done on stage); and at last Dixon's "You Shook Me."

The Zeppelin flew high, all right, and therein may be its problem; it has a tendency to soar, rather than keep on a straight flight plan. In short, many of the tunes wander, and some people feel the blues should be played only straight ahead.

But, after all, Zeppelins are flying machines. Even the kids on the hill must

(clockwise from top left) Phyllis Fox's friend gave Jimmy Page a blowjob, and told everyone about it; Elaine Bender was surprised that Zeppelin played an acoustic set; Robin Dexter saw Zep at the tented Carousel Theater in Framingham, Mass; Tom Blake recalls 'the worst concert I ever saw'; Dan Smith had tickets to see Zep on his eighteenth birthday but arrived as the show ended; George Boje recalls John Bonham being totally wasted

Jimmy Page at the New York State Pavilion, 30 August 1969 (Thom Lukas)

Robert Plant at the New York State Pavilion, 30 August 1969 (Thom Lukas)

(clockwise from top left) Kelly Craven watched the show from the front corner of the stage; Halldóra and her friends went to see Zeppelin when they played Reykjavik (top right & bottom middle); Jody Husseini saw Zep in Macon, Georgia from the front row; Dennis K Russell Snr can still feel the vibes over 50 years later; Wendy Nunez first heard Zeppelin at a head shop

(clockwise from top left) Jimmy and Robert on stage at the Bath Festival of Blues & Progressive Music 1969 (Peter Clinick)

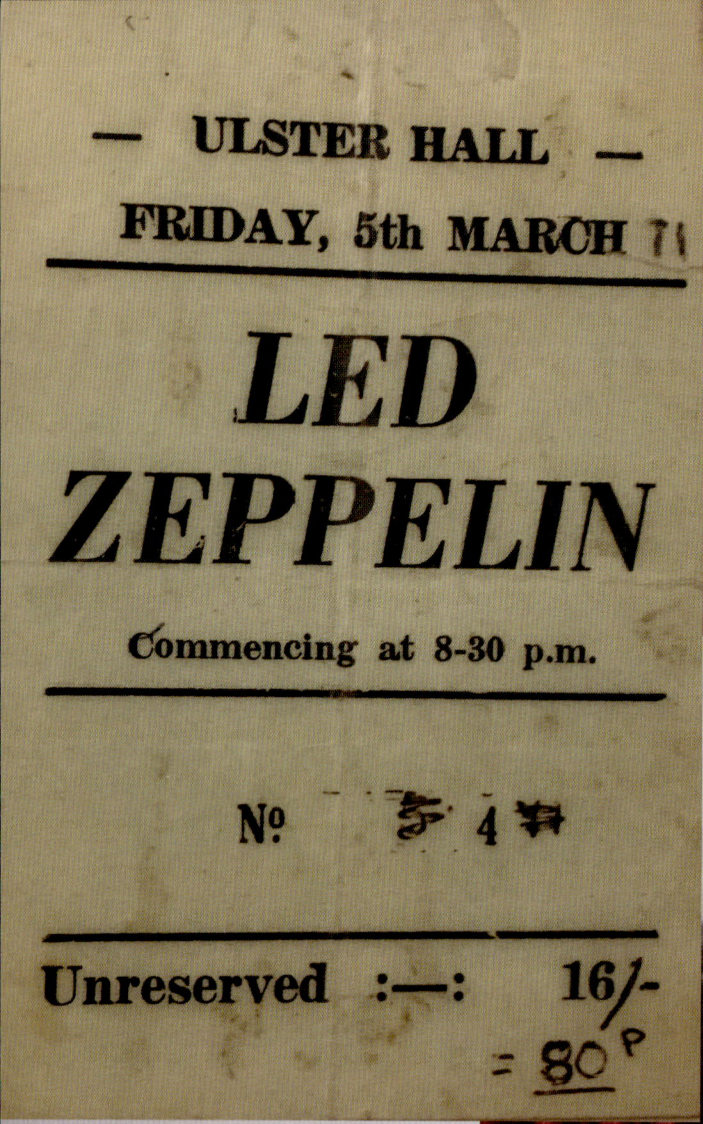

(clockwise from top left) Alan Beck's ticket for the Ulster Hall show, where 'Stairway To Heaven' was debuted; Jeff Crim paid $5 to see Zeppelin; Perry Dror was put off by Jimmy's facial expression; Peter Alcock saw two-and-a-half hours of Zeppelin at the top of their game; for Paul Sheppard, 75p was a big outlay; Jen McConnell queued for eight hours to get tickets

(clockwise from top left) Richard Turner roadied at Nottingham Boat Club; Roddie Gilliard saw Zep twice in the space of six months; Marcos Fernandes discovered Zep whilst living in Japan; Kathie Duvall Beach was a teenybopper until she heard Zeppelin; Robert and Jimmy in action (Ben Maska)

(clockwise from top left) Zeppelin in action in Dundee 1971 (all photos Graham Kennedy)

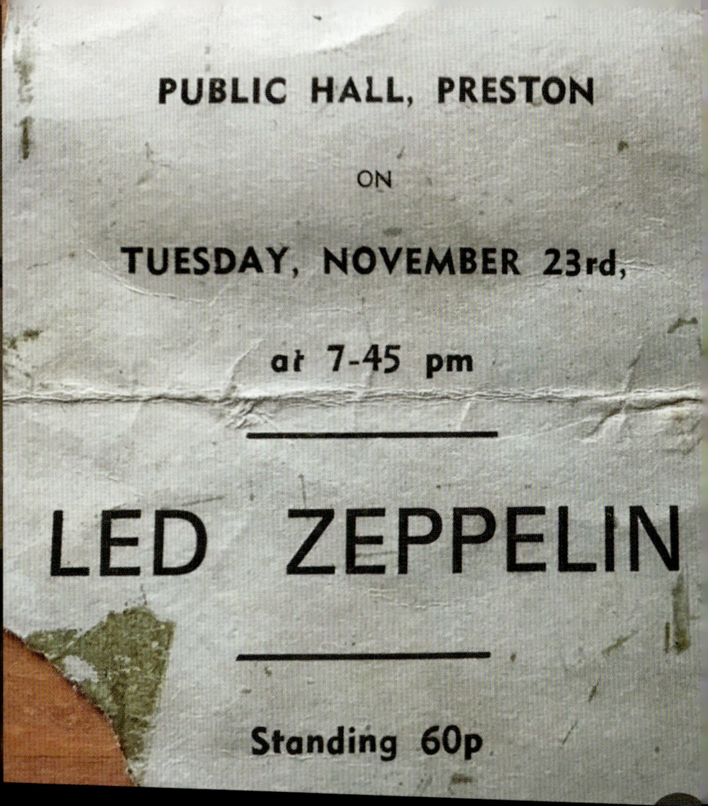

PUBLIC HALL, PRESTON

ON

TUESDAY, NOVEMBER 23rd,

at 7-45 pm

LED ZEPPELIN

Standing 60p

DAVID SIMONE AND

Leicester University
Entertainments Committee
present

LED ZEPPELIN

November 25th.

IN QUEEN'S HALL

TICKETS ON SALE FROM NOVEMBER 15TH, IN ADVANCE ONLY.
NO TICKETS WILL BE SOLD ON THE NIGHT, AND A S.U. CARD WILL BE REQUIRED TO BUY THEM FROM THE UNION.

Tickets £1

Leicester University Ents. Committee Presents

LED ZEPPELIN in Concert

Nov. 25th. Percy Gee Bldg. 8 p.m.

Tickets £1-00 in advance only

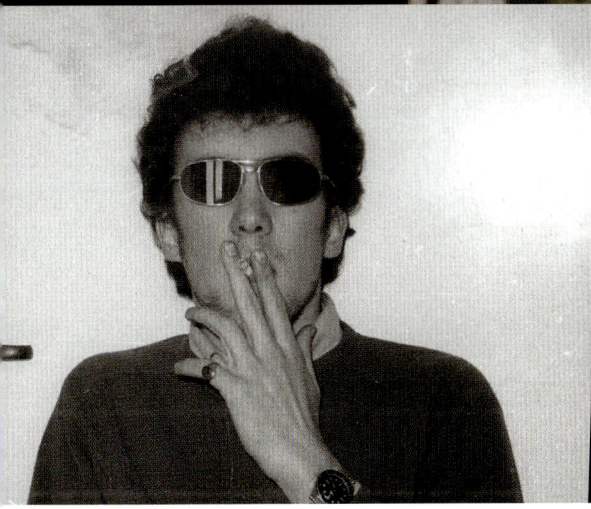

(clockwise from top left) Phil Oliver recalls the balcony at Sunderland's Mecca vibrating; Jim Long remembers Robert Plant strutting like a peacock; Steven Thorp saw Zeppelin twice in 18 months for just £1.60; Stuart Whitehead's Leicester Uni ticket; Graham Wilkins recalls Robert recommending 'bog paper' for earplugs; Jane Hall was scared the Baths Hall dance floor would cave in and she'd drown in the pool below

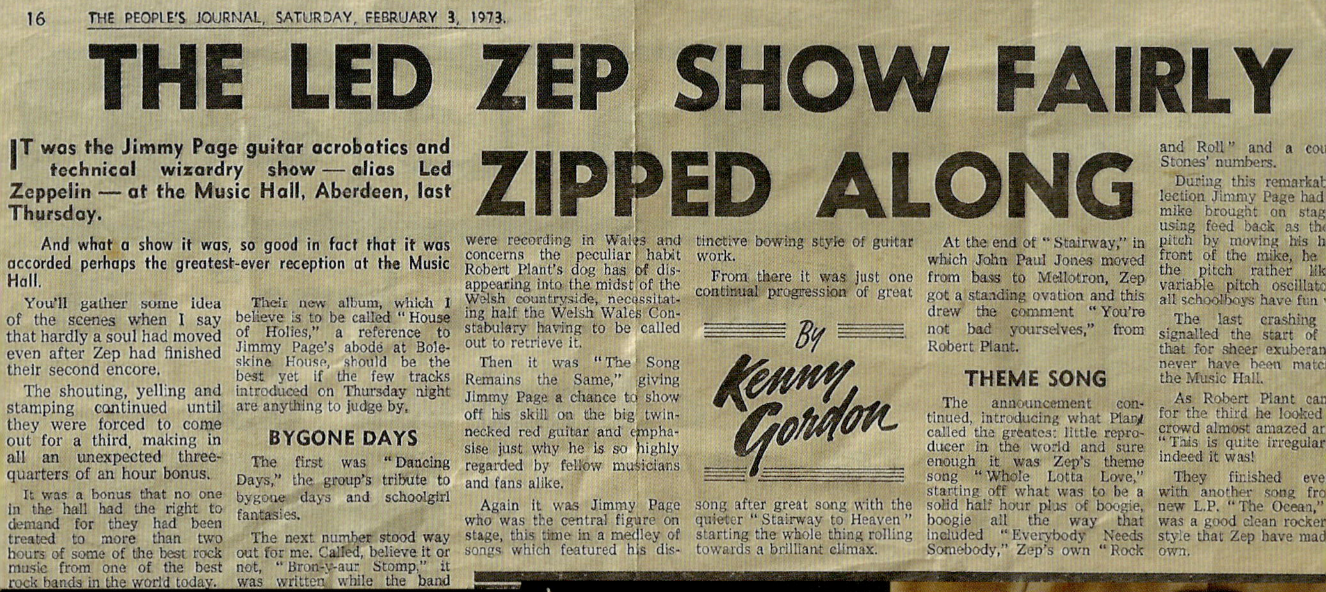

16 THE PEOPLE'S JOURNAL, SATURDAY, FEBRUARY 3, 1973.

THE LED ZEP SHOW FAIRLY ZIPPED ALONG

By Kenny Gordon

IT was the Jimmy Page guitar acrobatics and technical wizardry show — alias Led Zeppelin — at the Music Hall, Aberdeen, last Thursday.

And what a show it was, so good in fact that it was accorded perhaps the greatest-ever reception at the Music Hall.

You'll gather some idea of the scenes when I say that hardly a soul had moved even after Zep had finished their second encore.

The shouting, yelling and stamping continued until they were forced to come out for a third, making in all an unexpected three-quarters of an hour bonus.

It was a bonus that no one in the hall had the right to demand for they had been treated to more than two hours of some of the best rock music from one of the best rock bands in the world today.

Their new album, which I believe is to be called "House of Holies," a reference to Jimmy Page's abode at Boleskine House, should be the best yet if the few tracks introduced on Thursday night are anything to judge by.

BYGONE DAYS

The first was "Dancing Days," the group's tribute to bygone days and schoolgirl fantasies.

The next number stood way out for me. Called, believe it or not, "Bron-y-aur Stomp," it was written while the band were recording in Wales and concerns the peculiar habit Robert Plant's dog has of disappearing into the midst of the Welsh countryside, necessitating half the Welsh Wales Constabulary having to be called out to retrieve it.

Then it was "The Song Remains the Same," giving Jimmy Page a chance to show off his skill on the big twin-necked red guitar and emphasise just why he is so highly regarded by fellow musicians and fans alike.

Again it was Jimmy Page who was the central figure on stage, this time in a medley of songs which featured his distinctive bowing style of guitar work.

From there it was just one continual progression of great song after great song with the quieter "Stairway to Heaven" starting the whole thing rolling towards a brilliant climax.

At the end of "Stairway," in which John Paul Jones moved from bass to Mellotron, Zep got a standing ovation and this drew the comment "You're not bad yourselves," from Robert Plant.

THEME SONG

The announcement continued, introducing what Plant called the greatest little reproducer in the world and sure enough it was Zep's theme song "Whole Lotta Love," starting off what was to be a solid half hour plus of boogie, boogie all the way that included "Everybody Needs Somebody," Zep's own "Rock and Roll" and a cou Stones' numbers.

During this remarkab lection Jimmy Page had mike brought on stag using feed back as th pitch by moving his h front of the mike, he the pitch rather lik variable pitch oscillato all schoolboys have fun

The last crashing signalled the start of that for sheer exuberan never have been matc the Music Hall.

As Robert Plant can for the third he looked crowd almost amazed ar "This is quite irregular indeed it was!

They finished eve with another song fro new L.P. "The Ocean," was a good clean rocker style that Zep have mad own.

(clockwise from top left) Aberdeen press cutting; Charles Priestley saw Zeppelin with his wife, a Cliff Richard fan; Zeppelin in action in Dundee in 1973 (all photos Graham Kennedy)

(clockwise from top left) Zeppelin in action in Dundee in 1973 (all photos Graham Kennedy)

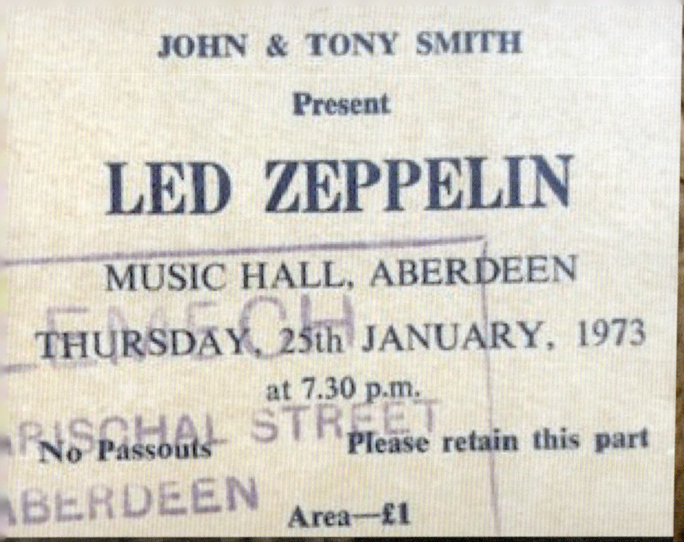

JOHN & TONY SMITH

Present

LED ZEPPELIN

MUSIC HALL, ABERDEEN

THURSDAY, 25th JANUARY, 1973

at 7.30 p.m.

No Passouts Please retain this part

Area—£1

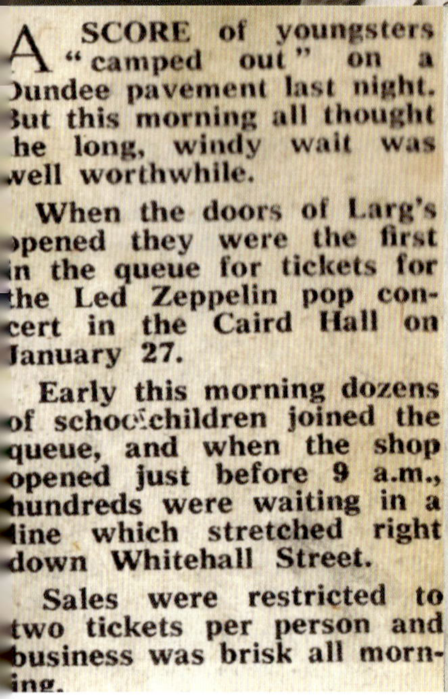

A SCORE of youngsters "camped out" on a Dundee pavement last night. But this morning all thought the long, windy wait was well worthwhile.

When the doors of Larg's opened they were the first in the queue for tickets for the Led Zeppelin pop concert in the Caird Hall on January 27.

Early this morning dozens of schoolchildren joined the queue, and when the shop opened just before 9 a.m., hundreds were waiting in a line which stretched right down Whitehall Street.

Sales were restricted to two tickets per person and business was brisk all morning.

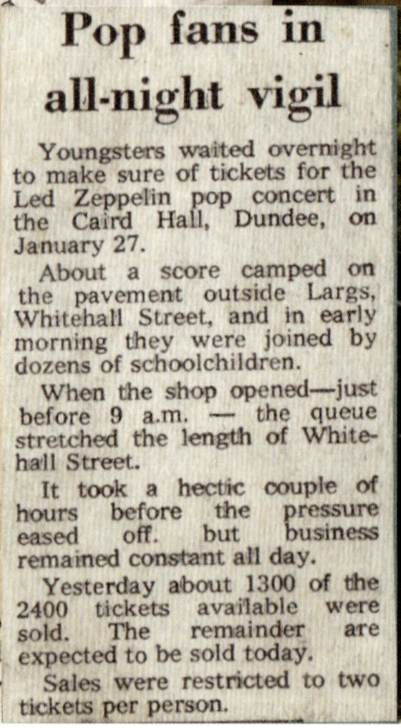

Pop fans in all-night vigil

Youngsters waited overnight to make sure of tickets for the Led Zeppelin pop concert in the Caird Hall, Dundee, on January 27.

About a score camped on the pavement outside Largs, Whitehall Street, and in early morning they were joined by dozens of schoolchildren.

When the shop opened—just before 9 a.m. — the queue stretched the length of Whitehall Street.

It took a hectic couple of hours before the pressure eased off, but business remained constant all day.

Yesterday about 1300 of the 2400 tickets available were sold. The remainder are expected to be sold today.

Sales were restricted to two tickets per person.

(clockwise from top left) Bob Douglas's ticket for the Aberdeen show; Grant Mackie bought his ticket from a Dundee record shop; Malcolm Wilson gets kudos by telling people he saw Zeppelin at Aberdeen's Music Hall; press cuttings from Dundee's *Courier* and *Telegraph*; Patsy Fraser-Mackenzie remembers an hour-long encore

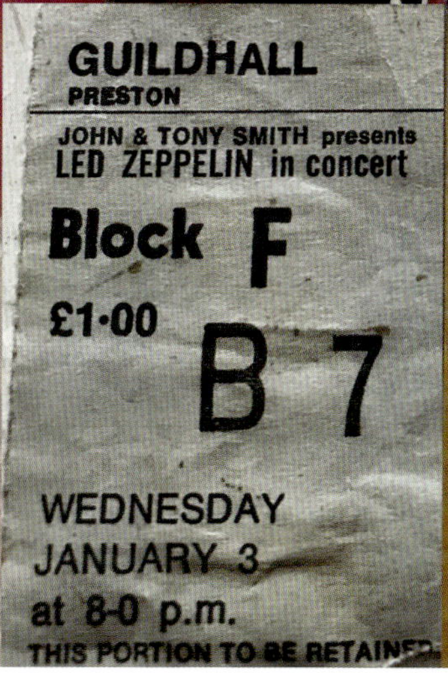

(clockwise from top left) Caz Kay wrote a letter to Zeppelin on a roll of wallpaper (*Lancashire Evening Post*); Nick Holme was at Preston's Guild Hall in 1973; Jimmy on double-neck guitar (Norman Wilson); Yvonne Nicol's Atlanta ticket; Stephen Thorp's Preston ticket from 1973; Ron Logan remembers crazy scenes at Atlanta's Fulton County Stadium

(clockwise from top left) Brett Bradshaw saw Zep just after his freshman year; Richard Burnett's Tuscaloosa ticket; Chuck Philipp saw Zep in Mobile, Alabama; Rick Powell saw Zep three times; Yoli Abud pictured with RP in Taos, New Mexico; Barbara Carlisle remembers Robert getting fed up with the crowd tossing fluorescent green wands around

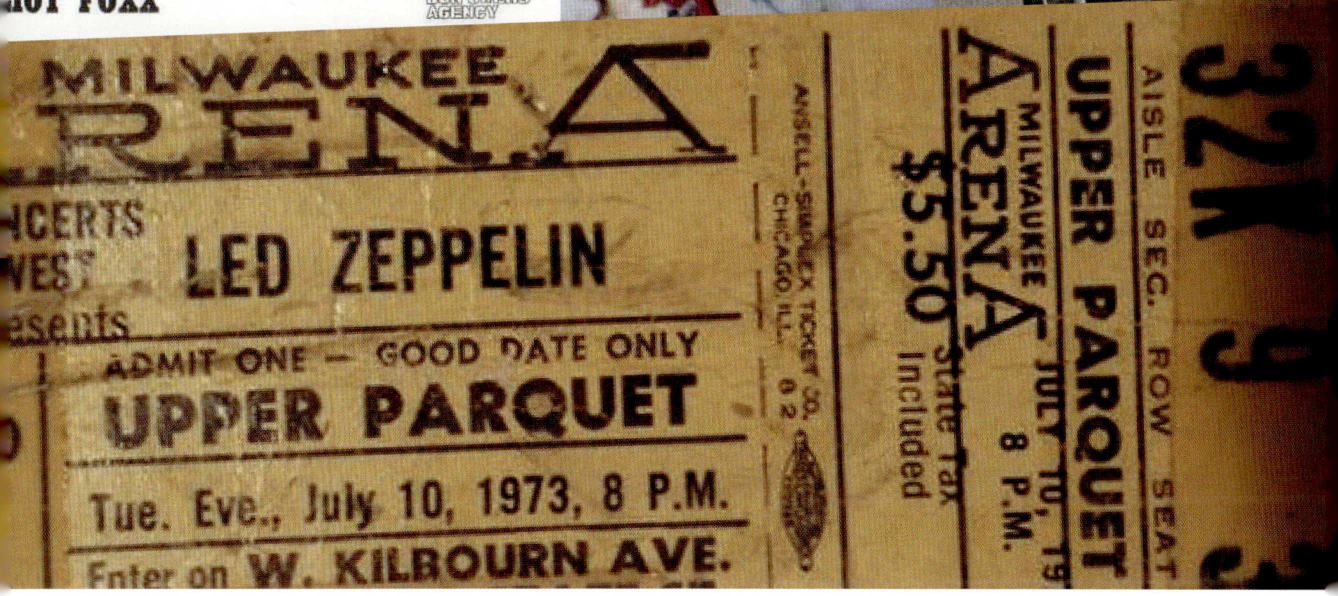

(clockwise from top left) Yoli Abud and her ticket; Darla Watlet remembers the pink smoke and the white doves; Mark Koenig's Milwaukee Arena ticket; Ed Vargas was at the Kezar Stadium show in 1973; Dennis Thomann took champagne and fireworks to the show

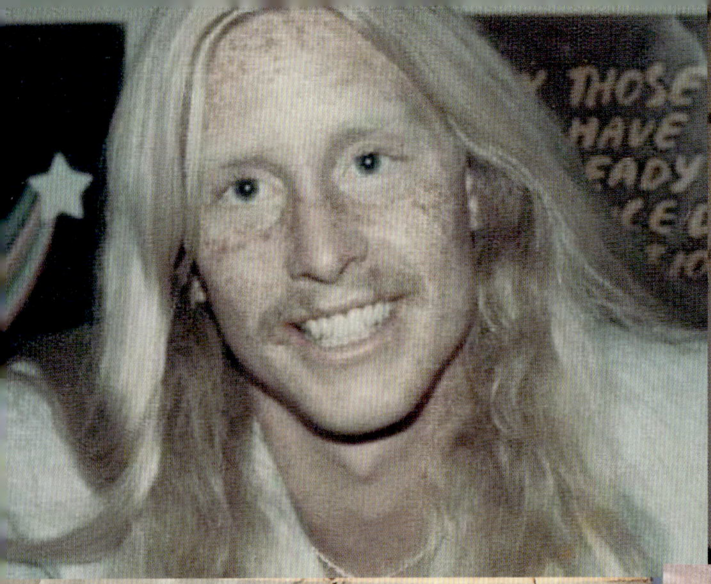

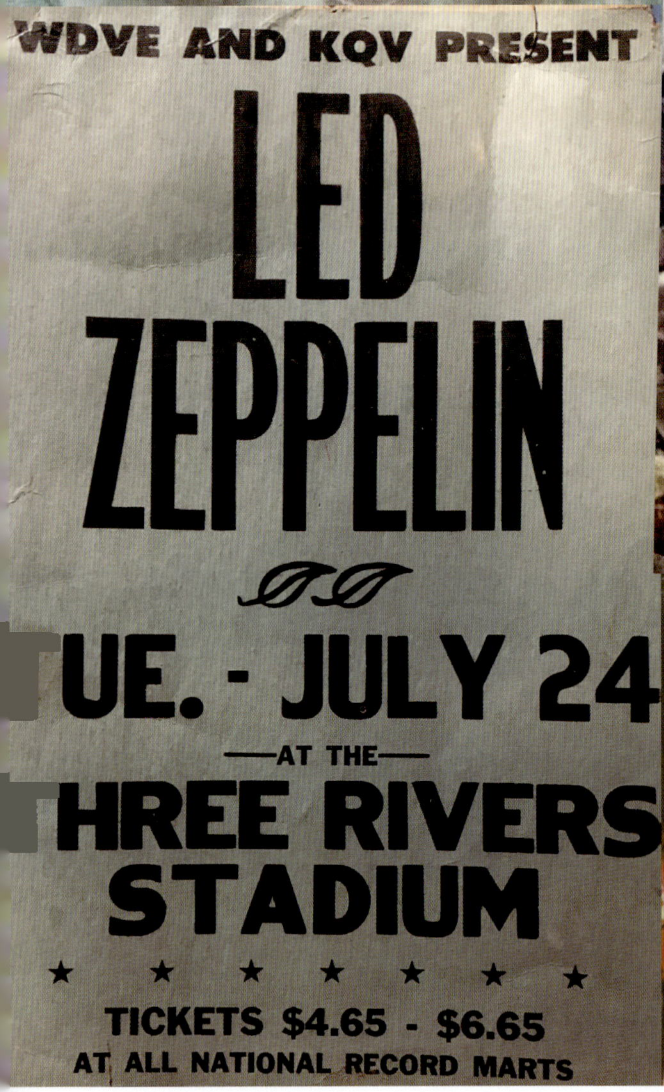

(clockwise from top left) Dave Livingston is a fan of *Houses Of The Holy*; Donna Loggia went to all the shows at Madison Square Garden; Deb Iarocci-Kempf recalls a once in a lifetime experience; Steve Acri saw Zep in Pittsburgh

(clockwise from top left) Steve Mazur's Olympia Stadium ticket; Michael Ruggieri had turned 13 just five days before seeing Zeppelin; Tom Ball was at the Pacific Coliseum; Bill Wilfong didn't need drugs to get high on Zeppelin; Jerry Brown recalls the coloured lights in Bonzo's drum kit; Georgia Vlahos recalls more about seeing Zeppelin than she does her own wedding day

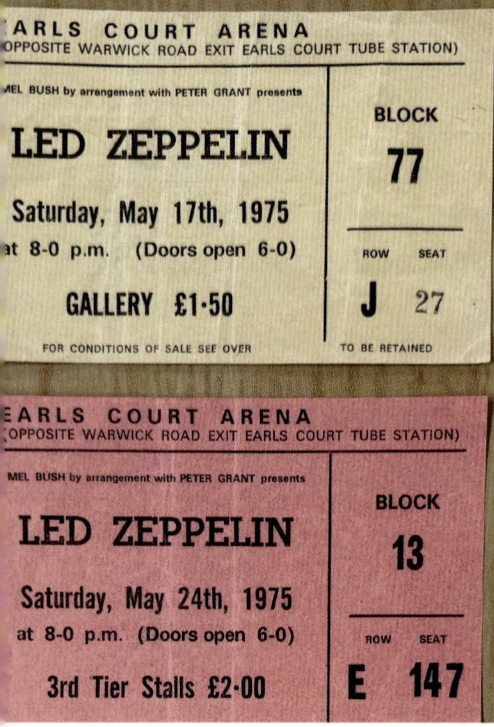

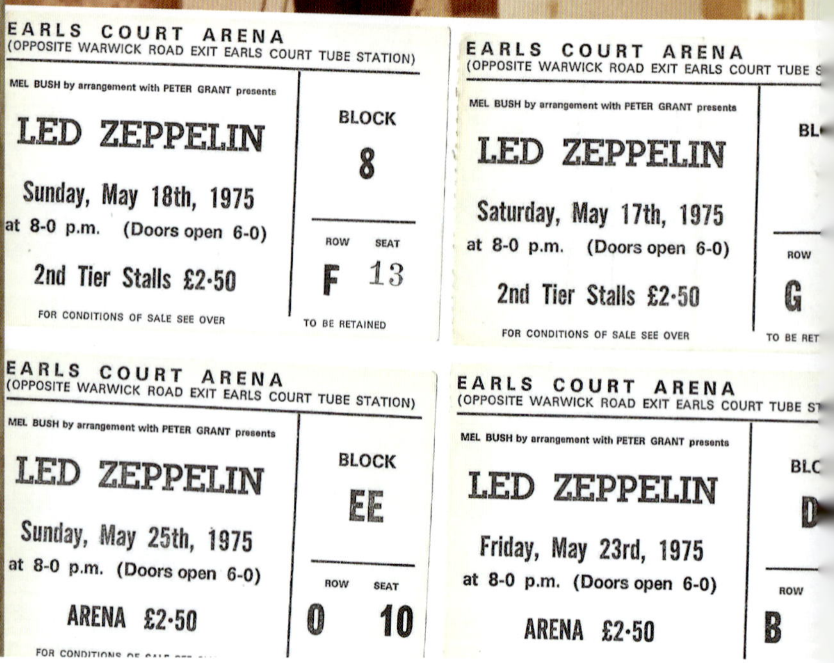

(clockwise from top left) Jon Berry got tickets for Earls Court, Derek Collison remembers smelling marijuana in the air; Nicky Roberts was at the show with his friend Derek Collinson; Dylan White in his bedroom aged 18; Ian Nicholson's Earls Court tickets; Dylan White's Earls Court tickets

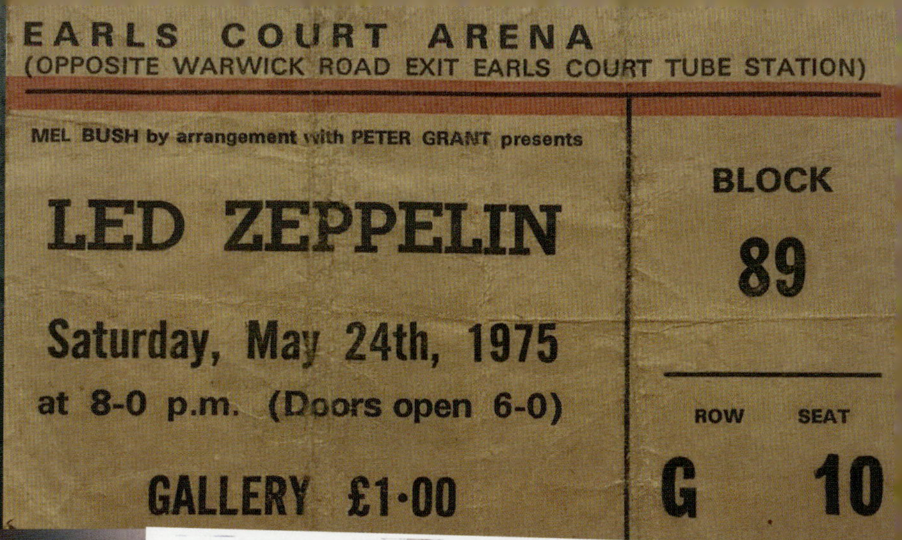

EARLS COURT ARENA
(OPPOSITE WARWICK ROAD EXIT EARLS COURT TUBE STATION)

MEL BUSH by arrangement with PETER GRANT presents

LED ZEPPELIN

Saturday, May 24th, 1975
at 8-0 p.m. (Doors open 6-0)

GALLERY £1·00

BLOCK
89

ROW G
SEAT 10

(clockwise from top left) John Griffiths was at Earls Court in Row G10; the Observer headline pondering whether Zep were bigger than The Beatles (Stuart Whitehead); Jimmy & Robert in action (all photos Stuart Whitehead)

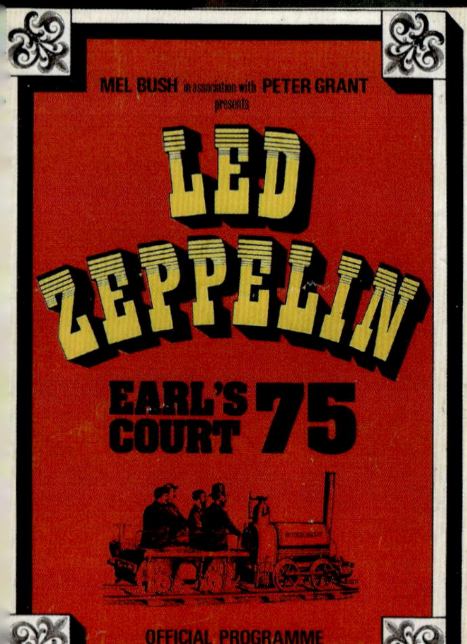

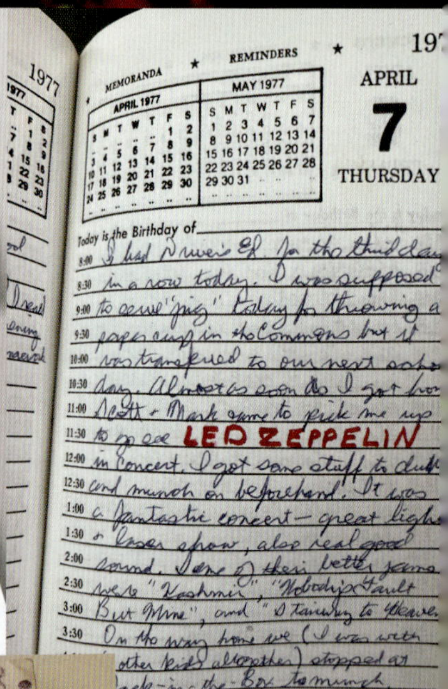

(clockwise from top left) RP & JP in action (Stuart Whitehead); Ed Ortiz's ticket for ASU; Tom Lynch's diary entry; Kevin Jarrell's Chicago ticket; Ian Nicholson's Earls Court programme

(clockwise from top left) Jonathan Smith was at Chicago Stadium; Zep in action in Chicago (Stacey Katsis); Tracey Rayfield (left) with his vomiting friend Mark (right) and AC/DC's Cliff Williams; Tracey Rayfield's St Louis ticket; Liz Dodson will die happy because she got to see Zeppelin; Phillip Solomonson was at the Chicago Stadium (Kent Kriegshauser)

(clockwise from top left) Zeppelin in Chicago, April 1977 (all photos Stacey Katsis)

(clockwise from top left) Stacey Katsis photographed Zeppelin in Chicago in April 1977 (two photos); Alan Tomasino's Pontiac ticket; John Roesli was at the Oakland Coliseum; Donald R Fuller's Greensboro ticket; Carmen Bindreiter Huston's now iconic 1977 tour t-shirt; Jay Allen Sanford's portrait of Robert Plant

(clockwise from top left) Robert & Jimmy in action (all photos Matt Meuser); Leonard Olivas's t-shirt

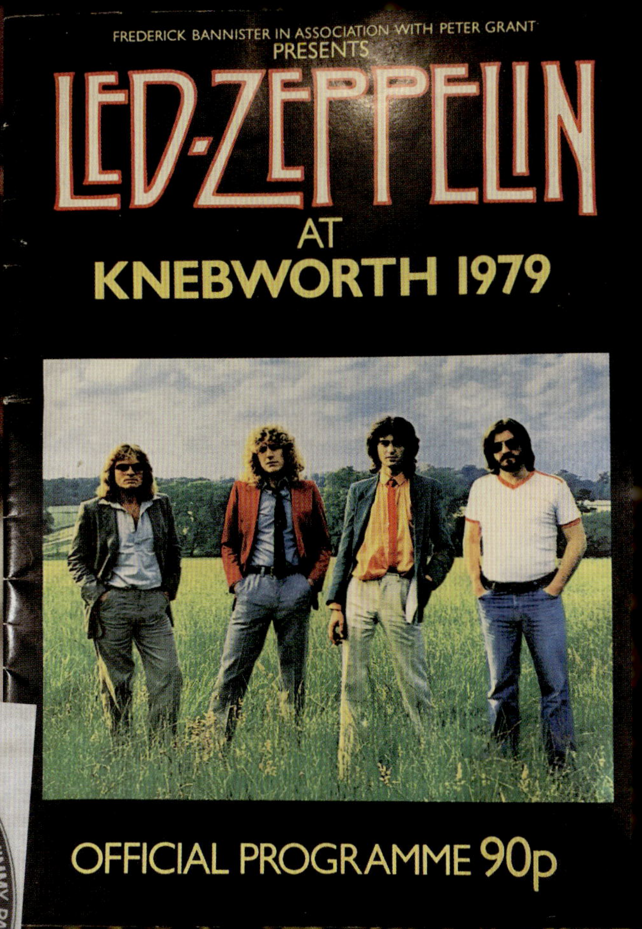

(clockwise from top left) Jimmy Page with Lee Spencer; Knebworth Festival programme (Lee Spencer); Nick Sharp got into the press zone; Michelle Mitch Ladyman went to both Knebworth shows; Robert captured on stage by Nick Sharp's friend; Knebworth t-shirt (Michelle Mitch Ladyman)

(clockwise from top left) Steve Sharpe's Eisstadion ticket; Robert and Jimmy in action on the Over Europe tour (all photos Dave Lewis)

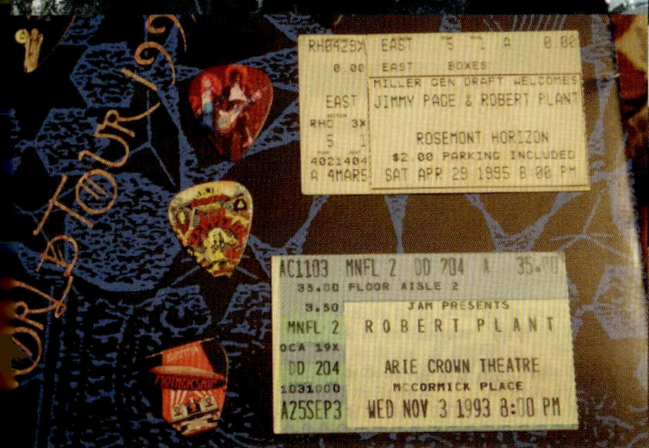

(clockwise from top left) Chris Beers was at the 2007 reunion show; Eric Chesnick's Auburn Hills ticket for Page & Plant; RP in action in the nineties (Helmut Ölschegel); Jimmy Page 1995 (Helmut Ölschegel); Daniel Rogers' tickets and plectrums; Jimmy Page 1995 (Helmut Ölschegel); John Griffith's wristband for the Ahmet Ertegün tribute show

(clockwise from top left) Jason Bonham 2004 (Helmut Ölschegel); Robert Plant 2006 (Helmut Ölschegel); John Paul Jones with Them Crooked Vultures (Helmut Ölschegel); Robert Plant live with The Sensational Space Shifters, June 18, 2018, Pritzker Pavilion, Chicago (Phillip A Solomonson); John Paul Jones with Them Crooked Vultures (Helmut Ölschegel); Robert Plant 2006 (Helmut Ölschegel)

GUILD HALL
30 JANUARY 1973, PRESTON, UK

I WAS THERE: NICK HOLME

I did my A levels at the Catholic College in Winckley Square, Preston. You could enter the college at the top of the square, clock in and then travel down interminable staircases in what were originally separate buildings until you came out at the bottom of the square and wind your way out through the college to spend a few hours at the Cedarwood Coffee bar.

Led Zep were appearing at the fairly newly-built Guild Hall in Preston. ELP were the first rock band to play there the previous November and we had managed to get on the front row for that. Ticketless for Led Zep, myself and friends Bernard Kehoe, Trev Eastham, John 'Tees' Taylor and Chris Kielthy decided to go along to the Guild Hall on the morning of the gig to see what was happening.

Vehicular access to the Guild Hall is a bit tight. An access road goes under the edge of the hall which is separated from the road by a set of railings. We watched by the railings as an artic backed down and a roadie opened the doors. A lift took equipment up to the level of the main hall, but access from it was down a corridor with a 90 degree turn to get to the back stage area. A single trolley could be used to cart heavy equipment but it wasn't going to be the easiest load-in for the road crew. We watched as the chief roadie fumed about the lack of help and then we offered our assistance, which was greatly accepted. We had free access to the back stage area and just helped carrying things as required.

Led Zep were apparently banned from the Guild Hall following their visit because the drum kit was fixed in place by nails being hammered into the stage. However, a contributory factor to the ban may have been that the easiest way to get a trolley full of equipment around the corner after coming out of the lift was to heave it against the plaster of the corner and drag it round, taking a large amount of plaster off in the process.

At one point, a roadie was testing a small effects unit. It didn't work so he hurled it across the stage in frustration. Someone asked what the problem was. He replied, 'I think it's broke, Brian.' Well, it definitely was after that! While the audience was coming in, a roadie had the job of putting a cassette tape of music into a player through the PA. He looked to one of his mates and said, 'Shall I put one of their albums on? That would fuck them up,' meaning to play one of their studio albums just before they were due to play the same tracks live. I don't think he was serious. John Paul Jones had a bass guitar back stage, I think a Fender Jazz bass, that was only partly finished as it had a plain unfinished mahogany wood body. We didn't get paid for our roadie work, but I did get one of Jimmy Page's plectrums! I've seen many bands but never one with the raw energy of that band.

The local newspaper carried a story about a girl, who was renowned in Preston as a major fan of the band, hand delivering a 30-foot long letter to the band that she'd written on the back of a roll of wallpaper. She disappeared into the dressing rooms with the band after the gig. Reputedly, Jimmy Page's trousers were thrown out of a changing room window.

The Guild Hall sound system when it first opened was far from adequate. It consisted of a number of column speakers (probably eight by eight-inch speakers) dangled above the stage at various angles and with what was probably a 100v line system which was popular in churches and halls back then but totally unsuitable for rock bands. They replaced these with a system using 'precision devices' speakers in square cabinets, again hung at various angles above the stage. More recently they have installed a 'line array' system.

We used to judge how good a gig had been back then by how many days our ears used to ring afterwards. I seem to remember this one only being beaten by Black Sabbath at the Hardrock in Manchester in March that year where a huge column of 4x12 speakers almost came crashing down and had to be held in place by a roadie for most of the gig.

I WAS THERE: CAZ KAY

The first time I heard Led Zeppelin it was like a bolt from the blue! I had always been into music but never really found my niche. Listening to that first album was like coming home. All I wanted to do from then on was to see the band play live. That opportunity came in 1970 when I hitched down to the legendary Bath Festival and got in through a hole in the fence for 50p. The next gig was 1971 at Preston's Public Hall, camping out on the street overnight outside the local music shop to get my ticket, price £1. I was totally and utterly hooked on Led Zeppelin and their music.

When it was announced that Zeppelin would return to Preston in 1973, I was determined to try and meet the band. Racking my brains to think of something that would attract their attention, I decided to write a letter using all the song titles from the first four albums, and just to make sure they didn't miss it, I wrote it on a 31-foot long piece of paper. Sending it off to Preston's Guild Hall, where they were due to appear, I crossed my fingers and hoped for the best. A few days later, I got a phone call from our local newspaper asking if I could go down to the Guild Hall to have my photo taken with my 'fan letter'. The venue manager was also there and promised that he would try and get me an introduction to the band. The newspaper printed the photos with an article headed 'Caz – the fan who stops at nothing'.

I thought the day of the gig would never come, but it did and Led Zeppelin were amazing. I had been told that when they had finished their set I was to go to the side of the stage and make myself known to the security guys. I nervously made my way down. As I reached the barriers the band came back for an encore, Robert ran across the front of the stage unfurling my letter as he went. I was helped over the barriers by a member of Zep's crew and led up the steps onto the edge of the stage. Standing with my ear two inches from Jimmy's amplifier, I watched the greatest band in the world play, just feet away from me. It was like a dream. I couldn't believe it was happening.

After the gig I was taken backstage to their dressing room. Jimmy, John Paul and John were there. They signed my albums and posed for photos. They had seen the newspaper article which mentioned that Robert was my favourite member of the band. Jimmy teased me about this and asked if I really wanted to meet him. I muttered something about being happy just to be there. Jimmy laughed and said that Robert was too shy (!) to meet me in the dressing room and that he was waiting on the stage.

I made my way back and there he was, the golden god himself! We chatted for about 15 minutes. Although most of it was a blur, I do recall that we discussed our mutual hatred of the dentist – very rock and roll! All too soon it was over but it was a night I will never forget. My only regrets about the night? That I didn't take enough photos and didn't have any photos taken with members of the band. Obviously, this was well before the days of mobiles and the ubiquitous selfie. I was so overawed by the whole experience and just happy to be there!

I went on to see Led Zeppelin at Earls Court, Knebworth and the reunion at the O2. I have also seen the individual remaining members live, in various guises, and continue to follow their careers, in particular my golden god, Robert Plant, who I have seen many, many times. Their music has been the soundtrack of my life and will continue to be so until the day I die.

I WAS THERE: ALAN BUDGE

They'd been to Preston the year before, playing the old Public Hall, which I'd missed. Apparently, the floor there had been on the verge of collapse during the concert, so moving to the new venue was probably not a bad idea! I remember Robert Plant saying, after the opening dual assault of 'Rock And Roll' and 'Black Dog', 'Well, we seem to have changed halls a bit since last time.'

They were, predicably, awesome, although I don't think I realised just *what* I was seeing. I caught them again at Earls Court a couple of years later, when the scale of the performance seemed more suited to their already near-mythical status. But there I was in Preston, with a couple of thousand other lucky souls, witnessing the band in all their intimate glory, on their determined march towards immortality.

Funnily enough, it wasn't 'Stairway To Heaven' or 'Whole Lotta Love' (the show's closers) that I recall best, or most fondly at any rate. I was there with Susan, my first proper girlfriend; she wasn't that into my heavy rock leanings, being more of a Cat Stevens/Paul Simon kind of girl, but she liked some of Led Zeppelin, one track in particular. When they'd finished delivering a rolling, rollicking performance of 'Misty Mountain Hop' (complete with Plant's coy pre-song references to Rizlas, police arrivals and the rest), she looked at me and said, 'It was worth coming just for that.'

It was worth being there, full stop.

I WAS THERE: BARRY 'FINBAR' KNIGHT

I don't remember them being overly loud! I do remember Robert Plant standing on the stage in his usual arrogant pose with what may have been a glass of whisky in one hand and a cigarette in the other. He said, 'I've been told there's no drinking (took a sip) and no smoking (took a drag) in the auditorium.' Everyone cheered. Oh, what rebels we were back then.

I WAS THERE: SUE MASON, AGE 21

It was over 50 years ago now… My main memory is of a brilliant version of 'Stairway To Heaven', all of which was very, very loud! But when you're only 21, excessive volume is the norm. I also remember that they were banned from appearing there ever again due to the excessive volume.

After the conclusion of the UK tour, Led Zeppelin undertake a 21-date tour of continental Europe, taking in eight countries.

MESSENHALLE
14 MARCH 1973, NUREMBERG, GERMANY

I WAS THERE: LEW CHARLES, AGE 18

It was my 18th birthday. Someone said, 'We got you tickets for this band.' One of the best concerts I ever saw. I also saw the concert where Jimmy got his hand caught in the elevator. All I can say is Jimmy was great with just two fingers playing the guitar!

28 MARCH 1973

Led Zeppelin's fifth album,* Houses Of The Holy, *is released. It tops both the UK and US album charts and goes on to be certified eleven times platinum by the Recording Industry Association of America in 1999.

The 1973 North American tour, the band's ninth, commences five weeks after the release of* Houses Of The Holy *on 4 May. Concluding on 29 July 1973, the tour breaks box office records across America, grossing $4 million in the process. The shows are a move away from the straightforward production of previous gigs, with the introduction of dry ice, laser effects, mirrors, mirror balls and pyrotechnics.

Jimmy Page: We really wanted to take the live performances as far as they could go.

ATLANTA FULTON COUNTY STADIUM
4 MAY 1973, ATLANTA, GEORGIA

I WAS THERE: PAUL FOSTER

I was working Atlanta Braves ground crew when they came to Fulton County Stadium. As a stadium employee I helped unload equipment and clean up the field the next day. I remember Robert Plant singing 'Take Good Care Of My Baby' during the sound check. I worked in front of the stage behind a huge wooden wall built for the concert as security. Three large speaker towers were built in the infield for additional sound.

I WAS THERE: LEON DOUGLAS HALL, AGE 17

The field was opened up for seating and they set the stage up at the centre field fence. There were 45,000 there and the acoustics were horrible where I sat due to the echo from the far side of the stadium. But it was an event. We got there in the early afternoon for an all-day party, seventies-style, and we had a great time. The poor acoustics didn't bother any of us!

I WAS THERE: SHAYNE BARRETT, AGE 14

It was the first date on the '73 tour. My mother let me check out of school early, as did a large majority of my high school, because I was going with my oldest brother, who was 20. It was one of the biggest concerts to ever happen in Atlanta at that time, and it was amazing.

I WAS THERE: JESSICA HANDLER, AGE 13

May 1973 was right around the end of my first year in high school. My friends and I listened to Led Zep on WQXI-FM in in Atlanta. We knew and loved Led Zeppelin's radio hits: 'Stairway To Heaven', 'Black Dog' and 'Dazed And Confused'. These days I'm more of a 'Fool In The Rain' person, but that's because as a teenager I didn't realise that a girl could be a drummer.

Our boyfriends played the Led Zep hits (or tried to) in their bands in their parents' garages, and the girls hung out and tried to sing. I looked in my diary from that year for some concrete memories and was surprised to find that I wrote nothing about that concert. But I read that I was grounded by my parents for bad behaviour about a week later, so that tells you something about the kind of kids my friends and I were.

Someone's parent must have driven my friends and I to the stadium in the afternoon and picked us up late at night. I remember that the music was super-loud, which was thrilling, and that most of the concert-goers in the massive crowd were older than us, which was thrilling and a little scary. This wasn't my first concert – I'd been to see Cat Stevens with my father the previous autumn – but this was the first full-on rock show I'd been to, on my own, with friends. I loved the crowd, the dancing, the waves of pot in the air and me and my closest friends being somehow on the loose amongst 40,000 people without the watchful eyes of parents. I remember sitting on the grass in the outfield, standing up to dance and craning my neck to try to see the stage. I loved the sensation of the hot Georgia spring day cooling into dark, cool night.

I WAS THERE: ALAN KAUFFMANN

The band had now perfected their musical skills along with an incomparable stage presence. They performed as the musical masters they had become and for that evening they controlled the universe. The sound quality was very good, considering it was in a round sports stadium and the audio system for baseball was inferior at best. Some sources state 40,000 were in attendance, others more than 50,000. I'm sticking with close to 50,000. I was fortunate enough to have an ideal spot directly on the field with a centre stage view. Perhaps my most vivid memory is of walking out of the stadium immediately after the show. Everyone was so stunned by the performance it seemed we all departed in total silence. It was eerie, yet amazing.

I WAS THERE: TERRY BARNES, AGE 16

I went with a couple of high school friends. This was a horrible place to hear music as the stadium was a round bowl. Led Zep played with a large screen beside them. Plant must have had a cold or something because he couldn't hit the high notes when singing. I also remember Page playing the double-neck guitar with a bow, which I wasn't a fan of. There was a lot of pot smoking going on, and I never did that, so it was quite an experience for me.

I WAS THERE: SUSAN WHALEY BELCHER, AGE 16

I went with a group of school friends. We purchased our tickets at a local Sears store in Marietta, Georgia. We paid around $15, which was a lot of money then. We were at the top of the stadium. There were big screens on each side of the stage so we could all see and the field was just covered in people. I remember there being so many messed up people. A guy who must have been doing some type of acid fell down about 15 concrete steps and then got right back up. It was an open baseball field and the sound wasn't that great. I heard after the show that the band said they would never come back to Atlanta and I don't think they ever did.

I WAS THERE: RON LOGAN

It was a pop festival setting. Many more people were there than anticipated – there must have been 80,000 there – and we were elbow to elbow. People were leaving their cars parked everywhere, including on the side of the expressway. Zep were incredible, and when they came onstage a bunch of doves were released. They played for about three hours, ended with 'Stairway' and Page was amazing.

I WAS THERE: MITZI FISHMAN, AGE 13

I was a precocious 13-year-old in love with her transistor radio and cassette recorder. 'Stairway To Heaven' was the song everyone wanted to hear and it got loads of air play on the radio. One of our flagship stations, WQXI radio, was having a ticket giveaway promotion for the upcoming Led Zeppelin concert. I happened to be the lucky thirteenth caller and was awarded two tickets as my prize. I invited my best friend Debbie to join me. Her mother drove us to the stadium. Traffic was at such a standstill near the stadium that passengers were just getting out of cars on the freeway and walking across lanes to get to the venue. I couldn't believe she'd allow it, but Debbie's mom told us to 'go ahead'.

When we got inside the stadium, our eyes were filled with the sights of what our older peers were up to, and our nostrils were bombarded with the smells of marijuana. There were long-haired males and females milling about the stadium. Some brought blankets and were caught up in the mantra of 'love the one you're with', while some were engaging in friendly chat and others were twirling around to the LSD-produced movies playing in their head. I was both fascinated and a little frightened by the things I saw.

No one was rude, mean or lascivious toward us. No one offered us drink or drugs. When Led Zeppelin came on the stage there was a migration of the crowd toward them, but I never feared being smashed or trampled. I thought the show was fabulous! I had nothing to compare it to. It was my first concert ever. The band were at their peak, and I was witnessing history.

I WAS THERE: BOBBY CARROLL

They weren't prepared for an event like this with a mega group like Led Zeppelin. The venue had a 50,000-seat capacity but only enough parking for 20,000 cars. and, by the time we got there, parking was already at capacity. Thousands of rabid, smiling Zep fans on their pilgrimage to see the fathers of metal and mayhem just pulled over and parked on the shoulders of the four-lane highway right next to the stadium. Nothing was going to stop us.

As we made our way from the car to the gates of purgatory to witness this extraordinary event, we were met with people begging for an extra ticket. Young and old, pleading for passage to the realm of the great ones know as Led Zeppelin. Finally, we were standing at the entry of the place at which the great ones were residing. We gingerly handed our tickets to the gatekeepers who had uniforms of gilded and burnished gold and platinum. We made our way to our seats that seemed to be in the clouds because they were so high up in the stands and thought to ourselves, 'We will never be able to witness the great ones from this altitude, much less hear their magical sounds.'

We waited and watched in great anticipation and then, like a great flash of lightning, we heard the sound and fury of the god of thunder himself, Jimmy Page. The roar of the crowd was deafening. The sound and fury of 'Black Dog' was emanating into the Coliseum and the unmistakable boom of the greatest drummer in the world was shaking the rafters, the mesmerising bassist was thundering and, finally, the golden locks of the wailer himself took centre stage – Robert Plant. All the beautiful young girls immediately lifted their blouses to pay homage to the great ones and the men trembled and bowed in their presence. It was by far the greatest musical experience of my lifetime and of everyone who was present.

I WAS THERE: GAIL TAYLOR, AGE 16

I skipped school that day. I arrived at the stadium about 8am for an evening show. It was very hot. People kept driving by during the day and it was like a street party, waiting all day. Being among the first five in line, my boyfriend got shoved from behind when the gates opened. He was stuck in the turnstile and people started being shoved on top of him. There probably would have been mass casualties had the turnstile not released him at the last millisecond. It was super scary. But I was in front against the barrier as I was one of the first in line. 'Whole Lotta Love' was my favourite song. We called it our 'candle song' as my girlfriends and I would lay on the floor between the speakers in the dark and watch the candles flicker. That was our bonding song. Zeppelin's albums were a constant soundtrack for the early to mid-seventies.

I WAS THERE: JOHN LEE DOZIER, AGE 18

Jimmy Page and John Bonham stole the show. They had festival seating and consequently it was a free for all on the field level where I was. The sound quality was fair at best. Tickets were cheap in those days. What I really remember is the overflowing rowdy crowd. Someone was actually shooting bottle rockets toward Robert Plant. I saw him duck a few.

I WAS THERE: RICK FREEMAN

I had tried to purchase tickets to see Led Zeppelin for the previous three years. Then they announced a stadium tour. Atlanta was the first stop, followed by Tampa. Being from the Tampa area I thought about it, but my girlfriend was going with me so we bought tickets for the Atlanta show. I had been to a few pop festivals but never a stadium show. What could go wrong, other than rain?

The stadium was used by the Atlanta Braves baseball team and the Atlanta Falcons football team and officials were concerned about the overflowing crowd that showed up at the stadium. What none of us expected was the management decision to herd the crowd through just a few gates to keep us under control. It would be six years before this crowd control measure was to cost the lives of eleven people (at The Who's concert in Cincinatti, Ohio) and how no one died on this day is still a mystery. From the moment they opened the gates, thousands surged forward wanting to reach the front of the stage.

My girlfriend and I had brought a blanket, food and water which we soon lost, both of us being off our feet for the duration of the push forward. People were falling, but everyone grabbed them and pulled them up. It was total chaos. I lost my girlfriend but a guy took hold of her and held on. It was getting harder and harder to breathe. Then suddenly we were inside. Out of exhaustion, I took my girlfriend's hand and pulled her up into the stands, thanking the guy who helped her. We stayed in the stands as the field quickly filled up. I looked back at the tunnel we had been carried through. It was full of discarded material. A few people were helping the ones who were exhausted from the ordeal.

After we watched the roadies working on the stage, out strolled the members of Led Zeppelin. It was still light but they kicked off with a triple whammy of 'Rock And Roll', 'Celebration Day' and 'Black Dog'. Page was all over the place and Plant was shaking his trademark hair. I felt that they sounded a little rusty since we were the first show after a break in touring. Then they seem to kick it into gear.

We all have bootlegs of the tour. The standouts were 'Over The Hills And Far Away' and 'Since I've Been Loving You'. Then we got a rather lengthy 'No Quarter', and as good as John Paul Jones is as a musician, I confess to growing bored during the song. Then we got 'The Song Remains The Same'/'The Rain Song', which was followed by another self-indulgence from Jimmy Page with 'Dazed And Confused'. It included a 30-minute solo, and as interesting as it was, I think it would have been better about half the length. 'Stairway To Heaven' was sublime but unfortunately another indulgence was to follow with 'Moby Dick'.

Things get a little blurred after that because people were moving around so much. With this being a general admission show, we found our way to the front of the stage. Plant was standing over me. The girl next to me was about to go after him but she couldn't get over the barrier. Seeing Page so close was the best part of the concert for me, and they closed with a glorious 'Communication Breakdown'.

It was a three-hour show. My only complaint was the three 30-minute solos, 90 minutes in all. I have been to concerts where the group played 14 songs in that time frame!

Flash forward to the nineties, where I saw Page and Plant on the two tours they did. No long solos. To be honest, I enjoyed them more, but the seventies was a different era.

The ordeal of the human tidal wave left a bad taste in my mouth, but nothing was mention in the newspapers about it.

I WAS THERE: LORIE FORTUNE

I only saw them the once. But I could only really see them on the big screens. It was my very first concert after graduating from high school the year before. I was young and naïve and the things I saw in broad daylight in that stadium shocked me. But then I heard the music. It was glorious! I'm so glad I got to experience that.

I WAS THERE: MARY BETH WILLIAMS, AGE 18

I was with friends. We were high school seniors, all aged about 18, and chose to attend the concert rather than Senior Night at Six Flags, a local amusement park that we could visit anytime. We made the right choice, don't you think? It was general seating, so we arrived early and sat on the grass somewhere in the middle. Eventually, the entire place filled up. The concert was wonderful. Their music was always on the radio. And it still is, as Atlanta has a classic rock station, 97.1, that plays them a lot. I still love their music.

I WAS THERE: MARY MCEWEN COWAN, AGE 16

I went with a date, David Wallace, and another couple, Hans Miller and Robin Messer. It was the first concert at the Atlanta Stadium where they opened the field for the concert and that's where we all sat. I was still somewhat sheltered until that point. I saw a little of everything that night!

I WAS THERE: MICHAEL MCMILLAN, AGE 14

Houses Of The Holy had just come out. It was the first big concert I went to and it was general admission. I got down to about the middle of the field. They had big black and white screens on either side of the stage, which were a new thing back then, so everybody felt like they were on the front row. That was the first time I heard 'The Rain Song', so as a keyboard player Jones's mellotron was a standout. That was also the first time I heard that instrument in person. I went out and got the album right after the concert.

They released doves at the end and I remember seeing them crawling around Bonham's drums on the big screens. I was in junior high school and it made quite an impression on me, I was on a high for weeks. I went with a buddy from school. His father gave us a ride and picked us up afterwards. To get my parents' permission to attend, I told them my buddy's father was going to the concert with us. Rock and roll corrupting the youth, making us lie to our parents! When we got in the stadium, my friend told me, 'Nope, my dad would not like this.'

I WAS THERE: YVONNE NICOL

This was the launch of their 1973 tour for *Houses Of The Holy*, my favourite album. I went with my friend Beth Earwood (nee Lacey). She remembers that my dad took us downtown to the Atlanta stadium and that, on the way, 'American Pie' came on the radio and Dad turned it off because, being military, he didn't like some of the song's lyrics. We had decided to meet some friends of mine at Gate D. We stood there for the longest time, waiting for them. Those were the days way before cell phones or pagers. I was getting nervous because I didn't want to miss Led Zeppelin. I figured they'd have a warm up band. Most bands back then did. When the music started playing, it was loud and clear. In about 30 seconds, I recognised 'Black Dog'. I said, 'Well, they'll just have to find us inside, because I'm not missing this!'

The stadium was very crowded. The show was sold out. We tried to get close to the stage, but since we were late going in, that was impossible. The sound in the stadium was not good and there was a lot of echo. Still, we enjoyed the show. I got close enough to Robert Plant's beautiful blond curls. He sure was a hunk back then. The next day, there was a front-page article in the paper, saying that the band had said they'd never play Atlanta again. Apparently, a few fans were throwing hypodermic needles on stage.

I WAS THERE: CINDY MCKEE RICHARDSON, AGE 16

Tickets were only $6.50 back then, and I went with a high school boyfriend. The seating was open and you could sit anywhere, including on the baseball field, where we sat on a blanket. I was in complete awe of everything. I remember seeing so many people being carried out on stretchers from overdoses and wondering why they would do that, before the band even came on to play? I didn't do drugs and relished every sound from Robert Plant's mystical voice and Jimmy Page's long guitar riffs. It was just so amazing. I also remember my parents waiting up on me on the front porch, worried about me after seeing the huge crowds at the stadium.

I WAS THERE: JUDY RITTENHOUSE GRIFFIN, AGE 16

I wish I had a great story about seeing them but unfortunately mine was cut short due to the police chasing me down for bringing two ounces of pot (and other things) into the stadium. I was 16 years stupid at that time. Back in the day, the police were fairly lenient and let me go, instructing me not to come back or they would throw me in jail. However, it was Zeppelin and I had to see them! So after waiting an extended amount of time I was able to sneak back in for the final few minutes. They were a significant part of my life then and now.

When I was just twelve or 13 years old, we took the record player down to the beach and the only album we brought was Zeppelin's. I hate to admit it, but my first sexual experience was listening to 'The Lemon Song' and it's something I will never forget. I have always said should they ever reunite, I don't care how much it costs – I am going!

I WAS THERE: BETTIE RUFFNER

There were screens on the sides of the stage, and when Jimmy Page played it was a delayed reaction from the music to the screen. Great show. Everyone was smoking, I think – everyone except us!

I WAS THERE: SHERRY CHISHOLM, AGE 18

It was one of the first six or seven concerts that I had ever been to. I loved them. I had just gotten their album, from the friend I went to the concert with, and I was excited to get to see them live. But I don't remember anything about the show except that we were far back. We were all familiar with their music for a few years beforehand. I first heard them in 1971. That's why I was so excited to get the new album and go see them. My graduating class song was 'Stairway To Heaven'.

I WAS THERE: TOMMY STONE, AGE 14

I went with a friend from next door. It was my first concert and the tickets were only $5. They estimated 50,000 plus in attendance. People started parking on the side of the Interstate and walking the rest of the way to the stadium. There were license plates from a bunch of different states. The Hari Krishnas were there dancing around, passing out incense and panhandling so the air was filled with the smell of reefer and incense. lt was a warm spring night and the stage was set up in front of the backstop at home plate on the baseball field. We were standing in the grass near the pitcher's mound. The show was awesome and when they started playing 'Stairway To Heaven', these giant boxes across the front of the scaffolding used for the stage set up opened and hundreds of white doves took flight. I tell people that whenever I hear 'Stairway To Heaven', for a few seconds I'm 14 again and standing in the grass on a warm spring night, watching all the white doves fly around the stadium with the air filled with the smell of reefer and incense.

I WAS THERE: MARK TUNNEY

Bottle rockets and firecrackers dogged security until the show got under way. I misplaced my car and couldn't find it afterwards. I had to hitchhike back to Biloxi to go to work in the morning at Keesler Air Force Base and come back the next night and locate my car.

I WAS THERE: TRACY BOWER

Me and some friends rode to the concert in a 1964 Chevy hippie van. It was a three-hour drive. The concert was right after *Houses Of The Holy* was released. It was a damn good concert and fucking dynamite marijuana. I was intensely stoned.

TAMPA STADIUM
5 MAY 1973, TAMPA, FLORIDA

I WAS THERE: RICK RYAN

I would have been satisfied with my life, having seen them twice on their first US tour, but we weren't finished yet. In 1973 my brother brought up a Tampa, Florida show and we all made plans to attend. The venue was 350 miles away. We made plans to leave early in the morning. I showed up a little late, blasted and very much on. It was contagious. Riding in the back of this panel truck with friends and family, we could feel the magic unfolding around us. The trip was every bit as epic as the show. The show started and just took over everyone. At the end of the show, we stood there, already amazed, when a thousand white doves were released into the black night. I never realised how fortunate I was to catch Zeppelin when I did. It's my claim to fame.

I WAS THERE: JEFF BAUER

This was the largest single concert by a band at the time, 70,000, bigger than The Beatles at Shea Stadium. They had four giant columns of quadraphonic four channel speakers and played songs from *Houses Of The Holy*. I think it was the first time they played 'Stairway To Heaven' live in this country.

I WAS THERE: WILLIAM PAUL

There were wildfires going on in California, and instead of following 'and the forests will echo with laughter' with 'does anyone remember laughter?' as he often did during 'Stairway', Robert Plant sang 'does anyone remember forests?'

I WAS THERE: RANDY BAILEY

I was at this show, which beat the Beatles Shea Stadium attendance record. I was there again in 1977 for the rained-out show, also in Tampa. Then by the grace of God I was at the O2 for the last show ever. A live Led Zeppelin show is an experience like no other act. They had fun and goofed off a bit, but it was real power and the lightest shade when it was time to be. When it was over, you felt drained but you knew you were at something special. I'm 68, but if they ever decide to give it one more go, I'll be there, any place on the planet.

I WAS THERE: RON YOUNG

Like most in attendance, I was 'flying high' on something and don't remember a whole lot except that it was a great concert. Drugs were a big no-no in my part of the country and even having longish hair brought unwanted attention from the police but people were passing around joints and bongs like it was no big deal. I first got into Led Zeppelin as The New Yardbirds while a senior in high school. Then, when they came out with first album, you just knew they were going to be great. But to most of the college crowd of the time, they were just strange in their style of music, being years ahead of themselves in their idea of southern blues with a hardcore, upbeat sound.

COLISEUM
7 MAY 1973, JACKSONVILLE, FLORIDA

I WAS THERE: DARBY RAYNOR, AGE 16

There were about 13,000 kids in a venue that only held 10,000. One of the kids in my neighbourhood punched a cop and started a free-for-all. All the lights came on and the concert was interrupted for a period while cops were arresting kids. After that show the city put a 10,000-ticket limit on any shows that followed. The concert really rocked.

There probably weren't ten kids in the house that were not wrecked. I remember being pretty stoned as well. Those were the days. Sid Drashin was the promoter and he was a friend of my buddy's older sister. It was weird getting high with him. Just for clarification, I gave up the pot smoking and getting high 40 years ago. I am currently a successful semi-retired business man. But I still love Zeppelin!

I WAS THERE: WALLY STEINHAUSER

The venue, which has since been torn down, held 12,000 and was circular, with the stage at one end and seats above. It was sold out. I was on the floor, very close to the stage and it was so loud. They opened with 'Rock And Roll' from *Led Zeppelin IV*. Someone fell from the upper level onto the floor, but wasn't hurt too seriously. Jerry Weintraub wrote a book with a section about promoting Zep and their sound and said something about how, at a sound check, Jimmy Page didn't think it was loud enough, when it was plenty loud according to Weintraub. So Jerry arranged for stacks of PA cabinets that were either unplugged or had no speakers at all to be installed. That night, Jimmy said the volume was great!

I had discovered Zep in 1969 when I listened to 'Good Times Bad Times' and 'Communication Breakdown' off their first album. I have followed them ever since. I have their entire back catalogue, I've seen *The Song Remains The Same* and I saw their performance for Amhet Ertegün at the O2 in London.

MEMORIAL COLISEUM
10 MAY 1973, TUSCALOOSA, ALABAMA

I WAS THERE: WILLIAM E BARNARD, AGE 19

It was their *Houses Of The Holy* tour. I was home on leave from Navy boot camp and went with my wife and another couple. It was a fantastic show even though I was not close to the stage. I guess Robert Plant gives his voice all he's got coming into the studio sessions as, on that night, he wasn't hitting those high notes.

I WAS THERE: BRETT BRADSHAW, AGE 19

I had picked up their first album at 15, soon after it came out and was an instant fan. This show was put on by the University Program Council. I had just finished my freshman year in college in Tuscaloosa so I stopped by the Student Center and paid my $5 cash for the general admission ticket the week before finals. I had already gone home to Huntsville after school and had to make the three-hour drive back to town by myself for the concert. Even though school was out, the Coliseum was packed.

I sat midway back, in the stands, and had a great view of the show. I remember being impressed with the sound system and was excited for each song. My most vivid memory is the opening moments of 'No Quarter', with foggy smoke billowing up from around John Paul Jones's keyboards. I still have my ticket stub. My best friend, Don Wise, worked for the University of Alabama student council and was the cartoonist for the school newspaper. He designed the posters for the show as well as the t-shirts that were sold. I wish that I had copies of those. Just weeks later, I transferred to the US Military Academy at West Point, so this was my last big concert until I saw David Bowie in NYC in 1971.

I WAS THERE: RICK POWELL, AGE 16

I was exposed to Led Zep through the first two albums and FM radio, although *Led Zeppelin II* seemed to be much more of a force than the first one, which didn't get much notice. I saw them three times, once at the University of Alabama in 1973 and then at Chicago Stadium in 1975 and 1977. I bought the first ticket for $10 at a record store in Columbus, Mississippi. It was the tour captured by the movie *The Song Remains The Same*. I am surprised my mom let me drive the nearly 60 miles by myself, and in her car. I was still in high school and hadn't ever gone on a trip of that length by myself before, and it was well after midnight when I returned. One thing I remember about 1973 in Tuscaloosa is that after Bonham's solo in 'Moby Dick', a blond-haired fellow took over on drums for one song before Bonham returned. I'm not sure if he was gassed, but when he returned, I didn't notice anything else unusual about his playing.

I WAS THERE: RICHARD BURNETT

It's one of the first major concerts I went to. What stands out is the length of time that they played for – three and a half hours – with no opening band. I was blown away by Jimmy Page, especially with the bow on 'Dazed And Confused', and by the acoustic portion of the concert with them all sitting on stools. The second and last time I saw them was in '77 at The Forum in LA. The ticket price had gone from $5 to $15. The wardrobe had changed and it was a bit more upscale, less raw. But both shows were electrifying and although I've seen many good shows over the years and afterwards said 'that was a great show', with Zeppelin it was 'whoa! Did I really see that?' I was numb for a couple of days afterwards and never had that experience since. I knew I had witnessed seeing something surreal. I felt the same when I first saw what happened on 9/11.

I know why they called it quits after Bonzo died.

ST LOUIS ARENA

11 MAY 1973, ST LOUIS, MISSOURI

I WAS THERE: MICHAEL GOSLIN

Four of us drove around 100 miles to this show. Our seats were a bit over half up and halfway back from the stage, stage right. Zeppelin had no backup that I remember – but we were stoned! I've played music my whole life and was playing it then, so I really liked the way they set up, tight together in the middle of the stage. These days it seems bands set up across the whole stage with extra gear and pile it high. Zep had the usual stuff you'd see them with: the three half stacks, the theremin for Jimmy and the whole Bonzo kit and gong. JPJ had his two Acoustic stacks and a keyboard with pedals for bass when he was playing it. They also had tall gold-tinted mirrors behind them which were maybe 20 feet or so high and eight feet across. They played all our favourites from the first four albums including 'Stairway', and about half of the *Houses Of The Holy* album. We'd heard rumours of sloppy, drunken performances by a couple of them at previous shows on the tour but thankfully we got none of that. They were tight and right on it!

I WAS THERE: BOB WALKER

They were 20 or 30 minutes late starting. They had a WEM PA with Leslie speakers and two Acoustic 360s, the drums and two Marshall stacks. John Paul got a wine bottle thrown at him – it missed. The songs from the first album were loud but the organ was not loud enough. It was a great show, though, and my friend recorded it on a Sears cassette recorder with mics in his hat. He has since lost the tape!

MUNICIPAL AUDITORIUM
13 MAY 1973, MOBILE, ALABAMA

I WAS THERE: CHUCK PHILIPP

In 1969 I was a student at Organic School in Fairhope, Alabama. This was a private school where all the hippies went back in the day. It was an open atmosphere and many of the classes were held outside. Many of us walked barefoot on campus and there was always someone playing acoustic guitar. Many students took guitar lessons from Mr Kirby after school, including me. I switched to bass in 1973 and was a huge fan of Led Zeppelin. My parents almost did not allow me to go to their concert, since it was on a Sunday and I had school the next day. However, my begging changed their mind. I also told them I was going with my Organic classmates. Since we did not have the luxury of the Internet, it was important to attend concerts, to see if you were playing their songs correctly.

Even though Plant's voice was cracking at times from the heavy tour schedule, I was amazed by the power of their performance. My parents most likely regretted letting me go, because after that I was begging them to buy me an Acoustic 360 bass rig. My begging never produced one since this cost as much as a car in those days: $1,400. I had to settle for a Fender Bassman 10. When I became an adult, I was able to afford one and now I have a set of twin 360s like John Paul. (JPJ's twin 360 rigs sold in London at Christie's auction house for £27,000 in 2008. I expected them to bring in more when you consider who they belonged to.) I currently play in a Lynyrd Skynyrd tribute band called Almost Skynard. In 2021, we played a show at my old Organic School, with me using my 1969 360 rig, the same year I took my first guitar lessons. I came close to being in a Led Zeppelin tribute band, but was not considered due to not being able to play a Fender Rhodes keyboard. However, I have not given up, so when I do find the right band, there will be a set of 1960s 360 rigs on stage.

I WAS THERE: GREGORY HEWITT

I remember 1969 fondly, as my girlfriend and I were often bonking to Led Zeppelin. I had not heard of the group before then, but between the moans and groans, I learned the song was 'Babe I'm Gonna Leave You'. Which happened to us a few months later. So the best thing that came out of that relationship was being introduced to the album, *Led Zeppelin I*. I ended up buying my first 8-track of it a month later. I was 17.

Over the next few years I was enamoured of Led Zeppelin and ended up recording some of their tunes on cassette. Those were the prehistoric days before Napster, and no one really knew it was illegal to do that sort of thing. I did end up making restitution to the group, as I bought many of Led Zeppelin's albums and cassettes legally. I still have grill burns from the many hamburgers I had to flip to earn the money to buy them.

I graduated in 1973. If you add up the years I was in school, I was an old man of 19 by the time I left high school. I was a drummer and was more interested in playing music than remembering information for tests. Anyways, a buddy of mine was head over heels in love with his girlfriend, who had just moved to Mobile, Alabama, and he was determined to go see the girl. Luckily enough, he asked me to ride shotgun and told me we would also be going to a Led Zeppelin concert while we were there.

How could I refuse? Even if I was the one having to fund the 'project'. Unfortunately, the week before we were to leave, the guy's radiator blew and I was forced to become an accomplice to him stealing one for his car. Yeah, that happened, but fortunately we didn't get caught, and were soon on our way to Alabama. By the way, I plead the Fifth!

Two hippie types cruising to Alabama with no banjos on our knees. Hell, I can't even remember if we had any blunts during the journey. Mostly what I remember about the week, outside of the Led Zeppelin concert, was we stayed at 'Hotel Car', met a lot of pretty girls and me being set up to screw one of them who was about to get married. Her reasoning was she wanted some 'strange' before she got hitched. As I was naïve, I felt it was wrong and didn't partake in the adventure. What a dumbass.

The day of the concert was pretty normal for back in the seventies. A car overloaded with hippie types getting smoked up a ways before we headed into the parking lot. Because the cops knew all of us kids would be partaking in the ritual of getting blown away before heading in to listen to Led Zeppelin, they were busy sticking their heads into the cars to catch a whiff to see if anyone was doing just that. To this day, I believe the cops had done this one too many times and were now as stoned as we were. Anyhow, we managed to reach the parking area without getting busted.

What can I say? The night was magical from the moment John Bonham led the group into 'Rock And Roll'. In fact, every eye and ear in the auditorium was drawn to the stage. If you could have physically taken the music away at any given second Led Zeppelin was playing, you could have probably heard a pin drop. After hearing 'Rock And Roll' being played over cheap speakers for so many years, my words are probably inadequate to express how great it sounded hearing it live with so much veracity and power. All I know for sure is that I fell in love with the group all over again. From John Bonham's mountain-sized back beat to John Paul

Jones' powerful, low-end bass, Jimmy Page's versatile guitar licks and, of course, Robert Plant's incredible voice. I was just completely fucking blown away.

Each musician pulled his weight to give the audience more than what they paid for. We were up in the nose bleed section, but with tickets being so cheap back then, I'm surprised Led Zeppelin could even make a living playing concerts. But times were a lot different back then, cost-wise, and I'm sure they managed to sustain themselves quite well.

One thing I noticed right away was that Robert Plant did not sing his high notes on any of the songs in the beginning. Of course, I didn't know they were going to be playing three hours straight. But as they began kicking ass through songs like 'Black Dog', 'Misty Mountain Hop' and 'Celebration Day', his voice seemed to free itself and he began to blossom before us like a beautiful rose. Man, I can still feel the goose bumps.

Although Led Zeppelin never played 'Babe I'm Gonna Leave You', that night, that concert remains permanently etched in my brain. And now that I'm older, I'm sure I will carry that memory with me as I fade into the void. But hey, not a bad way to go... 'cause it's been a long time...

I WAS THERE: DOMINIC LYONS, AGE 14

I knew their songs from sitting in the driveway, turning down my brother's car battery and listening on the 8-track player in his car. Friends would come over from the adjacent grammar school I attended, St Dominic's, to listen at recess as well. This was my first concert and it cost about $5. It was a full house, 10,000. I was in the balcony and as I looked down and around at the crowd, red dots appeared seemingly everywhere, as if I was staring at a galaxy of red stars. The accompanying odour indicated it was otherwise. Plant was as thin as the bow which Page applied to the strings of his Gibson SG. Zeppelin were awesome!

MUNICIPAL AUDITORIUM
14 MAY 1973, NEW ORLEANS, LOUISIANA

I WAS THERE: TERRENCE BUCKLEY

Tickets were $6 and it was my girlfriend's first concert. She was in high school and when Monday came around, she heard her friends talking about the concert. She floored them when she told them she went to it and how great it was. Her friends asked her who you went with and she said, 'Terry' (me). They were a great band and it was a great atmosphere, with beach balls bouncing all over the arena and frisbees being thrown from one side to the other and back again. The smokes were cheap and good and everyone was having a great time, with great vibes, no hate or fighting. They were great times with friends and family, when tickets were affordable and there were glow sticks and we all had long hair.

I WAS THERE: BARBARA CARLISLE

My hardcore Zeppelin boyfriend took me to my first Led Zeppelin experience! That's the second-best thing he did for me, besides giving me my son. We were in New Orleans and the

Superdome was sold out, as always. We had prepared for this mind altering experience and it was pure magic. Robert Plant had on those low-slung button-fly bellbottom jeans, with no shirt but a small bolero vest. Jimmy Page wore a black satin outfit with a pair of bellbottom satin pants and a black satin jacket with a long sequined dragon from his feet to his shoulder. He had a bottle of Jack Daniels in one hand, a splint on his little finger on his guitar hand and a cigarette hanging from his mouth – and they were abso-freakin-lutely amazing! When they played 'Stairway To Heaven', you could hear a pin drop!

I WAS THERE: CYRIL A RUTH

I saw them about eight times between 1971 and 1977. I'm from New Orleans and in 1973 I met them all but Bonzo. Zep loved New Orleans and wrote a song on *Presence* called 'Royal Orleans', about the hotel where they would stay in the French Quarter. I met them again later (except Bonzo, who was dead at this point). The three of them were super cool to talk with. I talked more to Jimmy about The Yardbirds and the sixties more than I did Zep. Robert was a big fan of New Orleans music, people like Fats Domino and Ernie K-Doe. Jimmy stayed in New Orleans awhile because he had a girlfriend here. I met him one night at a small bar with a woman. That was cool. John Paul was very interesting. He was a highlight of a Zep show. In '73, the ticket price was $6. No joke.

MEMORIAL AUDITORIUM
18 MAY 1973, DALLAS, TEXAS

I WAS THERE: JAMES DODSON, AGE 16

It was the first concert I ever went to. Me and a good friend, Indian Pat Martin, bought tickets. I had just gotten my driver's license and worked all summer at the County of Dallas District 3 Barn, saving up my money to buy a '62 Chevy Impala four-door on a Pleasant Grove used car lot for $150. It was a great old car. Me and Pat rolled up about ten joints and bought a pint of Southern Comfort whiskey and a pint of Bacardi rum. We got to sipping on that booze and smoking them joints and by the time the concert was done I was shit face drunk. I was too drunk and stoned to remember very much of the concert, except when they sang 'Stairway To Heaven' which I thought was the coolest song I'd ever heard.

DALLAS LOVE FIELD
19 MAY 1973, DALLAS, TEXAS

I WAS THERE: JESSE PEREZ

At Braniff Airlines, we worked charters and I remember their gold 707 arriving when they were performing in Fort Worth. There were six limos waiting for them and they came down carrying cold Heinekens.

TARRANT COUNTY CONVENTION CENTER
19 MAY 1973, FORT WORTH, TEXAS

I WAS THERE: DANNY WILKERSON

I had tickets for Alice Cooper's *Billion Dollar Babies* show on May 3, 1973 at Will Rogers Coliseum in Fort Worth, Texas, which was to be my first major concert to ever attend but the show got cancelled. The promoter, Concerts West, who years later I would end up working for, offered money back or tickets to another show. I exchanged my tickets for the Led Zeppelin show. I got excellent floor seats so the promoter must have been holding back seats. The venue, Tarrant County Convention Center, held 13,500 people and the show sold out. My aunt took me to the show as I was too young to drive. Everything about the experience was amazing to me from start to finish – the crowd, the stage, the electric atmosphere in the room. My favourite performance of the night was 'Misty Mountain Hop'. It sounded incredible, so powerful, and I have never forgotten it. From this show forward, if they came to town, I was there. I saw every tour that came through Fort Worth or Dallas.

I WAS THERE: KEN HIGGINBOTHAM

It was sold out. My seat was on the floor and up front. I went with friends in their car and we all dropped acid on the way. I was tripping pretty hard, and about halfway through I went up the aisle to the restroom. After doing my business I started back to my seat. Page was playing his guitar with a bow. I'd stopped at the entrance to the floor to watch. I leaned against the wall for support and listened. Out of nowhere a warlock-looking dude with a black hooded robe walked up to me and stuck out his hand as if to shake hands. I took his hand and shook it. He laughed a wicked laugh then turned and walked away, leaving his hand and arm with me. This blew my mind. I realised it was a fake arm and then I laughed. When I finally found my seat, my friends asked me where I got the hand. I just laughed again. It was a strange trip indeed that took me to the Houses of the Holy. I still have that extra arm.

UNIVERSITY OF NEW MEXICO
23 MAY 1973, ALBUQUERQUE, NEW MEXICO

I WAS THERE: VOLI ARAGON, AGE 14

When *Led Zeppelin II* came out my friends and I went crazy for their music. We had never heard such an amazing sound. We bought our tickets as soon as they went on sale, for $5, and a bunch of us went to the concert. Standing in line outside of the auditorium there was a mad rush to get in when the doors opened and one of my friends fell down and got trampled by the mob. We ran inside to the front of the stage on the right side and I remember just rocking out and being in heaven, listening to their music live for the first time. My friend remembers Jimmy making some mistakes but says that John Bonham played 'Moby Dick' flawlessly. We did not realise that we were watching rock and roll history being made.

I WAS THERE: RICK ELLIOT

We were all 14 or 15 and big Led Zeppelin fans (we still are). We always made a point to go to all the concerts early and this was no exception; we wanted to be first in line for this one. We got there at 2pm, although the concert didn't start until 8pm. It was all general admission, and the crowd was already starting to arrive when we got there. It got crazy. So many people were pushing that that our feet would almost come off the ground. When the doors opened, it took everything we had to stay on our feet. My girlfriend Rhonda Dawes fell and was almost trampled. Yoli Abud and Julie Wallis made it in alive, and Yoli was able to convince the door guy to let her keep both halves of her ticket. We headed right to the front on the floor, where we met our friends Lisa Huerta and Joe Lavato. Everyone around us was lighting up and the big party was on! Zep came out at 8pm and didn't disappoint.

It was amazing! Robert Plant was right in front of us, John Paul Jones on the left, JP on the right and Bonham with his massive drum set and gong in back. Did I say it was amazing? Jimmy Page's playing was a little sloppy, but still badass with his licks and his violin bow. JPJ was the backbone and multi-instrumentalist who kept it all together, Robert Plant was being Robert Plant (there's nobody better) and John Bonham was spot on perfect, with highlight of the show being 'Moby Dick'. Zeppelin played for three hours. There was no backup band, and although they might have taken a break, I don't remember it. I do know that my ears rang for two days. We saw all the best concerts back in the seventies and this one was the best of the best and the one I will always remember.

Yoli went to see Robert Plant with Alison Krauss in Taos, New Mexico recently and talked to him and have her picture taken with him, with his arm around her. It was all meant to be. And general admission at The Pit? This was the last concert they had that was general admission. All because of us, of course…

SPORTS ARENA
28 MAY 1973, SAN DIEGO, CALIFORNIA

I WAS THERE: BILL RENO REIDA

I had been chomping at the bit to see them since *Led Zep I* was released but there was no chance they were coming to Omaha, Nebraska. But I was serving in the US Navy in San Diego when they came there. They opened the show with 'Rock And Roll' and then it was off to the races. I copped a buzz on whiskey and hash.

I WAS THERE: ROBERTA PEINADO, AGE 18

My first husband was stationed in San Diego. As he was a naval officer, we were able to get tickets to any venue inexpensively. The tickets were $5 apiece, something we could afford! I was newly married and had one child. My 14-year-old brother, who was getting into trouble at home, was staying with us for the summer. Little did they know we raised more hell together than they ever knew existed!

The venue was a coliseum and we got there early enough to be able to sit in the front of the stage. All seating was general seating, which was on the floor. I remember getting pretty loaded because in those days you were able to sneak in alcohol and drugs. By the time Zeppelin came out on stage, I was feeling good and somehow got separated from my brother and husband. I was still in front of the stage and when Robert Plant walked out it was like God came out. He was glorious, wearing a tan crop top with puffed sleeves and *very* tight light rose hiphugger jeans. His pants were so tight, I could see the outline of his crotch area and I was just mesmerised. I couldn't take my eyes off him. Jimmy Page was hypnotic with his guitar playing and between the two of them, I was hypnotised.

By the middle of the concert, the music was making me move to dance. It wasn't easy because the standing room was tight. But I managed to start swaying with the music. Whoever was behind me decided to move with me. 'Okay, that's cool!' I had taken my wooden platform shoes off and had them in my hand. You could break a leg wearing those shoes. There was a very young naval officer behind me, swaying and dancing along with me. This went on for a few more songs. 'Stairway To Heaven' began playing, and this young man behind me felt free enough to grab me and began fondling me! I turned around and swatted him on top of his head with my wooden platform shoes. Unbeknownst to me, my brother, who is six feet four inches in height, was watching me from the middle of the floor. My brother parted the crowd with a few sweeps of his hand and came towards me. He got to this poor kid and told me to run out. I headed for the exit, looked back and could see my brother and husband beating this poor kid.

I didn't get to see the end of the concert, but I saw enough to say I did enjoy myself until Mr Touchy-Feely decided to put his hands on me. Every time I see Led Zeppelin, this memory of their concert pops up. Especially Robert Plant's outfit and the body that occupied those jeans. Wow!

FORUM
31 MAY 1973, LOS ANGELES, CALIFORNIA

I WAS THERE: DAVID FRESHMAN

John Bonham's 25th birthday. What a party! Like the 1972 show, this concert was also a bit over three hours long. What was on the bill here were quite a few songs from *Houses Of The Holy*. 'Over The Hills And Far Away', 'The Song Remains The Same' and 'The Rain Song' were played, showing just how far musically Zeppelin had grown and progressed. There were complex chordal attacks a la Pete Townshend, with one of the most incredible rhythm sections ever in rock. JPJ's gorgeous use of the mellotron textured the band's music in a way that moved it a bit closer to progressive. Other highlights were 'Misty Mountain Hop' and 'No Quarter', which was spacey and psychedelic and a great keyboard showcase for JPJ. I felt the show could have been trimmed down a bit, but it was still fantastic, especially when Page and Bonham came in with awesome modes that were Arabian, Celtic and Spanish with a flavour of being out on the Moors. This was also a great showcase for Robert, as he was starting to really stretch out into Middle Eastern/Indian modes and micro-tonal scales. Led Zeppelin were moving into a whole new style of music that western rock music had yet to really properly explore.

I WAS THERE: ELLEN BERMAN

I was a big fan of Led Zeppelin starting with their first two albums. I finally got to see them play live in 1973 at the Los Angeles Forum. On stage, they proved everything that a top rock 'n' roll band should be. Great musicianship together and, separately, attitude – and then there was lead singer Robert Plant, oozing such charisma and pure sexuality. I really thought that I was going to die! The band played such an exhilarating show, interweaving many genres of music into their sound: blues, early rock 'n' roll, celtic, jazz, funk and R&B.

When Led Zeppelin came to Los Angeles, they would stay at the Continental Hyatt House on the Sunset Strip, then becoming affectionately known as 'The Riot House' due to all the insane antics and excess debauchery by the rockers who stayed there. Led Zeppelin's actions contributed to this, as documented in the hotel's history.

I'd see the band in the evenings at the new Rainbow Bar and Grill on the Strip – a restaurant and bar catering to a young hip rocker crowd. After 46 years, this place is still as popular as ever and has rock memorabilia and photographs covering all the walls, but in those early days and years it didn't have this because its history was in the process of being made.

Led Zeppelin would sit in the back at a very big table, holding court. With them would be the very young underage LA groupies Sable Starr and Jimmy's girl, Lori Maddox. There would be a big electric buzz in the dining area whenever they were there. These rock gods were always having a jolly good old time with food, drink and women. They seemed on top of the world, which they were. One of the most interesting things that I saw was that, whenever patrons were finished, they would walk to the back and pass by Zeppelin's table to pay homage and respect to the band. I myself did so one night, along with my friends. Lori was cuddled up and laughing with Jimmy while Sable was under the table 'accommodating' Robert Plant! It was always very cool and exciting to see these rock gods whenever they landed in the City of Angels.

KEZAR STADIUM
2 JUNE 1973, SAN FRANCISCO, CALIFORNIA

I WAS THERE: THOMAS GRANT FILIATREAU

This was an awesome show, with naked women and a lot more! It had been cold and overcast all morning, but when they started 'Stairway To Heaven' the sun came out. The first beam of sunlight hit the stage right over Robert Plant and then the white doves were released from the stage. It was very surreal. At the the first break, they collected all the joints that had been thrown onto the stage and put them on the amp. I had bright pink rolling papers and rolled a three-paper joint. They grabbed *my* joint and said, 'Hope you don't mind, we're going to do something a little illegal right now.'

I WAS THERE: BRUCE TREADAWAY

Led Zeppelin were at the pinnacle of rock culture. They came to the San Francisco Bay Area and it was almost mystical, with the sheer power of Jimmy Page's runs on his double-neck guitar and the unshackled lyrical performance. 'Stairway To Heaven', when all the white birds were released over the crowd, was a dreamlike moment. 'No Quarter' was almost mythological, with smoke billowing over the crowd. This was the highlight of the hundreds of shows I saw living in the Bay Area, from Altamont to the Fillmore, Winterland and others. Led Zeppelin rocked the Bay.

I WAS THERE: JEFF BOOKSTAFF

My older cousin had a record collection that rivalled the suitcase underneath Cameron Crowe's sister's bed in the movie *Almost Famous*. She had *Led Zep I* and *II* in 1969. I was twelve years old and I had never heard anything like it. Zeppelin were like a religion to me. We were way back in the boondocks at this show. I went with a cute little colleague by the name of Jere. She was so young, so cute, so Bay Area seventies. She wanted to leave before it was over and so we walked a mile or so back to my mom's '67 Mustang as they were playing 'Dazed and Confused'. I never called her after that!

I WAS THERE: DARLA WATLET, AGE 27

I was a hippy and it was the days of love and peace, etc. I discovered their music on the radio and then bought their albums. I was a fan along with my group of friends. Their music sucked you in with the beautiful melodies. Some songs had no specific meaning and became 'whatever it meant to you'. The best example of that is 'Stairway To Heaven'. I will always remember Led Zeppelin at Kezar Stadium. The mystical ambience of pink smoke bombs with white doves flying in the air. The stadium was noticeably quiet with people swaying to the melody as they played 'Stairway'. My friends and I were finally able to see our favourite rock band and it did not disappoint. Such performances stay in the memory forever.

I WAS THERE: ED VARGAS

My brother Steve was a drummer and I played lead guitar in a local cover band growing up in what is now called Silicon Valley. We were amazed at the musicianship and the sound from only four people. Steve was so impressed with John Bonham's drum kit that he went to Don Weir's Music Store in SF and bought that Ludwig Vistalite drum set in blue. We had first seen Jimmy Page when he was rhythm guitarist for The Yardbirds. Steve and I heard so much about The Yardbirds and Jeff Beck on lead guitar and were disappointed to hear Jeff had decided to leave The Yardbirds right before their concert in San Jose, leaving Jimmy on one guitar. But he did not disappoint.

I WAS THERE: RUBEN TREJO, AGE 23

I was stoned and feeling good. John Bonham did 'Moby Dick' and they did 'Bring It On Home', like they did at the Fillmore West. I remember the sun was going down and the chicks on the left side of the stage took off their clothes. I thought I was in heaven!

I WAS THERE: PHYLLIS GUINN, AGE 15

I went with my friend Vicki. Her cousin drove us. I barfed out of the window on the way home.

THE FORUM
3 JUNE 1973, INGLEWOOD, CALIFORNIA

I WAS THERE: MIKE MCCOLLUM, AGE 18

l was in the Marine Corps stationed at Camp Pendleton. When the lights went out and the guys came on stage, pure magic appeared. The thing that sticks out in my mind is Jimmy Page pulling out what looked like a violin bow and using it to play his guitar. The highlight of the night was 'Stairway To Heaven'. There was marijuana smoke in the air, lighters were up in the air and everyone swayed to the music. The stage was engulfed in a cool fog that changed colours with the lights. I wish I still had the t-shirt I bought that day.

MILWAUKEE ARENA
10 JULY 1973, MILWAUKEE, WISCONSIN

I WAS THERE: MARK KOENIG, AGE 16

In 1969 I was a lad of twelve, and with sisters five and six years my senior, rock 'n' roll was a fixture in our home. My father had a reasonable stereo – a Sherwood receiver paired with Jensen speakers – and the first Zeppelin song which caught my ear was 'Whole Lotta Love' on the local AM station. My sister bought *Led Zeppelin II* and I wore the grooves of the vinyl out. I was mesmerised by the powerful brand of music they played. I was at the Milwaukee Arena for the ridiculous price of $5.50. My initial memory of that evening is my first whiff of weed as my sister rolled and smoked a joint with her friend on the 30-minute drive. But that wasn't the last whiff as the Arena was rather cloudy the entire evening.

I WAS THERE: JOHN GOFORTH, AGE 15

The first Led Zep song I ever heard was 'Whole Lotta Love' on a local radio station, WRIT 101.1FM. It was on this station that I heard they were corning to town and I bought four tickets as soon as I could. Since I wasn't old enough to drive, my cousin was supposed to pick my girlfriend and I up and he and his girlfriend would make it a double date. But he had lost his tickets and never showed up. As show time was getting near, my girlfriend's parents gave us a ride to the show. We made it on time and what a show! They opened up with 'No Quarter'. The floor of the stage was flooded with fog for effect. They played for three and a half hours and I think they played just about every song in their repertoire.

BUFFALO MEMORIAL AUDITORIUM
15 JULY 1973, BUFFALO, NEW YORK

I WAS THERE: PAMELA GROGAN

I saw Zeppelin twice at the Aud in Buffalo, in June 1972 and July 1973. I had a seat about five rows centre from the stage. Someone sitting in the upper seats had thrown an M-80 firecracker onto the stage. It made such a big bang that Jimmy walked offstage and was not going to play anymore. Then Jimmy came back on and the crowd went wild! They finished the concert and I had such a good time that I will never forget it. A guy who I knew back then got on stage twice and was hugging Robert. The second time he did it they threw him out.

I WAS THERE: PAUL BEECHLER

I saw Zep in concert in Buffalo on the *Houses of the Holy* tour. It was a great show! But my fondest memory is buying their first LP for $1.99 when albums routinely sold for $4.99. I got it at a local discount store when some clueless sales associate at the store put it in the 'cut out' bin. Cut outs were so named because a small notch was cut out of the cover and the price slashed to half or less. I already owned the recently released *Led Zeppelin II* and had to examine this cut out to confirm it was the real Led Zep. I was quite pleased to get a terrific album for a steal. I bought my most treasured 45 as a cut out at the same store – The Beatles' 'She Loves You' for 19 cents!

I WAS THERE: DENNIS THOMANN, AGE 21

My friends and I were close to the stage. We rolled about 20 joints before the show and snuck in a bottle of Dom Perignon champagne. We also shot off some fireworks. My favourite part of the concert was Jimmy Page playing his guitar with a violin bow and using the double-neck guitar.

I WAS THERE: MAX EDDY, AGE 17

I discovered Led Zeppelin's music in 1969 when I was 14 years old and heard 'Whole Lotta Love' on the radio, inspiring me to buy *Zeppelin II*. I had seen *Zeppelin I* in stores and thought it looked interesting but never heard it. I got tickets for this show from a friend who bought several at a local pharmacy that sold concert tickets. I had a station wagon and stopped at the local teen hangout to ask if anyone needed a ride to the Zeppelin show. I ended up with about twelve people squeezed into my car. I remember the show being excellent and Jimmy Page doing an amazing extended guitar solo.

Some idiot was throwing M-80s in the air. These were powerful fireworks and very dangerous. They were exploding and Robert Plant stopped the show and said that if the clown throwing fireworks didn't desist, Zeppelin would leave the stage. He said someone could be seriously hurt and that 'children should leave their toys at home' when they go to a concert! The crowd roared its approval. A friend of mine was hit in the head with an M-80 which bounced off him and exploded nearby. Luckily, he wasn't hurt. I saw the incident from a distance but didn't know it was him until he told me a few days later.

I WAS THERE: NIAGARA GREEN

I saw them seven times. In 1973, I was so close to the stage I could see that Robert Plant was sweating. Towards the end of the concert, he was spitting on those of us in the front few rows. Tired from so much touring, I guess.

PACIFIC COLISEUM

18 JULY 1973, VANCOUVER, CANADA

I WAS THERE: BILL FARRAND

Robert Plant only sang for about 20 minutes before he stopped and left the stage. After a few minutes he came back on and the band played 'Stairway To Heaven' and then they left for good. Some guy came on and announced that Robert was not feeling well and had to leave. The real reason Plant had to leave had nothing to do with the heat. That is a made up BS story. The Pacific Coliseum had a very good ventilation system so the temperature did not get as high as the outside temperature. There was no problem with humidity, as that is not an issue in Vancouver.

I just looked up the weather report for that day. It was an average summer day for Vancouver. Being located right beside the ocean, the temperature is more moderate and even on hot days the cool breeze off the water lowers temperatures quickly. By 7pm the temperature was about 23°C, which is about 74°F, and not what I would call a hot day for July. Vancouver only has around 50 per cent humidity in the summer, compared to cities like New York which has 99 per cent humidity at the same time.

My memory of the events is not perfectly clear, as I was also under the influence of recreational pharmaceuticals, but apparently someone spiked Robert Plant's drink with LSD just before the band came on stage. I remember being pissed off after paying $5 for my ticket.

BOSTON GARDEN

20 JULY 1973, BOSTON, MASSACHUSETTS

I WAS THERE: BRIAN MAHONEY, AGE 16

Boston Garden is a hockey arena that holds around 18,000 people and I went with a bunch of friends because one of them said we could sneak in. We tried everything to get indoors, including climbing up fire escapes. Finally, the ringleader left and got on the subway, saying we couldn't do it. I eventually bought a ticket for two joints and $5.50! It was a blast!

CIVIC CENTER
21 JULY 1973, PROVIDENCE, RHODE ISLAND

I WAS THERE: DAVE LIVINGSTON

l first heard *Led Zeppelin I* in my friend's basement and we thought it was a new kind of rock 'n' roll. It didn't sound like anyone else. Songs like 'The Lemon Song' were harder, grittier. I played rhythm guitarist in a garage band and we played 'Communication Breakdown' and 'Good Times Bad Times'. But my favourite song to play on guitar and sing is 'Babe l'm Gonna Leave You'. The slightly complex chord progressions are so much fun and how the song goes from mellow to hard and back to mellow is genius. We reacted the same way when *Led Zeppelin II* came out... they kept getting better. We knew at that time that they weren't a one album wonder. My personal favourite is *Houses Of The Holy*, because I listened to it quite a bit when, in 1973 and aged 18, I moved 1,300 miles from my parents to college in Florida. I was finally out on my own in the world as an adult. Surfing is my passion and the songs on *Houses Of The Holy* seem to be in touch with the rhythm of the ocean. l like the way the album flows – a concept LP!

I WAS THERE: WAYNE PIMENTAL

I saw them once in Providence, Rhode Island and once at Nassau Arena in the NYC area. The first show was just like the movie, *The Song Remains The Same*, but better. It was nothing like a live show. The 1975 show was really great. The boys played four new songs from *Physical Graffiti*, which had not been released here in the US at the time, and including 'Kashmir'.

THREE RIVERS STADIUM
24 JULY 1973, PITTSBURGH, PENNSYLVANIA

I WAS THERE: STEVE ACRI, AGE 16

I found a 45rpm copy of 'Communication Breakdown' b/w 'Good Times, Bad Times' in a bin of toss aways in a thrift store in 1969. I liked it enough to keep it but didn't bother to seek them out any further. Later that winter, under the influence of some older cousins, I had a chance to hear *Led Zeppelin II* and fell under the trance of 'Whole Lotta Love'. I was hugely disappointed when local AM radio started playing an edited version, removing the extended middle section. But from that point forward, Zep was on my musical radar and I duly picked up all their albums as they were released.

Led Zeppelin performed in concert in my hometown of Pittsburgh, Pennsylvania four times. I missed the first two shows but did see the next two. They were spectacular. Interestingly, and completely unbeknownst to me at the time, I saw Jimmy Page play lead guitar for The Yardbirds on the 1966 US tour that Jeff Beck bailed on.

I attended my first Zeppelin show with my best mate, Joe. We had neglected to buy tickets in advance but went to the venue to try our luck anyway. We chatted with some other folks who were also attempting to get in and someone suggested simply handing a ticket taker a few dollars instead of a ticket when moving through the turnstile. A brilliant idea. The smallest bill I had was five dollars, which was a lot of cash to me. I queued up and when I got to the taker, I handed him my five dollars. He glanced at the bill, looked at me and pushed me through. Joe was even luckier. When the taker went to take his currency, a surge of patrons from the rear pushed him through the entry without him having relinquished his bill!

Once inside the stadium, we had to decide where to sit. By another crazy stroke of luck, we each found ticket stubs on the ground that allowed us access to a largely empty seating section because, this being a stadium show, many had chosen to leave their seats and move down to the floor for a closer look. We ended up with a reasonably good vantage point, a few hundred feet from the stage, right of centre. Joe had binoculars that allowed us an even better view. As a 16-year-old under the influence, I recall being thrilled to hear 'Rock And Roll' as the opener, being bored to near death during 'Dazed And Confused' and really enjoying the extended keyboard into to 'No Quarter' and the spectacle of sounds, lights and doves that was 'Whole Lotta Love'. It was great night of rock music.

I WAS THERE: DEBBIE VOGEL

It was a terrible venue. The funnel-shaped open-air stadium spread the sound so that those up in peanut heaven got to hear only a portion of the music. I heard primarily drums the whole evening, and then the 20-minute drum solo. I can't even remember what songs were played. All I remember is the drums. I never went to another concert at that venue again.

I WAS THERE: ED HENDRICKS

Tickets cost \$6 or \$6.50. They started with 'Rock And Roll'. I think they played for three or four hours. It was one of the most amazing shows I ever saw. I was 23 or 24. I went with three friends – Mark, Frank, and Eel. Mark brought a 35mm camera, lens and an entire camera kit. We lied our way into the press box and Mark got some great photos. It was the first time I had seen a 35mm camera. 'No Quarter' brought the house down and Bonham did a 20-minute drum solo which was unlike anything any other drummer could do.

I WAS THERE: JANET SWANWICK CONANT, AGE 13

My father brought home *Led Zeppelin II*, lay down in front of our huge console stereo and played 'Whole Lotta Love'. I had never heard anything like it and thought it was terrible. But I remember going to school and hearing some of the cool kids talking about it and, since my dad was so impressed, I was too. When I heard that they were going to be at Three Rivers Stadium, I asked my Dad if we could go, knowing damn well he would say no, and to my astonishment he said yes! The tickets were the astronomical amount of \$6.50 and I had to give up my allowance for four weeks to pay for mine, but I was so excited.

I went with my sister Diane, who was 11. Once we got to the show, my father dropped us off in the parking lot, and the next thing I recall is rushing to the stage, the massive crowds and all the marijuana! The show was like nothing I have ever seen before or since and is still the best concert

I've ever seen. We had 'festival' seats, which meant no seats at all, and we were close enough to the stage to see the sweat flying off Jimmy Page. Robert Plant, of course, did not sweat.

I WAS THERE: SHAWN MARGARET COHEN

I was 16 going on 17 and my best girlfriends and I went to see them live. When Robert got up there with a girl's top on with his bare chest hanging out, it was unforgettable; the moves, the music, his wailing soulful voice blended with Jimmy's guitar, Bonzo's banging beat and John Paul Jones's bass line. We were tranced out! It was like a religious experience and when 'Stairway To Heaven' came on, not a sound was made as everyone listened intensely!

Who knew that in 1988 I would end up working in the Primrose Hill Healing Centre in London and dating the owner, a guy called Ken. One day after work, Ken says to me, 'Do you want to get a drink before we go home?' It was a particularly hard day and we both worked with patients, or clients, so I said, 'Yes, okay, where should we go?'

At the end of the drive and to the right was a pub and he suggested we go there. We went in and Ken sat down while I went to the bar to get the drinks. As I approached the bar, right smack in front of me there were two very tight and cute bums staring at me! One belonged to someone with long curly blond hair and the other someone with darker hair. They were leaning on the bar and I could only see them from behind. Suddenly the penny dropped as I saw the blond turn and speak to the other and I could see it was Robert Plant.

I was just about to go up to him and say 'hi' and could we buy them a drink and get an autograph and could I dump my dull boyfriend and run away with him – you know, the usual – when he seemed to get a vibe that someone was standing behind him with their mouth to the floor at seeing him, even from behind, and so he and his friend ran up the back stairs to another floor.

He did not see me but I was caught, absolutely caught. Should I run up the stairs after him and get an autograph and tell him how much I loved him and how I saw him in Pittsburgh a couple of times? Or should I be a good girl and just behave myself and get my boyfriend a drink and sit down? I stood frozen and then looked at my boyfriend and said, 'Is that who I think it is?' and he said nonchalantly, 'Robert Plant? Oh yeah. He comes in here all the time. He lives around the corner.'

I was outraged. How could he keep such precious information from me? His response? 'I didn't know you liked him.' I was still in shock as I sat down and had my glass of wine waiting, in vain, for Robert to come back down the stairs for the laws of gravity state: 'What goes UP must come DOWN!' But no, he never reappeared. Like a magician, he disappeared out of some trap door the pub must have created just for him! Of course, I was devastated, that was it. I ended up leaving the boring boyfriend for many reasons but always regretted not running up those stairs after Planty to see what would have happened... Oh well, my virtue is intact. Big deal!

I still love Led Zeppelin and in fact my friends and I have our very own Led Zep Facebook group called 'Led Zeppelin's Ladies' Club'. I am good friends with the promoter who brought them to Pittsburgh too, all those decades ago, and he has some great stories about them, hunting for Moët & Chandon for them in Pittsburgh with our liquor laws back then! I attended a lecture in Cadogan Hall in Chelsea a couple years back where Jimmy Page was interviewed, which was great. I loved every minute of it, but sadly no sign of Planty!

Filmed for posterity for the feature film* The Song Remains The Same*, Led Zeppelin perform three nights at Madison Square Garden in New York, although the film does not see the light of day until 1976. Several scenes were later reshot at Shepperton Studios just outside London, with the Garden mocked up on a British soundstage.

MADISON SQUARE GARDEN
27-29 JULY 1973, NEW YORK, NEW YORK

I WAS THERE: GERRY ANNE DIMARTINO DALTON

There was a lottery to get tickets and I was lucky enough to be chosen. I had tickets for a summer jam concert at Watkins Glen, New York, but when I received my Zep tickets it happened to be the same day so I got rid of those tickets real fast. It was the weekend they shot footage for *The Song Remains The Same* at Madison Square Garden. I went with my then boyfriend, now my husband. I still have my tickets. I paid $7.50. Zeppelin are still my number one.

I WAS THERE: DEB IAROCCI-KEMPF, AGE 17

I was at my local record store, checking out Don McClean's *American Pie* album, when the owner put LZ on the turntable. I purchased the first three albums that day and I've been a fan and follower ever since. A friend's mom gave her four tickets for two nights at Madison Square Garden for her birthday and let us use her car so we headed into the city. We had no idea that *The Song Remains The Same* movie was going to be filmed. We had great seats, pints of vodka and many joints. It was a once in a lifetime experience!

I WAS THERE: DONNA LOGGIA

I went to all the shows at MSG. I would go every night as they would play the full week. Each show was a little different. I was part of the shows when they got robbed! The shows were so magical and the weed smoking was so intense that you could hardly see the stage. Everyone just partied and passed pot around from row to row. The music was loud and certainly the best. The fantastic voice of Robert Plant was epic with Bonzo on the drums, Jimmy Page with the guitar bow and John Paul Jones on keyboards and guitar. In the nineties, I also saw the Page and Plant shows which were very exciting and, again, pure magic.

I WAS THERE: MICHAELS, AGE 15

I was a long-haired somewhat post-hippie kid. Back then it was easy to scalp a ticket for basically nothing and we did for all three consecutive nights. They filmed *The Song Remains The Same* at those concerts. Back then you could also smoke in venues and I remember the scent of sweet herb throughout the entire arena! Page, Plant, Bonham and Jones were an unbelievable band, and sounded like ten guitars were playing. They were just all so phenomenal that words can't explain it. Each member had a very special talent and I'll never forget the crowd and their chants.

I WAS THERE: ROY MEFFORD, AGE 16

This was my best concert ever. I took the train from South Jersey to the Garden and got off the train, which was full of hippies all going to the show and all high as kites. I walked up the stairs and in the front doors. This was it. Zeppelin were gods to me.

The 1975 North American tour is Led Zeppelin's tenth visit to the continent, comprising 39 shows in total. 18 months since the band last toured, some critics suggest the band are rusty and lacking dynamism. Jimmy Page breaks a finger prior to leaving England, forcing him to develop a three-finger playing technique for the first part of the tour. After warm up shows in Rotterdam in The Netherlands and Brussels in Belgium, the two-legged tour of North America starts in Bloomington, Minnesota in January 1975 followed by three nights in Chicago. A bout of flu for Robert Plant sees one show cancelled and subsequent suggestions that his singing ability on much of the tour is negatively impacted.

CHICAGO STADIUM

20-22 JANUARY 1975, CHICAGO, ILLINOIS

I WAS THERE: SCOTT SAMUELS

Zeppelin were in Chicago for three nights. I was at the second show. My ticket was $15. I was on the side, about half way back. It was a good seat, to the right of the stage, on Jimmy Page's side. This was their *Physical Graffiti* tour. There was no opening band. It was about a two-hour show. They started with 'Rock And Roll'. Plant was having some throat trouble and he mentioned it during the show. So his voice was a little off, but not bad. I remember they played 'Kashmir'. No one had heard it before. They played 'Over The Hills And Far Away', and for 'Stairway To Heaven', John Paul Jones put down his guitar and played keyboards. Robert picked up a joint someone threw up on the stage and took a couple of hits. He said that Jimmy hurt his hand or finger when he got it caught in a passing El train in Chicago.

I WAS THERE: NORM FOWLER, AGE 17

I celebrated my seventeenth birthday with 20,000 others that night. Robert was ill and the show was less than spectacular but it was still a special night. That show also featured new stuff from the as-yet-unreleased *Physical Graffiti*. And by not hearing anything from the first or third albums, it was a bit of a letdown. It was still a thrill to see the biggest rock band in the world, especially when Jimmy played the theremin for 'Whole Lotta Love'.

I WAS THERE: RICK POWELL

The second time I saw them, Page had a broken finger and wasn't playing up to his usual standards. It was the only time I heard the live version of 'When The Levee Breaks', which I think Page played on a black Danelectro guitar.

COLISEUM
24 JANUARY 1975, RICHFIELD, OHIO

I WAS THERE: RICHARD B KELLEY, AGE 17

I was a high school senior in Toledo, Ohio, a fading factory town near the southern Lake Erie shoreline, and lucky enough to parlay my art ability and my love of music into a job at the first 'underground' record store in town. We sold a lot of vinyl, 8-tracks and dope pipes and catered to the tastes of the young factory workers who laboured daily throughout the city. Heavy, hard rock was our staple. We sold a lot of Eagles and James Taylor and a bit of British prog and sixties stalwarts but our big sellers were music to cruise and smoke pot by. Aerosmith and Trower were huge. Kiss, UFO, Blue Öyster Cult and Foghat all sold in large numbers but absolutely no band whatsoever could hold a candle to Led Zeppelin. In towns throughout the midwest and the nation, Zep were mystic god heads of the first order. A bigger than life band well suited to their heavy sound and artistically minimalist and mysterious album packaging.

Theirs was another world's primal wail, providing the perfect soundtrack to the machine shop, an open road, a bong party or the bedroom. They were Celtic hoodoo shamen who rocked! In this era of diverse musical styles and tastes, it's hard to relate to the mindset of the baby boomer music consumer in his youth. In 1975, music consumption was much more ghettoised. With the baby boomer generation you had a large population bubble and, by and large, members of that population shared the same musical tastes.

With *Houses Of The Holy*, Led Zeppelin had made their audience wait nearly two years for fresh material. It had been well received and sold fantastically but it didn't have the huge panache of *IV* or the *Symbols* album (or whatever the hell you wanted to call it), primarily because it didn't have a smash equivalent to 'Stairway To Heaven.' After *Houses Of The Holy* settled down sales-wise, the fourth and second albums returned as our big Zep sellers.

It's hard to relate in this day and age, when a band can take over a decade to bring new material to market, but anything over a year back then was an eternity. By mid-1974, our store's phone would ring six to ten times a day and invariably there was a stoned-sounding voice at the other end asking about a new Led Zeppelin album.

It was into this atmosphere of massive anticipation that the 1975 tour was announced. The band had finished their previous US tour less than 16 months earlier but the 1975 run was received as roughly the equivalent of The Second Coming. Around the same time, it was leaked that the tour would coincide with a new album.

Later we learned the album would be a double and that it would be on Zep's own label imprint, Swan Song, whose only big release was Bad Company at the time. Finally, we found out it would have the mysterious title, *Physical Grafitti*.

In February of 1975, I was not a Led Zeppelin fan. I was much too cool. Working in the hip hippie record store I had access to the latest and greatest. Artists like Genesis and Roxy Music and the fledgling competition between rocking songwriters like Springsteen and Nils Lofgren were cool. Any blue-collar rock, which of course included Zep, was not. I was more than a bit of a snotty ass about it, and indifferent when many of our staff and customers excitedly reported that they'd got tickets for Zep's appearance at the newly opened 22,000 seat Richfield Coliseum, between Cleveland and Akron in north central Ohio.

Zep were also going to be at Detroit's Olympia Stadium but it was a huge, echoey old hockey rink notorious for bad sound and sight lines, located in a dodgy part of Detroit. Olympia was an easier ticket to get and was less than an hour away but Richfield was shiny and new, even if was over a two-hour trip. I wasn't going to either show and I didn't care.

Exactly a month before the release of *Physical Graffiti*, Led Zeppelin were scheduled to perform at the shiny new Richfield Coliseum just off Interstate 77, south of Cleveland and a bit northwest of Akron. The venue had hosted the likes of Sinatra, Neil Diamond and Stevie Wonder but its presence in the tiny enclave of Richfield was said not to be appreciated by the locals, who found their small town way of life disrupted by traffic jams, city people, rowdy basketball fans and the like. The building, less than a year old, had never hosted rock and roll before and certainly not a band with the huge and voracious fan base enjoyed by Led Zeppelin.

It was Friday and I was scheduled to work my shift at the store while a couple of my bosses and their friends were heading out that afternoon to Cleveland to witness the mighty Led Zeppelin in the flesh. The phone rang about 10am and it was one of my employers. He told me I was going with him and the others to see Led Zep that evening. I reiterated my distaste for the band but he insisted. Someone in their group couldn't go at the last minutes and I was to replace him. Boss's orders.

We left in the late afternoon and the journey down US 80/90 toward Cleveland was as boring and dreary as it could be on a dark, cold January day. A considerable amount of pot was smoked by the five of us during the two-hour trip and I suppose we passed around a wine bota as my long-haired bosses were wont to do in those days.

We arrived in plenty of time, found our seats in the back turn of the lower bowl and, lo and behold, they were padded and upholstered! This was a shiny new building unlike any we had ever experienced. Most sports and concert venues were either post war arenas, basketball field houses built during the WPA era or crumbling vaudeville theatres from the twenties.

The security guards attempted to stop people from smoking but it was impossible. Beer wasn't sold in those days and there was nothing else to do while waiting for the show.

We sat and we sat. We smoked pot and we sat some more, all 21,000 plus of us. Eventually a cloud of smoke hung from the ceiling, as was common in the era. It was oppressive nonetheless. Finally, a little after 9pm, the lights went down and a few of the lesser stage lights came on. The arena erupted in flashbulbs as fans tried to get a shot of Page and company as they entered the stage under cover of darkness. The roaring crowd, now mostly awakened from their THC and hallucinogenic stupors, began shouting louder as the band fiddled about, tuning and testing in the onstage murk and strobe effect of the camera flashes.

Suddenly a massive drum tattoo pierced the darkness followed by blinding stage lights and the massive eruption of a very loud and extremely distorted electronic sonic maelstrom. The sound was awful. It took until nearly the end of the opener, when some of the breaks would allow for better listening, to realise that the band was playing 'Rock And Roll.' The as yet unheard 'Sick Again' followed and was likewise an incomprehensible din, at least in the back of the bowl where we were seated. I decided my distaste for Zep was not unwarranted. 'Over The Hills And Far Away' followed and apparently allowed the sound crew to dial in a slight better godawful mix.

It was at this point that we realised the stories making the rounds about the band on this tour were accurate. We'd heard that Jimmy Page had broken a finger or two in a train door and as such couldn't play up to snuff and that Robert Plant had some kind of throat infection that reduced his voice to a hoarse growl. You felt pained in their honour listening to them, especially Plant, whose voice was more gurgle and grunt that his usual primal scream.

The show muddled along, with the setlist alternating between the yet-to-be-released *Physical Graffiti* and 1973's *Houses Of The Holy*. Plant spent a goodly portion of the show carrying a half gallon jug of Jack Daniels' bourbon, slung hillbilly style over his shoulder. He and Page shared it enthusiastically and the more Jack they consumed, the more Plant's voice cleared up and the better Jimmy played. By the time they stampeded through 'The Wanton Song', Led Zeppelin were firing on all eights and were damned impressive. Then it got dark, surreal and very ugly.

Just as the energy level was increasing, the band embarked upon their legendary over-the-top solo segments beginning with John Paul Jones and an interminable presentation of 'No Quarter'. Boring nearly from the onset, the song seemed to plod on and on. My other boss and I decided to get up and look around this cool new sports and music venue. As we casually strolled the concourse, we were suddenly startled by loud clanking and clunking sounds echoing through the area. Then it began. Rocks and bricks and pretty much anything anybody could pick up and throw started crashing, en masse, through the plate glass exterior windows into the arena concourse. Suddenly, huge shards of glass and heavy projectiles were hurtling down and literally landing at our feet as one large window after another exploded toward the folks inside!

A panicked usher ran towards us, gesturing furiously and screaming for everybody to get back into the arena and away from the storm of violence crashing from the outside into the building. We chose to hang out in the vomitorium near our seats and watch the mayhem unfold. The usher who had admonished us minutes earlier ran past again, still shouting for everybody to get inside, but now blood ran down his panicked face.

A whole lot of people outside of the venue were mad. Extremely mad. At this point we decided returning to our seats was a prudent move and so we did. The band was playing 'Trampled Underfoot' when we sat down, another new one. At the time, I didn't realise the irony of the title given what was happening outside. A too-long drum solo followed in the form of 'Moby Dick' after which 'How Many More Times' featuring Page and his Gibson and cello bow wank-a-thon filled more time until the finale. In the quiet portions, you could hear the glass crashing in the outer concourse.

If the band was aware of the violence they didn't say anything and no official warnings were issued from the stage or over the public address system. Led Zeppelin continued rocking, finishing with 'Stairway', during the soft opening segment of which occasional smashing glass and shouts were audible, and encores of 'Black Dog' and 'Communication Breakdown.'

Upon exiting the Richfield Coliseum, we were directed by ushers and staff members, some sporting bloody bandages, to stay near the inner walls as most of the broken glass and projectiles had now been swept toward the exterior. It seemed that every large plate glass window from the ground to about twenty feet up was hanging in shards. Here and there the floor and glass were spattered with blood. A riot had happened here.

We rode the two and a half hours home in abject silence. We were tired from the day and the dope and stunned by what we'd witnessed. News articles later claimed that the box office had sold out of tickets, leaving several hundred fans outside angry and empty handed and venting their frustration on the plate glass. The same papers had reported several weeks earlier that the show had totally sold out and there would be no tickets to be had at the box office. The venue was grossly oversold for the Led Zeppelin concert, a practice not unusual in the era, and the fire marshal had closed access while the last five hundred or so fans holding legitimately purchased tickets were still waiting to get in. These angry fans erupted in violence, either out of frustration or to try and gain access to the show. The venue management had allegedly called the local police to help quell the violence but none had responded, fearing they would be overwhelmed. It was also rumoured that the locals and their constabulary, who never wanted the arena built there in the first place, found grim satisfaction in the extensive destruction.

The promoters, venue and media downplayed the mayhem and were rewarded with a two-night stand when Led Zeppelin returned in 1977. Money can't buy happiness but it sure helps heal old wounds.

I WASN'T THERE: MARCI CONNELLY

My memory of the Led Zeppelin concert in January of 1975 is not actually of the show itself, because honestly, I wasn't there on the night of January 24, 1975. I was at the Coliseum on the following night, for a Cleveland Crusaders (WHA) hockey game.

I was only 14, and when I arrived at the game with my parents all we could see were the boarded-up windows and doors. This was the Crusaders' first season in their new home arena and in a matter of a couple hours, all the entrances and many of the plate glass windows had been completely broken or damaged by the hundreds of Zeppelin fans who stormed the building that had opened only three months earlier. None of these fans had purchased tickets for the concert; they just overpowered the ticket-takers and security.

Led Zeppelin had not played in Cleveland since they performed at Public Hall in October of 1969, and I guess these fans just wanted to find some way into the arena. Two years later in 1977, I was fortunate enough to see Zeppelin's return to the Coliseum for what ended up being the last time they would tour the US.

MARKET SQUARE ARENA
25 JANUARY 1975, INDIANAPOLIS, INDIANA

I WAS THERE: RANDY KEMP, AGE 19

The place was packed. It was a snowy winter night and they didn't sound that great, but it was a good experience and a rare opportunity to see a great band in action. It was a Saturday night. I went with my friend Jeff, his girlfriend and my then girlfriend Judy. On the way to the show there were threatening winds and near blizzard conditions. I'm surprised they didn't cancel the show. We sat centre, just off the main floor, and Zeppelin opened up with 'been a long time since I rock 'n' rolled...'.

The highlight of the night was 'Kashmir'. Overall, I wouldn't give them great marks but it was the seventies and the era of shitty sound reinforcement. John Bonham played a killer solo, Robert Plant and Jimmy Page both seemed fairly disconnected from the crowd and John Paul Jones was okay. Market Square was not a great place acoustically. Being the crossroads of America, Indianapolis had every band touring come through that town and play, so the crowds were quite discriminating but I remember the crowd being pretty appreciative. After all, they were Led Zeppelin and they are gods of rock, right?

OLYMPIA STADIUM
31 JANUARY 1975, DETROIT, MICHIGAN

I WAS THERE: DAVID L CARDEN, AGE 18

The Olympia was a hockey arena where the Detroit Red Wings played but also served as a venue for concerts. The tickets were general admission. The group I was with found a spot on the main floor along the wall, maybe 15 rows from the stage. I played drums in a band and pretty much just focused on John as he wailed on his set. The show seemed to last forever. The band even took an intermission. After they came back, it was all about Jimmy Page. He played on his double-neck guitar and was truly amazing. But what really blew my mind is when he started slamming his strings with a violin bow. There was a delay, so it was a few seconds after he struck his guitar that you would hear it through the speakers. Throw in an echo effect and the place was going crazy. The Old Red Barn was rocking!

I WAS THERE: TERRY FLETCHER, AGE 15

Like most 15-year-olds in the midwest, I was all raging hormones and crazy about Led Zeppelin. As the Christmas break dragged into January, winter in Detroit seemed like it would never end. My light at the end of the tunnel was Led Zep live. As the days went by, the excitement built as word was getting out that they had new material coming out. However, there was an undercurrent of tension as news began to circulate that Page had slammed his finger in a train door which at best might hamper his playing. This was before the internet so information was scarce, which just made the whole situation more tense.

Skipping school early the Friday of the show, we got to the old Olympia Stadium early. My mom worked there and I had brought her dinner as she was staying to see the show (I have a very cool mom!). There were hundreds of people milling around outside the stadium and there was a certain edge to the mood. After waiting what seemed like forever, it was finally time for 'Rock And Roll'! With Bonzo bashing into the intro, Plant wailing and Page with guitar slung low like a six-string killer, I was fully into the best concert experience of my life. We didn't have to wait long to hear the new stuff as they launched into 'Sick Again' and, shortly after, 'In My Time Of Dying', and I remember thinking how incredible these new tunes sounded. Plant then introduced a song they had never played live and Page, wielding his bow, started in with 'Kashmir'. The hypnotic music, lighting and audience-supplied smoke created this almost trance-like state.

Suddenly this mood was broken as the aisles quickly began to be jammed with people. The crowd that had gathered outside who didn't have tickets had broken down the heavy steel and glass entry doors and were streaming into the stadium. However, once inside, everyone was peaceful and didn't cause any trouble. It was a very festive atmosphere. Zep blazed through an amazing set, mixing more new material with older tunes including one of my favourites, 'How Many More Times'. I was fortunate enough to see Zeppelin one more time, April 1977 at the Pontiac Silverdome. That was another amazing show, but as with any love you always remember your first!

I WAS THERE: STEVE MAZUR

It was a cold winter night and driving there the streets were icy. When John Bonham started his drum solo in 'Moby Dick', I looked at the clock inside the arena and it read 10.10pm. When he finished the solo, it was just after 11pm. Quite an endurance test! The show began at 8pm and was just over four hours long, ending at just after midnight. Then they played two encores lasting another 45 minutes, so the total length of their performance was just under five hours without a break or intermission. Robert Plant's voice sounded a little off, like he was struggling with a cold or something. Maybe it was just the Detroit cold winter weather!

I WAS THERE: LOIS BOWEN, AGE 15

My mom drove myself and my boyfriend to Olympia Stadium. We had seats on the main floor on the seventh row. I remember Bonzo's insane drumming and the huge gong symbol behind him and – of course – 'Stairway To Heaven'. *Physical Graffiti* had come out so watching Jimmy Page with the double neck guitar and using his bow was insane to experience when they did 'Kashmir'. I still talk about this concert almost 50 years later when people talk about their concert memories. Led Zeppelin was a topper.

I WAS THERE: DAWN SHONER PETTY, AGE 15

It was a date with a guy I knew. It was absolutely the best concert ever and I've been to several since. Led Zeppelin is the greatest band and they always will be.

I WAS THERE: DOUG SCHNEIDER, AGE 17

My buddy and I lived in the suburbs, about 35 minutes away in Northville. His dad had to drop us off at the Old Barn as my car was out of commission. I paid over a hundred bucks for two tickets that weren't even together. As we were walking to our crappy seats, I saw two open seats with a good view. I sat there with the intention of leaving when asked. No one asked, so I stayed. I had brought an Instamatic camera, strapped to my leg, and I took pictures. It was great. I particularly remember the 'How Many More Times' medley with the violin bow and the quad PA speakers in the rafters. Jimmy was playing great with a finger sprain, likely with the benefit of self-medication. We froze our asses off waiting outside for our ride home late that night, only a couple of blocks from where the '67 riots took place eight years earlier.

I WAS THERE: RICK HANA

We watched from the risers as, two or three songs in, the entire main floor folded up their chairs and sat down on the cushions. Then the lighters started flashing, about the same time as the laser light show began. The lasers were shooting out from the stage over the main floor about three feet high. People were catching the lasers in their hands. Looking down from the risers, the beams lined up like sheet music. The air was heavily with smoke, music and the laser beams dancing back and forth. It looked like I was reading the sheet music as Jimmy was playing!

CIVIC ARENA

1 FEBRUARY 1975, PITTSBURGH, PENNSYLVANIA

I WAS THERE: BILL WILFONG, AGE 19

I went with three buddies and we bought tickets from the arena. Tickets were like $10. I remember Page bringing out the bow and thought this was way cool. Whoever thought that these guys would get me into the blues today? That is the Zep I loved. They blew my mind. Rock and roll was my life and seeing them was a great experience. Hearing Plant was magical. I didn't need drugs. My high that night was a band called Zeppelin.

I WAS THERE: JANET SWANWICK CONANT

This was the second time I saw them. These tickets were $8.50 – a small fortune – but again my sister Diane and I went. My dad took us. We sat behind the stage, at an angle, and they were not the best seats but the show was amazing. Robert Plant wore that little half-vest he was so famous for, and the tightest, lowest jeans I've ever seen. I especially remember John Bonham's 'Moby Dick'. I wish I could remember more, but I've smoked way too much weed since then.

I WAS THERE: DENI DEBAISE, AGE 18

My boyfriend at the time took me for my eighteenth birthday. We had a car load of friends and drove two hours to get there. Our tickets were $8.50. We didn't like our seats so we made our way down to the floor and ended up in really good seats. There was not much security in those days but there was lots of smoke, booze and drugs. This was the tour on which 'Kashmir' was played live for the first time and it has stuck with me all these years. It's still my very favourite song of all time.

I WAS THERE: VINCE DUNSWORTH

I thought I saw them in 1973, when I was eleven, but I checked the internet and it was the '75 show I saw. I guess the internet has a better memory than I do. One of our crew had a friend who was friends with someone from the production company that ran the concert locally. We got floor seats, and if memory serves me right the cost was $10. The weird thing was that the concert was an open secret. It was not advertised; you pretty much had to know someone. The box office at the Civic Arena denied the concert was happening for fear of gate crashers.

I WAS THERE: STEVE ACRI

I next got to see Led Zeppelin at the Civic Arena on a very cold February 1. I was with my guitarist friend Shook. He was a fiend for the British players, with Jeff Beck and Jimmy Page being at the top of the list. This tour was to support the *Physical Graffiti* album which was still two weeks away from being released so we had not heard a lot of the songs before. This put me off a bit and made me anxious to hear the stuff I knew already. My friend, on the other hand, loved the opportunity to hear Page play stuff that was completely new and fresh. Led Zeppelin were still the kings of rock and we knew we were fortunate to be in their presence (no pun intended).

SPECTRUM
8 FEBRUARY 1975, PHILADELPHIA, PENNSYLVANIA

I WAS THERE: FRANK GINOCCHIO, AGE 8

I vividly remember my dad coming home and playing the *Houses Of The Holy* album when it came out. Normally he played the Faces, Elton, Bowie, J Geils and Grand Funk. This was completely different. I was really into Slade and Alice Cooper, but Zep was in its own class. My dad went into a Bag and Baggage store with a Ticketron in it and bought two tickets for $4.50.

I remember the house lights being up and the funny smell. The lights went down and it was just mayhem. The show itself is a bit of a blur because it was just this sensory overload of sight and sound. My eight-year-old mind was officially blown. I remember Robert's blond hair in the lights, a lot of dancing and Jimmy with the bow. I vividly remember parts of 'Moby Dick'. I remember the Clockwork Orange outfit and that the drums were loud. It sounded like a trade-off between thunder and bombs going off. When he played with his hands, Bonham got so fast that his arms looked like lawn mower blades on one of those old push mowers. It was just incredible. The big footlights at the tip of the stage looked really cool. I was totally taken aback by the huge LED ZEPPELIN sign that lit up towards the end of the show.

MADISON SQUARE GARDEN
3 & 7 & 12 FEBRUARY 1975, NEW YORK, NEW YORK

I WAS THERE: GEORGIA VLAHOS, AGE 22

My boyfriend's brother was dating a girl who worked for their record company so we got comped seats. I had no idea what I'd be in for: sixth row centre at Madison Square Garden, right under Robert Plant! Their records didn't do them justice, because they were awesome musicians. They jammed a lot. You didn't get that on the records. Jimmy with his violin bow blew me away. He would bow the guitar, and then point the bow at the audience. A light would follow it. At one point, John Bonham was playing the drums with his hands. His drum solo was mesmerising. Robert Plant was the sexiest thing I'd ever seen.

My boyfriend wasn't too happy with me. What you don't usually hear about is the way Plant and Page played off each other. It was very sexual. I even noticed at one point that Plant was – well, hard. It seemed like they got sexually stimulated by the music. The music itself was very sexy and I think that's part of their appeal. But their biggest appeal is that all four were amazing musicians who were at the top of their game. Each one had a presence, even the quiet John Paul Jones. They played insanely loud. When we went outside, it took about two hours before I could hear again. It was a long concert, but you wanted even more. I remember it better than I remember my own wedding day!

I WAS THERE: JIM CHIRONNA, AGE 14

I saw Zep live in '75 and '77 at Madison Square Garden, two of the best shows I have seen. In 1975, I had to mail away for my tickets through the *New York Times* – and pray! I went with my music buddies. Everybody was in their seats by 7.30pm and the electricity going through the crowd was amazing. People were just yelling 'Zeppelin! Zeppelin!' as though they couldn't believe they were there. The show was amazing, the musicianship was spectacular and the light show was killer. Jimmy Page just killed every song. Bonzo was the most powerful drummer I have ever seen. John Paul Jones is an under-rated, amazing musician. He played keys, bass, stand-up bass, mandolin and, during 'Ten Years Gone', three-necked acoustic guitar. Plant, the consummate front man, was great, interjecting cool insights about the songs in between singing his ass off.

They played until 1.30am and the last train back to New Jersey was 12.15am. We all slept in the Hoboken train station until the next morning because, being high school kids, we didn't have any money to buy new tickets. We only had our round-trip tickets from the night before. The train conductor was cool and let us slide. During the night, the parents of the girls who were stranded came to pick them up and gave rides to whomever they could. The rest of us had to go straight to school and didn't make it home. I missed my English final exam, got an F and got benched for my championship baseball game because I missed the first three hours of school and my homeroom attendance. My father was an English teacher and football coach at the time. He was pissed! When he told me I should have left early to make the train back in time so I could make my final exam and the baseball game, I explained to him it was Zep and there was no way I could leave the show before the end. My response was, 'You would never leave the Super Bowl if it were tied and going into overtime, would you?'

I WAS THERE: MICHAEL S

My favourite Led Zeppelin concert was in 1975, once again in New York City at Madison Square Garden, where they played on three separate nights but not consecutively in February. The most memorable was when we had seventh row centre seats. My best friend and I were absolutely ecstatic and excited as the usher led us closer and closer to the stage. Once again, the sweet smell of pot lingered all around us and we joyfully partook. When the lights went out in the auditorium, the crowd exploded in thunderous applause, screaming and yelling. Zeppelin took the stage in an explosion of lights, breaking into 'Rock And Roll', and the Garden went berserk!

The night before we had used a typewriter to type on a piece of rolling paper, 'From Mick and Paul'. We rolled that joint perfectly so you could read what it said if you looked at it. I waited for that perfect moment to run up as close as I could to the stage to toss that carefully rolled joint up at Robert Plant, but unfortunately, when I did, my throw fell short and hit a police officer right in the face as he stood in front of the stage, staring back out at the crowd as they did on occasions. I high-tailed it back to my seat.

NASSAU COLISEUM
13 & 14 FEBRUARY 1975, UNIONDALE, NEW YORK

I WAS THERE: MIKE RUGGIERI, AGE 13

Five days after my 13th birthday, I saw Led Zeppelin for the first time. This concert changed my life. It was a rare show in that they had a guest join them for the encore of 'Communication Breakdown' – Ronnie Wood! Having just heard several songs from *Physical Graffiti* performed live, I was counting the days until its' release eleven days later. I remember riding my bicycle to our local department store – Korvettes in Yonkers/Scarsdale, NY – and being the very first customer to buy a copy of the album, just as they were opening the box. They hadn't even put the pricing sticker on it yet!

It was quite a thrill to take the album home and listen to it in all its rock and roll glory. It contains my favourite song of all time, 'Ten Years Gone', it's still my favourite album of all time and it's still ingrained in my brain. I got rid of most of my vinyl collection in the nineties, but I still have that LP and I plan to give it to my oldest grandson along with this story.

I would see Led Zeppelin one more time, in June 1977 at Madison Square Garden, when I was 15 years old. In the ensuing years, I've seen Jimmy and Robert many times solo and on the Page/Plant tours of the nineties. I've even seen Jimmy come out and join Robert's band at a Plant show in New Jersey in 1985, just a few weeks before the *Live Aid* reunion. Jimmy even wore the same shirt he would wear at *Live Aid*!

I WAS THERE: PATTY CUFFE, AGE 16

I discovered their music on the radio. I was in high school from 1972 to 1976 and radio was our most important tool to discovering music. There was no internet or MTV, just the radio and telling each other the albums we bought and played at parties. I waited in line all night in freezing weather to get tickets. We ended up in the tenth row. Everyone was really high. Back then, there were great concerts all the time at MSG, with either the Stones, Pink Floyd or The Who. It was a great time to be young. I still go to concerts. I went to Desert Trip and was in the pit, which was awesome. Being so much older, I can now afford those front of stage seats. It would be awesome if Led Zeppelin ever had another world tour. Why not? All the other bands are doing it.

I WAS THERE: WILLY PUIG

Led Zeppelin made me a tad deaf. My seat was too close to the PA. My eyebrows were singed and my hair was pressed back as if it was starched. Page played slide all night because he had broken his finger on the hotel door the day before. Still, he pulled it off and it was awesome.

MISSOURI ARENA
16 FEBRUARY 1975, ST LOUIS, MISSOURI

I WAS THERE: DOUG STOVERINK

I saw them three times. Myself, my girlfriend, my best friend and his girl had gone to get tickets to one of the shows. Just to get tickets was a major event. Crowds of people waited for hours on end to get tickets to the show at a later elate. The crowd was so jammed together that, when they did open the box office, the crowd pushed together at once and a young woman got shoved through the plate glass window and got cut pretty bad.

Physical Graffiti*, the band's sixth studio album, is released by Led Zeppelin on their own label,* **Swan Song***, on 24 February 1975.*

I WAS THERE: RICHARD B KELLEY

After a show on February 16 in St Louis, reputed to be the best bootleg recording of the entire '75 US run, the band took ten days off to prepare for the release of *Physical Graffiti*, their sixth album. Our store in Toledo had likewise been preparing for this momentous event. We had over 400 customers who'd signed a pre-order sheet (over a dozen pages on an eight and a half by 14-inch legal pad) to ensure they received a copy of the album on release day. Some customers made a special trip in just to add their name and be guaranteed first crack. In those days records didn't find their way to every market on the scheduled date of release. Monday usually meant Tuesday in a secondary market like Toledo. We didn't really have much competition for the new Zep album, but we figured we owed it to our customers to bring it in as soon as possible. We had another store in Akron, Ohio not far from the shipping hub in Cleveland. We could get our order of 500 *Physical Graffiti* LPs on the Monday if we picked them up in person at the UPS facility there. Otherwise, every Zep-addled rocker in Toledo would have to gnash their teeth another day until the UPS man brought their albums on Tuesday.

That Sunday, I travelled with one bossman to Akron to spend the night at the other bossman's apartment so we could rise early, drive to nearby Cleveland and pick up our Warner Bros order which consisted of hefty quantities of the new Zep and Robin Trower albums. We rose in a timely fashion on Monday morning and speeded to the Cleveland UPS facility. Literally, as one bossman had a penchant for classic cars, in this case an early '50s DeSoto with one of the first Hemis (V8) and we had to follow him because he knew the way. There we picked up our order of more than a dozen boxes of *Physical Graffiti* and *For Earth Below*.

I hit the turnpike heading west in bossman's pick-up truck. It takes about two hours to get from Cleveland to Toledo now. It took a little longer in 1975, when the national speed limit was 55mph, as the Ohio State Patrol was notoriously officious. The journey back could not be completed in time for the store's usual 10am opening and it was closer to noon as we exited I-75. Being an arty-farty guy, I was excited to see what the packaging on the Zep album would like.

We had yet to open a box but they sure were heavy. As we rounded the corner and our tiny store came into view, we were more than a little taken aback! A massive line of over 100 people streamed out of our front door, onto the sidewalk and down the block past a neighbouring lumber supply company. Co-workers later told us there were already several dozen people waiting when they arrived to open at 10am. A cheer erupted as we turned in.

Bossman and I each carried a crate of LPs through the back door to the front counter. Someone brandished a box cutter, opened the containers with a flourish and lo-and-behold there it was! We popped an 8-track tape into the store system for uninterrupted play and set about selling the long awaited two LP set as fast as we could for the next four hours. The line of long-haired customers, some of whom had skipped work, seemed endless. Shortly before 4pm every damned LP copy was sold. 500 copies gone in an afternoon!

Fortunately, we could see what was happening and the bossmen got on the phone to the founding branch of our store in Kalamazoo, Michigan, about three hours away. They had copies to spare, as did a nearby rack-jobber (a middle man distributor) who was also associated with the store. We cobbled together another order. Bossman and another employee drove to Jackson, Michigan to meet employees from the sister store and pick up another 500 copies. He was back by 6pm.

And then it happened. *Physical Graffiti* stiffed! After nearly 600 units sold in a single day, the major demand had been satiated. It didn't help that word had gotten around that the album wasn't very good. We now think of *Physical Graffiti* as a diverse, sprawling masterpiece in the tradition of *Exile on Main St* or the *White Album*. But at the time, its multiple styles and sources, with some songs newly recorded and others being outtakes dating back to the *III* album, was hard to grasp for fans wishing for 'Whole Lotta Love'/'Black Dog' redux.

We had 400 copies of the damned thing to get rid of. The 8-track continued to loop for over a week in our store until it broke, but I heard *Physical Graffiti* more in that time than I have since. I grew to love the album decades ago and still play it a lot. But we had so many copies of the elaborately packaged set that the display shelving at the front of the store collapsed under the weight. It took a couple of months, and we had to beg for a couple of return authorisations, but eventually we arrived at a manageable inventory. It continued to sell moderately well but soon enough the *Symbols* album (*IV*) and *Zep II* returned to their status as our top Zep sellers.

There was never the excited demand for Led Zeppelin after that. *The Song Remains The Same* live album was issued a few months later and did fine. It chronicled the tour previous to the one that had just finished, and was more of a companion piece to the ridiculously overwrought film of the same name making the midnight movie rounds at the time.

A little over a year after *Physical Graffiti*, *Presence* was issued. I think we'd put out a sign up sheet for it as well but it was more or less a forced issue. The album sold very well but lacked the hoopla of PG. It was the harbinger of a dark decline in the personal fortunes of Led Zeppelin. A decline from which they would never recover.

LSU ASSEMBLY CENTER
28 FEBRUARY 1975, BATON ROUGE, LOUISIANA

I WAS THERE: FRED YOUNG, AGE 22

It was wild. There were about twelve of us, men and women, doing window pane acid. We had all known each other for years and had driven from different places to meet up, which made it more special. Their encore was 'Whole Lotta Love'. I loved them and they didn't disappoint. We played cards after we got back from the concert and we all hollered the whole game because no one could hear!

I WAS THERE: BARBARA CARLISLE

This was another spiritual experience. People were out of control, throwing things on stage. Those flourescent green wands were first out and they were flying all around. Robert Plant stopped the show in the middle of an acoustic number and said he would shut the show down 'if one more of those green dicks is seen flying through the air!' Needless to say, it stopped!

TARRANT COUNTY CONVENTION CENTER
3 MARCH 1975, FORTH WORTH, TEXAS

I WAS THERE: JANET JOHNSON

On the day tickets went on sale my husband and I got in line at four in the morning. It was 16 degrees. There were about 50 others in the queue. By 8am there were over 800 and things began to happen. The crowd got tighter and tighter until I could barely breathe. Then all hell broke loose.

I WAS THERE: JACK SUGGS

The first time I saw Led Zep was in a non-airconditioned and very, very hot horse arena at Fair Park in Dallas in the summer of 1969. A couple of months later I saw them play the Texas International Pop Festival in my little town of Lewisville, north of Dallas. And in 1970 I saw them at the Dallas Memorial Auditorium in Dallas. I also saw them at Tarrant County Convention Center in Fort Worth in 1975 during the *Physical Graffiti* tour.

I WAS THERE: JERRY BROWN

There was no opening act. None was needed. They opened with 'Rock And Roll'. The stage was dark and then you heard Bonzo start with the drum intro. He had plexiglass drums with different coloured lights in each drum, so it looked like a strobe light with colour variations. As soon the intro was done, it seems like a couple of pods blew and when the smoke cleared, there was the rest of the band. Robert strutted out and said, 'Been a long time, Fort Worth' and it was on. They played for three hours, every song you wanted to hear. I think it was during 'Kashmir' where Jimmy pulled out a violin bow and played a solo until every horse hair on the bow was broken. John's drum solo was 15 minutes long. The encore had three, maybe four songs. I will never forget the start of that show.

MEMORIAL AUDITORIUM
5 MARCH 1975, DALLAS, TEXAS

I WAS THERE: FRED ESPINOZA, AGE 18

It was nice outside when we arrived three days early to the front ticket office for Memorial Auditorium. There were already two people holding spots in what was to become a very, very long line. But it was Texas, and the weather would change... quickly! We spent the next two and a half days as we had begun, partying! Three of us were taking shifts to ensure we didn't lose our place in line. Each time someone came for his shift he would bring the appropriate essential partyables – pot, booze and munchies. It went well all the way until a few hours before the gates to coolness would open.

The night before the opening doors stopped the chaos to come, the weather changed. It turned very cold. I felt good about our place in line – third. It was still dark when I noticed a little push. Everyone had their camp broken up. There was no sign people had been there for several days. Maybe a little trash. The camp had become a queue. People standing very close to each other. Then a little push. Then the pushing became rude.

The line formed to the north of the six double doors. Roughly one hour before opening, the push became mean. Then the sixth or seventh in line decided they should move to the other doors, bypassing the line. Soon all six double doors were filled with flesh and heavy coats. I was at the very front of the second set of doors, the door handles at my chest. I was assured up front tickets.

Then 30 minutes before, it began. Like the queue, a small push, then it turned rude. The people towards the front began reacting with a little noise. Pushing turned mean. The noise became a roar! The mean pushing coming from the rear of the crowd, to the middle, to the very front, at the glass locked doors, made the temperature rise. The ambient air was freezing. In the crushing front of the crowd, it had become hotter, the unseen sun had been replaced. There I was, violently pressed against the glass. I was drenched in sweat beneath my heavy coat. The air was becoming thin. Breathing was hard, not just because of the air, but the crowd had forced me so hard into the glass that it was becoming very hard to physically expand my lungs. I began to fear. I was next to panic when two key holding employees walk to the doors. Yea, it was over. Soon I would have tickets to the greatest pioneers of the upcoming rock 'n' roll age.

Nope! The employees totally disregarded the soon to be crushed kids in line. They stood there by the other side of the door, waiting for opening time, paying no attention to the screaming front line begging for relief from the crushing horde. When the screaming, pleading and tears finally reached their hearts they would merely point at their watches and shrug. Right as people were near needing medical attention, the clock saved them. The doors opened and the rush was so swift I didn't make it to the windows first. I was actually third in line to the middle of the fourth window!

I went with best friends. The day of the show we tripped acid. This was back in the day of clearlite window pane, the good CIA stuff. We dropped right before the show. We knew it took about 30 minutes to kick in. We also knew if you smoked a joint right when you took it – kapow! You were tripping. So the minute the lights went down we lit up. And so began one of the greatest memories of my life. If it weren't for Freddie Mercury I could honestly say this was the greatest concert ever. It was the *Physical Graffiti* tour. Need I say more? Oh yeah, front row second balcony. Best seats in the house.

SPORTS ARENA
10 & 14 MARCH 1975, SAN DIEGO, CALIFORNIA

I WAS THERE: LARRY JOHNSON, AGE 22

I saw them at San Diego Sports Arena, twice in 1975 and once in 1977. In '75 I bought tickets for the first date and it sold out really fast so they added a second show and I bought tickets for that too. I was turned on to them in high school. I was a fan of all the British bands. The Beatles and The Who were my favourites. Then this heavier raunchy sound came out. I bought all their records and had them on 8-track and cassette in my cars. They were so loud and raw. I remember Page bringing out the violin bow to play on the guitar, Bonham beating those drums to death and Plant's voice. It was in the days of open seating and everyone rushing the stage. Security was having to pull people out of the crowd so they wouldn't get crushed. Tickets were about $7. I went to so many concerts in those days, I probably have forgotten more than I remember. But Led Zeppelin was one of the stand outs.

SEATTLE CENTER COLISEUM
17 & 21 MARCH 1975, SEATTLE, WASHINGTON

I WAS THERE: CHRIS SINGLETERRY, AGE 17
I went with my 19-year-old boyfriend and some of his friends. I had discovered their music three years prior, when we all waited for every new album to come out. We have a little town about two hours away from Seattle called Cashmere. Can you guess what song they sang and that they mentioned the little Washington town? I also saw them in 1977 at the Kingdome in Seattle. It had bad acoustics and echoed quite a bit so was not as good as the 1975 concert. Have you seen that t-shirt that says, 'I may be old but at least I got to see all the best bands'?

I WAS THERE: WILSON O'NEAL
I was turned on to the second album in 1969 by my friend across the street. The song I remember most from that album was 'The Lemon Song'. I remember driving about 300 miles from college to Seattle to see this show. The tickets were $7 and I went with friends. They started off with 'Rock And Roll'. The green lasers duringJimmy's violin sequence in 'Dazed And Confused' were amazing, forming a pyramid over his head and slowly spinning around him, making it look like he was standing in a green fog.

I WAS THERE: MORLEY CURTIS
I went with three other guys. They all did coke. I didn't do drugs – I only drank, which is still true today. My recollection is that it was not good. The music was fantastic but the acoustics sucked and the band seemed drugged out of their minds and missing cues and beats. I was in my late teens and sang in a garage band. Although nothing ever came of it, I recognised when bands were on and when they weren't, and Led Zeppelin weren't. The neatest experience of the night was wandering around the stadium and meeting a lot of fun people and seeing a lot of puking and passing out. Overall, I wasn't impressed.

I WAS THERE: SUSAN KING
I was a fan from an early age, like 13 or so. The first song I ever heard was 'Dazed And Confused', and I listened to them daily, playing multiple albums every day from 1971 through to 1978. I was totally in awe of them and thought Robert Plant was so good looking. I saw them live in Seattle, first in 1975 and then again in 1977. The 1975 concert was the most memorable. I considered myself lucky to get a ticket because they were hard to come by. The concert was festival seating but I remember going to sit up in the seats because I thought the crowd in the front would be 'too rough'! From where we were sitting, we could see backstage.

They were the only band on the bill and were due to start at 8pm, but 8.15pm and then 8.45pm rolled around and – nothing. At 9.15pm I saw the limousines pull up behind the stage. They piled out and by 9.30pm they were performing. Jimmy Page was mad about someone in the entourage having been arrested. I could see Robert Plant backstage finishing off a half gallon of some brown whiskey. When Robert went offstage, there would be someone there to put a kingly robe on him.

They played for four hours! It was truly amazing… Seeing Jimmy Page play his guitar with a violin bow blew my mind. The music was phenomenal. And loud. I couldn't hear out of my left ear (which was closest to the stage) for four days. And I couldn't hear out of the right one for two!

PACIFIC COLISEUM
19 & 20 MARCH 1975, VANCOUVER, CANADA

I WAS THERE: TOM BALL

My buddy Brett and I headed over to the show. It's hard to believe you could get a ticket for $6.50. We had to wander around before they came on. All of a sudden the lights went down and then up again and the very first song was 'Black Dog'. The show was so good and they had total control of the packed house. They started off playing something fast and then something slow, and seeing the crowd go from high octane to mellow in one song was breathtaking. Before we knew it the last song was playing and of course it was 'Stairway To Heaven'. When they were playing it, if you could have stopped every sound the band made, you would have been able to hear a pin hit the floor.

I WAS THERE: GEOFFREY PROVERBS, AGE 16

I saw Zep in '72 and '75, and when they toured as Page and Plant. I was so stoned at this show that 'Kashmir' almost hypnotised me. My big bro slapped me awake or I would have fainted. Everyone was drunk too, with beer flying everywhere.

I WAS THERE: JIM WALKER, AGE 18

I lived in south central British Columbia so had an eight hour drive to get there. Myself, two brothers and a friend went to the show. Memories are a bit foggy as we had done some purple microdot. We met up with a couple of girls from my class that had done some windowpane acid, which was kind of rough for them as they spent most of the concert crying out Jimmy's name!

THE FORUM
24, 25 & 27 MARCH 1975, INGLEWOOD, CALIFORNIA

I WAS THERE: BONNIE GILBERT

I remember listening to 'You Shook Me' and went out and bought the album that day. I got a ticket for this show from a scalper. I was with my brother and another friend of ours, so they took the two seats together and I went off on my own. I had dropped acid and my seat was front row, just off the floor, so I had a great view of them all night. I remember they had stools up on the stage and were doing acoustic numbers from *Houses Of The Holy*. Some of the people near me were getting tired of the sound and wanted the hard driving electric sound back, but I was really grooving to the sound. What was funny was this one guy turned to me and said, 'Don't you think this is boring?' Just then they geared up into 'Kashmir' and I laughed, went 'noooo!' and started rocking out again.

I WAS THERE: MAMNER JAMMER

I sent my dad to get my Led Zep tickets at the Raspberry Roach in downtown Los Angeles, where he stood in line for two hours. Thanks, Dad. My car broke down on the way to the opening night show on the 24th. I hitchhiked and then had to take a bus. When I got there, I found my tickets were for the show on the 25th. I tried to get in every door without luck. On March 25 – the correct night – everything went off great. The show was stunning and mesmerising. I'm left with lifetime memories which are all in my head, as my memorabilia, photos and ticket stub did not make it through the past 44 years. I will never forget their shows – Jimmy with that bow move and that wonderful sound it made.

I WAS THERE: DAVID FRESHMAN

Zeppelin debuted *Physical Graffiti* – brilliant! 'Kashmir', 'Trampled Underfoot', 'Sick Again' and 'In My Time Of Dying' were given a fantastic showing. Other wonderful works were 'The Rain Song', 'Over The Hills And Far Away', 'The Song Remains The Same' and 'No Quarter'. As in '73, I felt that 'No Quarter', 'Moby Dick' and 'Dazed And Confused' had become a bit bloated and could have used a bit of a nip and tuck. But overall? This was a brilliant concert!

I WAS THERE: SUNNY ZÖLDI RIEHL

I'm a huge Zep fan. I saw them three times, in '75 (on my fifteenth birthday) and twice in '77, all at the LA Forum. We saw lots and lots of great bands back then, including a new local band called Van Halen, but no other band ever came close to Zeppelin. I grew up in Los Angeles, a Mecca for classic rock. Zeppelin was our religion in Southern California in the seventies. I got a hold of a copy of *Led Zeppelin III* when I was eleven years old. It had been out for a while and I was hooked. It would be four years before I would be gifted with Zeppelin tickets. To this day I believe that my history can be very nearly traced by listening to all the albums from *Led Zep I* to *Presence*. Robert and Jimmy agreed that Los Angeles was their spiritual home. It's the reason they needed the Starship, so that they could come back 'home' each night to LA. As a native Los Angeleno, I truly felt that Zep was my hometown band. What a wonderful time and place to be young!

I WAS THERE: LARRY HARVICK

I became a fan when *Zeppelin II* was released. It's crazy but I hadn't heard any of the first album. Zeppelin was my second favourite band, just an inch behind The Jimi Hendrix Experience. That's the best one-two punch there is in rock 'n' roll! All that being said, I desperately wanted to see Led Zeppelin in concert, so in '75, when they were on the *Physical Graffiti* tour, I able to get two tickets for one of the shows at the Fabulous Forum in Inglewood, California. My best friend Daniel (who named his German Shepherd Zeppelin) and I went to the second show. By the time I saw Zeppelin I'd already gone to around 100 concerts and the Zeppelin concert was the best concert I'd ever seen. Zeppelin came out late but before they came out, the DJ from KAOS came out and said for everybody stay calm: 'Zeppelin's gonna come out here in a few more minutes, there's no opening band and it's gonna be a long show.' The crowd went crazy! The guys finally came out and played two straight hours and then took about a half hour break and came back out and played for what seemed like about two more hours. It was frickin' awesome. The fellas were on top of their game and everything about the band was amazing. It's still all these years later one of the most memorable concerts I can remember! They were the pinnacle of rock 'n' roll music and they still are in my book. It's the one concert that I brag about the most to my friends.

Led Zeppelin return to England for a series of shows at the then largest indoor arena in the UK, the Earls Court Exhibition Centre in London. Three shows are initially booked but tickets sell out in four hours and two more are added, with 85,000 tickets sold in total, **The Observer** ***newspaper noting that no group in history had ever attracted such an audience in Britain. Footage from parts of the shows appear on the Led Zeppelin*** **DVD** ***released in 2003.***

EARLS COURT EXHIBITION CENTRE
17 MAY 1975, LONDON, UK

I WAS THERE: JIM LONG

I queued all night after seeing Grand Funk Railroad. It was an amazing night, waiting for the ticket box office to open. They didn't disappoint either. It's still my best memory and the best concert ever.

I WAS THERE: PAUL HINDESS, AGE 18

I was married to Linda but she didn't come with me. Me and a few friends bought tickets for the first of three nights. But then they added two extra nights, which they put in front of ours. We'd all gone down on what was called the Zeppelin Express – the train. None of us had been to London before so we headed to Soho and one of these strip joints. It wasn't like strip tease today. A woman would come on stage and every so often she would take an item of clothing off. The place was full of drunken Scotsmen. It was Scotland vs England and I think it was the game where they pulled the goalposts down at Wembley.

The gig itself was magic. We had the same problem as we would have at home in Newcastle. We had to leave the gig before the encores started to catch our train because of the timing of the show. We actually leapt over the barriers at the station and didn't stop to show the man on the barrier our tickets. We ran down the platform, got on the train, made it just in time and – it didn't move! A few minutes later, more people came and got in our carriage. They had stayed until the end of the gig.

I WAS THERE: LESTER MCILWAINE

Several of us made the journey down to London from Manchester for this one. There were five concerts in all. We went to the first one, which was on a Saturday night. One of my room mates who lived in London had got us tickets. We had really good seats, only five or six rows from the front and right in the middle. Bob Harris introduced the band. It was a long set, around three hours. Predictably, they opened with 'Rock And Roll' which blew the roof off straight away. As the concert progressed, I felt that Plant's voice wasn't all it could have been in places and I think he missed a few notes along the way. I remember he made several remarks about the tea he was drinking throughout the show so maybe he was struggling a bit. Also, I thought that Page's guitar sound was lacking a bit of oomph at times (and I never had much time for his tricks with the violin bow). And I have to say I wasn't really impressed with John Bonham's protracted drum solo which, in places, included him playing with his hands instead of drumsticks. However, all in all, it was still a great show, closing with 'Stairway To Heaven' followed by an encore of 'Whole Lotta Love' and 'Black Dog'. On the length of the show alone, it was good value for money.

I WAS THERE: PERRY RIDLEY, AGE 16

I was more of a Pink Floyd and Rolling Stones fan. I only had one Zeppelin album, *Zeppelin IV*, which I played to death. My closest school chums were not into Zeppelin at all, and we used to swap albums around and tape them. As a result, I did not know a lot of the Zeppelin material, other than a few on *Zeppelin II*. My old friend at WEA Records, Jimmy Mulvoy, who had seen them at Alexandra Palace in December 1972, was a big fan and had inside information on when the tickets were going on sale. He was able to get hold of some for us. We thought that we would be right up close to the stage, but ended up one row from the back in the upper tier!

I went with a crowd who were a couple of years older than myself, but really into their music. When John Bonham did his drum solo in 'Moby Dick', it was extremely long. Being a guitarist I have never been a fan of drum solos, but hey – it was the 1970s! Every time he whacked the snare there was a serious delay between the sound and the images on the video screen, an innovation which could well have been the first time any band or artist had used one.

My overall feeling after the show was that I enjoyed it less than the Pink Floyd show I had seen at Earls Court in 1973. On reflection now I realise they were two totally different bands, with totally different stage shows. It's a shame that the gigs have never been released as I would love to hear them again.

Soon after Earls Court, I got a copy of *Physical Graffiti* and that really kicked off my love for Zeppelin. I purchased all the albums and still play their stuff today, but mainly on my iPod. I particularly enjoyed the sequence devoted to Earls Court on the brilliant Zeppelin *DVD* set released in 2003.

When Knebworth came around in August 1979, I was getting married later in the same month. My wife-to-be did not fancy standing in a field listening to a rock band with all those 'smelly long-haired people'. After she moaned all the way through Pink Floyd performing *The Wall* at Earls Court in 1981, the writing was literally on the wall for our relationship!

I met my girlfriend, Tracy Russell, in 1986 and fortunately she is a Zeppelin fanatic. We spend many a good night indoors listening to their tunes cranked up over several bottles of red wine.

When I mention to some of the younger fans of rock music where I work that I saw Led Zeppelin, the envy is obvious. I also watch Chelsea FC. After every game we have a beer in a pub just a few hundred yards from where Earls Court stood, with bits of Earls Court memorabilia on the walls. One of the most prominent is a poster of the Zeppelin gigs, 'The Zeppelin Express'. Ticket prices were from £1 to £2.50. What would tickets cost today?

I was one of the zillions who applied for tickets for the O2 reunion. Like many others I was unsuccessful in the ballot, but felt really pissed off when celebrity scroungers like Kate Moss and Naomi Campbell were there. Where they were at Earls Court in 1975?

I WAS THERE: JON BERRY

I discovered Led Zeppelin in 1971 when l was 13. I was listening to Slade and T. Rex but a work friend of my mum's (who I had a massive crush on) lent me a couple of albums, one being *Led Zeppelin II*. l took it home and put it on our brand-new Dynatron stereo radiogram, which I was very proud of as we were quite poor. What came out of the speakers was like a sonic boom. It just seemed to connect to everything I was thinking and feeling at the time. I can still recall the after effect of listening to it for the first time: raw, ground breaking and dangerous with a sexual innuendo and swagger. This was the point that I discovered 'proper' rock music.

When they announced the 1975 Earls Court shows, I had to get a ticket. I was at school in the sixth form in Leeds and a couple of my friends were also interested in going. The only outlet we could find with tickets left was in Birmingham. We bunked off school and jumped on a train to Birmingham. By the time we got to the shop it had closed so we wrote a note and left cash in an envelope, posted through their door!

Luckily, we ended up getting our tickets and made the trip down to London for the Sunday. On the morning of the trip, I felt ill but nothing was going to stop me getting on that train. We had no idea how to get to Earls Court so ended up walking all the way from Kings Cross. By this stage, I had a bright red rash all over my body and my buddies persuaded me to call in at a local hospital A&E where I was diagnosed with German measles. 'Oh well, could be worse', I thought and we continued on our fateful journey.

Nothing could really have prepared me for the size of venue and scale of the production I was about to witness. This was Zeppelin at their absolute max in terms of sound production and lighting. It was one of the first shows to use the back projection screens and lasers. I was in awe as we made our way to the front and I could see a huge pile of upturned chairs in front of the stage covered with a tarpaulin to deter any would-be stage incursion. This only served to underline the untouchable and godlike status of the band.

We took our seats and it seemed like an age before the lights dimmed and Alan 'Fluff'

Freeman came on stage with the words, 'Ladies and gentlemen, you and I are here because we have taste'. He introduced the band and the lights dimmed to the sound of Bonham's iconic intro to 'Rock And Roll'. From then on it was like I was in a trance; my heroes were not only living up to the hype but exceeding it with every song. 'Kashmir' was epic, 'Trampled Underfoot' mesmeric, 'Dazed And Confused' and 'No Quarter' spine-chilling in their eeriness. I didn't realise it at the time but my mind was truly being bent. It all seemed to be over far too quickly as we were left with the glittering finale that was 'Stairway' with the huge ballroom mirror, the cascading light reflections hypnotising us into submission.

How we got home I will never know. As the adrenaline wore off, I was aware of how weak I was feeling and had to endure a return train journey standing up for most of the way. Looking back, I wouldn't have missed it for the world. I was lucky enough to see Zeppelin twice more, at Knebworth in 1979 and at the Ahmet Ertegün tribute in 2007, which moved me to tears. The Knebworth shows were good but in retrospect they were past their best. However, Led Zeppelin at their worst was still head and shoulders above any other band I have seen since, and I feel truly privileged to have witnessed them in all their glory.

I WAS THERE: DEREK COLLISON, AGE 14

I used to listen to my dad's type of music – Buddy Holly, Elvis, Bill Haley, etc. – as he was a Teddy Boy when he was younger. My best friend at the time, Nicky Roberts, had got two tickets to see Zeppelin for his birthday in December 1974 but only asked me a few weeks before if I wanted to go. I hadn't heard of them before but wanted to see what a rock concert was like for an eleven-year-old boy. I liked most of the music Nicky listened to at that time and I wasn't disappointed.

The first thing I recall was all the long-haired guys in denim everywhere and the sweet smell of what I now realise was marijuana. Once inside the arena, I saw that the stage had a huge TV screen above it. Being in the gallery was a godsend as we were able to see a lot more of the action than we would have from our seats.

The concert was amazing. The half time entertainment consisted of people folding the flyers that had been placed on the seats into paper planes and seeing how close to the stage they could get with the rest of the audience applauding their efforts. The planes continued throughout the rest of the show, but people were more interested in the band once they came back on. Shortly after there were hundreds of glow sticks, glow bracelets and lighters being held in the air. Now all you see is mobile phone lights being waved around.

That concert changed my main taste in music for ever. I went straight out the next day and bought *Physical Graffiti*. It is still one of my all-time top three albums and I still play it regularly.

I WAS THERE: JIM JOHNSON

I went to both the Saturday concerts at Earls Court. I was not a Zep fan as such but, wow, this changed my mind. On the first Saturday I went on the train with a load of my mates. It was about 100 miles away. I had a great day going on the train. I remember the headline in *The Sun* newspaper was about the Bay City Rollers, the 'number one band in the UK', having sold out two nights at the Rainbow Theatre. It held about 3,000. There was no mention of Zep playing to 17,500 people each night for five nights.

The following Saturday, I went down in a car and got there mid-morning. England were playing Scotland at Wembley and there were drunken Scotsmen everywhere. I believe two got killed that weekend – one falling off a lamppost and the other falling in front of a Tube train.

My mate went on to the game. Me and my then girlfriend went and did the shops and had a drink in the Chelsea Drug Store in the Kings Road before going on to Earls Court, where there were more drunken Scots. Inside the gig, a Scot and his girlfriend were behind us. She was well sitting over him and you could tell that it was full blown sex – she had a short skirt and all that.

When we came out, more drunken Scots started to rock our car and were banging on the roof. As luck would have it, the mate who had been to the game had given a couple of Scots a lift back as the Underground was on shut down and they had given him a Scotland rosette. He lifted the rosette out of the window, a big cheer went up amongst the football fans and they let us by.

I WAS THERE: JOHN GRIFFITHS

Not so long ago, I was wandering around Camden Market and found a vinyl record store. I haven't owned vinyl for years but I just stopped out of curiosity and fingered through the racks. I pulled back the first album, which was something from Frank Zappa, and there it was, *Houses Of The Holy*, the first Zep album I ever owned. Indeed, it was the first album of any description I had ever owned. It's a cliche to say that it sent a shiver down my spine but it did, as I was transported back 43 years. I could still recite the track list by heart.

I wasn't a rock music fan through my early and mid-teens. I had loads of singles, played on our family Dansette style record player, but they were mostly pop chart singles. There were some pretty cool ones though, Atomic Rooster with 'Devil's Answer' and Free's 'Alright Now'. I had the CCS version of 'Whole Lotta Love', famous as the *Top Of The Pops* theme tune, but otherwise only had a passing relationship with Zep. Most of my friends were into the same kind of thing and that didn't change until I got into the sixth form.

Our school had a sixth form common room with a record player much like my home one. Snobbery ruled and the stars who controlled the record player wouldn't entertain my pop singles. It was albums, and only albums, that got spin time. One day I walked in to hear the most amazing riff playing. 'What's that?' I asked the only two other guys in the room 'Led Zeppelin. *Houses Of The Holy*. 'The Ocean'. Dave's selling it,' said one guy, nodding to the other. I knew Dave pretty well since we were in the Air Cadets together. The deal was quickly done for the princely sum of £1, which was still a note in those days. I didn't have it on me but, as he knew me, Dave was happy to wait a couple of days for his money.

That night I took it home and played it for the first time. Then the second time, then the third and so on, with the volume gradually reaching full until my mum shouted up the stairs, 'If you don't turn it down, I'll come up there and break it!' It was mid spring and the sun was shining. To this day I still play 'Dancing Days' on the first sunny day after my birthday in March.

I didn't buy another Zep album for a long time after. Well, it was probably only six months, but that's a lifetime to a teenager. It was almost as if I didn't want to break the spell and end up being disappointed by anything else from the catalogue. I played *Houses Of The Holy* pretty much every day and it wasn't until my parents bought me a Phillips cassette recorder – one of the ones that looked like Spock's Tricorder in *Star Trek* – that I took a gamble and borrowed *Led Zep II* to rip off. It was so different, but so good, and again I played it every day for months. *IV* followed and then being a teenager, I didn't bother with *I* and *III* because the sixth form aficionados said they weren't a patch on *II* and *IV*. I properly had to defend my love of *Houses Of The Holy* and didn't want to be an outcast by owning two or three unfashionable albums.

My sister started going out with another friend from the Air Cadets who, as well as eventually turning out to be her husband, turned out to be an electronics wizard. He built her a full hi-fi from cannibalised parts with a stereo headphone socket. Not only could I now listen to records in stereo but I could listen to them as loud as I liked. He also left copies of *The Yes Album* and Deep Purple's *Made In Japan*. I was absolutely riveted by these two albums and for a while Led Zep took a back seat.

Which was a shame, because I managed to get a ticket for the legendary May '75 Earls Court concert from my mate Marv. Sadly, from Little Nicky Horne's intro to the second encore, I was sat there wishing I was listening to Deep Purple.

I WAS THERE: NICK PARRY

I was 14 years old in 1969 and my musical tastes were beginning to form. At school, you were either a soul fan/skinhead or rock/greaser and I fell into the latter camp. Jimi Hendrix was the main man and I had many a night with Jimi on the record player. Teenage parties were regular events and most we went to had the girls selecting the music, which was mainly Motown, so my mates and me were left out until one night one of the girls brought an album of her brother's, *Led Zeppelin II*. That night is etched on my mind as a new awakening. The music on that LP was what I had been wanting to hear all my life: soaring guitar work, amazing vocals, the loudest and most intricate drum playing I had ever heard and a bass line to die for. In essence, the complete group.

After playing the entire album (much to the disgust of the soulies) I was hooked. I saved the money for the LP out of my paper round and got the LP as soon as I could, closely followed by *Led Zeppelin I*. How could I have missed this masterpiece? Although we were well under age, we could get away with frequenting pubs in Stourbridge in the West Midlands and always looked for places to go that had juke boxes with our music on them. It wasn't always Led Zeppelin, but the rock side of things like Deep Purple. One night in the Seven Stars, we were talking to the landlord about music and asked why there was no Led Zeppelin on the jukebox. 'It's not down to me, it's down to the owners of the jukebox,' he said. Okay, we said, but then he went on to say that the lead singer of Led Zeppelin was from around this area and used to play at the Seven Stars. In fact, he thought the gig there was his first ever. This made the band even greater in our eyes. Not only were they an incredible band but one of them was a local guy. Robert Plant became a hero along with the others, but Planty was a Black Countryman so that made him special.

Led Zeppelin got me through some hard times, helping me to study and get good exam results. My love for them had stood firm and subsequent albums were purchased. Planty was always my favourite but this increased when I found out he supported the same football team as me – the mighty Wolverhampton Wanderers. Now somebody who can sing like that *and* he's a Wolves fan? Well, it doesn't get much better than that.

The next thing was to see them live, as I had started going to gigs in the area. There were plenty of venues so you could go to a gig sometimes two or three times a week. When I saw Zeppelin were playing Earls Court in May 1975, I just had to get a ticket. I sent off for my ticket, postal order and SAE enclosed. When the SAE arrived, I was so excited. Finally, I would get my chance to see the greatest band in the world live, after reading so many good reports of their gigs. I was shaking when I opened the envelope, but inside was my postal order. My application hadn't been successful. I could have cried. It was a crushing blow that upset me for a week or so.

I was in conversation with my cousin who lived in the Lake District about missing out and what he said was the most wonderful statement I had ever heard. 'I have a spare one if you want it.' Of course, I said yes and sent him the £2.50 the seat cost and he sent it me recorded delivery. I was going to see my heroes on stage…

I WAS THERE: MICHAEL BARBER, AGE 17

I went with mates from school. We sent off for tickets by post including a postal order and stamp addressed envelope. It was an exciting morning when you saw the returned envelope with your own writing, not knowing if it was tickets or a returned postal order. It was the first really big gig I had been to and Earls Court seemed huge. The things I most remember are the huge blast of 'Rock And Roll' to start, the acoustic part when they sat on stools – 'Going To California' remains a particular favourite – and Jimmy Page's bow on 'Dazed And Confused'. Do I remember lasers from behind him? I also remember John Bonham's drum solo and bursting for the bathroom towards the end but not going as I did not want to miss anything! The next day I went on a geography field trip with school for a few days and had big kudos for having been down to London from Bedford.

I WAS THERE: STEVE YOUNG, AGE 15

My sister had the second album and once I'd played it a few times I was totally bewitched by them and bought the first album soon after. I saw them at Earls Court and Knebworth, which was not as enjoyable as Earls Court, but you did what you had to do to see them. Being a bit impressionable at such a young age, I honestly almost worshipped them at the time. A friend of mine who worked for the Post Office was sent to Monmouth because of a staff shortage. Who should walk in but Robert Plant who I believe had a farm thereabouts at the time. My friend was totally gobsmacked, as was my sister, who has lived in Australia for 35 years, when I told her I saw Robert Plant and his band Priory of Brian at our local, small theatre in my hometown of Ebbw Vale.

It is so much easier nowadays to watch your heroes on various devices. Back then Zep didn't do TV or radio much and that added to the mysticism. I went 200 miles to London on the back of a motorbike just to see the film *The Song Remains The Same*. I must have been mad.

I WAS THERE: NORMAN WILSON

Of all of the guys with whom I attended the show in Sheffield in 1973, only my mate Howard was interested in travelling down to London for these gigs. I applied by post for the first of the original three shows announced and was fortunate to secure two tickets. We arrived in London and first headed to Leicester Square to see Ken Russell's film version of The Who's *Tommy*, which wasn't on national release at that time. The Who and Led Zeppelin were our favourite two bands so this was a nice double header. After the movie, we headed to Trafalgar Square where thousands of Scottish football fans had taken residence in advance of the England vs Scotland game at Wembley the next day.

When we arrived at Earls Court, we were amazed at the huge size of the venue and then further amazed at how far from the stage our seats were, just a few rows from the very back of the arena on the upper tier. We had both smuggled recording equipment into the venue and set our kit up in readiness for the show.

Thankfully, as the band entered the stage a huge video screen behind the band exploded into colour, and the close-up images and the first chords confirmed that the sound was going to be loud and clear. They played forever, ensuring we were never going to make the last train back north. They had a lot to play given that *Physical Graffiti* had been released earlier in the year. The set was almost four hours long and we each burned through tape after tape recording it all. Highlights for me were 'No Quarter' – Page's solo after the John Paul Jones keyboard interlude was sensational – and 'Trampled Underfoot', where all three musicians excelled. It was great to see such a complete show including a lengthy acoustic set and so many of their greatest songs. Despite the distance from the stage, we thoroughly enjoyed the band's performance.

We were able to get back to St Pancras train station to wait for the first train to Sheffield the next morning and we had our recordings to amuse us for the four hours or so we had to kill!

I WAS THERE: PETER SMITH

Led Zeppelin were initially booked to play for three nights on May 23rd, 24th and 25th at the massive Earls Court Arena in London, which had a capacity of 17,000. The venue had been used for concerts before, notably one by David Bowie, at which the sound was reportedly atrocious. Due to what Mel Bush described as 'unprecedented demand in the history of rock music', two further dates were added on May 17th and 18th. The total attendance for the five sold out shows was 85,000. Bush negotiated with British Rail to advertise the ease with which Inter City trains could bring fans in. 'The Zeppelin Express Physical Rocket' was how it was dubbed, and the posters for the event featured a picture of Zeppelin riding the express. There was no support act for the shows, and Zeppelin played a long set, around three hours, each night.

This was my first chance to see Zeppelin after an almost three year gap since I last saw them at Newcastle City Hall in 1972. I went with my friend John and a couple more mates. Tickets went on sale for personal applicants only at various points across the country. John and I queued all night at Virgin Records in Newcastle. We arrived late, just before the pubs closed, and the queue grew massively overnight. I took my car and parked it beside the queue, hoping to catch some sleep. Some of the guys in the queue took a dislike to this idea and threatened to turn my car over, so I quickly moved it, parked it a few streets away and rejoined the queue. When the box office opened, we were quite disappointed to find that all they had on sale were tickets with pretty poor views, up the back of the arena. This was often the case in those days, with the best seats being sold at the venue itself, in London.

When we arrived at Earls Court, we found that out seats did indeed have an obstructed view. We were sitting behind a wide pillar and literally could not see anything. However, we were able to sit on the stairs between the rows of seats for the whole show, which gave us a great view. This was one of the first shows to use video screens at either side of the stage which was very cool for the time, and the first time we had seen colour video screens. Before that, all the other screens were black and white, usually at outdoor festivals and using a projector. The screens were pretty low tech compared to today, but at the time they were streets ahead of anything seen before at a rock concert. The sound wasn't great, but was okay with a massive PA system, particularly given the size of the venue.

The compere for Saturday the 24th was Capital Radio DJ Nicky Horne, who opened the proceedings with something like 'welcome to Earls Court. For the next three hours… your mother wouldn't like it.' The Saturday night that we attended is often rated as the best night of the five shows, despite a couple of minor glitches such as Page's guitar cutting out during 'In My Time Of Dying'. 'Kashmir' was a particular highlight and Plant joked, 'If you go along the A449, past Droitwich, take the third turn on the right, Kashmir is just up there – it's got a white fence around it.'

'Tangerine' was dedicated to 'families and friends who have been close to us through a lot. It's a song of love in its most innocent stages.' 'Trampled Underfoot' was simply breathtaking and included Robert unaccompanied leading into 'Rip It Up' by Little Richard for a few bars. The entire set was great with 'In My Time Of Dying', 'Trampled Underfoot', the acoustic set and 'Stairway' being the highlights. 'Sick Again' was a surprising choice. I am not a big drum solo fan and 'Whole Lotta Love' was sounding a bit overplayed, but these were minor quibbles over what was a fantastic experience.

We all then went straight back home after the show on the midnight train. It was the day of the Scotland vs England match at Wembley and the train home was completely packed, full of very drunk (and disappointed) Scots fans (England had won 5-1), travelling home after the match. We couldn't get a seat and spent most of the night trying to sleep on the (cold metal) floor of the guard's van, which was pretty uncomfortable!

Like a lot of things, at the time it felt a bit special, but I now realise what a historic event it was. Sometimes the sun, moon and stars are aligned, I feel very fortunate to have been present.

I WAS THERE: BILL LOVETT

I was at Earls Court for four nights out of the five and had front row seats for two of them. They were fabulously fabulous, and the best band I ever saw by some distance. I saw them first at Alexandra Palace at Christmas 1972 and was so blown away that I went the next night. We didn't have tickets but got in. Then we travelled to Oxford later in January 1973. Again, we didn't have tickets but got in somehow. The New Theatre was a small venue and they were just a few feet away. It was absolutely stunning!

It was a long wait until the Earls Court gigs and we queued all night for tickets. Zeppelin were absolutely brilliant. Eight of us went up to Earls Court in a Transit van. Two of our party weren't Zep fans but they said they had never been so entertained and had never seen a band like them. These were definitely the best concerts I ever went to. The acoustic set was brilliant and 'Trampled Underfoot', 'In My Time Of Dying', 'Kashmir', 'No Quarter' and 'Dazed And Confused' were all absolutely outstanding. It all was – 'Whole Lotta Love', the theremin section, all of it. It's probably the best heavy rock experience of my life!

I WAS THERE: CARLY HORGAN

My dad worked with them a lot for his company Artist Services. He was in Oakland for their last US gig when tragically Robert's son suddenly passed. My dad was with Robert at England 5 v Scotland 1 at Wembley before getting him back to Blake's Hotel for one of the 1975 Earls Court gigs. I was lucky enough to see them at Earls Court in 1975 and at both Knebworth shows in 1979, which again my dad did security for. He was pals with them all. I also saw them at the O2 reunion gig. My dad is still alive but very unwell. He's well known in 'the game' and, as well as Zeppelin, worked with loads back in the day.

I WAS THERE: PAK JOHN

I missed out on tickets for the three concerts that were announced at Earls Court in 1975 but then two more nights were added and we scored. It was a fantastic concert. They used lasers and a big screen for the first time. I bought the big poster that was on sale and I still have it now, in my room in faraway New Zealand. I remember Jimmy used a violin bow and at one stage he, Planty and JPJ left the stage and Bonzo launched into about a 20-minute solo. It's the concert highlight of my life.

I WAS THERE: JOHN STARKEY

They announced three shows and they added another two later. As soon as the first shows were announced, me and two friends decided we'd sleep outside the venue the night before the box office opened. There weren't postal sales so it was turn up or lose out. I'm pretty sure tickets were limited to two per person. I'd seen them before in '73 and remember turning up to get tickets and the queue was all the way around the theatre! Anyway, there were loads of us sleeping on the street, plenty of canned beers and the odd spliff and a pretty good atmosphere. I'm pretty sure too that tickets were capped at £2.50; in 1973 they'd been £1.

We got tickets dead centre, three rows back from the stage on the final night. We figured they'd be pulling all the stops out by then. I remember bumping into Alan Freeman in the gents and having a brief chat. The next time I saw him he was introducing the band! My recollection is that it was a great show. It was the first time I saw lasers and the big back projecting screens.

Watching the bootleg films of the night you can hear how the touring had affected Robert's voice, but they really knew how to put on a show!

I WAS THERE: CHRIS GAYWOOD

As a young lad Led Zep were always my favourite band. I remember sneaking out at school lunchtimes to go round friends' houses to listen to just-released Zep albums where we'd all huddle around old record players. When Zep announced that they were going to play five nights at Earls Court, I just had to get a ticket. I can't remember how it was communicated – maybe in the music paper *Sounds* – but when we found out when the tickets were to go on sale we had to go to Earls Court. Myself and a friend got the first train and Tube to Earls Court. Immediately, we saw that people had been queuing all night and that the queue, which was three to four people wide, went the length of Earls Court.

Very quickly more and more people joined the queue. There were metal crash barriers and as soon as people from the back of the queue moved forward, the width of the queue got wider, with everyone crammed in and squeezed against the barriers. I have never been in such a solid mass of people before, or since. It was pretty unpleasant.

Some idiots decided to start swaying, which had the effect of causing this to spread out as we were so packed together. All this was happening before the ticket office was open, which was due to be 9am. I was only about 30 or 40 yards from the box office. There was only one person selling tickets and it took ages for each person to get served. Suddenly, my friend who was smaller than me 'disappeared', and at this point I decided to leave. I had been in the queue for five hours and was still about 20 or so yards from the box office. I managed to get out and after a while found my friend. He had been pushed and shoved between people's legs. Luckily, he was okay but we went home ticketless, knackered and disappointed. A few days later it was reported that all Zep tickets had been sold out.

Then we heard from another friend's parent that a tiny box office on one of the London bridges was selling Zep tickets. Apparently, there was a small advert amongst the adverts for theatre tickets! At the first opportunity we shot up there. It was correct: it was a tiny advert in the window. We went in, asked the bloke behind the counter if he still had tickets, to which he replied, 'I got loads – what night do you want to go?' We opted for the last night. Mission complete.

Finally, the day of the gig arrived. By that time, we knew the set list. We had seats about two thirds of the way back from the stage. After an age the lights went down and Alan 'Fluff' Freeman introduced them. Pretty much after that it was all a blur. I was totally lost in the music. Three hours quickly came and went and it seemed it was all over. We went to the loo before leaving and then heard sounds from the PA in the arena. We ran back in right up the front. Zep had come back on stage. Unlike the previous evenings, they had decided to do some extra encores. I was shouting at the top of my voice 'Communication Breakdown'! Robert Plant turned to Page and I am pretty sure he said something like 'shall we play it?' and they roared into 'Communication Breakdown'. What a great end to the night.

The gig in total lasted three hours and 45 minutes. What a night. My dad was due to pick us up. We found him, strangely inside the doors. As everyone was coming out, he just walked in, heard sound inside the arena and saw the final encores. He thought they were 'alright'!

This still rates as one of my best gigs, up there with Van Halen at Finsbury Park. I have a vinyl bootleg which I purchased shortly after the gig called *No Quarter* on the Red Devil label. It is the acoustic set part of the gig. Years later, I got a copy of the *Conquistador* bootleg. This is an excellent soundboard recording of that night. It captures the ambience of the Earls Court sound and echo, and I still get shivers down my spine when I put it through my Roksan amplifier and turn it up to stadium levels.

I WAS THERE: STEVE COBB

I discovered them via *Led Zep III* round a mate's house when I was 14 or 15 years old. 'Twas a new sound back then. They announced a week of shows at Earls Court and tickets were obtained. We went to the gig – my second – so it was huge event for us. The gig was played and we thought it was the bee's knees. Zep did the unheard of, an encore of 'Communication Breakdown' after most of the audience had left. I guess there was a thousand or so of the audience left. Plant explained that the band had made a loss on the gigs and couldn't afford to get their plane off the ground and passed a white top hat round to collect for fuel. I suspect that was a con!

We all got home to Kent in time to wash, get bollocked by our parents and get to school. I still have my ticket in my ticket books, and one of our number was Martin Everest. Who was Martin Everest? Well, he became Max Splodge and wrote 'Two Pints Of Lager And A Packet Of Crisps Please'.

Wind on 30 years or so and a friend of mine who worked in Beano's, a huge secondhand record shop in Croydon, and who was magically able to get bootlegs, met me for a pint one lunchtime and presented me with *Conquistador*, the multi-CD bootleg of the very night I was at Earls Court. When I listened to it, it rather burst the bubble as the reality was far less impressive than the memory. Hey-ho.

I WAS THERE: FRANKIE PAUL

I went to four of the five nights at Earls Court. I can remember queueing at the box office at the crack of dawn to buy the tickets. As soon as I purchased one set of tickets, I moved along to the next queue and purchased another set. That's how I managed to get tickets for the Friday, Saturday and Sunday shows. I remember it well because I had my car towed away whilst I was queueing. It cost me more to get the car back than the tickets cost.

The Friday show was brilliant. *My* band on stage for three hours. I'll never forget the buzz of that night. The Saturday show coincided with an England v Scotland football match. Some people had their tickets stolen off them. The band once again were superb, but unfortunately the atmosphere wasn't. The Sunday show always stood out for me. Every song seemed to mean something to me, I guess because I loved the music but there was also another reason that I would never work out. Bonham's drum solo was epic that night.

God, I loved the band. They were special. As always will be. Four musicians who touched my soul.

I WAS THERE: RONNIE HUNTER, AGE 19

I was lucky enough to see Zeppelin three times, first at Earls Court and twice at Knebworth. Me and my friend had gone to the Apollo in Glasgow to get tickets for Status Quo and noticed that Zeppelin had added another date at Earls Court in London so we bought two tickets for £2.50 each. That was the best move ever, and they were without a doubt the best band ever.

I WAS THERE: BILL SPEEDY

A gang of us went from Liverpool to Earls Court on a flat backed lorry. I sat in an armchair all the way. It was a great night and two of us decided to stay for another night. The rest went home but we met some Aussie girls and stayed in a squat and then went home two days later on the mail train as we had run out of money. Try doing that now…

I WAS THERE: PAUL BAKEWELL

I first recall seeing Zep at Wembley for 75p in November '71 supported by the superb Stone the Crows. Then I saw them at Earls Court in May '75. This was yet another fine concert, albeit tinged with bad memories of enduring a numb bum on hard plastic seat for three-plus hours and then a communication breakdown (!) afterwards when I was supposed to meet up with a pal and drive up to Scotland through the night. It was not a good plan after a day's work and a long concert. I failed dismally and, although dog tired, I couldn't get to sleep in a lay-by in North London.

I WAS THERE: DYLAN WHITE

I started the year seeing Slade and Wizzard but ended the year seeing The Who and Pink Floyd. By 1975, I wasn't going to see Slade any more. Me and my mates now had long hair and flares, and we weren't reading *Record Mirror*. We were reading the *NME* or *Sounds* or *Melody Maker*. I bought *Houses Of The Holy* and *Physical Graffiti* when they came out. But I had to find *Led Zeppelin I, II, III* and *IV*, and so every Saturday was spent in shops that either sold new records or secondhand ones. It became a Saturday ritual.

Led Zeppelin playing five nights at Earls Court was a big thing. They hadn't played in the UK for years. I went twice with mates – I don't know why! I must have queued up for tickets although I don't remember doing so, and I bought tickets for May 17th and 24th. We were all there in a mass of people in denim and long hair. I was in the gallery for one show and the third tier for the other. There were photographs of the shows in the music press the following week and they became posters and I had a big poster on my bedroom wall from one of the gigs. Zep were the heavyweights of rock 'n' roll, no question.

I WAS THERE: STUART WHITEHEAD

Can a concert be life changing? Sitting on a wall outside the Warwick Road hostel opposite Earls Court in mid-May 1975, having left most of my belongings in my £1-a-night room, I was fiddling with my new camera that I had purchased a couple of weeks before. I noticed a young lady on the opposite side of the road with a long hippy dress, embroidered waist coat, beads and about twenty wrist bangles. This was the standard dress code for lady Zeppelin fans in '75. The other thing that caught my attention was the cardboard poster from a news stand that she was carrying, the kind of 'read all about it' declaration that these days would be reserved to announce yet another scandal on the A-boards outside of any given newspaper stand or shop.

This one was different, as underneath the blue masthead of The Observer it said in huge bold red letters 'LED ZEPPELIN - BIGGER THAN THE BEATLES?' God how I wanted that poster! We exchanged glances, I asked her about the poster, and she asked why I had a camera bag. I told her that I had front row seats for Zeppelin and I wanted to get some close photos. She shyly asked if there was any way that she could have a photo or two if they turned out okay. I scribbled down her name, Susan Palmer, and her Derby address and I gave her my Spalding phone number.

Well, the shows were phenomenal and are more than adequately documented so I won't go down that route, other than to add that I had managed to get great seats for all five nights, including three nights in block AA row A. I could have probably had seat 01, but I figured that seat 01 would be on one side of the stage so I went for somewhere around seat 20-something, assuming that number would be somewhere near the middle of the row, but I wasn't really sure. Bingo! I could hardly believe my own judgement, I was smack-bang in the middle, front row.

Fast forward to the summer of '75. I had been playing *Physical Graffiti* virtually non-stop since February, interspersed with bootlegs from US dates, when I had a phone call. 'Hello, it's Sue from Derby. How did the photos turn out from Earls Court?' Embarrassed, I apologised for not having got in touch and promptly sent her some prints from the show. She rang again a couple of days later telling me how she had been showing her friends her new 'real' photos of Led Zeppelin.

Sue was in Derby and I was in the market town of Spalding, known for its flatness and lack of any landscape. To the sign that greeted you as you entered Spalding, someone had added the words 'twinned with the moon. No atmosphere'. That about sums the place up really, unless you happen to like tulips and flat fields. So it was that I arranged to meet Sue at Leicester train station, only a stone's throw from where I had seen Zeppelin at Leicester University on a cold November night in 1971.

Was it fate that I met Sue at Earls Court? Well, I carried on fiddling with cameras and became a photographer, and I got myself a lovely wife, so the answer to my opening question, 'can a concert be life changing?', is most definitely yes! Oh, and I got to share that *Observer* poster that Sue later told me she had bought from a newspaper vendor for 10p, so I guess I still owe her 5p.

Presence, *Led Zeppelin's seventh studio album, is released on 3 March 1976. It's the first time Zeppelin release an album and don't tour to promote it.*

CINEMA 1
20 OCTOBER 1976, NEW YORK, NEW YORK

Capturing the band on stage in July 1973 at New York's Madison Square Garden,* The Song Remains The Same *grosses an estimated $10 million but is panned by the critics. Atlantic boss Ahmet Ertegün reportedly falls asleep at a midnight screening, and Zep manager Peter Grant calls it 'the most expensive home movie ever made'.

I WAS THERE: KRISTINE NICHOLSON

I was a music writer in NYC and I met Robert Plant shortly after he did that Coca-Cola commercial and I gave him shit for it. But I guess the song 'Cool Tall One' was perfect for that.

The very first time I saw Led Zeppelin was in 1973. I'd seen plenty of rock bands by this time, because I'd started going to concerts when I was 13 and I was 21 or 22 by now. I'd go to concerts in my town or near where I lived in Pennsylvania. But my mom wasn't letting me get into a van with some boys to go all the way to upstate New York, so I missed out on Woodstock.

It was sold out. We travelled about 350 miles to go there but it was worth it. While it was taking place, I felt like I was in some other world. It was about a month before I was going to move to New York City to study journalism at NYU. I was never the same again. I'd written some concert reviews for the *Allentown Chronicle* but seeing Led Zeppelin reinforced my determination to become a published writer. I immediately connected with the NYU radio station. I would do interviews for the radio station and I had a radio programme there.

It was a couple of years before I went to see Zeppelin again. I saw them in '75 at Madison Square Garden and got tickets for every night bar one. I had a way of calling up the record company and saying 'I'm going to report on this for my radio station' and they'd give me tickets. I was never more than ten rows from the front. I don't know how my ears survived it.

The very first time I interviewed Robert Plant I was with a friend who was a writer. She was married to a rock star but she was also a groupie. We were sitting in the office at Atlantic Records and Robert was promoting the single 'Big Log'. She said to him 'what's a big log?' And Robert said, 'Why don't you reach under the desk and find out?' And she reached under the desk so fast that she nearly broke her hand. I slid down in my chair, covering my eyes in embarrassment. He just sat there and laughed!

My writer friend called me up at two in the morning and wanted me to come out with her because Led Zeppelin were hanging out at a club up town called Tracks. It was Robert hanging out in a club, having a drink and saying hello to everybody. He was always very gregarious.

When they debuted *The Song Remains The Same* movie in New York, it was a big thing. The whole band went to the theatre. It was mostly music writers and critics that were invited, and they had a big party in a really fancy room at a glorious old hotel with gold leaf everywhere. Everybody in the world was at the party – Carly Simon, Mick Jagger, a lot of famous people – and I was there with one of my editors. I hadn't interviewed Robert at this point.

I had really long strawberry blond hair down to my waist and I was dressed all in white. My editor said, 'You look like the character in the film who goes off on horseback with Robert.' Then he looked behind me and said, 'And I think somebody agrees with me.' I said, 'What are you talking about?' He stepped away and Robert Plant walked across the room. He walked right up to me and said 'hello'. I just froze. I was really in awe of him. I was just like, 'Ah, hello.' He said something like 'having a nice time?', realised I couldn't function – that I wasn't a professional groupie – and walked away. It was so embarrassing.

I ran off and cried, and all my friends were like 'what happened? What happened?'. I said, 'I blew it!' They all just rolled their eyes.

The band's 1977 North American tour is their eleventh and proves to be their final tour of that continent. Originally scheduled to commence in February 1977, it is pushed back to April when Plant is struck down by laryngitis. The band's equipment had already been shipped overseas, complicating any efforts to rehearse.

Jimmy Page: All the equipment was shipped over there five days before we were due to go. I didn't play guitar for a month. I was terrified at the prospect of the first few shows.

MEMORIAL AUDITORIUM
1 APRIL 1977, DALLAS, TEXAS

I WAS THERE: GREG DANIEL, AGE 15

It was the realisation of a dream for me as a teenager, and not long after the release of *The Song Remains The Same*, which was incredible. The band was at its peak. *Physical Graffiti* had been out maybe two years. It's funny to look back and see how special it was, how short it lasted and how it burned so bright. I saw Plant and Page in the nineties, also in Dallas and which was also fantastic. But it was not the same.

CHICAGO STADIUM
6, 7, 9 & 10 APRIL 1977, CHICAGO, ILLINOIS

I WAS THERE: JIM MESSINA, AGE 13

We got into every major concert during the seventies for free. My good friend, Uncle, was a Chicago policeman but also a Chicago mafia member. The last row on the main floor was always not sold and was used for free people. The towers of speakers stood out and the way Jimmy Page danced with his guitar amazed me. All of my old friends, many of whom I still see, lived in Little Italy in Chicago which was not far from the stadium. We could have walked but the stadium was in a black area and back then there was a lot of racial tension. But we did walk home. Sometimes there were 20 of us. I was at the last concert they played in Chicago. They walked off stage in the middle of the concert. I thought it was because they were throwing a lot of fluorescent things at the stage but next day in the newspaper they said someone got sick. Years later I heard someone had a bad heroin reaction. I didn't like hearing that. Plant always thanked the places they played. When he said 'thank you Chicago' the place just erupted!

I WAS THERE: KATHY COHEN

I waited on Foster Avenue in Chicago, outside of Flipside Records and Tapes, for tickets to see Led Zeppelin. My boyfriend, Eric, and I lined up at dusk the day before they went on sale and waited all night for the store to open. Now, if my kids wanted to wait outside of a record store overnight at the age of twelve, the answer would be a resounding 'no', but it was the seventies and a different time, different place. We were the ninth or tenth group of people waiting but, by the time the store opened and it was our turn to get tickets, all that was left were 'nosebleed' seats. We were literally in the last row of the top section in the Chicago Stadium. If you were behind us, you were standing up against a wall.

My 'boyfriend's' mom took us and although we had purchased four tickets, we only used three. I distinctly remember 'Nobody's Fault But Mine', and how the standard pause in the chorus seemed extremely long. I remember the band sitting on stools and playing 'Bron-Y-Aur Stomp' and I remember Robert Plant tossing the stool playfully at Jimmy Page's legs when the acoustic set was complete. And I remember that it was very loud, and that the slightly sweet smell of herb surrounded us. Again, it was the seventies. And I knew every word to every song.

My love of Led Zeppelin started out as a crush on Robert Plant which continues to this day. It's my longest relationship. And, as I get older, my love of the music continues to grow and has never stopped. Robert lost his son just a couple of months after I saw them. And that was sad. 25 years later, I lost my youngest daughter, and the words to 'All Of My Love' and the more recent 'When The World Was Young' took on a completely different meaning, and my love of their music took on a different aspect, and grew yet again.

I saw Page and Plant in 1998 during the *Walking Into Clarksdale* tour. It was wonderful! So many emotions flowed that night; my love for them is personal on many levels, and public on many more. As I sang along with 'Most High', I was in music heaven!

I saw Robert Plant in 2010 and although I'm not as well-versed in his newer music (although I love *Carry Fire*), it was magical and delightful. After all, I was seeing my guy, who I first fell in love with at the young age of twelve, and hearing that voice which sang to me during the fun times, the poignant times, the deeply sad times and the growing older times. It was an emotional reunion for me.

Nothing stirs my soul and literally makes the hair on my arms stand up like the opening drums of 'Rock And Roll' and the opening concert shot from behind in the movie, *The Song Remains The Same*. My kids have instructions to play and sing 'Kashmir' at my funeral, if they're able. They know it – I'm just not sure they'll be able to pull it off at such a time.

I dragged a friend to the Lincoln Village theatre to see *The Song Remains The Same* nine times. And we're still friends! No band has touched me like Led Zeppelin and I don't expect one to ever come close. Their music has mimicked my life frequently; the soundtrack to my experiences and my soul. Thanks for allowing this old lady to reminisce. For just a few minutes, dancing days were here again.

I WAS THERE: MICHELLE MURPHY, AGE 16

We brought binoculars and passed – or wrestled – them back and forth the whole time. The binoculars worked so well you could see that Jimmy Page was drinking bottles of Heineken. I was 16 and in love with Robert Plant. The show was phenomenal.

I WAS THERE: MARC PASSERO, AGE 16

I had just graduated from junior high school and my parents gave me a pair of tickets for a present. It was my first live show. What an intro! I took my friend Dan, we got dropped off and all I can say is… wow! It was also the first time we had ever smoked marijuana. The guy next to us at the show told us, 'Hey kids, this will make the show better' and handed me a joint. Ha – he was right. I can still hear and see Jimmy on stage playing, and what can I say about Bonham? Damn, the dude could play.

I WAS THERE: PETER RUDOFSKY

I felt they had lost their raw edge and all the M-80 fire crackers being thrown onto the main floor made it hard to concentrate on the show. But I love Led Zeppelin. I tried to record and listen to every Led Zeppelin concert on YouTube with a standalone CD recorder. I stopped after 300 CDs!

I WAS THERE: RICK POWELL

The third time I saw them, in 1977, I had gone up to the Chicago Stadium with a few friends. None of us had tickets, nor much money, but thought it was worth a shot to get in. One of the stadium workers, an older man nicknamed Blackie, recognised us and let us in a back door without paying. The 1977 show was most notable for some laser lights, an acoustic set where Jones played guitar and mandolin and Bonham playing hand percussion. They did four or five acoustic numbers, 'Going To California', 'Battle Of Evermore', 'That's The Way' and a version of 'Black Mountain Side'.

I WAS THERE: LARRY GRANAT

This show turned out to be their last concert in Chicago. When we ordered tickets, the only date left was Sunday, the last of their four-day stint at the Stadium. But we were lucky because the night before they had cut their show short because of Jimmy's 'stomach cramps'. The concert was amazing. They had so much energy. Most big name bands I had seen were doing one-and-a-half to two hour shows. Not Zep. They played non-stop for about three hours.

I WAS THERE: JEFF HORNSTEIN, AGE 15

I saw the first show of the four-night run they played in April 1977 at the Chicago Stadium. I was 15 years old and a huge Zep fan. Leading up to the show, people were in shock and complaining about ticket prices because these were some of the first ten-dollar tickets for a rock concert in Chicago. My memory is that it was very loud. The acoustics in the old Chicago Stadium were horrible and even though it was an indoor show, a lot of people were setting off fireworks in the stadium.

I went to the first show on Thursday night because of a family engagement that weekend. Many of my friends said I was a fool for not going to the Saturday night show, but the Saturday show turned out to be the night that Page got sick (ie. overdosed) and where the show ended after less than an hour. My friends who went said that they announced that the show was cancelled and 'to save your ticket stubs' because the show would be rescheduled. People were supposedly diving on the floor looking for ticket stubs. The show was never rescheduled because of the tragedy with Plant's child.

My next shot at seeing Zep was going to be in 1980, again at the Chicago Stadium. This time we ordered our tickets through mail order. Well, that tour was cancelled due to Bonzo passing away. I never got to see Zep again, but I saw Plant a few times in the eighties and again about ten years ago. I also saw Page and Paul Rodgers with The Firm at the Rosemont Horizon outside of Chicago.

I WAS THERE: JONATHAN SMITH

I went with my older brother. It was my 16th birthday present and for me it was a great show because they played two or three songs from *Physical Graffiti*, which I still think is a masterpiece. But this was the infamous show where they played for a little over an hour and with Jimmy sitting down for most of that time. Then he needed a potty break because he had gastroenteritis…

After a few minutes, Richard Cole came out and said that Jimmy couldn't go on any further and they would come back at a later date and do it over, which they never actually did because a few weeks later Robert's son Karac died in England (from an intestinal infection, ironically).

I WAS THERE: KEVIN JARRELL

Everything looked to be going great at Chicago Stadium but less than an hour into the concert, Jimmy just collapsed into a chair and couldn't play anymore. Robert walked over to check on him and helped him off stage. It was the only time I was able to witness the magic of Led Zeppelin and I was such a fan I didn't care. I'd convinced eight other 15-year-old friends to take a bus across town to see Zep and they didn't know what to think. I just said 'he got drunk, how cool was that?' The Stadium said another date would be added but that never happened. In later years, I felt more ripped off after reading more about Jimmy's heroin use because it was obvious that drugs played a part in this. I do understand the tremendous pressure on these guys to perform flawlessly on these long tour dates and Zeppelin were known for putting in one hundred per cent in three-hour concerts, which was unheard of at the time. I only wish I had had my fill at the time. And I'm glad Jimmy survived it all and lived to a ripe old age!

I WAS THERE: TOM LYNCH, AGE 15

I had a lot of friends and our favourite bands were Zep, Floyd, Rush, Yes and The Who. We got six Zep tickets for the second night of their four-night run at the Chicago Stadium. It was a great deal at about $10 each. My friend's 22-year-old brother drove the six of us to the show, bought beer for us and let us smoke weed in his car all the way there. We took a generous dose of orange microdot LSD in the parking lot and headed in. We were in way over our heads! Zep was more than just another concert – it was an event where people lost their fucking minds.

Some highlights: They opened with 'The Song Remains The Same' and the crowd went bezerk. 'Nobody's Fault But Mine' brought a shit-ton of their new *Presence* vibe to the Stadium. 'No Quarter' gave JPJ a spotlight and he jammed heavily on organ. 'Kashmir' represented the apotheosis of everybody's favourite double album, *Physical Graffiti*, and left us with mouths agape and our jaws on the floor. 'Moby Dick' pounded our eardrums in so hard that they touched inside our skulls. Jimmy Page soloed inside some kind of crazy laser pyramid. And 'Achilles Last Stand' was the most devastating song I had ever seen in concert up to that point in my life, exceeding my high expectations. Oh yeah, we got this little thing too: 'Stairway To Heaven'. The encore? A perfect 'Rock And Roll.

I WAS THERE: PHILLIP SOLOMONSON, AGE 14

While my mates excitedly chatted away, I was staring out the car window lost in my own world. Complete silence overtook me on the entire ride home. Talking would have shattered my euphoria. Pinch me, I had just seen Led-fuckin'-Zeppelin in concert. Pure afterglow. Ringing ears and all. Determined to remember all details, I brought my mom's instamatic camera. Of all those horrible frames, one still survives as my oldest concert snapshot.

Like the movie *Dazed And Confused*, in 1976 I was that 14-year-old freshman eager to fit in. Just as quick to avoid harassing upper classmates, I was caught between trying to be both cool and invisible at the same time. Lost amid 5,000 students, campus life was intimidating. I found the promised land with my guitar, my rock and roll album collection, a local record store, rock mags, poster-covered walls and concerts. Music my Shangri-La, Led Zeppelin my guild.

When the 1977 Led Zeppelin tour was announced, I followed up all leads to score a ticket. The most coveted ticket around, it was a long shot to get one for any of the four sold out concerts. On one misadventure I walked miles and waited hours in the winter chill for a ticket. Not only figuratively, my contact left me out in the cold when he never showed up. Since I came from the land of the ice and snow, I handled it stoically.

But persistence prevailed. Thanks to a classmate's father with venue connections, he got tickets. I now had my ten dollar seat. Aisle 9, section 23, row G, seat 6 was a great raised-main-floor view. And no scalper's fee to boot. My night to witness Robert Plant, Jimmy Page, John Paul Jones and John Bonham was like winning the lottery.

Yet more obstacles. Would my mom allow me to go to a concert on a school night, much less Easter Sunday? I recall pleading. Or did I wear her down? Too young to drive, we needed a sympathetic parent to chauffeur us the 60-mile round trip to a dodgy neighbourhood. Rock and roll providence prevailed. The hammer-of-the-gods shined favour.

This final concert was special. The previous night was cut short because Page got sick. But they played. Determined, the band made up for the earlier shortfall performing an explosive three-hour concert. Lighting in a bottle. Waiting for 8pm was an eternity. Finally, the house lights went out, the stage lit up, fans went wild. The stage lights were spectacular. A mystical view through the pot-smoke haze. It was a stark contrast to that morning's Easter service. Both sacred in opposite ways. Bare-chested with a stunning head of golden locks, Plant was the rock god we expected. He strutted the stage while wailing his full range falsetto voice. His ability to hit all those high notes without fail was amazing. Plant was both dynamic and grounding on stage.

Plant jokingly dismissed Page's earlier illness as a false pregnancy. Playing the song 'Sick Again' was in title only. Recovered from the previous night, Page was in great form. He swaggered about the stage with the guitar as a part of his very being, playing his signature double-neck Gibson guitar when not playing a sunburst Gibson Les Paul or black Les Paul Jr slung low to his body. Page changed wardrobes to his white poppy suit from knee-high black boots, military trousers, black tee-shirt and suspenders. This was all framed with a long white pilot's scarf and peaked officer's cap, like two sides of an alchemist straddling light and dark.

Jones stoically held down the bass, then commanded full attention when switching to the keyboards. Pure prowess with that haunting church-organ sound during 'No Quarter'. Perched on a tall drum riser with timpani drums to his side and a huge gong behind him, Bonham pounded his kit with raw power. Then in full glory during his extended drum solo midway through 'Moby Dick', he was as forceful as a pneumatic trip-hammer.

From the first frenetic strumming of 'The Song Remains The Same' to the encore's crashing drum fills of 'Rock And Roll', I was transported to an alternate place. It was the first and only US tour to hear 'Achilles Last Stand' and 'Nobody's Fault But Mine' live in concert. The hard-driving blues of 'Since I've Been Loving You' and the tasteful 'In My Time Of Dying' were spellbinding. The rhythmic clavinet beat of 'Trampled Underfoot' contrasted the haunting, mixolydian modality of 'Kashmir'. A much different setlist than earlier tours but all epic.

Mid-show they lined four abreast, sitting on stools for a short acoustic set and played my favourite song, 'The Battle Of Evermore'. Add in 'Going To California', 'Bron-Y-Aur Stomp', 'Black Mountain Side' and 'Black Country Woman'. Bonham played a hand drum, Page on an acoustic guitar, Jones strumming acoustic guitar and his unique tripled neck mandolin. It was an unexpected display of their unplugged musicianship.

Alone on stage, Page performed his epic guitar solo. Teetering on controlled chaos, he noodled other-worldly sounds with a theremin. Trilling notes on his guitar with violin bow, Page then hammered it across the fretboard. Power chords reverberated through the stadium assisted by echo effects. The maestro would pause, momentarily pointing his bow about like a conductor with an oversized baton. The bow's shredded horsehair was sacrificed to the music.

The explosive chords synced to a huge, wireframe laser pyramid surrounding Page. The green beams dramatically cut through the din. Building velocity, the lasers rotating 90 degrees to each rhythmic crash. The increased tempo spun out the laser beams until he was in a hazy tempest. Page was as badass as it gets. The crowd erupted upon those first iconic fingerpicking notes of Page's electric twelve strings. The grande finale: 'Stairway To Heaven'. It was everything I could ask for that night. 'Rock And Roll' was the only encore, punctuating both our night's purpose and celebration.

Back then we didn't know this was the last time that they would play Chicago. By the time I was in college, Bonham had died and they were disbanded. In hindsight, seeing them in concert at 14 was against all the odds and a great rock and roll fortune for anyone my age.

I WAS THERE: STACEY KATSIS

I was 15 years old and really starting to discover all sorts of music. It was 1971 and I had the radio on in my room when suddenly 'Stairway To Heaven' came on. I walked over to the radio to turn it up and thought to myself: 'Well now, who is this band?' They were not just your average rock and roll band. They had this heavy guitar-driven sound but they also had this crazy mix of blues, folk and even some classical orchestration. I went and bought *Zeppelin IV*, or 'Zoso' as it also came to be known, to hear more. I loved every minute of it! 'Black Dog', 'Rock And Roll', 'Going To California'… And when I got to 'When The Levee Breaks' – wow! An absolutely mesmerising tune. I wanted more. *Houses Of The Holy* came out in 1973 and I was floored. 'The Rain Song' is probably one of the most beautiful tunes ever written. At this point, I went backwards and bought the first three albums so that my collection could be complete.

I also got into photography right around this point in time and talked my parents into letting me go to see concerts. I started taking my camera to every concert I went to because I wanted to keep the memories of seeing my favourite musicians live. Zeppelin did not do many tours near me but I knew that if they did come close enough, I had to go check them out. Along came *Physical Graffiti* and one of the best rock tunes of all time, 'Kashmir'. OMG, nothing can beat that tune to this day for me as a Zep fan!

Then it happened – four nights at the Chicago Stadium in April of 1977. I went to the first and last shows. I had unreal seats for both nights, right up front, and the band were amazing. Even though those two shows would turn out to be my only time seeing them live together as a band, I feel so lucky to have been able to see these legends.

MET CENTER

12 APRIL 1977, BLOOMINGTON, MINNESOTA

I WAS THERE: LIZ DODSON

I saw them twice. It would have been three times but there was a blizzard in Minneapolis and they cancelled. I must have had a premonition that it would be their last tour. I cried all night, I was 16. The shows were always amazing. I was up in front for one and I will die happy. *Houses Of The Holy* was the first album I ever purchased. I went through three copies of the album on vinyl and am now on my second CD!

CIVIC CENTER

13 APRIL 1977, ST PAUL, MINNESOTA

I WAS THERE: MARK CHAPMAN, AGE 17

My mother was a waitress at the hotel they stayed at and she served their meals. She told me the band was staying there and even got Robert Plant's autograph for my sister. My friend wrote for our high school newspaper and thought it would be great to get an interview with Led Zep. We went to the hotel and the front desk gave us the phone number of the band's manager's room. We called and he declined an interview but asked if we'd seen the show the previous night in Bloomington. (They played back-to-back shows in Bloomington and St Paul). We hadn't been able to get tickets so he said there would be two tickets waiting for us at the St Paul show that night. He was good for his word and we saw the smoke-filled show. A highlight was the stage lighting during 'Kashmir'!

I WAS THERE: BILL LINDSEY

l was in tenth grade. My buddy Marty was a Led Zep fanatic and when they announced two shows on back-to-back days in April of that year, he took his paper route money and snatched up tickets for us both. It was the best eight bucks l ever owed a guy. We jumped on a bus after school and headed to downtown St Paul and the Civic Center Arena. As we approached the venue you could tell there was a festival, big event-type of vibe already in swing because the place was swarming with teenagers, many desperate to buy tickets for the sold-out event from scalpers or waiting around to 'pop a door', which meant get someone from inside to push a door open and then to rush inside in large numbers and immediately scatter to gain free admittance.

Marty and I were on the lower level when the guards started to raise the gates like garage doors to let people into the show. There was such a crush by all the people pushing from behind that the guards stopped raising the gate and told everyone to move back. Marty and I dropped to our hands and knees and crawled between people's legs and through the small opening between the floor and the gate. The ticket takers took our tickets and allowed us inside. This meant we were some of the first kids inside and had our pick of where to sit or stand. It was general admission and the stage was so high that front centre would block our view of Bonham, so we sat on John Paul Jones' side of the stage, right at stage level.

When the lights went out the auditorium went off. The opening chords for 'The Song Remains The Same' came slamming out of the PA and it was on full throttle. The lights flashed on to reveal Jimmy Page in his white silk dragon suit, Plant in his trademark open-chested shirt, jeans and snakeskin boots, Bonzo beating the hell out of his kit, sporting a silk screen tuxedo t-shirt and John Paul Jones holding down the fort on bass and keyboards. Yes, we were so close that we could make out all the details of their stage clothes and instruments.

Highlights from a show of highlights were 'Nobody's Fault But Mine', 'Achilles Last Stand' and 'No Quarter', with the dry ice creeping low around the band's knees. They played a cool acoustic set in the middle of the show predating the 'unplugged' concept by decades. 'Battle Of Evermore' was a highlight, as was 'Going To California'. The last song in the regular set was 'Stairway To Heaven' and I remember them playing it so dose to the version on the record. 'Rock And Roll' and 'Black Dog' were the encores. I would never get to see Zep again after Bonham's untimely death. Thanks for getting me that ticket, Marty. I'll never forget it.

I WAS THERE: LORI LEI DEMBROSKI

I took a handsome fella from college. He turned me on to Robin Trower's *Bridge Of Sighs*. I returned the favour by treating him to this concert. His equally handsome friend drove us the 300 plus mile round trip to the venue. I thought that was a good and fair trade.

I WAS THERE: ED LAWRENCE, AGE 15

I went with my older brother and his friend, 'The Doctor'. The gates were closed and people were pushing and we were getting smashed. Finally, when I thought we were going to die, they opened the door. We rushed in to get our seat which ended up being on the right side of the stage. Robert Plant had his denim vest on and took the show. Jimmy as usual rocked the house. Marijuana was being passed from every direction. Women were topless. It was amazing!

ARENA
15 APRIL 1977, ST LOUIS, MISSOURI

I WAS THERE: DARREN MCGOVERN

One day in 1975 my older brother came to me and said he had two tickets to see Zeppelin. He could not get out of work and, if I could get a ride, I could have them. I had never seen a concert and when I told my mom that I had an older friend who would take me, she refused to let me go. That was the big fish that got away. When Zeppelin returned in 1977, I was amped! My girlfriend knew how big a deal it was to me, so skipped school to get in line for tickets. Three days before the show, a massive delivery of gold marijuana showed up in town. To this day I think Zeppelin had something to do with it.

The day of the show my girlfriend and I, three other girls and my best friend crammed into a station wagon and drove to the St Louis Arena. They opened with 'The Song Remains The Same' and I was under their spell for the rest of the show. In hindsight, I wish I was less high. I have little memory of several of the songs. 'Ten Years Gone' and 'Out On The Tiles' stood out, but what really impressed me was 'Moby Dick'. I couldn't believe how entertaining a drum solo could be. Bonham's drums rolled out to the front of the stage, lit up from underneath, and he threw his sticks out into the audience and began to play with his hands. Of course, 'Stairway' caused the room to explode but when it was time for an encore the band didn't come back out. The lights were on for a long time, and the audience got upset. Then the house lights came on and people went crazy and started throwing chairs. It was a long show anyway, so we were not too upset.

Later, I spoke with a guy who had a photographer's pass who told me Jimmy was guzzling a fifth of Jack Daniels between songs and that it was nearly empty at the end. He then witnessed Jimmy stumbling as he walked away at the end of 'Stairway'. He made it to the stairs to go down from the stage, fell into the arms of someone and was carried away.

I later saw Plant three times, Page three times and JPJ with Them Crooked Vultures. But when I saw Page and Plant at lrvine Meadows in 1995, it was with clear mind and the full band they had really filled out the music and I recall all the details, but without Bonzo and Jonesy the full aura was dulled a bit.

I WAS THERE: GREG MUICH, AGE 16

The heat and humidity were oppressive that night in St Louis as we left the bowling alley where my friend worked. Right next door was the huge Checkerdome concert hall and we could hear and feel the music pulsing from within. We instantly figured out that it was the Led Zeppelin concert! We only knew that because the ticket sales made the news as fans had camped out to purchase them, something that was uncommon back then. As we explored outside of the arena, an exit door cracked opened and some guy asked if we wanted to come in. This was the first rock concert of my life and I had no idea what to expect. The arena was packed, smoked-filled, swelteringly hot and loud! My first view of the crowd was a sight to behold. We had to wander about as we had no tickets and the venue was sold out but we finally managed to find some empty seats, dead centre but at the very top row. I can clearly remember looking directly down and watching Jimmy Page playing his guitar. At one point they turned on a very fine beam of light, long before lasers, that pointed up from the stage to just above our heads. It was so brilliantly defined in the dark, smoky air that I remember thinking I could hold on to it and slide all the way down to the stage. We were pretty stoned and just a little drunk!

I entered a restroom to take a leak and almost ran into a guy in a white t-shirt covered with bloody spots. He was cleaning blood off his pocket knife onto his shirt. I quickly looked about but the bathroom was empty except for him. I should have immediately turned around and left but I just said 'hey!' when he looked up at me and he responded with a 'hey!' back. I really had to pee bad so no knife-wielding nut was gonna stop me from going.

It was all so long ago that I can barely remember Robert's singing but what I will never forget is the image of Jimmy Page playing that double-neck guitar and especially of him playing his guitar with a violin bow in the spotlight. That image is burned in my mind forever.

I WAS THERE: JOE BRITTIN, AGE 16

The line for tickets formed the night before they went on sale, with many people sleeping in line all night. There was a limit of four tickets per person and the St Louis police used horse patrols to help control the crowd. Some of the guys who were first in line only scored tenth row tickets. I skipped school for the day to purchase tickets with two of my buddies, driving the 100 miles down from Springfield, Illinois. I found out later that other groups from Springfield came down for the all night line party! At the show, I was able to sneak in a 35mm camera and a small telephoto lens and worked my way up to around the tenth row. I got some great photos!

I WAS THERE: MARK RICCI

I was a high school freshman in 1969/70 when I first heard their music. I got a tape deck with an AM-FM radio for Christmas that year and started buying 8-track tapes. My older sister was playing a Zep album one day so she's the one who got me started on Led Zeppelin. She also got me listening to Joe Cocker.

I saw them in 1977 at the St Louis Blues Hockey Arena. We were sitting just up on the side but close to the stage where you didn't need binoculars. The air smelled sweet as usual like at any concert. My recollection of which songs were played in what order is not good, but I do know that every time the first note from each song was started it was dead quiet in that arena. Of course, 'Kashmir' was the top song that everyone was waiting to hear and, of course, it wasn't heard until last, as they did it for the encore. All in all, it has to be one of the best – if not *the* best – concerts I have ever been to.

I had all their music on 8-track. That was the worst investment ever, the 8-track. Now I have all their albums on CD.

I WAS THERE: TRACEY RAYFIELD, AGE 15

St Louis is a mid-sized Midwestern US city, so we knew we would only get one show, unlike Chicago who secured four nights of the tour. The challenge was to obtain what would be high demand tickets. Fortunately, my brother Rick, who had seen their '75 show, had a car and was willing to skip school with his girlfriend (now wife) Denise to score the elusive prize. Tickets were $7.50, $8.50 and $9.50, by far the most expensive concert tickets to date. I went to school that day like any other and had not really thought too much about it until arriving back home to get the good news from Rick that we had tickets. The seats were in the upper deck yet in still close proximity to the stage. This was my first time in the big house – the Arena, which sat 18,000 to 19,000 – and used mainly as a sports arena.

When my brother told me about the 10,000 fans who turned up for the amount of tickets issued, I felt lucky to be going at all. The mob that brought out the riot police to the Arena box office was the lead story on the five o'clock news that night. Normally, concert tickets were dispersed between several retail outlets in addition to the box office and phone sales, but because of the anticipated intensity of this tour ticket sales were only available at the Arena box office, creating the human mass to converge on that location.

The concert took place on a Friday night, which meant party time before the show. In addition to my brother and his girlfriend, my friend Mark came along. We were gonna get good and messed up before and during this rare spectacle. We began the ritual by drinking beer shortly after dinner but before leaving for the concert. Of course, we were too young to buy drinks in the venue so we would slam as many beers as we could before entry. We were too young to have been exposed to many heavy drugs by this time but we were avid pot smokers, so we brought plenty of treats to smoke during the show. We freely smoked pot in the stands at concerts in the States back then, but I'm not sure if all areas of the world enjoyed such freedoms!

My knowledge of the band's catalogue consisted of the songs played on our beloved FM rock station, K-SHE 95, and the double live *The Song Remains The Same* that was on regular rotation in our party room in my parents' basement. Of course, the movie soundtrack was from a 1973 concert and did not represent today's set list, as I would soon find out. I was hoping for a large diet of the likes of 'Whole Lotta Love' and 'Black Dog' for three hours. When eight o'clock came and the lights dimmed, the crowd roared in anticipation as their heroes took the stage. In a blink of an eye we were surrounded by light and sound that most of us had not experienced before. They opened with the title track to the aforementioned *The Song Remains The Same* and continued to gallop through some fairly heavy numbers, most of which I was familiar with. With the accompaniment of the laser light show, most fans were dazzled by the spectacle. As the first set came to a close, I was satisfied with the song selection so far, although not all were familiar to me.

We took advantage of the break to spark up another joint, when I noticed my friend Mark was beginning to look a little green. I thought I had better keep an eye on him and reduce his further pot consumption. The lights dimmed for the second set when I noticed four chairs at the front of the stage, when I thought 'what's this all about?' As the band launched into an acoustic set of some 20 minutes, I was quite surprised and honestly disappointed. As I said earlier, I was not completely familiar with all of their material and also I liked the heavy stuff better. About this time I heard some strange noises coming from my friend in the next seat – unrelated to the song selections! Upon further inspection I noticed Mark beginning to vomit on the floor at our feet. Thanks Mark, you are officially cut off!

We got some dirty looks from our neighbours but I just kept rockin' and acted like I didn't know this guy. Fortunately, as my friend began to regain some colour in his face, Zeppelin kicked into some heavy, more familiar hits like 'Moby Dick' and 'Kashmir'.

Overall, I was satisfied with the song selections as they finished their second set with the mighty 'Stairway To Heaven', much to the delight of the onlookers. Almost three hours of the biggest band on the planet left most of us exhausted and pleased with the evening's entertainment. Of course, we would have no way of knowing that this would be their final appearance in St Louis and the last time for most of us to see such an iconic band live again.

As history would show, the 1977 North American tour was one of the most tumultuous in any band's career and would come to a sudden and abrupt end in New Orleans two months later when Robert Plant received the phone call that no parent ever wants to get. His son had died and the tour was understandably cancelled. Life marched on for most of us but the life of one of the greatest rock bands in history was about to be cut short. Those of us that were fortunate enough to get tickets for their final American tour should forever count themselves as the few lucky ones.

On 19 April 1977, over 70 people are arrested as about 1,000 ticketless fans try to gatecrash Cincinnati Riverfront Coliseum for two sold out festival seating/general admission concerts. Some gain entry by throwing rocks and bottles through glass entrance doors and some wall height, all-glass panes surrounding the outermost perimeter of the arena.

RIVERFRONT COLISEUM
19 & 20 APRIL 1977, CINCINNATI, OHIO

I WAS THERE: JEFF L CAMPBELL

I saw them twice in one month, in Cincinnati, Ohio and then in Louisville, Kentucky (April 25th). Bonham was so good as were Page on lead and Robert out front. I remember a very long 'Stairway To Heaven' and a rush at the doors and a few people getting knocked down and some stomping accidents, which was so unnecessary.

I WAS THERE: PETER MCCARTT, AGE 17

I saw consecutive nights at the Riverfront Coliseum. My dad had his own advertising agency and bought ad time from all the TV and radio stations, so I could go to any concert or ball game that I wanted, no problem. I had four free tickets for each night! The first night was with my girlfriend and another couple and the second night was with my buddies. The problem with the second night was that my mom said I couldn't go. I was a bit of track star, having the fastest mile in the States in high school for several months in 1978, and I had track practice. My friends waited for me to finish practice and I ran and jumped into the Ford Mustang and we were off to downtown Cincinnati with a cooler of Miller beer on the back seat. We were set. I was going to get in big trouble but I didn't care. Led Zeppelin!

The Riverfront Coliseum is where the Who disaster took place, with eleven dead, just two years later. They had what they called 'festival seating', meaning no reserved seating. You got in line and the first one in got the front row. In hindsight, this was total madness. For Paul McCartney, which was months before the Who disaster, the throng of fans jamming to get in to get good seats was so much that they didn't collect tickets but just opened the doors and let everyone in. The stairs and aisles were filled with people. It was a disaster waiting to happen.

On the first night for Led Zep, I had an amazing spot on the floor, not jammed up front but a sensible 40 rows back. I am tall so I can see from anywhere, and I had my girlfriend on my shoulders for nearly the whole show, so she had a direct line to Robert Plant. We were dead centre and it was just an amazing show, with great laser work.

Next night was with my three pals. We got all lit up that night – stoned immaculate. Again, it was festival seating but, since I wasn't with my petite girlfriend, we crushed up closer to the stage but this time a little to the right of the stage which is where Jimmy was set up, as I knew from the previous night. As I recall it was the same set list. It was certainly the same laser show. My hearing was shot when I went to school the next day and my ears were ringing for three to four days. Of course, I was grounded, because my mom had told me that after the first night I couldn't go the second night with my buds.

I WAS THERE: MARCI CONNELLY

After the fans' destruction to the outside of the Richfield Coliseum when Led Zeppelin last took its stage in 1975, I was shockingly surprised and extremely happy that I was able to attend the 1977 concert at the same venue. If the concert in 1975 was remembered by the locals for damage and broken glass, the 1977 show is remembered for being an epic and classic performance by Led Zeppelin. Plant, Page, Bonham and Jones kept the fans up and out of their seats and rockin' for nearly three solid hours. Opening with 'The Song Remains The Same', the band moved seamlessly through hits like 'Nobody's Fault But Mine', 'No Quarter', 'Achilles Last Stand', 'Since I've Been Loving You' and 'Kashmir', and finished with 'Stairway To Heaven' followed by an encore of 'Rock And Roll' and 'Trampled Underfoot'.

This concert was everything that you might imagine a Led Zeppelin performance would or could be. Jimmy Page was mesmerising and absolutely masterful; his solos were tight and paid tribute to Zeppelin's roots in blues music while reaching beyond into the world of psychedelic rock. As a bassist, John Paul Jones provided a consistent pace for the show. But it was his diversity as a musician that was so impressive as he played the keyboards, often while still playing the neck of the bass guitar. And as for Robert Plant, he was, well Robert Plant! His melodic voice was strong, smooth and sexy all at the same time and took the audience beyond the heights that Jones and Page had laid out. Finally, John Bonham owned the stage; Bonzo maintained a frenetic beat that was truly like no other I've ever seen or heard – as a percussionist, he created controlled chaos and was undoubtedly one of the most creative and ingenious drummers of our era.

After just over an hour of rocking the house, Led Zeppelin came to the front of the stage and played wonderful acoustic versions of their hits, including 'Going To California' and 'Bron-Yr-Aur Stomp', which used a variety of unique instruments and John Paul Jones playing an upright bass. In 'The Battle Of Evermore', which was undoubtedly my favourite from this set, Jimmy Page quite literally serenaded us with his mandolin.

At the closing of 'Kashmir', Bonham began his drum solo, aptly titled 'Over The Top' as it was over 15 minutes of pure percussion perfection. Toward the end, Page joined in and the musical image morphed from beats and sonic sound effects to a guitar solo complete with a harmonizer, arching echoes, a theremin and of course his infamous use of a bow to attain a signature sound. Closing with 'Stairway' and coming back out to a frenzied crowd with 'Rock And Roll' and 'Trampled Underfoot', Led Zeppelin once again left their audience wanting more!

I'm quite sure that none of us imagined that we were witnessing one of Led Zeppelin's final concerts in the United States, but also that these shows would later become the band's self-recorded bootleg album, Destroyer. Now these concerts have been meticulously remastered, it is possible to re-live a moment in time that we will never get back.

THE OMNI
23 APRIL 1977, ATLANTA, GEORGIA

I WAS THERE: TOMMY STONE

After Fulton County Stadium in 1973, I saw them again at the Omni. I went with friends from school and my sister and brother. We got very reasonable seats for just $10 each. They did the long versions of 'No Quarter' and 'Dazed And Confused', like on the *The Song Remains The Same* album. It was an amazing laser and light show. They came back for an encore song then left. A few of us were disappointed they hadn't done 'Kashmir', our favourite Zep song. We clapped, cheered and held our lighters up for a good while but gave up and started to leave. We had gotten out to the corridors when we heard a loud cheer going up. We rushed back in and stood on the steps for a killer encore of 'Kashmir'. They had saved the best for last.

I WAS THERE: TOM GRIFFITHS, AGE 17

The Omni was built in 1972 for the Atlanta Hawks and Atlanta Flames and was state of the art at the time. Pink Floyd toured *Animals* there three days later. I was a junior in high school. Imagine being 17 and seeing both bands in the same week. I also saw the Page and Plant shows in Atlanta in 1995 and Jacksonville, Florida in 1998, The Firm in Atlanta in 1984 and Robert a couple of times, the most memorable being 1993's *Fate of Nations* tour. I also met and drank with Jason Bonham after a *Zep Sets* tour in Jacksonville in 1996. He was a regular bloke. I guess I qualify as a fan.

RICHFIELD COLISEUM
27 APRIL 1977, CLEVELAND, OHIO

I WAS THERE: FLOYD BURRIS, AGE 16

It was a beautiful day and I went with my friends, Mike, who is not with us anymore, and Rick. Mike had a powder blue convertible and the concert was about an hour from our homes. It was a big party outside with cops on horseback and K9 German Shepherds. Not one person got out of line. I just remember that awesome music from Page, the drums from Bonham and Plant's angelic voice. Jones? He was always kind of hidden.

I WAS THERE: CARMEN BINDREITER HUSTON

Four of us high school kids – me, Cathy Mullins, Kathy McFee and Burch Nerhenz – had a great time watching Zeppelin for three hours. We were students at Springfield High School in Akron, Ohio, and the next morning we went to school proudly wearing our black Led Zeppelin t-shirts.

I WAS THERE: CINDI CAMPBELL, AGE 17

That was the only concert where I did not smoke weed or do anything else because I wanted to remember every single note. Which is not like me. I like to party!

I WAS THERE: CAROL BODENMILLER. AGE 16

I was invited to go to the show as a surprise by my boyfriend. My parents weren't thrilled but my boyfriend's father was wealthy and we were allowed to use his loge – the luxury boxes between the upper and lower levels of the Coliseum – for the show, so I was allowed to go as I wouldn't be mixed in with their well-known rowdy crowd. Our loge happened to be near the stage. This was my first concert and it was excellent. I was awestruck by Jimmy Page, his talent and his good looks. Robert Plant lived up to his nickname. His voice was true rock legend. John Paul Jones' bass was perfection, but the best part of the show was the longest, most amazing drum solo by John Bonham. His energy level was something to behold and I knew I had witnessed the best rock drummer, bar none.

SILVERDOME
30 APRIL 1977, PONTIAC, MICHIGAN

I WAS THERE: JOE MOORE, AGE 15

I was living just outside Detroit in the suburb of Steding Heights when the announcement came that Led Zeppelin would be doing a show at the Pontiac Silverdome. By now Led Zeppelin was the biggest act in an era of mega star bands. Getting tickets was pure insanity. The Silverdome had a ten-foot-high chainlink fence all around it and the ticket booths were well beyond the fence. A massive crowd waited outside for the fence gates to open. It was worse than any Black Friday video you've seen, with thousands of people trying to funnel in through the gates and in a very aggressive fashion. Some started to climb the fence and that was a big mistake. One of the hopeful ticket buyers lost their life falling from the fence and landing head first on the asphalt. Just getting my two tickets was a major accomplishment. All 77,000 plus tickets sold out in under three hours.

My best friend, Mark Grablowski, and I lived about 30 minutes from the Dome. It was a general admission show and we planned on being there when the doors opened at 5pm. The show was scheduled to start at 8pm and the crowd wasn't huge at the time the doors opened. We ran down onto the main floor and staked our claim, centre stage about 50 feet back. We thought we had it made but had no idea of the carnage that was coming.

I'd been to a few big name shows at the Dome but they didn't prepare us for this. By 7pm it was getting crowded on the floor, but we were holding our own. As it got closer to 8pm it started getting a bit rowdy, with a lot of pushing and shoving as people tried to force their way up front. 8pm came and went and there was no sign of Led Zeppelin. The crowd was really revving it up now. With all the people in the back pushing forward, huge waves of people would come crashing down around us. Bodies came flying by. I looked at Mark and said, 'Whatever you do, don't go down.' Bodies would just crash into you and many people fell to the ground. Several fights broke out and when that happened it really got crazy as the crowd would make a circle around the fighters, pushing even more people to the ground.

8.30pm came and went, and still no Led Zeppelin. It was now a full-blown madhouse, with fights all over, people being pushed to the ground and a lot of pissed off people. There were people in the upper deck throwing M-80s. Unfortunately, a young female concert goer in the lower deck seating got hit with one of these and had a good portion of her face blown off. This was not a concert. It was a riot.

At 9pm the lights went off. All the energy that was going in every direction suddenly focused forward and the pushing towards the front got even worse than before. Out they came and the crowd was going insane. They put up a gigantic screen and I was watching as a stage hand helped Jimmy strap on his guitar. He had a cigarette in his mouth and the coals hit the back of his guitar, splattering him with hot ashes. It didn't faze him.

They opened with 'The Song Remains The Same', just the kind of high energy opener that got the crowd even more fired up. It took a constant effort to stay upright. I was feeling crushed at times. Mark and I lasted through the first three or four songs, but the crowd kept getting stronger and more aggressive. We fought it, but it was a losing battle. It got so bad I was being pushed out to the right and Mark to the left. We saw each other but there was nothing we could do. We just kind of laughed and waved 'bye!' There were times my feet weren't even on the ground as I was spat out the side. I didn't see Mark the rest of the concert. We met later outside the Dome by my car.

I spent much of the show in different locations, just wandering around, looking for a good view. The Silverdome was notorious for horrible sound quality. I finally found a decent seat off to the side but close enough for decent sound, made some friends with those seated around me and enjoyed most of the rest of the show from there. It was a marathon show, nearly three hours. I decided later I'd give the floor another go of it. The crowd had tired by now and I was able to get near the front again, but off to the side. I fought for a few more songs and decided I'd just go to the side.

When they started playing 'Stairway To Heaven' I knew the show was ending soon. They had a giant glitterball and many in the crowd had their Bic lighters out. It was surreal. After the band left the stage, everyone was screaming for an encore. Out came the band and played 'Rock And Roll'. They left the stage again, only this time the house lights came on. People started leaving immediately. I was still feeling exhausted and I just leaned against the back wall of the main floor. I was going to catch my breath before dealing with any more of this crowd.

Then I heard 'Hey, where are you all going?' It was Plant! I had a sudden renewed energy and immediately ran towards the front. Many had left so it was easy going. This was my favourite part of the show. I was up front and centre stage, I didn't have anyone pushing and shoving on me, and Zeppelin were jamming. They played a great version of 'Trampled Underfoot', one of my favourites from *Physical Graffiti*. That was the last song and it was my favourite of the night.

For music quality it was far from the best show I've seen. But this was far and away the most epic concert experience of my life and it happened more than 40 years ago. At the time this was the largest audience ever – 77,000 plus – to see a single act. My favourite songs were from *Physical Graffiti* and *Presence* and I thought they were the tightest on those songs. I never liked the live versions of the older songs after Page ditched the Telecaster. The sound was too different from the originals for my liking. All in all, it was a once in a lifetime experience, much more than just a concert.

I was excited in the fall of 1980 as I had just got my tickets to see the mighty Zep again but this time at the new Joe Louis Arena in Detroit. It was a heartbreaking day when I learned of the passing of the great John Bonham and the cancellation of the show.

I WAS THERE: DEAN V RICCI

It was an epic night. They played for probably three hours and Jimmy performed 'White Summer' whilst standing in a laser-created pyramid which spun around real fast at times. We sat up near the roof of the stadium, but it was festival seating on the ground floor as was practised at many 1970s concerts at stadiums. Many concert-goers were injured by being trampled or by being hit by fireworks being thrown. There was a multitude of stupidity on the ground floor. One girl ultimately lost an eye and another lost hearing in one ear. At one point Robert asked the crowd to 'cool it with the fireworks.' It was simply insane.

I WAS THERE: ALAN TOMASINO, AGE 13

I was in seventh grade. My older brother and sister listened to all the great bands during the late sixties and seventies and my sister got the tickets for the show. They were only $10 a piece. This was my first concert ever. We had main floor festival seating but there were no seats. We started out in the back of the floor, which was the size of an NFL football field, and made our way to midfield. There were giant screens to see the band. I really only remember 'Dazed And Confused' because it was the longest jam ever. I also remember Jimmy Page with the dragons on his bell-bottom pants. I couldn't tell you how long the show was but I was there and that's what really counts for me. I've seen Robert solo, and with Jimmy, since that show but it wasn't the same as the experience that night at the Silverdome.

I WAS THERE: FRANCIS HANCHETT

The only part that was really scary was when my feet were no longer touching the ground for 15 minutes as I was carried by the crowd. That and the explosions from the M-80s raining down from the crowd above us. I was on the first balcony and at one point on the main floor, I watched 30 or 40 people just shed their clothes and start piling on in an impromptu orgy.

I WAS THERE: JOE SKI, AGE 19

I went with a few friends. I got my ticket at the local place in my area that sold concert tickets. I paid $15. I still have my ticket stub and a few newspaper clippings. I was smoking pot all day and night. There was a wall in front of the stage and I climbed it and, in between songs, Robert was talking to Jimmy and I yelled 'JIMMY PAGE!' and they both turned and looked at me. When the house lights came on, people started to leave but Zeppelin came back out and played a few more songs and then it was over. I had been waiting a long time for Zeppelin to perform, and when they did, nothing else mattered that day.

I WAS THERE: ANDRE BOYER

We took buses to the venue from Toronto. The place was packed to the roofs. Someone left a nicely faded jean jacket on the back of the seat in front of us when the concert ended, and we had one and a half hours to get to our buses so we waited until many had left and I grabbed it. We jumped onto the bus for the six-hour trip back to Toronto. I found two wonderful ounces of Panama Red reefer inside the pockets of that jacket. What a nice gift to take home!

JEFFERSON MEMORIAL COLISEUM
18 MAY 1977, BIRMINGHAM, ALABAMA

I WAS THERE: KAREN DILLARD BROWN, AGE 16

I had my mother write a note so I could skip my senior high school exams in order to go. General admission tickets were $8.50. My daddy took my boyfriend and I all the way there and back. It was four hours one way. I sing Zeppelin with my band now. I guess I have come full circle.

I WAS THERE: VIC BUFORD, AGE 21

I first heard the 'Immigrant Song' over AM radio in 1970 and bought the single. Then the *Untitled* album came out, the greatest recording of the rock era. I bought two $10 tickets for $30 from a friend in college. My brother and I drove a '71 Camaro the 100 miles to Birmingham. There was only street parking so we had walk many blocks to the venue. There was no opening act. Jimmy walked on to the stage first, waved to the crowd and strapped on the double-neck Gibson. He plucked one note and kicked off into 'The Song Remains The Same'. The smell of weed was very thick in the air. After a few more songs the acoustic set was next with all the band members seated. Jimmy did the 'Dazed And Confused' violin bow thing. It was just three hours of lunacy.

I WAS THERE: EDDIE CULPEPPER

I still have my ticket and there is a bootleg CD of the concert. I've met Robert Plant a couple of times, he hangs out in the south a lot. I was invited to a casual get together in Mobile, Alabama a few years ago while Robert was on tour. What was interesting is that I sat across the table talking to him for several hours and Led Zeppelin was never mentioned! I did get a couple of photos with him.

I WAS THERE: MICHAEL BAKER

My uncle gave me a heads up on Led Zeppelin in 1969. I was 13. Most kids that age are looking for something that speaks to them and Led Zeppelin were it for me. Their 1977 tour brought them to Birmingham, Alabama. I don't recall tickets being difficult to get, and I imagine they were bought directly at the box office. The day of the show, I was with my brother, our roommate, and two or three more friends. A number of people were lining the sidewalks holding up fingers, indicating how many tickets they were hoping to buy. We had to park blocks away from the Coliseum. Some of that was trying to avoid parking lot fees. We were young and broke; most of my friends were restaurant workers, line cooks and such like.

The concert itself was mesmerising. We had far away seats – again, what we could afford – but almost dead centre to the stage and raised enough to have a great view of the stage. The only drawback was the echo coming from the concrete overhang from the balcony above and behind us. It was a great light show with creative lasers. Of course it was a high that lasted a long, long time. Back then, none of us were thinking about bucket lists, as we were young and bulletproof. But as time went on, I really began to realise what a rare thing it was. I'm one of the lucky ones.

THE SUMMIT
21 MAY 1977, HOUSTON, TEXAS

I WAS THERE: MARK WHITE

I had become a Zeppelin fan in 1969 aged twelve after hearing 'Whole Lotta Love' being used in a commercial on my AM vacuum tube radio. People who showed up for this show without tickets turned into an unruly mob and the police were called in. The crowd behind pushed me and other ticket holders through the doors once they were opened. We waited for Led Zeppelin to show up. It was past time opening time. Finally, after 30 minutes Jimmy Page showed up onstage with sunglasses on and wearing his white dragon suit. The performance went on for about three-and-one-half hours. They weren't great but they were not bad. I did not realise that Jimmy was hooked on heroin at this time. He was skin and bone.

Fast forward to 1994. Robert Plant and Jimmy Page were on tour and performed at the Woodlands Pavilion, north of Houston. I didn't go but my nephew was a salesman at the time and took some clients to a gentleman's club in Houston called Centerfolds. They went up to the VIP room and spotted Jimmy sitting with some strippers. My nephew's friends wanted to talk to him but the bouncer said no. One of the girls knew my nephew and asked him if he would like to chat with Jimmy. My nephew said yes. The girl went over to Jimmy and pointed to my nephew. Jimmy waved to my nephew to come to his table and chatted with him for ten minutes. The result was I have a personalised autograph from Jimmy Page.

TARRANT COUNTY CONVENTION CENTER
22 MAY 1977, FORT WORTH, TEXAS

I WAS THERE: TERRY MOSELEY

I still have my ticket stub and a little bit of my memory. It was originally going to be the first show in their North American tour but Plant developed laryngitis, pushing the date back to May. The tickets were only sold at the TCCC box office and went on sale maybe late December or early January. I did not camp out on the sidewalk as many did. It was too freakin' cold!

I was elected to get the tickets out of the bunch of us planning on going. I arrived at TCCC very early in the morning, just as lots of folks arrived. The kids camped out were still snoozing and the people just arriving started walking around the campers, who started waking up and getting mad because, having braved the cold and camped on the sidewalk all night, others were now trying to get in front of them. The campers jumped up and then there was a mad rush and crush to get to the ticket windows. There were no lines, just a massive crushing crowd and a lot of pissed off campers. I was way back in the throng and you could not go anywhere. The crowd started to move and when it did, so did you! The people in front would push backward and then the entire crowd would move back, then the people in back would push forward and so on. It was like waves in the ocean. Everyone was being completely crushed.

At one point, I raised my feet off the ground and was kept in place by the mass of humanity. After a while of this, the people at the edges were still cold but the people at the front and middle were hot. Everyone was wearing coats and hats and wrapped in blankets. The heat of the crowd then became a factor. You started seeing blankets, jackets and coats appear over the throng. People were taking them off because they were getting too hot and the garments were thrown off to the sides. Then people, mostly young girls, started passing out and they were lifted overhead and passed to the sides of the crowd. There were paramedics and ambulances on site to treat people that were being overcome. I never made it to the ticket window. I saw a friend much closer to the front and managed to get my money to them and they bought our tickets. What an ordeal! I was thinking that some people were hurt because they were shoved through some windows by the ticket office. This led to no tickets being distributed this way again.

It was an ordeal but well worth it. The show was fantastic and everything I could hope for. Highlights for me were when the boys sat in chairs at the front of the stage and played a few tunes and when Jimmy was playing his guitar with a bow, when green laser lights formed a sort of pyramid over and around him. He would strike the guitar with the bow and the pyramid would rotate 90 degrees and stop with each strike. I remember Bonham's solo on 'Moby Dick' was amazingly long.

I own two bootleg copies of this show on CD. One is an abbreviated set but is a limited edition release single CD called *Song Of The South*. The other is a three CD set of the entire show called *It'll Be Zep*.

I WAS THERE: PHILLIP BERMEJO

I stood in line for tickets in 18 degrees Fahrenheit. It was so cold but it was so worth it by the time the concert came. It may have been the first time I had seen lasers being used. I remember Jimmy using his bow on his guitar. It had an ear-piercing high note.

I WAS THERE: ED GRAY, AGE 16

Fort Worth was originally slated to be the kick-off show for Led Zeppelin's 1977 North American tour but it was delayed a month due to Robert Plant's laryngitis and finally kicked off in Dallas on April 1, the Fort Worth show taking place on May 22. A buddy and I had secured tickets on the top row of the arena and it was quite hazy up there. It was a great show and I remember Jimmy Page breaking a string during the front end of 'Whole Lotta Love'. The band stopped and didn't finish the song. Bad Company had played over in Dallas a couple of nights earlier and Bad Company's Mick Ralphs joined the band onstage for the final song. I had the classic black '77 tour t-shirt for years before finally wearing it out.

I WAS THERE: WAYNE SALES

I saw them in 1975 and 1977. It was quite an experience, especially '77. Just buying tickets was quite a party. In '77 I bought 52 tickets for friends and family. I had a pair of binoculars that I wasn't watching through for the first song, 'The Song Remains The Same'. We were above and to the band's right, but not that far away. After the song, Jimmy still had his sunglasses on. He cupped his hands around his eyes, as if holding binoculars, and looked in my general direction. I can't say he was looking at me, but it sure felt like it.

CAPITAL CENTRE
25, 26, 28 & 30 MAY 1977, LANDOVER, MARYLAND

I WAS THERE: VINCE DUNSWORTH

My second Zep show. Ticket sales were announced in March for four shows in May. The announcement was only made on the evening before tickets went on sale. We called our friends (remember, no cell phones back then), ran all over town to gather the money together and two of us told our parents that we were skipping school to go buy tickets. We were seniors in high school and our parents realised that resistance was futile. Mine wrote an 'excused absence' for me. Next morning we headed for the Capital Centre with $140 for 14 tickets. My buddy Bill is paralysed and in a chair, and that worked in our favour as the security folks waved us past the line to get our tickets. We were in and out in 20 minutes while others waited for hours. The four shows sold out as fast as they could take the money!

We got back to school and got our passes to rejoin the classes. We went in to chorus class with 14 Zep tickets fanned like a deck of cards. I was behind Bill, popping a wheelie with his chair. The chorus stopped mid-song as most of the tickets were for that group. It was a moment worthy of a cheap high school movie. Good times. And the show? Once again, the show was really great.

I WAS THERE: WALT SWARTZ, AGE 18

My friends and I were planning a camping trip to Elkton, Maryland, just 20 minutes over the border of Paton Chester County. I was with them and had a copy of *Rolling Stone*. I saw Zep's upcoming tour dates and not knowing where Landover, Maryland was, I blurted out, 'Hey, Zep are going to be in Maryland the same time we are.' Upon finding out it was two hours south, next to Washington DC, I thought, 'Oh, well'. Two weeks later, we were driving a late sixties Pontiac to our camping reservation. When we got there we were told they were full, as were the next four or five campgrounds where we tried to lodge. They didn't like the look of five 18-year-olds with no supervision.

Around 10.30pm, I suggested we try to see Zep. After all, it was Friday and we had the whole weekend. We took a vote, those in favour won three-to-two and we began our trek south to DC. We got lost several times and that two-hour ride took us just over four hours. We got to the point on the Beltway where we could see a large building in the distance, but could not get to it. We asked a DC metro cop who said 'follow me', hit his light and pointed out to the left as the direction we should go. It was about 4am as we reached the parking lot and drove to the furthest corner to drain our bladders.

Shortly afterwards, a yellow Volkswagen Beetle came over. The 22-year-old driver told us in a loud voice, 'You can't be here, get lost'. I said to him, 'Fine, we're going, but one question... Is this the building Led Zeppelin is playing in this weekend?' He said it was and we started talking. Next thing we know, he's drinking vodkas and orange juices with us and smoking pot. He told us how to get tickets on the far end of the building.

Next day, after a rough night at a KOA campground, we showed up around 5pm to scalp some tickets and ended up with two tickets in row 16 and three in row 17, all for $40 and a nickel of weed. They played and jammed from about 8 pm until very close to midnight and it was fantastic. This was the *Presence* tour so they played 'Achilles Last Stand'.

I WAS THERE: JAMIE SEELEY, AGE 13

Led Zeppelin did a four-show run at the Capitol Centre. The night I attended was the second show. I lived in Martinsburg, West Virginia, which was two hours away from the venue. My older brother got me a ticket and my seat was surrounded by beautiful girls who were a few years older than me. It was absolutely perfect. Led Zeppelin opened with 'The Song Remains The Same'. It was an experience I shall never forget. I have a soundboard recorded bootleg CD of that show. The acoustic set contained a short segment of 'Dancing Days', which I've read somewhere was the only time on the 1977 tour that they played that song.

I WAS THERE: W DAN PATERSON JR

I was introduced to Led Zeppelin's music as a 14 or 15-year-old in 1973, by which time they'd already had five albums out. Older kids in my neighbourhood introduced me to a bunch of early seventies music I'd probably not have been exposed to otherwise. I was played the 45 single of 'Whole Lotta Love' and all other music was lame to me afterwards. I pretty much became a Zeppelectic, and I still have a scrapbook of articles and magazine covers, etc. *Physical Graffiti* was the album for our group as it was the first tour and record they released after we started following them. I lament to this day missing their February 1975 concert at the Capital Centre, near where I grew up. It was before I was driving and I had no way to get tickets.

I finally saw them in 1977. It was our senior year high school. They played four nights at the same venue, the old Capital Centre, and I got to see two of the four shows. They were supporting the live album, and I took pictures. They blew the roof off the place initially, and then the momentum and pace slowed down with the slower, bluesier numbers. These were long shows and we got our money's worth. The highlight for me was Bonham's drumming, especially on 'Achilles Last Stand'. He was just a workhorse power house.

I still listen to Zeppelin and have seen all the solo projects and tours including The Firm, Page and Plant solo (and together) and John Paul Jones's tour in the early 2000s. I'll see Plant with Alison Krauss when they tour. Their music is still a passion of mine.

GREENSBORO COLISEUM
31 MAY 1977, GREENSBORO, NORTH CAROLINA

I WAS THERE: DONALD R FULLER

I was born in 1957 in Maryland, a 'military brat' as we were called, as my father was a career enlisted sailor in the US Navy. We lived in Norfolk, Virginia until my father retired from the Navy, moving to Arkansas in 1966. The Beatles appeared on *The Ed Sullivan Show* when I was just a few weeks shy of seven years old, leaving an indelible mark. We didn't have a stereo system or LPs during my early childhood but I would play music from the local Norfolk radio station on the small portable radio that sat on a shelf next to my bed.

The year I turned 13, the Beatles disbanded. It hit me hard, but there was little time for mourning as I began to discover all these (relatively) new bands and sounds – Steppenwolf, Grand Funk Railroad, Pink Floyd. As I entered high school, I started listening to newer bands like Queen, Aerosmith, and the Eagles. By that time, we owned a small combination stereo turntable/radio, but had little money to purchase albums as we were dirt poor. The year I turned 13, my parents also divorced, and my mother had to support three boys on a licensed practical nurse's salary while attending college to earn a degree to become a registered nurse. My brothers, mother, and I ended up living in my grandfather's old farmhouse in the middle of nowhere in northeast Arkansas. We survived primarily on food my grandfather grew in a vegetable garden he kept (he had since retired from farming and rented out most of his land except for a small patch he used for growing vegetables. Having few albums, I got most of my exposure to rock and pop on the radio. We could pick up WMPS in Memphis, which was a great rock station in its day, and on a clear night with atmospheric condition being just right, we could even pick up WLS in Chicago.

I wasn't aware of Led Zeppelin except for a couple of songs I'd hear on radio such as 'Stairway To Heaven' or 'D'yer Mak'er'. We just didn't hear much of them while I was in high school, and their albums were not available at the local record store. The giant world of rock'n'roll and all it had to offer did not take hold of me until I graduated from high school in 1975 and entered the US Navy. This is the backdrop of what was soon to become my obsession with Led Zeppelin.

How exactly I found Zeppelin is lost to antiquity, but I do remember being stationed on the aircraft carrier USS Forrestal, stationed in my old childhood home of Norfolk, Virginia. Somehow, I discovered *Physical Graffiti* and from the moment I heard the opening riff to 'Custard Pie' I was hooked. I bought their entire back catalog and listened to their albums almost incessantly. In 1976, their movie *The Song Remains The Same* was released and I went to see it at a local theatre. This was the first time I had ever seen any concert footage of them, and it blew me away. I just *had* to see this band perform live! Within months, there was an announcement in *Rolling Stone* magazine. Led Zeppelin would be touring North America in 1977.

Finding out which bands were touring was mostly by word-of-mouth or an occasional announcement in a rock magazine or newspaper. Young people would line up outside a

Ticketmaster or Ticketron outlet (usually a Sears and Roebuck or a record store), sometimes as much as a week before the day tickets went on sale, as then the best seats were gotten by the first in line. The line could literally stretch for blocks in some cases! There was a certain air of adventure in getting to an outlet as early as possible to get the best tickets possible. For bands like Zeppelin, being at the front of the line didn't mean getting front row tickets, because in those days most concerts were general admission or 'festival style'. Getting in line early enough was the difference between seeing and not seeing a show as they tended to sell out within minutes.

So…a 1977 tour was announced and weeks later the itinerary was finally released. The closest show to me was going to be Greensboro (North Carolina) Coliseum on May 31. Greensboro is approximately 250 miles from Norfolk. I didn't have a car at the time, and tickets were most likely going to sell out quickly in Greensboro. How would I be able to get a ticket to the show? I also had to get special liberty (ie. vacation time) from my division chief to travel to the show, and that wasn't going to be easy as my chief didn't care much for me because I wasn't the most squared-away sailor in the Atlantic fleet. Despite these obstacles, I was bound and determined to find a way to see Led Zeppelin in Greensboro!

Getting permission from my division chief turned out to be much easier than I thought. I guess he wanted a couple of days break from me, so he put up no resistance to my request for two days liberty (in the Navy, liberty is basically days off without them being charged as leave, or vacation days). Now I needed to get airfare and somehow find a way to get a ticket to a show that most likely would be sold out before I got a chance to score one. The flight wouldn't be a problem, as air travel wasn't nearly as crowded as it is today and you could get an airline ticket the day of the flight back then. Plus you could walk straight from the terminal entrance to any gate, ticketed or not.

But how to get a concert ticket? I decided to get the address of the Greensboro Coliseum (a challenge, as there was no internet then) and mail a money order to the Coliseum, addressed to the venue's manager. Perhaps if I told a convincing story, he'd take my money and send me a ticket. I got a money order for $25 but left the 'Pay to the order of' line blank as I did not know to whom I was to make payment, and I had no idea how much a band the stature of Led Zeppelin would be charging for the pleasure of seeing them perform. Into an envelope went the money order along with a self-addressed, stamped envelope (postage was 13 cents) and a letter about how huge a Zeppelin fan I was and how I'd never had the chance to see them play live – you know, the old song and dance. Off it went the next day.

The show at the Greensboro Coliseum was set for May 31st, which happened to be John Bonham's birthday. I sent the letter and money order to the Coliseum in January, thinking that would give them plenty of time to return either my money order or a ticket. Weeks went by, and now we're in March. Not a word. No ticket. No money order. No nothing. I was starting to get antsy. I figured not only was I not going to get a ticket, but the manager had kept my $25 too. I wrote another letter to the Coliseum manager, this one a bit nasty and accusatory.

A couple of weeks later, I received a piece of mail from the Greensboro Coliseum. I opened the envelope and out fell my money order. My heart sank like a boulder rolled off a mountain top! Hands shaking, I unfolded the accompanying letter. It was from the Coliseum manager, telling me only an idiot would send a blank money order in the mail, as anyone could write in their name and cash it. But he went on to tell me to come to the Coliseum on the day of the show, knock on one of the entrance doors, ask for him by name (a name I have long forgotten) and he'd have a Zeppelin ticket waiting for me. I jumped out of my seat and started whooping and hollering like someone who had won the lottery!

Taking what the Coliseum manager wrote to me in faith, I boarded a plane to Greensboro where I headed straight to the Coliseum. I arrived around 1pm. A good-sized crowd was already starting to form around the main entrance doors. I walked about halfway around the venue and found a single metal door. I started banging on it, hoping someone inside would hear me. I must have banged on that door for 30 minutes, losing hope as each knock produced nothing. As I turned away, dejected, and almost as if on cue, the door opened and an older gentleman asked me what I wanted. I gave him my story, thinking he would tell me to buzz off, but he invited me in and asked me to wait there for a few minutes.

Ten minutes later he returned, reached out his hand and passed me a green ticket. 'Here, enjoy the show but don't tell anyone how you got this ticket.' The price was nine dollars, but I was getting to see Led Zeppelin for nothing.

By the time I got in the queue, I was about 25 feet from the doors. I thought about getting to the floor and possibly wiggling my way to the stage (I was quite thin in those days) but, waiting in the springtime sun, I decided the crush to get to the front would be more than I would want to handle. I would make a beeline to the first risers, stage left. When the doors opened at 6.30 pm, there was a maddening rush forward as everyone jockeyed for the prime real estate! But I headed straight to the section I had in mind and ended up in the fifth row from the floor.

There was a reason why I decided to go for the first risers, and it wasn't to avoid the crush of fans rushing the stage. In those days, not only were airports easy to access, but a person could just about smuggle anything onto an airplane. I had brought with me several joints of primo Columbian Gold and a little powdery substance we called 'tick' in high school (known by its more widely known moniker, PCP). I asked the guy sitting next to me to save my seat for me and he graciously agreed. I went to the men's room to take a whizz and to snort the tick I had on me. When I got back to my seat, I rewarded the guy (and his girlfriend) next to me by lighting up a J. Within minutes, I was high as a flippin' kite!

The 8pm showtime drew near. It came. It went. And went further. And went even further. At 8.30pm-ish we smoked another J. By this time, the PCP was really kicking in. As I looked out at the increasingly large audience, I saw a guy in a full body cast being hoisted up onto the soundboard platform in an old Radio Flyer wagon. They situated him so his head was elevated. After that, it went dark…

And I don't mean the Coliseum lights. I mean *me*! I passed out from the PCP, dope and Jack Daniels I had smuggled into the venue. (They didn't sell alcohol at rock shows in those days – it was all BYOB back then). I was out for what seemed like an eternity and had the band been on time, I would have likely missed most, if not all, of it. But they were late getting to Greensboro due to inclement weather in New York City, which they were using as their base of operations for the east coast.

So I was pretty much dead to the world. I didn't know what time it was, but I could hear the cheers start to get louder, almost like thunder. I heard the pop of a guitar being plugged into an amp turned to high volume, a clicking sound and then – BAM! – the first couple of notes of 'The Song Remains the Same'! The sound hit me like a ton of bricks, so hard it jarred me right out of my drug-induced stupor. I jumped straight up out of my seat, so high that I jumped over the back of my seat and landed on the guy in the row behind me! To this day, I haven't forgotten what the guy said to me: 'Go with it, dude!'

I crawled back down to my seat and it was Hammer of the Gods! I don't recall details about that night because I was buzzed out of my skull, but I do remember most of the songs and I also remember they did about an hour of electric music, took a break, did a 45-minute acoustic set (my favorite part of the night, actually), took another short break and came back to finish off with over an hour of an in-your-face electric blitzkrieg.

At one point during the show, Jimmy came to the microphone and told the crowd that it was Bonzo's birthday. Robert added that we should sing 'Happy Birthday' to him. He then led the crowd of approximately 17,500 in a beautiful rendition of that birthday classic. Bonzo took a bow to thunderous applause, sat back down behind the kit and the blitzkrieg continued.

Reading online the setlist for that show, I do remember Zeppelin playing the songs listed, but at the time of the show itself, I wouldn't have remembered them all. The excitement of seeing my favourite band for the first (and as it turned out, last) time, combined with the cocktail of potent liquid, powder and smoke, had me so hopped up I would have been hard-pressed to tell someone my own name!

After three hours of the Hammer, the show came to an end. I sat there for at least ten minutes, taking it all in and reminding myself repeatedly that, yes, I had indeed just seen Led Zeppelin. As the crowd started to thin out, I got up, staggered out to a taxi and headed back to the airport. I don't remember sleeping much that night. The ecstasy of seeing one of the greatest rock bands to ever play was the only thing I could think about for the next several days. My ears also rang for nearly a week.

I WAS THERE: DAN ALLEN, AGE 23

It was John Bonham's birthday and his drums were elevated and moved to the front of the stage as he played a really ass-kicking solo. The place was packed and it seemed they played everything.

I WAS THERE: JOHN WYATT

My friends and I decided to go and had tickets in hand when we went to Greensboro. We arrived two hours before the show and the parking lot was filling up. There were hippies and Southern rockers everywhere, with alluring young women in t-shirts and jeans and big hair adorning the place. We could see a big crowd outside the entrance. This was a 'festival seating' event, so everyone wanted to be in the front row. I found my way to the main foyer about the time the doors opened. As the line shortened, we saw people squeezing through three at a time and unstamped. Not being shy, I placed myself between two slim women just as we had to squeeze through the door. Fortunately, I was a skinny kid. It was a tight squeeze and close to painful, but we made it through. I never saw those young ladies again, but my hat is off to them for just movin' on through! Because I squeezed through the doorway, the ticket takers could not tear my ticket and so I still have my complete, although slightly wrinkled, ticket stub.

Inside, there was further pandemonium as people scurried for the best seats. By the time I got there it was a little over half full. I caught up with my buddies and proceeded to indulge in some music-enhancing smoking. Now the events get a little muddy, but I think the opening song was 'Rock And Roll'. A lot more followed but the highlight was 'Stairway To Heaven'. The lead up was really cool. After playing 'Misty Mountain Hop', Robert called out John Bonham and said 'it's Bonzo's birthday!' and gave him what looked like an unlabelled bottle of rum, from which Bonzo took a huge swig. After a hearty smile to all, he went to the drums and 'Stairway To Heaven' started. What an intense song live, with John Paul Jones laying the backdrop and Robert Plant wailing into the great solo by Jimmy Page.

My memory tends to fade after that until my buddies and I were stopped in a median outside Siler City, taking liberties and tossing out a few beer cans. A sheriff rolled up. Very quickly we started picking up the cans in time for the sheriff to see and he said, 'Thanks for cleaning up. Now, you boys might want to just head on down the road a ways before you stop again.'

I WAS THERE: MIKE NICHOLSON, AGE 14

I heard 'Rock And Roll' on the radio in early 1972 as a nine-year-old. I had my dad drive me to the drugstore where I bought the 45 with 'Four Sticks' on the B-side. I wore them out. My brother went away to uni in 1974 and left me all his rock LPs. *Houses Of the Holy* was one that I played daily. Then a friend gave me a cassette containing 'Whole Lotta Love' and a couple of other tunes about the time *Presence* came out and I was hooked. I worked my paper route and bought all the albums until I completed my collection on Christmas Day 1976.

I had already seen *The Song Remains The Same* in the theatre with the proper sound system and was completely gobsmacked. I was shaking with anticipation before the movie started. It gets a lot of guff these days but I still love it. I've probably seen it 200 times. I started collecting bootlegs not long after and had a bunch of that stuff on vinyl. Now I have every show on MP3 or Flac.

Just to be under the same roof as my idols, the titans of all that I hold dear in the world of rock and roll (and rock and roll is my world) is something I'll never forget. I went with a friend, Tommy Yow. We snuck up the side of the building and squatted out of sight of the cops that were pushing interlopers and gate crashers back. At 6.30pm the doors opened and we beelined it into the Coliseum for the best possible seating. The floor was already a quarter full and filling up fast. People were pushing up front and so Tommy and I decided to get the best seats on the side we could. What great seats they were too, on Page's side just a couple rows up from the floor.

Then the wait began. We waited. And waited. The crowd was restless and the pushing at the front became so bad that several people had to be lifted over the barricade at stage right and onto to the stage. I heard later there were broken ribs and a couple of people had to be hospitalised. There were no seats on the floor at rock concerts in those days, and this was a rowdy crowd, openly guzzling cheap booze out of milk cartons and smoking tons of weed with the lights on. There was not a cop in sight. The Greensboro Coliseum belonged to the freaks and the arena was like one huge bong.

Finally, at around 9.30pm the lights flickered off and though the roar came the giant fanfare 'D' chord to signal the beginning of 'The Song Remains The Same'. We got sudden flashes of light and there was Plant's golden locks at the front of the stage dressed – as the band teased him – in 'Grandma's old knickers'. And there was *the* Jimmy Page, resplendent in his white dragon outfit, twisting and bopping with his double-neck while peeling off astounding runs from the twelve-string neck. The lockstep rhythm section of Jones and Bonham was clicking into overdrive from the start.

I already knew, through *Hit Parader* leaking it, what the setlist was going to be, and that they would play either 'Over The Hills And Far Away' or 'In My Time Of Dying', but not both. During 'Nobody's Fault But Mine', Page broke a string and his guitar tech did an amazing mid-song guitar switch from his #1 '59 Les Paul to his #2 '60 Les Paul, the one Joe Walsh gave him a few years before. It was also around this time in the show that Jimmy rather elegantly vomited over his left shoulder onto the stage. Knowing what I know now, it was probably a reaction to a certain substance that Mr Page enjoyed in those days.

Plant's first words to the audience after 'Sick Again' were an apology for their lateness because they had someone in New York. As Page strapped on the Danelectro, I knew it was gonna be 'In My Time Of Dying'. Plant described it as having its roots in American Delta Blues. When he then introduced 'Since I've Been Loving You', he said it was more of an 'English Blues' not unlike vintage Fleetwood Mac, John Mayall and Alexis Korner.

'No Quarter' lasted what seemed like a half hour, with lasers dancing throughout the arena as well as on top of John Paul Jones' piano. The acoustic set had a slight snippet of 'Dancing Days'. The sudden segue from 'Black Mountain Side' into 'Kashmir' was perfectly executed and the highlight of the night. Page's solo section with the theremin, violin bow, more lasers, smoke and a ring modulator was essentially a shorter part of the mid-section of 'Dazed And Confused'.

Before 'Over The Top' it was announced that it was Bonzo's birthday and Plant led everyone in a chorus of 'Happy Birthday'. The home stretch of the show was 'Over The Top'/'Moby Dick' (which was longer than one could imagine), 'Achilles Last Stand' and the finale, 'Stairway'. They then took a pretty long break before returning with 'Whole Lotta Love' and then 'Rock And Roll'. I swear they also did 'Black Dog' during the encore but I could be wrong.

This show is the best thing I have ever seen. To my knowledge no recording of this show has ever surfaced. I am kind of glad, as I'd hate to have my bubble burst. I have heard the night before in Landover and I own the excellent bootleg of the July 17th Seattle show on DVD. I probably own every show on this tour in some form or another be it a CD, LP or cassette. You can plainly hear they are not at their live peak, owing mainly to Page's sloppy playing due to his lifestyle and Plant's voice was not in top form for most of the tour either. Still, if you can find a copy of *Listen To This Eddie*, a bootleg of the first LA Forum show, you can hear the old magic.

I saw Jimmy Page on the *Outrider* tour of 1988 in Landover, Maryland and many things about that show were holdovers from this show. A guy named Bonham on drums, a blond lead singer and the exact same stage set. He did some Zeppelin faves and even ended with an instrumental version of 'Stairway'.

TAMPA STADIUM
3 JUNE 1977, TAMPA, FLORIDA

I WAS THERE: BILL MOORMAN

This concert was cancelled after Led Zep had started playing because of a freak thunder storm. I believe Aerosmith were playing with them. Concerts then cost between $4 and $10. They were incredible, as always, with giant Cheech and Chong rolling paper joints passed up and down the rows. I loved going to concerts then. They were inexpensive and reefer was everywhere. The cops weren't hassling anybody for smoking weed. There was no violence and everyone was high and loving the music.

I WAS THERE: CATHY MOTTA LOVE

Led Zeppelin, live in concert at Tampa Stadium! We were all so excited leading up to that day: my best friend John; his date (whose name escapes me); Diana, the shy and isolated girl I met in school and had introduced to my group of friends; our friend Laura; and Eddy, a guy we all knew who had asked me out recently. I had anticipated this day for months. I picked up everyone in my freshly-washed-and-vacuumed handed-down-from-my-mom-to-my-bro-to me 1966 Pontiac LeMans with the white roof and Pontiac Blue body. We were stoked.

We flowed with the crowd into Tampa Stadium and found our assigned seats in the stadium, pausing only to get our bearings, and waited expectantly. We were so very hyped and when the band came on with 'The Song Remains The Same' we were all on our feet and immediately decided to head down to the field to try to get closer to the stage. It was spectacular, a sea of dancing and singing fans in utter bliss. We made it down to the field, barely 50 feet from the stage, when the skies opened in a deluge which caused the band to stop mid-song and run for cover and from the all-to-real electrocution danger.

We all did our best to shield each other from the rain and were more than willing to ride it out. Time seemed to come to a screeching halt however when an announcement was made cancelling the remainder of the show. Confusion was evident, with people pushing against the barrier at the foot of the stage for protection from the storm and beginning to scuffle. All of a sudden, the barrier fell forward onto the crowd. Police in riot gear scaled the wall onto the spectators below and began clubbing anyone they could reach.

I was separated from my friends as they turned to run away. I remember standing in shock watching as the police clubbed even those running away. I turned just in time to see one officer turn his club on a young pregnant woman not 20 feet away. It was then I realised that I was in immediate danger and had been separated from my friends in the melee.

My next recollection is sitting on a curb outside in a parking lot on the side of the stadium. I was oblivious as to how I got there and where I was. Suddenly, a car appeared in front of me and stopped; someone called my name and I looked up to see John smiling at me from the driver's seat through the passenger window. I didn't recognise anyone at first, and the girls had to talk me into getting into the car. I remember checking Diana's head for cuts and bumps which seemed to irritate her immensely; I was convinced everyone had been clubbed. We drove home in stunned silence, obviously in a collective state of shock.

The news over the next several days placed the blame for the chaos on the fans. Even so, we still hoped the band would return and reward us with a full concert. Those hopes were smashed, however, when news of the untimely death of Robert Plant's young son broke. We all understood. We all grieved. We all retained our broken hearts, as surely did Robert Plant, to this very day.

I WAS THERE: GARY BRIER

Most of my friends were older than me and were all into concerts and music so I got to see a lot of the bands that were before my time. We were into listening to our albums at home and getting high in our rooms, smoking pot or wherever. I was living in Oceanside, Long Island and Nassau Coliseum was only 20 minutes away from where I lived, so we got to see a lot of concerts there. I saw Yes, Jethro Tull, Johnny Winter, ELP, the Allman Brothers and so many bands. I probably saw the Dead a dozen times in '73. I saw Pink Floyd on the opening night of the US tour for *Dark Side Of The Moon* at Radio City Music Hall on March 17, 1973, with a showtime of 1am. I was 16.

Led Zeppelin were part of our musical journey. I went to see them at Nassau Coliseum with a friend of mine. He'd done too many drugs but I didn't take him to the infirmary. I ended up laying him down in the bathroom and going back and enjoying the rest of the show. We were 14 or 15 years old at the time. What do you do?

The second time I saw them was at Madison Square Garden. My friend drove us into the city and after the concert we went directly from the Garden to Watkins Glen, New York for the Watkins Glen *Summer Jam* festival that had the Allman Brothers, the Grateful Dead and The Band playing, one of the biggest festivals the country ever had. There were about 600,000 people there, twice the size of Woodstock. It was a crazy weekend.

The third time I saw them was at Tampa Stadium and that turned out to be a disaster because a giant rain cloud moved over the whole place right after the show started and it just let loose on everybody. The band was getting electrocuted on the stage so they played three songs and they had to stop and there ended up being a riot. So they cancelled the show and they put out a full page article apologising to everybody for what had happened at the show. Nobody got their money back. It was a good show while it lasted, but all you could see was these blankets and other coverings that people had put over themselves going up and down to the music, instead of the people's heads.

I saw Plant and Page in the nineties in Florida. It was the same sized venue as Nassau Coliseum and it was a very good show. It was basically Led Zeppelin.

I WAS THERE: DAVID PETRI, AGE 20

They only played two songs due to inclement weather. On the way out of the stadium there were ticket stubs all over the ground. Days later it was advertised in the newspaper that the promoter was offering a $10 refund for every ticket stub that was mailed into them. I kept mine.

I WAS THERE: GEOFF COTTRILL, AGE 14

They played two or three songs in the pouring rain. They then went backstage and cancelled the concert. There was a riot at the stadium when the fans found out they weren't coming back out. I got into the show by showing up early and selling Coca-Cola all day to fans in the stands. It was a fun day.

I WAS THERE: HERBIE ARRAYO

Zeppelin flew in by helicopter and played about three songs before a summer thunderstorm came in suddenly as they do in Florida. Storms come in fast and furious with hard rain and lots of lightning but in 15 minutes the sun is shining again. Zeppelin flew away and never came back and the crowd was very angry and started throwing beer cans, bottles of booze they had smuggled in and whatever they could get their hands on. I was bummed because I was about 20 yards from the stage, standing up.

I WAS THERE: PAT MIDDLETON

I smoked weed on the afternoon leading up to the 1973 Tampa concert and while I enjoyed the weed, I think it might have caused me not to have too many memories of the concert. I don't remember arriving or leaving the concert. I went back for their 1977 concert in Tampa. Shortly after the band came on stage the bottom fell out of the sky and sheets of rain poured down. They said there were riots, and we saw a few small groups of people who were not happy and they caused problems. The band said they would have a redo the following night but the police said there hadn't been enough time for people to cool off. Led Zeppelin never rescheduled. The friends I was with had tossed their ticket stubs into the trash and without the stubs couldn't get a refund. It was a mess.

I WAS THERE: SCOTT MARKS

I took my girlfriend to the '73 show at Tampa Stadium. I was with her up at the front of the stage when all the girls took off their shirts and bras. It was wild!

I was also at the '77 show when, during the fourth song, a huge black cloud appeared and it started pouring down rain and thunder. Robert Plant said, 'Hey guys, we're going to take a break until the rain stops.' I was seated up about ten rows to the upper right of the stage, watching everything, and saw a black helicopter appear. Robert, Jimmy, John and Jonesey got on it and it took off. I turned to my friend and said, 'Look, they took off in that helicopter!' About 45 minutes passed and the rain stopped. We waited about another hour and the crowd of about 65,000 people started screaming bloody murder. Then people started rushing the stage and the cops started beating people. It turned into a huge riot. Fans started throwing bottles of booze at the cops and the cops were beating people up and striking them with their batons. My friend and I remained seated because we didn't want to get involved. Sirens started blaring and loading up injured victims. Over 500 people were hospitalised! Needless to say, the band never returned. I eventually got a refund on the tickets I purchased.

I WAS THERE: MIKE MACRUM

'Mike, where ya been? We have a real cluster fuck going on here.'

'I've been hassling with the boneheads at the hotel and the cops. I guess that vending machine I destroyed last night is a bigger deal than I thought it would be. You know it's gonna cost me $1500 to straighten it out?'

'Yeah, Yeah, Yeah. You should have never knocked it over in the first place, you idiot. You know how crazed everyone was. And why in Hell did you tell them you did it?'

I looked at Masher. He was dressed in his normal Showco tee and the same jeans he wore every day. I always wondered if he had more than one pair of jeans. Or just four or five identical pairs that were torn and frayed in the same places. His face showed real concern. That was not like him. If anyone kept his cool usually, it was The Masher. I was going to fill him in on the idea of guilt and what it did to some of us. Share my experience learned the hard way, that a pre-emptive confession always seemed to result in punishment less severe. But I could tell he was not on the same page anymore. I skipped it and got to the point.

'So, what's up? After the hotel raped me, they got all nicey-nice and told me I had a message. A message from you. By the way, that Coke machine stole my money.'

'Look out at the crowd. They just got word the concert's been cancelled. By the governor, no less. We need all hands on deck. I think the whackos are going to rush the stage.'

I walked onto the stage and gazed out toward the stadium. That high falutin' custom-built portable security wall set in place to keep back the crazies at outdoor gigs looked like a black wave. One end would lift and then fall. The next section would rise and then fall, and so on down the line like a black snake wiggling in front of the stage. The sound of the people in the crowd was an ugly sound. 50,000 fans not happy that they would not see Led Zeppelin this day. Many had become a mob intent on getting revenge. The rest just seemed to hang out as if they had nowhere else to go.

A bottle landed near me and exploded into a thousand pieces covering my Chuck Taylors with what I hoped was beer or pale wine. Jumping back, I tripped on the bull dick cable taped down on the stage floor and fell on my ass. Still seated, I turned and looked over to Masher. 'So why was the concert cancelled?' More objects began to rain onto the stage. Bottles, cans, even someone's hash pipe. I scrambled back out of the way.

'Look up.' Masher's eyes drifted skyward and he pointed to the fabric canopy hung over the stage. 'We had a screamer of a thunderstorm an hour or so ago. The fire marshall came through and said if we couldn't get rid of the water, the show was done. He was not impressed with the scaffolding fix we came up with. And then he called his guys who then called their guys and now the damn governor is involved. We need to start loading everything up before the crowd breaks through and starts destroying stuff. Get your truck backed in ASAP. And then get back here to help security keep the crowd back.'

Above me the canopy erected to keep the hot Florida sun off the pasty faces of the band was filled with water. It looked like a swimming pool's worth of water. And to be fair to the fire marshall, I was not impressed with that scaffolding fix either.

Water dripped down at a steady pace right where the monitor board would normally be. The monitor board had been yanked as had everything else on the stage. Just the lights, a couple of lonely looking mic stands and the speaker stacks remained. Water dripped on a bare stage and pooled under the dead cables that connected nothing anymore. I had not been hired to be a head breaker. I was a truck driver. I didn't mess with sound. I didn't do lights. I drove trucks. Busting on poor drunken or drugged slobs definitely did not fit into my perception of my job description.

I began to run all this concern by Masher, when Bob, the head engineer on the tour, came over and roared, 'Get your fuckin' truck and back it in. Let's move!' I beat a hasty retreat. No one argued with Bob. He was lead engineer for a reason.

Outside behind the stadium, I was impressed with the calm compared to the anarchy I had just left. No irate fans, no tense roadies or security guys. All there was to indicate pandemonium inside the stadium was the roar of thousands of voices as if cheering a continuous touchdown or never-ending home run. The trouble was inside not out here in the real world. Outside the sun was shining, cars drove by and seagulls stood on the dumpsters next to a chain link fence near my truck.

Backing up to the gate, I did not have to get out to find someone to open it. It opened as if by remote by two security guys wearing their standard black security t-shirts. I backed in until Masher popped out in front of the mirror and jerked his hand in a halt kind of way. Before I even had a chance to get out and unlatch my ramp, it had been removed and I saw two roadies running with it towards the rear of my trailer. By the time I had walked back my doors were open, the ramp was down and the first piece of equipment was almost on the trailer.

I stood there considering the tense vibes all around me. My musing lasted but a moment when Dave, the new driver with the biker attitude, walked over and handed me a mic stand. 'Let's kick some ass.'

I stood holding this mic stand and looked at him. He was enjoying this. I don't know what made me more nervous, the out of control crowd or this maniac waiting with bated breath to lay into someone. But I kept quiet and followed him over to stage left.

Just then the barricade broke. The crowd had finally found a weak spot and quickly threw it to the side. A sea of long-haired fans streamed through the opening. They jumped on the stage. Several were more intent on the victory of the breach than paying attention to the defence mounted against them. A few danced in circles with arms raised. Dave laid into the closest one with his mic stand, catching the poor bastard right in the kidneys. He went down and Dave moved onto engage his next unlucky target. I looked over to stage right and two security guys were having their way with another fan. It was mayhem. Violent and instant mayhem. All I could do was stand there, mic stand in hand, and watch.

Where were the cops? I wondered. And why were our guys so damn violent? It just did not make sense to me. Any of it. It was then something solid sailed right at me. I turned but not quick enough. I felt the blow but adrenalin had kicked in. I turned back and looked for the source. All I saw were people in various states of grappling violence. Anger came in a flash. Tossing down the mic stand, I ran to Dave's rescue. I pulled two guys off him and kicked another one hard. Dave extricated himself and all he said was, 'I had it under control bud.'

And he was off again, rushing another fan who had violated our space. I threw up my hands in retreat and backed up to where a group of roadies and stage hands had gathered just outside the circle of pandemonium. If I had to guess, I would say we all stood there with the same thing on our minds. How crazy was this? Just look at those guys. They are beating people because they like it. What the fuck?

Wanting nothing more to do with this stupidity, I retreated towards the Green Room. On the way, one of the light roadies popped out of the bathroom and walked by me. 'Hey Mike, there's some chick in the men's room giving everyone head. Get in line!'

I shook my head and continued to where I knew food and hopefully some quiet place could be found for me to escape this day that had started so wrong for me. Finding the Green Room, I quickly filled a paper plate with leftovers and plopped into one of the over-stuffed chairs. All the while the noise outside the door continued unabated.

At some point I noticed it was not as loud as it had been. I figured the worst was over and I left the Green Room's false security. Back behind the stage, I saw cops streaming by and people in handcuffs being led away with body parts trickling blood. A whiff of tear gas lingered. The crowd had been controlled. The security barrier lay in ruins in front of the stage. And the bulging canopy continued its steady drip-drip-drip of water. Out in the stadium, riot cops were busy clearing the fans determined to hang out. There was no hitting, just determined lines of uniforms moving everyone towards the exits.

Masher found me. 'I had Mountain Boy pull your truck out. Are you okay? I saw that shot you took. I don't blame you for leaving. Find the ambulance, they'll fix you up.'

'What shot?' I looked at Masher. I had no clue what he was talking about.

'Feel the back of your head, Mike.' He turned and left. I reached back and felt my head. A large bump had formed. My hand came away red. I found the ambulance. They cleaned me up and cut me loose.

I sat in my truck, numb. I tried to digest what I had just witnessed. What I had just been part of. All I could do was think about that damn roadie coming out of the bathroom and informing me some chick was giving everyone head. And I started to laugh. Deep chuckles that started at my asshole and purged all the anger and fear built up over the last 30 minutes. In all the chaos, hate and discontent, life still moved in predictable ways. The flow of what was normal – SSDD – always found a way to coexist with any upheaval placed in its way. No matter what madness existed, people still ate, people still got head. Some parts of life just happened naturally, paying no mind to whatever else was going on. It was then I realised this business of rock 'n' roll was going to be one of the most memorable times of my life.

I WAS THERE: DONA LOCKWOOD

I discovered them when I lived in Clearwater, Florida. A friend of mine was from New York City and he turned me on to the music. I have loved them ever since! The first album I heard was probably *Zeppelin III*. I was supposed to go to my graduation for high school but a friend of ours pulled up in an MG Midget and said 'does anyone want to go to Zeppelin?' So I missed my high school graduation because I was seeing them… and then the show was rained off!

I WAS THERE: ERIC ENGAN

I first became aware of Led Zeppelin when I was around ten years old and after hearing 'Whole Lotta Love' and 'Communication Breakdown' on our crummy little AM radio station, WKXY 930 in Sarasota, Florida, which was the station to listen to for the rock 'n' roll set back then. Before getting a transistor radio, my main exposure to rock 'n' roll was hearing my mom play the first couple of Beatles albums over and over. She wasn't much of a fan of them post 'Love Me Do'. And although I liked The Beatles (and still do) they weren't the brash loud rock music this kid really wanted to hear. As a kid, digging up the funds to purchase an album was no easy feat. Seeing *II* in the Zayre's record department a few times, with that bizarre and enticing cover art, I finally scrounged up the three dollars and fifty-seven cents to score this album, the first album I had actually purchased myself. I felt on top of the world.

Even on the cheap and crummy stereo I could play it on, 'Whole Lotta Love' was a transitory experience, particularly the middle part and its stereo imaging. I had never heard anything like it, and neither had my mom, who, predictably, thought it was too loud and obnoxious and took the opportunity to criticise my budding tastes. This, of course, made it even more appealing to me. The brashness of the guitars and drums and the innate swagger of the songs were just the thing. I was hooked.

Of course, Zep were not just all fire-and-brimstone, and even the much more mellow 'Thank You' closing off the first side was still a treat. And 'The Lemon Song'? Even as a pre-pubescent I knew what that was about. When *III* came out, I might have been disappointed by the acoustic edge to that one, but I wasn't. To this day 'Since I've Been Loving You' gives me the shivers as some of the finest electric blues ever recorded. The album cover? You can't get stuff like that anymore.

In my school, we had the Stones camp, a little later the Floyd camp, and of course the Zeppelin camp. I liked the Stones and Floyd, and still do, but you can imagine which camp your narrator was in.

In 1975, Zeppelin came to Tampa Stadium, about 70 miles north of me. My school chum Joe K went – his mom took him. My mom (there she is again) nixed my attendance. One of the missed opportunities of my life. Joe got a full show, and the envy of the rest of us.

I finally got my crack at the live Zep experience in 1977. By this time I was driving and college-bound, and my mom couldn't say no, although she strongly encouraged me not to go. Not this time, Mom.

My buddy David K and I went to Tampa Stadium for the long-delayed experience. I had never seen nor smelled so much pot in my life, and still haven't to this day. The clouds were looking threatening, but so what? This was the day we would finally see Zep.

It got dark, and eventually the opening riff to 'Nobody's Fault But Mine' made its way to the seats at the 50-yard line, where David and I were sitting. Although the sound was pretty crummy – it would take ten or 15 seconds to figure out what song the boys were even playing – this was still top of the world for me. Then, it started raining. The band went off and the PA announcer told us to wait – they would come back out when the rain stopped. And, surely it would, right? Well, apparently God didn't get the memo, and after some delay, finally the crane holding up the gigantic mirror ball over the field began hoisting the ball higher and higher. Not a good sign. We were soaked and waiting.

Then the PA guy told us the show was being postponed to some future date and to hold onto our ticket stubs and go home. A riot ensued. People started wrecking stuff and raising hell. David and I left amid the chaos.

Later, and in college, I discover the Ramones and the Sex Pistols, and later Black Flag and the Circle Jerks, but I have never forsaken Zeppelin. Now I am north of 60 years old, but I can still tell people who have seen Guns N' Roses, Queen or Van Halen that I have seen Led Zeppelin… even if only for a bit.

I WASN'T THERE: MIKE ROYAL

They caused a riot because the ticket said 'rain or shine' and they walked off after one song because of lightning. In retrospect, they could have waited out the storm. Tampa banned concerts for three years at the stadium as a result. I'm glad I skipped it.

MADISON SQUARE GARDEN
7-8, 10-11, 13-14 JUNE 1977, NEW YORK, NEW YORK

I WAS THERE: JAY ALLEN SANFORD, AGE 17

In the middle of June 1977, I hitchhiked with my buddy Tommy Gray from rural coastal Connecticut to Madison Square Garden in New York City (about two hours by car, but eight to 24 by thumb) to see the mighty Led Zeppelin on one of their final US dates. I've told people for years what a crappy show it was, and now I have the proof, having found it bootlegged on YouTube! It was a trip hearing it again all these years later, and there are actually a few good bits like 'Kashmir' and 'Over The Hills And Far Away', mostly the parts where Jimmy Page was passed out on a chair behind the amp and letting everyone else play. Yes, Page slept through part of the show on what was the fifth of six nights. A stagehand had to wake him up to do the solo between 'Heartbeaker' and 'Achilles Last Stand', but if you listen to the noise he was making, I have doubts that he ever actually woke up until well into the latter number. I can't even pinpoint the spot where he dropped the guitar onto the stage, because most of the 'solo' sounds like someone was running it through a washing machine.

That said, the hitchhiking was a great adventure! We got garbage thrown on our heads walking through Harlem, but still got to the show just before the lights went down. And the only way my folks let me go on a school night on one of the last school days of the year was because I promised I'd still go to school the next day.

Sure enough, the last ride I thumbed got me right to the school doors just long enough before the bell rang. That gave me time to earn my rank as the coolest kid in the entire school that day, because I was wearing the concert shirt and carrying the programme I got at a Zep concert the night before! Never mind that the band played like crap…

I WAS THERE: DAVID MOORE AKA PROFESSOR P-SOOP, AGE 16

I grew up with five older siblings and besides the AM radio I mostly heard their music – Mountain, Crosby, Stills, Nash and Young, Motown and The Bee Gees. But when I was around twelve, my family moved to the suburbs. The kids out there were playing in garage bands (I soon joined in) and listening to stuff that was just revelatory to me – David Bowie, Alice Cooper, Kiss – and Led Zeppelin. This band did everything. They would serve up gentle, melodic acoustic ballads, barn-burning arena rock, mystical mood pieces and the rawest blues I'd ever heard, working several of those into the same song. They never seemed to be trying to prove anything either. When others were trying to be so heavy to 'out-Zeppelin' Zeppelin, they put out their immortal and classic third album. If they didn't feel like pounding out a hard rocker, they didn't. And if a song didn't call for a guitar solo, it didn't get one.

There were those who didn't encourage this daring, adventurous approach. One silly critic even lambasted their masterpiece album, *Houses Of The Holy*, suggesting they should stick to what they do best. Keep doing 'The Lemon Song' over and over and deny us the unprecedented genius of 'In The Light' or 'The Rain Song'? Thank heaven their minds were more open than ours. When the movie *The Song Remains The Same* came out I watched it, dumbfounded, at least six times. Fortunately, my mother was a movie theatre manager.

In 1977, I was in high school and the only way to get Led Zeppelin tickets was through a lottery, by mail. I remember coming home from school one day and finding my tickets had arrived. I actually jumped up and down, not believing I would get to see Led Zeppelin at Madison Square Garden. For a rock-crazed kid it was like a dream. With seven incredible albums to choose from, my mind reeled at the thought of the set list they would put together. I remember being in the Garden when the lights went down, hearing the first chord of 'The Song Remains the Same' and thinking my heart would burst. I still tear up and shiver thinking about it.

That was the tour that was documented the least. In fact, it's the only one the band really doesn't seem to have recorded at all. I marvelled at the incredible white dragon outfit Jimmy Page was wearing and how this skinny little man hit the stage like a hurricane, throwing that double-neck guitar around, letting it drag him on his knees across the stage. I simply couldn't believe the length and breadth of the show. There was the incredible acoustic set with John Paul Jones playing mandolin, guitar and singing. Beyond that, he worked his magic on the synthesizer, the piano and, of course, the bass, on which he can be poetic or pulverising with equal prowess.

And John Henry Bonham. What could ever be said? While often celebrated for the ultra-violence visited upon his modest drum kit, the man was as adept a brain surgeon as he was a butcher, as dictated by the song.

It was always the song with Led Zeppelin. There was no needless 'musical weightlifting exhibitions' – apart from the solos, which all but Plant had. And Plant? Robert Plant was simply incredible in his role as master of ceremonies and chief storyteller, guiding us through three-and-a-half hours of the most incredible musical journey on which a live audience has ever been taken. And Jimmy Page? Well, there aren't any words; he's simply the master. He is the greatest rock composer, performer and guitarist of all time by a wide margin. The fastest, cleanest, most precise or learned? He'd be the first to say 'that's not me.' But has anyone ever wrung more aching, lyrical, frightening or exhilarating tones from the neck of a six-string? Not before, not since, not ever.

There was also no shortage of visual treats – the laser pyramid, the mist, the flashpots, the mirror ball, the lights – but even in a high school gym, they'd still have been the greatest show on earth.

There were many highlights. One is the epically drawn out 'No Quarter' with explorations and improvisations ranging from classical to old school retro rock, during which I recall Robert Plant picking up a rose that had been thrown onto the stage and dancing with it in his teeth! All in one song, too, and that one of the heaviest and most atmospheric songs in the Led Zeppelin canon. But something else would yet be thrown at the stage that sixth and last night of their final stand in New York wouldn't be received so well.

It was the stuff of dreams; even now, 41 years later, it is still the greatest single night of entertainment and thrills I've ever spent. They had played six nights at the Garden and this was the last. Unfortunately, an incident somewhat marred the ending. When they returned for their encore, a firework of some kind was thrown and exploded very close to Jimmy Page. I saw that his hand was bleeding. I seem to remember him looking at it, incredulous and in shock. The momentum was broken; that rush when the band is ready to reclaim the stage was delayed a bit, at least. They did come back after a time and finish but it was a very unfortunate turn. I felt badly for poor Mr Page but that night, that astonishing show, was an experience that many younger musicians I know wish they had been around to have.

I'm not nostalgic for my silly youth; being a kid and getting high and doing stupid things. Not at all. And I don't care to hear all the legends of epic debauchery that often accompany that era and that especially involved this band. Art should be free of such seamy tabloid trash. It was and is about the music. The songs remain the same; unstained, pristine, impervious to the ravages of time. I'm as convinced as I ever was that there will never be a band like this again and I celebrate and cherish the countless hours of transcendent joy they've given me. I hope this generation comes along for the ride, over the hills and far away; to Mordor, to Valhalla, to the levee, to Kashmir and every magical place Led Zeppelin takes us.

I WAS THERE: JACK KOUSSEVITZKY

I saw Zep twice and have seen Robert Plant solo since. The electricity and intensity at the Zeppelin MSG shows I attended back in 1977 makes them stand alone on so many levels. Simply put, those shows come to mind every single time I've entered a venue in the last 45 years as a barometer to what a rock show can be. I've been to many shows by many artists over the years and none have ever come close.

I WAS THERE: JOHN PULICE, AGE 16

I was 16 and in high school and a friend came up with four tickets. I didn't know I was going until 4pm on the day of the concert but one of the guys, Greg, decided to go out with this girl Doris instead. So I paid 17 dollars for my ticket and enjoyed myself beyond belief. The only concert I'd been to before was Smokey Robinson in Atlantic City, aged ten, but getting the train from Long Island to Manhattan was routine. We arrived at MSG and people were all over the place. Someone was selling shirts for three bucks so I bought one for me and one for each of my two brothers. We people watched outside until 7.30pm and then decided to go in and people watch inside. At 8pm, the lights went out. There was no warm up band and the spotlight was immediately on Page and the infamous double neck, playing the opening to 'The Song Remains The Same'. I was at the show!

It was three hours long with no intermission. The crowd was very large and loud. There had to be about 20,000 people there. I had never seen anything like this ever. In the first hour we got a six-song acoustic section in which they played 'Gallows Pole', 'That's The Way', Boogie With Stu', Bron-y-Aur', Going To California' and 'Tangerine'. It was brilliant, with all the songs performed like the recordings. Each one of the band was seated up at the front of the stage and they changed instruments after every song. JPJ pulled out this triple neck guitar, which was the coolest thing I've ever seen. After that was over, we had a few more songs and then came the solos part, with everyone getting a 20 minute solo – JPJ first, then Bonham, and then Page.

Page pulled out this violin bow and was doing his thing. He was in the middle of this laser light pyramid and every time he hit the guitar the pyramid would spin. He'd hit it faster and the pyramid would spin faster. This led into 'Kashmir' from 'White Summer', where Page had shown his slide guitar skills, then the bow then everyone was back in the finish the final hour of the concert.

The ovations after the songs were immense. Top bands I've seen since just never compared. Zeppelin had more people in the audience and more women in the audience. The equipment that other bands had on the stage Zeppelin had suspended in the air. They had more lights too. Everything was bigger and better with Zeppelin. I've seen Queen, The Who. Deep Purple, Black Sabbath, Pink Floyd, Jethro Tull and the Rolling Stones and none compared to Zeppelin. The other groups had intermissions and warm up groups, playing for 90 minutes. Zeppelin played for 180 minutes. They were the best group ever.

And the guy who didn't go and chose the girl instead? The girl was sick so big mistake there…

I WAS THERE: JILL ELIZABETH, AGE 16

I went with my girlfriends to celebrate my friend Molly's 16th birthday. Lots of people were passing weed around and the cops right there did nothing. There were massive crowds when we were leaving, pushing us along. We couldn't hear anything because the music had been so loud and we had buzzing in our ears. It was a little overwhelming. Molly kept her ticket as a souvenir – and took her seat number as well!

I WAS THERE: EDWARD JENNINGS

As a senior in high school in 1968 I hung around in the cafeteria before school and at lunch to discuss who we were listening to on WNEW-FM radio. We devoured *Rolling Stone* magazine from cover to cover. One of our circle had friends in England who told him about Led Zeppelin. *Led Zeppelin I* was everything I had heard about and more. I played it relentlessly on my hi-fi system and in art class at school. Lots of people borrowed it from me.

I wanted to see Led Zeppelin live in concert. In July 1969, I bumped into two high school friends who were psyched about having seen Led Zeppelin at the Fillmore East and listened intently as they talked about sitting in the balcony with binoculars studying Jimmy Page's guitar mastery. They watched his hands the entire show, as they both played guitar in a band. They were knocked out by his musicianship and urged me to see Led Zeppelin if I ever got the chance. Eight years later I did.

I purchased tickets at a Ticketron ticketing terminal. Led Zeppelin had booked a six-night engagement and I scored tickets for the Saturday evening, June 11. My sister-in-law drove us from Norwalk, Connecticut in her Volvo. Travelling by car to the Garden added to the excitement of the evening. There is a thrill in witnessing the streets and atmosphere of New York City at night – the lights, the people and the stores. We parked at the Garden and joined our fellow Zep freaks as we headed into the venue. Our seats were fantastic for $10.50 each. We sat on the left side of the band as they faced out into the audience. We had a great view of Robert Plant, Jimmy Page and John Bonham. John Paul Jones was tucked behind Bonham so we couldn't see him as well.

I remember being tired that night and starting to drift off to sleep in my seat (who falls asleep at a Led Zeppelin concert?) as they played several acoustic numbers whilst seated at the front of the stage. I snapped awake after 'Black Mountainside' as I witnessed Jimmy Page kicking a three-legged stool as it slid fast behind him under Bonham's drum kit. He grabbed his double-neck guitar, launching us into 'Kashmir'. It was a powerful moment that swept me along for the ride. 'Kashmir' was followed by the greatest drum solo I ever saw. John Bonham played 'Moby Dick' with drum sticks, his hands and the gong. I realized years later, when he passed away, why Led Zeppelin did not want to reform, as Bonzo was integral to their sonic experience.

The evening ended with the encore of 'Stairway To Heaven'. Hearing Robert Plant's voice echo across the sea of people in Madison Square Garden as the huge disco ball cast its light on us was breathtaking to witness. His hair was golden, as was the memory.

I WAS THERE: TOM GIORNO, AGE 16

You had to mail in and it was a lottery system for tickets. I missed out on tickets but as luck would have it, a classmate got tickets but couldn't go so offered me his. I think they cost $8. WPLJ was the radio station promoting the show and they gave out buttons. I still have mine. Highlights include 'No Quarter'. There was just something about the groove of it. And when the band was playing 'Stairway', Jimmy was playing the double-neck and all of a sudden he looked down at the guitar, realised he'd broken a string, and next thing one of roadies came out with the Les Paul and Jimmy just ripped into the solo.

I WAS THERE: RE DERING, AGE 19

In 1975 I went with my best friend. In 1977, I went with my boyfriend and my best friend. Zep always opened with 'Rock And Roll'. Bonzo's drum set was huge! They were promoting *The*

Song Remains The Same movie and album. We had dyed our hair green with food colouring, and from all the sweating our faces turned green where the food colouring ran down. We screamed every word to every song right along with Robert, who looked like a god onstage.

I WAS THERE: JAMES MCCURRACH

I was born and raised in New York and from an early age I was exposed to a lot of great music, mostly via AM radio which always seemed to be on in the background everywhere. WABC in the city was great – so many memorable songs, lots of Motown and pop music. In the early seventies music making was prolific with all those one-hit wonders and the quality of music just multiplied. Then I discovered pot and a whole new level of music.

As a freshman in 1974, it was all about heavy metal like Deep Purple and Black Sabbath – and Zeppelin! The first record I bought was Bad Company and the next was *Zeppelin IV*. I thought they were the coolest, with the ZOSO symbols, etc. We played that record to death and loved the different music styles, things like 'The Battle Of Evermore' and 'When The Levee Breaks'.

I got a fake ID (we all had them back then) and my 'name' was James Patrick Page. I thought I was so clever! For the next three to four years, I was obsessed with all things Zep. Finally, I got my chance to see them. You had to mail in your order for tickets and it was basically a crap shoot as to what seats you got. I went with a school buddy. Tickets were $10 and we thought that was a lot. And wouldn't you know we got seats behind the stage? Not good!

But Madison Square Garden was a big place and we just decided we would take our chances and try and find better seats. We spent a lot of time sitting in someone else's seats and then getting kicked out when they showed up. I remember sitting in the aisle for part of the show. They did a great version of 'Kashmir' but it wasn't a great Zeppelin performance. By that time, the band had a lot of personal and health issues – Plant's accident, Page's heroin issue, etc. – plus all the excessive partying meant they weren't at the top of their game. It was still good, just not great.

I WAS THERE: JEFF GROSS

I attended the Saturday night show. I think we were fortunate to catch one of the very few performances of 'Heartbreaker' as an encore, but unfortunate to miss 'Rock And Roll', 'Whole Lotta Love' and 'Over The Hills And Far Away'. The Page and Bonham solos were lifeless and never-ending. Page and Plant in 1995 and 1998 were much better performances, as was Jimmy Page and The Black Crowes in 1999 and 2000. But at least I own the bragging rights. I'm not sure if my disappointment was due to the actual performance or overly inflated expectations.

The biggest surprise was 'Battle Of Evermore', probably the last song I expected to hear. The low point were the teasing riffs – the opening riff of 'The Rover' but going into 'Sick Again' instead, the opening riff to 'Out On The Tiles' but going into the drum solo. This was a fucked-up summer for NYC – The Summer of Sam, The Bronx was burning, blackouts, etc. – but it was unseasonably cold on Saturday June 11. There were lots of lasers on stage and, unfortunately, pyrotechnics in the audience.

I WAS THERE: MICHAEL S

I think we managed to see at least four of those shows. Back then it was so easy to move around the Garden. If you were two young agile and athletic boys you could scoot past security guards and ushers and run down stairs to better seats and sneak into sections that you didn't have tickets for. And light up whenever and wherever you wanted while the authorities just looked the other way. 50 years and many, many concerts all over the US and Europe later, those Zeppelin shows are without a doubt some of the best concert memories I have!

I WAS THERE: ROSEMARY REINERTSEN, AGE 18

We went with friends from the Locker Room bar. We met them and took the train into the city from New Jersey. We had bad seats way up high and I had to use my binoculars. It was a very cool experience. 'Stairway To Heaven' really stood out for me, with the light show and the halo above Robert Plant.

I WAS THERE: CHRIS O'LOUGHLIN, AGE 12

The mid-month moon of June hung lazily over Manhattan island. We had secured Zeppelin tickets by mail order four months previous. In my young perception of time, the calendar grinned and mocked me as it only begrudgingly tuned its pages en route to the eagerly anticipated date. The mail order limit was six tickets per customer. I use the word 'we' loosely, as I had nothing to do with the purchase. I was all of twelve years old but I was already a bona fide Led Zeppelin impresario. My big brother Greg had made a coordinated effort to ensure that a veritable gang of Bronx Zeppheads would be present at Madison Square Garden for the final performance of their six-night run. The greatest of Greg's efforts was made in the form of promises and oaths under God and all else that is holy that I would be kept from the pot-smoking hoodlums and their rock concert carryings-on. Well, he made sure I was safe. All other bets were off.

Greg had come to be amused at coming home each night from hanging out in the park and finding me asleep with *The Song Remains The Same* on the turntable, stuck on a bad groove on the record at the end of the live version of 'Dazed And Confused'. He was impressed that his little brother had dozed off each school night to the mystical strains of the dark mage casting his eerie spell with a violin bow on a 1958 Les Paul.

I will never forget the day many months earlier, while on newspaper reading assignment in my sixth grade class at P.S. 94, having turned the page of *The New York Daily News* to a full-page ad announcing the release of Presence, the unexpected follow-up to *Physical Graffiti*. Every day after school I played air guitar to 'Achilles Last Stand', never imagining that I would soon be in the same arena as the gods of Olympus as they played it before my awestruck eyes.

I am as eternally grateful for not knowing that June 14th 1977 would be the final time Led Zeppelin ever played in NYC as I am for having been there. No, I wasn't screaming like an infatuated schoolgirl at a Beatles show. I was in an altered state of consciousness. Silent and stunned in jaw-dropped, reverent awe. Truly, it was sublime. The three-hour concert came complete with an acoustic set, a green laser pyramid, misty smoke, a whale of a Bonzo solo, 'Stairway', 'No Quarter', 'The Song Remains The Same' as an opener, 'Kashmir' and 'Ten Years Gone' and – yes, prophetically – 'Achilles Last Stand'. Jesus. I was in paradise. My consciousness had pierced the veil of eternity and I was in perfect... well... presence.

After encores of a part of 'Whole Lotta Love' into 'Rock And Roll', things went sideways because some asshole threw a lit M80 onto the stage. By all accounts it hit Bonzo's massive bass drum. Now, which particular Les Paul-wielding Dark Mage was forever hugging that kick drum to feel its impact on his frail frame? You got it. Jimmy's hand caught the burst of the moronic firework. I will always remember the only time I saw the maestro's back that night from our second-tier seats, the dragon on the hind side of his white poppy suit.

The band doctor was tending to Jimmy's hand burn stage right and he made the decision. The rest of the encores were 'called' and the last night of Led Zeppelin in New York City was over.

Heading down the MSG escalators some lazy reluctant minutes later, there was no talking, no 'that was so awesome man!' A certain post-church-like silence held muted court. The stunned collective remnants of an agreement. We had just witnessed what words were too lame to describe. The vibe was such that talking would somehow be blasphemous. Until, in true New York City ZeppHead who has noted the every-other-year rhythm of touring fashion, some dude joked: 'Yo, I got two tickets for 1979, you guys.' He got a silence-breaking laugh that Peter Grant would've smilingly approved of. '79 seemed twelve eternities away.

And as fate would have it, it was not to be. There was a very good reason for our stunned, awe-stricken silence. God hold you, John Henry Bonham. And long live Led Fucking Zeppelin, ya cunt ya.

THE FORUM
21-23 & 25-27 JUNE 1977, INGLEWOOD, CALIFORNIA

I WAS THERE: KENNEY STARKEY

I remember four young men walking on stage full of confidence. I remember how loud and crisp 'The Song Remains The Same' was. I waited for 'Kashmir' and it sounded just like the album. Without a doubt it was one of the best nights of my life. Those guys were so good. It was hard to comprehend how four musicians could be so good but I saw it with my own eyes and they were better than I thought they could be.

I WAS THERE: EVE ON, AGE 24

I went with my husband. We had great seats to the side of the stage. I was so excited I hardly sat in my seat and instead stood through most of the concert. They put on an amazing performance. Jimmy Page is and always will be my favourite guitarist. One of my favourite Zep blues song is 'Since I've Been Loving You'. I have too many favourites to choose only one, but 'Stairway To Heaven' is not one of them.

I WAS THERE: BRUCE SNIVELY

I think I first heard them through my brother Jeff's 8-track tapes of the band's first two records. In May 1973, I was nearing the end of eleventh grade and I went to school that day with the excitement of the school year coming to an end. But the excitement in the air was not about school ending, it was everyone comparing notes from seeing Led Zeppelin at the old Tampa stadium the night before. It seemed that the entire school went and I was the only who missed it.

In 1976, I joined the Air Force and after basic training I spent six weeks on my job tech training at Lowery AFB in Denver, Colorado. I saw the movie *The Song Remains The Same* in Denver and it whetted my appetite for the real thing.

In 1977 Led Zeppelin were playing Los Angeles at the same time I was stationed at Nellis AFB, Las Vegas. My roommate Steve Coca and l headed to LA for the Inglewood show. I remember a lot of dry ice during 'No Quarter'. This was the night when Who drummer Keith Moon crashed their encore. Keith was quite funny and really cracked up Robert Plant. At the end, Keith went to the microphone and said that next year he would come back with his band and play for us. The audience cheered loudly at this promise, but sadly Keith passed away in 1978.

I WAS THERE: JEFFREY WEISSMAN. AGE 18

l had inherited my family's 19-inch Zenith colour TV and I wasn't making much money, but I wanted to go – it was the hottest ticket in town. I found a guy that would trade four tickets for the TV. He didn't tell me they were behind the stage. The band turned around and played one song to us. Bonham's 'Moby Dick' solo with the spinning holographic pyramid above was a highlight.

I WAS THERE: KEN DUFAULT

I was at the opening night at The Forum. A friend's mother owned a ticket service and we paid an unheard of $20 each for tickets. It was the first time I had ever seen a laser used at a concert. There was a green laser triangle spinning around Jimmy Page during his solos. Truly amazing.

I WAS THERE: LD MCCLURE

I remember sitting or possibly standing so far back on the floor that I really couldn't see and was unhappy. This was long before Jumbotron. Zep didn't play 'Whole Lotta Love' or 'Black Dog' that night and, again, I was unhappy. But I'm glad I went and I made up for it by seeing Page and Plant in 1995.

I WAS THERE: KIM DEBOLT. AGE 17

My mom was born in Smethwick in the Midlands but came to the States when she was 13. Most of my family are from the Black Country. I like to think I have a little connection with Percy! I grew up in the San Fernando Valley just north of Los Angeles. We had a rock radio station here, KMET, and in the early seventies I used to listen to Dr Demento on Sunday nights on the station. Then I started listening to it all the time and that's when I first heard the band. I bought two albums in the summer of 1973 – *Led Zep III* and *Brain Salad Surgery*. There was just something about Zep's sound that drew me in, even as a young teenager.

Jump ahead to 1975 when Zep announced an American tour. They were coming to the Forum in LA and my friends and I saved our cash so we could go to a show. Then Robert was injured in the car crash. I did go to my first concert that summer – Black Sabbath, Peter Frampton, Lynyrd Skynyrd and Brownsville Station. I continued to buy Led Zeppelin albums and listened to them on my stereo every day. 'Kashmir' is still my favourite song as it just transports me to another time and place.

I hung out with a friend who was into music and we heard that Zep were coming to the States again in 1977 and playing the Forum. I told him I was going and that I didn't care how much I had to pay or how I got there. He told me he would go with me so I started saving some cash again. The friend came over one day and I told him I had the money to buy my ticket and we could go to Ticketron any time. He looked at me and said, 'We don't have to. I already bought two tickets.' He showed me the tickets – 16th row floor seats at the Forum. I almost fainted. He had bought them from a ticket dealer but never told me what he paid for them. I found out later from another friend that the tickets were $40 each. I couldn't believe he paid that much!

We went during the week and on a school night but eleventh grade was almost over. Many of my friends were talking about and going to the shows. They would come to school the next day in their concert shirts and just be freaking out about how good the show was. Our seats were fantastic. I remember sitting down, looking at the stage and thinking, 'God, they're going to be right there!' We sat next to two guys who were so stoked. I wore feathers on leather strips in my hair, which was very trendy at the time, and the one guy kept singing, 'With love in her eyes and feathers in her hair.'

There was no announcement that the show was starting. The house lights just went out and everyone went nuts. The first song they played was 'The Song Remains The Same'. They did a whole acoustic set which was cool. And I remember the awesome drum kit for 'Moby Dick' and Bonzo's solo, 'Dazed And Confused' with Jimmy's solo and 'Stairway to Heaven' for Jonesy, and 'Kashmir'. The band just transfixed you. You couldn't look away because you didn't want to miss anything. And the guys all laughed and joked so I felt like I was a part of it and not just watching.

We all sang, people were dancing. They played for three hours, if not more, because I remember not getting home until about 1am and the Forum is not far from where I lived. On the way out, my friend bought me two t-shirts which was super cool of him because I didn't have to pay him for my ticket either. We listened to Zep cassettes on the way home.

The next day at school, so many people had Led Zeppelin t-shirts on. I saw a few friends at the concert and they were just manic the next day. People thought of Led Zeppelin as such a mega band and put them on a pedestal, like gods. They seemed almost unreachable, and folks thought they would never get to see them. Led Zeppelin was the band you had to see at least once.

I WAS THERE: FRAN HICKMAN, AGE 15

I was 15 years old and had to lie to my parents to go. I told them I was spending the night with a girlfriend and we loaded up and off a whole gang of us went to LA. Concert memories all these years later are a little hazy, but I do remember waiting to hear 'Kashmir' and being so happy when they played it. My friend, Karen, was there and was even a more avid Zeppelin fan and she kept copious notes on the concert. I wish I had. Robert Plant has been my man crush ever since. We were up in the nosebleed seats but I distinctly remember Robert Plant and what he had on.

I WAS THERE: ROBERT ROBERT

I saw Zep four times in their heyday… in 1973 at Madison Square Garden on *The Song Remains the Same* tour and again in 1975 on the *Physical Graffiti* tour, and twice in 1977 at the LA Forum. One of those LA shows was when Keith Moon showed up and did 'Moby Dick' with Bonham on side-by-side drum kits. That could very well be my fondest memory. What I particularly remember is how they never had an opening supporting act. There would always be someone who would come to the mic and say to the rumbling, hungry-for-Zeppelin audience: 'Ladies and gentlemen, there will be no supporting act tonight,' he'd wave his hand back and say 'Led Zeppelin!' and – bang – they would open up with 'Rock And Roll' with a vengeance. The buzz amongst Zep-heads when Zeppelin tickets went on sale and as the shows got close to the dates in your city (especially in NYC) would be overwhelming. Before the '73 show in New York, I saw a guy peel off five $100 dollar bills to a scalper for a ticket outside. $500 was a ton of money in '73!

I WAS THERE: PAUL ROJO

They were unbelievable. The best concert of my life and I've seen Floyd at the Hollywood Bowl doing *Dark Side Of The Moon*, Deep Purple on a *Made In Japan*-era tour and Cream (or was it Blind Faith?) at the Swing Auditorium. Zeppelin was the best ever. We drove to the concert in a Chrysler Imperial limo from the high desert. We smoked Panama gold and swilled cheap wine. The show opened with songs from *Zep I*. Plant and Page tore us up for well over an hour. With John Bonham shredding it up, and Page killing us slowly with his licks, they broke out with 'Stairway'. The entire Forum went dark. Page began those notes we all know so well and everyone lit their BIC lighters. The flames (yeah, back then there were lighters, not phones) swept slowly across the crowded stadium. Then a thin narrow beam of green laser light came on, pointed right at that double-neck Page was killing us with. That beam then began to oscillate slowly, first in circles, then triangles and then it began to strobe. Remember, the only other light was all our lighters. That laser reflected all through the clouds of reefer smoke drifting through it. It was transfixing. We all stood, dazed and confused. Was this really unfolding before our eyes?

Page was dressed in some kind of cream-coloured suit. As the beam enlarged, more of the stage was revealed. There they all stood, in all their glory, with driving bass lines and killer drumming from the legend. It was all so hypnotic. What a night to be almost straight on to the stage in a $40 seat. It seemed endless. They played straight through to *Presence*. All the greats then. All those legends now. What an amazing sensory pounding we all took. Never again will there be anything so raw, so brutal, yet so comfortingly tender.

I WAS THERE: DAVID FRESHMAN

There were times at this concert that I felt that the band was a bit off. Jimmy and the band seemed just not in sync at times. Page was struggling with personal issues. That being said, what I loved about the 1977 show were three songs specifically – 'Ten Years Gone', which was sheer Zeppelin brilliance, 'Battle of Evermore', which was getting its live debut, and the unstoppable force of 'Achilles Last Stand'. Sadly, parts of the show seemed deeply sloppy due to Jimmy's personal issues. Compared to the four shows I saw between 1971 and 1975, there was something missing. I noticed for the first time Jimmy and Bonzo starting to struggle with their drug addictions. It made me so sad. The music had moved into another realm with 'Achilles Last Stand' and other songs. Still, I could see instantly the effects the heroin was having on my heroes. It broke my heart.

Of the five shows I saw, the shows in 1971 to 1973 had the most fire of them all. What I loved about Zeppelin live is that they could very easily swing between heavy and light. Electric/acoustic duality was essential to their success. But what struck me the most was the immense power of the rhythm section of John Bonham and JPJ. It was like weaving, only with incredible polyrhythmic drive and funkiness. Always solid, yet the two men played off each other in such a unique and fascinating manner. Jimmy's work in the early years was always spot on. He could play all the modes at the drop of a hat. Mix them up, toss them in the air and find those psychedelic/blue notes and otherworldly musical concepts that only the best cats knew.

When I think back to the amazing good fortune I had seeing Zeppelin at the tender age of 15, in 1971, through to 1977, I was most blessed. I will always cherish those concerts.

KINGDOME
17 JULY 1977, SEATTLE, WASHINGTON

I WAS THERE: GARY ALLAN

My brother and I were just out driving around and noticed the crowds heading toward the Kingdome and checked it out. We found out tickets were something like $10 each and decided to attend. The venue held about 60,000 for concerts. Sound systems had improved in the intervening four years and Led Zeppelin were incredibly loud. I had to go out to the concession area halfway through the concert to save my eardrums. The images of Robert Plant moving about without his shirt and of Bonham beating the drums mercilessly stick in my mind, as well as that of Jimmy Page.

I WAS THERE: WILSON O'NEAL

The second time I saw them. Tickets were $10 through Ticketmaster. 'Since I've Been Loving You' was the song I remember the most from that show. The Kingdome wasn't the best venue and it echoed after a song was over and the acoustics weren't the best. But hey, it was Zeppelin, so who cares?

ARIZONA STATE UNIVERSITY
20 JULY 1977, TEMPE, ARIZONA

I WAS THERE: ED ORTIZ

On their best night no one could even come close to the performance level of Led Zeppelin. Except of course Wednesday evening July 20th 1977.

I had high expectations for this show that was originally scheduled for Sunday March 6th and which was rescheduled due to Robert Plant's illness. The show was due to begin at 8pm but the band didn't even leave their hotel until after 8pm. Beginning at approximately 9pm, the band tore into 'The Song Remains The Same'. Jimmy was dressed in a black t-shirt with the dragon pants that he would wear at the next gig in Oakland.

All seemed to be well to begin with. The first indication that this was going to be a low-key show was the fact that Jimmy wasn't moving around much… In fact, he seemed quite content standing perfectly still just to the left of Bonzo. As the show progressed, Jimmy seemed more and more out of it. During the solo in 'Over The Hills And Far Away' he was on the opposite side of the stage when he needed to activate his guitar's floor effect. Robert Plant, being in closer range, actually activated it for him.

After a very lacklustre acoustic set and a very unusual 'Trampled Underfoot' guitar solo, Jimmy strapped on the Danelectro and, instead of performing 'White Summer', played a few bars of 'Black Mountain Side' before going into 'Kashmir' with Bonzo and then John Paul Jones joining in. Some have said that the band was not aware that this was going to happen, but I would have to disagree as Jones was sitting at the keyboards, when normally he would have been off stage while Jimmy performed 'White Summer'.

There was no Bonham drum solo and a pyrotechnic miscue at the beginning of 'Achilles Last Stand' caught Jimmy off guard, sending him staggering back a few feet from the flashpots. This was a huge explosion with very blinding white light that the audience thought was part of the show. But Jimmy was quite upset as you could see him going over to the side of the stage and raising a closed fist, presumably to a roadie. Robert announced after the song that the explosion was not meant to happen and that the person responsible would shortly be castrated.

There were to be no encores to this performance, with 'Stairway To Heaven' being the last number played. John Bonham seemed in a hurry to get the show over with as he was up and gone off his drum stool before Robert finished the final lyric of the song and we didn't get the customary cymbal flurry at the end. It's been said that Bonzo's hand was hurting and that he wasn't feeling well.

All in all it was a very uneven performance. Robert's performance was good, as was John Paul Jones'. And Bonzo? Aah, what can you say about dear Bonzo? A drummer who literally rises up off his drum stool to come crashing down on his kit with such power. That was worth the price of admission alone.

I just wished Jimmy was more into it. It would have been a great night. I was certainly very happy with my seats as I was the 84th person in line when the tickets went on sale and I was sat very close to the stage. But I am extremely fortunate to be able to say that I got to see Led Zeppelin, even if it wasn't one of those 'magical' nights. Tempe, Arizona would sadly be the second-to-last US city the band would ever play.

The two Oakland shows that ultimately were to mark the end of Led Zeppelin's live performances in North America are mired in controversy when, after the Saturday show, the Zeppelin entourage beat up a member of promoter Bill Graham's staff, who had assaulted Peter Grant's son. The Sunday show only goes ahead when Bill Graham signs a letter absolving Zeppelin of any blame.

ALAMEDA COUNTY COLISEUM
23 JULY 1977, OAKLAND, CALIFORNIA

I WAS THERE: ROY TODD, AGE 17

I saw them on the second to last show they ever played in the United States. Tickets went on sale about a month before. Rick Derringer opened the show then Judas Priest and then Zeppelin. I couldn't go to sleep the night before because I was so excited. When Zeppelin came on, they opened with my favourite Zep tune, 'The Song Remains The Same'. Needless to say, I've seen the movie at least 200 times. And, to top it off, I went on my first date with my now wife that night I went to see Zeppelin.

I WAS THERE: STEVEN DEVORE, AGE 16

I was eight when their first album was released. I recall sitting next to a friend's wall unit with the stereo blasting to 'Your Time Is Gonna Come' and 'Communication Breakdown'. In California, bands would take out ads in the Sunday papers to announce shows and that's how you found out about them, unless you had friends in the industry, which I did. I was up in the Bay Area at the time and a friend called, telling me Zeppelin was corning to town. I had him buy me the ticket. During the summer it was like Christmas, waiting to see who was coming to town. I had a shoe box filled with concert tickets that I would trade, barter and sell. It was my currency during high school.

I saw them both Saturday and Sunday. We got there about 10pm the night before. Partying on the sidewalk, waiting to get in the parking lot on the morning of the show, was always a good time. We had chairs and a cooler; sprawled out on our blanket. I waited that evening with two friends, Sterling and Drew, high school friends. We were 16 and going to see Zeppelin, and we were on top of the world.

I WAS THERE: MARK STAUFFER, AGE 17

I went with seven of my best friends. It was a hot summer day and we waited in the line to get down onto the field, get our spot and spread our stuff out to mark our territory, only for some drunk ass that was walking through the crowd to barf all over our stuff! But we managed to deal with that. Then the show went off and was incredible. 1977 was almost the peak of Led Zeppelin and they just kicked ass!

I WAS THERE: JOHN ROESLI, AGE 16

My friend Rafael, myself and two other friends drove from South San Francisco on the other side of the Bay to the Coliseum early that morning. I remember waiting in line and then being in the Coliseum sitting at field level when Judas Priest began to play. Nobody really knew who they were. We walked up to the stage and watched them for a few minutes, unimpressed. Then Derringer came on and I remember the grating noise when they dragged their guitars on stage. They were somewhat well known and the place had really begun to fill up. Somewhere in the middle of all of that we had managed to acquire a bottle of Southern Comfort and we drank that until I was just about passed out. I remember waking up and puking, so we got up and moved to seats higher in the stadium. I dozed off again and then was woken by the sound of a cannon.

It was sound checking on Bonham's bass drum and it was loud. We were recent fans of the band, having seen *The Song Remains The Same*, but I was probably more familiar with the *Presence* album which had only been out a while, and *Led Zeppelin IV*, which was still on rotation on many Bay Area album-oriented rock radio stations.

I remember bits of music from that day. John had switched to an Alembic bass, which sounded great and you could hear a lot more of his playing, but I did miss the Fender Jazz sound that he always had. I remember 'No Quarter' and the extended solo he played on a grand piano. Robert's vocals sounded good and he wore the 'Nurses Do It Better' t-shirt. At some point he led the crowd in callisthenics (hand/arm signals) to the pattern of the music. I remember 'Achilles Last Stand' and the 'Whole Lotta Love' encore.

Seeing them outdoors on a sunny day years after the movie was a lot different from what I expected, but none the less enjoyable. Afterwards, I remember reading in the *Chronicle* about John Bonham being arrested or detained for beating up one of Bill Graham's bouncers. We all thought that was okay because he had a bit of a gangster reputation. A few years later, I was in college and excited that they were coming back on tour when I heard the news that John Bonham had passed away. Another tragedy and the end of an era. I don't remember having an appreciation for their place in music history or the transformational impact. I just remember we thought they were the baddest rock and roll band in the land.

Somewhere in the attic is the poster from the Oakland show and I come across it every once in while and spend a few minutes reminiscing, as to me it was more than just a music performance. It was a ritual of passage from youth to manhood.

I WAS THERE: JOHN CAITO

Tickets were $20. That show was the one where Bill Graham's crew went backstage and told Led Zeppelin to get back out and perform their second set and a huge brawl ensued. Of course, the audience didn't know until the next day. I remember it sure being a very long time in between sets. John Bonham was all Led Zeppelin needed to handle the scuffle.

I WAS THERE: MILES NEEDHAM, AGE 14

Our second period art teacher would let the class listen to albums while working on whatever the assigned project was. I was aware of 'Whole Lotta Love', 'Stairway To Heaven', 'Black Dog' and 'D'yer Mak'er'. Then someone brought in *The Song Remains The Same*. I heard a few songs every day for a few months and, around late February, got my own copy. I played it non-stop for the next few months, acquiring *Houses Of The Holy*, and then the first, second and fourth albums. It was a weekday in June and I was not in school when at about 10am the deejay on the radio announced the 'Day On The Green' Led Zeppelin show. It was going to be on a Saturday. This was a summer concert series at the Oakland Coliseum that over the years hosted all the bands, big and small, locals and legends. The year before, I had saw The Beach Boys with Brian Wilson's return to the stage; fat and deranged, but Brian nonetheless.

Zeppelin had been slated to play there two years earlier, with Joe Walsh and The Pretty Things opening, but Robert Plant's auto accident in Greece and subsequent convalescence forced the cancellation of the gig. Having last played Northern California in 1973, the Bay Area was chomping at the bit for the Zeppelin to ravage the land. By the time I called my mom at work to beg her to drive about 25 miles one way on her lunch hour in heavy traffic to spend $12.50 each for ticket – a lot of money for a concert at the time – the show sold out.

Devastation. Then elation, as a Sunday show was announced. It was still morning and I pleaded with my mom, promising the world, knowing the promises would never be kept. She relented and the afternoon radio, being monitored for news of a second sell out, brought no such news. Sometime after 5pm my mom gets home with the ticket. Singular. One ticket. I freaked out. 'You're supposed to get two! What about my buddy?' She gets back in the car and hauls butt back to Pacific Stereo, returning a while later, victorious.

On July 23, my buddy Rod and I took the city bus downtown to the Sacramento Greyhound station and the 80-mile bus ride to the Oakland California Greyhound depot, the last place two 14-year-old white boys should be on a Saturday night in July. Oblivious to the pimps and pushers, most likely negotiating a price for our white asses, we skipped off to the BART station which zipped us away to the Oakland Alameda County Coliseum, where Led Zeppelin had played just hours before and would do so again in several hours. We were here! After hanging with folks lined up all night, smoking and drinking, about 9am the gates opened. First up was an unknown band from Birmingham, England, a little boogie woogie combo with the foreboding name that my grandpa used as a swear instead of 'Jesus Christ!' He would say 'Judas Priest!' and for a couple of years my cousins and I would crack up every time he said it.

Priest's set was about 25 minutes long. I remember it being hard rock and them staying about 20 minutes too long – 'this is not what we are here for' – but within a year Priest would be one of my favourite bands.

Derringer was next up and the 'Rock and Roll, Hoochie Koo' band shredded, Rick Derringer and the other guitarist throwing their guitars back and forth across the stage to each other. They put on a great show and primed the crowd perfectly.

Then the wait. Three hours of no Zep. Where were they? What was taking so long? Of course, we had no idea about events behind the scenes causing the delay. Finally, activity on stage as techs begin to plug in, turn on and tune up. Then the boys hit the stage. The daytime outdoor show deprived us of the laser show or the house lights going down but there they were. Jimmy Page was wearing jodhpurs, the black stormtrooper boots from the Chicago show, a white shirt with a knee length black topcoat and sunglasses. He was cool as fuck. Robert Plant was wearing blue satin pants and a plain white t-shirt and was also cool as fuck. JPJ was all in white and Bonzo was in sunglasses and a leather coat. How the hell did he play drums in leather? Jimmy Page, with his double-neck SG slung low, fired the opening salvos of 'The Song Remains The Same' and the crowd went wild.

It was problematic being a relative newbie to Zep who didn't know all of their songs at a daytime outdoor stadium show, as the sound shifted and swirled and bounced around through no doing of the band. The second song was 'Sick Again', now one of my favourite Zep songs, but I didn't recognise it, did not get into it, had no idea what it was about. Basically, if it wasn't on the first, second or fourth albums or *Houses* or the live album, I didn't know it. So much for quite a portion of their set, although I had just heard 'Kashmir' a few weeks before. I recorded it off the radio and labelled it 'Cashmere' on the cassette. There was no 'Dazed And Confused', except the bow section, and no 'Moby Dick'.

So combine a lack of set familiarity, spending all day in the sun, Jimmy and Bonzo's substance issues, Mexican brown weed and little or no sleep with youthful inexperience and the last half of the show made it hard for me to stay awake. When 'Stairway' began signalling the end of the show, we were relieved. The 'Whole Lotta Love'/'Rock And Roll' encore revitalised us a bit for the trek home. Possibly the highlight of the show was the mysterious 'Oakland Dancer' who appeared on stage during 'No Quarter' and 'Stairway'. She was whirling and twirling all over the stage for no apparent reason. We didn't know who she was or why she was on the stage.

At the time, it was a disappointing afternoon. In retrospect I'm glad I was there and the bootleg recording of the show many years later doesn't sound as bad as I remember it, musically or otherwise. To this day I am a total Led Head, and I am proud to say that I saw the very last show Led Zeppelin ever played on American soil.

I WAS THERE: ANNIE ALLEN, AGE 14

It was so unreal – and exciting! It was my first concert. We got there early in the morning for the day-long event. The opening bands were Judas Priest and Rick Derringer. We waited a long time for Led Zeppelin to come out. It was late afternoon, almost evening, by the time they did. I had made my way through the huge, tightly packed crowd to almost the very front, in front of Jimmy, on the right side. (I'm a huge Jimmy fan.) It was a very hot day and I had brought no water or food – and I didn't pee all day either! I could never have gotten back up to the front if I had. This is before I ever smoked pot or drank so I remember everything clearly. There were so many people.

They played for three hours and played almost every song. It was amazing. Adrenaline was coursing through me. I had gotten up pretty close, and made eye contact with both Robert and Jimmy. One cute girl who had been up on a guy's shoulders was summoned to come up on the stage in the end. I was so jealous and wished I was sexy enough to be invited up. Midway through they did an acoustic set. It was unforgettable. My ticket was $11.50. I was elated for weeks afterwards!

I WAS THERE: LESLIE RILEY

I was in my early twenties and just a kid really. Back in the day the pot, alcohol and drugs flowed freely – it was the seventies, after all – and it was two days of awesomeness. And compared to today's concert prices it was practically free!

I WAS THERE: MICHAEL SHAVER

I was at the Saturday show – on acid – two days before my nineteenth birthday. It was better than the Sunday show. We booed Judas Priest off stage. Rick Derringer was the next act up. When the show started it was overcast and we wanted sunshine for Led Zeppelin. Rick played a killer set and his last song was 'Helter Skelter'. The clouds opened up at the end of the song and suddenly it was completely blue sky. He walked off stage with his right hand up in the air.

I WAS THERE: ROSS MCCALLEY

I was at the Saturday show. I was a senior in high school. The tour was in support of the *Presence* album, so they did a few songs from that album. I especially remember 'Nobody's Fault But Mine' and 'Achilles Last Stand' being outstanding live. Tickets were around $12.

I WAS THERE: JOHN BULLOCK

There were 60,000 to 70,000 people there. They were awesome. 'Stairway' blew me away. They covered the stage with grey smoke and released around 100 white doves which flew out through the smoke. What a sight to see!

I WAS THERE: KEVIN BARBER

I was at the second Day on the Green in Oakland in 1977, in the infield about 30 yards out. It was the last show they ever played in the US. We waited forever for them to come out but it was worth it. They came out and played 'The Song Remains The Same'. Everything was good after that. The sound setup was the best ever. Bonzo had some type of surround sound speaker setup above the stage for his drums. It really rocked during 'Kashmir'. An incredible amount of music was crammed into a three-hour set. I also saw Page and Plant in Memphis in 1995. They played 'Kashmir' with the orchestra. But that didn't make up for no Bonzo.

I WAS THERE: MARK JOHNSON

I won tickets through a local radio station. Judas Priest got booed big time and Rick Derringer was awesome. Wireless guitars were fairly new and Rick and Danny Johnson (Rick's other guitarist) were tossing guitars back and forth across the stage. After that, there was a two hour wait for Zep. Bill Graham announced they were having problems with Jimmy's double neck guitar, but actually they were negotiating whether to cancel the show due to the incident the day before. When they finally hit the stage, John Bonham seemed drunk and was messing with the drum tech, signalling that there was something wrong with the drum kit and then laughing. Their performance overall was unremarkable, but I'm glad I was there.

I WAS THERE: MATT MEUSER

The girls we took did all the coke and took off with some other guys. We waited for ever for the band to come out but they left me with a memory that will last a lifetime.

I WAS THERE: NILES R SHARIF

I remember sitting in line outside the Coliseum all night so that we could get close to the stage. I remember a rumour going around about some fight that had occurred the day before involving Peter Grant and John Bonham versus one of Bill Graham's backstage security guards. I don't recall JP looking as bad as photos later showed, but the Oakland Coliseum is huge and we weren't that close to the stage.

I WAS THERE: LYNNE FISK

I went to the 'Day on the Green' when they had the crush at Oakland Coliseum Stadium, which turned out to be the last US concert. Zeppelin's security got into a big fight with Bill Graham's security on the Saturday. On Sunday, they refused to come out and they only came out after two to three hours when he threatened them again.

I WAS THERE: ROBERT CANACARI

I had seen them five times before this tour, going all the way back to a show at the Berkeley Community Theater in Berkeley, California in 1971. I then saw them on June 23, 1977 at the Forum in LA, which was great. But at the Oakland show you could tell something was off. And Page sat down on a stool for at least half of the show, not just for the acoustic set, because he was so stoned. A sad ending to the greatest band ever.

I WAS THERE: SUSAN HARDIN

They took hours to come on. Jimmy was sloppy in a way only he could be. Judas Priest opened up unbilled and unscheduled, and actually Rick Derringer – who played in between – was awesome.

I WAS THERE: TOM KNOWLTON

I was there Sunday. I was a sophomore from Westmont High School. I made my way to the stage when they finally came out and I remember Jimmy had a full Heineken and was spilling it as he took a bow.

I WAS THERE: JEFF BOOKSTAFF

After Kezar Stadium in 1973, I also saw what was to be their final show on US soil, as Robert Plant's son died two days later. This was an awesome show. We were right up front. Jimmy was very translucent white, very stoned and very frail. He didn't have a monkey on his back – he had an ape!

The band's next planned show is at the New Orleans Superdome. On 26 July 1977, shortly after arriving in the city, Plant gets the news that his young son Karac, back home in the UK with Plant's wife Maureen, has died following a sudden illness. Plant flies home to be with his family and the remaining seven tour dates are cancelled. Led Zeppelin never tour North America again.

SUPERDOME
30 JULY 1977, NEW ORLEANS, LOUISIANA

I WASN'T THERE: LESLIE MILLS

I had my $10 Superdome ticket in my hand when Plant received the call that his son died. Their plane just took off again and the show never went off.

With Robert and his family mourning the loss of his son, the band do not tour in 1978 and when Plant does agree to appear live again, it is at two concerts at Knebworth Park in Hertfordshire, just north of London. Before the Knebworth shows, Zeppelin play two warm up gigs in Copenhagen, Denmark.

FALKONER THEATER
23 JUNE 1979, COPENHAGEN, DENMARK

I WAS THERE: JAN A PEDERSEN

I got to record the concert and take a lot of pictures, even though you weren't allowed to. Led Zeppelin used so much power that they had borrowed a compressor from the Danish Defence Force to supply power. Our row of chairs wasn't there, but we got some other seats. The members of Led Zeppelin didn't look at each other once. John Bonham practically hid behind the drum kit. The pauses between songs were far too long. It was very strange. They had made a laser cage for Jimmy Page, which he was to use for improvisations at the end of the set, and the laser cage exploded. I don't remember the concert as particularly good. Even 'Stairway To Heaven' was long drawn out and boring. I think that day may have made me less of a fan of Led Zeppelin. That year I also saw Kate Bush and Mike Oldfield. They were far better, and the musicians they had with them were far better. I hate to admit it, but that's how it was.

KNEBWORTH PARK
4 AUGUST 1979, STEVENAGE, UK

I WAS THERE: KEVIN CURRY, AGE 19

I either got a train from Kings Cross or Finsbury Park to Stevenage. The first thought that struck me was the sea of faces – it seemed it stretched for miles. I went on my own, which did not bother me. The opening act was Chas and Dave. God knows why. Also on the bill were Commander Cody, Southside Johnny and the Asbury Dukes (who I thought were very good), Fairport Convention (who flew in by helicopter, did their set and flew out again to play Cropedy) and Todd Rundgren, who took to the stage in a very revealing jumpsuit. He was good as well. We were told that Zeppelin would be on stage at 9pm. Half past nine came and went and the crowd was getting impatient, probably in anticipation. Finally, 10pm came and the band came on stage to the opening chords of 'The Song Remains The Same'. I'm not sure of the running order. I remember 'Sick Again', 'Over The Hills And Far Away' and 'Ten Years Gone', with JPJ playing with a three-neck guitar. I think it was a twelve-string and six-string guitar and a mandolin.

One of the highlights was Jimmy Page's violin bow solo. Four green laser lights surrounded him in the shape of a pyramid and, as he struck the guitar, it turned a quarter turn. He did this four times and then he just kept striking the guitar in a frenzy and the pyramid was spinning around. He then pointed the bow skyward and a red laser beam went up into the night sky – absolutely brilliant!

'Kashmir' and 'Stairway to Heaven' were also great. The show ended and they came back for an encore. Was it 'Whole Lotta Love'? They went off stage but the crowd wanted more and started singing, 'You'll Never Walk Alone', which Robert Plant joined in. I can't remember what song they did next. It might have been 'Heartbreaker'. Then they came back for a rousing rendition of 'Rock And Roll' and then it was all over at 1am on Sunday morning.

I remember following the crowd in the middle of the night in a field and miraculously we found ourselves at Stevenage station.

I had got into Zep at a late stage into their careers. A mate of mine had an older brother who was into them and my mate put on *Physical Graffiti* and after the opening track, 'Custard Pie', I thought, 'Yeah, this is good'. By the time I listened to 'The Rover', the second track, I was hooked. I have been lucky and have met Jimmy Page and Robert Plant, but that is another story.

I WAS THERE: PAUL HINDESS

Twelve of us went down to camp the night before in this camper van with no windows. Everybody was having a great time, sat outside the tent that night, singing along to 'Fluff' Freeman's radio show. At midnight it was the last song and we were all expecting 'Stairway To Heaven'. The whole campsite would have sung along. He didn't play it, the bastard. He played 'Freebird' by Lynyrd Skynyrd.

The next day is a bit foggy for me. We had a spare ticket because one of the guys couldn't make it so I hung around out front, where people were looking to buy tickets, and this guy did a deal with us – our ticket for a bag of dope. I don't think we'd even tried marijuana in them days. We learnt from other people to get a can of beer and put some in there and – well, anyway, everything's a bit foggy for me because of that. I remember being at the gig and not having to leave early this time. I was taping concerts by then. It was quite a big tape recorder, like a woman's handbag, and I taped the show. But it was rubbish. We were miles back. But we could see fine and the atmosphere was great. The whole event was fantastic. But what I really remember is swapping the ticket for drugs and getting stoned for the first time in my life!

I wish I'd got tickets for the second show but when you're only earning £8 a week and you've got to hire a van or go on the train *and* buy your tickets, you have other priorities, like living. We didn't have a lot of money. I came from a family of six. I had a paper round to get my money. You could scrape together 75p to see Mott the Hoople at the City Hall, or see Led Zeppelin and pay for the bus fares. Do it twice? We couldn't afford to do that.

I WAS THERE: CHARLIE THOMAS, AGE 17

I had been in England for less than a year and was working at Pitts Records and Bookshop in the High Street in Exeter. I had arrived back in England with my parents and siblings to see if England was any better than when we left for Australia a decade earlier, as is often the case with us Brits after emigrating. To my parents it was a big fat disappointment and, with all the money they had spent in relocating, it must have been soul destroying. They never recovered from it financially and only lasted about 18 months before fleeing back to Oz.

For a lad who had grown up in a small country town in South Australia, this was heaven. It was a fantastic time in England musically and fashion-wise. There were punks, Mods, Teds, skins, rockers and the beginning of the New Romantics, and there I was working in a place that catered to all.

It's long gone now but Pitts Records was a chart shop back then. We had a diary that we had to fill in for every record we sold which we submitted to whoever put together the national charts for that week. As a chart shop, the company reps would be in to see us several times a week and the number of freebies was a real sign that the record companies would do what it took to ensure a number one spot on the charts.

My record collection was second to none and with the number of free t-shirts, jumpers, etc. I was never without some kind of promotional wear! I had been eagerly awaiting the release of *In Through The Out Door* and, on the day, I got to listen to a pre-release copy – I wish I still had it!). The rep who brought it in asked me if I wanted to buy two tickets to see Led Zeppelin at Knebworth. He wanted £10 each for them, and I was earning £17 a week back then. I immediately said yes. I was nearly sick with excitement as I had been a huge Zep fan since a schoolmate had introduced me to a cassette version of *Led Zeppelin II* when it was first released. I sold the second ticket to a bloke I vaguely knew and awaited the day.

It was 3 August when we got on the train at Exeter St David's Station. It seemed to take forever to get to the end of our rail journey and begin our walk to the venue. It took bloody ages to get there and the excitement was palpable! I bought a t-shirt along the way. I had to buy something as a memento. It was yellow and listed all the names of the artists appearing on the day. Actually, I had no idea it was a full day of entertainment before the big event. They had spelled the name of one of the artists incorrectly and I later discovered the shirt was too small. Never mind. At least I had the memento I wanted – albeit cheap, shitty, yellow and with a spelling mistake!

As we got closer to the gates there were people everywhere. Some had camped. Some were dressed as the wizard from *Zep IV* and the smell of joints filled the air. So this is what a music festival was all about. Amazingly, we walked straight up to the gates and then people started queueing up behind us. We were going to be first in. As the night progressed into the early hours, people began to get restless and I was beginning to feel the crowd starting to push from behind. At first, it was only now and then, and not so bad, but as you'd expect with an enormous crowd of excited, tired and impatient Led Zeppelin fans, it progressed into quite a scary situation. The security on the other side of the fence were starting to look concerned and the guard dogs were barking and snarling until one big heave saw the gates swing open and an almighty rush from behind had me at one point moving with the crowd but with my feet not touching the ground. That part was scary but as soon as we had funnelled through the gates – the guard dogs had scarpered by this point – we found our footing and I followed those ahead of me to the stage.

We managed to find ourselves about ten rows from the front and settled in for the day. I seriously don't recall much of the day other than that The New Barbarians were a no show, which I was disappointed at, Chas and Dave were brilliant, Fairport Convention were excellent and Todd Rundgren was shite!

The crowd was enormous. I had never seen so many people in one place before, all there with a common purpose – to see the greatest band of all time. The concert itself was amazing – the sound, the light show. Plant was amazing and, of course, so was Page. I remember thinking to myself how well Page and Plant bounced off each other and, in turn, JPJ and Bonham held it all together brilliantly. The highlight of the show was 'Kashmir', which was real hair raising stuff. The low light? Actually, there were two – getting shit thrown at us from the people behind because we dared to stand up at a Led Zep concert (how could you not stand?) and then missing the train home and having to sleep on the cold station floor until the next train, five hours later. But it is, and will always be, the best concert I've ever seen. The memories of the smells, the crowd, the pushing, the shoving and, of course, the music will stick with me forever. There they were and there I was – in the presence of the best there ever have been.

I WAS THERE: CHRIS DRAKE, AGE 21

I went with my fiancée. I had to work when tickets were released so my mum had to queue up to buy them. It was the first all day festival I had been to and they were the only band on the bill I liked. It was a long day as I had slept in my Ford Escort the night before. But it was well worth it for the 'Dazed And Confused' guitar solo alone, with the spinning laser pyramid around Pagey. We ended up near the sound engineer's tower. I was flagging by the end but Zeppelin restored my energy which was lucky as I had a long drive home. It was a mindblowing spectacle of sight and sound, reinforcing them as my favourite band.

I WAS THERE: GARY COLLINS

I saw both Knebworth shows. I first 'found' Led Zeppelin when I stole a copy of *Led Zeppelin II* from my cousin. I loved the album and 'Livin' Lovin' Maid' was my favourite track at the time, probably because of its catchy tune, which would have appealed to a 14-year-old. As I grew older, I progressed through the albums as they were released, buying *Led Zeppelin I* last. I still have them, including the one I stole.

Having already seen Deep Purple live at around that time, I was dying to see Zeppelin but for one reason or another it never really happened. I was supposed to be at Earls Court in 1975 but that never happened and I can't even remember why. In 1979, I had the opportunity to travel up to Knebworth with a bunch of my mother's work colleagues. I was happy to go with a crowd of people that I didn't even know just to see them.

The show was so good that I bought a ticket while I was there for the second show a week later.

I WAS THERE: DAVE EARL, AGE 17

My best friend, Trevor Jones, and I were both 14. We'd become friends when we started primary school and are still friends today. He said to me one day, 'Shall we move away from listening to pop stuff, the chart stuff and all that?' 'If you want,' I replied. 'How about trying Led Zeppelin?' he threw at me. 'OK, can do!' And so on that day in 1976, we walked into a record shop in our home town of Seaford in East Sussex, the lady put the newly released *Presence* on the turntable and we stood there listening to 'Achilles Last Stand'. We thought it was great. And so began our love of the world's greatest band. We collected all their albums.

1979 and a college friend, Sharon Frost, finds herself in a long queue outside a Brighton record shop, finally securing three tickets for Zep's 4 August show at Knebworth. Trevor and I met at Seaford train station on the 3rd. Amazingly, given how many people were there, we bumped into Sharon and a male friend of hers who had travelled separately in a Mini. The four of us spent a cramped night in that car!

Come the morning, we went our separate ways and we settled down and enjoyed the support acts. That is, until I got stung by a bee for the first time ever. I went to the first aid tent. I was told, 'If you suffer a reaction, you're off to hospital.' I remember replying, 'I'm not missing Led Zeppelin!' Fortunately, I was fine. And then it was time. Time for Zep to make an appearance. And what a moment, and what a show too. There we were, seemingly a long way from home in those pre-mobile days, two 17 year olds appreciating seeing our favourites. We knew it was huge, that lots of people the world over would love to see Zep but had never had the chance. And, after all these years, it's still the same for people today who never got the chance to see them.

That night, we slept under the stars in sleeping bags on a grass verge in a tree-lined street near the venue. Arriving home around lunch time Sunday, we were tired and smelly but, more than anything, so proud we had seen Led Zeppelin in concert. Fast forward to 2007 and Zep, with Bonzo's son Jason on drums, announce a one-off reunion concert at the 02 Arena in London. Ticket applications were in the many thousands, maybe more. I didn't apply. I looked back to 1979 and was happy in the knowledge that I'd seen Led Zeppelin. I'd seen them.

I WAS THERE: SEBASTIAN FLYTE, AGE 16

Seeing them at Knebworth as a teenager was more of an accident than a planned affair but it was a great experience. I grew up in a tiny village in the north of Ireland in the sixties. My older brother by seven years collected music. I grew up with classic British pop and rock and first heard Zeppelin when I was eight years old. My brother had to go to Belfast to buy records, which in the seventies was taking your life in your hands. When I turned teenager, I got part time jobs and began my own record collection. I was at my friend Peter McClean's house one day when the gruff Scotsman who was dating his sister asked us if we liked Zeppelin. We said yes, and he produced two tickets for the Knebworth gig. He had got them as part of a corporate goodie bag but he hated Zeppelin. Birthday and Christmas had come at once.

The Irish have a horrible stereotype of being a bit thick. I went to a good grammar school but obviously flunked geography because I had packed my bag with a few essentials and flew to Gatwick, not knowing that Knebworth is just a bit further north. Feeling a bit dim-witted, we managed to thumb a lift with a truck driver and he let us off in the English countryside with nothing but fields and cows around. We walked for a couple of miles and, on the horizon, saw the denim and leather and long hair – the uniform of youth – and followed some guys. All of a sudden, it was a mass of people milling about, drinking, laughing and smoking weed. Music was everywhere and it all became a bit of a headspin. Being under age and having very little cash, my friend and I milled about. There always seemed to be a beer at hand and all sorts of debauchery going on in broad daylight.

We kept ourselves pretty straight and managed to squeeze as far up the field as we could, ending up about 15 rows from the front. I had heard Zeppelin were loud. I know a guy who lived about five miles away from where I grew up who had seen Zeppelin in the Ulster Hall in Belfast where the urban myth went that they were so loud that they broke the glasses in his top pocket.

We watched the opening acts and loved them but then evening came, and sitting in front of the biggest stage I had ever seen, with the lights and screens, the atmosphere was electric. They opened with 'The Song Remains The Same'. I have never heard anything so loud in my life – and I have been to Motörhead gigs! That mass of people erupted and all of a sudden I was part of something so much bigger than me. When you are a teenager you can feel very isolated. To sit in a field on an English summer evening, singing every note of your favourite songs with 200,000 other drunken lunatics, was the most incredible moment.

The concert that night was utterly amazing. I have read disparaging reports about it, but it really was a case of you had to be there. Tight but loose was the Zeppelin way and they lived up to all expectations.

I WAS THERE: JOHN GRIFFITHS

Every week we scoured the music press for news of a UK gig to no avail, only reading about Robert Plant's car crash and then the tragic loss of Karac. We'd been going to the Knebworth Festival on and off since its inception and had seen some great bands there. It was the closest our group of friends ever got to a festival, driving straight from the pub on the Friday night – it was the seventies, when drink driving was practically compulsory – to arrive at Knebworth in the early hours. Then we'd kip down in the cars, ready to be up at dawn to get in the queue to get in. Completely out of the blue it was announced that Zep would be doing not one but two consecutive weekend gigs. We booked to see both.

I've read reviews of these concerts and wonder if I was at the same gigs. I remember going mental from start to finish, wishing it would never end. I still feel sick with excitement at the recollection of Page, alone on the stage, going from the acoustic instrumental of 'Black Mountain Side' straight into 'Kashmir' with all the lights coming on and the others just being there. Wonderful. Magical. Incredible. Then of course came rumours of Jimmy's smack addiction, quickly followed by the death of Bonzo.

What a horrid day that was, like a great chunk of your life had gone AWOL, which was pretty soon afterwards followed by the news of the band splitting up. Again, another long period of scouring the music press in hope of a reconciliation. But Plant, as he has always done, seemed to move on quickly, and in no time was playing with Phil Collins, sporting an up-to-the-minute fashionable mullet haircut.

I WAS THERE: MELVIN HEMINGBROUGH

The last time we saw them was at Knebworth. We were actually on holiday in Skegness and I left the wife and little kid and went across to Knebworth with the tent to meet up with the rest of the lads. The critics said they weren't on form at Knebworth. I think Jimmy Page was a bit out of it. But we were quite near the front, and they could have sung 'Jingle Bells' and we would still have thought they were great.

I WAS THERE: DAVID HODGSON, AGE 18

We travelled down overnight from West Cumbria. It was a great gig in a big field. One of my mates who came to the gig with me was a future member of the band It Bites, who supported Robert Plant on one of his solo tours.

I WAS THERE: JOHNNIE GRIFFITHS

I was still at secondary school when a group of us bought tickets to see Led Zeppelin from *NME*, or possibly *Sounds*. Early in the day we all got on the train from where we lived in Horsham, West Sussex to Victoria, and thenceforth to Stevenage. It all meant a very long day's travelling just to see our favourite band, but that didn't matter to any of us. When we finally arrived at Knebworth Park, the crowds were like nothing I had ever seen. I remember being so transfixed with excitement and did my very best to gradually work my way to the closest possible position. This meant some real jostling, apologies and determination, but I eventually managed to reach a great position – about a mile away from the stage! There were so many people all trying to do exactly the same thing as our lot, ie. get to the front. We must have been about 50 feet from the stage by the time Led Zeppelin came onto the stage. We were close enough to see the sweat running down Jimmy Page's nose, but closer to Robert Plant. I remember thinking Jimmy looked almost nervous at the beginning, but he wowed us completely and smirked as we applauded. Everyone heard the latest songs from *In Through The Out Door*, and I tried my first joint during 'In The Evening'!

My ears were ringing all the way home and throughout most of the next day, but it was a truly awesome experience for me. In something over a year, John Bonham had died and the original continuity of Led Zeppelin could not, apparently, be maintained. I am just glad we all got there, saw the best band there will ever be and managed to return triumphantly, safe and (with ringing) sound. I purchased a (probably unofficial) Led Zeppelin scarf and I still have the original programme from the day. I still listen to Led Zeppelin often. Nothing will ever erase that day from my mind.

I WAS THERE: MICHAEL MCWILLIAM, AGE 16

I was the son of a bank manager in straight-laced leafy Purley. I knew nothing about music save for the stuff rolled out weekly on *Top Of The Pops* and Capital Radio. A school friend, who happened to be the cousin of Genesis guitarist Steve Hackett, asked me if I wanted to see the Led Zeppelin film, *The Song Remains The Same*. I hadn't heard of Led Zep or the film but went along, curious and glad to get out of the house. I was never the same again.

Two years later, with a small but growing record collection scratched together from Saturday jobs, I heard they were to play Knebworth. The buzz this news created was incredible and it was mine and my friends' mission to get tickets. The snag was that we were all 16 and I, for one, had never been to a gig, let alone disappear off on a train to Knebworth with – in my parents' eyes – a legion of subversive hippies and greasers. My pal James got his mum to phone mine to tell her James' older brother, Andy, would look after us. Luckily, that did the trick. The next high anxiety task was to get tickets before they sold out. We jumped on a train on the appointed day to London and stood in a queue outside Harlequin Records, which was selling tickets. The queue went right around the block. Despite the fear of them selling out, we managed to part with our £7 .50 each. Clutching those tickets was a glorious moment.

The three of us set off from Croydon station on Friday 3 August with a crap tent, sleeping bags, sandwiches, not enough tobacco and a few cans of beer nicked from home. Once on the train to Stevenage, the buzz grew and grew as the train packed out with denim and patch-clad Zeppelin fans. It was like a troop transport of rockers to the far fields of Knebworth.

Around dawn on Saturday, the whole campsite arose and I remember joining a procession of thousands of people snaking their way in a mighty column that stretched for hundreds of yards leading to the entrance gates. By sun up we were in. I will always regret chucking my ticket stub in one of the bins they had for that purpose.

It was a long day of waiting despite the string of support acts but, around 9pm, it was time! The stage went to black, the crowd started to stir, growing ever more noisy, the atmosphere just got more and more electric and then there was some noise from the stage, Bonzo hit a drum, one light came on, then all the lights and – smash-bang-wallop – they belted into 'The Song Remains The Same'. It was hard to get my head around being in the English countryside on a summer's evening, witnessing Led Zeppelin at full thrash with such a huge crowd. It was truly awesome – and it was my first gig!

My next memorable brush with Zeppelin was meeting Jimmy Page on a video shoot in 1988 for the single 'Wasting My Time' from his solo *Outrider* album. I managed to beg my place on that crew from some lighting sparks whose conversation about the shoot I overheard in a studio lot on some other job. I'd worked on scores of music promos before then, but when Jimmy Page walked onto the studio floor, there was a sea change in the air. He has a star's presence and that same fluidity of movement when he walks as he does when playing live.

I was a lowly, shy runner/general crew hand in those days but I'd made sure to wear my old denim jacket with Zoso on the back. He very sweetly came over to me at one point, knowing full well I was an unimportant grunt, and said 'nice jacket, man'. I was pretty much dumbstruck and don't remember what I blurted out in response. He didn't have to do that and he later generously signed bits and pieces of Zep memorabilia I'd brought with me.

I WAS THERE: ROGER KINSEY

In the mid to late seventies, I was working in London for what was then the world's largest American-owned advertising agency, McCann Erickson, within their specialist division of direct marketing and recruitment advertising. One day I was called out of the blue by a Chris Boger, who was a film producer and had recently produced the soft porn film, *The Awakening Of Emily*, featuring a then unknown actress Koo Stark.

He invited me to his West End office. Initially he was seeking my help as to how he could achieve better exposure for Koo. He later contacted me again, and again I went to his office, but this time he told me about this 'hush hush' concert that was being planned for a UK appearance of Led Zeppelin at Knebworth. He had been contracted by Peter Grant to film this event and they had asked him if he could source the necessary inflatable structure which could be duly wound up at the back of the stage as the group performed their monster hit number 'Stairway To Heaven'.

Chris charged me with this task of sourcing such a structure from an appropriate company. I have to come clean now and say I failed miserably and I had to have a face-to-face with Chris and tell him I had had not been able to get this 'Stairway' prop. With hindsight, I should have realised the guys who produced the inflatable flying pig for the Pink Floyd *Animals* album cover would have no doubt taken up the challenge with relish!

Chris was gracious enough to thank me for my efforts. He threw two black t-shirts across his desk at me and said, 'Please use these as a small thank you from us for at least trying to help us.' When I unfolded them, I could not believe my eyes. He had given me two Access All Areas backstage pass t-shirts for those two Knebworth concerts. I took them home safely and arranged baby sitters for our two young daughters so my wife and I could go to the first concert on August 4th.

We parked up and were walking across the grassy fields to the arena. Countless other fans, seeing what we were wearing, were shouting out and asking how much we would sell our t-shirts for. No way were we going to sell them! Throughout the afternoon and into the evening we sat on the edge of the stage, enjoying every moment and knowing that we were so lucky to have those passes.

Two weeks later the wife decided the car needed a wash and shampoo and, after rinsing off the suds, looked around for an appropriate cloth to dry and polish the bodywork. Guess what she decided to use for this mundane task? Yes, she took the two t-shirts, thinking 'well, we will not need those anymore.' If we still had them, those t-shirts might now be worth more than whatever people were prepared to pay us on the day of the concert.

I WAS THERE: NICK SHARP, AGE 17

We had a band at school. Everyone was bringing in Black Sabbath and Pink Floyd records and one day this guy turned up with *Led Zeppelin II*. We were converted. We mimed 'Whole Lotta Love' to an audience at school. When *The Song Remains the Same* came out we were just awe-struck. We thought, 'Wouldn't it be incredible to see these guys live?'

I was hook, line and sinker a Led Zeppelin fan. I bought every album and just loved them. Shortly after that my parents moved house to very near Knebworth. When I knew they were coming to Knebworth I couldn't believe it. Zeppelin were coming to my back garden. I could have walked there! I even heard them practising in the days leading up to the gigs. They played both weekends but I only had tickets for the first one, and I was a little bit worried because I'd never been to a big gig like that before. The girlfriend of an older friend said, 'I'll go with you. I've always wanted to see Led Zeppelin' so we bought a pair of tickets for £7.50 each.

We thought we'd better go early in the morning, around 10am, because Chas and Dave were going to be on at 12, kicking it all off. When we got there the place was already full. People were so keen to get in they had knocked down all the fences. The security was a waste of time. We walked into the middle of this enormous crowd, although you could barely 'walk'. You had to constantly step over people to get anywhere. We sat down and we stayed in the same spot for the rest of the day, watching all these bands.

It was a long old day. We'd taken some food but not enough. The trouble was, to get from the crowd into the areas where the refreshments were, and there weren't many of them like they have these days, you got lost on the way back. There were a lot of heavy Hell's Angel-looking groups around and being quite young I was a little bit scared.

It must have been at least 10pm before they came on. I remember it being very late. It was pitch black. You couldn't see anything. They started with 'Rock And Roll' and it was just electric. I've never heard sound like it. The bass was so loud. We were only about 50 yards from the front and I had to duck down below the people in front of me because I could feel that my body was moving with the bass. It was just ridiculous. I now suffer with tinnitus in both ears, but I'm not blaming John Bonham for that. I think that's just a product of far too many gigs.

The quality of the sound wasn't brilliant. The speakers kept cutting out and the guitar sound wasn't quite right. It wasn't like the slick productions you get these days. It was seat of your pants stuff and you could see roadies running around everywhere, trying to change amps and pull leads out and do this and do that. It was like that most of the night, but it did settle down. The bigger numbers were just incredible. It was quite remarkable to see Zeppelin play those live. It was just an amazing night and I could quite happily not have slept for another week.

I WAS THERE: LEE SPENCER. AGE 15

Led Zep II was the first album I listened to, and then *Zep IV*. Our school disco always played 'Stairway To Heaven' as the very last track. The big thing was headbanging to 'Stairway To Heaven'. Of course, there are parts you can't headbang to! When it was announced that Zeppelin were playing down at Knebworth, I went to Manchester Piccadilly with a friend and we queued up and bought tickets from Our Price Records. The ticket included a coach down to Knebworth. We were both 15 and we knew it was 'down south' but we had no idea where Knebworth was. Both of us lied to our parents, saying we were staying at each other's houses. He packed a rucksack, I packed a rucksack, and off we went to meet this coach.

We must have been the two youngest guys on it. There were people on that coach who looked like Hell's Angels, with leathers and cut offs, carrying slabs of beer with them. We were there with our sandwiches and a couple of bottles of Lucozade. We very quickly had our eyes opened to the world of the older man, with people smoking dope on the bus and all sorts of things that we'd never witnessed. Going down the motorway, we were all bursting for a pee. The bus driver wouldn't stop because if he did, we were going to be late. But he was willing to let people step down to the entrance of the coach and hold the handrail while he opened the doors. So people were peeing out of the doors as we travelled down the motorway!

Arriving down in Knebworth, he said, 'The coach leaves at 11 o'clock sharp. If you're not here, we'll go without you.' We followed the line of people going into the concert. I remember arriving, buying my t-shirt and my programme and very quickly losing my friend in the crowd. I found myself next to what I would describe as a wheelchair platform but there were press people on there, with lots of photographers. Because I'm only five foot seven and I was struggling to see, I was trying to stand on a bit of scaffold to get a little bit higher up and see over everybody's heads. I remember this arm coming over and this guy offered me his hand. And through a combination of me scrambling and him pulling, I clambered up onto this platform with him and watched the whole show from up there, which was amazing because I was then a good head and shoulders above everybody else and had this fantastic view of the show.

At the time I didn't appreciate the enormity of the actual show. It was Zeppelin, it was another gig. It was my third or fourth concert. But very shortly after that we lost John Bonham.

Zeppelin went on very late and I stayed for the encore, not wanting to miss anything. My coach had gone by the time I got there. I made my way to a by now abandoned Stevenage railway station. Looking very lost sitting on a station bench on the platform, the station master came and asked what I was doing. He took me into his office, sat me in front of the fire, gave me a cup of cocoa and proceeded to phone my father up at two o'clock in the morning which, as you can appreciate, was not a good thing. I stayed there overnight.

In the morning my dad went to Bolton railway station and paid for the ticket. Bolton then phoned down to Stevenage to say the ticket had been paid for, I was issued with a ticket and I got on the next train home. To a big rollicking.

My friend had got back on the coach so missed the end of the show. I suffer from FOMO – fear of missing out. When people talk about the biggest show they've been to, being able to say Zeppelin is quite a big rabbit to pull out of the hat.

It's funny how things work out. 20 years ago, I got into the music business doing video. I've got a car company and we're moving Robert about at the moment. I've met Jimmy at a couple of functions. Six or seven years ago, I met him at the TPI awards, an industry do for riggers, lighting crew and audio crew. My friend had made the Zeppelin *DVD* and was up for video director of the year. Jimmy came to present him with the award. What do you say to these guys? All I could say was 'thank you'. He said, 'What for?' And I said, 'Well, for the music and for the amount of pleasure I've got from listening to it.' And he said, 'Oh, thank you my friend, thank you.'

I WAS THERE: DUNCAN WILSON

In 1977 I was living in Kincardine, Fife and I got to start going to gigs, mostly at the Glasgow Apollo, the highlight being the gigs that came to be *If You Want Blood You've Got It* by AC/DC. I met a girl called Jeanette from Paisley at the Apollo and it was her that bought the two tickets for Zeppelin at Knebworth. £7.50 each!

We hitchhiked from Glasgow. It took two to three days. I remember talking to one of the rangers at Knebworth the night before and he told us that someone was going to be in trouble because the crowd was already way beyond the ticket allocation. I understood this later when the story about extra tickets came out. We were only about 100 yards from the stage. I remember amazing highlights: 'Nobody's Fault But Mine', 'Kashmir', 'In The Evening', 'Stairway To Heaven' and 'Achillies Last Stand'. One of my strongest memories is of 'All Of My Love', which brought out very powerful emotions on and off the stage. But it's not on the set list I found online, so I must have invented it!

The whole set was amazing. All of the individual solo highlights, from Jones in 'No Quarter' to Jimmy Page with the laser pyramid and bow. I remember thinking that they were going to split because Robert Plant in particular took so long to go off stage and kept returning to thank the fans over and over. I don't know what time we left, but I'm sure the set was around three hours. It confirmed what I believe to this day, that this was/is the greatest band ever to play rock and roll. There was no single star or stand out member. Each one was totally linked to the others, each one amazing at what they do. It was the best night of music of my life.

The release of the Led Zeppelin *DVD* was the first time l got to see some of the Knebworth gigs. I was in the ballot for the O2 gig along with the other 25 million requests but never got chosen. I totally agree with Robert Plant. Led Zeppelin don't need a reunion. They should be remembered and seen in their full awesome glory that can never be repeated.

I WAS THERE: ALIDA HAZELGROVE

I was in a plastic bag to keep warm and fell asleep. I woke up to them playing 'Stairway To Heaven'!

I WAS THERE: DAVID C WOOD, AGE 17

It began with the gig being announced on *The Old Grey Whistle Test* but I missed it, I think my brother wanted to see something else on TV. I was in my sixth year of high school and due to leave at the end of June and, next day at school, the news was shared amongst those of us who were fans.

I had thought Zeppelin would never play again in the UK. I had some great pictures from a French magazine of the '77 tour, and I often thought that maybe if I joined the Navy I might get to the US and see them that way. I found out the date and location of ticket sales for the Knebworth show in Scotland, went through by train to Edinburgh and queued up to buy, a king's ransom of £7.50. Only two of us were set to go, myself (Woody) and a good mate called Hugh, always called Shug.

School finished, I didn't get the grades for uni, and I really had no interest in it. I applied for jobs and got a labouring job in the meantime. Summer crawled along… We set ourselves up to travel overnight by train to London. On the Thursday, I packed up my job. (Young and stupid, I could have asked for the Friday and Monday off or pretended to be sick.) We travelled down, getting next to no sleep. In London we found out how to travel to Stevenage. This was all before the internet, mobile, GPS, etc…

We arrived in Stevenage on the Friday afternoon. The town was mobbed and everyone appeared to be loading up shopping trolleys with booze. We followed the snake of people towards the grounds. Remarkably, we bumped into a guy I knew from playing rugby and a couple of friends of his. Everyone was hanging about on grassland out with the perimeter. Police were politely but firmly trying to corral us. One copper got chatting to us and we discovered he was a fellow Scot. He remarked that his shift was finished and told us to do as we pleased and asked if we had a drink. A bottle of whisky was produced and he had a nip before leaving.

Tommy Vance was on many radios around us and there was a happy atmosphere. We just lay about on jackets, bags, etc. I nodded off and was awoken by Shug frantically telling me to get up as the gates had been forced open. The next wee while was a complete haze as I was disorientated. I recall getting my ticket checked and going through some form of wooden entrance into the arena, a big grassy field with a dip towards a huge stage. More snoozing, then someone spoke from the PA. He said he was just stage crew and that a DJ would be on once they arrived; in the meantime, he would fill in. The very first music of the day was 'Take The Long Way Home' by Supertramp.

The day warmed up. The crowd was huge. I looked at some of the catering; I'd never seen watermelon before. I also went to the crude toilets. My grandmother had told me to look out for my cousin Thomas who was going to be there. I thought it was highly unlikely I was going to meet him in such a huge crowd and yet I stumbled over his feet on the way back.

The bands on the support bill played, Chas and Dave first. As evening came in, Todd Rundgren and his band Utopia were great. He was wearing a yellow skin suit and when he took off his guitar, we all burst out laughing. I think he had jumbo sausage shoved down there!

He finished his set and in the gathering dark we waited: noises, drums being checked, mic checks, then a couple of guitar sounds and… eruption! The opening chord of 'The Song Remains The Same'. It was 9.40 pm.

Leaping about, grabbing each other shouting, 'I had a dream!' and Robert the Golden God was finally in my ears. This was followed by 'Celebration Day', and then Robert addressed the crowd, a moment I thought I'd never experience.

The rest of the gig is burned into my brain. One of our group had a ghetto blaster and recorded it all on cassette. I had copies for years, slowly losing them over various marriages and house moves. The main set ended and we screamed for more, singing 'you'll never walk alone'. We got our three-song encore and then it was over.

In the dark the crowd began to move out. Strange aliens appeared, people wearing glowstick-type stuff around their arms and heads, selling them obviously. We wandered back into Stevenage and slept in the station area, eventually getting on a train to London. We wandered around, slept in a public park and went to Soho. I bought an import copy of *Presence*. We also went in to a naughty cinema (I was only 17).

Finally, the overnight train home, an adventure I will always remember, until dementia robs me of it. How appropriate that I type this on the eve of August 4th, 45 years later. A special time.

I WAS THERE: JOHN TRUMAN

There were 250,000 people there that felt like going to say God. I thought we'd never get to see them. We had tickets for the first show. And they took the tickets off us at the gate on the way in, which was annoying because they were beautiful tickets with the Zepplin logo on. They didn't give us a stub or anything. But we enjoyed it so much that we decided to go up there again for the second one. We thought we'd see if we could just hang about outside and catch some of the music. When we arrived, a bit of the fencing had broken down and we just walked in. So we got to see them twice. The second time we saw them for nothing apart from the petrol money.

I WAS THERE: NICK PARRY

Eager to see Zeppelin live again, it was with great joy that I saw they were to play two gigs at Knebworth Park. I duly sent off my money for both gigs and this time – I guess due to the huge capacity of the venue – I got tickets quite easily. My sister was to come with me for the first one as I had probably turned Julie onto rock by keeping on playing it when the parents were out!

We set off on the Friday afternoon before the gig on the train to Euston. We spoke to a couple of other guys who were going there but they didn't know how to get there so we said they should come with us. After arriving at Euston, we walked the few hundred yards to Kings Cross for the train to Stevenage. The lads with us said 'no, it's Knebworth we have to get off at' but we knew it was Stevenage and a message over the tannoy confirmed this. We looked a bit out of place with the city types going home in rush hour but we didn't care – we were going to see Zeppelin so nothing else mattered.

We arrived at Stevenage station and to our surprise it seemed most of the train also go off and started walking towards the venue. It was like a march of disciples to see the highest deity. We were promised a shuttle bus to Knebworth Park but couldn't see where they were so we carried on walking. I think we walked to the entrances quicker than a shuttle bus could have got us there due to the heavy traffic.

As we approached, the campsites came into view with hundreds of multi-coloured tents and smoke rising from the fires. I was loving all this. This was what it was all about. We knew we were in for a long wait and as we approached the entrances to the campsite we found the back of the queue. By the gates there was a huge skip with a sign saying 'No Alcohol' allowed in the venue, so anybody with drinks had a choice. Either drink it or dump it in the skip. Many tried to drink all they had but most just dumped it. We didn't have any alcohol as drinking lots meant lots of visit to the toilet, and if we were in a great spot near the stage then it would be an horrendous walk out of the middle of the crowd to the toilets and back again. We settled down for some sleep, but with music blaring out from everywhere there was no chance of that, and around 4am we were surprised to see the gates opened and we were allowed into the arena. A mad rush ensued. As soon as we were inside, we picked our spot, not too near the stage but close enough to get a great view and the best sound. We finally managed to get some sleep, but with people walking by us and sometimes stepping on us as they tried to get nearer the front, it was a losing battle.

I WAS THERE: PAUL FULLER

This is still the best gig I've ever been to, and I was lucky enough to be at *Live Aid*. I remember a couple that had got married that day wandered down to the front (she was still in full wedding dress!), Robert crying while singing 'Nobody's Fault But Mine' and Jimmy in his pyramid of lasers. And I remember not being able to find my tent afterwards and wandering round for ages and then sleeping in one of the big communal tents!

I WAS THERE: RICHARD STUDERUS

I was part of the backstage crew and was a chief engineer working on the Eidophor projector giving the large screen projection at the rear of the stage during Zeppelin's performance. During their set I was seated on top of the main speaker stack stage left and looking down on them! It was an amazing, earth-shattering experience and I remember it like it was yesterday.

I WAS THERE: ANDREW RIGBY, AGE 17

There was lots of stuff about them being past their best, being dinosaurs and being rusty, but the sheer excitement and anticipation of seeing them aged 17 as I was at the time has never been matched. They blew me away.

I WAS THERE: TOMAS UMLAUF, AGE 16

The gig at Knebworth was a magic and unforgettable experience of divine music, and what a performance for almost four hours! I hitchhiked all the way to England from Switzerland and made it to 60 metres from the stage. The concert started at sunset and the sun just disappeared in the red and purple sky behind the stage when the show began. The scenery was breathtaking and everybody was paralysed and couldn't believe who all of a sudden was about to appear. It was mysterious and nearly unreal. This attitude changed within the third song and the riff of 'Black Dog', when Jimmy and his mates accelerated the tune and the night became a true rock 'n' roll fairytale that words cannot describe. It just blasted everyone's minds. My other memory is at the end, when everybody was singing 'You'll Never Walk Alone'.

I also saw them in Zurich in June 1980, and of course it was a great show, but it wasn't as phenomenal as the Knebworth gig because being a European tour show the performance was only a little over two hours and there was no 'Whole Lotta Love' to end on.

I WAS THERE: TONY MACINNES

I grew up in the same town as John Bonham and went to a memorial gig held in his name. There's now a monument to him in the town. I had become a Led Zeppelin fan at boarding school near Worcester in '69 or '70. I was about 15 years old. *Led Zeppelin I* and *II* were my eye openers. Their sound was original, punchy and exciting to hear. I was also waking up to early Deep Purple and Black Sabbath and to Atomic Rooster. All were playing nearby and we went to see them all.

I saw Zeppelin at Birmingham Town Hall in early 1970 but have very poor memories of it. I saw them again at Earls Court in 1975, where I sat over to the right of the stage. I went on my own, the set was really long – over three hours – and, as it was one of five nights, I thought that was amazing. But Knebworth was a big step up.

This was my fourth visit to Knebworth. I had seen Pink Floyd there in '75, and in '78 I saw Genesis and then Peter Gabriel and The Tubes. For Zeppelin, I went with about a dozen friends. I went to the first of the two weekends they played. It was a very long day after being sat in front of the stage from something like 7am. It's possibly the largest crowd I'd ever been in, with estimates as to the size of it varying between 110,000 and 250,000. I've been in many large crowds over the years and this in my opinion leaned towards the larger figure, of that I have no doubt.

It was a long set and the performance was awesome, including opener 'The Song Remains The Same' and a brilliant 'Nobody's Fault But Mine' and 'Kashmir'. They played three encores, ending with 'Heartbreaker'. The thing that really stood out for me was Bonham's drumming. It was unmissable, and clearly said to me why he was the best rock drummer in the world.

The following Saturday, Led Zeppelin play Knebworth Park again. The line-up is the same except no Fairport Convention and with the addition of The New Barbarians, Ronnie Wood's band featuring Keith Richards.

KNEBWORTH PARK
11 AUGUST 1979, STEVENAGE, UK

I WAS THERE: NICK SHARP

The second week, I went with a photographer friend of mine. We didn't have tickets. We just went along. We were quite keen amateur photographers and he was very keen to get up the front. I said, 'Whoa, I ain't going up there' and he said, 'No, no, I want to get some good shots. we've got to get right up the front.' I stayed where I was, about 100 yards back. The janmy git went right down to the press box and bumped into a press guy who was coming out and said, 'All right mate, do you want a press pass?' So my mate got a press pass and into the front of the press box, underneath the stage where Zeppelin were playing. Some of the shots he got were just incredible. We had a right laugh developing and enlarging them afterwards. I've still got a few of those prints.

I tried to get a ticket for the O2 reunion. The cheapest one I was offered was £470 and I thought, 'I'm just not prepared to pay that,' even though they are a bit special.

I WAS THERE: NEIL FLEMING

I actually made it onto the video of the gig during the crowd close up after 'Kashmir' on the Zep live DVD! I remember what a fantastic performance they put in, albeit after a very late start, and what incredible performers they all are. These days Jimmy lives about ten miles away from me but I still haven't managed to meet up yet or get a peek at his guitar collection!

I WAS THERE: RICK HAIMAN

It started at a friend's auto shop in California after work one day with four of us – Bill D, Bill W, John L and myself. Someone had heard on KMET that Led Zeppelin were having a concert in the forest at Knebworth Castle. We all went, 'Wow, wouldn't that be something?' Our friend Lynne, who was from the UK, was going home that summer so I said, 'Why don't we go and see them?' They all looked at me dumbfounded and then the 'why not?' bulb went off in their heads. Next thing you know I'm calling Lynne and asking her about her upcoming trip. Being a huge Zeppelin fan, she said, 'That's awesome – I can get things like a place to stay while I am there.' We were all a-buzz.

Then someone said, 'How the heck do we get concert tickets in a foreign country?' The next day I called Atlantic Records in New York to find out. It was after 5pm in Anaheim, California and keep in mind we were not worldly. I called the operator in New York and got the number. I called the number and after maybe ten rings a gentlemen answered: 'Atlantic Records'. I said hello, and began to explain why I called. He laughed and asked, 'Do you realise what time it is here?' It then dawned on me that they were three hours ahead. He said, 'You know, that idea is the craziest thing I've ever heard.' He explained he was an executive vice president working late and had decided to answer the phone.

He said, 'You know, I think I may be able to help you get those tickets.' He had a friend who owned Harlequin Records in the UK and he said he would call him and that I should call Harlequin Records on Monday at the right time, which was the middle of the night here. I told my friends what had happened. Some of them figured I was BSing. Others knew I didn't BS.

I set my alarm to wake me at 3am to make the call. A woman with an English accent answered. I told her I would like to speak with the owner. She said 'no one speaks to the owner' and that was that. That evening, everyone was excited to hear what happened and their faces just went limp when I told them. The next night I called again. This time the woman who answered screamed, 'We were hoping you would call back. Let me transfer you to the owner.' I told the owner my crazy story about us teenagers wanting to see Led Zep play in the forest and he said he would sell me the tickets but that I had to send him a cashier's check for the total amount in English pounds.

That night, many of my friends said, 'That's BS. You're making that up. No way am I giving you money.' But the ones who knew me well gave me the money and I got the cashier's check from Security Pacific National Bank and sent it off. A couple of weeks later I received five tickets. The others were sick they hadn't trusted me. A month or so later we were on our way via Freddie Laker Airways to the UK to see Led Zeppelin!

I WAS THERE: MICHELLE 'MITCH' LADYMAN, AGE 19

I was there for both weekends and I still have the shirt I bought, although it is far too small for me now. My boyfriend at the time and his older brother were into Led Zeppelin and I got to like the music through them. I had a serious motor bike accident in 1978 and got some money as compensation, which enabled us to afford the tickets for both weekends. It was a very long hot day with lots of other bands, including Ronnie Wood's new band. There was a lot of hype about The New Barbarians but we thought they were rubbish. They kept us waiting for ages and got booed when they came on. It was dark when Zeppelin appeared and they had the laser show for 'Dazed And Confused', which was magical. Both weekends were great and I have never forgotten them. We were devastated when John Bonham died. It made what we had seen even more special.

I WAS THERE: GARY COLLINS

Having seen them the week before, this time I went with my own friends. We travelled up in a Reliant three-wheeler which was terrifying. We were right at the back and the band look minuscule but it didn't matter. Everyone had plastic fluorescent tubes that glowed into the night. It was my first and worst experience of festival toilets. I go to the *Download Festival* every year with my son. Toilet-wise, things are much better now.

I WAS THERE: BERNARD BOOTH

They were mostly amazing, except for a couple of serious slip ups by Jimmy Page in 'Stairway' and on 'Over The Hills And Far Away'. He started the solo in 'Stairway' but it suddenly stopped and JPJ and Bonzo were left to carry on the backing. Plant looked at Page in disbelief until he came in with the end of the solo. Extremely embarrassing. I had to leave before the end of the concert, as The New Barbarians were an hour late coming on. As I walked away, I could hear the last encore in the distance, 'Communication Breakdown'. I could have wept!

I WAS THERE: DEREK COLLISON

I was playing a darts match with the lads in our local church team and two of them were talking about the Knebworth concert. My ears pricked up when I heard them say Led Zeppelin. When one of them said they needed one more in the car for petrol money to make it worth the trip, I naturally offered my services. We sorted out the tickets, met up and one of them drove.

When we arrived, I remember going into a fenced off area. In front of me was a huge field full of the same long-haired denim clad people I had seen at Earls Court four years before as a naive 14-year-old. But I was now one of them. They were all standing or sitting around drinking and smoking, with the now familiar smell of weed in the air and a huge stage at one end of the field. There were 'hubbly bubblies' nearly everywhere. People were seated on the ground and it was a free for all, if you were that way inclined, to take a puff on them or even a drag of a spliff. I was and never have been into any drugs but I still really enjoyed the concert, albeit I was a little tipsy on beer and probably a bit high with all the substances floating in the air.

There was no real hassle amongst the crowd but I did hear that a few Hell's Angels kicked off with some of the security. What I remember is a really great concert with an amazing line up. Led Zeppelin closed the show to the usual standing ovation and rocked the hell out of the evening.

I WAS THERE: DOUG LEWIS

Zeppelin came on just as the sun was setting. I wish I could have got closer, but they still gave me a great experience. I also saw Page and Plant with the Egyptian orchestra. Led Zeppelin is the finest thing music has given, and there have been many greats.

I WAS THERE: KAREN DAVIS, AGE 22

I'd been a Zeppelin fan since I was 17. I got into them purely by accident. A friend gave me a copy of *Zeppelin II* because he didn't like it and said they were crap. I went back the next week and gave him a good slap and said, 'Crap? I don't think so.' A friend took me to Knebworth because he knew I didn't have the money to go. We got to the festival site and I'd never seen so many people in all my life. I thought, 'Jesus Christ, this is going to be a gig, this is.' You only had to stand up and somebody threw a can at you: 'Get bloody down!' The mighty Zeppelin came on at 9pm and the rest is history. Zeppelin have got me out of some very dark times in my life, times when I wasn't very happy. The music still sounds just as good as it did yesterday. They had a chemistry like no other band has ever had. When John Bonham died, I was absolutely beside myself.

I WAS THERE: PETER SMITH

The band's fee for performing was reportedly the largest ever paid to one single act at the time. I applied for tickets by post and got tickets for the first day. However, when I saw that The New Barbarians (featuring Ronnie Wood and Keith Richards) were playing only at the second concert, I swapped my ticket with a mate for one for the second gig. This may have been a mistake, as the first gig is often reported as the better of the two. In hindsight I wish I'd gone to both! The festival involved the largest stage ever constructed, attracted at least 200,000 people over the two weekends, and these were the final shows Led Zeppelin performed in the United Kingdom until 2007.

I drove to the gig with a group of mates, four of us crammed into my little yellow Mini. We left early on the Saturday morning, arrived around lunchtime, pitched our tents and went into the arena, which was already crammed. I remember little about the support acts. Todd Rundgren was good, while The New Barbarians were okay but not as good as I had hoped.

There was a long wait before Zeppelin took to the stage and it got quite cold. They opened with 'The Song Remains The Same' and they played quite a few new songs, several of which were unfamiliar to me. Highlights were 'Nobody's Fault But Mine', 'Kashmir' and 'Stairway', which was accompanied by thousands of raised lighters. The crowd was quite reserved at first. There was some clever use of lasers with Page being surrounded by a laser pyramid. It was never going to equate to being a few feet away from the band as when I saw them in the early seventies, but it was a great concert and, moreover, a great event. Reviews at the time were mixed, partly because, given the emergence of punk, Zeppelin were seen as last year's thing by some elements of the press. But overall, it was seen to be a triumph, and a fitting showcase for the Zeppelin legend.

Indeed, I thought that the concert was just plain fantastic. There was a massive sense of occasion about the event. We all felt that we were witnessing something historic. The last memory I have is of walking out of the arena towards our tent, watching a lighting tower going up in flames… Sadly, a year later, John Bonham was dead and what was arguably the greatest rock band ever was no more.

I WAS THERE: KEITH MARTIN, AGE 16

My first records were three LPs that a friend of my parents left with them and which they weren't interested in so, aged eleven, I got *Crosby, Stills and Nash*, *Shades of Deep Purple* and *Led Zeppelin II*. I devoured them and still have them today. That first Deep Purple line up is still my favourite of their incarnations and CS&N's 'Marrakesh Express' was a part of my childhood. But the awesome power of every single track of *Led Zeppelin II* made me a committed fan. I used to go to a small music shop that sold guitars and records and I'd browse the albums most weekends, buying something if I could afford it. One day I saw a handwritten note taped to the glass counter: 'For sale: Led Zeppelin Knebworth ticket, £6.50.' Or it may have been £7.50. I'm not certain about the amount – all I do remember is that I could afford it!

I had no idea where Knebworth was, but I bought the ticket and ran home feeling like I'd just one-upped Charlie and his Wonka factory golden ticket. I turned 16 before the gig, and my parents paid for my train ticket up from London and packed some sandwiches. I went into central London with my dad on his way to work that morning and got the train to Knebworth from there. I was on my own. I was wearing a very 1970s green corduroy jacket and jeans. It was my first ever gig – and it was utterly incredible. I was roughly in the middle of the arena, totally happy although a little confused.

Nicky Horne, a Capital Radio deejay, was emcee and I remember him announcing a 'special guest' – Chas and Dave – to laughter and mild derision from the crowd. I thought The New Barbarians were loud but – oh my God – I reassessed that when Page, Plant, JPJ and Bonzo hit the stage! I felt like I was on another planet. The lasers were incredible – lasers! 'Dazed And Confused', 'Kashmir'... Wow! Looking back, the songs seemed to happen all at once as well as across the evening. It's hard to explain it in words, but it has remained the best, the most soul-shaking, the most awesome gig I have ever been to.

Afterwards, floating a few inches off the ground (I was clean and sober), I stumbled with the crowd back to the train station, where I eventually slept and got an early morning train back to London. The song remained the same but my world had changed.

Since the early 1990s, I've worked every summer at Cropredy Festival. Fairport Convention's annual 'home town' festival, helping run the ticket and fence crews, and I've met Robert Plant there a few times, just in passing. I don't want to be a fanboy and I'm sure he's heard it before, but one day if see him again and the moment is right, I'll tell him how much the Knebworth gig and everything they did meant to me.

I WAS THERE: STEVEN SCHOFIELD. AGE 17

I can't recall how my mate and I got the tickets, but it might have been by mail order, as we lived miles from any centre of civilization. It is hard to believe in this paranoid age that parents would knowingly allow two teenage boys to thumb a lift from strangers all the way from Lincolnshire down the A1 to Hertfordshire just to see a band. Why my mother agreed to this I'll never know, but me and my mate hitchhiked all the way to Knebworth and back again afterwards. We got a couple of lifts down the road pretty quickly before a temporary pause at the Bedford roundabout. But after a half an hour or so, a guy in a Ford Granada screeched to a halt. He was in a real hurry. He couldn't get to his appointment in London and read the A-Z at the same time whilst driving at 100 miles an hour. My mate sat in the front passenger seat reading out directions and the miles literally flew by. We got dropped off in Hatfield, where my cousin and her husband lived, and Granada guy sped off towards London.

My cousin fed us, gave us a floor to crash on and a lift to near Knebworth the following morning. I remember a massive hike to the arena, but it didn't really matter. I was with my mate, and we laughed a lot. We were having fun. The day went by as fast as that guy in the Granada. They ripped our tickets up as we went in. We pitched up at the back, which seemed like miles away from the stage. Chas and Dave opened the show and we ignored them. We drank the beer we had brought with us and the day got steadily hotter. Then a band with a brass section appeared and we ignored them. I really enjoyed Todd Rundgren's soaring guitar – he could really play – but it was no *Bat Out of Hell*. Our beer ran out late afternoon and there was no way to buy more. That was probably just as well. Strange-smelling smoke signals from the group next to us wafted past in the sweltering summer air.

When The New Barbarians left the stage, there followed a very long wait for the appearance of the main act, during which time we made our move. In the next hour and a bit, we employed what later became known at the festival gigs that followed in the early eighties as the 'Knebworth Elbow'. I ought to apologise to everyone who had waited patiently all day on their prize pitch, as my mate and l used every weaselly trick in the book to make our way from the back of the crowd to stage left, within a few metres of the front. That we didn't get chinned was, I believe, a testament to the amazing tranquilising powers of summer sun and cannabis. In mitigation, we were at least a foot shorter than most of the crowd, so couldn't exactly have blocked anyone's view. Perhaps the rest of the crowd thought we were lost children looking for their parents. I took loads of photos that day with my Praktika SLR and 50mm lens. I lost almost all of the photos and the programme I bought in a house move, but from the few photos I still have, it's clear how close we got to the front. We must have had some brass neck.

I recently viewed the whole gig via a popular video site. Zeppelin's performance was exactly as I remember it – very rough in places, but still utterly, utterly brilliant. The video footage of 'Dazed And Confused' doesn't do justice to how cool the green laser was on Jimmy's violin bow once the darkness had fallen. We stayed to the bitter end, through all the encores, and as we trudged the weary miles across the fields back towards the train station along with a load of similarly knackered, leather and denim-clad, floppy-hatted, long-haired fans, I could still hear music in my head. In fact, I still can.

I hitched back to Lincolnshire alone the following afternoon, as my mate had set off early for some reason. At no point did we even consider that this might be a daft idea. I got picked up from the A1 roadside almost immediately by a guy in a little Fiat. He thought I was a biker, as

I was wearing a leather jacket, blue jeans and a new white t-shirt. He was off to look at a new motorbike 'up North', but I couldn't really hear him as my ears were still singing Zeppelin songs to my brain. The guy wittered on for an hour or two and then said, 'This is it, I'll have to drop you off now.' We were just outside Retford, just twelve miles from my house. Result!

I then stood in the chilling evening air for two miserable hours as every single car and lorry drove past me, stubbornly refusing to stop and give me a lift the last few miles home. Eventually, I admitted defeat, found a phone box and a 5p piece and rang my mum. She sent my Dad out to pick me up in the family's Morris Marina.

I still have the leather jacket and the white t-shirt. The leather jacket is too small for me now by far. The white t-shirt is too small and fragile to risk trying it on. The material is so thin now it is almost transparent. It also has a few pin-hole burns in it and some dubious stains. I used to wear it all the time. It has a yellow and red roundel on the chest, with a winged man and four names around the circle: 'John Paul Jones - Jimmy Page - John Bonham - Robert Plant' and in the middle it says 'Led Zeppelin, Knebworth 1979'.

Thanks, Mum.

I WAS THERE: ELLIE POORE, AGE 20

The only significant, positive thing that my ex-husband ever did for me was to introduce me, at the age of 14 in 1972, to Led Zeppelin! I was quite simply blown away. With my pocket money, the first album (vinyl of course) I ever bought was *Led Zeppelin I*. In the seventies, it was virtually impossible to see much of Led Zeppelin on the telly. It was a case of watching *The Old Grey Whistle Test* in the hope of a rare sighting, buying *New Musical Express* or *Melody Maker* for any article with a passing reference or buying into the war of words with Charles Shaar Murray about the best band in the world, never for once agreeing with his view that it was The Who, when we all knew that gods that were Led Zep were by far the best in the whole wide world!

So I became the rock chick, went to my fair share of (mainly local) gigs, grew the shaggy hair with the hippy clothes and loved to listen to music pretty much above everything. I swapped albums with the boys at school – the girls were into pop music but I was into rock and roll! I had the older boyfriends, did what the older kids did... you get the picture. While the other girls plastered their bedroom walls with Donny and David, I collected every available poster I could lay my hands on of Robert and Jimmy, and bought every album.

I went to Knebworth with my then husband Ted and his best mate, Steve. It was my first ever festival. I'd never seen so many people in one space ever before and I found it quite overwhelming at first. It was a really hot day and I was dressed completely inappropriately for the weather. I had dressed in jeans and a light jumper and was way too hot. No hat, no sun lotion – no preparation! We found a space to sit where we could – there was no shade – and so I just burned in the sun. I remember so well, trying to find my way to the loos, tripping over a biker guy and him shouting at me. It was virtually impossible to find a way through the bodies lying and sitting everywhere.

It was the first time I'd ever seen a trench dug for the toilet, with a piece of cloth for a door – if you were lucky! I felt quite intimidated and tried to make sure that I didn't land on top of somebody. I can remember also that so many of the girls just stripped off – completely. I didn't have the confidence then to do that, plus I had a very dominant, jealous man in tow. It all felt totally surreal to me, and in many ways I was still very innocent then.

The music was amazing all day long; bands that I'd never heard of before – Southside Johnny and the Asbury Jukes – and those that we had, Chas and Dave and Todd Rundgren. I remember The New Barbarians, being Ronnie Wood and Keith Richards, being totally pissed (and probably stoned too) on stage and not really performing well.

Once I had relaxed about the alien surroundings, I really loved just lying back and listening to the music and people watching. By the time the guys came on stage, we were soooooooo ready for them. It felt beyond ecstasy. I certainly was so happy to see them and hear them play live for the very first time. Of course, by then the temperature was dropping and it was getting dark. I must admit that I was a little disappointed with the publicity for the Knebworth programme. They didn't look like Led Zeppelin – but they sure sounded like them!

I WAS THERE: STEVE RAYWOOD

My brother got me a ticket. Me, Mike, Tony (another loon) and my brother got a train to London and another out to Stevenage, some way outside London. It was a seriously hot humid day, one I would have avoided like the plague any other time, but this was special. The crowd were totally wrecked even by early morning and the smell of dope wafted across the huge arena along with the nauseating stench of the makeshift toilets in the form of a trench at one side of the arena. Loads of fans were sprawled out in all kinds of makeshift protection from the elements. It all looked pretty chaotic apart from the huge stage in front of us.

I felt sorry for the acts that came before Zeppelin as they were in the shade and only filling time until Zeppelin took to the stage. I thought Todd Rungren did okay, although he looked a bit ridiculous the way he was dressed. Chas and Dave were surprising tight and entertaining. I don't remember much about the other bands though, apart from Ronnie Wood and The New Barbarians. They sounded wasted – and looked it! Their last number was a meandering and never-ending 'Jumpin' Jack Flash'. A lot of fans were getting restless as we all knew this mess was holding up Zeppelin taking the stage.

A visibly irate Peter Grant was seen pacing the side of the stage while Zep's road crew loitered about waiting. Eventually Ronnie (or was it Keith Richards?) and his cohorts left the stage. Almost immediately, Zep's crew got to work setting up Zeppelin's stage gear. I was fascinated to see Bonzo's stainless steel kit wheeled in on a podium complete with gong and tympani drums, Jonesy's keyboards on a podium and Page's guitar army to the left and his amps with the strange mystic symbol on.

You got a feeling this was going to be out of this world. Nicky Horne, who introduced Zep at Earls Court, did the introductions after which huge curtains parted and four figures could just be made out walking on stage. A few noises from the guitar and – bang! There they were playing 'The Song Remains The Same'. All eyes were on Page who looked rake thin and not at all in great shape, and sadly his playing was rough as well and deteriorated as the evening proceeded. It struck me how pedestrian they looked. Gone were the mystical trappings, apart from Page's symbol on his Marshall.

I soon realised there was no chance of a 35-minute plus 'Dazed And Confused' as it was pretty obvious Page was in no state to perform such feats any more. But Bonzo was spot on throughout even though, as we learnt later, he was ravaged with drugs and drink. Plant played the jovial emcee, but you could hear some sarcastic bitterness in his comments. Jonesy floated through the whole show as professionally as he always had.

Standout tracks of the evening were 'The Rain Song', 'Kashmir', 'Achilles Last Stand' (even if Page did break the first E on his Les Paul) and 'No Quarter', for Jonesy's great solo, even with speakers blowing during his solo. Sadly, many of the rest of the songs sounded rusty and under rehearsed.

The real high point for many was Page's violin bow theremin antics. Bathed in an eerie light, he proceeded to assault the ears with his weird effects and the theremin. This was truly jaw dropping to experience live, but it was to get even better as Pagey wandered centre stage under a green pyramid of green lasers. Standing there, bow raised, it suddenly glowed orange and, as the bow was waved about, it shot a green laser beam in the sky (rumour has it aircraft coming into Heathrow were aware of the green laser firing in the sky from below). Suddenly the pyramid of light was in time with the crescendo of sounds and started revolving faster and faster. The end result was green and orange lasers firing everywhere, across the stage and in the sky. Page the magi in full flight.

It was all over before you knew it. Page looked exhausted and ready to collapse by the end. It's incredible he didn't collapse during the show. Although I can say I was there at the time, I was stunned at how lacking the show was and how worn out the band sounded. Even the three remaining members have little to say about both shows, which to me speaks volumes.

I WAS THERE: NICK RAYBOULD, AGE 19

Just a couple of weeks before the Knebworth dates were announced, I bumped into Robert Plant in the music shop-cum-studio where our band had just recorded our single. I was very starstruck, yet managed to hold a relatively stutter free conversation with him. He was asking Sean the proprietor about those GPO telephone exchange sockets you see on old sixties films where the operator plugs a jack into to connect a caller. He was building a home studio at the time and such things weren't as readily available as they are now, I suppose. As luck would have it my dad, a former GPO telecoms engineer, had several squirrelled away in our garage. Plant was very interested in getting them if I could retrieve them. I never did get them to him, sadly. (It didn't seem to hamper his post-Zep solo career.)

With some mates I booked Knebworth tickets from Meade Gold Enterprises, a company who ran coach trips to various music events across the UK and into Europe via regular adverts in *Sounds*. We were picked up in central Birmingham, opposite the law courts. The coach was full of very excitable rockers, most of whom seemed to be of similar age to me and my tribe.

Stretching our legs on arrival, we set about finding a good spot to set up our little area amid the sea of denim-dad yetis. Whether by prior arrangement or sheer chance, we hooked up with a couple from our small Warwickshire town and through them I had my first go at smoking weed! I was the only one of our small-town group to accept their invitation and I recall the dirty look from our straight-laced bass player.

I'd never been to a large open-air event like this before and during the risible support acts had a wander about. The toilet facilities? Well, the gents' urinal area was a large metal bathtub. Nobody wanted to stand too close to this after a while as the ground around it had become quite saturated and, as the afternoon dragged on, became a wider and wider swamp. We just pissed in the general vicinity in the end.

Refreshments, as I recall, consisted of warm flat scrumpy. On returning to our little spot in the middle of the sea of hippies and rockers, I found the older couple were now nicely stoned and a pair of breasts had popped out! The others were grumpily enduring Commander Cody and His Lost Airshipmen or whatever they were called. I was more into post punk and ska music and had initially hoped such new music was to be in some way represented in the supporting programme. Led Zeppelin and Black Sabbath, whilst dearly cherished, were already a kind of nostalgia thing to me. I've always thought the supporting bill of Chas and Dave et al a real cop out. Did someone fear the very exciting and vibrant post punk new wave would challenge Zeppelin's dominance of this weekend?

After Keith Richards and Ronnie Wood's jam session with various session hacks had fizzled out, our enthusiasm and excitement were revived. The road crew seemed to take forever to prepare the stage. A large white grand piano was wheeled out and the thousands of fans had to try and keep buoyant whilst what looked like an old college professor painstakingly tuned the thing. At this preamble was starting to make me angry. A few isolated glass throwing outbursts occurred. The light was now fading. This, I think is what the production crew were waiting for. Eventually, all the stage was immersed in darkness.

And then – boom – Led Zeppelin were on! There before us all was the band many had feared would never play live again. In fact, many of us had pretty much given up on ever actually witnessing this huge musical phenomenon. They were loud and truly majestic. An enormous video screen filled the entire width of the stage and showed multi camera close-up details of the band. Backlit, Plant's masses of corkscrew blond hair resembled a rock god's halo. Bonham was on a monster chrome drum kit and Jimmy Page and John Paul Jones looked lean and up for it. The sound quality was superb – loud, dynamic and crystal clear. All the irksome build up to this moment evaporated as that first guitar note echoed in the valley bowl and beyond us.

We were stunned into silence and just stood agog. All the classics were pounded out, and from the new album, 'In the Evening'. An ambient synthesised drone, that mournful cry of the title from Plant and then I remember the echo in the night air as the drums thundered in. Awesome. A guitar solo from Jimmy Page within a rotating mysterious neon pyramid, then lasers fired from his violin bow. And then, as the last note rang out, faded and the stage sunk into darkness, 'Kashmir'! The lights were back up but the huge screen was off, allowing a spectacular spiral of smoke to fill the air above the band as they thundered through their anthem of anthems. I still have my t-shirt. I can report that it fits me like a glove. Not like a t-shirt. A glove.

I WAS THERE: NORMAN WILSON

I initially bought a ticket for the first Knebworth show, on 4th August 1979, but I didn't know another person who wanted to attend. Then a second show was announced for the 11th, with the same line-up plus Keef and Ronnie's band, The New Barbarians, and some friends then decided they would go to this event. I was able to switch my ticket at Harlequin Records on Oxford Street in London without any trouble or cost (try that on Ticketmaster now) and bum a lift with Pete, Sally and Ralph up to the gig.

We arrived after a very early morning drive in the wet and seeing the gates were already open secured a place some distance from the stage. It was a long, long day with only Todd Rundgren for me to enlighten proceedings. The huge delays before both The New Barbarians and Zeppelin could have killed the atmosphere, but as Zeppelin hit the stage and with the huge video screen behind them and a loud and clear sound system, the place exploded.

I thought the setlist was a good selection of their best but needed more from the still unreleased *In Through The Out Door.* They needed to show the New Wave that they could still cut it and produce new material that counted. Although material from *Presence* had never been performed in the UK, the album was released over three years earlier.

There were some problems both with the equipment and some sloppy playing from Page, but it was clear the band was desperate to prove the naysayers wrong. The press from the previous week's show had not been complimentary. I really wanted them to be great so that my friends would appreciate what I saw in them, but other than for the classics – 'Stairway' and 'Whole Lotta Love' – I don't think they really got it. The band had stripped down some of the more self-indulgent parts of their 1977 shows, but as the 1980 European dates showed, they really could cut it when limited to just two hours.

In Through The Out Door, ***Led Zeppelin's final studio album, is released shortly after the Knebworth shows. It reaches number one on the*** **Billboard** ***chart in the USA and triggers the entire back catalogue re-entering the*** **Billboard 200** ***in October 1979.***

BLUNDELL PARK
11 DECEMBER 1979, CLEETHORPES, UK

I WAS THERE: NICK PARRY

Like me, Robert is a Wolverhampton Wanderers fan. One night my brother and I had gone to a League Cup replay at Grimsby. After another draw, we were on our way out of the ground when I said to my brother, 'Well that means we have another match to play so our match versus Liverpool will be postponed.' The chap walking alongside me in the half-light said, 'Bloody good job, the way we are playing.' I was about to agree with him when I realised who it was – Robert Plant! I was speechless. The funny thing was the guy in front of us had a Led Zeppelin sew on badge on his jacket and little did he know who was behind him.

1980 sees Led Zeppelin's **Tour Over Europe** *run from 17 June to 7 July 1980 and focus primarily on West Germany. After rehearsals at London's Rainbow and Victoria Theatres and Shepperton Studios, the band play a (for them) short two hour set in small venues, with a scaled-down PA and a more modest stage and lighting set up.*

WESTFALEN HALLE
17 JUNE 1980, DORTMUND, GERMANY

I WAS THERE: HELMUT KUCKY KUBERKA

I saw Led Zeppelin in my home town. The concert was a dream come true for me. They played their big hits such as 'Whole Lotta Love' but also a cross-section of their albums. I was in the first row and was hypnotised. When they played my favourite song, 'Since I've Been Loving You', I had tears in my eyes and I wasn't ashamed of it. I also saw Page and Plant live in Oberhausen. It was a great concert, but it wasn't Led Zeppelin.

STADTHALLE
26 JUNE 1980, VIENNA, AUSTRIA

I WAS THERE: ANDREAS REISMANN, AGE 15

For months Flo, my best schoolmate, and I were completely excited about the prospect of seeing one of our god-like bands live on stage. In Vienna. In the Stadthalle. We sat together for hours in our homes in the suburbs of Vienna, listening to our favourite bands like Queen, Pink Floyd, Deep Purple and of course Led Zeppelin. Flo's mother drove us to a cinema in Vienna to see the film *The Song Remains The Same*, a distant taste of what it was like to see the band live on stage. But Madison Square Garden in New York City seemed so far away.

But then they were coming to Vienna. We couldn't believe it! We ordered the tickets by telephone. They cost 200 Austrian schillings, around £13 in today's money. The day of the gig arrived and my father drove us to the Stadthalle in Vienna's 15th district. Our parents had given us some money, so we each bought a tour t-shirt and a shiny badge and went in. Surprisingly, the concert wasn't sold out. We were a bit disappointed about that. Their latest album, *In Through The Out Door*, hadn't sold very well here in Austria.

When they entered the stage we just stood there, mouths open and mesmerised. But although ecstatic at having our musical heroes performing live in front of us, one could tell this was 1980 for Led Zeppelin and not 1973. They played well but not perfectly, and at one point it seemed as though John was yawning while playing his drums. Still brilliantly, but routinely. You could recognise he wasn't in the best shape and condition and, four months later, he would sadly pass away. Another memorable moment was when Robert, John Paul and John had just left the stage for Jimmy to start his solo guitar piece on a bar stool. A small fire cracker was thrown by someone onto the stage and exploded next to the guitar god. Jimmy immediately left the stage, the lights went on in the Stadthalle and everybody stood there in disbelief.

We waited for some 20 minutes for something to happen before Gotthard Rieger, a deejay on Austrian radio, appeared to say the band would only reappear on stage if the culprit with the fire cracker revealed themselves. 20 minutes later, Gotthard came on stage again and told us the culprit, an Armenian student, had been found and the concert would proceed.

Robert, John Paul, John and Jimmy came back on stage and played for approximately another 40 minutes. They weren't exactly in a very jolly mood after what had happened, but my schoolmate and I were extremely happy to have them up there on stage again.

There was plenty to talk about after that night in Vienna – Led Zep live and the fire cracker incident – and the next morning at school we told our stories like soldiers coming home from war. Seeing Led Zeppelin live? I am very grateful to have had that privilege and, whenever I listen to 'Since I've Been Loving You' or 'In The Evening', I am back there in the Stadthalle.

MESSEZENTRUM-HALLE
JUNE 27, 1980, NUREMBERG, GERMANY

I WAS THERE: DON SHEPARD

I saw Led Zeppelin three times on this tour, all in West Germany prior to the Wall being removed. I was stationed in Geibelstadt Air Base with the US Army. As soon as these shows were announced, I knew I would be on military leave for a few days. I was planning on going to Berlin and see an old friend. I asked him to purchase two tickets. My friends at my duty station also wanted tickets for the Nuremberg show. We all travelled down to Würzburg to get our tickets at the PX (the air force retail outlet).

Five of us travelled by train early on the day of the gig to Nuremberg to drink some beer and get a good spot in the venue. We knew that Messe Halle was a very small venue, about the size of a high school gymnasium. We arrived at the venue two hours before the doors opened. When they did, we made it to the front just left of centre stage, about four people back. There was a group of girls in front of us. The crowd was getting really rowdy and pushing to the front against the stage. Peter Grant came out and told us all 'to fucking back up from the stage'. It didn't happen. We felt the 'squeeze' from the crowd pushing forward and it was getting crazy.

The band members starting coming on stage. John Bonham was first. He started for his drum kit and stumbled into one of his cymbals stands, knocking it over trying to catch his balance, and sat down. I remember John Paul Jones looking at him and kind of shaking his head. Jimmy Page was facing his amps and strumming a couple of notes, and then he turned around and walked up to middle of the stage. The crowd was going crazy at this time, screaming, yelling and still pushing forward. Robert Plant walked out and the venue exploded. They immediately went into playing 'Train Kept A-Rollin''. As they were playing, I told my buddy that the sound was terrible with a lot of feedback and distortion. By the end of the song, the sound was adjusted and sounded much better.

At the end of the song, John Bonham stood up from his kit shaking his head and said something to Plant. He staggered a little and again grabbed his cymbal stand and knocked it over. The stage hand helped him to his stool and set the stand back up. Bonham did not look well, and we said as much to each other as they went into playing 'Nobody's Fault but Mine'. John Paul walked over to the drum kit and was watching Bonham. The timing was really off. Plant kept turning around looking at Bonham. Page just kept playing. At the end of the song, John Paul and Plant walked back to the drum kit and talked briefly with Bonham, who appeared to be unbalanced. Plant apologised to the crowd, saying that a couple of them weren't feeling well but they would play on.

The intro to 'Out On The Tiles' started but with no drums for a bit and then Bonham came in. Bonham started into 'Black Dog' really hard, but after a few bars he appeared to be swaying behind his kit. At one point he stopped playing completely and looked over at the stage hand. They made it through the song and Bonham yelled 'no way!' Plant introduced the next song while looking back at Bonham and talking to the crowd at the same time. Bonham appeared to try and get up from his kit and fell to his knees and the stage hand grabbed his arm. He half-sat and half-lay there and several folks went to him, including the other band members. Plant got on the mic and said, 'Hang on, we are having some technical problems.' They walked Bonham off stage. He appeared to be drunk, but other reasons for his appearance given afterwards include saying he had eaten too many bananas and was sick from that.

About ten minutes later Peter Grant came out and said that they would be right back out. Five minutes after that he came back and said that they could not continue and that that was the end of the show. The crowd started to yell at him, with a few things being thrown up front. The girls standing in front of us started to cry. Peter announced that the ticket stubs should be kept and they would be honoured for the Frankfurt show. That didn't do us any good, although we were later able to get tickets for the Munich show after a lot of persuasion of a clerk at the PX in Würzburg.

The crowd was mad but everybody made their way out of the venue somewhat peacefully. We had a disappointed train ride back to our base. We had waited a long time to see Led Zeppelin live and were smacked in the face with what the show turned into. I noticed a concert poster hanging in a window at a shop and went in asking the owner if I could have it. She gave it to me with no questions asked.

I WAS THERE: JEFFREY CAMP, AGE 20

I was down front with four or five friends. We were all in the army. Tickets were bought through the army, which had a morale support fund. I'm sure they were at a discount but I can't remember what they cost. We were 20 years old at the time and we had what we called a 'sex, drugs and rock and roll' day. We bought a bunch of hash. In Nuremberg they have the walled city, which is the old part of the city, and right inside that wall they have these prostitutes in storefront windows, so we stopped there on the way. That was the sex part. Zeppelin was the rock and roll. It was memorable. Mostly for the Zeppelin part, but you put in the extracurriculars and it was a great day for a 20-year-old in Germany!

They played three songs and John Bonham passed out on the drums. It was about a month before he died. We got some great pictures. Jimmy Page was real thin. We were quite bummed when the concert got cancelled, because Peter Grant came out and said they would try and come back on a free day. Which they didn't. In hindsight, once Bonham had died, I realised how lucky I was to see them.

I WAS THERE: JERRY MICHALAK

I was back to Germany for the third time in my Army career, this time stationed in Bad Kissingen with G Troop 2nd Squadron 11th Armored Cavalry Regiment. Our mission was to provide surveillance and report any activity along the border in our sector. We did not have much idle time for things like rock concerts but this show was on the horizon and we would not be in the field training on 27 June. We had a group big enough to fill a large bus and it was on: we were going to see Led Zeppelin. The night before the show some moron broke into our motor pool shop and office. They took a shit in our water buffalo (water trailer) and tore up the office, also slinging shit in there. At formation in the morning our First Sergeant was livid. If he had known who did the dirty deed at that point, he would have killed him right then and there. That almost derailed our trip to see the show but we made it out of there.

We arrived at the Messe Halle in Nuremberg. As we were walking up the stairs to the hall, some dude was drunk, high or wasted up toward the top of the stairs. His pants were down around his ankles and he lost his balance and we watched him tumble down a whole lot of stairs, I don't think he made it into the show.

Once inside, we had spot on the right side of the stage in what seemed to be awful small for the biggest band on the planet. The band came out and opened with 'Train Kept A Rollin'', but the acoustics in that place sucked and it took a while to even understand what they were playing. Robert said a few words and then they played 'Nobody's Fault But Mine', which sounded better but still not great. We could see somebody by the drums. It looked like they may have been repositioning some things. Robert told the crowd that he and another member weren't feeling well with stomach trouble. Then they broke into the intro to 'Out On The Tiles' and right into 'Black Dog'. After that Robert introduced the next song, 'In The Evening', there was a bit of commotion on stage and it was then announced the show was cancelled.

Later we found out that, during 'Black Dog', Bonzo fell on his drums. He was drunk on his ass and could not continue. It was a major bummer because it wasn't very often we would get the time to go to a show. Almost three months to the day, John Bonham was dead. So sad for his family and Zep's millions of fans. The biggest show of my life turned into one of the biggest disappointments!

I WAS THERE: MICHAEL FABER

I saw them in Frankfurt on 30 June. I had tickets for the Nuremberg show first and switched them out after Bonham fell off his stool during the second song and the show was over. The place got trashed.

I WAS THERE: PETER NEUHAUSER, AGE 17

I saw Led Zeppelin live – or should I say I saw Led Zeppelin playing three songs? It was a lousy evening. The venue was a convention centre – definitely not build for loud rock music – and the sound was miserable. What was absolutely not usual at that time was that the concert began at 8pm, and I thought to myself, 'What a shitty opening act'. I read years later that Led Zeppelin started with 'Train Kept-A-Rollin'', but there was no way to recognise it. It sounded like a no-name opening act. Song number two was 'Nobody's Fault But Mine', and again it was impossible to recognise it as Led Zeppelin. The third song was 'Black Dog'. Okay, at that point of the show it was clear that this was not a covers band trying to play Zeppelin songs, but the masters themselves having a terrible day. Robert Plant just talked to the audience for the first time, and was about to announce 'In The Evening' from the *In Through The Out Door* album, which was relatively new, when Bonzo collapsed.

They tried to claim that there were technical difficulties, but minutes later, the house lights in the arena went on and we were told to go home. For me it was a remarkable weekend, because the day before I saw Frank Zappa with a monster performance of his *Sheik Yerbouti* show and the next day, I saw one of the greatest bands in rock history. In disastrous shape.

HALLENSTADION
29 JUNE 1980, ZURICH, SWITZERLAND

I WAS THERE: DANIELE VINCENTI, AGE 22

I discovered them in 1973. Zep for me was the biggest band of all of times and I love every single song of theirs. I saw them at the Hallenstadion in Zurich, one of their last ever concerts, because a couple of months later Bonzo died. I'm Italian. During that period concerts by foreign bands in Italy were banned. There was an agency that organised travel to see concerts in other countries and I applied for Zeppelin tickets, but they were instantly sold out. I was very sad, but then at the last minute the agency called me to say that one customer had cancelled their reservation so I got a ticket and my dream – to see them – was fulfilled.

Outside the Hallenstadion, there were buses from the whole of Italy and from Sicily and Sardinia too. I read later that the concert was organised just for Italian fans at the explicit wish of Jimmy Page. And, at the start of the concert, Robert said 'hello' in Italian. Obviously, it's the best concert I've seen in my whole life!

FESTHALLE
30 JUNE 1980, FRANKFURT, GERMANY

I WAS THERE: DAVE LEWIS

I am in the confines of the backstage area within the grand Festhalle venue in the heart of Frankfurt and I am standing no more than ten feet away from the four members of Led

Zeppelin. Tonight, they are playing one of the larger venues on the tour. Ten years ago, Led Zeppelin became the first band ever to play this venue and their return is much anticipated by the German audience. Tonight's crowd is also boosted by the presence of a number of US servicemen based at the nearby army base where Elvis Presley did some of his time for Uncle Sam way back when.

I am extremely fortunate to be viewing all this action unfold just a few feet from them by the side of the stage. Watching Led Zeppelin from this ultimate vantage point is, unsurprisingly, a thrilling experience and one that I will repeat in Mannheim and Munich later in the week.

The lights are dimmed and road manager Phil Carlo shines a torch through the dark and leads them up to the stage. John Bonham climbs the rostrum to the drums, John Paul Jones turns right where his tech assistant Andy Ledbetter straps on his Alembic bass and Jimmy Page walks onto the stage to the left, followed by Robert Plant.

As they walk into the glare of the spotlights, those assembled in the Frankfurt Festhalle finally view all four members of Led Zeppelin and the place erupts.

Guitar tech Ray Thomas straps on the Gibson and Jimmy moves to the effects pedals. A few snare shots and bass shuffles from Bonzo are the signal for the guitarist to lean back and exhort a fierce moaning wail from the Gibson. Robert takes a stance to his immediate right, the spotlights pick out the pair in regal splendour and then – WHAM! – they launch into 'Train Kept A-Rollin'', the old Johnny Burnette barnstormer The Yardbirds used in their heyday, and indeed which Zep played on their first US tours. Now it is being revived to kick-start what will be two hours of full-on power and excitement. This performance will include a unique encore delivery of Barrett Strong's 'Money (That's What I Want)', with Atlantic Records exec Phil Carson jamming on bass.

At the end of the show at around 10.30pm Robert Plant, with microphone in hands held aloft, is shaded by a single spotlight. Jimmy Page is showered in sweat but still grinning as his guitar tech takes the Gibson. To his right, John Paul Jones is dapper and cool as ever after driving the Zeppelin rhythm section for nigh on two hours. John Bonham, happy and smiling, jumps from the drum rostrum and strides over to the side of the stage where manager Peter Grant, promoter Harvey Goldsmith and Ahmet Ertegün, the esteemed head of Atlantic Records, are ready to receive them in a joyous celebration. So keen is Harvey to preserve this moment that he duly hands me his camera and asks me to take a photo of him and Ahmet by the side of the stage.

I was lucky enough to witness Led Zeppelin perform live on 15 occasions. Of those, that night in Frankfurt stands out. Tragically, in less than three months, the band would grind to a halt following the tragic death of John Bonham. Nearly 45 years from that final tour, my memories of this extraordinary band on stage in all their glory grow ever stronger.

EISSTADION
2 JULY 1980, MANNHEIM, GERMANY

I WAS THERE: STEVE SHARPE

I was stationed in Herford, West Germany when the tour was announced. We anxiously looked for which venues would be available and the Hannover gig seemed the best bet. However, the Army had different ideas and sent me on Operation Crusader 80, the largest NATO exercise since the Second World War. Mannheim was now the nearest venue I could attend, some 400 kilometres or four and a half hours away. The ticket was bought from a shop that sold concert tickets and there was no great demand for them, so that was a relief (unlike the 2007 reunion show).

On the day of the gig three of us drove down to Mannheim, arriving in good time for the show. I didn't recognise the opening number and only 20 or so years later, when the bootlegs appeared and the internet was available, did I discover that it was 'Train Kept A Rollin'', which of course was the first song they ever played together. They played a few songs from the new album, *In Through The Out Door*, as well as the standards so overall I think we were well pleased. Straight after the show we drove back to Herford, t-shirts loaded. I still have one of the two I bought that day – although I think it has shrunk in the wash! Having acquired several versions of the show over the last ten years, it's nice to hear it again and relive the day I was there.

OLYMPIA HALLE
5 JULY 1980, MUNICH, GERMANY

I WAS THERE: CARMEN, AGE 17

I was almost 18. We had been hanging around the Olympic Park all day. I was going to college in Munich at the time. We did not have tickets for the show because it sold out too quickly. I was living by the Chiemsee, which is about an hour east of Munich. I normally took the train in every day. We stayed with friends overnight on that day. Of course I knew 'Whole Lotta Love' before I was fully introduced to Led Zeppelin by my boyfriend, Joe, but through him I was introduced properly, because he was pretty much a Zeppelin fanatic and there was no way he wasn't going to see them. I was always up for a concert, but didn't really care that much – before the show!

One of my boyfriend's friends was working backstage as a roadie. He wasn't part of Led Zeppelin's road crew but was working for the venue, and he had promised us tickets to the concert. It turned out he was wrong and he was not able to get us in. However, due to the insane demand for tickets the venue started selling tickets for behind the stage, as in behind the curtain, so we'd be in the building and the auditorium with awful sound and not being able to see the band.

My boyfriend was quite the trickster, so we just went to one of the entrances to the arena to see if there was any way at all to get down there. The people going down the steps ahead of us did not have general admission arena tickets either. But they bribed the guard and the guard thought we were part of that group and so let us just follow them onto the coveted arena floor. This then meant we could not leave until after the concert and so there were no pee or beer breaks because we wouldn't have been able to get back down there.

We ended up about three metres from the barrier, right in front of Robert Plant. Oh my God, what an amazing experience. I had not been a huge Led Zeppelin fan before, but after the concert, I was a convert. The crowd was so thick and dense we could not move. I am assuming our guard, and the other guards, made quite a bit of money that night by letting people onto the floor and getting some extra cash for it because the place was so full. At one point, Jimmy Page had sweat dripping from the cigarette in his mouth. This was back when you could smoke inside venues. We ended up completely drenched and exhausted.

When it was all over, we waited for the crowd to disperse and in the stands, a few rows up, I spotted some friends from my high school. I had no idea they were going. They said that from where they were, they couldn't even see the people on the floor because of the thick cloud of hashish smoke hovering over us and the steam from our sweat evaporating. Everybody was exhausted, but in a good way. My boyfriend said he 'saw God' at this concert (one of his catch phrases at the time).

I was just mesmerised by Robert Plant on stage. Picture an almost 18-year old young woman in that setting, that close to Robert Plant. Yeah – ha ha! My favourite song that night was definitely 'Kashmir'. We 'felt' the music, and especially John Bonham's drums. To this day, I still don't think there is a drummer as powerful as he was.

I WAS THERE: DON SHEPHARD

After the Nuremberg show, we made attempt number two to catch Led Zeppelin live, and hopefully for a full concert this time. We decided to drive to Munich for this show because a couple of the guys had to report for duty the next morning. I would take the train from Munich straight to Frankfurt to catch the troop train to Berlin.

We arrived in Munich later than expected. There was already a long line outside the venue entrances. Unlike Messe Halle a few days earlier, the Olympia Halle is a full-sized indoor arena. Getting up front was not going to be possible. The seating was all around and the open floor was standing only. We were about three quarters of the way back from the stage. The first thing I noticed was that the pre-music show did not sound very good and appeared to only be coming from the front. My group agreed that we hoped the sound would be better for the show. I also noticed a second drum kit set up off stage and wondered what was going on with that.

The crowd was jumping, whistling and clapping very loudly, with a few screams of 'Led Zep'. The arena lights went down and the very loud crowd erupted into a frenzy. The crowd started to push forward and packed the floor, so little free movement was going to happen. Jimmy Page was illuminated on stage in a spotlight wearing a blazer over a dark shirt and white tie. He started playing 'Train Kept A-Rollin''. The stage lit up when all the band started in. The sound was very low so we had a hard time understanding the words.

After the unfortunate events at Nuremberg, we were very excited when they broke into 'Black

Dog' and I held my breath, hoping that they would make it past the song. They did and I knew we were in for a full show at that point. Bonham showed no signs of letting us down tonight. He went into a little drum solo at the end of a song and Plant just stood there, smiling and shaking his head. I was so excited to see Page bring out his Danelectro guitar and play the solo to 'White Summer/Black Mountainside' and then go right into 'Kashmir'. When Page pulled out the double-neck Gibson and started 'Stairway To Heaven', the whole place sang along.

Throughout the show, Robert and Jimmy both addressed the unruly crowd. There seemed to be a lot of hecklers that kept yelling at the stage and Jimmy and Robert asked for quiet and waited for them to stop. The crowd was being pushed forward to the front again.

They made it through the playlist and then Robert asked the crowd to welcome Simon Kirke from Bad Company to the stage and the crew pushed out a second drum kit, the one I'd spotted earlier, setting it up between John Paul and Plant's mic. The crowd went crazy when Kirke and Bonham went into a drumming master piece to start the song 'Whole Lotta Love'. It was an amazing performance. That number ended the show and all five guys came to the stage and waved and exited. The crowd kept screaming and yelling until the house lights came on.

We headed out of the arena and the crowd kept cheering, 'Led Zep! Led Zep!' My friends dropped me off at the Bahnhof, envious that I was heading to Berlin to see the show there again and they headed back to the base. Little did I know that it would be the last time I would see a couple of my buddies.

I WAS THERE: CRAIG HIGGINS

I was working at the Hilton Hotel in Munich in room service. We got tickets for the gig at the Olympiahalle from Zep's roadies, and the morning after I served Robert Plant, Jimmy Page and John Bonham breakfast in their suite. They were all really friendly and took time to talk to us about the gig.

EISSPORTHALLE

7 JULY 1980, BERLIN, GERMANY

I WAS THERE: ALASTAIR G MUIR

I got into them through albums while I was living at home, aged about 16. Later I joined the Royal Air Force and, aged 28, was posted to Berlin. When I saw they'd be performing their *Over Europe* tour in Berlin, I had to get a ticket. My wife wasn't happy because it was the same date as my son's second birthday. I saw them with a work colleague. The venue was packed solid, the sound very loud but brilliant and there was very little deviation from the albums. My lasting memory is of the sea of lit lighters held aloft when they played 'Stairway To Heaven'. My ears rang for hours afterwards but it was worth it. It was a brilliant night. Sadly, Bonzo died about six weeks later and after finishing the tour. I'm so pleased I grabbed the opportunity to see them complete and live. To this day I'm the only person in my town that can say that I saw the complete Led Zep live!

I WAS THERE: DON SHEPARD

After 14 hours of travelling from Munich to Berlin by train with a little lay over in Frankfurt, I finally reached Berlin in the early morning. The Berlin troop train only travelled under the cover of darkness as per the agreement of the governments. I had several hours to kill so played tourist around Berlin. I met my buddy Mike at his barracks and headed to the venue. We had some beer and food across the street and got in line around 6pm. After a little wait, the doors opened and we made it to the front stage against the barricade, about five feet from the stage edge. We were just to the right side, which we planned on, so we could be close to Page. The Eissporthalle was a rather smaller venue that held about 6,000 people, with seating on one side and the stage set up at the end of the building.

After a wait of over an hour, a spokesman came out and asked the crowd to move back from the stage. They didn't listen. A couple of girls were being pushed against the bars and the concert crew pulled them over the barricade and had them sit down there for the entire show. The announcer came out and announced the band and again told the crowd to move back, in German and English.

The house lights went down, the stage lights went up and Bonham and Jones came out with Page following them. They started playing 'Train Kept A-Rollin'' and Plant walked out to the front. Page went into 'Black Dog' and just tore up the guitar solos. The crowd was just crazy over this until they went into 'In The Evening', which was one of the best live performances of any song I had heard. They played it so hard that they seemed to lighten up when 'Rain Song' started because Page seemed to be fighting his riffs. When they got to 'White Summer/Black Mountainside', he switched from his Gibson to his Danelectro, started to play and stopped and walked to the side of the stage.

Plant started talking to the crowd about some technical problems and they were working on it. It looked like the guitar was not tuned for the song but the guitar tech did it real fast for Page. He started out on a stool centre stage and then stood up when they went into 'Kashmir'. When Page grabbed his double-neck Gibson, I knew it was time for the crowd to go crazy again. Page went into the opening of 'Stairway To Heaven' and the crowd exploded and started pushing forward. As at Munich, there was a 6,000 strong choir singing along with Plant.

The last song they played was 'Whole Lotta Love'. The crowd was so excited for the last couple of numbers. The energy was just crazy. Little did anybody know that we had just witnessed the last live show ever by Led Zeppelin. About the mid-point of the show, Robert Plant said, 'We've done 16 towns in 21 days and it's, that's dyno movement, that is. This is, uh, we've had a good time. This is the last concert so we intend to have a better time now perhaps than we have done before.'

I originally planned on seeing Led Zeppelin only once during their tour in Germany but ended up attending three. Well, two plus four songs. Every one of these shows had some significant history to the band and music that I was able to witness first hand, including the short concert at Nuremberg where John Bonham passed out behind the drums from 'eating too many bananas'. Simon Kirke from Bad Company waiting in the wings to play at Munich and then coming out and playing a duet with John Bonham on 'Whole Lotta Love' was a masterpiece.

I am honoured to have witnessed the final show of the original members in Berlin before the passing of John 'Bonzo' Bonham. Of the three I attended, Berlin was the best show. The saddest part of this experience was not anything to do with Led Zeppelin, but learning that my buddies were killed in a vehicle accident on their way back from the Munich show. Led Zeppelin will always be one of the greatest bands ever. I feel privileged to have had the opportunity to see them live and to be able to rock to their music to this day. Long Live Led Zep!

Rehearsals for the 1980 North American tour begin at Bray Studios. The tour is due to commence on 17 October in Montreal, Canada.

OLD MILL HOUSE, CLEWER
25 SEPTEMBER 1980, WINDSOR, UK

John Bonham falls asleep on 24 September 1980 at Jimmy Page's house after a day's rehearsals. Bonham had been drinking heavily since the morning and is found dead the next day.

I WAS THERE: ALAN KAUFFMANN

I was a student at Georgia State University from 1975 to 1980 and a deejay at the college radio station. I was in the middle of an air shift on Wednesday evening, 25 September 1980. As I pulled the news feed for the next newscast, I realised the unfortunate words that l would have to broadcast only a few minutes later – John Bonham had just died.

The death of John Bonham leads the surviving members of the band and their manager Peter Grant, after a short period of reflection, to issue a statement: 'We wish it to be known that the loss of our dear friend, and the deep sense of undivided harmony felt by ourselves and our manager, have led us to decide that we could not continue as we were.' It is the end of Led Zeppelin as a touring and recording entity.

INGLEWOOD FORUM
27 SEPTEMBER 1983, LOS ANGELES, CALIFORNIA

I WAS THERE: TOM COYNE, AGE 16

Sadly, I missed Zeppelin by about two years. I did see both Plant and Page at the LA Forum in 1983, but at separate shows. Plant played there on his first solo tour, and Page played there at the Ronnie Lane ARMS show. I was 16 and in awe. I also caught Page three times with The Firm, once on his *Outrider* tour and again on the Page/Plant tour. He was in fine form by '88. And I caught Plant in '85 and '88 solo, with Page in '95 and with Alison Krauss in 2023 at the

Greek Theatre. I've never seen John Paul Jones. In January of 2008, I met Jason Bonham at the NAMM Show in Anaheim, California. He was signing publicity photos for Ludwig Drums. By then I already had a bootleg of the O2 concert from December 2007. I asked him what happened at the end of the guitar solo section of 'Dazed And Confused'. He laughed and said 'it was Jimmy!' Jimmy had gotten lost coming out of the solo and played the wrong part over Jason's big drum fill. Oops! They fixed it on *Celebration Day*.

NATIONAL EXHIBITION CENTRE
18 MAY 1985, BIRMINGHAM, UK

I WAS THERE: PAUL HINDESS

When Zeppelin ended, and Robert and Jimmy did their own things, I did nearly every gig. By then I had a company vehicle, fuel, an understanding wife and off I just went. For The Firm's first tour, when Jimmy toured with Paul Rodgers as his lead vocalist, I did every gig. They were playing at the NEC in Birmingham. I drove down for that one and went in the bar of the hotel at the NEC and who should be sat there, with hardly anyone else in it, but Jimmy Page? It was the first time I'd met Jimmy. I went over to talk to him and he bought me a drink and signed the receipt 'rock on' which I've now had framed. I then went to the loo and who should walk in the door but Robert Plant? I knew Robert, because during his solo career I'd done a lot of his gigs with a friend of mine, who was a close friend of his, so I always used to get backstage and meet the band.

So there's Robert and I said 'hi Robert.' I went back in the bar and said to Jimmy, 'Robert was just in the loo.' He didn't play the show that night and I don't think he was at the after show do either. He'd obviously turned up at the NEC, gone to the hotel where he knew Jimmy was but then had never come in to the bar to meet him. It was those days when they were handbags at ten paces, you know? They were sort of getting on but not getting on. That's where they were and, to be honest, that's really where they are now. Some of it is about Robert having moved on musically, and Jimmy wanting to re-edit and remaster a new Led Zeppelin CD and put that out. And some of it is deeper than we'll ever understand, about Jimmy's reaction to Robert's son's death and about Bonzo's death. Some of it stems from that. The great thing is they did get together from time to time and whenever they did it was brilliant. It was magical meeting Jimmy that one time.

I went to Robert's last gig at the City Hall in Newcastle and I walked out of there with it not having touched a nerve of me. It did absolutely nothing. I was down in the front and I looked at him, gave him the thumbs down and he wasn't very happy. What he's doing just didn't do it for me. He does Zeppelin songs but he destroys them. I wish he'd leave 'Black Dog' and stuff alone. He does stupid things with them and it just pisses me off.

LIVE AID, JOHN F KENNEDY STADIUM
13 JULY 1985, PHILADELPHIA, PENNSYLVANIA

I WAS THERE: SAM MCCLAFFERTY

My Led Zep concerts are what could have been. For the *Physical Graffiti* tour I waited in line on a freezing February night from midnight to noon, only to have the guy in front of me get the last tickets. I then had tickets at JFK when Plant's son died and the tour was cancelled. But I saw them at *Live Aid* and then Page and Plant on the *No Quarter* tour. I can't believe they didn't tour after the O2 show in 2007. They would have killed it.

I WAS THERE: TONY PAULINE

I'd seen Plant three or four times up and down the East Coast, on his first solo tour in September '83, and then I saw Page at the ARMS concert. When they announced the *Live Aid* concert in London and then Philadelphia, and then said that Jimmy Page was going to be there, I said 'well, I haven't seen Jimmy Page in a couple of years' and then they announced separately that Robert Plant was gonna be there. That's when my radar went up and I picked up the phone and said to my father, 'Dad, you gotta get me tickets for this.' And my dad said 'how many tickets do you want?' It was going to be me and my buddy. And this guy Steve said he wanted four tickets and my college roommate's brother wanted four tickets, so ten tickets at $75 apiece.

Bill Graham was running the Philadelphia portion of the show out of New York City, so my father said to me 'you've got to go to the office on 77th Street with $750, pay the cash and the girl will give you the tickets.' But when it comes to time to pony up the money, eight of the ten people decide that they're not going to go. So it's just me and my buddy Steve, and I go down to the office on the West Side and the woman pulls out an envelope and says 'here's your tickets'. I said, 'I only need two.' She was very upset. She said, 'I'll be right back.' In the back office I could hear Bill Graham on the phone screaming and yelling at somebody. And he's saying 'Rod Stewart will be on the stage at 4.30pm in the afternoon in Philadelphia if he wants to play *Live Aid*.' Rod's name was splashed everywhere and his name was even in the official programme. He didn't play *Live Aid*.

I didn't believe Zeppelin were going to get back together. I'd had my heart broken too many times. My buddy and I used to work at the golf course. He went out caddying before me so I had to hitchhike to meet him because we were going to drive home and get ready for the show. And another caddy happened to see me and he picked me up and we were talking in his car and he said 'it's official. Zeppelin are getting back together for *Live Aid*.' I felt such a rush of emotion when I realised it was going to happen.

We got into the stadium about eight o'clock in the morning and I had no idea what time they were going to come on, or what the running order was. They had these fibreglass benches and I was stood up on one of them. When Phil Collins started announcing the names, you could see the crowd go crazy. I was so excited that I was jumping up and down on this bench and then, all of a sudden, I heard – crack! – and the bench had cracked beneath me.

The performance was not good. Plant's voice was not good. You saw Jimmy Page fumbling around, with his wires getting caught in the microphone. I didn't care. I went absolutely out of my mind. At the very end, Page and Plant came to the middle of the stage and hugged each other and the crowd went crazy. I went and sat in the back where the concessions were. I sat there wth a jug of water for, like, 40 minutes. *Live Aid* was over for me. Zeppelin at *Live Aid*? It was a slice of heaven.

Billed as Page and Plant, Jimmy and Robert begin working together again in 1994.

FRANK ERWIN CENTER
13 MARCH 1995, AUSTIN, TEXAS

I WAS THERE: STEPHANIE RENEE HILT, AGE 32

I saw Jimmy Page and Robert Plant when they toured with the Egyptian back up band. It was incredible. Robert Plant's voice was spectacular and the whole show was fabulous. They played Led Zeppelin songs and songs from Plant's solo album. I never heard 'Kashmir' sound so alive.

SKYDOME
27 MARCH 1995, TORONTO, CANADA

I WAS THERE: JENNIFER PRYCE

In 1995 my best friend and I made a pact to see Page and Plant as many times as we could. The first show was at the Skydome. The whole show was magical. It wasn't always easy to acquire tickets and rides. One time we even rode in the trunk of a car to get to a show!

BRENDAN BYRNE ARENA
6 & 7 APRIL 1995, EAST RUTHERFORD, NEW JERSEY

I WAS THERE: SUZY SOLTIS

My teenaged kids did not want to attend this show. But this was as close to seeing Led Zeppelin as anyone was going to get since the passing of John. The show was filled with amazing energy. My son, who was 13, turned around and asked me for a lighter. That's what we did back in the days of old. The teen in front of him told him he was 16 and this was his first concert too. All my three kids rocked to the music they were hearing at home, but now hearing live. They thanked us for 'forcing' them to go!

OLYMPIASTADION
2 JULY 1995, MUNICH, GERMANY

I WAS THERE: HELMUT ÖLSCHLEGEL

I've never seen Led Zeppelin, but I've seen Page and Plant at *Rock Over Germany* in Munich, Robert with UFO in Neumarkt, Jason Bonham with UFO and JPJ with Them Crooked Vultures and got to photograph them all.

CORNWALL COLISEUM
15 JULY 1995, ST AUSTELL, UK

I WAS THERE: DEREK THOMAS

They had the Moroccan orchestra and it was absolutely fantastic. We booked seats in the upper circle and we were right in line with the side of the stage so as the artists were coming off – ie. Jimmy Page getting a drink, getting another guitar or whatever – you could almost touch them. But the guys without seats on the floor were having a great time whereas it was almost like a tea party up in the circle, with no clapping or dancing. I said to my missus, 'Come on, let's go down on the floor.' Robert was saying, 'I love Cornwall. My parents used to bring me here for summer holidays when I was a kid.' He repeated it a couple of times and said, 'Oh I've already said that, haven't I?' I was going to try and get to the front of the stage and say, 'Remember Stourbridge? Remember Frosty?' But I was too embarrassed.

SHORELINE AMPHITHEATRE
7 OCTOBER 1995, MOUNTAIN VIEW, CALIFORNIA

I WAS THERE: DAVE STUBER

It was just like a Zep show, but with the San Jose Symphony Orchestra. Very cool.

UNITED CENTER
13 OCTOBER 1995, CHICAGO, ILLINOIS

I WAS THERE: DANIEL J ROGERS

We had hardcore Led Zeppelin fanatics on the south side of Chicago where I grew up. My father was blessed a couple of times to see Zeppelin and it was him who turned me onto Zeppelin. He had the *Zeppelin IV* album, a Thorens turntable with a diamond tip needle, four JBL speakers and an Akai reel-to-reel tape recorder. My parents divorced young so I'd stay with him on the weekends and take advantage of his record collection. I was exposed to a myriad of stuff: The Who, the Stones, Robin Trower, the Moody Blues, the original Fleetwood Mac.

I was a senior in high school when Jimmy Page came to Chicago on the *Outrider* tour. Jimmy Page, Jeff Beck and Clapton were the first three influences on my own guitar technique before I moved on to Hendrix and Robin Trower and, later, Stevie Ray Vaughan. Seeing Jimmy Page for the first time was absolutely phenomenal. We knew that Jason Bonham was going to be on drums and we'd never heard any of his stuff, although friends had said I should check him out in Virginia Wolf, the band he played in before playing with Jimmy. The whole band were phenomenal. The vocalist, John Miles, was unbelievable.

I was in eighth grade when he came through with The Firm. I really wanted to see that but I was only 14 and I was sick. My mother wasn't keen on me going out with these older high school kids.

When Robert's first solo album came out, it was almost like the nail in the coffin to a possible Zeppelin reunion. My dad was saying, 'Danny, John Bonham has passed away!', but this was confirmation that Robert was going his own way. Looking back, he's been true to himself. He's kept the creative output going by making sure that he works with other musicians. When they did the Page and Plant shows, I went to several of those to get my fix and I loved every single one of them. I saw the O2 reunion with a full surround sound in a theatre. I thought that was fabulous and I couldn't believe how rehearsed they were.

A lot of people attacked Jimmy for *Live Aid* because his playing was off that day, but Jimmy has been an excellent carrier of the torch with the rereleases of the albums and the outtakes. He always seems very affable and willing to speak about Zeppelin, whereas it seems Robert is almost ready to throw up when that question comes up. It irritates him. But I think Robert is now enjoying incorporating some Zeppelin stuff into his new musicians and his new band arrangements.

THE CITY
1986, NEW YORK, NEW YORK

I WAS THERE: MARK DELGUIDICE

Robert was alone in the corner of the club's VIP section all by himself. Everyone was scared of his celebrity and trying to impress each other by ignoring him. He was taking up three spaces on a bench so, being a cocky punk and an aspiring rock star (it never happened), I said, 'Hey rock star, can ya move ya ass over so I can sit down?' He loved that I did so and said, 'yes mate, sit, sit.' He asked me if had any weed. 'Of course, I'm from Chicago!' After a bit he said, 'Let's get outta here – these sycophants are so boring.' He had a huge roll of drink tickets so we went into the real club with the lights and disco and he suggested we give the tickets away to all these groups of girls. He and I then talked fishing and NYC stuff. Having grown up near the Kingston Mines I admitted I'd played there a lot and he only wanted to hear about that. We didn't talk Zep except at the end, when I thanked him for his music. Two tall gorgeous black girls came up and asked us if we could dance at all. They had no idea who he was. He looked at me with a boyish grin and said 'oh yes, we can dance!' And we did, for an hour. It was such fun. At the end he offered me a ride 'in the limo' but I had to go get my celeb girlfriend so declined. He and the girls headed out together, and he threw me a big smile and waved!

SHEPHERDS BUSH EMPIRE
25 MARCH 1998, LONDON, UK

I WAS THERE: ROB WHITMARSH

I was just a couple of years too young to see them first time around. I never thought Led Zeppelin would reunite, so when Jimmy Page and Robert Plant got together for their *No Quarter: Unledded* tour, I managed to go to five of their UK shows. The vibe of those gigs was quite acoustic and the Led Zeppelin songs they performed were reworked versions of the music I loved. A big part of me really wanted to see Jimmy Page and Robert Plant rock out with a full electric performance. My wish was finally granted in March 1998, when the magazine *Kerrang!* had a small article announcing: 'Zep pair play one-off show. Page and Plant will play a one off UK show at a secret London venue on March 25. Tickets for this show will only be on sale for one day – Saturday March 14 – at the Virgin Megastore in London's Oxford Street.'

Before the internet, acquiring tickets had to be done the old school way. On the evening of 13 March, I duly took the train to London to camp out on the street and snag myself a golden ticket to this mysterious show. Arriving at the Virgin Megastore at 11pm, the queue was already snaking from the store's side entrance on Tottenham Court Road and about to continue into the back lane of Hanway Street. I joined the happy campers. As the night wore on, I was pleased I didn't end up in Hanway Street – we all needed to pee during the night and this lane became the perfect place. It stank to high heaven and I'll always think of Hanway Street as Piss Alley. There is a bootleg of this show called *Queuing By The Sick*!

The doors to the Virgin Megastore finally opened at 8am and, 25 minutes later, I had my ticket in my hand. I was cold and tired but very happy. The queue had been speculating which mystery venue would be hosting the gig – Hackney Empire and Shepherds Bush Empire were strongly rumoured. As the first tickets were sold, we were told that it was to be the Shepherds Bush Empire. I had breakfast straight after and then made my weary way back to Waterloo to catch the train back home.

Eleven days later I was back in London. Shepherds Bush was perfect for me, as that's where I always parked my car when I visit the capital. I joined the line to get in and knew that I was about to see the two front men of Led Zeppelin up close and personal, playing what was basically a club show and a proper electric gig with an acoustic interlude. There was a new album coming out about a month later, so we were bound to hear a couple of new tracks, but this was to be a very Led Zeppelin gig. I was three rows from the stage, right in front of where Jimmy Page was to be.

The band had warmed up by playing a handful of shows in Eastern Europe the previous month, but this was their big homecoming gig. The band was now stripped back to a five piece – Jimmy Page, Robert Plant, Charlie Jones (bass), Michael Lee (drums) and Phil Andrews (keyboards and mandolin). There was no support band so, as the house lights dimmed, their Egyptian intro music was played through the PA. There was no gap. Just an instant flash of the stage lights and the band hammered straight into 'The Wanton Song', fully rocked up and very powerful indeed. Robert Plant was spinning around and giving it maximum. This was going to be a very lively performance from Page and Plant. It was also going to be a very lively performance from the audience, which was going berserk, as was I.

They played a triple opener as the band went straight into 'Bring It On Home' and continued with 'Heartbreaker', which featured Jimmy Page's first solo of the night. Both Jimmy and Robert were on top form. Their set continued with 'Ramble On' before the first new song of the night, 'Walking Into Clarksdale'. Later we had an acoustic set including 'Going To California' and a personal favourite of mine, 'Tangerine'.

Throughout the show, we had plenty of 'Plantations' as Robert chatted to us. The whole band seemed to be having great fun whilst giving a very energetic performance. After the acoustic section, we were back to the rocked up performance. I remember how wonderful 'How Many More Times' was. This track included a part of 'In The Light' and featured Jimmy Page with his violin bow. Jimmy was completely in another place and totally in the zone and we witnessed some true magic from him.

'Most High' was the only song from their forthcoming album that had been released at that moment and fitted in well with the Led Zeppelin songs. The main set finished with a high energy 'Whole Lotta Love', but the night wasn't to end there. We were treated to four more songs over two encores. The first of these songs, 'Burning Up', was only ever played in concert at this show, while 'Crossroads' only got played four times. The second encore gave us 'Thank You' and they closed the night with an immense 'Rock And Roll'. I was to see the fully rocked up Page and Plant another two times on this tour. Those other performances were superb in their own right, but there was an added bit of magic at this Shepherds Bush gig. Maybe it was the fact that the whole audience went the extra mile just to get a ticket. Maybe it was that the band was truly on fire that night. It was the first time I had seen what was basically a Led Zeppelin show in a small venue. And all for the princely sum of £22.50.

I WAS THERE: JOHN GRIFFITHS

The nineties brought a reconciliation of sorts, with Page and Plant releasing a new album and touring. My best mate Mark was working in the import/export side of the business and got the contract for shifting the gear about. The week before the gig at Shepherds Bush Empire, he announced he had tickets for anyone who wanted to go. We all piled in. I had retrained and was working as a teacher at the time, with a class of children to get up to the next day, so mid-week outings were a rarity.

The set list was pretty much Zeppelin and utterly brilliant. Then, as the encore faded, Mark doled out credentials for the back stage party! The whole thing took on the air of the surreal as we waved our passes at the huge bouncers who smilingly allowed us through, only to scowl menacingly at the punters who tried following us. When we got in, Mark calmly announced the bar was free. I was well on the way to being shit-faced (it would have been rude not to) when I heard a commotion behind me and turned to come face to face with Percy himself I wanted to fall on the floor in true *Wayne's World* 'I'm not worthy' fashion but pulled myself together, thrust out my hand and said, 'Great gig, Bob'. Without hesitation, he shook my hand and after a micro-second of assessing who I was and realising I was just another face in the crowd, he generously grinned back and said 'glad you could come' in his Brummie accent before moving on. I looked around to see all my mates were wide-eyed and drop-jawed. Fame at last. The hangover was a monster, but having to deal with it and a class of four-year-olds next day was worth it.

PALACE OF AUBURN HILLS
26 JUNE 1998, AUBURN HILLS, MICHIGAN

I WAS THERE: ERIC CHESNICK

They played for over two and a half hours and covered almost all material on all Zeppelin albums, including a lot off of *Physical Graffiti*.

CIVIC ARENA
1 JULY 1998, PITTSBURGH, PENNSYLVANIA

I WAS THERE: CHUCK J SBERNA

I was surprised by the songs they played. They had two drummers to keep up with the playing style of Bonham. The sound was really great and they played songs you would have never thought, like 'Tangerine'. They played at least one song from every album, except *In Through The Out Door*.

WEMBLEY ARENA
5 & 6 NOVEMBER 1998, LONDON, UK

I WAS THERE: MARTIN NOKE

I never saw Zep unfortunately. We went to see Page and Plant twice. At Wembley I remember thinking if you just squinted your eyes, you could imagine it was 1973, but of course no Bonzo. I did go to the ARMS charity concern for MS at the Royal Albert Hall in 1983 which was staged as much as a tribute to Ronnie Lane. Jimmy was there and played an instrumental version of 'Stairway'. He was whip thin and swaying around the stage, probably right in the middle of his heroin phase. We had seats up and behind the stage with a sideways view. It was great to see him on stage with Jeff Beck.

My wife Caroline and I came across Robert at Covent Garden sometime in the late eighties. I don't really look at people but Caroline recognised him and nudged me. I sidled across and said to him, 'I don't suppose you are who I think you are, are you?' and he said, 'Well, depends who you think I am,' at which point I should have said 'David Coverdale' and he would have probably have punched me in the face. But I said 'Robert Plant' and he said 'yes'. I just said I had been a fan of his music for 20 years and shook his hand and left it at that. He seemed to have such a big face and a great mane of hair like a lion.

Jimmy, I met by luck. I had a meeting for work in Kensington and I had an idea to walk past the Tower House. I was just taking pictures of the gargoyles when I heard the lock turn on the door. I thought, 'Wouldn't it be weird if Jimmy came out?' and in a way I knew it would be him. Sure enough, out comes Jimmy Page in jogging bottoms and an old t-shirt. I just said 'you must be Jimmy Page' and he said 'yeah man, yeah' in that distinctive voice of his. So it was the same conversation really about being a fan for years, etc. but he was in a hurry and so we just shook hands and he wandered off towards Kensington High Street. It was obvious that he was just popping out so I could have hung around but I didn't want to appear to be a weirdo so I went on to my meeting. The phone I had at the time did not do selfies but I did get a picture of him walking away as an afterthought.

John Paul Jones I've never met. When it comes to Bonzo, I've been to the grave a couple of times. The second time we were driving to Clitheroe in a hired van to play a gig for my mate's 20th wedding anniversary and I took a detour to the village church without telling the other guys why. They were moaning at me for getting them lost when I pulled up at the church and said, 'Boys, we have to make a pilgrimage.' They were quite surprised when we got round the back of the church to find the name on the headstone with all the broken drumsticks and other paraphernalia.

In December 2007, the surviving members of Led Zeppelin reunite for a concert to celebrate the life of Ahmet Ertegün, co-founder of Atlantic Records.

O2 ARENA
10 DECEMBER 2007, LONDON, UK

I WAS THERE: PETER SMITH

There had been rumours for some time that Zeppelin might reform, and in September 2007, Harvey Goldsmith confirmed at a press conference that a reunion concert was indeed going to take place. This was a benefit concert held in memory of music executive Ahmet Ertegün, who had been involved in breaking Zeppelin in the USA. It was to be the first full Zeppelin concert since the death of John Bonham in 1980. Bonham's son Jason Bonham took his dad's place at the drum stool. As soon as I heard about the show, I was determined to do my best to attend.

Tickets were made available via a lottery system. I entered my details several times into the website, hoping against the odds that I would score tickets. Apparently one million people registered for the 20,000 available tickets, so the odds of success were, to say the least, low. When the results of the lottery were released, I was on every Zeppelin online forum that I could find, and soon realised I hadn't been successful. Those who had won were emailed a passcode which enabled them to buy two tickets via Ticketmaster. I looked on eBay, and to my dismay, found passcodes on sale. It was clear that some enterprising individuals had managed to make multiple entries to ensure success. I decided to take the risk and bought two passcodes which enabled me to buy two pairs of tickets, the plan being that my wife, two of my children and I would all attend the show.

I went straight to Ticketmaster and bought two tickets in my name and two in my wife's name, using different credit cards. The rules said that one individual could only buy two tickets, and that orders on the same card would be cancelled. We received our confirmation emails immediately, and were told that my wife and I would have to collect our tickets from the O2, along with photographic ID. We were in! Or so I thought. I was so excited, and looking forward to seeing Zeppelin again.

Over the next few weeks there was a lot of talk in the press and on the internet about the method of ticket allocation, and the fact that some touts had managed to get hold of tickets. Harvey Goldsmith announced that he would cancel any tickets that had been bought by anyone other than those drawn in the lottery. This resulted in several guys who had obtained tickets in a similar manner to me, particularly from the USA, threatening legal action. In the end, I'm not sure if any tickets were actually cancelled, but I was pretty stressed and worried at the time, in case Harvey carried out his threat.

On 1st November 2007 it was announced that Page had broken his little finger after a fall in his garden and the show was postponed to 10th December. Panic! We had trains and hotel rooms booked. We cancelled those and rebooked, which cost us considerably, but my excitement at seeing such a legendary band reform meant that I didn't mind too much.

We were advised to turn up early to collect our tickets, and the O2 opened the day before to issue tickets and wristbands for the show. We went down to London a day early, joined the queue and collected our tickets and wristbands. It was obvious from talking to people in the queue that many had travelled from all over the world for this historic gig. The USA contingent was particularly strong.

We went along to the O2 on the night of the gig with my whole family very excited about the prospect of seeing Zeppelin, particularly my children who were too young to have ever had the chance to see Zeppelin live. We had standing tickets, but my late wife, Marie, wanted a seat so we went upstairs to the box office and asked if we could swap our seats for standing tickets. Miraculously, there were some tickets left and we were allocated seats in two pairs upstairs in the same block, with a reasonable view of the stage.

The show opened with a performance by a supergroup consisting of Keith Emerson (ELP), Chris Squire and Alan White (Yes) and Simon Kirke (Free, Bad Company) with the brass section from Bill Wyman's Rhythm Kings. The show also featured Bill Wyman's Rhythm Kings, Paul Rodgers, Paolo Nutini, and Foreigner. Other guests were Maggie Bell and Alvin

Lee. We watched the start of the set and caught Paul Rodgers and Foreigner, but spent much of the time having a look around the arena, taking in the atmosphere. We saw Bob Geldof and Joe Elliott from Def Leppard in the bar. Many other stars attended the gig, including (reportedly) Paul McCartney.

There was a short interval and then we took our seats. You could feel the anticipation in the air. What would they be like? What would they start with? The entrance of Led Zeppelin was preceded by a short film, taken from TV reports of a seventies US tour. And then there were on stage, and the familiar opening riff of 'Good Times, Bad Times' – the first song from the first album; a very strict order appropriate start – echoed across the massive arena. The sound was a little patchy at first, but that was soon sorted out.

The atmosphere was strange; the crowd seemed subdued, as if they were completely awestruck, and couldn't believe what they were experiencing. This developed as the evening progressed, with later songs getting rapturous audience receptions. They were everything I could have hoped for. The performance of each band member was stunning, the weeks of rehearsal paid off. Plant sang songs in a lower key, and his scream wasn't as piercing as it had been, but then how could it be? I also reckon that Page fluffed some of the notes at the start of 'Stairway'. But these were minor points.

Overall it was a great performance, and Zeppelin reclaimed their legacy. Highlights for me were 'Since I've Been Loving You', 'Dazed And Confused', 'Stairway To Heaven' (although I've heard it so many times that the magic it held for me in the seventies has dimmed), and 'Kashmir'. Encores were 'Whole Lotta Love' and 'Rock And Roll'. I was hoping for a further encore of 'Communication Breakdown', which they had apparently rehearsed, but – hey – you can't have everything.

The whole family felt privileged to have seen such a special gig and we all thought it was just great. It's probably not the best time I've seen Zeppelin, but it was still a momentous, unforgettable and emotional event. My kids still talk about it today and are so pleased that they got the chance to see this legendary band. Few people of their age had the opportunity to do so. Many of their friends hardly believe that they saw Led Zeppelin and are very jealous. And so they should be.

It's something I will remember for the rest of my life. Magic, pure magic.

I WAS THERE: JOHN GRIFFITHS

We're scouring the internet for our music news and still praying a reunion can be accomplished, with almost no hope. And then it happens. Led Zeppelin are getting together again to celebrate the life of Ahmet Ertegün, who had recently passed. Along with almost everyone I knew, I went into the ballot for tickets and spent a whole week checking my email every five minutes. Nothing. Soon after, I saw with almost complete indifference the news that Page had broken his finger and the concert would have to be postponed, little realising the significance.

A couple of weeks later, I yawningly opened my email over my pre-work toast and then went into complete meltdown when I saw an email offering me the chance to buy two tickets for the re-scheduled date. Oddly, there were some people who had had to return their tickets as a result of the re-scheduling (to this day I don't understand why you would do that) and the returns had been put into a further ballot of the original unsuccessful applications. The next half hour as I completed the transaction – online ticketing was still a bit flaky at this time and it was never a done deal until you had the confirmation email – was so nerve wracking that, to this day, I have palpitations thinking about it.

My son Mike says I practically kicked the door down to his room to tell him the news and I frantically left messages for my friend Mark to call me as soon as he could. I kept my phone on me at school, which is a big no-no, and surreptitiously took his return call whilst pretending to look for equipment in the outside play storage shed. 'Mate, what's up?' 'Do you want to go to Led Zeppelin?'

Mark and I have been best friends for most of our lives and there is no-one else I would have wanted to share the experience with. Thankfully the wife has never been a Zeppelin fan (she fell asleep at the first Knebworth concert and never actually saw them – something that doesn't trouble her in the least) so there was no conflict there.

We drove down to the O2 at Greenwich to pick up our wristbands the day before the actual concert. It was like a massive party, with people from all over the planet talking and sharing experiences. The queue hardly moved at all for hours and the rumours inevitably began flying that they would run out of time and those at the back of the queue would lose out, but that proved false as suddenly it started flying and, before we knew it, we had the wristbands.

Mark and I turned up the next day with plenty of time to spare and had to pace ourselves drinks-wise so as not to be out of it for this once in a lifetime experience. We cut it fine, as we decided to have one more pint (we never liked Paolo Nutini anyway) and only just got back as the house lights were going down. I had doubts that Zep could cut it. They were men in their sixties attempting to do things they were famous for in their twenties without the years of constant touring and consolidation that other bands who hadn't split up had fortified themselves with. All that went out the window as 'Good Times Bad Times' pounded out with all the sass and sheer rock gold that Zep had always been. As it finished, Mark and I fell into each other's arms with absolute joy. We were straight back into our teens as though we had never been away and the next couple of hours were 24 carat bliss. 'My, my, my, I'm so happy, I'm gonna join the band. We gonna sing and dance and in celebration…'.

I WAS THERE: CHRIS BEERS

I had long resigned myself that a Zeppelin reunion would never take place. In early September 2007 the radio was on as I fell asleep on the sofa. It was about 5am and I heard 'Stairway' playing. I stirred and heard them announce that Zep were to do a one-off full show in London for charity, with Jason Bonham on drums. By midday, everybody I knew had either texted, emailed or phoned to tell me, as they knew what a fan I had been since I was a teenager. I had to be there by hook or by crook.

I put myself into the ballot but, like thousands, didn't get pulled out of the hat. Then nearer the time it transpired that Jimmy had injured a finger and the date was put back from November to December. There was to be another chance to get tickets from another ballot.

Again, I wasn't lucky enough.

Myself and a friend composed a letter to send to Harvey Goldsmith the promoter, almost begging to clean the floors, make tea or anything, just to see if I could bag a ticket, or at least get him to screen the show live in cinemas for all the people who missed out. It kept my spirits up, but I never got a reply.

On a Zeppelin forum, I talked about how I hadn't got a ticket and that I was still going up, just to be there outside. I told them about the letter to Harvey, etc. About ten days before the show, I got an email from Steve on the forum, who I had been talking to for months. He said, 'I have two tickets for the gig.' He was going to take his missus but she felt the spare should go to a true fan. I couldn't believe it.

Three days before the gig I got another message from Steve saying he had managed to bag himself a backstage pass. The other ticket was now up for grabs. It was agreed that my missus would buy this ticket as she wanted to witness the gig with me.

The day of the gig was filled with anticipation, with people queuing up from the night before. We got into the Arena and found a good spot just in front of the mixing desk. The first half passed seeing other acts. By the time Zep hit the stage with 'Good Times Bad Times', I had a tear in my eye. Okay, it wasn't Bonzo, but by the time the third number had been played, it dawned on me that they were on top form. They were owning the stage, with none of the so-called debacle of *Live Aid* or the Atlantic reunion in the eighties. It was epic. If this was half as good as the seventies, how good were they then?

Highlights were 'For Your Life' and that awesome riff, Page swaggering around looking all the rock god, and the glances to each other, almost reliving their youth. By the time 'Kashmir' was played, they had reclaimed their crown as the best live act of them all. 'Kashmir' thundered, the walls and floor shook to the monolithic riff and, to this day, this was the most exciting live moment at a concert I have had the pleasure to witness.

Then it was over. The buzz leaving the arena was like nothing else. I even gave up going to gigs for a few years because I knew I could never ever top that one gig. One part of me wanted them to tour – it would have been incredible – but in hindsight I am glad they left it there as a statement, a one off and leaving at the top. And it saved me remortgaging the house to finance following them around America.

I WAS THERE: JOHN STOREY

I'm an Acton Boy. My brother was in the same year as Entwistle and Townshend at school. I heard *Zeppelin I* and *Zeppelin II* back in the late sixties. My mum and dad ran a boys' hostel in Camberwell in south east London, and there were 50 boys from the ages of 15 to 21. One of them was a mad Zeppelin fan and had the albums and was playing them and I thought, 'Well, this is good stuff.' The first time we went to see Zeppelin was '75 at Earls Court. It was a Saturday night and I remember Jimmy Page playing the guitar with his bow and the lasers going everywhere and all the hieroglyphics they used to have in those days. At the time we didn't think it was that big a deal.

I started at a printing company when I was 16 but ended up owning that printing company 25,

30 years later. It was a great little company, and we managed to look after our clients which meant we used to get boxes at the Royal Albert Hall, Wembley and stuff like that for pretty much anybody and everybody that was worth going to see. The hospitality companies would phone me up before something was announced and say, 'We've got this concert coming up. We know you're a fan.'

When the Zeppelin one was announced, I got a call from the hospitality suppliers. It was £1,000 a ticket. A lot of money but, obviously, needs must. So I phoned a good client and said, 'Do you fancy coming to see Zeppelin?' Because obviously I had to justify spending the money and I couldn't go on my own or with my wife. It had to be a business thing.

We went to the O2. Hospitality was set up around the back of the stage and above it. It was full of people from the music business – I saw the Gallagher brothers, McCartney, Jeremy Clarkson, Madonna. According to the papers, everyone was there. There was an aftershow party as well. Although it was billed as Zeppelin's reunion, it was a big tribute to Ahmet Ertegün, the founder of Atlantic Records. As a result, there was quite a load of other people on beforehand – Foreigner, Keith Emerson, Paul Rodgers. Pete Townshend was billed to play and I was quite excited about that, because he's on the Atlantic label in America, but he didn't appear in the end. Then it was time for the big event.

Zeppelin came on and just blew everybody away. They started off with 'Rock And Roll' and it was just a wonderful, wonderful concert. To this day, no one can understand why they rehearsed for it and set it all up and didn't then come back in three weeks' time and do five nights or whatever. But I don't think Robert Plant is interested.

I WAS THERE: TONY UNWIN

I was one of the 20 million or so individuals who optimistically applied for tickets for the one off Led Zeppelin gig at the O2 Arena. I duly checked my emails on the day the lucky recipients were announced and... Nothing.

Ten days later an email appeared in thick black type which stood out from the others. 'Ahmet Ertegün Tribute Concert' was the headline. I'd 'won' two tickets to the hottest gig of the century after all. I can only assume they were initially issued to someone else who failed to claim them within the given timescale. I had to claim them within five days. After ascertaining that this was not a scam, I duly applied for two standing tickets. All tickets were priced at £120, standing or seated.

I thought collecting the tickets may prove to be a problem as all of them were issued on the Sunday afternoon or the Monday night of the gig, and only issued to the cardholder who had purchased the tickets. You had to provide photographic ID and correspondence confirming name and address. I was armed to the teeth with utility bills, bank statements and anything else I could lay my hands on. I was not taking any chances!

Despite their long stage absence, Zeppelin put on an awesome show. A few well-known numbers were omitted, including 'The Immigrant Song', simply because Robert Plant could no longer reach the required notes. This did not detract from the performance. They all looked as if they were really enjoying themselves. It was a one-off gig so they didn't have the thought of planes to catch and 30 more concerts to perform. Looking back, I consider myself to have been so very fortunate to have been one of the lucky ones to be able to purchase a ticket. The fact that all these years on Led Zeppelin have no plans to play together again makes the concert even more exclusive...

I WAS THERE: ROB WHITMARSH

I entered the ballot but was unsuccessful. I decided to purchase a ticket on eBay. My wife knew how much this meant to me and gave her blessing, so I found a perfect seller and placed my bid. I won the auction on 25 October and knew I was going to have one of the most expensive nights of my life, at £1,550 for a single golden ticket. I'm only a regular working man and couldn't really justify spending that much money, but this would be a lifelong dream fulfilled. After contacting the seller, I felt confident I was dealing with someone genuine. He sent a copy of all the ticket information he had received. There were emails with his passcode, Ticketmaster's ticket purchase confirmation, contact details and even a photo so I could recognise him when we collected our tickets. Then the news broke that Jimmy Page had injured his finger and the show would be rescheduled. Panic set in and I contacted the seller the moment I heard the news. Fortunately, it wasn't a problem for either of us.

We arranged to meet at the venue the day before the show as tickets and wristbands could be collected from the O2 Arena box office ahead of time. I drove to London, parked up and got the Tube to the O2. Between the Tube station and the venue, I noticed a large wall covered with some lyrics from 'Kashmir'. It helped to set the mood. I got there early and joined the biggest merchandise queue ever. I was there for about an hour, where my ticket buddy joined me in line for our programmes and posters. After buying our goodies, we joined the ticket collection line. Signatures were taken, wristbands were fitted and tickets were handed over. At that moment I knew it was guaranteed. After a lifetime of waiting, I would finally see Led Zeppelin.

On show day, we joined the large queue for entry to the show around 4.30pm. This was the moment I realised just how truly multi-national the audience was, with people from America, Colombia, Germany, Australia and another pair of fellow English fans. Television crews were filming us all and the atmosphere was incredible. As we had standing tickets, we had to decide on the best spot to enjoy the show. We ended up leaning against the front of the mixing desk on its righthand side, as we faced the stage.

At 9.04pm the Tampa newsreel footage was shown above the darkened stage and then 'Good Times Bad Times' roared out. The energy level lifted in stages throughout the show, noticeably before 'In My Time Of Dying' and 'For Your Life'. Would 'Stairway To Heaven' be played? Of course it was. It all built towards the magnificent 'Kashmir'. The visuals and the sound for the whole event were exceptional, but it was the sheer energy of the musicians on stage that surpassed everything. After the last notes of 'Rock And Roll' had faded, I knew I would never experience a show like that again. I left the venue with 20,000 other people who had just witnessed a bit of history being made on that special night in London.

I WAS THERE: OLE TOLLANES

We were queuing up in front of the ticket booths. The BBC was interviewing fans from all over the world. I picked up my tickets and wristband, showing my passport and credit card used for the purchase as ID. Inside the arena, the security measures taken were strict. We had to go through a metal detector. I hid my small pocket camera in my pants, between my legs, and luckily no alarm went off. I went to buy a t-shirt which I still have, and will have to my death!

The seating was pretty good, on the stand to the right of the stage. We did not pay much attention to the artists such as Bill Wyman and his Rhythm Kings, a band consisting of names like Keith Emerson, Alan White, Chris Squire, Paul Rodgers, etc. We were waiting for the headliners. A movie with bits and pieces of their past was shown on the big screen and a huge roar went through the audience. And then they just entered the stage and started to play. I could not believe my eyes. From 'Good Times Bad Times', it's hard to explain what I felt. I was just the happiest man on the planet. The sound was perfect, the band was fantastic, Jason on drums was outstanding and Robert, Jimmy and John Paul were out of this world. The set list was just what I hoped it was going to be.

When it was over I was pretty much speechless. When 'Rock And Roll' faded out, it was like an empty space was created. People around me were probably in the same state of mind. Time went so fast and suddenly they had left the stage. No more encores, no more rock 'n' roll. But the memories of this fantastic gig will follow me to the grave.

I WAS THERE: IVAN ANDREWS

I arrived at work one morning and a co-worker informed me that he just heard on the radio that Led Zeppelin were going to play a concert in London and you had to enter an online worldwide lottery for a chance of being selected to be able to purchase tickets. I called my daughter, Megan, and told her to enter my name in the draw. Later at the draw date, I received an email notifying me that I was selected and could purchase two tickets. I bought those tickets right at that moment. My thoughts after that were, 'I have to get off work now and book hotels and flights!' It was a rush of excitement. The show was in November and Sinead O'Connor was playing in Dublin around the same time, so I bought tickets to her concert too. Then we heard that the Zep concert was being postponed to December because of an injury Page received.

We decided to fly to London from Vancouver, British Columbia in November and went to see Sinead in Dublin, then fly back home for a week and then back to London again to see Zeppelin at the O2.

It had been thirty years since I last saw Zeppelin. My daughter Megan and I were in the crowd waiting for them to come onstage at the O2. When they came on stage, I must admit I had tears in my eyes. I didn't think I would ever see them live on stage again. The show was extraordinary and I wanted them to keep playing forever. It was one of the best Led Zeppelin performances I've seen in my life. As we left the O2 that night, I felt that if that was the last concert I would see in my lifetime, it would be okay. I was so happy and totally satisfied. Thank you, Led Zeppelin!

I WAS THERE: MICHAEL MCWILLIAM

After literally hours of trying to log on to the ticket site I finally got on, slightly less a bag of nerves than I was when I first booted up the computer. Form filled out, computer switched off and all promptly forgotten about as I knew I had sweet FA chance of getting a ticket. It was weeks or months later that I was at my computer looking at emails when I saw one that said I'd won the chance to buy two tickets. So certain was I that there was no chance of getting tickets, and thus so switched off to it all, I hadn't even noticed that the original concert date had passed and that no gig had happened.

For a while I absolutely thought a friend had pranked me with this email. Gradually it became clear that the email was real and that the gig date had changed – Page apparently had injured a finger forcing cancellation – and that some ticket winners for the original date couldn't make the new date and so their tickets went back into the hat. I had got two of them. It's an obvious thing to say but I could not believe my luck – I had just won a lottery!

I was never one for elbowing my way to the front of a gig but this was different and never to be repeated so elbow I did, leaving my wife and I about six deep from the front of the stage. Taking my wife Carmel was an issue of deep contention. Should I give the other ticket to a fellow die-hard Zep fan mate or take Carmel? I think my friends have just about forgiven me. Nowadays, I continue to collect anything that says Led Zeppelin on it and I even named my micropub in Whitstable The Black Dog. The toilet in the pub is called 'The Jimmy Page Suite' and has an original 1970s poster of Jimmy letting rip on the double-neck. All that time ago it could have been the Bay City Rollers. Fortunately, the path that I went by was the mighty Zep.

I WAS THERE: FRANK SMITH

I heard rumours (again) of Led Zeppelin reuniting in June 2007. I didn't think much of them until September when I received a cryptic email from my Zeppelin associate saying it was definitely on. I had to promise not to repeat this information to anybody until it was officially announced, at which point the Zeppelin world on the internet exploded. There was to be a concert in honour of Ahmet Ertegün, with Jason Bonham on drums. Like 20 million other fans around the world, I registered for a ticket online although I didn't seriously consider having a chance at winning a ticket. However, a few weeks later I got an email from my Zeppelin associate saying 'pack your bags'. I thought he was playing some sort of practical joke so replied to his email asking 'is this what I think it is?' He said it was and that it came from 'The Source', a reference to his connection with Jimmy Page's manager, who he'd met in 2003 at the New York premiere of *DVD*.

I flew to England and met up with my two fellow Zep friends, Nech and Mike, at Heathrow Airport, which was swarming with Zeppelin fans from all over the world. The atmosphere was buzzing with Led Zeppelin magic. We took a train to the hotel from where we were to collect our tickets and were given a room number. We excitedly knocked on the door. On entering, we found the room filled with hangers-on, roadies and assistants. We identified Jimmy's road manager on the cell phone and then sitting at a table making plans about tickets and passes. We sat on the sofa as not to intrude on the proceedings. Finally, my buddy spoke with the manager and was told to wait.

30 minutes later, we were each given an envelope spilling over with tickets, passes, and multi-coloured wristbands. Were we given the right envelopes? These apparently were for VIPs as the passes were for rehearsal access, multiple after parties and everything a fan could possibly want and more. I could only say 'thank you, thank you.'

We checked in to our hotel, the $600-a-night West India Quay Marriott. I thought that rather steep but figured we were getting the tickets and passes for free so it was worth the expense. But the girl at the desk said 'it's taken care of.' I looked at my buddy and didn't say a thing. We gathered in the lobby and asked, 'Did she mean what I thought she meant?' He thought so. Apparently, we were 'comped' by the band. All three of us were staying at the hotel for three days for free. Unbelievable!

One of the passes we were given was for the soundcheck/rehearsal. The O2 was only a mile away but we had to take a train to get there. We boarded the train and made it to the venue. We immediately met familiar faces and spent time with the Zep tribute band, Led Zepagain. While in line, we could hear the rumblings of 'No Quarter' coming through the doors.

After a 30-minute wait, we were escorted into the stage area where we saw Robert, Jimmy, John Paul and Jason on stage casually working through 'No Quarter', 'Nobody's Fault But Mine', 'In My Time Of Dying' and a loose jam. There were maybe 100 people among the audience – mostly crew, charity people and contest winners. Robert got down from the stage and wandered around on the floor to listen to the sound and socialise with the crew and fans.

During the rehearsal, Jason's son did a little drum solo which was met with a nice round of applause. Robert's voice sounded great and Jimmy's guitar sound was powerful! It was amazing to see the band rehearsing and in such a casual mood. It was the best of both worlds where they were the famous rock stars but also casual enough to just be themselves hanging out and enjoying the chemistry. All four band members seemed relaxed and upbeat. After about an hour, we were all asked to leave and we were back into the O2 corridors. From the performance we had just witnessed, we anticipated a powerful concert.

That afternoon back at the hotel, I got a call from one of my buddies who said, 'Quick, get to the lobby. Jimmy's guitars are down in the lobby in cases!' I jumped on the elevator and made it to the lobby but the gear had disappeared as fast as it had arrived. Apparently, the road crew was staying at our hotel.

On the day of the concert, we all met up in the one hotel room and did multiple checks for tickets, passes, wristbands and the identification that we were told would be required to get into the building. After a frantic search for a misplaced ticket, we headed to the train station.

Arriving at the O2, the atmosphere was cold but electric with anticipation. Fans spilled in and were spread out all over the place. The news media had camped out all over the grounds of the enormous venue grounds, covering the hottest news story all over the world for that day and days afterward. I said to nobody in particular 'I wonder if there will be any celebrities here?', not realising that this event was *the* social event throughout all of Europe, for everybody including non-Zeppelin fans. Models and celebrities from all over had descended on the event as the place to see and be seen.

We arrived at the door and were let in just on showing our wristbands. Security was not enforcing the identity checks put in place, at least not as strictly as had been announced. It would have just taken too long. We made our way up the ramp to where our seats were and realised the seats were in the VIP area. At this security checkpoint, they were looking for cameras and recording devices with a metal detecting wand. Jimmy's road manager was there and came over said to security, 'It's OK, these guys are OK,' and we were let through the line without any bother. The seats could not have been better. We were up about half way up of the first section on Jimmy's side of the stage.

The warm-up acts were given polite applause but nobody was interested in hearing them. Everybody was only there to see Led Zeppelin, and it was painfully obvious to fans and support acts alike. There was a filmed tribute to Ahmet and a very nice filmed documentary of the band. Then I noticed Jimmy come to the side of the stage and begin stretching his legs, limbering up before the show. Finally, the lights went down and a roar came up through the crowd. The first chords of 'Good Times Bad' Times raised the roof. It was a powerful, palpable sound! They played 'Ramble On' and 'Black Dog' and Robert said 'good evening'. He commented on Ahmet and the fact that there were fans from 129 countries at the show. A powerful 'In My Time of Dying' followed while 'For Your Life' was met with a huge roar. We got 'Trampled Underfoot', 'Nobody's Fault But Mine', a very powerful 'No Quarter' and 'Since I've Been Loving You'.

'Dazed And Confused' was great, with Jimmy using his bow and the laser pyramid. 'Stairway To Heaven' was introduced by Robert as 'this is for you, Ahmet' followed by 'we did it, Ahmet' afterwards. 'Kashmir' was the highlight of the night. Robert's vocals were great and the visuals were perfect and mesmerising. The crowd reacted to this song the most. Someone threw a bowler hat up on stage at this point, in dedication to John Bonham.

Jason Bonham came to the front of the stage and turned around to face Robert, Jimmy and JPJ in an 'I'm not worthy' gesture. And they encored with 'Whole Lotta Love' and 'Rock And Roll'.

I WAS THERE: JEFF LOUDON

I registered for the ticket lottery and had several friends and family members register for me, but no one won so I purchased a code on eBay with a 'Buy It Now' option. Most of the codes had lots of bids on them already, but this one had just been posted when I came across it so I took a chance on it being legitimate and lucked out. My girlfriend at the time convinced me to buy the code. She knew what a fan I was and said 'if you don't try, you'll be kicking yourself for the rest of your life.' She was right – I couldn't turn down my only opportunity to see them play together. The code cost me $400, which was a lot of money for a young guy working at Guitar Center, and then each ticket was $250. I wasn't 100 per cent positive I'd be able to get in until the day before the show, when everyone was supposed to pick up their tickets and wristbands. I lived in New York at the time so this was my first (and only) time in London, and there were rumours that they would be cancelling tickets if the name on the order didn't match the person who applied for the code, but thankfully that never happened.

When I got to the venue, I expected there to be thousands of people in line already but there were only 15-20 people ahead of me. I waited in line most of the day. I met people from all over the world in line and we looked out for each other that day, saving spots in line for people who needed food or a bathroom break. All of us were interviewed by several news outlets. My picture was in a few newspapers the next day. It was all pretty surreal. At one point, someone came down the line offering £10,000 in cash to anyone who would give up their ticket and their spot in line. I think they eventually found someone a few hundred people back.

It's funny what I remember about the show. I particularly remember Jimmy Page drooling a lot while he played and there being some bad feedback issues early on that they ended up figuring out. Thankfully, most of the audio was salvageable as the feedback didn't really come through in the *Celebration Day* recording. 'Kashmir' was easily the best song of the night, but the whole concert was simply incredible. Jason Bonham made his father proud with a perfect performance, and aside from Robert Plant understandably struggling to hit a few of the highest notes they far exceeded expectations.

I WAS THERE: PAUL HINDESS

I had my own business so I applied for a ticket online and got all the girls in the office who worked for me to apply as well. I was praying to get a ticket. And we got two. I had two options and took one of them. I invited my friend Malcolm to come with me, who was at that Zeppelin concert at Newcastle City Hall with me in 1972 and who was my best man in 1975. It was a really emotional time. When they came on stage, he was crying. We were both crying.

Led Zeppelin live was it for me. Do I think Robert and Jimmy will get back together and work together? Yes, I do. Blood's thicker than water and those two are welded together. They have commercial differences and personal differences but if the right little thing came up, they would do it. I don't think they'd do a tour again but I wouldn't be surprised if they did another O2-type one-off thing. I hope it's soon. I'd go along. Just bloody do it, man.

ACKNOWLEDGEMENTS

I should like to thank everyone who contributed their memories for this book but in particular: Dave Lewis, who kindly agreed to write the foreword to this book and who is the author of several Led Zeppelin books and editor of the long running Led Zeppelin magazine and website *Tight But Loose* (www.tightbutloose.co.uk); Henry Race, who contributed memories to my Who and Pink Floyd books and provided me with some great Led Zeppelin images; Sonny Casale; Dave Barber (coda-uk.co.uk); Nigel Molden, author of *The Centre of a Revolution – Live Events at The Polytechnic 1965-73;* Paul Welsh, Paul May; *Asbury Park Press* and Jean Mikle for permission to quote from her article of 23 August 2014; Gregory Hewitt, for permission to quote from his essay, 'Led Zeppelin – Back in the Daze'; Mike Macrum, for permission to quote from his blog; Benjamin Salisbury for background material; and Thom Lukas, Graham Kennedy, Stuart Whitehead, Jody Husseini, Phillip Solomonson, Stacey Katsis, Peter Clinick, Dave Lewis and Helmut Ölschegel for use of various photographs of Zep in action (all rights reserved).

I also made use of various reference materials to check and double check dates and research the Led Zeppelin story. No self-respecting Led Zeppelin fan will be unaware of the website ledzeppelin.com or several excellent books on the band, notably Mick Wall's *When Giants Walked The Earth*, Stephen Davis's *Hammer Of The Gods*, *Jimmy Page: The Definitive Biography* by Chris Salewicz and *Robert Plant: A Life* by Paul Rees. Finally, I should also like to thank Kate Sullivan. Since I've been loving you, babe.

Body Cast Doesn't Stop Zeppelin Fan

Tim Lee, an ingenious 19-year-old from Knightdale, made it to the Led Zeppelin concert, despite being in a body cast. He arrived at the Coliseum via a Radio Flyer, a little red wagon pulled from the parking lot by his girlfriend, Anne Sullivan, a student nurse from Raleigh.

Because of Tim's condition, he and Anne were allowed into the Coliseum a bit before the thundering herd of 17,500 poured into the building to vie for the choice spots. Trouble was, the promoters wouldn't chance letting Tim lie in his wagon among the shoving fans on the floor.

An English Knight came to the rescue. Ian Knight, the show's lighting designer, invited Tim and Anne to join him on the small auxiliary stage used for special effects. Knight helped lift Tim, wagon and all, to the stage. And, he provided crates to elevate the incapacitated rock fan's head.

Commiserating with Tim Lee was Jim Clark, whose arm was in a cast. Clark, who works with the show, broke his arm Saturday in a fall from the spot on which Tim's wagon was parked for the concert.

Tim Lee, Anne Sullivan, Jim Clark At Zeppelin Concert

Zeppelin Sends Crowd Flying